IN SEARCH OF
HERITAGE
as Pilgrim or Tourist?

THE
ROBERT GORDON UNIVERSITY
HERITAGE LIBRARY

IN SEARCH OF
HERITAGE
as Pilgrim or Tourist?

Edited by
J. M. FLADMARK

Papers presented at
The Robert Gordon University
Heritage Convention 1998

DONHEAD

First published in the United Kingdom
in 1998 by
Donhead Publishing Ltd
Lower Coombe
Donhead St Mary
Shaftesbury
Dorset SP7 9LY
Tel. 01747 828422

ISBN 1 873394 24 1

A CIP catalogue for this book is available
from the British Library.

Printed in Great Britain by
T J International Ltd, Padstow.

In order to produce this book quickly for conference delegates,
the publishers have used camera copy
provided by the editor.

CONTENTS

Foreword   ix
Thor Heyerdahl
Acknowledgements   xiii
William Stevely
Introduction   xvii
Magnus Fladmark

1   **HOW IT ALL STARTED**   1
Early Routes of Merchants and Soldiers
Anne Mustoe

2   **IN SEARCH OF HOLY PLACES**   15
Then and Now
John Wilkinson

3   **THE APOSTLE OF SCOTLAND**   25
Is it Ninian or Columba?
Ian Bradley

4   **TWO PILGRIM TOWNS**   37
A Quest for St Andrew and St Margaret
Jurek Alexander Putter

5   **VOICES OF THE CHERUBIM**   55
A Musical Odyssey to Scotland
John Purser

6   **TO SANTIAGO DE COMPOSTELA**   77
A Journey of Remembrance
Nicholas Luard

7   **SAINT OLAV OF NORWAY**   91
Reviving Pilgrim Ways to Trondheim
Mari Kollandsrud

8 **MEMENTOS TO TAKE HOME**   105
   The Ancient Trade in Souvenirs
   Godfrey Evans

9 **FROM INDIA TO JAPAN**   127
   Buddhism Then and Now
   Brian Burke-Gaffney

10 **JAPANESE PILGRIMS TO THE WEST**   141
   Their Impact Since the 16th Century
   Paul Akira Kadota

11 **FROM ABERDEEN TO NAGASAKI**   153
   Thomas Blake Glover in Japan
   Alexander McKay

12 **THE ARTS AND IDENTITY**   163
   From Pilgrimage to Grand Tour
   Duncan Macmillan

13 **HERALDRY AND IDENTITY**   179
   From Knights to Corporate Branding
   Gordon Casely

14 **LANGUAGE AND IDENTITY**   193
   Modern Sources of Written Scots
   William Donaldson

15 **ACTION IN A LANGUAGE WAR**   205
   How The Kist/A' Chiste was Won
   Robbie Robertson

16 **CULTURAL CAPITAL AND IDENTITY**   219
   Scotland's Democratic Intellect
   Magnus Fladmark

17 **FOOD IN FOLK TRADITION**   235
   How Scotland Celebrates the Seasons
   Catherine Brown

18 THE MEETING OF CULTURES   253
El Pueblo de Los Angeles
Jean Bruce Poole

19 RELIGIOUS LIFE AND ART   263
St Mungo Museum in Glasgow
Harry Dunlop

20 A MUSEUM CHALLENGE   271
The Iconography of New Zealand
William Tramposch

21 A REGIMENTAL SHRINE   283
The Gordon Higlanders Museum
Stuart Allan

22 A CITY HARVESTING THE SEA   295
Aberdeen Maritime Museum
John Edwards

23 SOUTH INDIAN FOLK HERITAGE   311
Breaking New Ground at Dakshinachitra
Deborah Thiagarajan

24 AFRICAN HERITAGE   319
The Assets of Sierra Leone
Arthur Abraham

25 ECHOES OF AFRICA   337
Jamaica's Musical Heritage
Olive Lewin

26 MAKING MINOR PLACES   351
Dilemmas in Modern Tourism
Dean MacCannell

27 SERIAL SOAP ADDICTION   363
From Screen Viewing to Pilgrimage
Patricia Sterry

28 **IN SEARCH OF BRAND IDENTITY**   375
The Makers of Wales Campaign
John Carr

29 **THE IMAGE OF ALSACE**   395
Trails for Imbibing Tourists
Dragan Crnjanski

30 **HISTORIC NORWAY**   405
Identity and Issues in Heritage Policy
Hild Sørby

31 **POLAND IN TRANSITION**   417
The Spirit and Identity of Cracow
Jacek Purchla

32 **SIR PATRICK GEDDES**   431
Pilgrimage and Place
Murdo Macdonald

33 **NEW PILGRIMS OLD TOWNS**   445
The Historic Burghs of Scotland
David Cameron

34 **SCOTTISH MERCAT CROCES**   461
Their Spiritual and Secular Significance
Lindsey Thomson and Dennis Urquhart

35 **READING THE CITY**   473
Approach and Orientation
Brian Evans

FOREWORD

From my own vantage point of a lifetime in search of cultural connections in human history, I welcome this volume which represents a timely contribution to questions of immense importance. Its fundamental precept is that understanding ourselves as cultural beings is an essential prerequisite for both spiritual and environmental survival. The authors deal with subjects in urgent need of public debate, and study of the history of travel and pilgrimage is an illuminating way to inform such debate.

Our attempt at preserving heritage has increased on a global scale throughout the twentieth century, and has become an urgent issue as we approach the threshold of a new millennium. Our ability to cope intelligently and immediately with this problem will decide how long mankind can remain the master of life and culture on this planet before nature itself takes over to prevent humanity from causing environmental collapse.

Human heritage spans over a vast number of generations: from remote times when our first common ancestors were able to enjoy the freedom of prospering on the natural resources bestowed upon them by the animal kingdom, to whatever each and every one of us today have inherited as personal property from our nearest relatives. In this we can draw a clear line between two categories: natural and man made.

The pleasure and benefits from preserving man made heritage go back to early Antiquity, although it seems to have been almost lost in Medieval Europe until it returned with increased intensity at the end of last century, when people who could afford a hobby began to preserve and collect antiquities.

The motives for preserving heritage among early non-European peoples in other continents, including Oceania, were totally different and mainly based on religious beliefs. Whereas Darwin's theory of evolution stimulated a belief in a continuous progress of the human body and brain, earlier cultures and some advanced civilisations had a strong element of ancestor cult in their religion, and the ruling families and elite claimed descent from the divine sun or some other mythical god or legendary semi-god.

Ancient temples, monuments and images were therefore held in higher veneration than those of contemporary architects and artists. Their royal genealogies were kept in written or oral traditions as far back as memories reached. Where memories were lost, symbolic deities and hierarchical representatives of the sun on earth took over. Always, the past was more glorious than the present, and the kings were of higher rank the further back and closer to the gods they appeared.

Today, western civilisation has literally eliminated ancestor worship, and the pendulum has instead swung too far the other way. Modem youth feel greatly superior to their grandparents who had neither transistor radios nor television. Further back, when there was neither electricity nor cars, people must have been closer to the apes than to us today.

In spite of our unreasonable and unfounded feeling of superiority over former generations, we do now at long last witness an increased understanding of the importance of preserving heritage. Ancient buildings, furniture, art and manuscripts, as well as all sorts of oral information on bygone customs and events are recorded and saved for posterity. Even more important is that political and economic interests are added to the cultural and aesthetic interest in preserving man made heritage. Tourism all over the world is a major sponsor for the preservation of immobile and indigenous heritage.

Fortunately, tourism attracted by cultural heritage involves an educated clientele interested in preservation more than abuse and destruction.

From personal experience, I have seen how tourism based on cultural heritage can help protect and preserve assets which would otherwise have had little chance of survival. My own experience derives principally from two sites, where I was personally instrumental in unearthing archaeological remains, and thereby indirectly also in opening mass tourism potential. These were Easter Island in Polynesia, and the Tucume pyramid complex in the coastal plains of northern Peru.

On arrival of our Norwegian Archaeological Expedition to Easter Island in 1955, there was no tourism, no harbour and no airport. There was a population of less than one thousand people living in utter poverty, and their only regular contact with the outside world was an annual four-day visit by a warship from the Chilean Navy.

A spontaneous change came when books and broadcast documentaries about the giant ancestral statues brought attention to this lonely island. There are now harbour facilities for cruise ships and an airport, where twice weekly, tourists pour in from all corners of the world. The population has increased fourfold and every family is prospering on lodging, catering, transporting and guiding tourists. Strict laws for protection and supervision of the monuments have been introduced by the Chilean government, and UNESCO has recently designated the island as a World Heritage Site.

A similar economic transformation is now well under way among the poverty stricken population of Tucume in northern Peru. A disastrous flood had reduced the present day local descendants of a pre-Inca culture to misery by the time we started an archaeological excavation project of the large pyramid complex in 1989. Ignored by the rest of the nation and unknown to tourists, more than ten thousand village people lived in the shadow of the eroded remains of the then unexplored and yet largest pyramid complex in South America.

Excavations brought to light amazing cultural remains from their maritime pre-Inca ancestry, and the Peruvian government built a local museum for this national heritage. Books and publications brought public attention to Tucume, and thereby funds for rebuilding the collapsed schools, dams, roads and bridges, as well as providing new systems for sewerage and the supply of drinking water and electricity. Together with excavations conducted by the Peruvians and exhibitions of the art treasures from neighbouring Sipan, the whole area of coastal northern Peru is now becoming a tourist area rivalling the Inca ruins of Cusco and Machu Pichu in the High Andes, international tourism being its principal source of future economic growth.

The benefit of tourism to local economies is only one of many issues dealt with in this book. Its theme ranges widely to explore the history of travel which shows that tourism has also been a positive cultural force over the centuries, but the advent of mass travel is beginning to raise concerns about environmental impact. Indeed, more important than any kind of regional or national heritage, is the one and only global heritage which we all share and depend upon for survival, today as much as in the past. Our inherited ecosystem is threatened and can never again be excavated by future generations if we allow it to be destroyed.

Thor Heyerdahl
Tenerife 1998

ACKNOWLEDGEMENTS

The Glover Institute is founded on the seminal values
which governed the life and work of Thomas Blake Glover.
These values are about the interaction between nations
which build civilised societies on cultural exchange and trade.
The Institute's mission is to study how these interactions
shape cultural identity and sustain economic activity.

Among the assets for which I became responsible on coming to Aberdeen in the middle of last year was an initiative called the Heritage Unit. Like the University itself, its successes had been built on a strong commitment to partnership in the community, where the relevance of our academic endeavours can be tested against the real world. Especially through the international Heritage Conventions, staff had demonstrated the mutual benefits of working closely together with government, industry and voluntary bodies, as borne out by the creative partnerships behind the previous three events and their associated publications.

The fourth volume in the series is now launched under a new banner. It has been my privilege in the months since my arrival to help put the whole initiative on a new footing by transforming the Heritage Unit into The Glover Institute. Following consideration of several options, we concluded that there was no talismanic Aberdonian more fitting than Thomas Blake Glover to grace our new Institute with his name. He enbraced the culture of his adopted country, and his contribution to the renaissance of modern Japan earned him admission to The Order of the Rising Sun in 1908.

Since the last Convention in Inverness, the University has introduced a MSc in Heritage Management. It is based on similar principles to the conferences, and I am grateful to colleagues for embracing so enthusiastically the need to work across sector boundaries within a multidisciplinary framework, and for their dedication to the promotion of scholarly exchange across national boundaries. Central questions at the heart of the Institute's programmes are whether culture can prosper without commercial enterprise, and whether modern consumerism erodes cultural identity.

The contents of this volume bear witness to the University's commitment to international collaboration, and I am especially grateful to the contributors from overseas. It is their willingness to enter into the spirit of what we are trying to do which makes it worth while to make the enormous effort required by our staff to mount the conference and to produce the book. Their contributions, alongside the wide range of talents we were able to call upon from the UK, represent fertile ground for international comparison of policy and practice. At a practical level, I thank each author for finding time to write the papers so that they could be published in time for delegates arriving in Aberdeen.

Active encouragement by several members of our Advisory Board has been a source of strength, and I am particularly grateful to Lord and Lady Balfour of Burleigh and John Foster for their enthusiastic support, as well as for their insistence on the pursuit of excellence at all times.

We were greatly encouraged by those who came forward with helpful suggestion on various matter relating to both the conference and the contents of this book. They are too many to list, but we would like to mention Tom Band, Sheila Brock, Alan Dick, Leonard Forman, Anne Malcolm and Michael Turnbull. Special thanks go Michael Glen for making the initial suggestion that we use the 'Window on Pilgrimage' at the Carfin Pilgrim Centre in Lanarkshire for the cover picure, and we are grateful for support from the the Centre Manager, James McCrossan, the stained glass artist herself, Shona McInnes, and the photographer, Michael Wolchover. We are likewise grateful to Jessica Brown and the Sano Foundation for allowing us to use the painting of Thomas Blake Glover.

The keen eye of staff directly involved is also clearly reflected in the high standard of papers to have found their way into this book. In addition to being Editor, Professor Magnus Fladmark has also had to cope with teaching and leading the work associated with establishing the new Institute. Like Glover, he left his country of birth to contribute to the affairs of another, and we are all grateful to him for the vision, energy and enthusiasm applied during long hours well beyond the call of duty.

On both our behalves, thanks go to others who were willing to put in the extra hours required to meet the high standards achieved, especially Alison Wood and Caroline Martin, as well as Margaret Wood and Samantha Groves who kindly volunteered their services. Other colleagues who have in one way or another helped sustain the core team, include Professors Seaton Baxter, Eric Spiller and Robin Webster, Dr Christopher Andrew, Dr Stuart Hannabuss, William Lonsdale, Dr Keith Maguire, Katherine Pacitti, Martin Parker, Dr David Silbergh, Andrew Turnbull and Ben Morton Wright.

On behalf of the University, I extend special thanks to Dr Thor Heyerdhal for writing the Foreword. His expression of support for the University's work has been a source of pride and inspiration for all staff concerned with this project. We are likewise indebted to Jill Pearce and Lindy Cornforth at Donhead. Without their support, collaboration and input, the quality of this volume would not have been possible.

I am grateful to Lord Provost Margaret Farquhar for opening the conference proceedings which were greatly enhanced by a distinguished array of personalities who attended and kindly agreed to chair sessions at the conference: Dr Gordon Adams of the Scottish Tourist Board, Tom Band, Peter Cockhead of Aberdeen City Council, Kåre Hauge the Consul General of Norway, Tsatsuaki Iwata the Consul General of Japan, David Kingsley, Katrina Morrison of Grampian Enterprise, Dr Graeme Roberts of Aberdeen University and Robbie Shepherd. Amongst those directly associated with the University, I thank our Chancellor Sir Bob Reid and Governors Dr Howard Fisher and Andrew Lewis, as well as David Caldwell, David Kingsley and my predecessor Dr David Kennedy.

Professor William Stevely
Principal & Vice Chancellor
The Robert Gordon University

INTRODUCTION

The past is everywhere. All around us lie features which, like ourselves and our thoughts, have more or less recognizable antecedents. Relics, histories, memories suffuse human experience. Each particular trace of the past ultimately perishes, but collectively they are immortal. Whether it is celebrated or rejected, attended to or ignored, the past is omnipresent.

from *The Past is a Foreign Country* by David Lowenthal, 1985

The aim of our heritage conventions is to promote international exchange among policy makers, professionals and academics. As reflected in this and previous books, our philosophical approach to the subject of heritage management is multi-dimensional, in the sense of extending across the boundaries of both disciplines and national cultures. Therefore, to see the whole picture, and to give this international exchange full meaning, it is necessary to paint on a big canvas.

The size of the canvas and the picture painted are also governed by the dimension of time. To make sense of the future, it is necessary to understand the past. This is true of life generally, as reflected in the above quotation from Lowenthal, as well as in heritage management, where it is a fundamental precept. The rhetorical question behind the general theme of the conference, which elicited the contributions to this volume, was simply: are there lessons to be learned from the history of early travel which can inform future tourism policy?

We invited speakers of distinction from around the world to explore issues associated with this question. It is rooted in the conundrum that the motivation for holiday travel may be moving in new directions, whilst accepting that cheap international air travel, which made mass tourism possible in the first place, is here to stay. Speakers from ten different countries accepted the challenge of speculating on whether the trend is towards a more timeless desire for cross-cultural experience rather than the mindless trek to concrete jungles by sunny beaches.

They were asked to be visionary and provocative, and in this spirit they accepted the challenge of examining the conference hypothesis that the medieval boom in pilgrimage was the start of modern tourism. The contributors who addressed this proposition directly confirm that it was triggered by religious motivation, but they acknowledge that pilgrims were also motivated by a desire for adventure and discovery, some seeking both cultural and material enrichment.

If so, can it then be argued that the history of pilgrim routes and saintly destinations promoted by our ancestors holds lessons for today? We did not set out to give definitive answers. Indeed, readers will not find panaceas for the future between these two covers, but the question has been asked and this volume will have served its purpose if it simulates interest in the hypothesis and encourages others to explore further the vistas opened up by some of the authors.

The answers found in these pages are generally in the affirmative. The past is indeed omnipresent, and the future depends on whether we have the humility to look back and to understand. Sustainable tourism is not a late 20th-century invention. The Vatican decreed the size of a medieval pilgrim town in line with the productive capacity of surrounding land so that pilgrims could be adequately fed, and there were rules for security and welfare of travellers. But their purchasing power and gullibility were also targets, and the international trade in souvenirs which started then is still with us today.

Cultural identity is an issue addressed by several authors, showing that the hand of history can give interesting pointers. Indeed, collective identity is embedded in time, and Lowenthal says that each 'trace of the past ultimately perishes, but collectively they are immortal.' This was the notion of identity applied by medieval kings and clergy when branding places to attract pilgrims, not to be confused with the instant and transient images of modern marketing. The problem today is that policy makers tend to treat promotion of cultural identity as if dealing with product branding of mass consumption items. The evidence from history indicates that collective identity is a product of more enduring quality with a strong spiritual dimension.

The most compelling issue to emerge from this volume relates to the identity crisis caused by today's burgeoning theme park industry, referred to as 'dreamworks' by Dean MacCannell. This has given rise to the two-nation syndrome, presenting both policy makers and visitors with the dilemma of having to choose between places of dreamworks or places of real people, sights, sounds and smells. The Editor's money is placed on the latter to win, as in Dragan Crnjanski's concept of 'terroir', which is essentially about timeless authenticity.

Professor Magnus Fladmark
Director, The Glover Institute
The Robert Gordon University

1

HOW IT ALL STARTED
Early Routes of Merchants and Soldiers

Anne Mustoe

My interest in historical roads was awakened in the winter of 1982 when I was a headmistress on a fortnight's holiday in India. One morning in Rajastan, I looked out of the coach window and saw a man on a bicycle, a solitary European pedalling across the immensity of the Great Thar Desert. To my surprise, because I was not a cyclist and had never been the least bit sporty, I was seized with sudden envy. I wanted to be out there myself, alone on a bicycle, passing through small villages, living among the people and really experiencing India, not just staying in tourist hotels and watching the country through a plate-glass window.

Not being one for half measures, my idea of cycling across India soon became a scheme for cycling round the world, and I began to plan it in earnest. I decided to travel from west to east, so that I should start off in France, Switzerland and Italy, gaining confidence in countries I knew and loved, where I spoke the languages, before I had to cope with unfamiliar places and peoples.

I am a classicist by training and have always needed some historical or cultural background to my travels. Looking at the globe, I realised that I could combine my intellectual interests with my cycling by following historical routes: the Roman road network across Europe; Alexander the Great from Macedonia to the Indus Valley; the Moghuls along their Imperial Road (later to become the Grand Trunk Road of the British Raj) from the Hindu Kush across Pakistan and India to Calcutta; the British Raj again on Highway One connecting the States Settlements of Malaysia's west coast with Singapore; then, across the Pacific, the great pioneer trails, such as the Oregon and the Pony Express, which had opened up the

American West. Finally, I could fly from New York to Dublin, cross over to Anglesea and pick up the Roman roads again. The journey which began on the southern section of Roman Watling Street, between London Bridge and Dover, would end on the northern section of that very same road, between Chester and Marble Arch, a neat completion of the circle.

The staff and girls at school clubbed together to buy me a bicycle, and in 1987 I set off on my first adventure. It was a fascinating ride, because I was conscious of following, in the wake of armies, the progress of ideas and cultures from west to east. But I realised that it was only half of the story. There was an equally important progression of ideas from east to west, from Rome to the Atlantic, from the Hispanic countries to South-America, and from China along the Silk Road into Europe. I have completed that second circuit, Rome to Rome, east to west. I have also cycled, since I began my new career from the north to the south of India, across Australia, along the Pilgrim Way to Santiago de Compostela and along most of the Roman Roads in Britain and Spain. So I may not be a professional historian, but I have certainly got to know every inch of the roads I shall be talking about, the hard way.

With such a wealth of material, I shall need to narrow down my topic. I shall do that by starting with a few general remarks on the development of roads. I shall then go on to consider two road systems in particular: the Silk Road which, despite its singular title, is in fact a whole tangle of interconnecting routes, and the Roman road network. Finally, I shall throw in a few ideas on the part these historical roads might play in the tourism of the future.

THE ORIGIN OF ROUTES

Roads began as short paths between agricultural settlements, used by the inhabitants for the exchange of local goods. As these settlements became more secure, some of their members took up and refined such crafts as weaving, pottery-making and metalwork, all of which required special raw materials. This was probably the origin of the long distance trade route. Nomadic peoples, who followed regular patterns of migration, were ideally placed to collect the raw materials needed by the craftsmen. These they exchanged for the finished artefacts and produce of the settlements. In time, some of the nomads gave up herding altogether and became full-time traders, moving from settlement to settlement with a variety of materials and finished goods.

As civilisation advanced and powerful states arose, requirements became more specific. In Egypt, for example, a route was already in existence as early as 3000 BC to carry copper and turquoise from the mines of the Sinai Peninsula to the Nile. By 2000 BC, jade, 'the jewel of Heaven', was travelling from the Khotan region, south of the Taklamakan Desert, eastwards into China and westwards to the Iranian Plateau. Jade tools, weapons, sculptures and jewellery have been found the whole way along this 5000 mile route between China and Western Asia. Of course, no individual merchant travelled the whole distance; each one carried the jade across his own territory, then sold it on to the next in one continuous chain.

Long distance routes would never have been developed beyond precarious merchant tracks had they not been put to military use. Good roads need good government. They are expensive to build and maintain. They must be well policed and well provided with amenities for travellers. In the 19th and 20th centuries, we have been preoccupied with commerce and have built roads specifically to service industry. In the past, the only justification for such heavy investment was the strategic one.

THE SILK ROAD

The fabled Silk Road from Xi'an, the ancient capital of China, to the Mediterranean, began with just such a military purpose. In the second century BC, the Chinese were under attack from the Huns. The Chin Emperor, Shi Huangdi, (the Emperor of the Terracotta Army) had already built the Great Wall in an attempt to keep them out. In 138 BC, the Han Emperor, Wudi, sent his General Zhang Qian on a mission to the West to try to recruit allies against them. He was unsuccessful in his quest, but he brought back useful intelligence on 36 kingdoms along the ancient jade route, as far West as Samarkand and Bokhara. More importantly, he brought back tales of the astonishing horses of the Fergana Valley, 'the Heavenly Horses' which were to feature so prominently in Chinese Art. They were so superior to the short-legged Chinese variety, that their acquisition enabled the Hans to rout the Huns and preserve China for the Chinese. Sericulture was a closely guarded Chinese secret and it was bales of this coveted silk which were sent to Fergana in exchange for the all-important horses. According to contemporary accounts, gravel was laid, streams were bridged and wooden trestle-paths constructed on dizzy heights through the mountains to facilitate this traffic. And that was the origin of the Silk Road, at least from the Chinese end.

The Mediterranean end of the road was Roman. By one of history's coincidences, at the same time as the Chinese Han Dynasty (206 BC – 8 AD) was growing in strength and pushing westwards, the Romans were

3

on the march towards the East. The two greatest powers the world had so far seen were exact contemporaries.

The Romans first saw silk in 53 BC. They had advanced into the Middle East with no significant opposition until they met the Parthians, whose superb archery and horsemanship at the Battle of Carrhae put the Roman legions under Crassus to shame. When the Roman lines had been broken and their army was in disarray, the Parthians produced their final weapon. They unfurled gigantic banners of red silk, which billowed out and filled the heavens, shimmering in the desert sun. The Roman horses panicked and the army was routed. They lost the battle, but they managed to obtain samples of this magical material, which the Parthians said they had got in exchange for an ostrich egg and some conjurers.

It was the beginning of the Roman passion for silk, and the beginning of great wealth for the Parthians, Sogdians, Kushans and Indians, who acted as middlemen in the silk trade. There was never, as far as we know, any direct contact between the Chinese and the Romans. They never even identified each other with any accuracy, owing perhaps to the grandiose names which each empire bestowed upon itself and its location. The Romans called the Mediterranean simply 'mare nostrum' (our sea), while the Chinese gave the name to China which is still in use today, Zhongguo (Middle Kingdom, or the middle of the world). Neither title was very specific geographically.

The Roman stretch of the Silk Road, where it crossed the Middle East, had existed for centuries. The chronicles of the Assyrian King Tiglath-Pileser I describe in detail a campaign against the Kurds in 1115 BC: 'I hewed a way with pickaxes of bronze and made passable a road for the passage of my chariot and troops'. The road network, which held together his empire, was organised with remarkable efficiency. There were road signs, guard-posts at six-mile intervals, wells and forts. The road surface was packed earth, paving being too expensive to use, except on the approaches to temples.

The Persians took over the Assyrian network and improved on it. They built rest-houses along the way and relays of royal couriers carried mail from one end of the Empire to the other. The Greek historian, Herodotus, says of this service: 'These men neither snow nor rain nor heat nor gloom of night stay from the swiftest possible completion of their appointed stage', a statement adopted centuries later as their motto by the United States Postal Service.

These excellent roads were still in use when the Romans took over the Middle East. Their empire spread across the Levant from the Black Sea to the Red Sea, so the eastern silks and spices which they craved had safe passage to Rome, once they had crossed the desert to Palmyra or reached the Gulf of Aqaba by sea.

4

China held and policed the eastern end of the Silk Road, maintaining caravanserais for the merchants and their camels; and Rome did the same for the western end. Between the two spheres of influence lay Iran, Southern Russia and the steppes of Central Asia, which neither power ever succeeded in taming. There was just one short period in its history, the century of the Pax Mongolica (AD 1260–1368), when the entire road was under the control of a single authority. When the writ of the Mongols ran from China to the shores of the Mediterranean, Marco Polo and traders like him could set out from Venice and travel in safety across half the world to the court of Kubla Khan.

Travellers before and since have not been so lucky. Throughout its history, they have had to take the branch of the Silk Road which was politically possible at any given time. Nothing has changed. When I cycled the Silk Road last year, the route I really wanted to take, through the Fergana Valley and Samarkand, was out of bounds, as my bicycle and I failed to meet Uzbekistan's complicated visa requirements. There was civil war in Afganistan; and Kashmir's Muslim separatists were in revolt against the Indian Government. So I was left with only one possible overland exit from China: the Khunjerab Pass over the Karakorams into Pakistan, at 15,500 feet (roughly the height of the summit of Mont Blanc), the highest paved road in the world. It was a punishing route, not at all the one I would have chosen, but I had no other option. The steppes of Central Asia have always been a seething no-man's land; and the mountain ranges bordering China are the world's highest. I could quite understand why both the Chinese and the Romans left these troublesome regions to their own devices and relied on middlemen for their trade.

ROMAN ROADS

Like the Chinese Han, the Romans moved outwards from their heartland on the fertile plains on Latium in self-defence. They were an agricultural people, who had settled in a good central position, protected to the north by the river Tiber, to the east by the Apennines, to the south by the Alban Hills and to the West by the Mediterranean with its convenient little port of Ostia. They had everything they needed. They were not interested in trade, nor were they looking for territorial expansion.

If the Romans however were not covetous, their neighbours were. They were attacked by one Italian tribe after another, and in 391 BC, they had to buy off the Gauls, who swept down over the Alps to besiege Rome. It seemed that the only way they could protect themselves in the long term was by taking control of the whole Italian Peninsula, which they accomplished by 264 BC.

Then it was the turn of the Phoenicians, who dominated trade in the Mediterranean and were growing anxious about the rising star on their horizon. Hannibal and his Carthaginians crossed into Spain and moved overland to attack the Romans in Italy. By the end of the Third Punic War in 146 BC, Carthage lay in ruins and the Romans held North Africa and Spain.

The pattern repeated itself throughout Europe and the Middle East. The Romans annexed country after country, but each time a new border was established, it was attacked by the next tribe along the line. Most empires feel the need for moral justification. Cicero and Livy both claim that the Romans never fought a battle which was not in their own or their allies' defence, and the facts do give considerable support to that claim. There is little sign of spontaneous aggression. The Romans were swept along by force of circumstance and seem to have acquired their vast empire almost by accident.

Having acquired it, they had to administer it, and they realised that good communications were the key to control. They set about building all-weather roads with the same discipline and meticulous care which they applied to the business of war. In fact, the roads were built by the Roman legions, to keep them fit and out of mischief between engagements. The very term for road-building, 'viam munire' (to fortify a road, from the same root as 'moenia' meaning ramparts) is an indication of their military purpose.

Like their predecessors, the Romans took existing roads and improved them for their own use. The Via Aurelia, which follows the western coast of Italy up to Genoa and the Riviera, started life as an Etruscan highway. The Gauls had smoothly laid tracks, along which their chariots could bowl at great speed, tracks which Julius Caesar exploited to make his quick conquest of their country. The Middle East, as we have seen, already had its own splendid network. Rome's contribution was to elevate road-building to an art, to create an overwhelming monument which would withstand centuries of wear and tear. From the Golden Milestone, whose ruined remainder still stands in the Forum today, 19 separate roads radiated out from Rome. Each of these 19 developed offshoots and continuations, until their tentacles spread throughout the whole empire. By the reign of Diocletian in the third century, the Romans were administering 372 distinct roads, covering an estimated 53000 miles through 34 countries.

Technically, the roads had no precedent. No earlier examples have been found anywhere of the deeply laid road beds and cambered surfaces of the Roman roads. Even the undersides of their interlocking polygonal surface stones were cut like diamonds, so that they lodged firmly in the final layer of sand and gravel beneath. They were raised above the surrounding land and their foundations were so strong that they could in fact double up as ramparts, defining boundaries. The Fosse Way from Lincoln to Axmouth is a good example. It was an early border-line drawn across Britain, before the Romans moved north to Hadrian's Wall and the Antonine Wall across Scotland.

No natural obstacle was too great for the Roman road-makers. Embankments were built across marshes, bridges over rivers and tunnels bored through mountains. When Gaius Julius Lacer built a bridge to carry the road over the River Tagus in Portugal, he dedicated it to the Emperor Trajan (98–117 AD) and inscribed it with the words: 'Pontem Perpetui Mansurum in Saecula', I have built a bridge which will last throughout the centuries. How right he was. The six arches of that giant bridge still tower 158 feet above the River Tagus and they still carry the road.

MOTIVATION FOR TRAVEL

In the centuries before the laying of the Roman roads, people's motives for travel fell into five main categories:

1. They travelled on business, their own or their government's. I include military service under this heading.
2. They travelled to shrines and spas for health reasons. The temple of Aesculapius, the Greek god of healing, in Pergamum was particularly popular, especially during the period when the great physician Galen held his surgeries there.
3. They travelled to attend festivals and games, such as the Olympics and the great dramatic competitions in honour of Dionysius in Athens. As these festivals were religious, as well as sporting and dramatic, their appeal was enormous, the equivalent of combining today's World Cup with the Easter Celebrations in Rome. In fact, the crowds at these ancient gatherings were so notorious that one master threatened his recalcitrant slave: 'If you don't behave yourself, I'll take you to the Olympic Games!'
4. They travelled as pilgrims to temples, to sacrifice, to pray and to seek the guidance of oracles.
5. Finally, they travelled for cultural enlightenment, for academic purposes or simply out of curiosity. They were tourists, as we know from their graffiti. One of the earliest, on a pyramid wall, is dated 1244 BC. It reads: 'Hadnakhte, scribe of the treasury, came to make an excursion and amuse himself to the west of Memphis, together with his brother, Panakhti, scribe to the Vizier.'

All those who scratched their names on monuments were scribes, as scribes were the only people who knew how to write. The Greeks were keen on sight-seeing too, and they used the excellent Persian roads to travel as far as India. Even Alexander the Great, whose main purpose was war, took cartographers and draughtsmen in his train to record what they saw, and botanists to collect specimens for his old tutor, Aristotle, in his retirement in Athens. Herodotus, the Father of History, carried out his researches in Egypt and possibly the Sudan, across large parts of Asia Minor, and in the north as far as the Black Sea and Scythia. He delighted in his travels, as is clear from the verve of his writing.

Overland travel was arduous and longer journeys were undertaken wherever possible by river and sea, despite the expense of voyages and their attendant perils. Once the Roman roads were in place and well policed, travel became possible for any free man with modest resources and the necessary time. Latin was spoken from the Atlantic to the shores of the Black Sea, and Greek from there to Babylon. Roman law protected the traveller and Roman coinage was honoured throughout the empire and even beyond. The world had never known such security.

The Romans built their roads to serve their own strategic ends. It is only in the light of history that we realise their full significance. By these roads, the Romans gave the world its freedom, the freedom to move about in safety, for work or pleasure. A man had only to tie his sandals and pick up his scrip, and the civilised world was his oyster.

As a result, there was a boom in all the five categories of travel, and the Romans added a sixth. They invented the holiday. Their favourite resorts were the Bay of Naples, Sorrento and Capri, where they spent their summers fishing, sailing, bathing in the thermal springs, riding along the sands in litters, watching the gladiators and giving dinner parties. So many of the wealthy built villas out over the sea that, according to the poet Horace, the fish were cramped for space. Poorer Romans would take a room in a boarding-house. They all wanted souvenirs: excavations have revealed large numbers of drinking-glasses, engraved with the sights of the bay. Some Roman holiday-makers even travelled as far as the coast of Spain, Tarragona being the smartest resort, especially for a winter break. Then there were the spas at Vichy, Aix-en-Provence, Bath and Wiesbaden. All had their devotees. The Romans travelled extensively and enjoyed it.

To help them on their journeys, they had guide books and maps. 'There is but one entrance to the Acropolis,' wrote Pausanias in the second century. 'The monumental gateway has a roof of white marble, and for the beauty and size of the blocks it has never yet been matched. On the right of the gateway is a temple of Wingless Victory.' It could be Baedecker or the Guide Bleu. By great good fortune, a medieval copy of a Roman map has come down to us, the Tabula Peutingeria. Drawn on a sheet of parchment over twenty-two feet long, it gives a schematic picture of the Roman road system with distances marked and symbols for easy reference. For example, there was a square for a high-class inn; a twin-peaked roof for a more modest one; and a single-peaked box for a flea-pit. Sometimes, map and souvenir were combined in one article. Travellers along Rome's longest continuous road, the Via Herculanea to Cadiz, could buy small silver beakers, which listed the towns on their route and served as their guide.

Going on a pilgrimage was always popular. In the early days, the Romans visited Troy and followed the fortunes of the Greeks and Trojans with the aid of their copies of the Iliad; and they travelled to the temples and oracles of Classical Greece. When the Empire turned Christian, the tradition of pilgrimage survived, though the destinations changed. What had once been a trickle of sightseers to the Holy Land became a flood of the devout, led by Constantine's mother, Helena, who discovered the True Cross. They walked to Jerusalem, Bethlehem, the Mount of Olives and even the Sinai Desert. In the Middle Ages, pilgrims also travelled towards Rome, and they journeyed on foot or horseback to the great cathedrals and shrines of Christian Europe. However they still tramped the Roman roads to get there.

PILGRIMS ON THE SILK ROAD

The Silk Road did not lend itself so readily to mass travel. It passed through some of the world's most inhospitable regions, the Gobi and Taklamakan Deserts with their howling winds and their reputation for evil spirits, the steppes of Central Asia, the Pamirs and the Himalayas. No one risked it without a serious purpose and its main uses were always those for which it was originally designed: military and commercial. Even today, it is not a journey to be undertaken lightly.

Yet, despite all its hardships, the Silk Road became a major pilgrim route. Buddhism began to filter through from India to China in the first century, and by the fourth century it was well established there. But the Chinese worried about the authenticity of their Buddhist teaching. In 399 AD the first Buddhist pilgrim to have left a record of his journey, the monk Fa-hsien, braved the Taklamakan and the Himalayas to visit the sites sacred to the Buddha and to bring back Buddhist texts for translation from their original Pali. He was the first of a steady flow from China to India. Along another branch of the Silk Road, Nestorian Christians, Jews, Manichaeans and Zoroastrians entered China and even made a few converts. The religion which finally superseded Buddhism was Islam. It was introduced by Arab traders during the Tang Dynasty (618–907 AD) and today the minority peoples of Western China are Muslim. As the pilgrimage to Mecca is one of the Pillars of Islam, the Silk Road acquired another flock of devout travellers.

It was not only religions and luxury goods which travelled between east and west. The Silk Road was the channel for cross-cultural exchange on a grand scale, for the sharing of advances in mathematics, astronomy, architecture, medicine and the skills of war, fashions in art, the development of musical instruments, ceramics and glass; even the dissemination of many flowers and fruits which today we take for granted. The Chinese were generous with most of their inventions; their paper, printing and gunpowder transformed the western world. Wisely they clung on to the secrets of silk, their greatest source of wealth. Even when the Middle East began to produce it, around the sixth century, it was rough in texture and there was still a ready market for 'Chinese woven wind' as the Indians so poetically called it.

By the end of the eighth century, the Arabs had mastered the sea-routes from the Red Sea and the Persian Gulf to the port of Canton. In the late fifteenth century, the Portuguese rounded the Cape of Good Hope and opened up a direct sea-passage from Europe to China. That was the end of the perilous Silk Road as a transcontinental highway. The Roman roads fared better. They continued in use as the unchallenged communications network of Northern Europe and the countries of the Mediterranean seaboard until the advent of railways and commercial airlines.

FUTURE PILGRIMS ON OLD ROADS

And what of the future? It seems to me that tourism is in crisis. Florence now attracts 50,000 visitors a day in 500 coaches, which are triple-parked along the banks of the Arno. Farmers in Goa and Thailand are deprived of water for their fields, so that holiday hotels may provide unlimited showers. Firms are advertising inexpensive five-day trips to Petra, where the crowds, trampling over that confined and vulnerable site, turn it daily into a sort of Wembley Stadium. Early retirement, redundancy on generous terms and longer holidays for those in employment have all increased the amount of time available for travel and most people, unfortunately, flock to the same places. We are in danger of loving our cultural and environmental heritage to death.

Yet there are faint, but encouraging, signs of change. Parties of schoolchildren on visits to stately homes dress up in the costumes of the period and do its chores. Historical theme parks take visitors back in time to get a taste of what life was really like in a medieval dungeon or an Elizabethan dockyard. There is a growing wish to participate, to

10

empathise, to be something more than an alien observer, peering at landscapes and buildings through a coach window.

There are signs too that the seaside holiday is losing its appeal. Mindless roasting on the beach has suffered a blow from the growing incidence of skin-cancer. Even the young Apollos of Bondai Beach have taken to surfing in wet suits and their girlfriends have left the sands for their own, more active pursuits. We are becoming more health-conscious.

We are also beginning to discern a spiritual vacuum in our lives. Religious pilgrimages to Lourdes and Santiago de Compostela are attracting ever larger numbers; India and its religions draw seekers after enlightenment; retreats and work amongst the dispossessed are seen as meaningful alternatives to traditional holidays. We live in a secular age, so we have added the cultural and environmental pilgrimage: walking through the Cevennes in the steps of Stevenson, following the development of Italian Renaissance art through Tuscany, sailing with Captain Cook across the Pacific, or going on expeditions to save the rain forests.

Against this background, the great roads of the world could take on a new significance. They are resonant with history, with the struggles, the faith and the aspirations of those who built them and trod them. Only the slow, thoughtful traveller is in tune with those resonances. To travel their roads in the old ways, on foot, on a horse, or its modern equivalent, the bicycle, is to participate to some extent in the struggles of our ancestors and their great achievements. It takes an hour to fly the California Trail over the Utah and Nevada Deserts and the snow-capped Sierra Nevada, an hour in a plane with in-flight entertainment and food and drink on a tray. Three hours suffice for the Gobi, the Taklamakan and the Himalayas, a five-month ordeal on a camel. I have travelled both those routes on a bicycle, through desert heat and mountain blizzard, and I feel that I have to some extent shared the experience of those early settlers and traders, in a way which would not have been possible by any other means.

Those are perhaps extreme examples which would never appeal to the public at large. The Roman roads of Europe are less taxing and could be made attractive to the growing numbers of people who want participation. I can think of nothing more delightful than the winter ride I took round the shores of the Mediterranean, following the Via Herculanea from Rome to Cadiz. There was sunshine all the way, flowers and blossoms along the Riviera, vineyards and Roman cities in Provence, the craggy shoulder of the Pyrenees and the Spanish Costas out of season. All that, plus the excitement of setting out from the Forum, like a Roman traveller with his silver mug in his hand, and the satisfaction of finally wheeling across the causeway into Cadiz, once the greatest port in the world. The thought that I was making the journey on the world's greenest and most energy-efficient machine added greatly to the pleasure.

Apart from its intrinsic merits, the modern pilgrimage has the virtue of dispersal. The 50,000 tourists who pour into Florence every day would cause scarcely a ripple if they were spread along the 1,745 miles between Rome and Cadiz. The life of the people would continue without disruption; the country would be unspoilt; and local provision would be adequate without the need to build monster hotels.

Of course, there are practical problems. The simplest one to address is the cost of travel to and from the beginning and end of routes. Linear travel is at present punished by exorbitant single fares and carriers would need to be encouraged to adapt their price-structures.

Then there is the problem of financial incentive. It is obviously more profitable, as well as logistically simpler, to funnel large groups of tourists into one resort, in one conveyance, and keep them there. The next best thing is to contain them in a coach and send them off on a well-worn tourist circuit. Only a few travel firms have so far risen to the challenge of arranging tours for cyclists and walkers. Yet, in the new millennium, it is just this kind of niche market which may well be the salvation of the tour-operators. Cultural pilgrims do not need to mortify the flesh and there is no reason why walkers and cyclists should not be accommodated, wined and dined in style; the returns for the operator on quality packages could be quite acceptable. A few people, like myself, relish the complete freedom of setting out with no plans, no schedule, no bookings, and taking each day as it comes. Most people prefer a guaranteed bed for the night and a courier to solve their problems. There will always be a need for the tour-operator, but he may have to be more flexible.

Then there is the matter of promotion. The Council of Europe is promoting cultural itineraries, UNESCO is working on the Silk Road, and private organisations like the Confraternity of St James of Compostela and the Friends of the Pony Express Trail, are helping prospective pilgrims. So far, the potential of these long journeys has not attracted the attention of the paid image makers.

Modern pilgrimage is an exciting possibility, of benefit both to the pilgrim and to our cultural and environmental heritage. Much work needs to be done if it is to take its rightful place in the tourism of the future, and that is work for the experts. I just ride my bicycle.

The Author

Anne Mustoe has a degree in Classics from the University of Cambridge. She has pursued a varied career in industry, education and as an independent tour operator, specialising in visits to Classical sites in Italy, Greece, Turkey and North Africa. She has served as President of the Girls' Schools Association, Chairman of the Independent Schools Information Service and as a Justice of the Peace in Suffolk. In 1987, she gave up her post as Headmistress of St Flex School, Southward, to cycle alone round the world from west to east, following historical routes. She has since cycled from the north to the south of India; and round the world a second time, from east to west, always on historical tracks. Between journeys, she combines educational consultancy with work as a travel writer and lecturer.

References

Carry, M., *A History of Rome*, MacMillan, 1935

Casein, L., *Travel in the Ancient World*, George Allen and Unwin, 1974

Frank, I. X. and Brownstone, D. M., *The Silk Road*, Facts on File Publications, 1986

Herodotus, *The Histories*, Penguin Books, 1954

Mustoe, A., *A Bike Ride: 12,000 miles around the World*, Virgin Books, 1991

Mustoe, A., *Lone Traveller*, Swan Hill, 1998

Polo, M., *The Travels*, Penguin Books, 1958

Von Hagen, V. W., *The Roads that led to Rome*, Wiedenfeld and Nicholson, 1967

The Garden of Gethsemane as seen by pilgrims to the Holy Land in the 1860s.

2

IN SEARCH OF HOLY PLACES
Then and Now

John Wilkinson

For the purpose of this paper, I wish I could present myself as a prophet or a philosopher. I regret to say that I am neither, but I do have some practical experience as a former member of staff of St George's College in Jerusalem. There we ran adult short courses about the Holy Land, and I got a lot of experience as a guide. Then a war broke out and the courses had to stop. During this time I also translated some early accounts of pilgrimage, which gave me a glimpse into the mind of the traveller in those days. The human mind and our motivation for travel have not changed much since, and my general conclusion is that there are some general principles of good guiding which are equally applicable now as they were then.

REAL OR IMAGINED AUTHENTICITY

When thinking about Holy Places there seems to be a competition between what is true and what is acceptable. Let us start by examining a poster, written almost nine centuries ago. It was to be displayed in a port like Brindisi, from which ships sailed towards Jerusalem. It started with these words:

> Any one who may wish to go to Jerusalem, the Holy City, should continue to travel eastwards, the direction in which, by God's guidance, he will reach Jerusalem.

So far this is simply transport doing its public relations, with the emphasis on the other end of the journey. The rest of the poster-text is an itinerary, and here is a sample passage:

> And south of Jerusalem, about four miles away, is Bethlehem, the city of David in which Christ was born, and the Well over which the star descended, which had led the Magi to worship the Child.

It was quite easy for would-be travellers to check the truth about the journey. They had only to consult those who had returned from pilgrimage. What about the poster's historical truth? Christ was certainly born in Bethlehem, but what about 'the Well over which the star descended'? Modern biblical scholars might find this detail doubtful. In 1100, the year when the poster was compiled, all the Churches in the Holy Land thought the well was authentic. So in 1100 this statement of fact was acceptable, and quite harmless too, if it simply served to recall the Magi.

CUSTOMER CARE AND CUSTOMER CONTROL

The first holy places, mentioned in the second century AD, are the cave where Christ was born and Golgotha where he was crucified. There are some brief reports of pilgrimage to Jerusalem in the third century. It is only from the fourth century that fuller accounts of pilgrimage have been preserved for us.

Strictly speaking, at this early date we cannot yet call the journeys 'pilgrimages'. The modern word 'pilgrim' derives from the Latin, *peregrinus*, which only meant 'traveller', and it simply meant this till the late twelfth century. Before that date one could of course have differentiated between a traveller and a pilgrim, for a pilgrim was a person who 'went to a place in order to pray there'. It was only in the late twelfth century that the word *peregrinus* came to have the additional meaning of 'pilgrim'.

The churches took great care of people who 'went to a place in order to pray there'. In the fourth century Egeria, possibly a nun, wrote a marvellous account of her pilgrimage. She went to various ecclesiastical districts to visit the Holy Places. In each of them she seems to have been met by a clergyman who showed her round, and conducted the bible readings and prayers there.

For instance, Egeria went to the place on the River Jordan where John had been baptising. She was taken there by a clergyman. He said a prayer and then read the piece of the Bible which begins: 'John also was baptising at Aenon near to Salim'. Then he said a psalm and perhaps another prayer.

Egeria was constantly delighted that the clergy were present in all the Holy Places. They would welcome people and show them the sites. They would pray with them and perhaps give them a small present known as a 'blessing'. This must have been the result of agreement among the church authorities to be benevolent hosts to the pilgrims.

Coming to today, I think that the people most like the pilgrims of Egeria's time are the Orthodox villagers who come from Cyprus. They stick to Orthodoxy and do not take much notice of other Churches. They are chiefly concerned with the discipline of prayer at the Holy Places and meeting the monks. A priest from the Greek Orthodox Church in Jerusalem knows the right places. He goes round with them and says the prayers.

They travel by bus, but apart from this method of transport, they might well have been doing the same things five hundred or a thousand years ago. They take back to Cyprus various gifts from the Holy Land, including the shroud in which they will be buried, with pictures of the crucifixon, the taking down from the Cross, and the Holy Sepulchre.

Today's pilgrims from western Europe or from the USA between them have many forms of belief and devotional systems. So, like the Cypriots choice of an Orthodox priest they naturally want a leader whose views about Christianity they can respect. So one of the features of the travel agents' publicity is the choice of a guide. Here is an example:

> April 25 led by the Rev. Ann
> May 30 led by Fr McCabe
> June 3 led by the Rev. James

The fact that Christians have a choice of their leaders is a sign that in their own small way they are trying to continue the discipline of prayer in places they anticipate as being solemn and holy.

And it should not be forgotten that we, like the early pilgrims in the Holy Land, have to travel to a place which we are bound to find is foreign. It is not so out-of-the-way that our journey is threatened, like the pilgrims of long ago, by pirates or highwaymen. We have to come to terms with the fact that a place, very familiar from the Bible, somehow looks very different in real life.

So an extra important person on your pilgrimage is the guide. He or she should be friendly enough to make you think of the guide as one of the few people you can turn to in his strange country. He should explain the foreignness of the place. And this is a task which a guide has to do over and over again with each new group.

Being hospitable to the newcomer is not simply good professional conduct, but it is essential to the educational value of guiding. Only in this way can a guide get to know the group well enough to judge what message they are likely to welcome. Good Holy Land guides have these skills. Even so there are others. Tourists complain that some Holy Land guides are bored with the sites, discourage prayer, and are only anxious to push their political propaganda.

A Holy Land guide has to be every bit as expert as a guide in any other country. A Holy Land guide has to choose between explaining, or deliberately not explaining, archaeological excavations. Of course the guides have been taught about archaeology, and may be tempted to talk about it. Not many newcomers can judge what the site was like by seeing an excavation. For instance, the excavation at Jericho, now forty years old, is very hard to understand. So perhaps, if there are a few things which are intelligible, the guide might concentrate on them. Where the site is totally unintelligible it is best to concentrate on something other than archaeology like its geographical position, which will enable visitors to understand, and identify with, what to them is a foreign setting.

PRAYER VERSUS HISTORY

Let us look more closely at the tradition of prayer. In Jerusalem some people claim that Jesus Christ was buried at the Holy Sepulchre and others say at the Garden Tomb. What effect does this have on prayer? The Garden Tomb is outside the present walled city of Jerusalem, and is an old rock tomb in a quiet garden. The Holy Sepulchre has no garden. It is an unattractive church inside the city, hemmed in by town buildings.

Small wonder that many people, left to themselves, would choose to pray at the Garden Tomb. To them it looks and feels right, and they do not particularly mind whether it is or is not historically authentic. This is the opposite of the situation with the guides. In their case an unintelligible archaeological site had to be side-stepped or bypassed. In this particular case the very attractive Garden Tomb is a wonderful place for prayer. Nevertheless, as the wardens of the place are legally bound to tell you, it is improbable that it was Christ's tomb. The unattractive Church of the Holy Sepulchre certainly goes back to the second century AD, and very likely back to the Gospels themselves. It is extremely hard to visualise the place of Christ's tomb as being there, and so crowded that it may be hard to find a quiet place to pray.

ELASTICITY OF TRADITION

I once guided a group of New Testament professors round the Holy Land. In Galilee I pointed out the village called Meshhed. There, I told them, was Nebi Yunis, the Tomb of the Prophet Jonah. On our way southward I showed them dozens of other things. When we reached a point 85 miles from Meshhed I pointed out in the village of Halhul Nebi Yunis, another Tomb of the same Prophet Jonah.

Are these two Tombs of Jonah competing with each other, like the Holy Sepulchre and the Garden Tomb? The local residents do not look at them this way. These two Tombs are among the places held holy by the local people. Certainly at present they are venerated by people who are nominally Muslims, and Muslims commonly venerate the tombs of notable people, whether they are prophets, teachers or martyrs. Tombs were there in the Holy Land a long time before the dawn of Islam. Jerome speaks of them two hundred years before the birth of Muhammad.

In fact a similar reverence for tombs goes back into the Old Testament. People then could venerate tombs of the same person in two different places, So the Book of Samuel said that the Tomb of Rachel was 'at Zelzah in the territory of Benjamin'. Genesis places Rachel's death at Ephratah in Judah, where the present tomb is now pointed out.

In the Holy Land it is very easy to find tombs with biblical names inscribed on them. For instance, about two years ago some bone-boxes were discovered, with the names of Jesus, Mary and Joseph, however biblical names are extremely common. An equivalent discovery in England might be tombs with the names Smith, Jones, Robinson and Brown.

Nevertheless from the fourth century we have solemnly-told accounts of similar discoveries. When Egeria was in the city called Carneas, she heard of a desert monk who was given a message from God. He went to tell it to the Bishop of Carneas who collected some men. The monk showed them where to dig.

> As they dug they at first discovered a cave, then, following it in for about a hundred yards they suddenly came upon a piece of stone. When they had thoroughly uncovered it they found carved on its lid the name JOB. *Travels 16, 6.*

In my view, one takes a wild chance if one identifies an inscribed biblical name with a biblical figure.

The desire to pray at biblical places sometimes overrides accurate history. How often is *sometimes*? Is a pilgrimage to Jerusalem an exercise in pure imagination, like a trip to Disneyland? There are some undoubtedly real places, like the Pools of Bethesda, where Jesus healed the paralytic. Unfortunately only the two plastered pools are left, the parts which were underground, and we cannot tell where the healing took place.

We also know that Jesus was in the Temple. The outer perimeter walls are still there as they were built by the Herods. Even a gate has been left. We can thus judge what the disciples meant when they said: 'Master, see what manner of stones and buildings are here'. However these walls only surrounded the temple court. The Temple itself has been thoroughly destroyed, and has been replaced by Muslim monuments.

During his time as Prefect, Pontius Pilate was the supreme authority in Judaea and Samaria, and in that sense succeeded to the authority of the Jewish kings like Herod the Great. Pilate's main residence was at Caesarea. When he was in Jerusalem he chose as his Praetorium the palace of Herod the Great. We know exactly where this was. Somewhere here he tried Jesus. Apart from one great tower, the palace too has been deliberately destroyed.

Anyone who has tried to present heritage sites in the most effective way, will understand these difficulties. You are bound to ask what kind of archaeological and material traces a famous man might leave behind him.

I can answer this in one way for the Holy Land, but no doubt there are others. I shall use the words of the first pilgrim to describe his journey, the Pilgrim of Bordeaux, writing in 333 AD. He is leaving the city of Jerusalem, and about to cross the Kidron Valley and climb the Mount of Olives. I would like you to attend particularly to the humble objects which mark the Holy Places:

> Arriving at the gate of Jerusalem which faces the east, on your way to go up the Mount of Olives, you come to what is called the Valley of Jehoshaphat. On the left is a vineyard, where is also the rock where Judas Iscariot betrayed Christ; and on the right is the palm-tree from which the children took branches and strewed them in Christ's path.

The gate from which the journey starts is today in the same place as when the Bordeaux pilgrim had seen it. As you go down the path you first see a rock in a vineyard. The vineyard was identified as biblical Gethsemane and the rock as the place where the Gospels say Judas kissed Jesus and betrayed him. On the right is the palm-tree, identified as the very tree from which the Gospels say the branches were laid before Jesus, riding into Jerusalem on his donkey. It would be too much to suppose that that rock and that vineyard and that palm-tree were in the correct biblical places. Indeed this area had been devastated by the Roman army in 70 AD. The Bible also gives us a rough idea about their location. They were at least quite close to the right places.

GUIDING THEN AND NOW

When I started work at St George's College, the first thing I wanted to do was to find out which traditional holy places were real. The course members wanted something different. It was OK to pray at the Holy Places, but not painstakingly to analyse them. They were more interested in the strange country in which they found themselves. They wanted to know about its seasons, its animals and its harvests.

Was this really pilgrimage? A description of Egeria's pilgrimage gave me an answer:

> First, with great industry, Egeria perused all the books of the Old and New Testaments, and discovered all its descriptions of the holy wonders of the world, its regions, provinces, cities, mountains and deserts. Then in eager haste (though it was to take many years) she set out with God's help to explore them.

Egeria's range moved on beyond the Holy Places in the direction of bible study. I now agree that the ideal modern pilgrimage should contain prayer at the Holy Places and bible study, a combination of acceptability and, as far as we can get it, of truth.

I started pursuing my interest in early pilgrimage to Jerusalem as a historical subject, but soon I discovered that being a good guide is more than being an objective historian. I now realise that guiding visitors successfully depends on some permanent values. I have so far identified three such values from my experience in the Holy Land which seem to me to be equally applicable to sites in any other country. Egeria says what a great effort it was to climb Mount Sinai:

> You don't go round and round the mountains, spiralling up gently, but straight at each one as if you were going up a wall. Though I had to go up them on foot I was not conscious of the effort – in fact I hardly noticed it because, by God's will, I was seeing my hopes coming true.

Her hopes were to see the places which she had read about in the Bible and to pray in them. She was serious about these places and regarded them with respect. The same can be said about people who visit heritage sites. They are usually respectful enough of history to take the places where it happened seriously.

This is a warning to me as a guide. The group will not judge me mercifully unless I show respect for the places I am describing. This does not mean I should not make any jokes, but ideally I should love the place. If I do not respect the places, I am likely to disappoint the aspirations and legitimate hopes of those who are in the place for the first time.

Earlier this year, my wife went away for a week to look at some gardens in Italy. She wanted to make the most of her visit, and for two weeks before she boarded the aeroplane she read books about the gardens. She was like Egeria, who, as you remember, had prepared her ground by reading the whole Bible. The message after 'respect the places' then is 'respect the history'.

As a guide with a new group, I cannot tell what academic or technical experience the members might have. There may be experts on geography or botany or rainfall – let alone history. Egeria gives a splendid example of this when she goes to Edessa. The Bishop gave her a copy of the letter which Abgar, King of Edessa, wrote to Jesus, and Jesus' reply, which converted the city. Egeria was already an expert:

> One thing specially please me. I received from this holy man the copies of Abgar's letter to the Lord, and the Lord's letter to Abgar, which during the prayers the holy man had read to us. I have copies of them at home... And it may be that what we have at home is not complete, because what I was given here was certainly longer. So, dearest ladies, you yourselves must read them when I come home, if such is the will of Jesus our God.

As a guide, I can never know too much about the places I explain, and, whether I know it or not, mistakes will be picked up.

The good guide goes a bit further than this. He soon sees the level at which the group as a whole displays interest, and he starts at that level. He might go forward from there, but it depends on the group. There may well be an expert in the group who interests the guide, but if his contributions bore the group, the guide should make time to discuss with the expert on his own. On the job the guide is not a researcher but a teacher. He is not there to reel out a long list of facts, but rather to set a tinder to the mind and imagination of the group.

Egeria was not a great expert in describing views. Her main interest is in the people. They knew a lot about the places. In addition, she constantly says how kind they were. The Bishop of the city of Arabia, Egeria tells us:

> is now a man of some age, of a godly life since the time when he became a monk, and an approachable man, who is very good at welcoming pilgrims, and very knowledgeable about God's Scriptures.

So, to me, as a guide, the third message is 'respect the customer'. Egeria speaks so warmly about her guides that she must have been a model customer. You and I have often seen more difficult ones, so I have to remind myself of the status of the guide. On a purely material level the difficult ones are contributing as much money to the guide as the easy ones. The guide is not equal to the group. He is being paid to serve them.

So, however learned he or she may be, and however dedicated to educating the group, the guide is there to give sensitive service. This is appreciated more than anything. Here is what Egeria says about the monk of Mount Sinai:

> I cannot do enough to express my gratitude to all the holy men who so kindly and willingly welcomed to their cells a person of such little importance as me, and, what more, took me all round the biblical sites I wanted to see.

My study of early pilgrimage has given me three values: respect the places, respect the history, respect the visitor. These three are still the values of a successful travel business.

The Author

John Wilkinson read classics and theology at Merton College, Oxford. He was ordained a priest of the Church of England, and was sent by the Archbishop of Canterbury to the Catholic University of Louvain. In 1961, he went to teach at the new adult education college in Jerusalem, and spent altogether nine years there, with a break of six years as a missionary society editor. He wrote translations of early pilgrim writings, and a book called *Jerusalem as Jesus knew it*. During his teaching, he took an interest in the art and architecture of the Holy Land, and on return to London, studied for another degree at the Courtauld Institute. His final post in Jerusalem was as a Director of the British School of Archaeology for six years, followed by a fellowship in Byzantine

Studies at Dumbarton Oaks, Washington DC. He is presently writing a book on the design of synagogues and churches.

References

Avigad, N., *Discovering Jerusalem,* Thomas Nelson, Nashville Tennessee, 1983 (for an account of the Jewish Quarter excavation)

Benoit, P., *Jesus and the Gospel,* Darton, Longman and Todd, London, 1973 (for the Praetorium)

Ousterhout, R. (ed.), *The Blessings of Pilgrimage,* University of Illinois Press, 1990

Wilkinson, J., *Egeria's Travels to the Holy Land,* Translations of Egeria and the pilgrim of Bordeaux, Ariel Press, Jerusalem, revised 1981

Wilkinson, J., Hill, J. and Ryan, W.F., *Jerusalem Pilgrimage 1099–1185,* Translation of Qualiter, Hakluyt Society, 2.167, London, 1988

3

THE APOSTLE OF SCOTLAND
Was it Ninian or Columba?

Ian Bradley

Those of you brought up in a less politically correct culture may conceivably share my view that the greatest show ever given us by the BBC Light Entertainment Department was the Black and White Minstrels. While their removal from our television screens in the mid 1970s was, perhaps, understandable, their removal from the airwaves was bizarre. You may recall that the signature tune of their weekly programme on what then still rejoiced in the name of the Light Programme was a particularly fine slow and syncopated antiphonal version of 'When the saints go marching in'. What I propose to offer you here is, in a sense, an account of the slow and antiphonal battle as to whom should be regarded as the evangelist of Scotland? Specifically, I want to examine the claims of the two who are normally accorded that accolade: Ninian of Galloway and Columba of Iona.

In looking at the claims of these two undoubtedly great founding fathers in the early story of Christianity in Northern Britain, let us begin by reminding ourselves of what is perhaps the best known early account of their activities: a passage that has been the foundation for many of the claims that have subsequently been made about them. It comes from *The Ecclesiastical History of the English Nation* written around 730 by the Northumbrian monk, the Venerable Bede, from his monastery in Jarrow:

> In the year of our Lord 565 there came from Ireland to Britain a priest and abbot named Columba, a true monk in life no less than in habit; he came to Britain to preach the word of God to the kingdoms of the northern Picts which are separated from the southern part of their land by steep and rugged mountains. The southern Picts who

25

live on this side of the mountains had, so it is said, long ago given up the errors of idolatry and received the true faith through the preaching of the Word by that most reverend and holy man Bishop Ninian, a Briton who had received orthodox instruction at Rome in the faith and the mysteries of the truth. His episcopal see is celebrated for its church, dedicated to St Martin, where his body rests, together with those of many other saints. This place which is in the kingdom of Bernicia is commonly called Whithorn, the White House, because Ninian built a church of stone there, using a method unusual among the Britons.[1]

Bede's words, which were written at least 100 years after Columba's death, have been highly influential in determining the popular impression of how Scotland was evangelised. They suggest that Columba was responsible for bringing Christianity to the northern Picts, ie those living in the northern and western Highlands and in Aberdeenshire north of the Mounth (the upland ridge which skirts the Dee Valley from Lochnagar to Aberdeen). The southern Picts, inhabiting Perthshire, Angus, Fife and the lands around the Forth, had earlier been converted by Ninian, a shadowy figure for whom our only sources apart from Bede, are an eighth century poem and a twelfth century life by Ailred of Rievaulx. As a result of Bede's account, Columba and Ninian have posthumously vied for the accolade of being hailed as the True Apostle of Scotland. Scholars have championed one or the other in a somewhat unedifying academic wrangle which has often owed more to sectarian prejudices and ecclesiastical partisanship than to the interests of historical truth.

Columba has found favour with enthusiasts for all things Celtic and with those who have seen him as establishing a proto-Presbyterian church, clearly distinguishable from the episcopally governed church favoured by the Rome-educated Bishop Ninian. Ninian's champions, on the other hand, have been drawn particularly from those with an anti-Irish agenda who have wanted to stress the Britishness of the native Galloway saint and emphasise the indigenous nature of early missionary activity in Scotland.

The debate over which Saint should be seen as the principal evangelist of Scotland was particularly lively in the early decades of this century. Leading the pro-Columban camp was William Watson, Professor of Celtic at Edinburgh University, who underlined the Irish contribution in the Christianising of Scotland and enthusiastically followed Bede in crediting the conversion of the northern Picts to Columba. Ranged against him were a trio of Presbyterian scholars. Dr Douglas Simpson, librarian of the University of Aberdeen, Archibald Scott, Church of Scotland minister in Kildonan (Helmsdale) and Frank Knight, United Free Church minister and keen archaeologist. Scott, who could not forgive the Irish for failing to fight with the British in the First World War, in which his brother had been killed, was in no doubt as to the primacy of 'Ninian the Great' over Columba. He regarded the 'great mission' undertaken by the Briton as the key event in the early Christian history of Scotland, leading directly to the establishment of what was to remain the sole church of the Picts until the time of Kenneth MacAlpin in the mid-ninth century.[2]

Douglas Simpson was even more enthusiastic in his championship of Ninian and his dismissal of Columba. Holding that the Irish saint's political activities were 'consistently directed against the Pictish King and people', he held that 'long before Columba's time, Christianity was widely spread among the Picts'.[3] The key agent of this early evangelisation of Highland and northern Scotland had been Ninian. On the basis of church dedications Simpson argued that the British saint had travelled from Galloway via Glasgow and Stirling to Dunottar and Methlick in the north east and Glenurquhart in the Highlands. In his view, indeed, Ninian got as far north as Caithness and Shetland.

More recent and less partisan scholarship has seriously challenged, if not completely exploded, the arguments of Scott and Simpson and has suggested a much more limited role for Ninian. Charles Thomas, Professor of Archaeology at Leicester and one of the leading contemporary authorities on Christianity in Britain in the period between 300 and 700 has cast grave doubts on Simpson's assertions about the extent of Ninian's travels by demonstrating that many of the church dedications which he took to be contemporary were in fact made several centuries after the Saint's death.[4]

In a recent book John MacQueen, former Director of the School of Scottish Studies at Edinburgh University has argued that Ninian was largely active in the areas of Dumfries, Bernicia (the Borders) and possibly in Renfrewshire and Stirling and that he did not penetrate significantly into areas occupied by the Picts. There is some literary evidence from relatively earlier sources that Ninian may have got to Glasgow, specifically to Cadder, and it is also quite possible that he penetrated into the Forth Valley as far as the Stirling area. It seems very unlikely, to say the least, that he got any further north or east than this. Certainly archaeological finds show no evidence for Christianity in the Pictish heartlands of the Highlands, the north east and the north of Scotland until the sixth century at the very earliest.

The dating of Ninian and the nature of the church with which he was involved have also been the subject of considerable controversy over the last few years. There is uncertainty as to how soon after the departure of the Romans from Britain he appeared on the scene and whether the church in Galloway of which he appears to have been a bishop, with its centre at

Whithorn, was a surviving offshoot of Roman Christianity, possibly linked to ecclesiastical centres further south such as Carlisle or even York, or an early example of indigenous British Christianity. We know from archaeological evidence that a Christian settlement existed at Whithorn at least from the mid-fifth century: the Latinus stone, apparently marking the grave of a father and daughter, which was found there, can be dated to this period and is, in fact, the earliest Christian memorial in Scotland. What is not clear, even from Bede's account, is whether Ninian actually founded the church at Whithorn, which is certainly an earlier ecclesiastical and monastic site than Iona, or how long before Columba he lived.

For long it was thought that Ninian was a contemporary of Martin of Tours, the Hungarian-born saint who brought Eastern monasticism to the West and who died in 397. This date was traditionally taken for the foundation of Whithorn, largely on the basis of a remark in the twelfth century *Life of Ninian* by Ailred of Rievaulx (written 500 or 600 years after his death) that news came through of Martin's death as the church there was being built. This gave rise to the idea that Ninian had visited St Martin's monastery in Gaul on the way back from his training and ordination in Rome and had dedicated his own monastic foundation to him when he returned to his native Galloway in the last days of the Roman occupation of Britain.

Modern scholars are almost all of the view that this is too early a dating for Ninian. John MacQueen places him in the first half of the fifth century while still holding on to the traditional view that he founded the church at Whithorn. However, a more recent and highly persuasive article by the Glasgow-based scholar, Dr Alan Macquarrie, argues that Ninian almost certainly belonged to the first half of the sixth century and, as such, overlapped with Columba. In his view, Whithorn was already a thriving monastery and Christian centre when Ninian, who had been born around 493 from the same British Christian stock as Patrick, went there to train. He possibly travelled to Rome, coming back to Britain as a missionary bishop working predominantly south of the Forth, notably in the Borders area around Peebles. Later he possibly returned to Whithorn as Bishop of Galloway, rebuilding the church there and dedicating it to St Martin of Tours, whose cult seems to have been strong among North British Christians.

Several early sources mention Ninian as coming into conflict with Tudwal, a king of Dumbarton, whose reign Dr Macquarrie reckons can be dated fairly accurately to the mid-sixth century. On this interpretation, Ninian died around 563, just 30 years or so before Columba. Like Dr MacQueen and other modern scholars, Dr Macquarrie is convinced that Ninian did not venture beyond southern Scotland. If he did do any preaching or evangelistic work among the Pictish people, then it was with an extreme southern offshoot who lived south of the Forth.[5]

If this recent work somewhat diminishes the importance and primacy of Ninian, it does not establish Columba as the unchallenged Apostle of Scotland. Bede's apparent assertion that Columba evangelised the northern Picts from his base in Iona has also come under a good deal of scholarly attack. It is far from clear whether Columba did in fact spend much of the last 35 years of his life between his arrival on Iona around 563 and his death in 597 traversing Highland and north Scotland, or whether he was based on Iona administering his rapidly growing family of monasteries, exercising a pastoral ministry to the many visitors who came to the island and making occasional forays into the mainland, and indeed back to Ireland.

Was Columba an ecclesiastical administrator or a missionary? Once again, the evidence is conflicting. Some sources portray Columba in the years after 563 as largely remaining on Iona and dividing his time between priestly and pastoral duties, scholarly pursuits and the leadership of the monastic community. This is broadly the picture given by Adamnan although his life records the Saint making frequent trips to Hinba, possibly for regular periods of solitary retreat, and also visits to Skye and Ardnamurchan. On a number of occasions Adamnan describes Columba as journeying to the other side of *Druim Alban* ('the Spine of Scotland' and thought to refer to the Grampian Mountains) and being among the Picts.

There is, in fact, considerable debate among scholars as to how many journeys into Pictish territory Adamnan reports Columba as making. Some are inclined to put the number as high as seven, although Marjorie Anderson, editor of an important edition of Adomnan's Life which first came out in 1961, takes the view that all of his accounts relate to one single expedition made up the Great Glen to Brude's court. Although Adamnan describes a number of individual conversions secured by Columba on his travels, the overall impression is not of missionary activity and certainly not of mass evangelism.

Other sources make much more of Columba's missionary endeavours and portray him as being constantly on the move, converting the heathen people of North Britain. *The Irish Life* perhaps conveys this impression most strongly: 'When Colum Cille had founded Iona he went on a preaching circuit among the Scots and Britons and Saxons, and converted them to faith and belief after he had performed many miracles and raised the dead to life'.[6] The *Amra Choluimb Chille* suggests more specifically that his main missionary field lay among the Picts in central and eastern Scotland (modern Angus and Perthshire), describing him as 'the teacher who would teach the tribes of the Tay' and commenting that:

'His blessing turned them, the mouth of the fierce ones
Who lived on the Tay, to the will of the king.' [7]

This, one has to say, seems very unlikely as does the story in the 12th Century life of Kentigern, that Kentigern and Columba meet on the shores of the Tay and exchanged staffs. We really have no evidence at all that Columba came this far east. Virtually all of Columba's missionary activities, if such they be, seem to have been confined to the Irish colony of Dal Riada, covering modern Argyllshire. If we are assessing Columba's role in the Christianising of what was to become the modern nation of Scotland, I think we should follow his early biographers and regard him less as a missionary or evangelist and more as a planter of churches. This is certainly how Adamnan saw him. In the second preface to his Life he describes Columba as 'the father and founder of monasteries'.

The elegy that appeared a few years after his death refers to him as *cet cell custoit* (the guardian of a hundred churches). This may be an exaggeration but there seems little doubt that he was personally responsible for founding a number of monasteries. In Scotland, apart from Iona, these included communities on Tiree, Hinba and the island of Elen, which has been tentatively identified by Sally Foster as Jura, and on the shores of Loch Awe, significantly all of them within the kingdom of *Dal Riata*. There is also strong evidence that he returned from Iona to Ireland to found a monastery at Durrow around 587. Columba almost certainly established other communities in Ireland, notably at Derry which may well have served as a port of communication between Iona and his monasteries in Ulster.

My remarks so far may seem to have had the effect of downgrading the roles of Ninian and Columba as they have traditionally been portrayed. I would rather see them as placing both men in the context of a more gradual and fragmented process of Christianisation in which many others also took part. The Ninian versus Columba debate has at least produced one beneficial result in reminding us that there were two different movements at work bringing Christianity to 7th century Scotland. The older one came from the British church, centred possibly on Carlisle and with its missionary base in Strathclyde. It sent missionaries westwards into Dumfries and Galloway, eastwards into the Northumbrian controlled Lothians, northwards towards Stirling and possibly into the Pictish lands of Perthshire and Fife.

The other more recent missionary movement came in the wake of the Irish push into western Scotland and spread from its base in *Dal Riata* westwards into the central Highlands and Tayside and north into the Highlands and the north east. Place names can give us much information as to the progress of these two movements. Names with 'eccles' (deriving from the Latin *ecclesia* and the British eglwys) suggest early Christian churches founded under British influence. They are found in considerable numbers across southern Scotland, with a particular concentration in the South West, and up the east coast between the Forth and the Mounth but are hardly found north of the Mounth or west of the Great Glen. Other place names give evidence of early Irish penetration. A good example is Atholl in north Perthshire which derives from *Ath Fthoda*, meaning 'a second Ireland'.

The extent to which these two movements had their early headquarters at Whithorn and Iona respectively is by no means certain. Although Bede states that 'Iona was long the head of all the monasteries of the Picts' there is little evidence that Columba himself planted any monastic communities or churches in the Pictish regions of Perthshire, the Highlands and the north and north east. Bede's remarks probably apply to the period a hundred years or more after the Saint's death when his followers had established communities in Pictish territory and possibly also when churches founded by missionaries not associated with Iona had become absorbed into the increasingly powerful Columban families. It may well be, in fact, that there was a third important movement bringing Christianity to the Picts in the late sixth and early seventh century, quite independent of the British mission from Whithorn and the Irish mission from Iona.

The conversion of those who lived in the region of the Tay may well have been brought about by monks and nuns based at Abernethy. The origins of the monastery there, of which the fine round tower still survives, are shrouded in mystery and it is not clear whether it was founded by British or Irish evangelists, or even as an indigenous Pictish initiative. Three of the lists of Pictish kings assign the foundation of Abernethy to 463, which would conceivably make it earlier than both Whithorn and Iona, but others put it later. Most scholars are inclined to opt for a date during the reign of either Gartnait, who died around 601, or Nechtan, who ruled in the 620s. This later dating is probably the more likely.

There is a tradition that Nechtan founded a church dedicated to St Brigit at Abernethy in the presence of Darlugdach, abbess of Kildare. Alfred Smyth has suggested that this Nechtan also ruled Strathclyde and that he may have founded the house with Irish nuns from Kildare around 625. Whenever it was established, and whether its first members were Irish, British or Picts, there is no doubt that the monastery at Abernethy played a very important role in the evangelisation of Perthshire, Fife and Tayside from at least the early seventh century onwards. I have heard it argued very persuasively that it, rather than Iona, should be regarded as the true cradle of Christianity in Scotland.

What cannot be gainsaid, however, is that Columba (and Ninian if we accept the later dating) were by no means the only Christian missionaries to be active in the vast areas of central and northern Scotland which were occupied by the Picts in the sixth century. Nor were they the first to penetrate these pagan realms. In his seminal two volume study of the archaeological evidence for the early Christianising of Scotland, Frank Knight identified eighty men and women who were actively evangelising the country before Columba had left his native Ireland and 'who had literally covered the land with hundreds of churches before the Iona Mission began.' [8] It is difficult to avoid the conclusion that had they been fortunate enough to have royal blood, find a biographer like Adamnan and forge close links with the family that was to provide Scotland with its ruling dynasty, they too might have become famous names.

Among these early pioneers were several near-contemporaries of Columba who, like him, came from Ireland, apparently on *pergrinatio,* and established monasteries in *Dal Riata.* St Catan, St Moluag and St Blane all hailed from the monastery at Bangor in County Down. Catan founded a community at Kilchattan Bay at the south end of Bute and was possibly also associated with foundations on Colonsay, Islay and Jura. Moluag founded an important monastery at Lismore before working in the Hebrides, notably on Skye and Tiree, and then moving to the mainland where he died possibly at Rosemarkie in Ross-shire in 592.

Blane is traditionally credited with establishing the church at Dunblane, after first setting up a monastery at Kingarth on Bute. According to some accounts, St Machar, associated with preaching to the Picts of Aberdeenshire and founding the church and city of Aberdeen, was one of Columba's original companions on his journey from Donegal. Another of his original companions, if an equally unlikely story is to be believed, was St Donnan, who seems to have evangelised much of Skye and became one of the first Christian martyrs in Scotland, when Pictish raiders massacred all 150 members of the community that he had established on the island of Eigg in 617.

Curiously, Adamnan makes no reference in his life to any of these Irish monks despite the fact that they were apparently living and working so close to Iona. However, he does, refer to Columba's friendship with a number of others who seem to have been operating quite independently of Iona and its daughter foundations. In one chapter he describes 'four saints who had founded monasteries in Ireland' visiting Columba on Hinba.[9] Significantly, two of them seem also to have established monastic communities in Scotland, although Adamnan does not mention these, presumably out of a concern not to detract from the primacy of the Columban *familia.*

St Comgall of Bangor seems to have set up a monastery on Tiree and St Brendan of Clonfert at Eileach an Naoimh in the or at the mouth of the Firth of Lorne. The other two Irish saints mentioned as making the visit to Hinba, were St Cainnech of Aghaboe and St Cormac, who is also portrayed by Adamnan as being commended by Columba to King Brude and voyaging to Orkney. This reference has led some scholars to suggest that Columba 'sub-contracted' evangelistic work among the Picts, especially those in the northern isles, to Cormac.

A number of other monks of both Irish and British extraction, were also preaching to the Picts during Columba's lifetime. They included St Kessog, who supposedly evangelised the Trossachs from his base on Monk's Island in Loch Lomond and St Serf who seems to have been active in the Ochil hills and Fife and had a similar island retreat on Loch Leven. St Ternan, a shadowy figure, possibly based at Abernethy, is associated with the Christianising of the Dee valley in Aberdeenshire. St Columba's best known evangelist contemporary, the British born St Kentigern, who is traditionally portrayed as the first bishop of the Strathclyde Britons, did most of his missionary work in Strathclyde, although an almost certainly apocryphal story in Jocelyn's twelfth century life describes him meeting the Saint of Iona near the banks of the Tay.

There were undoubtedly many other monks whose pioneering work in bringing Christianity to the remoter parts of Scotland has gone unsung, while their better-connected contemporary continues to receive honour and attention. As Dr Alexander McBain, a distinguished Gaelic philologist, noted more than a hundred years ago, Columba 'swallowed up into his own fame all the work of his predecessors, companions and contemporaries, and deprived generations of pioneers and missionaries of their just fame'.[10]

It certainly seems, on the basis of the best available evidence, we now have that Columba does not, any more than Ninian, deserve the accolade of Apostle to the Picts. His forays into Pictish territory seem to have been few and far between and it is highly doubtful, as we have seen, if he himself felt any evangelistic impulse to convert this particular people to Christianity. Rather his missionary efforts, such as they were, seem to have been concentrated almost entirely among the *Scoti* in *Dal Riata*. Although Adamnan describes him as founding monasteries on both sides of Druim Alban, among the Irish and the Picts, but there is no evidence of any Columban foundations in areas occupied by the Picts. All those that we know of are either in Scot's *Dal Riata* or Ireland. It seems likely that Columba's missionary work among the Picts was confined to isolated individual instances of conversion and baptism of the kind described by Adomnan. More concerted evangelism almost certainly did not come until the seventh century when it was undertaken by such figures as St

Maelrubha, a possible relative of Columba who lived from 642 to 722 and made a series of journeys from his base at Applecross into Invernesshire, Banffshire, Skye and Harris and as far north as Cape Wrath. Archaeological evidence suggesting that the area around the Moray Firth was not converted to Christianity until the late seventh or early eighth century would certainly tend to favour Maelrubha, rather than his better known predecessor from Iona, as the true evangelist of the northern Picts.

The Author

The Rev. Dr Ian Bradley holds first class degrees from Oxford (history) and St Andrews University (theology), and obtained his doctorate from Oxford. His career has included full-time journalism with *The Times* in London, serving as Head of Religious Broadcasting for BBC Scotland, school teaching and parish ministry. Since 1992, he has lectured in church history and practial theology at Aberdeen University. He is the author of more than 20 books on subjects ranging from Gilbert and Sullivan to the theology of sacrifice via studies of hymnody, modern liberalism and numerous nineteenth century topics. His books on Celtic Christianity include 'The Celtic Way' (translated into Dutch and German) and 'Columba, Pilgrim and Penitent'. He has just completed a major publication for Edinburgh University Press entitled 'Chasing Dreams: 1300 Years of Celtic Christianity'. A frequent broadcaster, he was last heard in 1997 on Radio 4 in his four part series 'On the steps of Columba'.

References

1. Bede, *The Ecclesiastical History of the English People*, Oxford University Press, 1994 pp. 114–5
2. Scott, A., *The Pictish Nation: Its People and Its Church*,T.N. Foulis, Edinburgh, 1918 p. 1
3. Simpson, W.D., *The Historical Saint Columba* ,Milne & Hutchison, Aberdeen, 1927, p. 1
4. Thomas C., *The Evidence for North Britain* in *Christianity in Britain, 300–700*, edited by M.W. Barley and R.P.C.Hanson, Leicester University Press, Leicester, 1968, pp. 94–116
5. Macquarrie, A., *The Date of St Ninian's Mission: A Reappraisal* in *Records of the Scottish Church History Society*, Vol.XXIII, Part 1, 1987
6. Herbert,.M. *Iona: Kells & Derry*, Oxford University Press, 1988, p. 261
7. Harkus G. & Clancy T. (eds), *Iona: The Earliest Poetry*, Edinburgh University Press, 1996, pp. 111–113

8. Knight G.F., *Archaeological Light on the Early Christianising of Scotland*, James Clarke, London, 1933, p. 7
9. Adomnan of Iona, *Life of Columba*, Book Three, Chapter 17
10. Quoted in Galbraith, J.D., *St Machar's Cathedral: the Celtic Antecedents*, Friends of St Machar's Cathedral, Aberdeen, 1982, p. 1

The two great cathedral churches of St Andrews on the cliffs above the grand harbour, where international pilgrims would arrive and depart. Drawing by Jurek Alexander Putter of what it might have looked like in 1546.

4

TWO PILGRIM TOWNS
A Quest for St Andrew and St Margaret

Jurek Alexander Putter

Since opening a studio in St Andrews in the 1960s, the author has concentrated his work on the task of visual recreating of Scotland's glorious period of pilgrimage during the Middle Ages. This task has been accomplished through historical research and the making of pictures which show in great detail what life might have been like for pilgrims and the places they visited, mainly focused on the pilgrim towns of St Andrews and Dunfermline.

The inspiration behind the work, and the modus operandi adopted, has come from a study of how artists in the Middle Ages developed a prosperous industry in response to a demand for 'pious pictures', both by clergymen and by private individuals as patrons. Like today, there was an 'agent' who acted as intermediary between client and artist. The agent would find out the client's requirements and negotiate a fee for the artist to undertake the research and do the painting. The great painters and studios at the time were mainly Italian, French and Dutch, each with a master and a supporting cast of painters and apprentices.

The genre style of these studios embodied the symbolism of the late Middle Ages with a growing interest in realism as ideas moved towards the Renaissance. The studio master would direct operations and decide the grand strategy of composition and execution, based on drawings and sketches provided by the agent. He would himself paint the principal characters and elements of the picture. His assistants would handle the landscape and architectural setting based on research of the patron's life and circumstances. Apprentices at various stages of learning would be allocated specific tasks, including test pieces for approval by the master or agent. In other words, a whole team would be engaged at different times on the execution of a single commission.

Pictures commissioned by a patron were on completion gifted to the Church, either by hanging in a particular building at a religious centre or for peripatetic loan to smaller religious foundations in remote parts of the country which were too poor to own their own paintings. An interesting form of this peripatetic system was an arrangement of small picture theatres on wheels which were dispatched on tour by an appointed priest. The intention was to reach deep into scattered communities of rural parishes to give people experience at first hand of Christian images and culture.

The arrival of such stunning paintings into isolated communities would have been an inspiring event, stimulating the desire to 'go and see for onesself'. The pilgrimages that ensued, reduced the effects of isolation, helped to spread new ideas, and drew people into national and European culture. From the evidence of the few surviving travelling pictures, such as the great Crucifixion painting in the Parish Church of Fowlis Easter, two miles north west of Dundee, they were executed in oils on wooden panels, measuring about eleven feet by seven feet. The remarkable feature of the Fowlis Easter picture is that it was not painted on the Continent, as one would expect, but in Scotland by a 'national school of art' in the year 1472.

St Andrews and Dunfermline stood out in medieval Scotland because of pilgrimage, which brought income and wealth. Their designation by the Church as pilgrim centres, advertised them throughout Europe, and the visitors flocked there by the thousands. The great shrines gave them a competitive edge which was to benefit their appearance and attractions. Pilgrim destinations had not only to give visitors an edifying spiritual reward, but also to provide a host of secular attractions and entertainments. The tragedy for many parts of Britain, was that the great sites of pilgrimage were to be either destroyed or so down-graded as to lose their former status and meaning forever. To realise what Scotland lost, one only has to look to the sites which survived on the Continent: Santiago de Compostela, Mainz, Bruges, Czestochowa and Rome itself.

It has been said that there were as many reasons for pilgrimage as there were pilgrims. Regardless of the prestige of a pilgrim place, no false promise was ever made for cures of the body or mind. Miracles did happen, as they still continue to do in places like Lourdes and Fatima, but they were the exception rather than the rule. Much depended on the faith of the individual concerned. Pilgrimage was, and remains, that innate desire of the heart to visit a special place, even only once in a person's lifetime. The notion is as ancient as human history. It is practised today, even by people of no particular religious persuasion. There are various 'Meccas', especially in sport, that magnetically attract devotees repeatedly, with an intensity and fervour of 'faith' that is impressive. Wimbledon is the Mecca of Tennis, St Andrews the Mecca of Golf, Hampden and Murrayfield the Meccas of Scottish football and rugby.

In the Dark Ages, as Christianity blossomed amidst the fall of empires, the sanctity and importance of special sacred places grew. The classical pilgrim place is one associated with the martyrdom of a Saint: Rome for St Peter and Paul, Patras in the Gulf of Corinth for St Andrew, and Jerusalem for St Stephen. In modern times, this concept survives at a personal level. It is not uncommon for people to journey to the site of a battle. Monte Cassino, the beaches of Normandy, Arnhem, and an endless list of others. The site of a fatal accident often attracts a lone bouquet of flowers years after the event. What is important is that the 'place' assumes an extra meaning: a special sight or a memory which provokes a multitude of emotions, usually ones of deep reflection and profound enrichment.

THE DESTINY OF ST ANDREW

As it emerged from the Dark Ages, it was the Apostle Andrew who gave Scotland its true identity. Yet no matter how powerful and dynamic a symbol he became, and no matter how enduring the symbol of the X-shaped cross, which became the Saltire of the Scots, the origins of his cult in Scotland has been shrouded in the fog of myth and legend. Many people seem content to accept the mythical inventions found in many history books, but the author has undertaken research for his pictures which provides evidence to assist in unravelling the real story.

St Andrew came from the town of Bethsaida and was a simple fisherman, like his brother Peter. They had abandoned that life to follow John, and Andrew is known to have 'chosen' Christ, before Christ chose him. He stands out as the follower of John the Baptist, who had chosen to believe in Christ before meeting him. It demonstrates the great difference between his belief and the doubts of St Thomas, who was chided by Christ after the Resurrection with the words: 'Blessed are those who have not seen and yet have believed'.

The Apostles were sent to spread the Gospels outside Palestine: St Peter to Rome; St Paul to Asia Minor and finally to martyrdom in Rome; St James to Spain; the doubting St Thomas to India; and St Andrew to Greece, the lower Balkans, and to Southern Russia. In the year 60AD, Andrew was in a town called Patras in the province of Achaea, when there was an outbreak of persecution of the Christians. These persecutions are well documented, and the decrees against them were carried out to the letter by provincial officials. It was inevitable, given the nature and the mission of the apostles, that they would fall foul of the local authorities. Andrew was not destined to escape this persecution, but the exact manner of his crucifixion will never be fully resolved. Lagnon and Cazelles (1969) have this to say about the matter:

> Brother of Simon Peter, Andrew is said to have preached in Palestine and then in Scythia, Thrace and Achaia. In Patras in Greece, he converted the wife of proconsul, Aegeus, with whom he had a number of profound discussions. Upon refusing to obey the proconsul's order to make a sacrifice to the pagan gods, Andrew was imprisoned and bound to an X-shaped cross. *The Golden Legend* relates that he remained crucified for two days before a crowd of 20,000 people to whom he continued to preach during his suffering. He refused to be removed from the cross and expired on the third day in a blinding flash from heaven.

The Romans became great practitioners of crucifixion as a form of capital punishment, and they elevated it to a great art of cruelty calculated to inflict pain and degradation. It was designed to inflict the maximum humiliation and to draw out the suffering of the victim. Only two of the Apostles were crucified, Andrew and Peter. As a Roman citizen, Paul was beheaded. This is what differentiates them from the others, and gives them a special status. Indeed, every aspect of crucifixion was developed and refined to a calculated degree. The humiliation at court, followed by the horrors of flogging. The 'Flagellum', the Roman whip with two cords which terminated in twin balls of lead, inflicted severe wounds of broken skin and ripped flesh where applied. It was calculated to break the spirit and weaken the victim.

It is disturbing to dwell upon the details of such suffering, but it makes us realise the implications of what it was like in those days to lay down your life for the faith. Individuals like Andrew, were keenly aware of the penalties meted out by Roman despots for the crimes of heretical opposition to the established Roman religion. They had witnessed such executions as part of daily life. Therefore, to persist in the proclamation of Christ took courage and fortitude. Andrew was presumably about sixty when he was martyred, and this factor would have added to his suffering. Yet it may have been a blessing in disguise, as he probably weakened quicker than a younger man and succumbed earlier. It became the custom, after the death of a martyr, to preserve carefully the mortal remains. The site of death and burial often became especially revered as a place of pilgrimage, and Patras was one of the great sites of early Christian pilgrimage.

The position of the Christians was to be reversed dramatically through the intervention of Constantine the Great who was proclaimed Emperor in 306, and who was eventually responsible for legalising Christianity. His mother was the Empress Helena. A convert to Christianity, she is attributed with the discovery of the 'True Cross' at Golgotha, and her great piety and work to preserve the holy sites were to earn her the title of St Helena. Her son Constantine created a new capital in the East, which he called Constantinople. A programme of church building ensured that his city would survive him as a truly Christian capital. Influenced by his pious mother, he saw advantage in eclipsing the ancient capital of Rome, by concentrating as many as possible of the known corporeal relics of the Apostles in his new metropolis. Under him, the Empire was systematically swept for relics so that they could be brought to Constantinople. In a way it was an act of preservation, and St Andrew's body was reinterred in a custom built church named St Andrew in Krisei.

A story relevant to a later incident in Scottish history, at Athelstaneford in 750, is what happened when Maxentius challenged Constantine's position as Emperor. Camped near Rome on the eve of the Battle of Milvan Bridge, Constantine had a vision in which a fiery X-shaped cross appeared in the sky. He duly ordered his soldiers to paint this symbol on their shields, and later attributed his victory over Maxentius to this providential vision. It was a connection used effectively by his public relations department to emphasise the Emperor's association with the cult of St Andrew.

THE RELICS TRAVEL TO SCOTLAND

It is to Pope Gregory that we can give credit for first bringing the relics of St Andrew to Britain. A Prefect of Rome, he abandoned a promising political career for Christian devotion and converted his palace into a monastery dedicated to St Andrew. Dispatched to Constantinople as a Papal Envoy, he was able to obtain relics from the Church of St Andrew in Krisei. On returning to Rome, he became Abbot of the monastery he had founded, and in 590 was elevated to the throne of St Peter.

Augustine reached the Isle of Thanet in Kent in 597, receiving a sympathetic welcome from the local monarch Ethelbert. He provided protection and permitted Augustine to preach, and was himself later converted to the faith. A Holy See was established at Canterbury in 601, and Augustine was given ecclesiastical jurisdiction over what could loosely be described as England. There is some evidence that the relics of St Andrew were among the various sacred treasures brought to Britain by Augustine.

There is an interesting story that, on arrival in Kent, various sealed chests were opened, and great disappointment was expressed about the quality of the relics. They were found to be in the main 'incorporeal', such as small items of cloth, sandal straps and the like. Mindful of their tenuous footing amongst a fierce and warlike folk, the mission considered that their chances of success could be enhanced by the presence of 'real and corporeal relics'. A delegation was hastily dispatched back to Rome, and some 'real' relics were duly supplied. It is important to remember that at this time, real relics were rare and greatly prized in the West, since the bulk was held in Byzantium, and the most substantial relics to exist at the time were Gregory's fragments of St Andrew.

The next piece of action moves north to Northumbria, where more conclusive mention is made of the relics. The Holy See at York was founded in 601 by Paulinius, a Roman who became the first Bishop of York. In this expansion northwards, the spiritual tide reached Hexham, and St Wilfrid (634–709) was granted the ecclesiastical territory by Queen Etheldreda. He set about building a magnificent church and monastery at Hexham dedicated to St Andrew. Eddius, in his *Life of St Wilfrid,* enthuses about the splendour of the structure, with its complex of vaults and passages, staircases and columns, and states that there was nothing finer to be found 'North of the Alps'.

We know from Eddius that Wilfrid made two pilgrimages to Rome, where he went round the shrines of the saints to make a collection of relics, each labelled and named. There is repeated mention in early documents of the great care taken to determine the authenticity of relics, and to ensure that even the smallest fragment was correctly identified. In Wilfrid's time, Hexham had become the richest and most influential centre in the North, and it was there that the northern cult of St Andrew started, which would not have been possible without the relics being present. We know that Bishop Acca, who followed St Wilfrid, added to the collection of relics at Hexham, extended the library there, and encouraged Gregorian Chant to be sung by inviting Maban, an Italian who had taught at the Canterbury choir.

Acca is the most important link we have as regards the spread of the cult and the relics to Scotland. In the year 732, for reasons most likely caused by a conflict with the local monarch, he was forced to flee Hexham, bringing with him the relics of St Andrew in a reliquary, referred to as 'The Morbrac'. The records show that he travelled north to the ecclesiastical centre we know today as St Andrews, then called Righmonaidth. What we know about the place is gleaned from the old Irish Annals. The Irish missionaries who poured into Scotland during the 6th century to convert the pagan people targetted existing sacred sites like Righmonaidth to convert the local Druid priest. If you could turn him, then you were more likely to reach and influence the local king, and then turn the tribe.

Raighll, who became St Rule, was an Irish missionary and friend of St Columba. He targeted Righmonaidth which was easily the most important of the pagan sacred sites on the eastern seaboard of Scotland. The name Righmonaidth translates as 'the Mount where Kings are crowned' or simply the Mount of Kings. It referred to the headland at St Andrews overlooking the harbour, now dominated by the sprawling ruins of the great Cathedral Church. The pagan tradition throughout Northern Europe held that kings had to have their investiture validated by being 'crowned beneath a Crann Bethadh (the Tree of Life), and the Oak Tree is one of the keys to understanding the history of St Andrews.

In the sacred grove of trees, the high priests of pagan times performed their rituals of purification and coronation. The Tree of Life was placed above all the other things as a source of good fortune. At Righmonaidth, the sacred grove of oaks stood half way between the east gable of the great Cathedral and the old Church of St Rule. This we know due to yet another tradition. In order to preserve the sacred continuity of the site after conversion to Christianity, the dead tree was carefully cut down and the timbers symbolically incorporated into the rafters of the first Christian church to stand on the site. This is how the Oak survived from the Dark Ages into the Middle Ages in all the heraldic seals of the City.

Raighll reached Righmonaidth around 580. His missionary work was successful, and he left behind a thriving Christian community which was to prevail. He returned to Ireland, where he was to preserve a memory of Scotland in the name of his small monastic cell. He called it Muckross, which means 'the promontory of the boars', and this was the name of the ancient secular community beside the sacred trees at Righmonaidth.

The adoption of the Saltire cross as a national emblem was confirmed in 750, when the Picts and the Scots were mired in a catastrophic military incursion against the Saxons deep inside Northumberland. Driven back into the Lothians by Athelstane, General of the Northumbrian forces, the Scots under King Angus were beginning to succumb to something akin to panic. During prayer, Angus fell into a deep sleep, and a vision of St Andrew appeared in a dream, granting him victory. Armed with this inspiring news, the Scots rallied, and routed their enemy at Athelstaneford near Haddington. There is another version which states that during the course of the battle, when defeat seemed imminent, Angus observed a gigantic X-shaped cloud in the blue sky. Taking succour from the providential appearance of the symbolic cross of their Patron Saint, the Scots gained courage and finally won the day.

NATIONAL IDENTITY AND PILGRIMAGE

No single event so profoundly transformed the subsequent history of Scotland as did the arrival of the relics of St Andrew. Christianity introduced the building blocks of theological order and awakened an interest in intellectual discipline and scholarship. It was the powerful magnet which was starting to draw the Scots out of pagan chaos and into European culture, but it needed a final ingredient, the last piece of the spiritual jigsaw puzzle to give it a national focus with a sense of local ownership. The relics satisfied this last requirement. The turning point was the year 732 when Acca travelled north from Hexham to the place which in pre-Christian times had been called Righmonaiddth (Rymont), the Mount of Kings, and which the Irish monks renamed Cennighmonaidh (Kilrymont), the Church on the Mount of Kings.

Saint Andrew's relics were regarded as a divine reward for embracing and sustaining the faith in the face of great difficulty. It was seen as evidence of God's compassion for those inhabiting the far flung fringes of civilisation, having providentially permitted the safe passage of sacred relics into the keeping of such a remote people. It was this accepted notion of a gift to a distant people that began the long road towards national identity. St Andrews the place and St Andrew the martyr represented the undisputed focal point of national consciousness. To the Scots, even his name bore the hallmark of attraction. In Greek, his name was Andreas which means 'manly'.

The Dark Ages were passing, the Age of the Irish was only a memory, and the great Age of Faith with the building of enormous Cathedral Churches was about to begin. The Cathedral Church of St Andrews was the largest building ever built in Scotland until the Victorians started to construct their enormous hospitals, hotels and railway stations. 'Gloriosa Domus Sanct Andree' (The Glorious House of Saint Andrew), as it was known, came to represent not simply a great spiritual exercise, but also a national enterprise of profound significance.

Building started in 1160, and it was completed in 1318, when it was consecrated with the presence of Robert the Bruce. Its construction spanned the Wars of Independence, and became a physical symbol of resistance to English schemes of annexation. Under the determined guidance of the great Bishop Lamberton it became the rallying point for the Scots during the difficult years of occupation. Even prior to its completion, it had become the 'Treasure House for the Scots', the greatest treasure being the relics of St Andrew. They were recorded as follow: the bones of the first three fingers of the right hand, the bones which made up the forearm, a kneecap, a small piece of the skull and a tooth.

So what really did make Dunfermline so special throughout the Middle Ages? It was Saint Margaret, the other Saint who contributed greatly to the shaping of Scotland's identity. An Anglo Saxon Princess who was to become Queen of the Scots in 1070, she is best known for her work in Dunfermline. She was raised to the status of Universal Saint in 1250 by Pope Innocent IV.

Born to exiled parents in Hungary at Rekvar Castle around 1046, she returned with her entire family to the Court of Edward the Confessor in 1057. Her father was Edward the Exile, the Lost King of England. Her younger brother Edgar was technically and dynastically speaking the rightful heir to the throne of England. After the conquest of England by the Normans in 1066, the Royal credentials of the family placed their safety in jeopardy, and her brother Edgar, real heir to the English throne, fled North to the court of Malcom Canmore at Dunfermline. From this sanctuary, he had participated in abortive military expeditions against William the Conqueror. The subsequent trek northwards by Margaret's family is perhaps indicative of a feeling of mounting insecurity. It was from Northumberland, in the year 1069, that the family finally fled to Edgar and Scotland.

By 1070, Margaret the Princess, had married the widower Malcolm. The next 23 years were to see Margaret almost single handedly set in motion the process of national transformation. This highly educated woman devoted the rest of her life to dragging Scotland from the disorder of the Dark Ages into mainstream European culture. She set an example to Crown and commoner alike with her practical piety. This cosmopolitan woman employed her formidable talents to confronting and overcoming basket of National ills. Using Christ as her example she highlighted the chronic problems of poverty and deprivation among the poor and sought means and a will to provide for those afflicted. The orphans and the abandoned, prisoners of war, those held in bondage and servitude, their plight she addressed and their liberty secured.

She was the catalyst of real change and improvement. Her actions were motivated by genuine concern and compassion for all her subjects. During her 24 years as Queen, she transformed a parochial court with primitive manners into one where a semblance of real culture began to be expected and was encouraged to develop. She bore her husband eight children, and thereby knew the problems and difficulties of motherhood. There is some evidence to suggest that she died from cancer of the bowel, an affliction that was at work for at least two years prior to her death. One does not need a vivid imagination to realise what that meant in a society without any real form of medical care. On her deathbed, she embraced and accepted the distressing news of the violent death of her husband and eldest son at the battle of Alnwick in 1093.

Her body was taken to Dunfermline and interred in the Abbey. Her lifelong devotion to the plight of others and her works of great charity inspired an enduring love. Her grave rapidly became an unofficial shrine, and pilgrims en route to St Andrews paused there for a few days to pay their respects to her memory. It is of interest to note that the main qualification of sainthood for women in Medieval times was virginity and chastity. St Margaret is all the more exceptional because she was a mother.

She was very aware of the civilising influence of the Benedictines. Their work was in the main educational and agricultural. They founded schools, drained swamps and brought land under cultivation. Many of the older Universities grew out of Benedictine schools. Their habits were commonly black and hence they are known as black monks. Benedictine convents of nuns date from the end of the 6th century and were as widespread as the monasteries. It is known that St Margaret was brought under the educational influence of the Benedictines both in Hungary as a child and at the English Court of Edward the Confessor as an adolescent. Their influence upon her was profound and lasting.

Queen Margaret herself was to revive and encourage pilgrimage to St Andrews. She improved and expanded the facilities available to pilgrims throughout Scotland by building 'stations' along the principal pilgrim routes. These stations provided rudimentary welfare, security and accommodation not just for pilgrims, but for other travellers. The most enduring testimony to improvements implemented by her were the two great pilgrim stations at North and South Queensferry.

It would be an exaggeration to give her sole credit for the transformation of Scotland, but her example set a precedent for a more modern code of behaviour and attitudes which embraced the whole spectrum of national life: political, social, industrial and religious, both at court and among the people of Scotland. It was how she articulated these hopes that endured. Her legacy was her personal qualities and compassionate persuasion, and she possessed a powerful and original personality not witnessed since the arrival of the Irish missionaries in the 6th century.

What is significant, is that the memory of her activities did not fade with her death, but that it was enhanced with the passage of time. It is not disputed that Scotland appeared to lose its progressive momentum and totter on the precipice of destructive disorder immediately after her passing. The fact that this did not happen, was largely due to the embryonic mechanisms of meaningful stability that she had fashioned both at court and in the countryside. Many of her aspirations were to be fulfilled during the reign of her illustrious son, King David I. When he too passed away, the accolade accorded him was an echo of Imperial Roman antiquity. With reference to Scotland's built heritage, it is said that 'he found a nation of wood, and left it in stone.'

She was the great unforeseen catalyst, the foreigner armed with a 'global mentality'. She witnessed the use and misuse of power, and she shattered the mired complacency and hopelessness of the 'old order'. It was due to her that the 'ancien régime' was finally consigned to the past with remarkable ease and lack of regret. Like the biblical Noah, she was a bridge from the old to the new. In death she triumphed and her message endured. The gift of Innocent IV, by making her the 'second' Patron Saint of Scotland, was as much an accolade for the Scots as it was for their Queen.

REDEMPTION THROUGH PILGRIMAGE

Pilgrimage is to be found in all religions and is normally centred around a single god or prophet. From a spiritual point of view, it is the innate desire of the human heart to visit places made holy by the birth, life or death of the god or prophet. The Egyptians journeyed to Sekket's shrine at Buastis or to Ammon's oracle at Thebes; the Greeks sought council from Apollo at Delphi and for cures from Asclepius at Epidaurus; the Mexicans gathered at the huge temple of Quetzal; the Peruvians massed in sun-worship at Cuzzo and the Bolivians at Titicaca. Buddhism and Islam are especially famous for their attachment to this method of devotion. At certain times of the year, enormous gatherings of people visit Kapilavatsu where Buddha began his life, at Benares where he opened his sacred mission, and at Kasingara where he died. Mecca and Medina are today among the greatest sites of pilgrimage in the world for those following the prophet of Islam.

The crusades were a manifestation of this human desire to visit and venerate all the places, personalities and things associated with the birth, life and death of Christ. This was extended to the disciples, especially those who were martyred, as their passion and death stamped certain localities with a special spiritual significance. Another influence was to amplify this through a privilege invented by the early Church to grant remission of canonical penance to those who could bear witness of a martyr. It is certain that this practice was highly organised at an early date, so much so that there was a libellus or warrant of reconciliation granted to re-admit sinners to Christian worship. Not only had the martyrs this power to absolve people from ecclesiastical penalties in their last dying moments, but their tombs and scenes of martyrdom were also considered to be capable of removing the taints and penalties of sin.

Accordingly, it became looked upon as a purifying act to visit the sites and relics of the Saints.

As the early Church developed its penitential system centred on the sacrament of confession, it established a legal and authoritative framework where pilgrimages were considered as adequate punishment for certain crimes. The hardships of the journey, the garb worn and the mendacity entailed, made a pilgrimage a real and efficient penance. The guilty person was ordered to make a specific pilgrimage to some distant shrine, and bring back a certificate stating the fulfilment of the sentence prescribed by the ecclesiastical court.

In the city archives of St Omer in North East France, there survives an illustrative example of this practice in a certificate of expiation issued to William Bondolf in the City of St Andrews by John of Gowrie, Augustinian Prior of the Cathedral Church and the third most powerful 'Guardian of the Realm.'

Bondolf was a cleric of Dunkirk who had killed a man called André d'Esquerdes and was tried by an ecclesiastical court. There is evidence that he was originally brought before the civil court which assessed the case and, taking into account the fact that the accused was a cleric, saw fit to arraign him before an ecclesiastic court which was considered better suited to try and sentence him. The sentence imposed was a requirement to travel on a pilgrimage of expiation to St Andrews in Scotland, to pay a fine of twelve livres, and to commission thirteen sung requiem masses in St Andrews for the repose of the soul of the deceased.

The pilgrimage to St Andrews was presumably chosen because St Andrew was the Patron Saint of the deceased, and also because the pilgrimage had to be a difficult one. There is no evidence in the surviving certificate as to whether Bonfolf came by sea or walked. Taking into account the seriousness of the original crime, it might be deduced that in all probability he made the trip alone and on foot. It was in fact tantamount to writing Bodolf's death sentence. Indeed, the purpose of penitential pilgrimage was that it had to be difficult, even to the point of placing the penitent in a position of mortal risk. The accused under sentence would be encouraged, with due regard to the real dangers, to visit all the major devotional shrines along the pilgrim route, and there pray for his own safety, as well as to reflect upon the death of his victim and pray for the repose of the victim's soul.

Bondolf duly reached St Andrews. On 29 May 1333, the Saturday before Trinity Sunday, he received his certificate confirming the fulfilment of his pilgrimage and the court's sentence. It was duly signed by John of Gowrie, in his capacity as the Augustine Prior. A little less than a month later, on 26 June, he was back in St Omer, presenting his certificate to the judicial authorities and being absolved from his crime. The four weeks interval suggests a direct passage by sea, one would imagine direct from St Andrews to Dunkirk.

Redemption through gifts was another tradition important to pilgrims. Rich visitors would bring gifts which reflected their status. These could be devotional pictures, Missals, liturgical books, richly fashioned gold crucifixes embellished with precious and semi precious stones and money was also given to the Abbey for its upkeep. There existed within any pilgrim town an industry complete with highly skilled craftsmen capable of manufacturing items that could be presented to the Abbot or to the many charitable organisations.

If a pilgrim did not possess the wealth to provide a gift in the physical sense, then the gift of labour or skill or craft was donated. It is amazing just how many great Medieval institutions were maintained and sustained in this manner. Building of bridges, roads, ditches, walls, churches and pilgrim stations were assisted in this way. The Church would also raise what was known as a 'Plenary Indulgence' for such offerings of labour. For example, there are records surviving which show that the Priors of the great Augustinian Priory of St Andrews raised such Indulgences for the building of the massive stone bridge spanning the river Eden at Guardbridge. The Indulgence did not buy the remission of sins, rather the charitable offering was seen to reduce the level of suffering that an individual might in theory experience in Purgatory. It is not important whether we today believe in this religious notion, but it was believed at the time. It was what motivated men and women during the Middle Ages, and this is important to our understanding of their times.

It is also important to state that people's good faith was rarely abused by this concept of 'remission through suffering'. It was a concept almost akin to a Sacrament which was freely available to all. People were not forced or manipulated into such Indulgences, just as people were under no pressure to embark upon pilgrimages. A person could live his or her life out within the confines of their parish or town, without being spiritually penalised in any way. Pilgrimage was and to a large extent remains the innate desire of the heart to visit a special place to venerate whatever makes that place special. The act of journeying there and the emotion of veneration remain as powerful means to satisfy an inner spiritual needs.

PILGRIM TOWNS AND STATIONS

Pilgrim destinations, were by their very nature, furnished with facilities to accommodate the needs of travellers. The name 'statio', the original Latin word for 'station', was a place on the pilgrim highways, which provided welfare and sanctuary. Some were modest in size and housed all of the facilities under one roof. Then, there were the major 'assembly stations', placed in orbit around the main pilgrim towns, usually about three or four miles distant. By tradition, pilgrims stayed there until their numbers were sufficiently large to justify dispatching them in groups into the town or sacred place where the ecclesiastical authorities had the opportunity of providing an official welcome.

This time lag for rest and reflection served another purpose. It heightened that sense of anticipation. It enhanced the sense of accomplishment felt by the pilgrims on having reached to within the sight and sound of their destination. The stations provided people with a sense of fellowship and belonging. Safely ensconced within the walls of the great courtyard of buildings, pilgrims could ponder upon the hardships experienced and triumphed over, especially by those from far afield. The stations also provided facilities for washing their tired bodies and dirty clothes so that they could appear at their best for making the final walk to the holy sites.

All major pilgrim destinations had orbital assembly stations. In the case of St Andrews, there was Guardbridge and St Ayles, as well as smaller rest stations at Strathkinness and Peat Inn. The latter often became the site of coaching inns after the Reformation. The main assembly station for Dunfermline was North Queensferry, with rest stations at Milesmark and Hillend, as well as at South Queensferry. For Whithorn, there was a major station at Bladnoch on the River Bladnock. Then there was the renowned rest station with an infirmary, located on the edge of the Lammermuir Hills at Soutra Mains. There, pilgrims travelling north, gained a first view of their destinations at Edinburgh, Dunfermline or St Ayles on the Fife coast at Anstruther.

The medieval philosophy was that no pilgrim should need to enter a sacred site unwelcome or unannounced. The arrrangement was for pilgrims to move in procession in large groups towards their final destination from an assembly station, and they would be welcomed at the town gates. Indeed, there were specific ceremonies devised to receive the 'holy visitor'. Thereafter, it was customary, once officially received, for pilgrims to be housed within the day of their arrival. They were usually accommodated at the large guest halls within the walls of the town, or even within the walled enclave of the ecclesiatical complex. The stations were administered by the Augustinians at St Andrews and by the Benedictines at Dunfermline.

After the Reformation in 1559, pilgrimage was outlawed, and two generations later, the memory of its associated industries and activity had been entirely erased. When the term 'bed and breakfast' industry is mentioned in the context of the Middle Ages, there is a sceptical response. The author would argue that it is an unassailable historical fact that the

Scottish tourist industry started during the great 'Age of Faith'. This answers many questions about urban growth, as pilgrimage generated development and business. In any pilgrim town, visitors had to be accommodated, fed, entertained, shod, clothed, the ill nursed, horses shod and carriages repaired. Visitors purchased pilgrim tokens and printed ephemera such as broadsheets of the Gospels, the parables and text on herbal remedies. Pilgrimage was also instrumental in the development of the postal services. Pilgrims kept in touch with families and relatives back home by regularly sending items and letters 'down the line' of the long established pilgrim highways.

As mentioned elsewhere in this paper, the towns designated by the ecclesiastical authorities as principal pilgrim destinations had their populations 'capped'. The reason for this was simple. The town had to be able to feed and accommodate its indigenous population as well as the large numbers of visitors. If the designated town were permitted to grow out of control, then especially in times of poor harvest there would be great logistical difficulty in feeding everyone. Dunfermline seems to have had a resident population of around 2,000 souls. Bearing in mind the number of pilgrims arriving annually, one sees the need for prudent restraint on urban expansion.

If one seeks some idea of the numbers of pilgrims reaching Dunfermline annually in the Middle Ages, it is possible to construct a model based on St Andrews. During a good year, it received about quarter of a million pilgrims. In bad years, there were about 150000. The comparative figures for Canterbury were 750000, and Santiago de Compostela, 2 million. There is also evidence to suggest that Walsingham in Norfolk received around one million. From this, it is not unreasonable to assume that Dunfermline probably attracted around 200000 annually, or an average of 4000 per week spread over the year, although there could be as many as 10000 to 20000 people at peak periods. It was therefore of paramount importance that the agricultural infrastructure be capable of sustaining that volume of traffic.

Once again the importance of the Benedictines emerges as an influential factor. We must remember that they were in the Middle Ages regarded as 'the levellers of land, the clearers of forests, the creators of fields'. The Church saw its responsibility as being to ensure that the productive capacity of the areas surrounding St Andrews and Dunfermline was sufficient to be basically self-sustaining. They were also conveniently situated by the sea, with harbour facilities, for trade and import of produce from the other fertile parts of Scotland and from Continental Europe.

What happened to St Andrews in 1140 is reminiscent of today's system for 'European City of Culture' designations. This was the year when the

Pope designated St Andrews as a 'European City of Pilgrimage', and Bishop Rodger issued instructions for the building of the second and greater of the Cathedral Churches as a 'national enterprise'. According to his instructions, it was to be a pilgrim city laid out with processional streets of boulevard proportion, each capable of accommodating large processions of the faithful on pilgrimage. In addition, it was to be a garden city of spacious graciousness, which when complete, would mirror the majesty of the Cathedral Church. So here was a holistic concept of town building which held that the entire project be conceived, planned and constructed as an integrated operation. As the largest urban building project in northern Europe of its time, it became the pride of Scotland, and the planned pattern of these streets has remained unaltered since 1140.

The Author

Jurek Alexander Putter attended Madras College in St Andrews and graduated in graphic design from Edinburgh College of Art in 1966. He then founded the Grafik Orzel Design Studio in his home town, where he has sought to revive the 'Patronage and Art' model from the Middle Ages. Rigorous historical research, such as in the Vatican Archives, has enabled him to recreate medieval Scotland in a series of unique pictures, showing in great detail what life was like when St Andrews and Dunfermline were major centres of European pilgrimage. Now valuable heritage assets in their own right, these pictures have been shown at touring exhibitions in several European countries, and his St Andrews studio has in turn become a popular place of pilgrimage in Fife. His services as a lecturer are widely sought, especially his series entitled *A Feast of Images*, from which this paper has been culled.

References

Baxter, J. H., *Copiale Prioratus Sanctiandree: the Letterbook of James Haldenstane Prior of St Andrews 148–1450,* St Andrews University Publications, No XXX1, 1930

Dunlop, A., *Life and Times of Bishop James Kennedy,* Oliver and Tweed, Edinburgh, 1950

Encyclopaedia Britannica, *Pilgrimage,* Vol. 17, pp. 925–928

Goodall, W. (ed), *Scotchronicon Johannis de Fordum cum supplimentis et continuatione Walteri Boweri,* Edinburgh, 1759

Hendry, D., *The Knights of St John,* W.C. Henderson, University Press, 1912

Jarret, B., *Pilgrimage,* Catholic Encyclopaedia, pp. 85–99

Jusserand (tr. Smith), *English Wayfaring Life in the Middle Ages*, London, 1852

Lindsay, E.R. and Cameron, A.I. (ed), *Calendar of Scottsish Supplications to Rome*, Scottish History Society, 1934

Longnon, J. & Cazelles, R., *Les Très Riches Heures du Duc de Berry*, Thames & Hudson, 1969

McRoberts, D. (ed), *The Medieval Church of St Andrew*, Scottish Catholic Historical Association, 1976

Marx, *Das Wallfahren in der Katholische Kirche*, Trier, 1842

Miller, A. H., *Fife, Historical and Pictorial*, Vols 1 & 2, John Menzies, 1895

More, T., *A Dyalogue of the Veneration and Worshyp of Images and Relyques, praying to Sai nts and goyng on pylgrymage*, London, 1520

Paul. J.B., *Royal Pilgrimages in Scotland*, Transaction of the Scottish Ecclesiological Society, 1905

Sivry and Champagnac, *Dictionnaire des pelerinages*, Paris, 1859

Springer, O., *Medieval Pilgrim Routes from Scandinavia to Rome*, Medieval Studies, XII, 1950

Sumption, J., *Pilgrimage, an Image of Medieval Religion*, Faber & Faber, 1975

The pilgrim station at Guardbridge on the River Eden, where pilgrims assembled before entering St Andrews, as it might have looked like in the 14th century. Drawing by Jurek Alexander Putter.

5

VOICES OF THE CHERUBIM
A Musical Odyssey to Scotland

John Purser

The creation and origin myths of many cultures involve the element of sound, whether it be the perfect accordance of the affairs of the Chinese empire with the pitch of the *huang chung*, or the philosophical longings of such as Kepler and Newton to discover the music of the spheres. For a mucisian, the role of musical sound in the shaping and projection of cultural identity is of fundamental interest.

An Odyssey is a homecoming, a homecoming fraught with difficulty and requiring heroic feats, the greatest of which is the forcible removal of other suitors for one's long-neglected, yet faithful wife. I do not put Pierre Boulez in the role of suitor, however, but rather that of accepted lover, when he said, after reading *Scotland's Music*: 'I really believe that the only untouched music left in the world is Scotland's. Everything else has become the language of tourism.'

Of course it is not true. Scotland's music has been part of cultural tourism for at least two centuries, all across the globe where Scots have travelled, but there is an element of truth in what Boulez said. What makes us and our music different from most western music is that the pure running stream of it remains in a few places cherished and unpolluted, a source from which all may drink: to which both the most sophisiticated and the most commercial of us can return, as Odysseus returned to his Penelope, perhaps little deserving of such fidelity.

In inviting the reader to join me in this 'Musical Odyssey', it is not with the intention of prostituting the Scottish muse to touring suitors, but rather to invite you to share with me the story of both the survival and the recovery of the music associated with some of the centres of pilgrimage in Scotland. These centres are Iona, Glasgow Cathedral, St Andrews Cathedral, Stirling Castle, and the Hamilton Mausoleum. We will be calling in on other centres of pilgrimage by the way, including Egypt and the Panama isthmus. In all of these, the destiny of our nation is in some way involved, and at the heart of them is an Egyptian stone: the 'Lia Fail' or Stone of Destiny. A stone bearing that name is currently housed in Edinburgh Castle, and is itself the focus of pilgrimage, as it was when it resided in Westminster Abbey, where English and British monarchs have been crowned sitting ignorantly upon a chair into which the stone was incorporated.

I say ignorantly, because this is certainly not the true Stone of Destiny, for it is a piece of Scottish sandstone with no footprints carved upon it. The ignorance is compounded by the fact that all these pretending monarchs, from Edward II to the present incumbent, have failed to legitimise their succession, for they should have stood barefoot upon it. The stone itself has failed to legitimise them. It cannot, as it is not the true stone. Even if it were, it has not, for the true stone always uttered a cry of recognition or acceptance. The stone now in Edinburgh, and formerly in the hands of thieves in the form of the Church of England, has remained decently silent for centuries. This much can be accorded to it, as a mere imposter of a stone, that it has been honest and modest.

The legend is that the true stone was Jacob's pillow, and it was brought to Ireland out of Egypt by Scota and Gaythelos, her Greek husband. It is claimed that she was a daughter of Rameses II, and some believe that the stone came to Scotland at the time of the Gaelic settlement of Dalriada in the 5th century AD. This legend was and remains part of the origin myth of the Scots, being first published abroad by the seminal Scottish historian, John of Fordun, in the mid 14th century; and it is fundamental to an understanding of the Hamilton Mausoleum, which is the largest personal tomb in the Western world since the pyramids.

RINGING ROCKS AND BELLS

So what has this got to do with music? It will be revealed when discussing the Hamilton Mausoleum in the concluding part of the paper. As for sounding stones, close to one of our most frequented sites of pilgrimage, St Columba's abbey on Iona, is an object of greater antiquity than anything else on the island. It is a naturally resonant rock, ringing rock, bell rock or sangelstein. Call it what you will, but no map records it, no guidebook speaks of it, and few visit it. But it has been sounded and recorded by members of the Order of Bards, Ovates and Druids, and more recently accompanied by a replica bronze age horn.

Did the Lia Fail sound like a ringing stone, or was the cry it uttered more unearthly? Surely not, for the Lia Fail represented the earth goddess to whom the King was married symbolically. It is indeed the cry of the earth. There are also several other ringing stones in Scotland. One of them is the central recumbent stone in an early bronze age recumbent stone circle in Aberdeenshire. Another, with prehistoric cup-marks, is on the island of Tiree. It is said, were it ever to be moved, the island would sink. In a hollow on its top, pilgrims have placed their votive offerings of coins. Thus we can see and hear even today how the natural sounds inherent in the substance of the land have been linked into ritual and belief and have acted as a focus for local pilgrimage for literally thousands of years.

It would be nice at this point to consider the acoustic properties of the stone circles and megalithic chambers in Scotland, but there is space only to hint at these properties, for we are only now taking on board what should have been obvious from the start, that some of these structures managed sound, as well as space and light.

The interior of Maes Howe in the Orkney Islands off the north coast of Scotland dates from before 2700 BC. Its entrance is aligned with the setting sun at the winter solstice. Like the pyramids, it manages light, and sound, and we shall come to the significance of these below. Maes Howe, and its many counterparts on the Celtic fringe of Europe, share with the pyramids the function of tomb and ritual space to offer contact between this world and the next. In many respects, it is no different from any cathedral which is aligned east-west, with sound and light carefully managed and replete with burials and often built on the site of an earlier significant burial.

No doubt some of these megalithic structures were still in use at the time of the development of the bronze age horn during the period leading up to the 7th century BC, which is the usual date given for them. I have myself experienced replica bronze age horns invoking a standing wave in the central chamber of New Grange in Ireland, and finding a particular focus to the sound when played beside the central stone at Callanish. This is an area of musical archaeology only just opening up, and 1 return to the bronze age later. In the meantime, apart from a ringing rock, what else is available to connect us to Iona through sound? The answer is bells, and Scotland can boast several surviving from the 7th–9th centuries, but which have scarcely been used as a focus for anything.

The bells have interesting connections with rock gongs. Gildas, a 6th century saint from Strathclyde, reputedly used a rock gong rather than a bell to summon the faithful in Brittany. His rock gong has been recorded and is so resonant that its sound is not far removed from that of an iron bell. Indeed, the process of smelting ore and refining it into iron, which is then fashioned into a bell, can be seen as a releasing of the sound in the rock. The use of a rock gong for purposes of Christian assembly is a straightforward continuation of the pre-Christian functions these ringing rocks are assumed to have fulfilled.

Back in 1994, I made reference to the failure of our centres of pilgrimage to address their own heritage. Alas, little has changed. Just as it was my privilege to be the first in centuries to record the Iona ringing rock, so it was my privilege to be the first to sound one of these early bells in Iona Abbey. It was also my privilege to obtain the recording of chants specifically for St Columba in his own Abbey for the first time, all in the space of the last two years. I would have thought any one of these fascinating enough to have drawn crowds for centuries. Iona is a place of pilgrimage, and thousands upon thousands go there every year. But visitors cannot buy a recording of these early bells; the shop does not sell the only CD available of chants for St Columba; the ringing rock is uncharted and unvisited; they cannot even buy a replica of an early bell, or a photograph of the Inchcolm antiphoner, or a photograph of the ringing rock.

I have no desire to commercialise Iona. But I do have a sense of shame that the visitors come and go and miss half of the essential material, because nobody cares to provide it. The same can be said for the St Mungo Museum in Glasgow, to which I also referred in 1994. Where are the images or postcards of the Sprouston Breviary? Why have they not made a selected recording, including some of the chants for its patron Saint Mungo, and the sound of an early bell or two? Pluralism and breadth of treatment are fine, but when you are operating right on the site of a great cathedral and you have named your museum after its patron saint, and you choose to ignore some of the most relevant cultural representations of the place and the man, then we are entitled to ask questions.

IONA

For the early Christians in the Celtic-speaking West, pilgrimage was fundamental in a particular sense. They chose the white martyrdom. It was considered more gruelling than red martyrdom. It was easy to die, but to exile yourself, that was hard, and that was what they did. All across Europe, these Celtic speaking monks and saints made an indelible impression. St Columbanus, St Gall, St Killian, St Gildas, St Cuthbert, St Finnian, St Sillan, and so on, names recognisable to the devout on the Continent, but known to very few in Scotland. Even St Columba, who should be our patron saint and for whom there were many celebrations last year, is shadowy to most Scots.

These men were on a search far beyond any money-sucking millemial dome stitched together by spin doctors. Their search was for an ideal beyond the here and now, beyond even the golden Cherubim, whose great wings of solid gold spanned the perfect cube of the Holy of Holies in

Solomon's Temple, guarding at its heart, the ark of the covenant and the tablets of law. Their ideal acknowledged these, but went beyond to that which they represent. The Cherubim did not only defend the land east of Eden, they also celebrate the glory of the godhead. Above all, they did sing fanciful stuff, but not so fanciful that it was not truly sought after by the first Christian pilgrims to Scotland.

> Three matchless birds on the chair before the King, and their minds set on their Creator through all time; that is their part. The eight hours of prayer, these they celebrate by praising and acclaiming the Lord, with chanting of Archangels joining in harmony. The birds and the Archangels lead the song, and all Heaven's family, both saints and holy virgins, answer in antiphony.

Fis Adamnan, Adamnan of Iona's vision 11th century.

It is natural to think of the birds singing in heaven, it is precisely what they do, and only a small flight of imagination is required to raise them high enough to join the Seraphim and Cherubim. So much for hierarchy in Celtic Christianity in which the birds lead one to eternal joy. The story of the little bird is the classical example in which a monk follows the sweet song of a bird until dusk, but on returning finds the orchard gone, the brothers in different habits, for two hundred years have passed in the beauty of the song.

That pilgrimage, following the beauty of the sound of the bird through time into eternity, is a kind of spiritual migration. But the early Christians who came from Ireland to Scotland, and moved out eventually as far north as Iceland and as far east as the Danube, made a unity of the physical and the spiritual by their pursuit of the white martyrdom of exile for Christ. Brendan, like the birds, was a superb singer, but having heard a heavenly bird singing on the altar, he would listen to no mortal music. He was guided often by the birds, even reaching America; and Columcille, whose name is that of a bird and who was also a renowned singer was indeed a dove over the ocean.

Whether these saints were conscious of the 'opinion of Pythagoras concerning wild fowl, that the soul of my grandam might haply inhabit a bird', I cannot say, but Columba would probably have agreed with Malvolio's reaction, 'I think nobly of the soul and in no wise approve his opinion', for Columba specifically rejects worship of the birds.

And yet, time after time we find these references to birdsong and to the beauty and innocence and wisdom of birds, and I cannot help feeling, after reading much of the early literature of the western Celtic Christians, that while they would not have accepted the theory of the transmigration of souls, their orthodoxy did not prevent them from having a deep feeling for the living creatures, which included the trees and the mountains, and attributed to these creatures a kind of sentience which was not far removed from the pantheism which they had but recently replaced with the gospels. Indeed, shape-changing was a recurrent element in the stories they themselves transcribed.

In Scotland, the study of bird-song goes deep, for the Gaelic version of Nennius reports that the Picts were reputed to have brought to Ireland: 'every spell, charm, sneeze and augury by the voices of the birds, and every omen. The Scots and the Irish share the music of the pre-Christian lament, the pilililiu, with the redshank, a subject I have covered in previous volumes in this series.

As for the question of the motivation for birds to sing, I see no reason for supposing that swollen gonads and pure joy are mutually exclusive. Au contraire. If the dove of the Holy Spirit can brood over the creation, there must have been swollen gonads in heaven too, and no doubt the 'three matchless birds' of the Holy Trinity sang us into existence, full of the joy and high hopes that are the lot of uninstructed parenthood.

So, how have we, their Scottish musical children, responded to our inheritance? Not badly, I believe, for my criticisms are primarily levelled at the provision for tourists. As musicians was have done our best over the centuries to keep the resonance of our song in tune with nature as the uncorrupted link between humanity and heaven, and we have, on occasion, attempted to evoke the heavenly chorus as a reminder that our earthly music is but a faint pre-echo of the song of the birds and the Archangels and all Heaven's family. However, what of the voices with which we ourselves are endowed? We too, might we not also have natural gifts that link us to heaven?

COLUMBA THE DOVE

I have made it a practice never to discount my sources as mere fancy, or foolish hagiography. I read such texts of the lives of the saints as attempts to fill out the effects of experiences that may well have been genuine, and repeated from life to life; and miraculous account to miraculous account because they actually occurred, and occurred more than once. Take this account of St Columba, written by St Adomnan in the late 7th century. Adomnan knew people who had known Columba and his account, miracles and all, deserves the closest attention. This story refers to a fortress near Inverness belonging to the Pictish King Brude whom Columba had converted to Christianity, to the dismay of the Druids;

When the saint himself was chanting the evening hymns with a few of the brethren, as usual, outside the king's fortifications, some Druids, coming near to them, did all they could to prevent God's praises being sung in the midst of a pagan nation. On seeing this, the saint began to sing the 44th psalm, and at the same moment so wonderfully loud, like pealing thunder, did his voice become, that king and people were struck with terror and amazement.

'What is stranger still', writes Adamnan of other occasions, 'to those with him in the church his voice did not sound louder than that of others; and yet at the same time persons more than a mile away heard it so distinctly that they could mark each syllable.'

A gothic text states that Columba had a carrying voice heard at 1500 paces and that it was like a melodious lion. Mere fancy, one might say. But one voice only, can sing Psalm 44 in a way that might well frighten a credulous audience. The sound is indeed like a melodious lion. Adamnan admits that Columba rarely performed his vocal feats, and only when he was inspired. I am not saying that these sounds recorded today are what Columba actually did. I am sure he did much better. What if Adamnan had written that Columba sang with two voices simultaneously, one so high that it sounded as though it was the call of the Cherubim from heaven itself? Rubbish, I would have said. Impossible! This is Adamnan endowing his hero-saint with heavenly, not earthly powers. The song of the Cherubim maybe, but not the voice of man.

For those of you familiar with harmonic singing, there is nothing so very startling about such claims, but try and describe the effects in words and even the most extravagant hagiography would be hard put to it to explain this sound. However, it is real. It was and is a widespread technique in religious worship in the middle and far east, and was probably used in mediaeval churches. Indeed, really good chanting naturally produces it and, in the case of the deep sounds, some Tibetan monks lose the power of speech by over-use of the technique. They dedicate their voices to God.

I say this to give an idea of the vocal threads that may be drawn between earth and heaven without using any text. I trust it gives greater meaning and credence to texts that tend to be treated with indulgence rather than respect. We have music and poetry of our principal saints which still remains little studied, although it is from at least as early as the 13th century and some of it may be very much older. This is all the sadder because these are in fact some of the very oldest literary manifestations to be found in any Scottish manuscripts, and the poetry and ornate prose they contain is fascinating, not just for its linguistic interest, but for its artistic beauty both in sound and sense. What is also of peculiar importance to these texts is that we have music for them, music which can give a clue to stress, rhyme, metre, emphasis, meaning and symbolism. There should be nests of scholars working on them. Here is a chant for St Columbals feast day. It is full of elaborate assonance and rhyme, within a syllabic structure which is reflected in musical rhymes and assonances:

> O mira regis Christi
> clementia nam tota
> refulget ecclesia
> signis et preludiis
> Columbe mirabilibus
> certat plebs magnivoca
> felici memoria
> patris pii precibus
> Gloria Patri et Filio
> et Spiritui sancto.

O wondrous clemency of Christ the King! The whole church gleams with the signs and wondrous portents of Columba. The people vie with full voices in blessed remembrance and prayers to the devoted father.

Not perhaps the Cherubim, but imagine this sung at vespers at the vigil on the eve of 9th June on Inchcolm, the twenty lighted candles at the high altar, the people singing with full voices in blessed remembrance, the sweet tones of the clarsach accompanying the chant (as we know was common practice among Celtic monks), and one feels a little closer to the company of angels. I was on Iona on the eve of 9th June 1996, on pilgrimage for Radio Scotland. Apart from my producer, I was the only person in the Abbey, both of us agnostics, alone keeping vigil for the greatest of our saints.

It is important to recollect that chants such as 'O Mira Regis' may even have been in use in the late 15th century and actively encouraged, as suggested by the following quotation from the licence granted to Chapman and Millar for the first printing press in Scotland:

And als it is divisit and thocht expedient be us and our counsall that in tyme cuming mess bukis, manualis, matyne bukis and portuus bukis efter our awin Scottis use and with legendis of Scottis sanctis as is now gaderit and ekit be ane reverend fader in God and our traist counsalour Williame, bischop of Abirdene, and utheris, be usit generaly within al our realme als sone as the sammyn may be imprentit and providit; and that na maner of sic bukis of Salusbery use be brocht to be sauld within our realme in tym cuming under pane of escheting of the bukis and punising of thair persons, bringaris thairof within our realme in contrar this our statut, with al rigour as efferis.

GLASGOW

Like St Columba, St Kentigern or St Mungo, was also widely venerated. He is buried underneath Glasgow Cathedral in one of the finest crypts in Europe. A forest of stone surrounding him, sacred, and almost as dark and Druidic as the encounter he was supposed to have had with Merlin. 'The Sprouston Breviary' contains a complete set of services for Mungo.

Two further manuscripts containing musical offices for St Kentigern have been lost in this century. One by the Bolandistes Library, the other by a dealer in London. But who cares in Glasgow for such losses, when they will not even bring to public notice St Mungo's miracles in 13th century song. For example, the miracle of the fish and the ring. In this story the Queen of Cadzow's husband, finding a ring he gave her on the finger of another man, removes it when the man is asleep, throws it into the Clyde and then demands it of his wife, most uncivilly. Finding she cannot oblige, but protesting her innocence, she goes to St Mungo, who promptly goes fishing and catches a salmon with the Queen's ring in its mouth. It is duly returned and the King who chooses to accept the return as token of his wife's innocence.

The chant likens this miracle to the story of Peter finding the coin in the fish's belly. It is a subtle way of side-stepping the moral dilemma posed by the Queen's questionable behaviour. After all, how come another man was wearing it? To whom should it be returned? To the King who first gave it, to the Queen who apparently passed it on, to the knight who was wearing it?

To whom does it belong? asks Peter of Christ with respect to his coin. Whose image is upon it, asks Christ? Caesar's, says Peter. Render unto Caesar that which is Caesar's says Christ. And so in like manner, the ring is returned to its rightful owner, she who claims it as her own image of her unbroken fidelity. The chant rises to its highest point at the mention of Kentigern, and the beautiful melismas coil around the vowels like the water round the fish in the shallows of the Clyde. This is a responsory for the third nocturn of Matins, St Mungo's Matins, mentioned by Lindsay in the Papingo as still being sung in the 1530s, but not to be heard in his Museum and not to be publicised in the city whose coat of arms refers to this very miracle.

There is nothing of the Cherubim in this music, but to the ears of the adulterer it must sound as sweet to hear a saint reaching out towards heavenly justification, by a symbolic as well as miraculous sympathetic relationship with nature.

ST ANDREWS

It is not hard to make the connection between Glasgow and St Andrews, for it is very probable that the Precentor at Glasgow Cathedral in the early 13th century, and who became bishop of St Andrews, was the commissioner, possibly even the compiler of the great 'St Andrews Music Book', known to musicologists as Wl because it is now in Wolfenbuttel, whence I made my own recent pilgrimage.

About half a century before the chants for St Kentigern were written down, the great St Andrews manuscript was compiled, containing some of the works from the period of Leonin and Perotin. However, at the ends of the fascicles of this manuscript and in the whole of fascicle 11, the scribes added material which is without Parisian concordances, but which shows traits broadly known as 'insular', a disgraceful term which buries Scotland and Wales and Ireland under England in the hope that they will Go Away.

If we could identify the 'Walter' who copied much of the St Andrews Music Book, we might find out its exact date; but of Walter we know nothing whatever except that when he finished his laborious business at the end of the tenth fascicle of the manuscript, on the verso side of folio number 191 Walter signed his name in music: 'May Walter, the writer of this book, be blessed.'

The manuscript can not be definitively dated, nor is it possible to determine the original date of the music. However, there is one piece which seems likely to date from between 1164 and 1170. It is a planctus or lament, *In Rama Sonat Gemitus*, and when Walter wrote it out, he shaped the initial letter I into the form of a bishop's staff. That was because the lament was for the Archbishop Thomas a Beckett's exile in France. Perhaps Beckett, who was a Norman, had a colleague in France with Scottish connections who wrote this piece that appears uniquely in the manuscript. Another closely related Scottish manuscript appears to be the only insular source for a history of the office for Thomas a Beckett. So Beckett, source of one of the greatest pilgrimages in these islands, may have had Scottish connections. The poem is a sort of biblical allegory for the relationship between Beckett and King Henry II of England, which was not a good one. The church is Rachel, Henry is Herod. The sinuous beauty of the descending phrases and the perfect placing of the intense climax of the lament make this one of the most deeply felt vocal lines from any time or place:

> In Rama the English Rachel weeps, for a descendant of Herod has covered her in ignominy. Behold, her first-born, the Joseph of Canterbury is exiled to the Egypt of France.

For how long this music remained in regular use we cannot say. What it establishes is that Scotland, far from being peripheral, was thoroughly aware of the musical world around it. However, it was a nation battling for its existence against the English and it was some sixty years after the compilation of the St Andrews Manuscript, before the Battle of Bannockburn gave Scotland a brief opportunity to turn its energies away from politics and fighting.

The victory at Bannockburn must have given a reat impetus to Scottish culture generally, one of which was the completion of St Andrews Cathedral by Bishop Lamberton. A building such as this, with its holy-of-holies containing the shrine with the bones of St Andrew, required music to match. When pilgrims were finally conducted into the inner darkness, lit perhaps by subtle arrangements of candles, waiting for the great moment of revelation as the reliquary was revealed, the shutters opened, and the whole purpoose of their pilgrimage brought to its climax, there must have been a musical preparation. The one I am proposing might have been heard on such an occasion, but could not have been used for every group of pilgrims, it is too demanding vocally for that, but had a prince or a queen, a bishop or a visiting singer of quality been in the group, then surely they would have brought out their best soloists.

In one of the sections of the St Andrews Music Book, with unique music of likely Scottish origin, we can hear what such a performance would have been like. It is indeed the voice of the Cherubim, because it says it is. It is virtuosic, extravagant, and almost certainly Scottish, despite having been used to supplement a reconstruction of a Notre Dame Easter mass possibly because they did not have such exciting music in Paris. It is a Sanctus trope, describing the melody of heaven, the song of the Cherubim, resonating in the church. It is as near as a trained voice can get to the extended song of a bird.

But what of counterpoint, the art of singing more than one tune at a time and which was only just developing when this manuscript was made? Imagine yourself one of the countless European pilgrims to St Andrews. Perhaps you have never heard two-part singing, if you come from the provinces. You enter the cathedral to attend mass. An introductory church drama is performed, a visitatio sepulchri, sinuous lovely single lines searching out the architecture of one of the great buildings of Europe. But now the mass proper begins. The old familiar Greek words, so perfectly designed for singing, just nothing but vowels and vowels and vowels, Kyrie eleison, Christe eleison, kyrie eleison, but magically, incredibly, the line divides into two. The effect is ethereal, an exquisite blend of decoration and simplicity as text and chant are troped.

This music comes from the eleventh fascicle of the St Andrews music Book. It is again almost certainly Scottish, though clearly based on the

Parisian tradition. Hierarchy? Well yes and no. The parts cross and recross, though the cantus firmus (the underlying plain chant) is mostly the lower of the two. But the text for both is a trope, a non-liturgical addition. Here, the musical pilgrim is permitted to add a secular element to the chant that bore the sacred text.

The secular and the sacred meet with particularly touching intimacy in the idea that men and angels could converse in music, an idea primarily associated with the shepherds in the Christmas story. Bach symbolises the two in the Christmas oratorio, the shepherds playing pipes. In Scotland, it was illustrated with delightful naivetee in the Christmas medley 'All Sons Of Adam':

> All sons of Adam rise up with me,
>
> Go love the blissed Trinitie
> Sing we now-ell, nowell, nowell,
>
> Cry Kyrie with Hosanna,
> Sing Sabaoth, sing Alleluja,
> Now save us all Emanuel.

At this point the music changes because Gabriel is going to speak. The first statement: 'Then spak archangel Gabriel' is straightforward, but when Gabriel himself said: 'Ave Mary mild, the Lord of Lords is with thee, now sall thou go with child, Ecce ancilla Domini.' then the part writing becomes more strictly and obviously imitative and closer to the kind of music one would have heard in church. Mary's reply takes up this style for 'Then said the virgin young As thou hes said so mot it be.'But as soon as her own thought enters, 'Welcom be heavin's king' the music is simplified and leads into a lovely passage which is probably the earliest known version of 'I saw three ships'. The picture is a musical one:

> Then cam a ship fair sailland then,
> St Michael was the stiersman,
> Sanct John sat in the horn.
>
> Our Lord harpit, our Lady sang,
> And all the bells of heavln they rang
> On Christsonday at morn.

Now the angels join in and the music changes again. They sing in Latin, of course, and they use an improvisatory but well established technique of part-singing known as faburdon in which the main voice is parallelled by the others. Then the sons of Adam round it all off joyously 'with honor and perpetual joll'. The whole thing operates at at least three different levels of register for mankind and Mary, for the Archangel, and for the Angels all and sum. However, though delicious and charming, this is not the sophisticated concept of hierarchical yet mystical dialogue that is ultimately sought by the pilgrim. For that we have to go to Robert Carver's ten part mass.

THE CHAPEL ROYAL AT STIRLING

The darkness of the fall of man. Human speech a mere Babel. All words but shadows of that which they signify. The hierarchy established with God, angels, mankind, animals and plants in that order. Remember the birds? So close to God all you have to do is follow the song of a little bird as the old monk in the Celtic folk tale did, and he passed beyond time into an eternity of joy. The mediaeval mind no doubt had its schemes and its orders of rhetoric and argument. But music and poetry and story skip across these boundaries even while honouring them. When God set up the hierarchy of heaven there were ten orders within it:

> Seraphim, Cherubim, Thrones in the first circle.
> Dominions, Virtues and Powers in the second circle.
> Principalities, Archangels and Angels in the third circle.

That makes nine. The tenth order was the order of Satan: the fallen angels. Mankind was created in the fond parental hope that we would make up for the failure of Heaven's first parturition which was to create hell. One hell of a responsibility, one might, with justice protest.

This is not just speculation. It was part and parcel of religious observance. In the Chapel Royal, dedicated to St Michael and the Virgin, the devil was under direct assault. St Michael as the warrior archangel, the dragon-slayer: the Virgin as the mother of Christ whose heel would bruise Satan's head. Not far away a few miles down the river Forth, was built the Great Michael, launched on 10th October 1511. She was Europe's biggest warship. She was probably intended to lead a crusade against the Turks: the devil incarnate. One is tempted to suggest that the launch was eleven days late, St Michaells day being 29th September. Perhaps weather, or the usual delays in such projects, were the cause. James Reld Baxter has suggested fascinating connections with the Burgundian court and the order of the golden fleece. But it appears to have been earlier, in 1506, that Carver's ten part mass was completed. The music is based on a cantus firmus drawn from a Magnificat Antiphon with these words: 'Dum sacrum mysterium cerneret Johannes, Archangelus Michael tuba cecinit' (while John behold the sacred mystery, Michael the Archangel sounded the trumpet), and it goes on: 'Forgive oh Lord, our God Thou who openest the Book and loosest the seals thereof.'

This is apocalyptic stuff, but why not nine parts like Wylkynsong's Salve Regina' in the Eton Choirbook, almost certainly known to Carver, and in which each voice part was given the name of one of the orders of angels? Because, in Carver's work, mankind has a place too. The sequence for St Michael's day enumerates the nine orders of angels and then continues 'The angels are the work of Thy primeval hand, we the latest in Thine image fashioned.'

What we have in this great work, is not just the heavenly chorus itself, but mankind joining in it. Not a dialogue between shepherds and angels, each holding their proper musical stations, but a hierarchy in which mankind has a potential place and to which we may aspire. In the *Oui sedes*, who sittest on the right hand of the Father, we have a vision (we have no single word for a hearing experience, one of the greatest single omissions in the English language), so it is a vision in sound of the heavenly chorus, the great waves of sound beating on the ear drums like vast wingbeats. In part of the *Agnus Dei*, James Ross has suggested that, if the voiceparts do correspond to the hierarchy of angels in detail as well as in general, then we are about to hear the Seraphim and Cherubim as they float on the soprano voices above the altos of Thrones and Dominions.

This work is connected to others by Carver. To the *Missa L'Homme Armee* by its warlike subject matter. To the six-part mass through musical links and possibly links with the launch of the Great Michael. To his great 19 part motet, *O Bone Jesu*, by direct quotation with the Seraphim and Cherubim above the Thrones and Dominions, leading to the final part of the prayer on these words:

> O dulcia Jesu,
> recognosce quod tuum est, et absterge quod alienumest
> O amantissime Jesu,
> O desideratissime Jesu,
> O mitissime Jesu,
> O Jesu admitte me intrare regnum tuum, dulcis Jesu.

This is a personal request on behalf of James the IV, already occupying the earthly parallel of Thrones and Dominions, to enter truly into that community of heaven. This composition was probably commissioned by the King as part of his elaborate penance for his involvement in his father's death. A king who dethroned his own monarch, his own father, seeking expiation. The iron links around his waist and the intended crusade: 'Admitte me intrare regnum tuum.' Permit me to enter thy kingdom.

What ironies lie there for the young king. If the sound of ten parts, humans joining the angels was already stupendous, what is one to say of this immense 19 part texture: the maximum the Chapel Royal choir could achieve with their sixteen men and six boys, two each to the three top parts? Or is it a deep numerical allegory, not just the nine choirs of angels, but the ninth hour, the hour of crucifixion: not just the ten choirs when mankind is included, but the Roman ten: the X for Christus in Greek, the X for the cross of St Andrew. These two combined, who is to say?

One thing is certain, in this monumental work the name of Jesu is reiterated over and over, and every time in the score, Carver places above it a Corona, the Latin name for a musical pause, a crown. And before that crown the music pauses to allow the congregation to genuflect at the holy name. So here in Scotland, we can perform a musical pilgrimage, feeling a close contact with holy sites such as Iona, Glasgow Cathedral, the ruins of St Andrews cathedral, and with the Chapel Royal in Stirling, but above all it is the soul's pilgrimage and this supreme music sounds the chord of creative genius that draws us into the eternally sounding chord of the creation itself.

TO PANAMA AND THE USA

It is in the search for that chord, both as a people and as musicians that we must make our excursion to Panama and the USA. Take a look at the pyramid on the dollar bill: its level egalitarian base, its four quarters of the compass and its apex pointing to the stars. It represents one side of the Great Seal of the USA and it is a masonic symbol. The pyramids are younger than the great megalithic tombs and stone circles of Western Europe; but their significance as structures binding the earth to the stars has dominated our imagination for millenia. Note the divine light, emanating from the eye at the apex of the pyramid, the all-seeing eye of God and of undivided truth. And the mottos? '*Annuit coeptis*', the Creator is favourable to our undertaking.

These idealistic new world sentiments might well have formed the motto of the Scottish company which in the late 1690s proposed and briefly achieved the settlement of Darien on the Panama isthmus, with the intention of setting up a free port and controlling trade between the world's two greatest oceans. They weren not the only ones with that idea and eventually the canal zone became the territory of the USA in 1911, when Theodore Roosevelt boasted 'I took Panama'.

The time I speak of is 1698–1700, and at that time it belonged partly to the native Indians, partly to the Spanish, and a teensy-weensy bit to the Scots. However there is an extraordinary connection, between the Scottish

Darien scheme and Roosevelt's ultimate achievement, for Roosevelt was the direct descendent of The Rev Stobo, one of the colonists in the Scottish fleet which had retreated from Darien, and whose wife was drowned off the coast of America. Stobo survived and settled in Carolina and his daughter Jean married the Scot, James Bulloch, whose great-great-grandson was Roosevelt's grandfather. Roosevelt's proud boast 'I took Panama' was made in the knowledge that he was making good a defeat suffered by his family at the hands of the Spanish over 200 years before. His great-great-great-great grandmother, Jean Bulloch, had nearly drowned in the Scottish retreat. There is a poetic justice in the fact that next year the USA will be handing the canal zone back to the Panamanians exactly 300 years after the Scots had established Fort St Andrew in Darien, and just as Scotland itself takes its first steps towards reestablishing its democratic parliamentary independence.

The whole Scottish enterprise in Darien was motivated by one man, William Paterson. He was an idealist who believed that world-wide commerce should be open to all without regard to nationality, religion, or race; that paper currency should be redeemable in gold and that governments should eliminate their national debts. He was the founder of the Bank of England. But his Darien scheme was a total failure, though it started out with high hopes and ideals: hopes and ideals which a young Scottish aristocrat expressed through music.

John Clerk of Penicuik was 19 when he wrote his cantata *Leo Scotiae Irritatus*, The Lion of Scotland Angered, setting a Latin text by his Dutch friend Hermann Booerhaave. Why angered? Because the Spanish and English were mucking about with the glorious Scottish colony in Darien. The fact that the colony was underfunded, under-provisioned, ignorant of the threat of disease to white men in Central America, and generally naive, did not deter the moral outrage of these two young idealists, Clerk and Booerhaave. They had envisioned an ideal state of perfect social harmony: another Eden or a New Jerusalem. They were supported by the native Indians whose canoes were to-ing and fro-ing with Scottish flags waving proudly, looking for a better deal than the Spanish offered.

This music is history, not just in its text, but in its very structure. The first aria comes to a close 33 bars on from the first vocal entry, the call to arms having commenced at bar 22. So the first sections of the work are built up out of multiples of eleven bar units. This is unheard of in music which, was settling down into multiples of four, by the late 17th century. These remain standard units of length as in 8 and 12 bar blues. So what do these multiples of 11 mean? The answer is that they are deeply symbolic of the ideals which motivated the colony, and they are profoundly associated with pilgrimage.

Clerk's symbolism starts with the 11 bar instrumental opening, for the number 11 represents the number of the tribes of Israel given land. The 12th tribe was the priestly one, and was distributed among the other 11. So the Scottish colony in Darien would be a new Promised Land, the Scottish clan system being a natural parallel to the tribal system of the Jews. Indeed, many Scots regarded themselves as one of the lost tribes of Israel, their history first surfacing in the land of the pyramids.

The whole opening aria adds up to 44 bars, indicating (via Hebrew numerology) that it is in essence a psalm of David. The next section of the Cantata is 22 bars long and represents the number of kings in Chronicles II, the first (Solomon) and last of whom (Cyrus) respectively built and rebuilt the Temple of Solomon in Jerusalem. Its inner sanctum, the Holy of Holies where the tablets of law were housed, was a perfect cube and represented the New Jerusalem, the Heavenly City to come.

> The enemy are confounded and destroyed, these plagues on Scottish land are scattered. God's anger will not rest until many are slaughtered, and the envious who injure us are overcome. May Mars and War destroy those who harry the Darien colony.

The total length of the cantata so far is 66 bars, underlining the Biblical justification, 66 being the number of books in the protestant Bible. Clerk knew all this. He was training as a lawyer and became a leading mason. That is why the number scheme is broken for the passage describing the horror of war with the words 'Illos arma sonora, illos horrida bella'.

Clerk's use of number symbolism should not surprise us. His slightly younger contemporary, Johann Sebastian Bach used it. In any case Clerk was the great-great-grandfather of James Clerk, better known as James Clerk Maxwell, one of the greatest mathematical geniuses of all time.

The next movement, acknowledging that Fortune's wheel is turning against the Scots, asks for it to be reversed. Clerk uses a ground bass shaped to imitate the repeating rise and fall of the wheel. Against this, the voice sings in broken phrases, vainly enumerating Scotland's virtues, righteousness, law, religion, justice and equity. These were the very things enshrined on the tablets of law in the ark of the covenant, in the perfect cube of the Holy of Holies, and so Clerk made this aria 27 bars long, 3x3x3 being a perfect cube. The ground bass itself is 3 bars long and occurs 9 times, 3x3x3 again.

The last surviving movement looks forward to the gentle peacefulness of a Scottish pastoral idyll in the new colony, but the remaining pages of the score are missing, though we have the complete text. Did Clerk remove their triumphant vision, when he learnt of the failure of the colony? Clerk himself became a signatory of the Treaty and Act of Union between

Scotland and England, signed in 1707. It brought the English and Scottish Parliaments to an end, creating a new parliament of the United Kingdom. But the Kings were not truly ours any more. The Stewarts were ousted and no stone would ever cry with joy for the Houses of Hanover or Windsor.

THE HAMILTON MAUSOLEUM

What follows is in a sense the wildest fantasy imaginable, but it is not my fantasy, and it has living reality in the form of the most remarkable personal tomb since the pyramids. It has the most remarkable acoustic in the world, and the most gloriously eccentric ambition I have ever encountered. It was the acoustic that drew me to it, so it has musical relevance, but it goes beyond music into the infinite, the infinite that is also represented by the point of the pyramid.

Lurking behind it all is the origin myth of the Scots, the widely held belief that they were descended from the daughter of a Pharaoh. Her father was drowned in the Red Sea, and her subsequent emigration via Spain and Ireland to the land now called Scotland, was a parallel to, (if not in point of fact), a search of one of the tribes of Israel for the Promised Land. For Scota was the name of the daughter, her husband was a renegade Greek prince, and they supported the Israelites against her father. She and her consort were therefore not permitted to succeed to the throne, so the myth goes, and she took her royal Egyptian eggs and he his Royal Greek seed, westward. This is a myth. There is no proof behind it, but that does not matter. It is the myth which was believed. It was the myth published by Scottish historians from as early as Fordun in the 14th century. William Wallace and Robert the Bruce probably knew of it.

It is interesting to note that Franklin and Jefferson's original proposal for the Great Seal of the USA was to show Moses crossing the Red Sea, and to bear the motto 'Rebellion to tyrants is obedience to God.' It was a tough decision, what to put on the Great Seal. It took them six years to come up with the pyramid and the eagle, the eagle being the symbol of the Scottish masonic rite.

It was not just the high and the mighty who thought in these ancient biblical terms. One Scot who led a group of highlanders from Glengarry, northward over the Adirondacks, told his story in later years to a new Scottish settler in Glengarry County. The pioneer told of climbing over mountain slopes, following trails through uncut forests, crossing muskegs, evading hostile Indians and angry revolutionaries. The listener exclaimed: 'Well, well! The only example I can think of like that is when Moses led the Israelites into the Promised Land.' 'Ach, Moses' said the pioneer, 'Moses be damned. He lost half his army in the Red Sea. I brought my party through without a single loss.'

However, death comes to all, as the pyramid on the dollar bill, and the Hamilton Mausoleum near Glasgow remind us: and the kingdoms of the gods are not the kingdoms of this world, not that is, unless you are a Pharaoh and descended from the gods. That is precisely what Alexander, 10th Duke of Hamilton believed himself to be. The Hamiltons had long held a claim on the Scottish throne. They believed that the Scottish monarchy was 'Imperial and Independent' and directly descended from Scota, a disinherited Pharaoh's daughter, so said the old Scottish historians. Being a Pharaoh, therefore, Alexander Hamilton, 10th Duke, Baron of this and Lord of that, needed a proper burial. But being a Scot, a pyramid was not good enough. He reverted to the more ancient Phallus. The Pillars of the upper and lower kingdoms, the Cleopatra's needles that adorn many a masonic burial place. So the Duke had built for himself a gigantic circumcised penis, 120 feet high, and designed to be flooded annually at its base by the river Clyde. This represented the Nile, and the fertile tears of Isis for her murdered brother, the God Osiris, whereby she caused his dead flesh to rise and impregnate her with their son Horus. The Duke's cylinder emerges from a perfect cube, the cube being the shape of the Holy of Holies in Solomon's Temple, signifying the shape of the New Jerusalem to come, itself an image of the cosmos.

Consider the significance of one little patch of snow on the glans of the Duke's metaphorical penis. Fantastic? Yes. Boloney? No. In 1822, for 600 pounds sterling, the Duke purchased a superb Egyptian coffin carved from green porphyry, discovered in Memphis and containing the embalmed body of Maaru, an unmarried girl believed to have been the daughter of a Pharaoh. She died in 610 BC. Some rumours say she was pregnant. The Duke had her removed and, the coffin being too small, had grooves cut in the interior to take the lower parts of his legs which were dislocated before his body was embalmed and placed where once had lain a girl. Her coffin was carved with the symbols and names of Isis and Osiria.

Many papers could be written on the subject of this building alone but I will have to confine myself. That the crypt below was designed to be flooded, I can prove by its architecture. That it symbolised the transition to the eternal life is carved upon it. And that it also symbolises the entrance of divine light into the darkness of death is manifest in the single light at the very top of the structure, the all-seeing eye of the Creator, diffusing its divine light evenly within the regenerative organ that the structure represents. So, like Maes Howe and other megalithic tombs, and like the pyramids, this is an elaborate tomb and ritual space which manipulates light and sound. The megalithic tombs and the pyramids are designed to admit light at a specific time, mostly annually. This tomb is designed to admit water annually.

I came to it for a different reason: for its acoustics. This has the longest reverberation of any building in the world. When its bronze doors were in place it was about 30 seconds, now it is 151 seconds, and still a world beater. Its nearest rival is the Taj Mahal, another mausoleum. Running close to them is the great pyramid.

Why have such an acoustic? Even the masons I have spoken to, thought it was an architectural error, an acoustic catastrophe. I think otherwise. Many cathedrals attempt to produce similar acoustic effects. What is remarkable about this structure is that it outdoes them all with a fraction of the space. I believe what was aimed at was a kind of eternal prayer, because we are in search of eternity, the infinite point of the pyramid, infinity of eternal music of the spheres. That is what a Tibetan prayer wheel is for, to pray eternally, if not turned by the passer-by, then turned by the wind. That is why in some mediaeval monasteries they had teams of monks to sing the *laus perennis* uninterrupted song 24 hours a day every day of the year. Perhaps also in the Duke's mind, this vast stone edifice represented the legitimising stone of destiny that would call out its acknowledgment of his rightful claim for ever and ever amen.

Had the architect succeeded, any sound made in this space would never cease. It would be heard forever. The architect of the Hamilton Mausoleum achieved 93% efficiency, and what it sounds like with one bronze age horn, and one voice harmonic singing, nothing added, is hard to believe. And why harmonic singing and bronze age horn, rather than flute? Because the bronze age horn, like that oldest of instruments, the didgeridoo, is designed not to produce a complex scale of different notes, but to explore the fundamental harmonics and rhythms in a single note, just as harmonic singing explores the natural harmonics that exist in every human voice. These values are the absolute fundamental values upon which all music ultimately depends, and they thrive in this kind of Pythagorean acoustic, in which architectural proportion and acoustic become one and the same thing.

We have come a long way. From Egypt and the children of Israel, to the Promised Land and the Great Seal of the United States of America. From birth to death and life hereafter. Our pilgrimage has taken us to some of the most important sites in Scotland. In scarcely one of them will you find more than a token reference to what was their first and fundamental function: to house sound. The ear is a pilgrim too, and if Scotland's music has been a faithful Penelope in this vast Odyssey, then it is about time her Odysseus came home and claimed his own.

The Author

Dr John Purser is a graduate of Glasgow University and the Royal Scottish Academy of Music and Drama. A polymath of Renaissance stature, his distinguished career has embraced work as a composer, musician, poet, dramatist, broadcaster, writer and university lecturer. He is best known for his energetic campaigning for Scottish culture, which has included a major BBC Radio Scotland programme on the history of Scottish musical traditions, associated with the publication of his book, *Scotland's Music* (1991).

References

Purser, J., *Scotlands Music: A History of the Traditional and Classical Music of Scotland from Early Times to the Present Day*, Mainstream, 1992

Purser, J., *Homecoming of the Deskford Carnyx: After 2000 Years of Silence*, in Fladmark, J.M. (ed), Cultural Tourism, Donhead, 1994

Purser, J., *On the Trail of Music: Origins of the Scottish Triple Pipes*, in Fladmark, J.M. (ed), *Sharing the Earth: Local Identity in Global Culture*, Dohead, 1995

6

TO SANTIAGO DE COMPOSTELA
A Journey of Rememberance

Nicholas Luard

The energetic and visionary Magnus Fladmark, like his fishermen ancestors casts his net wide. In 1995 he scooped me up to write on two of the subjects closest to my heart wilderness and survival. Dipping his net back into the waters, he has hauled me into his longboat again. This year's volume is devoted to pilgrimage and tourism. Like all good Norwegians, I am sure both pilgrimage and tourism run deep in the Fladmark blood. His compatriot Leif Eriksson has a fair claim to be called one of the world's first great pilgrims and tourists for his epic voyage across the Atlantic. Like Leif Eriksson, although in a much more modest and less hazardous way, I have also been a pilgrim.

Eriksson was following the cod shoals, the white sea-borne winter gold of the Norwegian coast. In that sense he was a mercantile tourist. Like countless others after him, like Marco Polo, like the gentlemen Indian adventurers and the dour African traders, many of them Scots, he was in it for the protein and the money. Being a good Viking, was not quite enough. He had the Norse gods to answer to. He needed their protection and approval.

Eriksson has left us no records of his voyages, but given the bleak evidence of the Norse Sagas, it is not fanciful to imagine that the gods concerned him as much as the Atlantic waves. The two were inseparable. Make your peace with one, the gods, and the storms would make their peace with you. In pursuit of cod, he had to settle accounts with God.

ON PILGRIMAGE

Leif Eriksson was a pilgrim. So, I believe, adventuring, exploring humanity has always been a pilgrimage. We are natural nomads, witness the world's oldest people, the constantly travelling San hunter-gatherers of the Kalahari. Like them, the impetus to roam is encoded in our genes. Herding, tilling, and settlement come very late in man's evolution. They are last night's messages. We were designed long before last night. We are not programmed to be settlers, we were made to wander. On that level, pilgrimage is nothing more than an expression of a primal instinct. It is one we rationalise in a wide range of ways: as penance, a promise honoured, divine benison sought for some future venture, the stock-taking of a life as a defining moment approaches, a prudent storing-up of brownie points against the years ahead or the world beyond. It may be simple curiosity to find out what it is like to travel the long, winding road so many have spoken of, to escape from seemingly intolerable pressures at home, for monetary gain or even theft. Many a villain has taken the pilgrim way and returned chuckling with his pockets bulging.

Everyone who sets out is by definition a tourist, a traveller. Everyone, at whatever level of consciousness, is exploring their innerself, and attempting a reconciliation with their Maker. Even the bandits, pickpockets, and confidence tricksters still go, as they have always done, to mass at stages along the way. Quite properly. As the Palestinian carpenter said: 'In my father's house are many mansions'. Now, as for a thousand years, several of those mansions are used to store stolen goods. The police of at least two countries would dearly like to know their addresses. Perhaps if they too went on pilgrimage they would meet some copper's nark who would tell them.

I went on foot as a pilgrim to Santiago de Compostela. I had two companions, my younger sister and another woman, Hilary, a close friend of my sister and now a companion of my heart too. Both are bold, learned and strong, the first and last essential requirements of pilgrimage. 'Amazonion' was a frequent and not unkind description applied to them. As I do, both speak fluent French and Spanish. It immeasurably enriched the experience for all three of us. The one thousand mile journey took us in stages, three weeks each in successive seasons, three years to complete. We started in 1993, and finished the journey in 1995.

What follows is a highly personal account of the nature of pilgrimage today. It is inevitably personal. Much has changed since the Middle Ages, but much more remains the same. What will never change, for the devout, the sceptic and the thief, is the essence of being a pilgrim. That will always hold its singularity and its privacy.

The external journey through Europe's landscape is also the pilgrim's own internal journey through the landscape of his or her mind. The past is examined, the present tramped through day by day in snow and wind and sun, the future considered at night by the fire.

By the early Middle Ages, Central Europe had become the theatre or staging post for the emerging modern world's three great pilgrimages: to Jerusalem, the focus for the Palestinian carpenter's short life; to Rome, where after the carpenter's crucifixion, the fisherman Peter, the 'rock' who followed him, raised the banner of his beliefs; and to Santiago de Compostela: 'St James of the Field of the Star'. Jerusalem and Rome are obvious enough destinations in the context of Christianity's history. But Santiago, swiftly eclipsed both Jerusalem and Rome.

WHY SANTIAGO?

Santiago was a village in north-western Spain, perched on a lofty stretch of plain close to what was then the edge of the world, the wind and wave-battered coastline of Cape Finisterre. It had nothing. It was not a trading-post nor at a cross-roads. It had no traditions, no past, and no associations with Europe's history. It was simply a hamlet of rough stone-built cottages surrounded by outlying peasant farms. The earth was sour and hard to work, and the Atlantic gales raged over it throughout the long Iberian winters.

In 814 AD, the priest of Santiago had a dream. He saw a boat made of stone beaching in a cove beneath Finisterre's cliffs. Lying in the boat was a body, the body of St James. James, murdered by Herod, was the first of the Carpenter's apostles to be martyred. James's own followers used the stone boat to bring him to Spain. They carried him up from the shore and, taking their signal from a bright star shining over a field beside the little hamlet, they buried him there.

While they were dragging the boat to land, a horseman passed by. The horse bolted in terror and plunged with his rider into the sea. When the two emerged from the waves, both the horse and rider were covered in scallop shells. A strange migrant creature, a pilgrim of the ocean, the scallop became the emblem of the millions who later made their way to Santiago.

The priest recounted his dream to his bishop, with the request that he was allowed to dig in the field of the star for the Saint's body. The bishop passed the request to Rome. Eventually Rome granted permission. The priest dug, he found the remains of St James, a shrine was built to hold them, and what is often called the cult of Santiago began. Cult has become an ugly and debased word, mainly used today to describe American fundamentalist movements which often end in scandal and violence. It does little justice to the passion and courage of those who have set out across the centuries on the long and dangerous journey to Santiago.

What is the appeal of the way of St James. The French call it *le chemin*, the Spanish *el camino*. Both mean the same and require a definition, an explanation. For hundreds of years, the Santiago pilgrimage was the greatest event in Europe, a constantly-rolling celebration of the human mind and spirit, a quest that embraced partying and fornication, asceticism and deprivation, endurance, companionship and loneliness. Historians have estimated that in certain years as much as one fifth of Europe's entire population was either on pilgrimage or engaged in servicing the pilgrims. Why particularly to Santiago?

In 711 AD, the Arabs, the Moros or Blackamoors as they later became known in medieval England, crossed the straits of Gibraltar and started their conquest of Europe. A fanatical and disciplined warrior race, hungry for land with fertile earth and water to irrigate it, they advanced up the Iberian peninsula with devastating speed. Within a few years they reached the Pyrenees and were poised to extend their empire beyond the mountains. The Pyreneean passes, their overstretched supply lines, and Charlemagne's Frankish armies checked them.

The Arabs made a short tactical retreat, and set about building and consolidating their empire in Spain. In many ways, they were excellent and tolerant, if somewhat austere, colonists. The problem was that they were colonists nonetheless, and utterly alien ones at that. They worshipped a different and unknown God, and shared nothing of Europe's Christian culture. And their subjects were the notoriously stubborn, independent, and difficult Iberian Celts.

The Celts began their long and bitterly contested campaign to oust the invaders. There was no cohesive idea of modern *hispanidad*, (Spanishness) to link them, only a mosaic of ancient kingdoms and tribal territories which shared the same peninsula. They did not even have a common language. Today's Spanish, Castilian: 'the tongue of the castles', only came into being as a Lingua Franca as the line of the reconquest advanced. They needed an emblem to wear, a banner to march under, an ancestral heritage to unite them. They found it in St James.

The Church of Rome embraced Santiago and made him its own when they became aware of his talismanic power. The strangeness of the legends surrounding him, the stone boat, the terrified horse and the scallop shells support the view that James came from a much older world. Long pre-Christian, it was a pagan world of spirits and heroes, of magic springs and forests, of Gawain's green knight and the giant wolfmen of the mountains.

Often when the Christian armies, or more accurately the fragile coalition of Celtic tribal warrior bands, were facing defeat by the Moros in battle, a ghostly horseman would appear in their ranks and scythe down the enemy. In one epic encounter he is credited with slaying 50,000 Arabs. St James, the gentlest of Christ's disciples, is also Santiago-Matamoros, the vengeful and triumphant blackamoor killer.

Santiago is the spirit, the *anima*, of Iberia. When Ferdinand and Isabel finally entered Granada in 1492, and the long Arab occupation was over, Columbus, the half-mad Genovese-Jewish navigator and would-be tycoon, was waiting fretfully a few miles away for the queen to honour her promise and give him the money for his planned voyage. He had to wait a further frustrating twenty-four hours. On Isabel's mind was one matter more important than the possible discovery of a western route to the riches of India. She had to give thanks not to God, but to St James.

Santiago reached out to and expressed the soul not just of Spain, but all Europe. Pilgrimages to Rome and Jerusalem were important and the dedication of those who embarked on them was often fervent. At heart, though, they were essentially reverential and passive. A pilgrimage to the Field of the Star was not. It was dynamic and real.

St James had challenged the common enemy at the gates of Europe and hurled the enemy back. He was heroic. He wore the mantle of the new religion, Christianity, but he was rooted in the old, in the tales children heard whispered round the fire at night when, in deep midwinter, branches of evergreen fir framed the hearth to encourage the return of spring.

The carpenter's son preached peace and died on a cross. Santiago wielded a sword, rode a magic horse, and lived. Europe flocked to the Field of the Star.

STARTING OUR PILGRIMAGE

As the cult of Santiago grew throughout the Middle Ages, four main gathering points developed for the bands of pilgrims who wished to make the journey to Compostela. All four were in France. They were at Paris, Vezelay, Arles in Provence, and the modest town of Le Puy close to Lyons and not far from the Swiss border. We, my two companions and I, chose Le Puy. The reason was straightforward. The traditional pilgrim routes from the other three points have largely been concreted in as modern highways. From Le Puy the way still wanders as a virtually trackless path over mountains, across rivers, and through little villages now often deserted.

It is not, as we discovered, the easiest route to take. In fact it remains, as it always was, the most challenging. But for the pilgrim on foot it is also the most rewarding. None of us ever regretted the choice. On a bright April morning in 1993 we paid our respects to the black virgin of Le Puy, and set off. The sun shone, the fields were bright with spring flowers, the air was warm and scented. We strode along, pausing at midday for a sturdy and excellent lunch at a little restaurant thronged with local farmers. In the golden light of evening we reached our planned stopping-point for the night, the village of Saint-Privat-d'Allier.

Over dinner, another equally good and robust French country meal, we all agreed the hazards and ardours of pilgrimage had been greatly exaggerated. The way to St James, we decided, was no more than a vigorous tramp in sunlight through some of the loveliest countryside in Europe.

By next morning the temperature had plunged, the skies were black, and rain was sheeting down through the icy gusts of a north-easterly wind. Shivering, we headed out onto the path again. The rain and the bitter bone-chilling wind lasted for five days. Then as we climbed up into the mountains of the Auvergne, the weather worsened. The rain turned first to sleet and then snow, the wind became a howling winter gale, and the temperature dropped even further.

At one stage, high up on a mountain pass, we were wading sightlessly through waist-high snow drifts. Navigation was almost impossible. Although the path is notionally way-marked for pilgrims with occasional little red and white painted bands, on trees and rocks, the trees had often fallen in storms and the rocks had been washed away in the spring torrents. We frequently lost our way. We had to cast back and try, through the driving snow, to pick up our track again. It could take hours. More than once we stumbled into our lodging for the night long after darkness had fallen.

All we wanted then was a fire. We slumped before it, numbed and chapped and shaking with cold, and with a steaming bowl of Auvergne gruel. Hungry as we were, we were too tired to eat anything else. One evening I saw my sister make an immense effort after eating and scrawl an entry in her journal. My sister is tall, fit, and formidably strong, a Highland hill walker and a veteran of many long mountain treks. I asked her what she had written: that 'I've never been so cold or tired in my life', she replied. That 'I'm not sure I can go on, although of course I will'. And that 'I'm starting to learn the sheer bloody price the pilgrimage way makes you pay.'

It was a lesson all three of us were learning. I mention our experience of the tempests and snows of the Auvergne mountains, not because they were peculiar to us, but because they were typical of what Santiago pilgrims underwent throughout the centuries.

As the 20th century comes to an end, we had several advantages over those who trod the way over the thousand or more years before us. Our boots and clothes, for instance, were better-equipped to protect us against the violent and unpredictable mountain weather. Alexander Graham Bell had devised the telephone. If we had had an accident in the high drifts, and at times I felt one was close, and if one of us had managed to make their way to one of the lonely upland farms, we could have called for another modern invention, the four-wheel drive vehicle, to rescue the casualty. A horse or waggon might have taken a day and a night to make the journey. A Landrover could have been there in a couple of hours.

It could have been, but Landrovers can get trapped in deep snowdrifts almost as easily as pilgrims on foot, as had almost happened to us. Telephone lines too, can buckle and break under the assault of the mountain weather. Only the rocks remain impervious to whatever is hurled at them. Painful and demanding as it was, it was also in a strange way comforting to know we were experiencing and enduring the same conditions as Santiago's pilgrims had always endured.

On the twelfth day, a fitful sun came out again, and we continued under blue skies patched for a while longer with racing clouds. Our legs were weary, our feet blistered, our eyes still glazed and streaming from the snow. But our staffs were in our hands, our scrips (the leather pouches, in our case canvas backpacks) on our shoulders, and our scallop shells hung from our necks. Compostela was still 850 miles away, but none of us doubted we would get there. When the first three-week stage of the journey was finished, we returned to Britain and parted.

STARTING AGAIN

In the autumn we gathered again at the point in south-western France where we had left off, and continued. So it went on, in episodes over three years. We walked across Gascony, into Acquitaine, and then Navarre. We reached the foot of the Pyrenees, and climbed up the pass of Roncesvalles, following the wild and almost lost track Napoleon chose for his invading army in his attempt, as futile as that of the Arabs, to subjugate the Celts on the other side of the ramparts. We had seen the snow-capped peaks from afar. On the day we set foot on the roof of Europe, freak weather conditions raised the temperature to 54°C, the hottest ever recorded. By midday, we had drunk the two litres of water we each carried with us every day. That evening, as we descended the jagged rock-faces, we were all reeling like meths-sodden derelicts, giddy and hallucinating with dehydration. It took a week to shake off the effects. Even in the mountains, we were being tested close to the limits of our endurance.

We made our way to Pamplona and arrived during the great bull-running Feria of San Fermin. As all good pilgrims do, we dressed in white, tied red sashes round our waists, and partied, drank, and sang the night away to choruses of Basque anthems, and we were still up at dawn to watch the bulls being raced through the streets to the *plaza*. We headed across the harsh dried bull's hide of the Castilian plain. In its bristling thorny ferocity, the landscape could have been pegged out from the salt-cured skins of the great wild-eyed animals we'd seen raging with tossing horns across Pamplona's cobbles.

We reached Burgos with its majestic cathedral, and the fragrant partridge stews in the restaurants in the narrow streets of the old town. Then the extraordinarily elegant city of Leon. Finally we headed up into highlands again for the last stage towards Compostela.

Along the way we lodged at night, both in France and Spain, in farms, in monasteries, in convents, in the local priest's house, in pilgrim hostels and in tiny hotels. Sometimes when the nights were warm, we slept under the stars beneath the overhanging eaves of a haystack. We carried all our belongings on our backs. It made us self-sufficient and flexible. We could accommodate any detour or halt suggested by our fellow pilgrims and others we met along the path, and we met many: rogues, believers, travellers, and the folk of the countryside.

In the jostling night-time streets of Pamplona, smiling pickpockets 'accidentally' poured glasses of water over us to distract our attention, and then, as they apologised, their hands would wander through our pockets in search of our cash and valuables. They had been doing the same for hundreds of years. Jugglers entertained us and troubadours sang us songs. We put Francs and Pesetas in their hats. A con-artist relieved my generous sister and our companion of enough money to see him home after telling a heart-rending and totally convincing story of having all his possessions stolen. We discovered later he had been working the way of St James with the same scam for years.

Priests cursed us in most-unchristian language when we arrived late looking for lodging. Father Abbots in monasteries bewailed the erosion of faith over flagons of the good black wine of Cahors. Innkeepers diluted our wine or, far more often with the characteristic generosity of those who have seen generations of pilgrims pass by, insisted we drank a carafe of their finest vintage as a gift. Peasant farmers gave us milk and baskets of fruit. Dogs chased us, children giggled at us, weary policemen with cynical faces managed a smile and a wave as we passed.

We were walking through the landscape of Breughel's paintings. *The News of the World* used to boast that all of human life could be found in its pages, in the days of truly naughty vicars and scoundrels with pomaded hair, when 'intimacy' took place on several occasions and the mayor skipped off with the pensioners's savings. They could have saved themselves their large and expensive staff. A couple of cub-reporters posted along the way of St James would have assembled enough material to fill the paper for years.

END OF THE JOURNEY

Finally late on a clear May evening, with the stars appropriately coming out over the Field of the Star, we came to the end of the journey. We reached the cathedral in Santiago, climbed the steps, and walked along the great darkened nave. We lit candles for all the many and tangled reasons and for people who had brought us there across the three years and along the one thousand miles. Then we went outside and briefly embraced each other. It was over.

It was not over, although where the way would lead next none of us knew. 'El camino es una droga'(The way is a drug), the Spaniards say. It enters the body, it fills the veins, it floods the heart and mind. The way, of course, is nothing more than a daunting physical metaphor for life itself. Perhaps for many of us it requires the experience of travelling the way to start to understand that each day in all our lives is a journey, a pilgrimage. For wandering and searching humanity everywhere, it has always been so.

'Where next?' My sister demanded that evening as we sat over a bone-and-beans stew in a little hosteria off Santiago's main square. I closed my eyes. My feet had held up this time but only just. They were starting to bleed again, and like the other two, I was immensely tired. They were both limping, my sister's hip was painful, our companion Hilary's recurrent back problems had come back. I shook my head and opened my eyes. The two women were studying maps. 'What do you favour?' Hilary asked me. 'How about the Silk Road to China?', I said vaguely. I reached for the heavy earthenware pitcher of Navarran wine.

There are maps of the ground and maps of the spirit. We believe they are distinct. They are not. They weave and thread together. I was caught up somewhere in the knots where they join. So on his own journey, which took him out into the wilderness and then back, was the Palestinian carpenter. It was a friendly, companionable realisation. The son of God and I had much more in common than I had ever imagined. We will have many travellers' tales to exchange when we eventually meet.

PILGRIMAGE TODAY

An account of what it is like to embark on pilgrimage, as the 20th century nears its end, can only be a highly personal and fragmentary story. That is inevitable. Pilgrimage is very personal. The experience it provides is far too diverse and rich to be more than tokenly summarised in a paper of this length. There are huge areas I have not touched on. Many are simply outside the range of my knowledge, like the styles and traditions that nurtured the ancient built environment which frames so much of the way. Others, such as agricultural practices and their effect on southern Europe's ecology, I know something about, but have not the space to examine here.

Theologians, scholars and academics have provided learned and penetrating contributions found in libraries to give academic ballast to the study of our European tradition of Christian pilgrimage. They are the men and women from the ministry of higher knowledge. I am simply the man with muddy boots who walked the way. I debated with scowling French curés, drank deep with Spanish Franciscan monks, almost (but not quite) got skinned by Breughel tricksters, guided my companions through Auvergne snowstorms, gave alms to beggars, gathered crops with farmers' lads, studied orchids and eagles, wore the scallop shell, wondered and considered and prayed in some of Europe's loveliest chapels, and eventually reached the Field of the Star.

In short, I was a pilgrim. I stood, humbly, in the proud old tradition that Bunyan hymned, Dame Juliana of Norwich and St Teresa of Avila chronicled, and which bewitched St Francis of Assisi all his life. I even had the same scars on my feet and the same frost-bite on my face that marked theirs. The experience provided many lessons and insights.

Most, and here again I have to refer to the internal dimension of pilgrimage, are inevitably private. They are stored safely out of sight in the attics and cellars of the mind. Others can be shared. I used to think I knew Europe well. I have lived for long periods in several of its countries, and speak a number of its languages. What I discovered, what only the traveller on foot can discover, is quite how little one knows of Europe: how extraordinarily rich, diverse, and strange it is, and I refer only to two of its countries.

On the maps France is coloured, say, red, and Spain yellow. In both cases the traveller tends to assume he is dealing with long-defined homogenous areas. The traveller is wrong. On the ground, one threads one's way through an intricate tapestry of cultures, nations, languages, historical pasts, climates, cuisines (perhaps the best and oldest indices of national identity), cultivation methods, vernacular architectural traditions, religious attitudes, regional dress styles, and social organisations. A hat and a sausage say as much about a people's individuality as an emperor

86

and a thousand legions. There are plenty of hats and sausages along the Santiago way. They are all different and they are all emblems of a much deeper distinctness.

Except for cartographers' and beaurocrats' convenience, Europe has little to do with maps. Europe is a state of mind, or rather myriad states of mind. It cannot be neatly crammed into an atlas. It is a cornucopia fed by subversive spirits from below. Ceres is its goddess, and poets like Verlaine, Cervantes, Schiller, Yeats, and Dylan Thomas, the celebrant wordsmiths of its soul. Like all cornucopias it overflows, it spills out in a cataract scattering its strange ripe fruits at random everywhere.

The way of St James which interweaves Europe's landscape, utilising the prehistoric transhumance tracks and the drovers' roads of druidical times, has been travelled for more than ten centuries. Wolf packs may no longer hunt the high meadows it crosses, but only a 20th century muttonhead would claim the green giant does not still make his bed of fir and leaves in its dark and lonely copses.

What is comforting and intriguing, as I have mentioned above, is how little the *Camino's* own culture has changed. The rogues and grumbling priests, the patient nuns and taciturn smallholders, the devout, the lost souls, the wicked innkeepers, and the bold adventurers, they have always, of course, been part of the caravan. But other unchanged echoes from the past came to us. A monk would ask for news of the recently restored monastery of his parent order in Paris. Photographs gave no real idea. What did it really look like now? I promised to write and tell him. A lacemaker in a little Galician town asked my sister what were the favourite designs in the Madrid shops. My sister said she would find out and let her know. And so it went on.

We, the pilgrims, were sources of revenue, a lifeline to fragile rural economies. We were also even in an age of television, radio, and the Internet, still conduits of information: of gossip, of intellectual exchange, of the distribution of trade initiatives and political ideas. Where we passed, people gathered. They took our money, they talked, they learnt from us. No communication is as potent as between people meeting and discussing face to face soil, crops, and eternity. Of course, as we worked through those hard matters, we learnt far more from them than they did from us.

WHY?

At the end I suppose I should answer the question that, as a pilgrim, is insistently put to me again and again. Yes, but why after everything you have said and explained, why did you 'really' set out on pilgrimage, why did you walk a thousand miles to the Field of the Star?

The answer is simple. To light candles. Candles for my daughter, Francesca. All along the way, all along my life and hers, the years past and the years ahead when I shall still be lighting candles. To explore where we met and how we laughed at each other as we parted when she died. What great venture is worth undertaking, as Dylan Thomas said, except one in praise of God and for love of man. In this case it was for my love of a bold, beautiful and fearsome young woman.

Passion is the wellspring of pilgrimage, reconciliation its goal. The way of St James made peace between my rare turbulent daughter and me. Like her, I can sleep well now. The detail and the footnotes I leave to Fladmark's pen. Meanwhile, I finish with the medieval pilgrim's traditional call of encouragement to his companions along the way. 'Utrera'– further, always further! That is where I am heading. I still have the memories. I still have unfinished business with life and Francesca yet.

The Author

Nicholas Luard was born in London but raised on the Isle of Mull. He went to school at Winchester, and studied at the Sorbonne and Cambridge Universities. He held a graduate fellowship, at the University of Pennsylvania. He was educated by himself and the British Army. A co-founder of *Private Eye* magazine and The Establishment Theatre Club, he subsequently became a writer, naturalist, and explorer. He has led expeditions across the Kalahari and Namib deserts, and in the Himalayas, and has also travelled widely in many other parts of the world. The author of 18 books, he is married to the writer Elizabeth Luard, and divides his time between London and his hill farm in Wales. He is chairman of the John Muir Trust, the Wilderness Trust, the Gaia Trust, the Hebridean Whale and Dolphin Trust, and is a Council Member of WWF. He is also advisor to the British Joint Services mountaineering expeditions.

Before starting the journey, the author knew that his beloved daughter Francesca had been diagnosed as carrying the HIV virus which causes Aids. She died before the journey was completed, and in the concluding part of the paper Luard shares with the reader how he walked together with his memory of her life to light candles for her soul at Saniago de Compostela. His book, *The Field of the Star: A Pilgrim's Journey to Santiago de Compostela*, was published in 1998.

References

Arribas Briones, P., *El Camino de Santiago en Castilla y Leon*, Burgos, 1982

Bolen, J., *Crossing the Avalon*, New York, 1994

Bottineau, Y., *El Camino de Santiago*, Barcelona, 1965

Domke, H., *Spanien Norden: der Weg nach Santiago*, Munich, 1973

Hanbury-Tenison, *Spanish Pilgrimage: A Canter to St James*, London, 1990

King, G. G., *The Way of St James*, New York, 1920, 3 vols.

Lambert, E., *Le Pelerinage de Compostelle*, Paris–Toulouse, 1957–58

Luard, E., *European Peasant Cookery*, London, 1989

Luard, E., *Family Life: Birth Death and the Whole DamnThing*, Bantam Press, 1996

Luard, N., *Andalucia: A Portrait of Southern Spain*

Luard, N., *The Field of the Star*, Michael Joseph, 1997

Prescott, H., *Jerusalem Journey*, London, 1954

Selby, B., *Pilgrim's Road*, London, 1994

Tate, B. M., *The Pilgrim Route to Santiago*, Oxford, 1987

Toibin, C., *The Sign of the Cross*, London, 1994

7

SAINT OLAV OF NORWAY
Reviving Pilgrim Ways to Trondheim

Mari Kollandsrud

Those of us who are concerned with the protection of natural and cultural heritage assets as part of our daily work have become accustomed to meeting objections, and sometimes strong opposition. We have learnt that persuasion is necessary in order to put our points of view across, and that the general public may have opinions that differ substantially from ours as professionals.

It was thus a surprise and a pleasure to be able to take part in a project that has met with an interested and positive response, as we did when we began to register and restore the old pilgrim ways to the city of Trondheim, known in the Middle Ages as Nidaros. Here lies the world's northernmost cathedral, where the earthly remains of King Olav Haraldsson, or St Olav, were kept during the Middle Ages, and which was a place of pilgrimage.

THE PATRON SAINT OF NORWAY

Olav Haraldsson was a direct descendant of King Harald Fairhair, the first king to reign over the united nation known today as Norway. Olav was born in 995, and is said to have been only twelve years old when he went on his first Viking expedition. This took him to England and France, where he is said to have been christened in Rouen. On his return to Norway in 1015, at the age of twenty, he saw a chance to seize power. Within two years he had managed to oust the two brothers who were ruling the country, the Earls Svein and Haakon, and become king himself. Olav was a harsh ruler, and made a number of powerful enemies. These allied themselves with King Canute of Denmark, and forced Olav to leave the country in 1028. He fled to Gardarike, as Russia was then known, where he was well received by King Yaroslav and Queen Ingegerd. They offered him the Kingdom of Bulgaria, then still a heathen country according to the Sages, but his wish was to return to Norway where Earl Haakon had again taken the helm.

Shortly after this, Haakon was lost at sea, so Olav made another attempt to regain power. In 1030 he marched across Sweden at the head of an army and at Stiklestad, just north of Trondheim, he met a large army led by three of his old enemies. On 29, July the two forces joined battle, and Olav and many of his men were killed.

Olav was a devout Christian and very determined to establish Christianity in Norway. He saw as his responsibility, the completion of the work of his predecessor, Olav Tryggvason, who had been brought up at the Russian court and was baptised and taught the Bible by a hermit in the Scilly Isles. He is said to have brought priests and other learned men from Britain to Norway. As the country turned away from the old gods and became converted to the new faith, churches were built and priests and scholars were brought in, mostly from the Celtic Church in Scotland in the early years. For the general population this represented a revolutionary change that did not go unopposed, but Olav Haraldsson is now generally regarded as being the true founder of the Church in Norway.

While all this was going on, King Canute was conquering England. The population of the British Isles had long since become acquainted with the Vikings, and although they were a source of fear, a good deal of trade and cultural exchange also went on across the North Sea. Indeed, the son of Harold Fairhair, who became King Håkon the Good, was fostered and brought up in the Christian faith by King Athelstan of Northumbria, but he sought in vain to persuade his subjects to abandon their heathen gods.

After the Battle of Stiklestad Olav's body was rescued by his closest followers and buried at a secret place outside Trondheim. However, rumours of miracles occurring near the grave soon began to spread, and it was said that Olav was a holy man with special powers. A year after his death the grave was opened. Miraculously, the king still looked as if he had just fallen asleep, and it is said that his hair and beard had to be trimmed and nails cut before he was reinterred. On 3 August the same year, Olav was canonised by the English bishop Grimkell. The date was not a coincidence as it is also the anniversary of the martyrdom of St Stephen. Thus, St Olav was Norway's first martyr and became its patron saint, and all through the Middle Ages pilgrims visited his shrine in Christ Church in Nidaros.

During this period, Trondheim lay at the northernmost corner of a square formed by the four other principal pilgrim shrines of the Middle Ages: Jerusalem to the East, Rome to the South, Santiago de Compostela and St Andrews to the West. Whether the pilgrim traffic to Trondheim was great enough to warrant calling the town a pilgrim shrine is debatable, but there is no doubt that St Olav was known and revered well beyond the borders of his native land. In Norway there were 56 churches and seven cloisters dedicated to St Olav, in Sweden 115 and a further 162 churches and chapels in the rest of Europe.

Pilgrim traffic ceased after the Reformation, which reached Norway in 1537. But certain traditions connected with St Olav have remained alive right up to the present day, and currently there is a strong and widespread interest in the Middle Ages and medieval ideals. Thus, when a request was addressed to the Ministry of the Environment that the old pilgrim routes should be retraced and reconstructed, with all the waymarking and information work that this would involve, the proposal met with a positive response.

In 1992, the Ministry gave the responsibility for carrying out this task to the two Directorates for Natural and Cultural Heritage, and they established a joint 'pilgrim way project' with a secretariat under the Directorate for Natural Heritage. We know that the pilgrims took several different routes to Trondheim, and the project encompasses two of them: the route from Oslo through Gudbrandsdalen and over the Dovre mountains, and the route from Sweden via Stiklestad. A steering group was appointed, with additional members from the Church of Norway, the public roads authorities, representatives of landowners, the Ministry of Agriculture and four of the counties through which the routes pass. The project was completed in 1997, the year Trondheim celebrates its millenium as a town.

THE OPERATIONAL STRATEGY

The Directorate for Natural Heritage in Trondheim and the Directorate for Cultural Heritage in Oslo are both responsible to the Ministry of the Environment. This illustrates the way in which the protection of the natural environment and the cultural heritage are regarded as two sides of the same coin in Norway, and thereby integrated into a coherent environmental protection policy. The two Directorates co-operate closely with one another and have interests in common across several areas. The pilgrim way project was an excellent example of practical and constructive collaboration between the two organisations. The Directorate for Natural Heritage wishes to create favourable conditions for meaningful outdoor recreation. The Directorate for Cultural Heritage wishes to help people become familiar with their cultural legacy wherever they are. Accordingly, there was complete agreement on the goals and conditions for work on the pilgrim way.

The Directorate for Natural Heritage was responsible for the financial and practical administration of the project, for providing maps, and for the major part of the funding. Three people from the Directorate were involved: the project co-ordinator, a landscape architect and a lawyer.

The Directorate for Cultural Heritage was responsible for approving the actual route, administering matters relating to the logo, information, and the practical work of developing and producing the signposts. Two employees from the Directorate's department of information and one from the landscape department were involved. The latter was responsible for approving the use of the logo.

Right from the beginning it was obvious that, at the level of the Directorates, it was neither possible nor desirable to do more than be responsible for the overall management of the project. In this type of effort, it is important to mobilise the local population and give them a sense of involvement and ownership. Not only do people's enthusiasm and their interest in and knowledge of local traditions constitute a valuable resource, but the project is heavily dependent on local funding and voluntary help.

Thus, we chose a decentralised model of organisation. Funds were transferred to the counties through which the routes run so that they could each employ a person to co-ordinate the project at local level. The co-ordinator had recourse to a network of local experts and was responsible for administering and advising the 29 municipalities that are involved in the project. The co-ordinator was also in charge of transferring funds to the municipalities for restoration and signposting. The latter choose their own form of organisation, usually by appointing one person to be in charge with a network of advisory experts, as the counties did.

There was naturally a good deal of suspense as to whether the project would generate enough local support, but the response exceeded our expectations. Although the initial response in some municipalities was rather reserved, others showed such enthusiasm and commitment that we have almost had to restrain their creative zeal. We found that in general, the Middle Ages, and especially the pilgrim tradition, fires people's imagination, and that there are still tales and legends from this period that have been kept alive. In many of the hamlets and valleys where we know that pilgrims used to stay, people had already started registering the routes, and wanted to reconstruct and signpost them. Local historians examined written sources and provided us with valuable information and comments on our choice of route. It cannot, of course, be denied that the prospect of income from a burgeoning tourist industry may lie behind much of the municipal goodwill.

IMPLEMENTATION STRATEGY

The pilgrim way extends for over 450 miles, and the intention was to make it possible to follow it on foot all the way. It was not possible to trace the exact routes taken by the original pilgrims as they were often buried under modern roadways or cultivated land, or they had become overgrown. In some places, boats were used to ferry the pilgrims, which is no longer a practicable solution. In cases where it was very difficult to know where the route went, we followed ancient highways that are still in use. Sometimes new paths have been constructed to link up established routes. Thus the course of the route was determined by historical knowledge, current conditions, the nature of the landscape and existing historical monuments. Helping the municipalities make decisions involved a great deal of work on the part of the project co-ordinators at county level.

Each municipality applied first to have the main route approved before planning the details. The pilgrim way was to be linked by the still visible traces of the Middle Ages, and it was the task of the Directorate for Cultural Heritage to approve them. Guidelines were laid down by the project co-ordination team, explaining that applications had to be well documented, with a list of the relevant literature and source references. When the application was approved, the pilgrim logo could be used for signposting and on printed material. The project co-ordinators at county level acted as managers and advisers during the detailed planning.

The municipalities involved spent most of 1994–95 in registration and documentation work and in preparing specific proposals. Some of them even managed to start signposting the way, but most of this was done in 1996. The whole way was completed and signposted by 29 July the following year, the date of the Battle of Stiklestad and the Feast of St Olav, when the country's patron saint is commemorated.

When the two Directorates began the project, they had to start from scratch. The Directorate for Natural Heritage had experience of establishing hiking trails with a cultural or natural beauty theme, and my own Directorate possessed the requisite historical knowledge. But neither of us had any experience in recreating a historical route based on events with associations that cannot all be acquired from written sources. The most important, and also the most difficult, part of this process was to predict the kind of situations that might arise and decide how to tackle them. We achieved a certain amount of success in this, and managed not to lose control of the process or to depart from the original aims, but a good deal of improvisation was necessary along the way.

Sufficient funding is essential to the success of any project. It would be unreasonable, and probably impossible, to expect the municipalities to find the money for work that is more or less imposed on them.

Both Directorates allocated funds to the way during the initial year of the project, and this budget was totalling NKr 4,8 million, channelled through the counties to the municipalities. These funds were not enough to cover all the costs, but they encouraged the municipalities to cover some of the costs themselves. Much of the work was done as part of unemployment schemes and some by volunteers.

QUALITY ASSURANCE

The first step was to organise a competition among Norwegian graphic designers and illustrators for the symbol that would identify the pilgrim way. As we hoped it would be, the winning design was a visual description of the message we wanted to convey: a combination of traditional motifs in modern dress. The same designer was also used to design the products for which we were responsible. The Directorate for Cultural Heritage 'owns' the logo, which is a symbol of quality. It has been patented and may only be used for products that are either produced under the auspices of the project or by special licence.

Our function was to make the pilgrim way accessible to the public. When it was finished and in use, our task was over. How it is used, and by whom, is not our concern. However, the choices we made about signposting and information along the route were based on certain perceptions of what a pilgrim way represents. During the planning we were guided by the idea of the pilgrim way as the way to self-knowledge through a spiritual encounter with God or with nature, and thus by the need to provide an atmosphere of stillness and contemplation.

We therefore felt that the signposting should be discreet and of high quality as regards design and materials. We also felt that on a route like this, wayfarers would be more interested in what they were seeing than an ordinary hiker would be. The theme was established early, and there was to be no signboards explaining the sights along the way. Instead these are now marked by a simple wooden post, and wayfarers are expected to make use of the printed guide that is available through the municipalities involved. In each municipality, a milestone was erected to show the remaining distance to Nidaros.

The signposting is intended to show that the pilgrim way is different from all other trails. This will be appreciated by those with a sense of design, while others will be entirely oblivious to the message being conveyed, and they will only judge it according to practical criteria. However, we hope that all wayfarers will consciously or unconsciously feel that the nature of the symbol pointing the way and the understated information material enhance the uniqueness of the experience.

A PILGRIM WAY FOR WHOM?

We were given the task of doing whatever was necessary to make the pilgrim way accessible. The final product was the result of a good deal of discussion and debate, especially about for whom the way was intended. Were we making a route for those we 'hoped' would use it, for those we 'thought' would use it, or for those who really 'would' use it? Was the image we were intending to project one that would influence the type of user, attracting some and excluding others?

The pilgrim way was designed to be used for recreation, for the enjoyment of nature and as an encounter with the past through the historical monuments that line the route. The monuments are not only connected with medieval pilgrimages. The route has been used from time immemorial, and it passes monuments that are even older than those the medieval pilgrims must have passed: burial mounds, traces of ancient settlements, and rock carvings that are thousands of years old. And during the centuries since the Reformation, houses and other architectural features have been erected along the way. We felt it was right to include these buildings. They are part of our past, and part of the original pilgrims' future.

The pilgrim way in Norway does not offer the traveller great and famous historical monuments, as does, for example, the way to Santiago de Compostela, where even the smallest village has a church worth visiting. Here everything is of modest dimensions, all the way to the great Cathedral of Nidaros. Thus it was for the pilgrims of the Middle Ages, who after a long and hard journey finally reached their goal, to be dazzled by the size and beauty of the great cathedral.

Although modest in terms of architecture, the pilgrim way offers a rich and contrasting variety of natural beauty, running as it does, past fields of grain, through narrow river valleys , and across open and treeless uplands. Much has changed since the first pilgrims made their way along it, but the setting and the landscape are in essence the same. It is thus still possible for us to imagine what the medieval pilgrims saw on their journey.

We know little about the medieval pilgrims, but we do know that not all of them were inspired by religious motives. The same applies to today's pilgrims, but today we are unlikely to find the adventurers and hangers-on that often accompanied the original pilgrims. The project's aim was to provide a spiritual experience. We avoided the word 'religious'. Nowadays, nature itself is many people's cathedral. A spiritual experience may be cultural, religious, emotional or aesthetic, and it was important to create an atmosphere that favoured quiet contemplation, where people are not disturbed by a bombardment of information or a chaos of visual symbols.

When the project was completed and the way was ready for use, it took on a life of its own, which will be influenced by many different factors. For example, The Church of Norway has been an active participant since the beginning. The three bishops whose dioceses are involved showed great enthusiasm for the project and followed its progress closely. The Church appointed a special priest at Nidaros Cathedral to provide information about the pilgrim tradition and guidance for wayfarers on the religious aspects. In connection with the completion of the project in 1997, the Church arranged a pilgrimage from Oslo to Trondheim, which was joined by many groups at different points along the way.

The municipalities that have invested in the route are also naturally interested in seeing it used. The pilgrim way undoubtedly represents a tourist attraction for those who want a holiday with a difference. Norway's tourist appeal abroad is linked to an increasing extent with natural beauty, and this combination of natural beauty with cultural interest should prove very attractive. This will no doubt be exploited by the tourist industry.

What can the pilgrim way offer in addition to nature and culture? Products for sale, of course: souvenirs, pilgrim robes and copies of other pilgrim articles, many manufacturers knocked on the door, but here our influence ended, and this was how it should be. A number of original designs were produced under the auspices of the project, but apart from these the only control we have is over the use of the pilgrim logo, which will be restrictive, since it is an indication of quality. And here we come back to the original aim of the project: the pilgrim way was revived for the sake of modern wayfarers, and the pilgrim robe and staff have been replaced by the anorak and backpack. In all honesty, it would not be right to interpret today's pilgrim tradition in any other way. The pilgrims of the past were a product of their time, and no amount of dressing up in pilgrim robes can reproduce this.

For most people, a pilgrimage is a golden opportunity to exercise hidden talents and creativity. Local processions have been held of people dressed in what they imagine to be pilgrims' clothes. Plays and concerts have been performed with amateur and professional participants. This is an expression of an interest that, while genuine, may not always go very deep, historically speaking; the trainers, so to speak, will always stick out from under the robe, and there is a danger that this pilgrim worship will become very artificial. However, this is an inevitable consequence of local commitment and initiative.

LOOKING AHEAD

High priority was given to stimulate local initiative, and there was a great deal of activity in all 29 participating municipalities.

Publicity events were arranged and promoted throughout the project. In 1995, they were linked with the millennium of the birth of St Olav, which was commemorated at the place where he was born, and at Stiklestad where he was killed. In 1996, there was a major event in the Dovre mountains, and in 1997 a stone marking the end of the route was laid outside Nidaros Cathedral. The project was officially completed on European Heritage Day in mid-September of that year.

However, having completing this project does not mean that we have finished with pilgrim routes in Norway. The route covered by this project is only one of many leading to Nidaros, and already an alternative route is being implemented through the Østerdalen valley. In order to be able to use the logo, the organisers will have to apply for approval according to the rules that apply to the present project. This route is scheduled to be finished by the turn of the century.

Nidaros was the most important, but it was not the only shrine that attracted pilgrims during the Middle Ages. On the coast of western Norway lie the ruins of the monastery of Selje. The church is dedicated to St Sunniva, the daughter of an Irish king who is said to have been forced to flee her country after refusing a royal suitor. Together with her companions, she crossed the sea in a boat that had neither sail nor oars, and landed at Selje. Here Sunniva and her followers took refuge in a cave, but the entrance was blocked by an avalanche of rocks, and the whole company died. Other places of pilgrimage were the stave church in Røldal, which had a miracle-working crucifix, and St Thomas's church on the mountain of Filefjell, both of them in the southern half of the country.

All these places are likely to want to revive the pilgrim tradition, but the two Directorates are only involved in pilgrim routes leading to Nidaros, and the pilgrim logo will only be approved for use in this connection.

The pilgrim way to Trondheim through Østerdalen was used by pilgrims from Sweden, and it joins the main pilgrim way at several places along the route. The route on the Swedish side of the border is being reconstructed and linked up with the Norwegian route, and the Swedish authorities have been allowed to use the Norwegian logo for the sake of coherence and unity.

All over Norway and in the other Nordic countries, historians and public roads authorities are collaborating on the registration of ancient highways. The pilgrim ways followed the contemporary roads which later became the king's highway, post roads and military roads. This means that the pilgrim way is likely to become part of a whole network of ancient roads and highways that are being restored.

And finally, what was probably the most significant pilgrim way of all has not yet been revived: the sea route along the coast. Boats were the major means of transport in the old days, especially so in a mountainous country like Norway where overland travel was slow and difficult before good roads and the coming of the railway. Thus, the pilgrim way initiative is only the first of a whole series of exciting new projects. We have only just begun, and it is a promising start.

The Author

Mari Kollandsrud was an Information Adviser at the Directorate for Cultural Heritage in Norway (Riksantikvaren), where she was responsible for revitalising the pilgrim routes to Trondheim in co-operation with the Directorate for Natural Heritage. She graduated as an architect from the University of Trondheim in 1956, and practised architecture until 1979. She was for 10 years Secretary General for the Society for the Preservation of Monuments and Sites and Editor of the quarterly journal *Fortidsvern*. She administered the 'Plant a Tree' campaign in Norway in 1977 and a year later she took the initiative to found the society 'Friends of the Tree'. She is the author of the official guide for the Pilgrim Way to Nidaros, and now works free lanse as a consultant.

References

Bakken, A., *Pilegrim til Nidaros i 1995*, in *Årbok for den Norske kirke*,
    1995, Vol. 44 , pp 70–72
Bakken, A.,*Pilegrimsvandring før og nå: På vei mot Nidaros*, Nidaros Domkirkes
    Restaureringsarbeider, 1994
Blom, G. A., *Nidaros som pilegrimsby: et utslag av den alleuropeiske
    pilegrimskulturen*, Nidaros Domkirkes Restaureringsarbeider, 1992

Direktoratet for naturforvaltning, *Gamle veger og vegfar: Bruk-vern-vedlikehold*, in *DN-håndbok*, nr 5

Riksantikvaren, *Informasjon om pilegrimsleden*, in *Meldingsblad for Prosjekt Pilegrimsleden*, Riksantikvaren, 1994

Kollandsrud, M., *På pilegrimsvandring igjen*, in *Fortidsvern*, 1994, Vol. 20, no.1 pp 33–35

Kollandsrud, M., *Pilegrimsleden tar form*, in: *Fortidsvern*, 1995, Vol. 21, no. 4,

Kollandsrud, M., *Pilgrimsleden til Nadaros, En Guide til Bandrere*, Gyldendal, 1997

Langslet, L.R.,*Olav den Hellige*, Gyldendal, 1995

Luthen, E., *I pilegrimenes fotspor til Nidaros*, Cappelen, 1992

Luthen, E., *På pilegrimsferd*, Pilegrimsforlaget, 1996

Direktoratet for naturforvaltning, *Pilegrimsleden: Godkjenning, merking og skilting*, 1995

Selnes, A., *Vandring langs gamle veier fra sagatid til nær fortid*, Tapir, 1995

Sturlason, S., *From the Sagas of the Norse Kings*, Dreyers Forlag, 1967

Thomsen, P., *Happy Norway to You: Moving around in Norway*, JW Eides Forlag, 1949

One of the granite milestones erected in every municipality along the route,
showing the distance to Trondheim. Photo by the author.

Map showing the pilgrim route from Oslo to Trondheim, and from there via Stiklestad to the Swedish border. There is a spur from the old cathedral town of Hamar via Lillehammer.

8

MEMENTOES TO TAKE HOME
The Ancient Trade in Souvenirs

Godfrey Evans

The first Christian souvenirs were the earth and loose stones gathered at the holy places associated with Christ and the early saints. These and other Late Roman and early Byzantine souvenirs were referred to as 'blessings' (eulogiae) meaning that they conveyed and transferred a spiritual blessing, and many Christians thought they also had the power to cure and protect. This created a very real problem for the early guardians of the holy places. On the one hand, they were faced with the danger that fervent pilgrims might damage a shrine to obtain a semi-relic or 'blessing', even breaking off bits of rock from Calvary or Christ's tomb in the Church of the Holy Sepulchre in Jerusalem. On the other, there was very little that pilgrims could take from many of the sites. The response was the production of mementoes which can be regarded as the beginnings of the manufacture and trade in souvenirs, and to what has become an important aspect of tourism.

AMPULLAE

Over the years, but mainly in the 4th and 5th centuries and thereafter, the guardians of the holy places sought to prevent damage and to satisfy the rising demand for souvenirs and secondary relics by controlling the supply of what could be given away: the hallowed earth, dust, oil and water. Pilgrims were only allowed a small amount, which was placed in a small container, an ampulla or pilgrim-flask, and sealed up. At some stage, there may have been a ceremony involving a blessing. Early surviving examples are generally made of clay or earthenware, with flattened oval bodies and two holes or loops for suspension around a person's neck or body. Many are decorated with the Egyptian soldier-saint Menas, whose shrine was at Abu Mena, near Alexandria. Another group shows a man writing. Most scholars accept that he represents St John the Evangelist and link these flasks with the huge shrine of St John at Ephesus, where it was believed the saint was blowing holy dust (manna), from his tomb and that this was particularly potent, able to ensure the happy outcome to a difficult childbirth or to stop storms at sea.

Much higher in quality, and even more interesting, are the 16 metal ampullae in Monza Cathedral, which are reputed to have been presented by Queen Theodolinda (d.625), and the 20 fragments of similar ampullae at Bobbio Cathedral, also in north Italy. These are richly decorated in relief with the Holy Sepulchre, the Cross of Golgotha and scenes from the Life of Christ and bear Greek inscriptions: 'Oil [of the] Tree of Life from the Holy Places of Chris' and Blessing [of the] Lord from the Holy Places of Christ'. They were probably made in Jerusalem in the late 6th or early 7th century and contained oil from lamps burning in the Church of the Holy Sepulchre. The inscriptions and accounts by pilgrims suggest that they were blessed with relics of the 'True Cross', possibly during Easter Week.

Around this time, pilgrims to the Holy Land and Syria would also have been able to obtain circular tokens of clay, earthenware and other materials decorated with scenes from the Life of Christ, St Symeon Stylites the Younger (d.592) and other religious subject-matter. These tokens are comparable to Late Classical doctors' pills and some were definitely intended to be equally, if not more, beneficial. The tokens relating to the Syrian pillar saint St Symeon would have been made from the reddish earth around his column, which was used as a miraculous medicine, and some are actually inscribed with an invocation to the saint to *heal* or simply with the word *health*.

Ampullae, tokens and holy medals continued to be made in the Byzantine Empire after the Muslim occupation of the Holy Land and Syria in the early 7th century. Byzantine output influenced European churchmen and craftsmen, but there seem to be relatively few European examples prior to the mid-12th century. When it came, large-scale European production was directly associated with church rebuilding on a colossal scale throughout Europe. This saw the establishment and development of regional shrines, in many cases competing with each other, and the attendant growth of mass pilgrimage.

European ampullae were also regarded as thaumaturgic and talismanic. Pewter ampullae were being made for the shrine of St Thomas Becket at Canterbury shortly after Thomas's death in December 1170, and before his canonisation in 1173. They were filled with 'Canterbury water', which was said to be tinged with the dying martyr's blood and able to effect miraculous cures. The healing and protective powers of the water are indicated and underlined by the Latin inscriptions on surviving 13th-century ampullae. Many claim 'Thomas is the best doctor of the worthy sick', while another reads 'All weakness and pain is removed, the healed man eats and drinks, and evil and death pass away'.

PILGRIM BADGES

Pilgrim badges, which generally represent the saint associated with a particular shrine, were being produced on the Continent during the second half of the 12th century. They became increasingly popular throughout Europe over the following two centuries and were eventually made for most European shrines, replacing and virtually eliminating the ampulla as a souvenir. The majority were cast in tin-lead. Sales figures are hard to come by, but great shrines such as Canterbury and Aachen must have sold tens if not hundreds of thousands of badges each year. In 1466, 130,000 were sold in a fortnight at the Swiss monastery of Einsiedeln.

These were the first popular and mass-produced souvenirs. Wealthy pilgrims would also have been able to buy silver or gold badges from goldsmiths. The badges would have been worn on the hat or clothing as a clear sign that the wearer had been on a praiseworthy pilgrimage to a particular shrine. Some owners cherished their badges, taking them with them to the grave, bequeathing them or presenting them to their church or another shrine. Some definitely regarded their badges as amulets and prophylactics, placing them at entrances, at the footings of buildings, on walls, above beds, with their animals or on drinking-troughs. Both badges and ampullae have been found in arable land, suggesting that some may have been purposely placed on or in the ground to help achieve good crops. That said, some of the most elaborate and later openwork badges may well have been made and purchased primarily as attractive, affordable jewellery which reflected well on the wearer's taste and character.

Although the Reformation ended the manufacture of religious souvenirs in Britain, they continued to be produced in huge quantities on the Continent, where they were seen as one way of strengthening Catholic faith. Badges developed into medals and continued to be enormously popular, as is evident from the large number of different medals showing the Madonna of Loreto. These were made between the 16th century and the present day, and are represented in the collection of the famous shrine of the Holy House at Loreto, in central Italy. Basically, religious medals are of two main types: light-weight medals for wearing, and more substantial pieces, closely related to secular commemorative medals, which celebrate and commemorate anniversaries and events.

PRINTS

From the mid-15th century, badges and medals were challenged, as souvenirs, by woodcuts and, later, other types of prints. Among the earliest significant cheap picture souvenirs are the 'faces of Christ' or 'veronicas', which were supposed to represent the face of Christ on the handkerchief of St Veronica, one of the principal relics in St Peter's in Rome. These were being sold by Germans, the originators of the woodcut, from booths on both sides of the main door of St Peter's in the mid-1470s. Woodcuts were still being produced in the 18th and 19th centuries. This is clearly illustrated by the surviving prints of St Anthony of Padua and the woodblocks in the Museo Civico, Bassano del Grappa. However, from the early 16th century, pilgrims were able to buy copperplate engravings of religious images, views of shrines and centres, and illustrated lists of relics and treasures owned by cathedrals and churches. In the 19th century, there was a major shift to small, easily portable images, printed from copper or steel plates, and to colour lithographs of devotional subjects and, especially, topographical views.

JET, CERAMICS AND BRASS

Three groups of items stand out from all the later European religious souvenirs. The most important consists of the carved jet made for pilgrims to the shrine of St James Major at Santiago de Compostela in north-west Spain. By the 12th century this had become one of the principal shrines in Christendom, and was drawing an estimated half-million visitors each year at the height of its popularity in the Middle Ages. Originally, people had collected scallop shells from the shores of Galicia as souvenirs, and these had become the internationally recognised symbol of a pilgrim and of pilgrimage. Few of the 13th and 14th-century jet pieces survive. The most common later items are the small statuettes of St James, either alone or with one or more diminutive flanking figures, and the small amulets in the shape of a clenched hand. Much rarer are the small carvings of St James as Santiago Matamoros (St James the Moor-Slayer), which represent the saint's alleged intervention at the unrecorded Battle of Clavijo in 844, when he is said to have miraculously appeared on a horse, rallied the Christian troops and defeated the Muslims.

Jet carvings are difficult to date with any precision: the statuettes of St James are generally assigned to the 15th or 16th century, while some of the examples of St James the Moor-Slayer have been published as belonging to the 17th century. A key item, both in its own right and in helping to date other work, is the pilgrim's hat of Stephan Praun of Nuremberg. This is in the Germanisches Nationalmuseum at Nuremberg, and is decorated with small jet figures of St James, bone staves and shells acquired by Praun during his visit to Santiago in 1571.

The second group of noteworthy items are the small maiolica (tin-glazed earthenware) bowls sold to pilgrims to the sanctuary of Loreto, near Ancona. Inside the basilica the faithful were able to see what was supposed to be the house of the Virgin Mary at Nazareth, allegedly transported there by angels; a venerated statue of the Virgin, and a bowl – the Santa Scodella – said to have been used by Mary. The souvenir maiolica bowls allude to the holy bowl. They depict the Virgin of Loreto and purport to have some dust from the Holy House, and possibly some water from the holy bowl, mixed in the actual ceramic body. Most of the cheap pilgrims' bowls appear to be inscribed in Italian with an abbreviated version of *'Con Polvere Di Santa Casa'* or *'Con Polvere Et Aqva Di Santa Casa'* (with dust and water of the Holy House). These bowls were made in the 18th and 19th centuries and are assumed to have been produced locally, either in or around Loreto or at a nearby centre in the Marches. There are also some much better quality maiolica bowls decorated with the Virgin of Loreto, mostly dating from the first half of the 18th century. They are inscribed in Latin: *'Ex Pvlvere Parietvm Et Aqva Sacrae Scvtellae Almae Domvs Lavretanae'*. Some may have been made by potters in Castelli and sold to pilgrims, but further research is needed into these more expensive pieces.

The third corpus of items relate to a small copperplate engraving of the Virgin of Luxembourg, dated 1640, which was set up in a small shrine, then in a chapel, at Kevelaer in the 1640s. Kevelaer is situated in the Lower Rhineland, near the border with the Netherlands, and became the premier place of pilgrimage in Germany. According to some accounts, it was already attracting 100,000 visitors a year during the first half of the 18th century. Most of the early surviving souvenirs date from the 18th century. During this period, local potters to the south-east of Kevelaer, at places such as Sonsbeck, Sevelen and Tönisberg, produced many 'folk art' plates and bowls of coloured, glazed earthenware, decorated with the Virgin of Kevelaer, and also small statuettes and shrines.

In the late 18th century, those with more sophisticated tastes, and probably more money, were able to buy cream-coloured earthenware plates and tea services, painted in polychrome enamels with the Virgin of Kevelaer. The bases of some of these items are either impressed 'TURNER' for the Staffordshire potter John Turner (1738–86) of Lane End, or his sons, or with one of the Leeds Pottery marks. Other pieces can be attributed to Staffordshire or Leeds on the basis of their pattern, the colour of the earthenware and the appearance of the glaze. The enamel colours and style of decoration indicate that these ceramics were exported plain to the Netherlands and decorated there. It seems likely that Dutch merchants played a key role in producing these souvenirs and transporting them to Kevelaer. This is not as surprising as one might think: Kevelaer lies on the trade route between Amsterdam and Cologne, and many Amsterdamers and other Netherlanders made processional and less regimented pilgrimages to Kevelaer.

Among the other Kevelaer souvenirs are items for smoking and snuff-taking. The most common are the oval tobacco boxes engraved with the Virgin of Kevelaer on the lid and St Anthony of Padua on the base. They are stylistically 'Dutch' and are engraved in Dutch with the identities of the two figures and the inscription (below the Virgin): 'Come pilgrims, honour this Virgin with diligence; then she will hear your prayer before you return. She is the advocate for us all, therefore visit her at Kevelaer'. The shape and engraving of the boxes suggest they were designed and made in the first half of the 18th century, but they have been published, and are exhibited, at Kevelaer as 'second half of the 18th century'. It looks as though Dutch merchants were also involved with this type of souvenir. However, caution is needed, as very little seems to be known about the manufacture of small base metal boxes in the Lower Rhineland in the 18th century.

Nineteenth-century pilgrims were able to buy clay pipes with the Virgin of Kevelaer either moulded or represented on the front of the bowl, and small snuff-boxes of papier-mâché and wood, with the lids press-moulded with a representation of the Virgin above the basilica of Kevelaer. These boxes can be dated approximately, as the basilica was begun in 1858, consecrated in 1864 and had its tower completed in 1884.

THE HOLY LAND

Visitors to the Holy Land in post-medieval times continued to collect bits of rock allegedly from the Holy Sepulchre and other sacred sites. A good example is William Wey in 1458, but purpose-made souvenirs were certainly available to 15th and 16th-century pilgrims, including those who came on the 'package tours' organised by Venetians. Regrettably little is known about the 15th and 16th-century models of the Church of the Holy Sepulchre, but from at least the 1660s onwards, there are dozens of surviving large wooden models of the Church, which are decorated with inlaid mother-of-pearl and bone in the tradition of Islamic, and particularly Syrian, intarsia work. Most have the arms of Jerusalem on the courtyard and the Sacred Monogram IHS on the bell tower.

Other related items include small models of the Cave of the Nativity in Bethlehem; hundreds of 18th and 19th-century altar or table crosses; and thousands of wooden crucifixes and rosaries with mother-of-pearl decoration. Some are decorated with the arms of the Franciscan Order, as well as with the Sacred Monogram and arms of Jerusalem. The majority would have been made by Arab-Christian craftsmen and their families in Jerusalem and Bethlehem, either working directly for the Franciscans, the Latin or western custodians of the Christian places in the Holy Land since the 14th century, or with much looser links with the Order. Other 19th-century souvenirs include pearl-oyster shells carved with scenes from the Life of Christ and other religious subject-matter, and crosses, cups and bowls made of bitumen.

These and many other items could have been purchased in the vicinity of the Church of the Holy Sepulchre and elsewhere in Jerusalem and Bethlehem, but there is also abundant evidence that the Franciscans and others were engaged in a well developed and profitable export trade. Constantin Volney, who visited the Holy Land in 1784, states that 'about three hundred boxes' of rosaries, reliquaries, shrines, crosses, crucifixes, Agnus Dei's, scapulars, etc, were exported from Jerusalem each year to Turkey, Italy, Portugal, Spain and its colonies. Writing of his visit in 1806, the German Ulrich Jasper Seetzen refers specifically to a warehouse in the convent of St Saviour in Jerusalem, the Franciscans' main base. He records that it contained 'religious articles such as rosaries, crucifixes, Madonna's Milk, models of the Holy Sepulchre, etc', which were sent through agents to Italy, Spain and Portugal. This trade continued through the 19th century. Around 1853, according to the English engraver W. H. Bartlett, items worth several thousands of pounds were shipped each year to France, Italy, Spain and Austria.

This brief review of religious souvenirs throws up three general points which need to be considered in subsequent work. First, many souvenirs are directly related to local or regional craft activities. Secondly, there are clear signs of some international trade and sophisticated merchant /entrepreneurial involvement in the production and supply of religious souvenirs in the 18th century, if not earlier. Thirdly, there was definitely an international trade in finished *souvenirs* well before this. In some cases, this was almost the equivalent of today's mail order.

SECULAR SOUVENIRS

Some of the earliest purpose-made secular souvenirs were produced for visitors to the spas, where aristocrats and others could purchase luxury items and mementoes between drinking the waters. At Spa itself, to the south-east of Liège, the souvenir industry seems to have developed from the production of walking sticks or staves. By the 1680s, there are references to caskets, boxes, bowls, brushes, bellows, mirrors and other items. Some of these are clearly described in the local archive as being decorated with mother-of-pearl and tin or pewter and brass. In 1672, for example, there is an early account 'Pour une belle eschouvette travaillée de nacre de perles. 4 florins 10 patars'. In 1703 another account refers to 'deux cassettes travaillées d'estain et de perles que j'ai achetées à l'Echevin Xhrouet pour 15 escus'. This is of considerable interest because it proves that the Xhrouet family did produce this type of work.

The English physician Edmond Nessel provides some very useful information about late 17th-century Spa products. He writes:

> They work also very nicely with all sorts of colours as well as with mother-of-pearl, ivory, tortoiseshell, tin of Cornwall, copper and silver; they are also imitating there, and they produce also just as cleverly as in any other place, works of marquetry representing all sorts of figures, of men and animals, insects, flowers, foliages and all that one can desire

It is possible to couple these references with a few examples in the local museum at Spa and to assemble a large body of rectangular caskets and other items with inlaid brass wire and painted mother-of-pearl.

During the 1680s and '90s, there is also clear evidence that boxes and other items were being made which imitated Chinese lacquer. Nessel notes that they were gilded and had 'the finest possible polish'. Like the inlaid items, the Chinese-style lacquered pieces continued to be produced into the 18th century; they had a revival in the mid-18th century.

Both types of work were superseded by boxes painted and varnished with mythological, romantic, rustic or topographical scenes. The Xhrouet family are said to have excelled at scenes of fables and histories, the Leloup at landscapes, and the Dagly at flowers and figures of China. Contemporary accounts and letters reveal that the most valued 18th-century acquisition was a complete toilet service, with boxes of various sizes. But a broad range of items was available, including boxes for gambling counters and tobacco, cases for watches, scissors and tweezers, work boxes, and even tables and other items of furniture.

The most common souvenirs are the small rectangular boxes decorated, on the lid, with a view of a scene in or around Spa. They were made in the second half of the 18th century and the early 19th century. The views are generally painted in monochrome or a very restricted number of pale colours, and are surrounded by matching pale colours. On the more expensive boxes, these pale surrounds are sometimes painted to imitate wood grain or coloured marble. Subsequent 19th-century decorators employed a much richer palette and endeavoured to create miniature oil paintings on the pieces.

TUNBRIDGE WARE

Wooden souvenirs were also available at the 'courtiers' spa' of Tunbridge Wells in Kent. Although easily reached from London, it was comparatively isolated and spartan before the 1680s. After a fire in 1687, the rebuilding of the Upper Walk created a continuous colonnade with shops under cover behind it. In 1697 that indefatigable traveller Celia Fiennes discovered 'shops full of all sorts of toys, silver, china, milliners, and all sorts of curious wooden ware, which this place is noted for'. She describes the latter as a 'delicate neat and thin ware of wood both white and Lignum vitae wood'.

Until recently, it had been thought that these pieces were made by George Wise, a turner and the founder of a dynasty of Tunbridge ware makers. However, it is now known that he was not born until 1703, and the working theory is that most of the early wares were made by London craftsmen and brought to Tunbridge by Londoners. This is reasonable. Lignum vitae is a hardwood imported from the West Indies or tropical America and the sort of wood one would expect a London turner to use. Moreover, two Londoners – Thomas Ashenhurst of Lambeth and Sir Thomas Janson of St Martin's-in-the Fields – were heavily involved with the building of several assembly rooms, at least 17 of the shops on the Walks, and house development. Furthermore, we know that Londoners rented some of the shops.

In the 18th century, the local makers produced a wide variety of turned items; goblets, bowls, cups, ladles, pepper and spice mills, and small cabinet work, some of which was inlaid. The woods used included the whitewoods holly and sycamore and the fruitwoods cherry, plum and yew. In his History of Tunbridge Wells, published in 1766, Benge Burr observes:

> The trade of Tunbridge-Wells is similar to that of the Spa in Germany [ie Spa, in Belgium], and chiefly consists in a variety of

toys of wood, such as tea-chests, dressing-boxes, snuff-boxes, punch-ladles and numerous other little articles of the same kind. Of these great quantities are sold to the company in the summer, and especially at their leaving the place, when it is customary for them to take Tunbridge fairings to their friends at home

Late 18th- and early 19th-century production included pieces veneered with marquetry or parquetry and whitewood items decorated with paint, prints or penwork.

In the 1830s, Tunbridge ware underwent a radical metamorphosis and became synonymous with pieces decorated with veneers of patterns or pictures, cut from blocks assembled from sticks of different colours.

A basic point to note about the souvenirs produced at Spa and Tunbridge is that they almost literally grew from the rich woodlands surrounding them. Other spa souvenirs also tend to be closely related to a local resource, craft or industry. At the great spa at Karlsbad (now Karlovy Vary in the Czech Republic), 18th-century visitors were able to buy folding knives, forks and spoons made of iron. These were damascened with gold and silver and are clearly associated with the local weapons industry. At Cheltenham, Isaac Cook, Thomas Rich and other retailers were able to obtain tumblers, mugs, cups, spill vases, bough or bulb pots and other items decorated with views of Cheltenham and its spas from the Chamberlain porcelain factory at Worcester, about 20 miles away. Similarly, many of the Central European spas were supplied by the Bohemian glass houses and wheel-engravers, with some of the engravers working in the spa towns.

ITALY

Visitors to Italy in the 18th and 19th centuries were particularly well catered for with souvenirs. Most tourists were aristocrats or members of the professional classes, and had come primarily to see the architecture and antiquities of Rome. They may also have visited Naples and the recently discovered Roman towns of Pompeii and Herculaneum.

The souvenirs naturally reflected and matched the interests of the visitors. 'Grand Tourists' passing through Florence in the late 17th and early 18th century would have been able to acquire small bronze copies of some classical and modern sculptures from Massimiliano Soldani Benzi (1656–1740), the Master of the Florentine Mint. But a much wider range of items relating to Roman antiquities was available to their successors who visited Rome in the second half of the 18th century.

A number of Roman foundries were engaged in casting bronze miniature replicas of classical sculptures. In the context of souvenirs, the most important was probably that run by Giacomo (c.1731–85) and Giovanni Zoffoli (c.1745–1794), situated above a spaghetti factory in the Via degli Avignonesi, off the Strada Felice. Their works are found in many British collections and are sometimes signed GIAo: ZOFFOLI: Fc: for Giacomo. More commonly, they are signed G. ZOFFOLI F. or G.Z.F., which could refer to either man. Dated and semi-documented pieces indicate that production must have been well underway by 1763.

A single page list in Italian, circulated by Giovanni in the 1790s, helps explain the success of the enterprise. It reveals that the firm was only offering 59 statuettes, busts and vases and that the prices were relatively low, beginning at 5 Roman zecchini (£2 12s 6d at the then current rate of exchange of 10s 6d to the sequin) and rising to 80 zecchini (£42).

The Zoffoli's main competitor was Francesco Righetti (1749–1819), who had a much bigger business. When Pope Pius VI visited Righetti's workshop in 1782, the diarist Chracas records that he was able to see a copious collection of statuettes copied from the most celebrated classical works in Rome and Florence, and that these were being produced in abundance to satisfy the desires of the erudite dilettante.

In 1794, Righetti published a four-page catalogue of his copies in French, entitled Aux Amateurs de l'Antiquité et des Beaux Arts. This confirms that Righetti was making many more items than the Zoffoli's, including full-scale copies as well as small reductions, and that his pieces were more expensive. Prices started at 12 zecchini (£6 6s) for a small bust and went as high as 1300 zecchini (£682 10s) for a large copy of the Vatican Apollo. Other bronzes could be obtained from the Valadier family of goldsmiths and the obscure Giuseppe Boschi.

Visitors to Rome were also able to acquire models of the Colosseum and other classical buildings. Antonio Chichi (1743–1816) was making impressive cork models, which are often signed, but almost invariably left undated. These could be purchased individually or as a 'complete series' of 36 models of buildings in and around Rome. The best-selling models in the 19th century seem to have been the marble copies of the restored remains of the Temples of Castor and Pollux and of Vespasian in the Forum Romanum.

The most popular later souvenirs were unquestionably micro mosaics: pictures built up of hundreds or thousands of tiny cubes or chips cut from threads of coloured glass. Credit for advancing and commercialising, if not actually inventing, this type of work is generally given to Giacomo Raffaelli (1753–1836), a member of the Vatican Mosaic Studio, who is said to have exhibited examples in his private studio in 1775. Micromosaic workshops began to be established in and around Piazza di Spagna, where tourists were plentiful and the British traditionally stayed when in Rome. A guidebook of 1874 records at least twenty mosaic workshops or retailers in the vicinity, frequented by tourists.

Visitors could choose from small circular or rectangular micromosaics, either 'loose' and simply on their metal supports or mounted on the lids of boxes; necklaces, bracelets, earrings and brooches set with very small oval or circular micromosaics; and even painting-like plaques or tables decorated with separate scenes, a panorama or a floral composition. These large items could take anything from a few weeks to five years to complete and may have had to be ordered. Many souvenirs show views of classical buildings or St Peter's. A favourite late 18th/ early 19th-century subject was the Roman mosaic called The Doves of Pliny, which represents four doves drinking from a bowl. Discovered at Tivoli in 1737, this had subsequently been installed in the Capitoline Museum in Rome. Micromosaics of animals are also common, and many reproduce compositions after the Bohemian animal-painter Wenceslaus Peter, who was active in Rome from 1774 until his death in 1829.

Among the other souvenirs on sale in the Eternal City in the 18th and 19th centuries were specimen marble table tops, plaster casts of sculptures, 'books' or stacking trays of impressions of engraved gems, shell cameos, and classically-inspired jewellery and items decorated with the Chi-Rho monogram and other references to the Early Christian Church by Castellani and other jewellery firms.

Visitors to Naples in the 18th century had the opportunity to buy tortoiseshell toilet sets, snuff-boxes and other items decorated with gold wire. Much more was on offer in the 19th century: carved coral, shell cameos, 'Pompeian' and Etruscan archaeological-revival jewellery by Casalta-Morabito and others, so-called 'lava' jewellery and other small items carved from coloured limestone, and Sorrento ware, which is similar to 19th- century Tunbridge ware. It was also possible to buy good copper alloy copies (and some silver copies) of items excavated from Pompeii and Herculaneum from Sabatino de Angelis, J. Chiurazzi and G. Sommer.

Fewer souvenirs seem to have been on offer in the other Italian cities. Since at least the 15th century, visitors to Venice had been buying glass made on the island of Murano. The outstanding 18th-century souvenirs are the three dispersed sets of white glass plates painted in red with views of the Grand Canal, copied from prints after Canaletto. They appear to have been acquired or commissioned, as sets of 24 plates, by Horace Walpole, John Chute (the owner of The Vyne, near Basingstoke in Hampshire) and the 9th Earl of Lincoln (who became the 2nd Duke of Newcastle) during their stay in Venice in 1741. Unfortunately, Venetian glass-making went into decline after this. Quality and choice improved dramatically after the revival of the industry by Antonio Salviati (1816–90) in the 1860s–70s.

The most noteworthy souvenirs in Florence in the 19th century were the plaques and other items decorated with mosaic pictures pieced together, like a jig-saw puzzle, from shaped slices of pietre dure (hard stones).

ELSEWHERE IN EUROPE

Wealthy visitors to other European capitals and cities in the first half of the 19th century were frequently able to buy porcelain tea services and other ceramics painted with townscapes or important buildings. This fashion for veduta painting developed in porcelain factories throughout Europe in the 18th century and reached a climax in the services and vases produced in Vienna and Berlin in the first half of the 19th century. The highest quality pieces were generally commissioned for the court or as official gifts, but many items were on sale as normal luxury goods/upmarket souvenirs.

Glass souvenirs were also available. In Vienna, Gottlob Samuel Mohn (1789–1825), Anton Kothgasser (1769–1851) and others painted glass beakers with views of St Stephen's Cathedral or the streets of Vienna. In Berlin, Carl von Scheidt (active 1812–21) painted beakers with the Brandenburg Gate or other local scenes. Between about 1830 and 1860, the Bohemians produced a wide range of glass cased with an outer layer of coloured glass or painted with red enamel, which was wheel-engraved with views of Aachen or other great centres. They also exported glass painted with red, yellow or green enamel, which was wheel-engraved with views of London, York and Edinburgh.

In the early 19th century, the Russians were beginning to produce large quantities of small rectangular boxes and other items decorated with views of Russian monuments and buildings in niello (a black mix used to fill and emphasize engraved lines). Falconet's equestrian statue of Tsar Peter the Great in St Petersburg appears on thousands of snuff-boxes. Over the course of the century, the Kremlin and St Basil's Cathedral in Moscow became increasingly popular and feature prominently on snuff-boxes, beakers, tea services, cigarette cases and caviar containers. Most of these nielloed pieces were made in St Petersburg or Moscow, and many must have been acquired by Russian and non-Russian visitors.

Aristocratic and professional families visiting Brighton, the first major seaside resort, in the early 19th century would have been able to buy whitewood boxes and other items decorated with views of the town. These were made either in Brighton or Tunbridge Wells. Painted ceramics were also available. Bohemian glass wheel-engraved with Brighton Pavilion or the Chain Pier appears to have been on sale in quite large quantities in the middle of the century. Visitors could also have had portraits of themselves made by a number of silhouettists, including two – J. Gapp (active 1827–40) and Edward Haines (active late 1820s–d.c.1896) – who worked in booths under the towers on the Chain Pier. (The bearded French artist Huardel Bly was still making silhouettes on Brighton's West Pier before the First World War, and was succeeded by another cutter, Hubert Leslie.)

MASS PRODUCTION

Almost all the items discussed up to this point were made by skilled craftsmen for the prosperous upper and middle classes. There is little evidence of the concerted production of 'popular', purpose-made secular souvenirs, other than printed ones, before 1850. The great watershed was, of course, the Great Exhibition, held in South Kensington in 1851, which drew over six million visitors from all walks of life to the Crystal Palace. Many were avid for commemorative mementoes and this massive demand could only be met by mass-production. As far as the 1851 Exhibition was concerned, this chiefly meant printing on paper or textiles, transfer-printing ceramics, and die-striking medals. Over the next fifty years, the manufacture of ceramics and glass using moulds, transfer-printing on wood, and the acid-etching of glass would become increasingly important. In the 20th century, the main technological developments have been the production of moulded plastics and the printing of ceramics and glass with a wide range of deep, intense colours.

The Great Exhibition demonstrated to manufacturers and retailers that there was a mass market for certain types of souvenirs and commemorative items. However, the Great Exhibition and its successors were short-term events, which did not lead to long-term sales.

In retrospect, one can see that large-scale souvenir production was held back by two factors. First, relatively weak demand before the lower middle class and working classes began to take short breaks and holidays at the seaside and elsewhere in the late 19th and early 20th centuries. Secondly, the determination of many manufacturers to produce large, high quality items, which could either be viewed as 'Art' or as eminently respectable objects. Small, cheap items were anathema to many Victorian firms.

Many souvenirs have been made by firms which embarked on large production and were then obliged to diversify and sell more widely – both in geographical and socio-economic terms – in order to maintain their sales and continued existence. One can see this diversification and geographical expansionism in the late 18th-early 19th centuries, as the makers of small oval enamel boxes in South Staffordshire seized the opportunity to add souvenir boxes for Cheltenham and other spas and Scarborough, Weymouth and other seaside resorts to the range of their products.

One of the best 19th-century British examples is W. & A. Smith of Mauchline, Ayrshire, which widened its range in the mid-19th century to include varnished sycamore boxes and other items decorated with transfer prints of Robert Burns and other Scottish subjects. These were followed by an avalanche of articles transfer-printed with views of towns, cities and seaside resorts in England and Wales and, in turn, by scenes in Europe, Australia, India and North America, for these markets.

On the Continent, the large number of Bohemian glass houses, wheel-engravers and sellers saturated the domestic market and were forced to export or cease operating. They sent huge quantities of glass further and further afield, until they were supplying throughout Europe and into North America. The Germans and Bohemians also had many porcelain factories and were quick to meet the demand for cheap ceramic souvenirs. They produced porcelain plates and other items decorated with transfer-printed views of British cities, towns and resorts when British companies failed to provide appropriate pieces at the right prices. These ceramics are generally referred to as pink souvenir ware because they are decorated with washes of pink enamel around the sides. German and Bohemian companies also competed with British firms in supplying 'crested china'.

W H GOSS AND CRESTED CHINA

Porcelain decorated with coats of arms, so-called 'crested china',was one of the most important types of mass-produced souvenirs available in Britain between about 1890 and 1930. Its introduction is credited to William Henry Goss (1833–1906), the owner of the Falcon Works, Stoke-on-Trent. In the biography of her father written after his death, Adeline Goss records that, in his early days, W.H. Goss produced ceramics decorated with coats of arms for 'the universities and some of the more noted public schools'. Later, apparently in the 1880s, he began to make small porcelain copies of ewers, jugs, urns and other artefacts found in Britain. Many of these were based on sketches by his son Adolphus, who was the main traveller for the firm, securing orders from retailers. Adolphus also sketched views of towns and buildings for the transfer prints which were used to decorate the 'viewwares'. It seems that Adolphus was the real driving force behind the production of early crested china and related viewware souvenirs. Although Adolphus left the firm after his father's death, his brothers Victor and Huntley continued and expanded the business he had developed.

The Goss factory's miniature models were transfer-printed in black with a coat of arms, which could be coloured in by hand, and were sold through agents. Initially, it was intended that a model would only bear its appropriate coat of arms: thus a copy of the Aberdeen bronze pot would only be emblazoned with the arms of Aberdeen and would only be sold in the Granite City. However, this was much too restrictive and it was soon possible to buy a wide range of items decorated with the arms of the agent's town. The number of Goss models went up from 136 in 1900 to 400 in 1921. In 1900, Goss had 481 British agents. Two years later, there were 601 and 1,378 by 1921.

Crested china was produced by many other Staffordshire potteries. The two most important were Arkinstall & Son Ltd, founded by Harold Taylor Robinson in 1903, and Wiltshaw & Robinson Ltd, which was founded before 1890 and advertised 'Heraldic China' in 1902. Arkinstall items were made at the Arcadian Works in Stoke-on-Trent and marketed as Arcadian China. Wiltshaw & Robinson's pieces were produced at their Carlton Works, also in Stoke, and sold as Carlton Ware. Among the Continental firms making crested china was Schmidt & Co. of Karlsbad, which used the 'Gemma' trademark.

Basically, the thousands of models produced by the various firms fall into five major categories. First, there are the serious subjects: the busts and figures of great men and women, the cottages or houses of famous individuals, and historic buildings. Some are represented among W.H. Goss's early products, while others are a logical development of them. They are followed by two predictable groups: obvious seaside souvenirs, such as copies of shells, crab ashtrays, lobster pin trays, bathing machines, lifebelts and lighthouses, etc, and all manner of animals and birds. The fourth group is a little shocking today, but British manufacturers produced a remarkable range of items associated with the First World War, including miniature models of bullets, bombs, guns, tanks, ships, submarines, airships, aircraft, soldiers and nurses. Later, there were reduced copies of the Cenotaph and other war memorials.

In the 1920s and '30s, manufacturers and buyers understandably turned their backs on the horrors of the Great War and indulged themselves with cute, escapist kitsch groups and animals, modelled in the rounded forms of the new Art Deco style.

The person running the crested china stall at the foot of Brighton's West Pier would simply place an order, giving pattern details and quantities, and the items would be supplied, decorated with the arms of Brighton.

Customers would make their selection and go off with a souvenir of Brighton, however inappropriate it might be.

AMERICAN SOUVENIRS

It is impossible to consider the history of modern souvenirs without referring to the United States. Americans have been much more enterprising than the Europeans, and have marketed a much wider range of souvenirs than their European counterparts.

The Americans pioneered a new type of souvenir, the souvenir spoon, which enjoyed enormous popularity between about 1890 and 1910. Souvenir spoons were made by over two dozen American firms and were die-struck in silver or base metal, which was electroplated. They were produced in large numbers to commemorate the Columbian Exposition in Chicago in 1893 and many later exhibitions; visits to New York and other cities; and holidays and excursions to Atlantic City, Niagara Falls, Coney Island and other resorts. European spoonmakers never matched the imaginative designs and quality of workmanship of the American spoons.

While the first great exhibitions in Europe had been almost entirely educational, with largely static displays, the Americans added spectacle, entertainment and amusements to theirs. At the Centennial Exhibition in Philadelphia in 1876, for example, Gillinder & Sons of Philadelphia built a small glass factory, which produced paperweights and other pressed glass as souvenirs. The Libbey Glass Company, which had just been established at Toledo, Ohio, followed their example at the 1893 Chicago Exposition, making and distributing miniature glass hatchets, paperweights and other items as souvenirs. Thomas Webb & Sons of Stourbridge would respond to these ventures by constructing a glass works at the 1908 Franco-British Exhibition in London, and turning out miniature glass pigs and teddy bears for sale as souvenirs.

The Americans also appear to have led the way with official and licensed souvenirs. Many souvenirs of the 1893 Chicago Exposition incorporate the seal of the exhibition. A wide variety of items relating to the 1904 Louisiana Purchase Exposition, held in St Louis, are marked as 'official souvenirs' and some actually bear the signature of the exhibition secretary, W.B. Stevens. Licensing was a very major business by the time of the 1939 New York World's Fair, with a large number of licences and licence numbers recorded on the souvenirs or their mounts or packing.

At the 1939 New York World's Fair, the organizers and architect-designers succeeded in creating a very impressive central, focal construction, the 700 ft high Trylon and the 200 ft wide Perisphere, which could also be used as an arresting symbol of the exhibition and reproduced, under licence, in a very wide range of attractive souvenirs. The success of the Trylon and Perisphere and the related souvenirs led to the Atomium at the 1958 Brussels Exhibition, the Space Needle at the 1962 Seattle World's Fair and the Unisphere at the 1964–65 New York World's Fair, and the production of millions of souvenirs representing them.

The study of American souvenirs also reveals that imported Japanese souvenirs have a long history. The Japanese were exporting porcelain tablewares and novelties to the United States before the First World War. By 1934, they had 85% of the market in imported dinnerware. Among the Japanese ceramic souvenirs for the 1939–40 New York World's Fair are large quantities of imitation Wedgwood blue jasper vases and ashtrays, with white representations of the Trylon and Perisphere or other buildings at the Fair, and tea services, vases and dishes with painted decoration showing the principal features of the Fair. In the 1930s, the Japanese were also supplying large numbers of dishes, crumb scoops, jugs, boxes and other items in thin, die-stamped metal. Many are decorated with views of the 1933 Chicago Fair, the 1939 New York Fair or Coney Island.

After the Second World War was over, and Japan occupied, American firms placed orders with Japanese companies for ceramics and cast and die-stamped metalwork. Among the Japanese ceramic souvenirs are plates, based on early 20th-century German or Bohemian models, which were transfer-printed and hand-painted in Japan with the Parachute Jump and other rides at Coney Island. They were ordered by Enco, Incorporated, of New York City, probably in the 1950s. In the 1950s and '60s, the Japanese supplied a high percentage of the pressed and plated metal souvenirs sold in the States. They include condiment sets and dishes relating to cities and States and models of the Space Needle at the 1962 Seattle Fair.

THE FUTURE

Having looked briefly at the past, what of the future?

Three factors will profoundly affect the production of souvenirs over the next few decades. In the first place, the manufacture of many ceramic, plastic and other souvenirs now takes place in the Far East, where labour is cheap. For many years, Japan has been superseded by Korea, Taiwan and, now, above all, by China. The strength of the Western currencies and the recent collapse of the Far Eastern economies will lead to more and more items being made in China and developing Far Eastern countries. Western firms will be unable to compete unless they produce first-rate products and adopt advanced specialist technologies.

Secondly, ever rising personal wealth and aspirations, coupled with the high requirements set by the leading firms in the entertainment sector (such as Disney), will necessitate the production of very good quality souvenirs from now on. Bad souvenirs just won't sell. The corollary of this is that investment costs and unit and retail prices will rise.

Thirdly, there will be more and more 'themed' souvenirs, as amusement parks, heritage centres and exhibitions increasingly concentrate on themes. Disney obviously sets the pace, but this year, for instance, Expo 98 in Lisbon will focus on 'The Oceans: a Heritage for the Future'. The centrepiece will be the Ocean Pavilion, with a gigantic central tank the size of four Olympic swimming pools, and no less than 25,000 fish, birds and mammals on view. Many souvenirs for the projected 15 million visitors will be manufactured to link up with and cash in on this.

All this is fairly self-evident. What we will look forward to discovering, over the next 20 to 30 years, is whether companies and entrepreneurs will merely produce slightly better quality mugs, fridge magnets and T-shirts, or whether they will come up with original ideas and designs.

The Millenium will be the next great challenge. It offers tremendous scope for souvenirs and it will be very interesting to see what will be on sale at the Dome in Greenwich and at the celebrations in Rome and elsewhere.

The Author

Godfrey Evans graduated in history from the university of Hull in 1975, with the university prizes in history and history of art, and undertook an MA at the Courtauld Institute, University of London. After receiving a distinction in Museum and Gallery Studies at Manchester University, he worked for four years at the Walker Art Gallery, Liverpool, and Aberdeen Art Gallery and Museums. In 1982 he was appointed Curator of European Metalwork and Sculpture in the National Museums of Scotland, Edinburgh. Since 1996 he has been Curator or European Art in the National Museums of Scotland. He was responsible for organising the 1985 Edinburgh Festival Exhibition *French Connections: Scotland and the Arts of France* and the gallery of *European Art 1200–1800* in the Royal Museum of Scotland, which opened in 1987. Over the years he has secured many important items for the national collection, including the great travelling service of Napoleon's sister, the Princess Pauline Borghese, and the Chesterfield wine cooler by Paul De Lamerie and Paul Crespin. At the present he is preparing a catalogue of the Continental silver in the National Museums of Scotland and an exhibition and book on souvenirs.

References

Alexander, J. & Binski, P. (eds.), *Age of Chivalry. Art in Plantagenet England* 1200–1400, Royal Academy of Arts, London, 1987

Andrews, S., *Crested China. The History of Heraldic Souvenir Ware*, Milestone Publications, Horndean, 1980

Austen, B., Tunbridge *Ware and related European Decorative Woodwares*, W. Foulsham & Co. Ltd., Cippenham, 1992

Buckton, D. (ed.), *Byzantium. Treasures of Byzantine Art and Culture from British Collections*, British Museum Press, London, 1994

Büttner, A., *Korkmodelle von Antonio Chichi, Entstehung und Nachfolge*, in: Kunst in Hessen und am Mittelrhein, Vol.9, 1969, pp 2–35

Canoy, J.L., *À la Découverte du Bois de Spa*, Spa, 1990.

Charleston, R.J., *Souvenirs of the Grand Tour*, Journal of Glass Studies, Vol. 1, 1959, pp 62–82

Emery, N., *William Henry Goss and Goss Heraldic China*, Journal of Ceramic History, No.4, 1971

Gonzalez-Palacios, A, & Röttgen, S., *The Art of Mosaics*. Selections from the Gilbert Collection, Los Angeles County Museum of Art, Los Angeles, 1982

Grimaldi, F., *Mostra di Medaglie Lauretane*, Archivio Storico Santa Casa, Loreto, 1977

Haskell, F. and Penny, N., *Taste and the Antique*. The Lure of Classical Sculpture 1500–1900, Yale University Press, 1981

Hembry, P., *The English Spa 1560–1815. A Social History*, The Athlone Press, London, 1990

Huth, H., *Lacquer of the West. The History of a Craft and Industry*, 1550–1950, University of Chicago Press, 1971

Osma, G.J. de, *Catálogo de Azabaches Compostelanos*, Madrid, 1916

Padua, Museo al Santo, *Antonio ritrovato. Il culto del Santo tra collezionismo religioso e privato*, Padua, 1995

Peters, F.E., Jerusalem. *The Holy City in the Eyes of Chroniclers, Visitors, Pilgrims, and Prophets from the Days of Abraham to the Beginnings of Modern Times*, Princeton University Press, 1995

Petochi, D., with Alfieri, M. & Branchetti, M.G, *I Mosaici Minuti Romani dei secoli XVIII e XIX*, Rome, 1981

Pine, L. & N., *William Henry Goss*: The story of the Staffordshire family of potters who invented Heraldic Porcelain, Milestone Publications, Horndean, 1987

Pinto, E. H. & E.R., *Tunbridge and Scottish Souvenir Woodware*, G. Bell & Sons, London, 1970

Rossen, H.M., *World's Fair Collectibles*: Chicago, 1933 and New York, 1939, Schiffer Publishing Ltd., Atglen, Pennsylvania, 1998

Solodkoff, A.von, *Russian Gold and Silver*, Trefoil Books, London, 1981

Vikan, G., *Art, Medicine, and Magic in Early Byzantium*, Dumbarton Oaks Papers, Vol.38, 1984, pp 65–86

Collection of religious souvenirs showing jet statuette of James from Santiago de Compostela, a plate and brass tobacco box decorated with the Virgin of Kevelaer, a bowl from Lorento, and a model of the Cave of the Nativity made in Bethlehem or Jerusalem.

Collection of American silver souvenir spoons (l to r): World's Columbian
Exposition in Chicago 1893, and Baltimore, New York, Washington, and
Louisiana Purchase Exposition in St Louis in 1904.

9

FROM INDIA TO JAPAN
Buddhism Then and Now

Brian Burke-Gaffney

India was on the verge of an intellectual revolution in the sixth century BC The division of Indian society into four distinct castes, *brahmans* (priests), *kshatriyas* (warriors and aristocrats), *vaishyas* (merchants and professionals) and *shudras* (cultivators), was firmly entrenched, and the Brahmans enjoyed not only tremendous social prestige but also exclusive control over a complicated system of philosophy and religious ritual based on ancient Hindu scriptures called the Vedas. A new wave of sceptical inquiry and disillusionment with authority and material wealth was bringing the Vedic period to a close.

One of the great reformers during this period was Siddhartha Gautama, known today as the 'Buddha' or 'Shakyamuni' (Sage of the Shakya Clan), Siddhartha is said to have been born around 560BC to the wife of Suddhodana, king of a region located in what is today, the southern part of Nepal. Legend has it that the prince grew into a brilliant child who excelled at hunting, sports and academic pursuits, but who worried his father with his tendency toward bouts of gloomy introspection. The king tried to shield him from the pain and sorrow of the world by preventing him from leaving home. However Siddhartha eventually saw an old man, a sick man and a corpse outside the palace and, when told that this was the fate of all human beings, he renounced his princely life and set out alone in search of truth and liberation from suffering.

After leaving home he visited holy men and engaged in all the ascetic practices of the day. After six years he abandoned this as futile and made his monumental decision to sit under the papala tree in Bodhgaya until attaining enlightenment. This attainment was made, legend tells us, eight days later when Siddhartha looked up and saw a star in the early morning sky. Immediately after this event he proceeded to the deer park in Sarnath, near Varanasi, and laid out the first simple points of his spiritual discovery for five ascetics resting there. The sermon which has been passed down from generation to generation as the cornerstone of Buddhism. It dwelt upon what Siddhartha called the 'four noble truths' and the 'eightfold noble path' to liberation from suffering.

The first truth is that all things are transient and therefore full of misery. Disease, separation, old age and death are inevitable. Even worldly happiness is tinged with pain because it is impermanent. The second truth is that suffering results from craving, in a futile attempt to grasp things that are transitory. The third truth, which is a logical extension of the second, is that to overcome suffering the fires of craving have to be extinguished. The fourth truth is that there is a way to get rid of craving and therefore to overcome suffering, namely the eightfold noble path consisting of the right view, right resolve, right speech, right action, right livelihood, right effort, right remembrance and right contemplation. In this, 'right' is taken to mean perfect or highest.

Siddhartha subsequently led the life of a wandering mendicant until his death in Kushinagar at the age of eighty. In the interim he gained a wide and zealous following, not only among religious aspirants, but also among the wealthy classes of northern India. However, he did not, limit himself to any one base of activity, preferring to rest during the monsoon season and to travel when weather permitted. The students who gathered around him during these rest periods certainly shared a common reverence for their teacher, but they were not bound together under any of the rules of conduct and organisation that characterised the later Buddhist community. Similarly, although the Buddhist *sutras* (scriptures) are derived from sermons attributed to him, Siddhartha did not try to enlist students, to have his utterances compiled or to establish a religion. He simply lived and wandered, profoundly influencing people he met along the way.

The above is the universally accepted account. The fact is that we have no hard evidence to support it because the teachings were transmitted orally for three or four centuries before being committed to writing and none contained a biography of Siddhartha or a historical account in the Western sense. The oldest existing collection of scriptures is the Pancha-nikaya or 'Five Sections.' Among these, the fifth section or Khuddaka-nikaya is treated with special reverence because it contains elements, in particular the Sutta-nipata, written in an older form of Pali than that used in the other nikaya, and thus considered to be the closest possible approximation to the actual words of Siddhartha. The following are excerpts:

Not abstaining from the flesh of fish and animals, nor fasting, nor going naked, nor shaving the head, nor tangling the hair, nor smearing the body with dirt, nor wearing the rough hide of the deer, nor making offerings to the god of fire, nor punishing the body to overcome death, nor reciting the mystic formulas of the Vedas, nor making sacrifices, not conducting rituals, nor exposing the body to the elements can purify the mind of a person who is not free from doubt.[1]

A person does not become a Brahman by birth, nor does he fail to become a Brahman by birth. A person becomes a Brahman by actions, and he fails to become a Brahman also by actions.[2]

Aside from the radical rejection of asceticism, class privilege and other aspects of the status quo, the most striking feature of these scriptures is their simplicity: nowhere is there an idea that strains comprehension or rises out of the terms of daily existence. By far the most famous and widely translated portion of the Khuddaka-nikaya is the Dhammapada, or 'Footsteps on the Path of Truth', a collection of 423 phrases selected from the early scriptures as expressive of the essence of Shakyamuni's teachings. For example:

He insulted me, he hurt me, he defeated me, he robbed me. Those who think such thoughts will not be free from hate. For hate is not conquered by hate: hate is conquered by love. This is an eternal law.[3]

All beings tremble before danger, all fear death. When a man considers this, he does not kill or cause to kill.[4]

It was precisely this philosophy of love and non-violence that struck a chord in the heart of Ashoka (273–232 BC), the Mauryan emperor who viciously extended his rule through virtually all of India, but who took to Buddhism after witnessing the carnage and misery caused by his military campaigns. Under his direction, edicts urging compassion and social harmony were inscribed on rocks and pillars throughout India, nature reserves were established, and the teachings of Buddhism spread to lands as distant as Syria, Egypt and Macedonia. In short, it was Ashoka's burst of contrition and devotion that catapulted Siddhartha's simple teachings onto the level of a world religion.

BUDDHISM LEAVES HOME

Unfortunately, Siddhartha's spiritual heirs did not follow the maxim of harmony as assiduously as Ashoka. Soon after the death of their beloved teacher, the former students gathered in the town of Rajagriha, capital of the kingdom of Magadha, to confirm the essence of the teachings before dispersing to various regions of northern India. Almost as soon as the council adjourned, opinions began to differ about the correct interpretation of the teachings and the ideal approach to their implementation. By the time of the second council at Vaisali 100 years later, the monks were breaking squares with each other over questions like what did or did not constitute an infraction of some minor monastic rule.

The various schools of thought fell basically into either the conservative or progressive camp. The former insisted on a strict literal interpretation of the teachings and simple emulation of Shakyamuni's lifestyle. However, the latter, condemned this as shallow, and instead advocated a wide interpretation and practice based on, not only a desire for personal salvation, but also on compassion for other living beings.

Geographically, the conservative school spread southward, treasuring the original Pali scriptures and sinking roots as *Theravada* or 'School of Elders' Buddhism in Sri Lanka and later in Burma and other Southeast Asian countries. It was in Sri Lanka during the first century BC that the scriptures were committed to writing, finally overturning the long-standing conviction that the teachings should be learned by heart and practiced rather than written down and institutionalised.

The progressive school meanwhile transmitted the scriptures in Sanskrit and spread along the trade routes into northwestern India, where it encountered cultural influences from Europe and Persia. Severed from its southern counterpart, the progressive school began to refer to itself as Mahayana, or 'Great Vehicle' and to apply the derogatory term Hinayana, or 'Small Vehicle', to the conservative school.

One of the most important figures in the exportation of Buddhism to China and Japan was the Chinese monk-pilgrim Xuanzang (602–664), who left the Tang Dynasty capital of Chang'an (now Xi'an) in 627 and embarked on an epic journey along the Silk Road to India. Xuanzang spent more than a decade studying at the Nalanda Mahavihara north of Rajagriha[5], and after returning to China he devoted his life to a government-subsidised translation project that produced Chinese versions of the six hundred volume Prajnaparamita Sutra and numerous other scriptures. These works paved the way for the development of Chinese, Korean and Japanese Buddhism and are still in use today.

Xuanzang also wrote a detailed travelogue that remains as one of the most important sources of information about the Silk Road and Buddhist holy sites in India. In it, he provides a rare glimpse into the lifestyle of the Nalanda Monastery, which by the time of his sojourn had grown into the hub of Buddhist studies, not only in India, but throughout the Buddhist world:

> The priests, to the number of several thousands, are men of the highest ability and talent. Their distinction is very great at the present time, and there are many hundreds whose fame has rapidly spread through distant regions. Their conduct is pure and unblamable. They follow in sincerity the precepts of the moral law. The rules of this convent are severe, and all the priests are bound to observe them. The countries of India respect them and follow them. The day is not sufficient for asking and answering profound questions. From morning till night they engage in discussion; the old and the young mutually help one another. Those who cannot discuss questions out of the Tripitaka are little esteemed, and are obliged to hide themselves for shame. Learned men from different cities, on this account, who desire to acquire quickly a renown in discussion, come here in multitudes to settle their doubts, and then the streams of their wisdom spread far and wide. . . If men of other quarters desire to enter and take part in the discussions, the keeper of the gate proposes some hard questions; many are unable to answer, and retire. One must have studied deeply both old and new books before getting admission. Those students, therefore, who come here as strangers, have to show their ability by hard discussion.[6]

Xuanzang's description shows clearly that, unlike the early Buddhist communities where memorisation of the oral tradition and simple emulation of Siddhartha's lifestyle were emphasised, the Nalanda monks and their Mahayana colleagues engaged to a considerable extent in book study and philosophical debate. As a result of this jettisoning of old values, Mahayana literature tended to gallop off on its own, incorporating lofty philosophical notions like 'emptiness' and 'consciousness-only' and embellishing its writings with countless miracles, legends and other artifacts that had no place in the Theravada scriptures.

Buddhist art followed a similar course into the supernatural. Siddhartha had been depicted only by symbols such as footprints, wheels and trees during the first few centuries after his death. The artists of Gandhara in northwestern India, under the influence of both contemporary trends in Hindu art and graphic European techniques introduced by Greek invaders, concocted a glorified image of Siddhartha in sculpture and paintings from the second century AD. These renderings were of course based entirely on fantasy, but with time a prototype emerged and artists soon found themselves obliged to include a full set of the 'thirty-two marks of a great man' in their creations. The incorporation of all these marks, which include bizarre features such as webbed fingers and wheels engraved on the feet, is the figure that we know today as the 'Buddha.'

Indian Buddhism was in fact already in decline by the time of Xuanzang's visit. The Theravada tradition had drained out of India to the south and east, and the Mahayana school was staggering under pressure from a revival in Hinduism. By the tenth century, Nalanda was one of the few remaining Buddhist centers in India, but the studies had digressed widely from the early teachings, devolving into a belief in the power of charms and spells and the practice of esoteric rituals. Even this would have quickly died out, if it had not been for the continuing patronage of local kings. The death blow came in the thirteenth century when Muslim invaders trampled northern India, destroying every Hindu and Buddhist temple they could find and of course making no exception of the monasteries and libraries at Nalanda. Subsequently, the relics of Indian Buddhism's age of glory either blended into the background of Hinduism or sank under the dust of time, not to be seen again until European archaeologists hacked their way through the jungle in the eighteenth and nineteenth centuries.

BUDDHISM REACHES JAPAN

There are two particularly important points to note when considering Japanese Buddhism. One is the fact that it was introduced through the filter of China and Korea, not through direct contact with India, and therefore that the whole spectrum of Japanese Buddhism, from philosophy to architecture, ritual and dress, is deeply tinted by Chinese and Korean culture. The second point is that after its arrival in Japan, Buddhism underwent enormous changes while adapting to the indigenous spiritual tradition, namely the system of animism and ancestor worship referred to today as 'Shinto'.

Although Buddhist ideas had no doubt found their way to Japan much earlier, the Nihon Shoki[7] states that the official introduction occurred in the year 552 when the king of Paechke (one of the three early kingdoms of Korea) sent a mission to Japan with presents including written sutras and a gilded statue. Prince Shotoku (574–622) became Japan's first imperial proponent of Buddhist by promulgating a set of injunctions based on Confucian and Buddhism doctrines, calling for national harmony and loyalty to the emperor, and issuing an imperial edict for the promotion of Buddhism and the building of temples. As a result of this royal support, several schools of Chinese Buddhism were introduced in the late seventh and early eighth centuries and systematic Buddhist studies and monastic practices began in earnest.

The Nara Period (710–794) witnessed a rush to import not only Buddhism as a court and state religion, but all the artifacts of continental culture from urban design to architecture, language, calligraphy, clothing and food. Even the name of the capital, Nara, was borrowed from the Korean word meaning 'country'.

The next infusion of Buddhism came during the Heian Period (794–1185), when the Tendai and Shingon teachings arrived from China and gained support from the ruling aristocracy and imperial court. This period also saw the rise of several noted priests who laid the foundations for several modern Japanese sects and who are revered today as saints among Japanese Buddhists. These include Saicho and Kukai, founders of the famous Tendai monastery at Mt Hiei and Shingon (Tantric) monastery at Mt Koya, respectively.

One of the most important developments in the history of Japanese Buddhism is undoubtedly the popularity enjoyed by Zen Buddhism and the influence it exerted on Japanese culture after the establishment of the Kamakura shogunate in 1192. Zen appealed greatly to the *samurai* or warrior class because it emphasized concrete action over speculation and was thought to provide a way to overcome fear of death on the battlefield. Although certainly a sharp diversion from early Buddhism, this association with *Bushido* or 'the way of the warrior' imbued Japanese Zen with warrior ideals such as stoic endurance and unbending loyalty and spearheaded a surge of creativity that brought about the flowering of ink drawing, tea ceremony and other arts that the world knows today as the quintessence of Japanese culture.

BUDDHISM IN JAPAN TODAY

Buddhism was able to prosper and spread across a diverse palette of Asian countries because it adapted readily to different cultural settings, like water to the contours of differently shaped jugs. As mentioned above, the contour it faced in Japan was the indigenous system of ancestor worship and nature reverence in what is known today as Shinto or 'the way of the gods'. Buddhism did not try to negate Shinto or to relegate it to secondary status. On the contrary, the two religions joined in a symbiotic relationship that ensured their mutual survival. This is evident today in the amiable co-existence of Buddhist temples and Shinto shrines in the Japanese townscape and in the compatibility of the two systems in the spiritual life of the people. Simply stated, Buddhism took responsibility for the 'dark' side: funerals, burials, death commemorations and other rituals for the deceased, while Shinto kept the 'light' side: the blessing of newborn infants, weddings, purification ceremonies and prayers for worldly success.[8]

This division of labour was further strengthened by the visit of Christianity to Japanese shores in the sixteenth and early seventeenth centuries. Although tolerated at first, the foreign religion was banned because of its supposed threat to national security, and a variety of measures were taken to expropriate all memory of it from Japanese hearts. One of these measures was the famous anti-Christian edict of 1614 which stipulated that every last Japanese citizen must become a member of one of the principal Buddhist sects and that it was the responsibility of the Buddhist priests to ensure the strict observation of the edict by paying regular visits to the parishioners' homes and by submitting an annual report to a body of religious commissioners.[9] Subsequently, Japan enjoyed a period of peace, security and national isolation lasting up to the Meiji Restoration of 1868, but during this long hibernation the fires of creativity were snuffed out and Japanese Buddhism lapsed into an era marked mostly by stagnation and lethargy.

Today, suspicion toward Christianity and enforcement of religious affiliation are of course long gone. The *danka* (parishioner) system created in the wake of the 1614 edict continues more or less unchanged, and Buddhism's role as *mundus morti* is so solidly established that Buddhist temples have little more significance to most Japanese people than funeral parlors or grave keeper's houses.

The typical Japanese 'Buddhist' is a person who can claim membership to a certain Buddhist sect but probably knows very little about the founder, tenets or practices of the sect, because the only time he or she has occasion to visit the temple is to attend funerals and *hoji* [10] or to pay respects at the family grave. If particularly devout, the parishioner may attend other ceremonies at the temple on special occasions, but these will be devoted far more frequently to prayers for dead ancestors than to activities such as meditation or studies on Buddhist doctrine.

The association of Buddhism with death manifests itself in odd and unexpected places as well, such as the ban on Zen monks walking on Kyoto streets during the auspicious New Year holiday, and the custom of sprinkling salt in the footsteps of priests to dispel the aura of death. It can even be seen in police-gangster jargon: a hard-boiled detective at the scene of a murder will call the 'stiff' a *hotoke*, the Japanese word for 'Buddha'.

As shown by the above, the principal function of Buddhist priests in Japanese society is not spiritual leader or icon of religious virtue, but minister of the dead. One significant consolation for this morbid duty, however, is that it pays well. Priests collect enormous sums of money for conducting funerals, conferring *kaimyo* (posthumous names), and allotting temple space for effigies to aborted fetuses. Exempt from taxation and blessed with spacious property, they are also able to dabble in less traditional enterprises like the operation of parking lots, restaurants and kindergartens. It is no wonder that they are chided sarcastically with the term *marumoke* ('clear profit'), a pun on the word *marubozu* meaning 'shaved head'.

As the priests will be quick to point out, the mercenary activity is justified to some extent by the high cost of temple upkeep, especially the maintenance of aging wooden buildings prone to the predations of termites and rainy weather. The dwindling of Buddhism into a funeral business and art receivership has distanced it from the spiritual needs of modern Japan and indeed turned many of the country's great temples into mere tourist attractions. The search for something more significant in Buddhism is behind the emergence of numerous *shinko shukyo* or 'new religions' like Soka Gakkai and Reiyu Kai in recent decades, a phenomenon that has few parallels in other Buddhist countries. Even the notorious Aum Shinrikyo (the members of which killed or injured hundreds of people by releasing deadly sarin gas on the Tokyo subway in 1995) attracted followers by skillfully exploiting traditional Buddhist concepts and methods of practice.

If there is a lesson to be learned from this, it is that traditional forms, whether tangible objects like buildings and gardens or intangible phenomena such as rituals and festivals, are quickly distorted and devalued if not accompanied by the spirit that created them in the first place.

The traditional practices of Buddhism have also changed in Japan, so drastically in fact that one has to search hard to find similarities between the Indian and Japanese systems. Siddhartha did not say anything about the afterlife, and he expressly rejected ascetic practices. But modern Japanese Buddhism has everything to do with the afterlife, and, partly because of the link between Zen and Bushido, *shugyo* the Japanese word for religious training, bristles with images of naked people standing under the icy torrent of a waterfall or sitting in a meditation session policed by a person carrying a 'warning stick' flattened out at one end and used to slap drowsy shoulders. However this does not mean, that the light of Buddhism has died out in Japan.

In his English introduction to the book *Zen no Shiki* (The Four Seasons of Zen), Professor Eshin Nishimura of Hanazono College, Kyoto says:

> Zen monastic life reflects the ideal of Zen practice. Zen Buddhism is essentially a religion of Self-seeking, concentrating on the inner life by cutting off all secular involvement. Zen monks have without

exception left their families for the sake of the individual pursuit of the Way and started anew in an entirely different form of community life where individuality is carefully guarded.[11]

This is misleading because the vast majority of Zen monks are the sons of temple priests who are merely putting in a few years of obligatory training in order to take over the family temple. Like their counterparts in all the other sects of Japanese Buddhism, most of them will marry after leaving the monastery, raise children and lead a life different in very few respects from that of a businessman or company employee.

However, Nishimura's comment is true in the sense that the Japanese Rinzai Monastery has adhered to traditional values more tenaciously than the other monastic systems of Japanese Buddhism. To this day, training Rinzai monks follows a strict schedule that has changed little in 500 years, eating simple healthy meals, keeping living quarters immaculately clean, and relinquishing most of the conveniences of modern civilisation. They also maintain a high degree of self-sufficiency and what might today be called 'eco-friendliness' by assiduously avoiding waste and unnecessary consumption. Food is cooked and the bath warmed with firewood cut from abandoned lumber or pine needles collected from the garden; water comes from centuries-old wells; tea dregs and vegetable scraps are used as compost; the wash water from the rice, ashes from the fireplace and contents of the toilets are similarly dispatched to the roots of plants and trees; and every bit of discarded paper is either burned as kindling in the fireplace or bath fire or, if unmarked, used to repair holes in the paper doors or to make memo pads. Even the embers from the fireplace are carefully extinguished in water, dried in the sunlight, then reused as fuel in braziers.

The guiding principle behind this frugal lifestyle is not mortification of the flesh or even thriftiness but simply the traditional Zen spirit of 'devotion to the living moment'. However obscure to the vast majority of Japanese people today, it is undoubtedly this spirit that rises above the barrier of East and West, that transcends the gap between the tenets of an ancient religion and the reality of a modern society, and that links Japanese Buddhism with its mother teaching in India.

Hanging outside the Rinzai meditation hall is a thick board called a *zenpan* that is hammered every evening to announce the beginning of meditation sessions. This board is usually inscribed with the following sixteen-character Chinese poem:

> Life and death are the great issues
> Days and nights pass like arrows
> Nothing is permanent; everything changes

136

Strive, and do not give in to listlessness.

The sound of the board echoes, not just across the gardens of Zen monasteries and the rooftops of Japanese towns, but also down the corridor of time to ancient India when a man named Siddhartha Gautama said:

> A house of bones is this body, bones covered with flesh and with blood. Pride and hypocrisy dwell in this house and also old age and death. Make therefore an island for yourself. Hasten and strive. Be wise. With the dust of impurities and passions blown off, you will be free from birth that must die, and you will be free from old age that ends in death.[12]

The Author

Professor Brian Burke-Gaffney was born in Winnipeg and studied at St Mary's and Carleton Universities in Canada. Following ordainment as a monk in 1973 at Busshinji, a temple of the Rinzai sect of Japanese Zen Buddhism, he spent eight years as a training monk at the Myoshinji Monastery in Kyoto. Left the Buddhist priesthood in 1982 and moved to Nagasaki where he was appointed advisor and translation consultant to the city government. Served as simultaneous interpreter for the Mayor of Nagasaki at the UN General Assembly special session on disarmament in 1988. Received the Nagasaki Prefecture 1992 Citizens' Award, as first non-Japanese recipient in history. Currently Professor of international studies at Nagasaki Institute of Applied Science, advisor on international affairs to Nagasaki City, and co-editor of the annual Journal *Crossroads*. He is an authority on the life of Thomas Blake Glover and has written a book on the subject.

References

1. Sutta-nipata, 249.
2. Sutta-nipata, 650.
3. Dhammapada, 3, 5. For a complete English translation see: Mascaro, *The Dhammapada*, Middlesex: Penguin Classics, 1973.
4. Dhammapada, 129.
5. The *Great Monastery of Nalanda* was India's center of Buddhist learning from the fifth to the twelfth centuries. With the patronage of the Gupta kings, the monastery grew into a sprawling university complex with some

2000 teachers and 10000 students from all over the East, and with a curriculum that included subjects such as art, medicine and metaphysics in addition to Buddhist studies and training.

6. Beal, *Buddhist Records of the Western World*,Delhi: Motilal Banarsidass Publishers, 1981, II 171–2.

7. *Chronicle of Japan* The oldest official history of Japan, this is a collection of works written in classical Chinese and based on ancient documents of various origins. It is thought to have reached completion in the year 720.

8. For a detailed description of Shinto and its practices see: Nelson, *A Year in the Life of a Shinto Shrine*, Seattle: University of Washington Press, 1996.

9. Boxer, *The Christian Century in Japan*, Berkeley: University of California Press, 1951, 317–9.

10. The *hoji* (literally 'dharma service') is a ceremony held at a Buddhist temple to pray for the souls of deceased relatives, usually on the 3rd, 7th, 13th, 17th and 25th (sometimes even the 50th or 100th) anniversary of death. Unique to Japanese Buddhism, these services are often accompanied by meals and alcoholic drinks and, if nothing else, provide an opportunity for scattered family members to enjoy a reunion.

11. Zen no Shiki *The Four Seasons of Zen*, ed. Zen Bunka Kenkyusho/Rinzai Kai Tokyo: Kosei Shuppansha, 1988, 248.

12. Dhammapada, 150, 238.

Engraving on one of the gates of the Sanchi Stupa at Madhya Pradesh, the oldest remaining stone structure in India and one of the earliest known specimens of Buddhist art. Photo by the author.

Top: the Sensoji Buddhist Temple (left) and the Asakusa Shinto Shrine stand side by side on the same plot of land in downtown Tokyo. Bottom: an advertisement for a shop selling Buddhist paraphernalia stands alongside other billboards in a Tokyo train station. Photo by the author.

10

JAPANESE PILGRIMS TO THE WEST
Their Impact Since the 16th Century

Paul Akira Kadota

A historical document entitled *Teppo-ki* (on guns) tells us that several Portuguese landed on Tanegashima Island in 1543 (in the south of Kagoshima Prefecture), where they introduced guns into the country. As far as is known, they were the first Europeans to come to Japan

In 1549, a Jesuit priest, by the name of Francis Xavier, landed in Kagoshima with two other Jesuit priests. They stayed in Japan for about two years, and the Christian population grew to about one hundred thousand during this time.

When Xavier left Japan, he took a young Kagoshima man with him, called Bernard. He was the first Japanese to visit Europe, and was presented to Pope Paul IV at the Vatican in January 1555.

From 1616 to 1854, Japan was closed to all foreigners except those from China, Korea and Holland. In 1854, the Tokugawa government of central Japan concluded a treaty of friendship with the United States, sending a delegation to the US in 1860. Japanese began travelling to the West again, but under the strict control of the Tokugawa government.

Some rich and powerful local governments contravened the controls by secretly sending students to the West. The first to do so was the Choshu clan, now Yamaguchi Prefecture, by sent five students to London in the autumn of 1863.

This was followed by 19 from the better organised Satsuma region, present-day Kagoshima. Four were diplomatic Satsuma representatives to the British Government, and the others went to pursue scientific studies.

The purpose of this paper is to give an account of both kinds of cultural pilgrimage to the West.

FRANCIS XAVIER AND BERNARD OF KAGOSHIMA

Francis Xavier's letters and Georg Schurhammer's *Francis Xavier: His Life, His Times* provide a good account of his life and works. He was born on 7 April 1506 at the Xavier Castle in the Kingdom of Navara. When he was 19 years old, he left Navara for Paris, where he entered the St Barbara Institute of the University of Paris. In 1530, he started lecturing on the philosophy of Aristotle. Under the influence of Ignatius of Loyola, one of his friends, he became a member of a religious group which later came to be called Jesuits.

In 1541, at the request of the King of Portugal, he was appointed apostolic delegate for Asia, and he left Lisbon for Goa in India, which was then a Portuguese colony. He settled there and performed missionary work for the Portuguese, spreading Christianity to the native people of countries in South East Asia as far as Malacca.

On 7 December, 1547, he met a Japanese named Anjiro. He was a samurai and trader from Satsuma. He had killed a man, was running away from his avengers and asked a Portuguese trading friend to let him on board his ship to take him abroad. He mistakenly boarded the wrong ship, the captain of which was a friend of Xavier, named Alvares. Anjiro told Alvares of his misdeed, and was advised to ask forgiveness from God by making a confession to Father Xavier. After a long dangerous voyage, Anjiro arrived at Xavier's Church in Malacca.

Xavier learned much about Japan from Anjiro, which stimulated his interest in the country, and he eventually decided to go there to preach the Christian gospel. He found the Japanese a well educated people, having colleges and universities like those in European countries, and there were some schools for Buddhism and Confucian higher learning. Xavier was enthusiastic about the prospect of a good harvest of Christian converts.

He left Malacca on 24 June 1549, and arrived in Kagoshima on 15 August of the same year. Anjiro seems not to have been a criminal, as he was soon presented to Lord Shimadzu, Prince of Satsuma. Arrangements were made for Xavier to be received by Lord Shimaduz at the castle of Ijyuin on 29 September, and permission was given for Xavier to preach. He made friends with Ninjitsu, a Buddhist Priest of Fukushoji Temple in Kagoshima, and it is said he preached there under the main temple gate.

Xavier lived in Kagoshima for one year, and it is said that about one hundred people were baptised. He completed a catechism and a translation of the Gospel of St Matthew, although the texts of these no longer exist. Lord Shimadzu had hoped for an opportunity to trade with Portugal during Xavier's stay, but this did not happen and no Portuguese trading ships came to Satsuma. Instead, they went to northern Kyushu, where it was more convenient for them to gain access to central Japan.

Xavier wanted to go to the capital Kyoto to be presented to the Tenno Emperor so that he could seek permission to do missionary work throughout the whole country. Lord Shimadzu allowed him to leave Satsuma for Kyoto, along with his disciple Bernard, and the Satsuma Christians were committed to the care of Anjiro.

Bernard of Kagoshima was the first Japanese to go to Europe. He was born in Kagoshima, but nothing is known about his personal history there, and we do not know his Japanese name.

When Xavier left Satsuma for Kyoto, Bernard accompanied him. The exact place from where they departed is unknown, but they left in August 1550. They went to Kyoto via Hirado, Hakata, Kurosaki, Shimonoseki, Yamaguchi, Iwakuni and Sakai. They travelled on foot for the first part of the journey, and then from Iwakuni to Sakai by sea.

Xavier had little luck at the imperial court with his request to preach throughout Japan. In those days, Kyoto was often a battle field of rival clans, and the Tenno Emperor had neither the interest in nor the power to give such permission.

Xavier also wanted to meet scholars of the Hieizan Temple, but he was first requested to present an expensive tribute. This he was unable and unwilling to do, staying there in vain for about a month in the knowledge that a tribute was necessity to see any high ranked person in Japan.

He returned to Sakai, and boarded a ship at Osaka for Hirado, where he arrived in the middle of March 1552. There he prepared a big tribute with letters of credit from the King of Portugal and the Governor of Goa. Not as an apostle of Jesus, but as an envoy of Portugal, he went with this to Yamaguchi for an audience with the Daimyo Prince Ouchi. This time he had better luck in obtaining permission to spread the word of Christ. In the middle September, he went to Fudai, present-day Oita, and successfully converted many people to the Christian faith.

After this series of successes, he went back to Malacca with Bernard and one Mateo, a young Yamaguchi man. He wanted to send both of them to Europe to study Christianity and to acquire a knowledge of Western culture.

In February 1552, Xavier decided to dispatch a young Portuguese Jesuit to Rome, who was asked to take Bernard and Mateo. Xavier left Goa in April for mainland China in order to convert the Chinese. His experience in Japan had taught him that the Japanese would be more ready to accept Christianity when they saw China adopting the new faith. Several months later Mateo died of disease, and Xavier himself died an epidemic on Sancian Island in southern China on 3 December 1552.

Around March the following year, Bernard left Goa for Lisbon, arriving there in September. At the end of February 1554, he became a member of the Jesuits. In July, he left Portugal for Rome, and arrived there in early January. After presenting himself to Pope Paul IV, he returned to Portugal in October.

In February of 1556, he arrived at Lisbon, and then returned to the Jesuit Institute in Coinbra. His health had been weakened by the extensive travelling, and he took ill and died in February the next year.

We know about his personality from *Bernard: the first Japanese to visit Rome in 1555* by Pasquale M. D'Elia. Several letters and memoranda quoted by the author confirms that Bernard was a deeply religious man. A letter addressed to Ignatius of Loyola from a Jesuit father, dated 14 February 1554, tells us that Bernard 'is a very reliable person. He seemed as if he had been educated by us since he was very young. He is now being disciplined at Coinbra. We earnestly desire that he is being one of God's excellent servants. He is very good at his study, too'

The last material D'Elia quotes on Bernard is dated 14 February 1558. It is from a letter written by a Jesuit father remembering his death, where he tells us 'Bernard died as a saint does. While he was alive and living with us, he always served as our model. And then he impressed us very much on his deathbed, too.'

MISSION TO EUROPE IN 1582

Xavier's visit to Japan was the start of many, as after that many Catholic missionaries went there. The population of Christians increased, especially in western Japan. A great volume of correspondence was exchanged between Japan and Europe, with the result that people on both sides of the world came to know much more than before about each other. At long last, Europeans knew that Japan was not an island full of gold.

Japan's struggle between clans came to an end when Oda-Nobunaga unified the nation. It was a rather short period of peace, and under his rule economic development was encouraged. He protected Christian missionary work to promote foreign trade, and reduced the strength of Buddhist Temples, which wielded considerable military power at this time in Japan's history.

This is how Catholic churches came to be built in Kyoto and in Azuchi, where Oda-Nobunaga had a large castle as his headquarters. In 1579, he allowed an Italian priest called Valignano to establish a seminary, the first European type school ever established in Japan.

Following of the Christian religion increased mainly in the Kyushu district, with the support of the so called 'Daimyo Christians': Lord

Otomo-Sorin of Oita, Lord Arima-Harunobu and Lord Omura-Sumitada of Nagasaki. On Valignano's advice, four boys were sent as envoys to Rome to pay respects to the Pope. The boys were Ito-Mansio, Chijiwa-Migel, Nakaura-Juriao and Hara-Martinho. The travelled with six other attendants, and arrived in Rome in February 1582, where they were given a very warm welcome. They were called the 'Tensho Boys' Envoy to Europe', and returned to Japan in 1590.

Sadly, Oda-Nobunaga had been killed just after the envoys left Japan, and friendly relationships with the Christian church was thereby completely lost. Nobunaga's successor, Toyotomi-Hideyoshi, was suspicious of the foreign priests and their spiritual ambition to conquer Japan. Hideyoshi expelled all foreign Catholic missionaries from Japan in 1587, and persecution became commonplace. In 1597, 26 Christians were crucified in Nagasaki in 1597, representing the first Christian martyrdom in Japan.

From the 16th to the middle of 19th Century, Japan was a closed country for almost all European countries, and the Christian faith was forbidden.

Today, there are two Christian Pilgrimage roads in Japan. One is the way from Kyoto to Nagasaki, commemorating the 26 martyrs and following the same route the martyrs walked. The other is Xavier's road, commemorating his journey from Kagoshima to Kyoto. The latter is not completed yet, but with the coming of the 450th anniversary of Xavier's landing, Japanese Catholics have begun walking from Kagoshima. Voluntary groups are making brochures, maps, guidebooks, and have already started internet services.

NINETEENTH CENTURY PILGRIMS TO BRITAIN

The closed country policy was broken by the American Admiral Perry in 1854. In March of that year, the Tokugawa Shogunate government was forced by Perry to conclude a peace treaty, first with the US, and then gradually with other nations. In 1858, a commercial treaty was also concluded. Foreign traders came to Japan, some having settled to establish branch offices, and among them was the Jardine Matheson Company in Yokohama.

It was true that Japan opened the gate, but the Tokugawa government was the gatekeeper, and did not allow other feudal daimyo lords to have free and direct relations with foreign countries. The Tokugawa Shogunate monopolised all profits from trade, whilst on the other hand, Tenno did not allow concluding treaties with European countries.

The spirit of 'sonno', loyalty to Tenno, spread through Japan at this time. The advocates of this philosophy, which originated from studying Japan's old history and mythology, insisted that Tenno should be regarded as the only true sovereign of Japan. Shogunate or 'Seiitaishogun' means 'commander-in-chief against foreign invaders'. According to sonno opinion, the Shogun did not have the authority to conclude a treaty, as this could only be done with the express permission of Tenno.

The news of the Opium War in China and the invasion of Asia by European countries was already well known in Japan. This encouraged 'joi', a strong dislike of foreigners. As Tenno and his chief retainers were advocators of joi, it was natural for sonnoism and joiism to become unified into sonno-joiism. Big feudal daimyo lords who were dissatisfied with Shogunate monopolistic policy, tended to support sonno-joi policy. Among such daimyo lords was Prince Choshu (present-day Yamaguchi prefecture), and Prince Satsuma.

Whilst some of their retainers supported the anti-foreign lobby, others felt it important for the country to be opened up, referred to as the 'kaikoku' policy. This included the introduction of European scientific knowledge to Japan, and thereby making the country wealthy through foreign trade. These were the opposing views held within both the Choshu and Satsuma clans in the 1860s, when groups of young men were sent to Britain for their training and education.

THE FIVE CHOSHU STUDENTS

After Japan was opened to foreign countries, some senior members of the Choshu clan thought they should turn out men of ability for foreign diplomacy. On the other hand, some thought they should have a powerful navy to support the anti-foreign movement.

A Choshu man of 'joi' inclination, Kaoru Inoue, who had been studying nautical science in Yedo (present-day Tokyo) wanted to go to Europe to obtain the latest knowledge available there. He approached the highest authority of the Choshu government, asking them to fund five young men to study in the West. Permission and funds were granted, and the selected men were: Kaoru Inoue himself, Yozo Yamao, Yakichi Nomura, Shunsuke Ito and Kinsuke Endo.

They left Japan for Shanghai with the help of Abel Anthony James Gower, British Consul, and William Keswick of the Jardine Matheson Company in Yokohama. On their arrival at Shanghai, they saw another Keswick, brother of the Yokohama Keswick who was the Shanghai manager of the company. He was asked to arrange passage for them by ship to Britain. Their English language ability was so poor that Keswick only understood the word 'navigation' uttered by one of them, and he guessed that they wanted to be employed as sailors. Consequently, he put

146

them on board two of their ships, The Pegasus and The White Adder as members of the crew.

After more than four months of hard labour at sea, they arrived in London in the autumn of 1863. Hue Matheson, London chairman of the company, introduced them to Dr Alexander Williamson of London University, where they began learning English. Inoue and Ito studied military science, politics and law. Nomura, Yamao and Endo studied natural science.

The five Choshu students learned about the Bombardment of Kagoshima by a British squadron on 15 August 1863 from a newspaper article. The also learned from reading the news that the Choshu clan had fought a battle against European allied forces at Shimonoseki on 5 September 1864. They were all worried about the future of their clan and wanted a stop to such hostilities. Inoue and Ito returned to Japan to explain to the Choshu authorities about the military power of European countries and how foolish it was to engage them in war.

In 1865, the remaining three Choshu students met the Satsuma men who had come to study at London University. In September of 1868, the remaining Choshu scholars finished their studies in Britain and returned to Japan.

THE SATSUMA STUDENTS

The Bombardment of Kagoshima destroyed almost all the batteries of Satsuma, and most of Kagoshima town was burnt down. Some of the 'joi' supporters persisted in continuing the fight, but many knew British military power was too strong to resist. It was eventually decided to negotiate a peaceful solution, and advocates of war were swept out of top positions.

The Satsuma clan concluded a peace treaty with Britain, using the Shogunate government as a intermediary. This involved having to pay indemnity for the victims of the 'Namamugi Affair', including the murder of a British businessman by Satsuma 'joi-ist' samurai. Satsuma borrowed the required sum from the Shogunate, but the money was never repaid.

After this, the Satsuma authorities established a school on European lines, mainly for the teaching of military subjects, but one year later it was thought better for the students to go to Europe for western knowledge rather than to study it in Kagoshima.

The Satsuma representative in Nagasaki discussed this matter with Thomas Blake Glover, and he helped the clan to organise a whole programme of sending students to Britain. This student programme was far better organised from the outset than the one initiated by the Choshu clan.

The Satsuma agent in Nagasaki had maintained a good trading relationship with Glover since long before the Bombardment of Kagoshima took place. When the Namamugi Affair occurred, Satsuma's Nagasaki agent discussed the matter with Glover at once, even seeking his opinion about a plan for secret payment to the British so that they would not retaliate. However, this plan was not acted upon.

The most influential person on the Satsuma side was Tomoatsu Godai, who later went to Britain with the students as a commercial representative. After the bombardment, he sent a representation to Satsuma's top officials, saying it would be a necessity for the clan to send students to Britain as a matter of priority.

The 15 students selected to go were: Mimbu Machida, Naoe Murahashi, Yoshinari Hatakeyama, Heima Nagoya, Naonobu Sameshima, Seishuu Tanaka, Hakuai Nakamura, Arinori Mori, Kiyonari Yoshida, Kanjyuro Ichiki, Yaichi Takami, Shinshiro Machida, Seijiro Machida and Hikosuke Isonaga. With them went Keibu Nilro as superintendent, and Koan Matsuki (later Munenori Terashima) as diplomatic representative. One of the group, Tomoatsu Godai, was economic representative, and Takayuki Hori acted as interpreter.

The party left Hashima harbour, north-west of Kagoshima, on 17 April in 1865 and arrived at Southampton on 21 June. They the travelled to London and settled there. A senior representative of Glover accompanied them all the way, and one of his brothers helped arrange things for them in Britain, in regard to both domestic and educational matters. The first priority was to improve their English language skills, and in October they became 'non-matriculated' students at London University.

There are some records on their daily life immediately following their arrival. On 2 July, one of Choshu five, Yamao, called and made himself available as their guide for visits around London. On 29 June, both the Choshu and Satsuma students made a joint trip to Bedford where they inspected Britannia Iron Works. On 10 August, Niiro, Godai and Hori left London for other places in Britain and continental Europe, mainly for commercial purposes. On 11 February, the following year, they left Marseille for home, and arrived in Kagoshima on 25 April.

On 19 August 1865, Kanaye Nagasawa (formerly Hikosuke Isonaga), who was then 13 years old, left London for Aberdeen to enter The Gymnasium School where Thomas Blake Glover had been educated. Nagasawa's memoirs, recorded by the Japanese-American newspaperman Shakuma Washizu, reported that he stayed with Glover's parents and that he attended school as a day student. He studied there for two years, and then moved to United States with five fellow Satsuma clansmen in 1867.

In March 1866, Matsuki had his first meeting with the Earl of Clarendon, then Britain's Foreign Minister, through the good offices of Lawrence Oliphant who was a Member of Parliament and formerly a member of the British legation to Japan. Matsuki explained Satsuma's situation, saying that the clan wanted to promote free trade under the rule of the Tenno government in opposition to the monopolistic policy being pursued by the Shogunate. It is said Clarendon was sympathetic, and a second meeting took place. After these talks, Matsuki and Murahashi returned home, and they arrived in Kagoshima on 6 July.

In the summer of 1866, each student undertook a study tour. Some travelled to countries in continental Europe, and others to North America. Sameshima and Yoshida went to the United States in the company of Oliphant who was a follower of Thomas Lake Harris, a religious leader of an American cult. Oliphant introduced Harris to Sameshi ma and Yoshida, who were immediately influenced by Harris and became cult followers.

By autumn 1867, the students' situation changed because there was prospects of a civil war in Japan, and the Satsuma government could not continue to support their overseas expenses any longer. Machida and the five remaining students decided to return in May 1867, while six others moved to the United States where Harris had promised to help them continue their studies.

SIX SATSUMAS IN THE UNITED STATES

The students who moved to the US in August 1867 were Yoshida, Sameshima, Mori, Matsumura (once Ichiki), Hatakeyama and Nagasawa. Initially, they settled in a cult colony run by Harris named 'the Brotherhood of the Newlife', with a base in the State of New York. In December, they moved to a new colony established in Brocton, where they led a monastic life of hard labour. The State of New York was one of the main US wine producing areas at that time, and Nagasawa, who later became a wine producer in California, learned how to make wine in Brocton.

Harris was partner in the establishment of a bank, and managed some businesses, including wine production and distribution. He intended to establish a school for Japanese students in Brocton, but doubts about the cult among some of the Satsuma students caused a split and the plans came to nothing.

The issue for the students centred around the problem: which side are we to support, if war breaks out between Japan and the United States? The argument became more and more heated without any conclusion. Then they asked Harris for his opinion. He answered that there should be no war between Japan and the US, but if there were to be one, they should fight for the righteousness of God, no matter what nationality they belonged to.

Yoshida, Hatakeyama and Matsumura left the colony at once, while Mori, Sameshima and Nagasawa did not change their faith in Harris and remained with the cult. However, a month after the argument, Harris told Mori and Sameshima to return to Japan and the two left immediately for home.

Yoshida, Hatakeyama and Matsumura entered Rutgers College, and Matsumura entered the US Naval Academy in 1869. Yoshida returned to Japan in 1871, and Hatakeyama later became a member of Tomomi Iwakura's delegation to the US and Europe. Hatakeyama arrived back in Japan in 1873, the same year that Matsumura graduated from the Naval Academy and returned home.

Now only Nagasawa remained with the cult, and he moved to California with Harris in February 1875. When Harris passed away in 1906, this Japanese disciple became the owner of the Fountain Grove Winery, one of the biggest and most prosperous wineries in California. But the prohibition law of 1920–33 and anti-Japanese feeling at the time made his life and business difficult. He died in 1934, and the winery was sold.

THE SIGNIFICANCE OF WESTERN PILGRIMAGE

There were two kinds of Japanese pilgrimage to the West. One was planned and supported by Portuguese and Spanish traders and missionaries. The other was planned by the Japanese clan governments and made possible through help from British traders, especially those from Scotland.

The first pilgrimage of Japanese to the West did not bear any direct fruit. However, Christian missionaries converted many Japanese to Catholicism. Some of them secretly kept and observed their Christian faith throughout the 200 years when the country was closed and there was policy of persecuting those who belonged to the Christian church.

Although the new Tenno government opened the country to foreigners, it continued to forbid Christian worship and to promote Shinto as the state religion. Shortly after the Meiji Restoration in January 1870, the new government arrested about three thousand Catholics in Nagasaki and exiled them to about thirty clan territories. This Japanese policy was so severely censured by Christian countries that the Tenno government decided to allow religious freedom, and this represented a very important turning point in the history of Japanese thought.

The fruits of the second pilgrimage are essentially worldly. Japan started its cabinet system of government in 1885. The first prime minister was Hirobumi Itoh, one of the Choshu students. The Foreign Minister was Kaoru Inoue, also one of the Choshu students, and the Minister of Education was Arinori Mori of Satsuma. Another Choshu man was Yozo Yamo, who served as Director of the Law Bureau at the Ministry of Justice.

Before the cabinet system was introduced, during the period 1867–85, traditional style of Japanese government gradually changed to follow a Western pattern. Matsuki, who changed his name to Terashima, always stayed at the top level in the Foreign Ministry, he holding the post of Foreign Minister 1873–79. Sameshima was deputy minister 1875–78.

In the early stage of developing diplomatic relations with the US and European countries, almost all senior officials belonged to the Satsuma group of students who went to Britain. Mori was the first Japanese Charge d'Affairs in the US. Sameshima was the first diplomatic representative in Britain, who at various times also carried responsibility for France, Germany, Portugal and Spain. Others worked in many different fields, and it can certainly be said that the education they received in Britain was used to full advantage in the modernisation of Japan.

The Author

Professor Paul Akira Kadota read economics and educational studies at Kobe University. His broad interest in history embraces the cultural influence of early travel, both by Westerners who came to Japan and by Japanese who travelled abroad. A former Visiting Scholar at St Edmond College Cambridge, he has undertaken extensive research on the group of Satsuma students described above, especially on the life of Kanaye Nagasawa. This research took him to Aberdeen, where Nagasawa attended school, and he has written books on the subject, including *Kanaye Nagasawa: A Biography of a Satsuma Student*, published by Kagoshima Junior Prefectural College in 1990. He won the 1987 Minami Nippon Broadcasting Company Prize and the 1992 Toyota Minoru Prize, and he is a member of the Historical Society of English Studies.

Thomas Blake Glover with the insignia of the Order of the Rising Sun, conferred on him in 1908 by Emperor Maiji for his contribution to the modern renaissance of Japan. Painting by Jessica Brown courtesy of the Sano Foundation.

11

FROM ABERDEEN TO NAGASAKI
Thomas Blake Glover in Japan

Alexander McKay

Thomas Glover's fifty-year residence in Japan coincided with that country's rise from mysterious obscurity to world power status. His contribution to that rise was recognised by Emperor Meiji when he honored Glover in 1908 with the prestigious Order of the Rising Sun. That occasion was the high point of Thomas Glover's life and career in Japan; photographs taken at the time show an elegant, proud, still handsome seventy-year-old, seemingly basking in the glory of the occasion. For him, it must have been a time for reflection. A time also for remembering his early days and how his pilgrimage to Japan began.

He was born, almost certainly in a house in Fraserburgh's Commerce Street, on 6 June 1838, the fourth son in a family of six surviving boys and one girl. His early years were spent in that windswept fishing town on the coast of the Moray Firth, about forty miles north of Aberdeen. His father, a career officer in the Coastguard, was later posted to the bigger and more prestigious Bridge of Don station just north of Aberdeen. Young Tom's secondary education was at the Gymnasium in Old Aberdeen, a private school with a reputation for producing ministers for the Church of Scotland. His father was an English-born Episcopalian, his mother an Aberdeenshire farming Presbyterian, but young Tom was not a particularly religious person and, in fact, later warned against over zealous Christian missionaries in Japan.

What we can be certain did develop in his childhood in Scotland, though, was the go-getting, occasionally ruthless character of the successful entrepreneur. He had the sexual energy and the succession of lovers that, psychologists tell us, often is in the nature of people driven, as he was, to succeed. Perhaps, in the Far East, he was liberated from the straight-laced, sometimes hypocritical behaviour of the Victorian British middle classes in which he grew up. After completing his secondary schooling, there is no record of any higher education, it can be assumed that he spent some years learning the ropes of the shipping and insurance business in which his family were involved in Aberdeen.

Arriving in Shanghai in his late teens, his next two years were spent as a clerk with Jardine, Matheson & Co. There, he learned the basics of trading in the Far East, certainly absorbing the routine and meticulous paper work on which his company insisted. Inevitably, the excitement of the volatile political situation in China, almost permanently in a state of unrest, and a company struggling with the moral and technical problems of the highly profitable opium trade registered with him. Whatever the case, he took the chance when it came, to go to the mysterious and newly opened Japan.

It took courage to go Japan in 1859. If China had complicated political problems, Japan was even more difficult and few Westerners fully grasped the situation there. The country was split in much the same way as Glover's native Scotland had been into regions dominated by basically feudal clans, or han, ruled by clan lords, or daimyo. From his stronghold in Edo (present-day Tokyo) the hereditary military dictator of Japan, or shogun, ruled through his government, the bakufu, but relied on the support of various clans.

A delicate balancing act was required to run the country. Many clans were traditionally anti-bakufu, but reluctantly accepted the status quo. For the Japanese emperor had been little more than a figurehead controlled by the bakufu, but emperor, shogun, bakufu and daimyo were all agreed on one point. They watched the ongoing Western expansion into Asia with alarm and wanted it stopped. For some time, it had been clear that Japan's long exclusion from the world would have to end, most likely by force, and some young modernist samurai in the less conservative clans actually welcomed this development. Yet there were many hard-liners, totally opposed to any dealings with the foreigners as they feared Japan would suffer colonisation or be divided and broken as was happening in China.

Groups of terrorist samurai were formed, extremists violently opposed to any foreign presence and ready to fight the Westerners, no matter their military strength. The unrest was palpable at the time of Glover's arrival and, in the first years after the opening of Japan, there was a series of horrific attacks and murders; it was a very dangerous place in which to live and work.

Paradoxically it was only in Japan that Glover would get the freedom and opportunity to shine, opportunities he would not have had by remaining in Aberdeen. In Japan, despite the dangers, were the ideal conditions for a young entrepreneur brimming over with ideas and determination;in Japan he could defy convention and, sometimes, break the law with relative impunity. Here, later, would come his chance to influence decision making at the highest levels of government and industry.

Glover was a fascinating, complex, enigmatic character. He loved, apparently, all the trappings that went with success: the big house, the servants, the lavish entertainments and the clothes. In period photographs he is always immaculately dressed and he was photographed at the turn of the century driving what must have been one of the first cars in Japan. For a publicity stunt, he imported and ran Japan's first locomotive a few hundred yards along the Nagasaki waterfront in 1865, at one point driving the train himself and it is hard today to imagine the excitement these events caused.

Still in his twenties, he had assumed the leadership of the expatriate community in Nagasaki. A photograph exists of Glover lying, rifle cradled in his arms, at the centre of a group of Westerners, many of whom were older and more experienced, posing on a picnic. Yet this same man could display the humility and simplicity of a schoolboy. This was a tall, handsome man who could reject lovers, abandon the mother of his son: and, incidentally, in the process most likely inspire the Madam Butterfly. story. Despite his many infidelities he was a family man, a devoted father and grandfather who would pull out all the stops for his own. He was a complex, difficult man, a considerate man with a virulent temper who could beat a non-performing miner or get in trouble with the law for killing a dog in anger. This same man would not let down a friend and would risk, quite literally, his life for a cause he believed in.

His mission was to commercialise Japan for Jardine Matheson and make himself rich in the process. As a businessman, he was ruthless, energetic and determined, for example he boasted of bribing the Dutch engineers trusted by the Japanese to give his ships a clean bill of health. He would illegally import arms and export rice and eager young samurai desperate to learn the secrets of the West. He would, in his own words, 'nail the coffin' of a leading rival, Charles De Montblanc. Having said that, he was perhaps alone among the Westerners in the early days to see the potential of a new, industrialised Japan and at all times treated his Japanese allies respectfully and insisted on quality products.

His built-in-Aberdeen dock at Kosuge in Nagasaki Bay is an indication of that quality and his coal mine on Takashima Island is another example. It was on Glover's advice that both of these enterprises were later sold on to and prospered under Mitsubishi. On Takashima, he installed the latest British technology which provided the exports to bring in crucial foreign currency for Mitsubishi and the new Japan during their first years of existence. Most of these major business enterprises took place in the 1860s and 70s. His Kirin Beer project was a later development, but another example of encouraging the Japanese to go for quality and to do-it-yourself.

In all of Glover's later business exploits he was successful. In the beginning, though, it was not so easy.

It started with tea, perhaps influenced by an old China tea-hand, his fellow Scot and partner, Kenneth MacKenzie. It was a struggle he endured for years with no real success. Only after similar problems with silk, did Thomas Glover became involved in arms, docks, ships and shipping. Apart from the far greater profits, and of course danger, this move to arms and ships would seem a logical progression: his father and brothers were all involved in the shipping business in one way or another. Aberdeen in this period of change from sail to steam was a major shipbuilding centre and Glover had a series of first class ships built there for the Japanese, culminating in the state-of-the-art warship, the Jho Sho Maru, which later became Emperor Meiji's royal vessel.

Dealing with ship and arms buyers led to Glover the rebel. As Japan lurched towards civil war, access to modern ships and arms, only available through the hated westerners, became of paramount importance to the various clans as they lined up to fight and settle the problems of who would govern Japan. Glover had few scruples, and his initial meetings with rebel samurai determined to bring down the shogun were all geared towards developing trade and profit for his company.

There was no commitment to anyone at this stage. At the same time he was selling ships and arms to pro-shogun clans and the bakufu itself. His was a gradual conversion to a cause, perhaps in the beginning influenced by seeing an important and profitable position for his own company in a 'new' Japan, a Japan dominated by the rebel clans. He got to know, intimately, many of the leading rebels, Ito Hirobumi, Inoue Kaoru, Kido Takayoshi, Godai Taomatsu, Terashima Munenori, Saigo Takamori, Iwasaki Yataro, founder of Mitsubishi, and his brothers, Sakamoto Ryoma and others, all about his own age and all eager for change. He was influenced by them and in turn exerted his own influence and enthusiasm on them and, perhaps more importantly, on the British diplomats.

In a modern analogy, a rebel movement in a developing country would be immeasurably boosted by the approval of the superpower, the USA. In the 1860s and 70s, British approval was crucial, the help and encouragement given to the rebels by Glover bringing, for example, the British Minister in Japan, Harry Parkes, to the rebel capital of Kagoshima in 1866 is incalculable.

Of his own part in the rebellion which brought down the last shogun, he said: 'I was the Greatest Rebel.' This is a typically bombastic remark, but certainly his help was an important factor. There were several recorded attempts on his life in this period, all of which he survived. In one case, he even named the attempted assassin, and in the later stages of the rebellion he was totally absorbed in the struggle. It is a measure of his commitment that he bankrupted his own company in extending loans and credits to the rebels. His business and profit making interests were forgotten in a rush for rebel success. At the end of this period, Glover was thinking and acting like a Samurai, totally caught up in the movement to unseat the shogun. Fortunately for him, when the rebels took over the running of Japan, they did not forget the help given to them by their British friend.

His love life was as turbulent as his business and politics. Within months of landing in Japan, and beginning with Hiranaga Sono, Glover had a series of romantic liaisons with Japanese women. There are four recorded children born to different mothers and strong anecdotal evidence which suggests more. His only surviving son, Tomisaburo, was recorded on the koseki, the family register of an unknown woman named Kaga Maki. Although the theory put forward in my book, 'Scottish Samurai', that this Kaga Maki is the model for the Madam Butterfly of the short story, play and opera, a fact strongly disputed by some sources in Japan, the argument stands. Certainly, what cannot be in dispute, is that some elements of the Glover story found their way into Puccini's classic opera. In his later years, Glover settled into a steady relationship with his partner, Tsuru. No marriage certificate of any kind involving Thomas Glover has ever been located.

Yet during the dangers and turbulence of the rebellion, the trade war with his arch rival Montblanc and a complicated love life, Glover found time to make perhaps his biggest contribution to the development of the new Japan. It is clear that he believed that simply telling the young rebel samurai about the advancements of the West was not enough. Books and lectures alone would not do. In his opinion it was essential that the brightest and best of them went and saw for themselves. There is a lesson here that perhaps is still valid for any pilgrim of the late 20th Century: only by personal experience can another way of life be really appreciated.

By helping in the escape of 'the Choshu Five' in 1863, and two years later 'the Satsuma Nineteen', Thomas Glover accelerated the modernisation of Japan. The young samurai he assisted to the West included a future prime minister, a foreign minister, the father of the Japanese railway system, ambassadors, consuls, leading businessmen and industrialists. This group of then unknown rebels, became a virtual Who's Who of the leading lights of Meiji Japan. Yet it seems at the time of their leaving, only Glover of all the Westerners saw the potential of these young men.

Professor Paul Kadota has written an account of the life of one of these young samurai, Nagasawa Kanaye, who stayed at Braehead House for some years and was educated in Glover's old school, the Gymnasium in

Old Aberdeen. However, there were others. One contemporary newspaper report mentions the son of the chief minister of the daimyo of Shimonoseki, presumably a boy with high connections in the Choshu clan, whose capital was the city of Shimonoseki. The Gymnasium School records from this time, 'five boys from Japan'. What cannot be in doubt, is that Braehead House in Aberdeen was for some years the base for several young Japanese. There is also reason to believe that Ito Hirobumi and Inoue Kaoru of the Choshu Five visited the Glover family during their stay in the UK two years before Nagasawa.

By early 1868, Glover had returned from a long business trip to Aberdeen and was once again deeply embroiled in Japanese politics and business. The demise of the shogun and the 'restoration' of the emperor that year did not bring the instant rewards he had perhaps imagined. His company lurched into bankruptcy. The civil war had weakened Japan's currency and the few daimyo who could pay him at all paid in devalued money. He struggled on with the development of his mine and dock and other interests, but his comet had burned brightest during the years of turbulence. Certainly, by the mid-1870s, the young samurai he had helped began to move into positions of power in government and industry and they did not forget Thomas Glover.

One of the Japanese, Iwasaki Yataro, with whom Glover had dealt in Nagasaki, brought him to Tokyo to advise him on the company he had formed, Mitsubishi Shokai. Among Glover's first recommended acquisitions for this company were the mine and dock at Nagasaki, moneyspinners he had nurtured and that were much appreciated by the Japanese. As the years passed and Mitsubishi and Japan grew, these early projects were perhaps dwarfed by others, but it was Thomas Glover who had shown the foresight and blazed the trail.

He settled into the adviser's role with ease, spending time in Yokohama, Tokyo and Nagasaki. He had retained his beautiful home in Nagasaki overlooking the harbour and where for a time he managed the Takashima Mine for Mitsubishi. It would seem that he had had his fill of the violence, plotting and intrigue of the 1860s and was content to take a back seat. This was a pattern he followed till the end of his long life.

The Japanese government, too, used his expertise and the official record of his achievements for Japan presented to him with his medal in 1908, runs to more than twenty pages of Japanese script. As the new Japan began to flex its military muscle, especially in the 1894 war with China, Glover almost certainly eased the worries of the British and other diplomats who were concerned at the aggressive nature of this new power in the Far East. In the war with Russian in 1904–5, Japan became established on the world stage, an ally of Britain, and Thomas Glover was pictured with the victorious Admiral Togo, Japan's Nelson, at a victory reception in the garden of the Mitsubishi president. That photograph by itself tells us much of Glover's status during this period.

His twilight years were spent in quiet ease. The magnificent Tokyo house, apparently gifted to him by Ito Hirobumi, became a centre for both expatriates and progressive Japanese and there are many photographs of him entertaining both. A flavour of Glover as an old man can be had from the reading of a letter he sent to an old friend, Captain Albert Richard Brown in January, 1911, the year Glover died. Brown, ex-Mitsubishi, then recovering from illness, worked in Glasgow where he was serving as Japanese Consul:

> You cannot imagine what an immense relief I experienced on receipt of your long genial letter of 3rd December. All your friends were anxious including the two Barons [the Iwasaki brothers who owned Mitsubishi] ... I am keeping very well and go to the Mitsubishi office every day although my house is 3 miles out in the country, and I use a jinrikisha over wretched roads and this morning the snow was eight inches deep .... I am writing to Ted [Captain Brown's son who lived in Helensburgh near Glasgow] to thank him for sending that cask of Special Blend [Scotch Whisky] to Baron Koyota.
> PS When I was in Australia I saw posted up in a hotel this notice to Business Men: If you find smoking and Whisky drinking interfere with your business, give up your business!

Brown, who had spent many years in Japan and was a senior figure in the Mitsubishi shipping division, was given the authority to open a Japanese consulate in Glasgow's St Vincent Place, and he was appointed the first consul. The consulate was necessary to look after the numbers of Japanese, both businessmen and students, studying and working there: then the Mecca of heavy engineering and shipbuilding. Opened in the 1890s, the Glasgow consulate remained in operation, run by members of Brown's family until the outbreak of the second world war. The very existence of this consulate and the extensive Japanese presence in the UK at this time again illustrates the strides taken by that country in a phenomenally short time. Thomas Glover must take some of the credit for accelerating this learning process.

He died in his palatial Tokyo home in December 1911. His funeral was attended by hundreds of VIP mourners and his legacy remains. Paraphrasing the words dedicated to Sir Christopher Wren, a look around at the success of modern Japan is his real monument.

In the first half of this century, the aggressiveness of the new Japan he had helped create, perhaps hindered Thomas Glover's recognition outside the expatriate communities of his adopted country. In the era after the second world war, some critics called him a 'merchant of death'. Certainly he dealt in arms, but there was much more to Thomas Glover than that. Recently his role in the Meiji restoration has been re-examined and perhaps is beginning to be more appreciated.

His only son, Tomisaburo, was a quieter, more introverted character than his famous father. Though a Japanese citizen, the childless Tomisaburo was kept under house arrest during the second world war and suspected of spying for the British. He hung himself in the bathroom of his home in Nagasaki a few days after the atomic bomb was dropped in August 1945. He was seventy five years old. Descendants of Glover's daughter by Tsuru, Hana, survive today in the USA.

In the 1960s, Glover's Nagasaki home, which survived the atomic blast of 1945, was developed as part of a bigger tourist complex: Guraba-Tei or Glover Garden. It is visited by close to two million people every year. Recent developments suggest that he is at long last starting to become recognised as a man of achievement in is own country of birth.

The Author

Alexander McKay spent part of his childhood in Aberdeen and trained as an engineer in Glasgow. Following service in the merchant navy, he moved to the offshore oil and gas industry and worked for a spell in Brazil before going to Japan, where he met and married a Japanese girl. After a visit to Glover House in Nagasaki, he became fascinated with the story of Thomas Blake Glover, about whom little was known in his native country. He has carried out extensive research on the life of Glover and is now an authority on the subject. The first edition of his book, Scottish Samurai: Thomas Blake Glover 1838–1911, was quickly sold out and attracted publicity which caused new material to come to light.

The Glover family consisted of:
Thomas Berry Glover Father, born 'in England' 1805, Coast Guard Officer, m. Mary Findlay 1829, in Fordyce, d.1878 in Braehead House, Aberdeen.
Mary Findlay Glover Mother, born Fordyce, 1807, d.1887 in Braehead House, Aberdeen.

The children were as follows:
Charles Thomas, b. 1830, Fordyce, shipbroker, d.1877, Aberdeen.
William Jacob, b. 1832, Fordyce, ship's captain, d.1877, South Africa.
James Lindley, b.1833, Fordyce, shipbroker/businessman, d.1867, Braehead House, Aberdeen.

Henry Martin, b.1836, Fraserburgh, d.1837, Fraserburgh.

Thomas Blake, b.1838, Fraserburgh, businessman, d.1911, Tokyo.

Alexander Johnston, b.1840, Fraserburgh, businessman, d., unknown, in USA.

Martha Anne, b.1842, Fraserburgh, m. Charles George 1861, d.1903, in Nagasaki.

Alfred Berry, b.1850, Aberdeen, businessman, d.1904, en route to Aberdeen from Nagasaki, body returned to and buried in Nagasaki.

Charles and James Glover were involved with a shipbroking firm, Glover Brothers, trading from Marischal Street in Aberdeen during the 1860s (See Aberdeen Post Office Directories). William Glover was a ship's captain and commanded several of Thomas's Japan-bound vessels. The husband of Martha Glover, Charles George, also traded as an insurance broker from the same address. James, Alex, Alfred and Martha Glover followed Thomas to Japan; James, whom some consider the real brains behind Glover and Company, died, aged 33, while on a business trip to Aberdeen in 1867; Alex later left Japan for the USA; Alfred was a Nagasaki resident for more than three decades; after several years based there, Martha died in Glover House, Nagasaki, 1903.

The Jardine Matheson Archives at Cambridge University Library contain much of the period correspondence between Glover and the Jardine Matheson offices in Hong Kong and Shanghai.

Glover's made-in-Aberdeen ships were as follows: Owari, John Smith & Co. [shipyard], 1865; Kagoshima, John Humphrey & Co., 1866; Helen Black (specially constructed for and used to transport Glover's slip dock from Aberdeen to Japan) Alexander Hall, 1868; Ho Sho Maru, Hall, Russell & Co., 1868; Jho Sho Maru (later renamed Ryujo [Whirlwind]), Alexander Hall & Co., 1869; Wen Yu Maru, Hall, Russell & Co., 1869.

See the interview given by Glover (in Japanese), shortly before he died, to Choshu clan historian, Nakahara Kunehei and published in an article in Bocho Shidan-kai Zasshi (Choshu Historical Society Magazine, No.27.,1912, 'Cho-Satsu-Ei No kankei' ('Choshu-Satsuma-Great Britain Relations'), pp 49–72.

Glover's recorded children were: 1861, a son, Umekichi, mother Hiranaga Sono (the child died the following year); 1870, a son, Tomisaburo, mother Kaga Maki; 1876, daughter, Hana, mother Tsuru; 1878, a second child born to Tsuru (died the same year); a fifth child, unknown mother, but almost certainly a mistress of Glover, was a son, 'John, son of Thomas D [sic] Glover' recorded in the Nagasaki British Consulate Records. There is evidence of at least one further child of Glover being born in Yokohama.

Noda Kazuko, a great-great granddaughter of Tsuru, for example, hotly disputes the Kaga Maki connection and in Japan has written extensively on her own theory of the events surrounding Tomisaburo's birth and the Madam Butterfly-Glover connections, claiming Tsuru was the model for the tragic heroine.

See Kadota, Paul Akira and Jones, Terry Earl, Kanaye Nagasawa: A Biography of a Satsuma Student, Kagoshima Prefectural Junior College, 1990.

Braehead House, a two-storey granite mansion situated above the historic Brig o' Balgownie, about a mile upriver from the Coastguard Station house at the mouth of the River Don where Thomas Glover grew up, was the Glover family home from 1864 until c1890. Nagasawa Kanaye stayed there as well as, almost certainly, several other young Japanese (one former owner of the house told the present author that for some unknown reason the cellar area of Braehead had always been known as the 'students' room' so it is at least possible that the Japanese boys lived in that part of the house). Thomas Glover returned to Aberdeen on a business-cum-holiday trip in 1867 and stayed there(a Japanese walnut tree in the garden dates back to that year); certainly there was a strong Japanese influence – the Glover family wills (Scottish Record Office, Edinburgh) show that the house contents included, among other things, 'a Japanese case of coins, a Japanese sword stand with four swords and two daggers, a folding screen, Japanese Armour'.

For example see the Aberdeen Herald, 5 Oct 1867.

Also see the Record of the Gym, Spirit Adhuc Amor, A Shewan, Aberdeen,1923.

WB Mason, writing in the New East magazine, February, 1918 'Thomas B. Glover, A Pioneer of Anglo-Japanese Commerce' made this claim. In the same article Mason – no admirer of Glover – says 'Glover was one of the few [Western] men who found admission to the inner shrine of Japanese life'.

Professor Kadota quotes one Japanese historian as saying that the relationship between Glover and Iwasaki was, 'as if they had been real brothers'. The Iwasaki family kept the close links with Glover and Glover's son, Tomisaburo, stayed with them in Tokyo while attending school there.

Quoted in The Life and Times of the Illustrious Captain Brown, Lewis Bush, Charles E Tuttle, Tokyo, 1969.

References

Burke-Gaffney, *Hana To Shimo Gurabake No Hitobito* (Blossoms and Frost Members of the Glover family)(in Japanese) Nagasaki, 1989

Checkland, O., *Britain's Encounter with Meiji Japan 1868–1912*, MacMillan, London, 1989.

Fox, G., *Britain and Japan 1858–1883*, Clarendon Press, Oxford, 1969

Kadota, P. A. & Jones, T. E., Kanaye Nagasawa, *A Biography of a Satsuma Student*, Kagoshima, 1990.

McKay, A., *Scottish Samurai Thomas Blake Glover 1838–1911* (2nd edition), Canongate, Edinburgh, 1997.

12

THE ARTS AND IDENTITY
From Pilgrimage to Grand Tour

Duncan Macmillan

Art is a witness whose testimony is usually reliable, and properly interrogated it can yield much information. St Andrews was a great pilgrimage centre from earliest Christian times until the Reformation, drawing pilgrims from all of Europe. The art of the great sarcophagus in the cathedral that once held the saint's relics also bears witness to a pilgrimage in the opposite direction.

Looking at the formality of the structure of the St Andrews sarcophagus and at the three–dimensional vigour of the sculpture that decorates it, especially the figure of David, we see a native Pictish artist incorporating into his own free and inventive tradition lessons that he could only have learnt from seeing the formal grandeur of the art of ancient Rome.

The artist's awe in the face of the grandeur of antiquity is tempered by self–confidence. He must have travelled to learn at first hand from the great examples that he knew by reputation. Perhaps this was as far as Rome itself, but it was certainly to somewhere where the myth of the Eternal City and the potency of its example were still tangible. The date of the sarcophagus is a matter of conjecture. Scholars are mostly agreed that it belongs in the eight or early ninth centuries, and at the turn of the ninth century, not far away on mainland Europe, Charlemagne established a new Roman Empire. Rome was topical. The city was also the shrine of St Peter. For St Andrews, the shrine of Peter's brother, the comparison was especially pertinent.

There is sometimes corroboration for art's witness too. The Pictish king Nechtan had renewed ties with Rome, and though he did not go there himself, his emissaries certainly did. The journey to Rome seems to have been undertaken regularly. Several centuries later the Scottish king himself travelled to Rome. When Macbeth ruled the Scottish kingdom and in spite of his evil reputation, perhaps because of it, he made the pilgrimage. That an artist should have made the journey, perhaps with one of these embassies, would have been quite natural.

Travelling to Rome, the artist was a pilgrim and the pilgrim was an artist. The same journey was still being made by artist–pilgrims a thousand years later when Rome became the central destination in the Grand Tour, a cultural pilgrimage in an increasingly secular world. But had the deeper motivation changed so much?

Though it is easy to see the Grand Tour as a product of the secularisation of art, sceptical North Europeans apparently indifferent to the way in which this long continuity had been driven for a thousand years by the engine of religion, it may be that the function had not changed, only the focus. As the religious motive faded, art took its place. Art itself took on the spiritual power that had driven the pilgrims. Indeed, until the Reformation, it had always been part of it. This was so much so that it was to purify religion, to free it from the distractions offered by this glamorous sibling, and it was the reason why the iconoclasts went about their work with such dreadful thoroughness. It is ironic that art survived this destruction in far better shape than religion and, as it did so, its devotees still travelled the same routes that had been established in the days of religion's dominance.

Indeed, when art and religion were split by Protestantism, now independent, art actually gained in status. By the end of the 17th century, the journey to Italy and Rome was an essential ingredient in the education of two classes in society, artists and aristocrats, and especially in Protestant Northern Europe. These travellers must have been driven by some sense that their journey was a search, a pilgrimage, and that that search might reveal something that repaid their effort. Art had come to be seen as a vessel that holds the substance of civilisation in tangible form. Did this pilgrimage become a search for civilisation itself?

Certainly the extraordinary continuity of the pull of Rome reflects something more than a reputation. It was an instinctive sense that for all the diversions along the road of history, in Rome one could confront the roots of Western civilisation. No exotic culture could ever hold such sway. Nor has it ever done so, even now in these days of global travel. Rome's authority was only challenged when the 18th century artists started to look, not further afield, but even deeper for the roots of their own culture, their civilisation, deeper and closer to home.

When the popularity of the Grand Tour was at its peak, the source of its decline was already apparent. It lay in a change of focus towards a new, modern psychological idea of civilisation that was born in the

Enlightenment. An idea that eventually substituted for the great unifying force of classicism, the solipsism of our modern world ruled by the absolutism of the individual.

Throughout the Middle Ages, Rome's reputation never faded. The draw of the Roman church meant that travellers from all over Europe continued to be exposed to such mighty witnesses of its greatness as the Colosseum, the Pantheon, or the Baths of Caracalla. Rome was not the only destination, of course. Especially at the time of the Crusades, many went beyond Italy to Asia Minor and the Holy Land where there were other things to give inspiration. But the peculiar power of the Roman myth survived all competition.

What is most remarkable, though, is that, in Northern Europe at least, the direct and imaginative inspiration from the human idea at the heart of classical civilisation, as we see it in the St Andrews sarcophagus, is unusual. It is not the norm, though it does reappear from time to time at moments of special intellectual excitement as in Sicily under Frederick II or in Chartres at the beginning of the Gothic period.

It is testimony to the creative energy of Pictish culture that it had appeared there too. In most of the centuries that followed, even as they marvelled at the splendour of its ruins, it was religion and politics that absorbed visitors to Rome. But the artist at St Andrews had understood the grandeur of the human image, an ideal of humanity, that had developed in the Mediterranean civilisations of Greece and Rome. In the change in European self–awareness that we call the Renaissance and which eventually convulsed Northern Europe in the Reformation, it was this vision of humanity that was once again the issue.

The Reformation was a cataclysm and it split Europe. When Scotland came down so firmly on the anti–Roman side, it put Rome pretty well out of bounds. But though they are generally seen as so different, even antithetical, it is actually difficult to disentangle the Reformation from the Renaissance. Looking at Scotland in the century before the crisis, there are striking signs of the self–awareness and curiosity that we associate with the Renaissance. There are signs, too, of the belief in the importance of art and architecture that is its most distinctive characteristic. The transition from religious to artistic pilgrim was not brought about so abruptly and by the Reformation alone. Things were already changing before Scotland decisively took the Protestant road. But these changes were also clear signs of the mental attitudes that eventually made the Roman Church's claim to authority seem intolerable.

In Edinburgh, the extraordinary centrally planned building, now called St Triduana's Well, suggests that James III and his architect were conscious of current debate in Italy about the special symbolic suitability of such a shape for a church in spite of its liturgical disadvantages. But remarkably it seems they may also have been aware of the much earlier Byzantine tradition of centrally planned churches whose existence underlay this debate, especially the Dome of the Rock in Jerusalem. This is not only speculation. That extraordinary individual, Sir Anselm Adornes, had been to Jerusalem, very much it seems on James's behalf, and if he went as a pilgrim, he certainly went too as an artistic investigator, an art–pilgrim in fact.[1]

Of course many people from the court and church of the three Renaissance Stuarts travelled to Rome, and Roman visitors came to Scotland too. In 1433, the future Pope Pius VI, Aeneas Silvius Piccolomini came on a mission. Rather a secret service mission it seems, but he left a vivid diary of his impressions and experiences. He was impressed by the sight of coal, and by the fact that the country was divided in two. The northern half where they spoke a different language was entirely covered in forest. The women he found comely and of easy virtue, though how he knew this as a priest is not clear. He was shipwrecked on the way in. So he insisted on going home overland in spite of the risk he faced in England as a hostile spy, and resting in Alnwick he experienced a Scottish Border raid from the receiving end.[2]

Later in the century the sceptre gifted by Pope Alexander VI to James IV in 1494 and the sword gifted by Julius II in 1507 are both Italian Renaissance art of the highest quality and are the product of this diplomatic traffic. The carved roof of the great hall of Stirling also suggests a self–confident familiarity with classical models. Recent research into the building of the Palace of Linlithgow offers up–to–date Italian models for that building too.[3] The courtyard and stair of Crichton Castle are another example of this. Francis Stewart built the remarkable, palazzo–like north range of the castle after he had returned from a journey to Italy in 1581.

In the 15th and 16th centuries, Italy's Renaissance certainly made it a magnet for artists, a magnet whose power was in contemporary culture and in the wealth that made it flower. In the centuries that followed, this modern reputation became enrolled with Italy's ancient history. The reputation of the great artists of the Renaissance was explicitly integrated with that of the ancients. There was now twice the reason to visit Italy, and especially Rome where Raphael and Michelangelo had made their greatest works.

After Dürer's two journeys to Italy, if not before and if he could find the means, such travel became a necessary part of any artist's education. Flemish and Dutch artists left a record of the impact of both aspects, ancient and modern, of the art they saw on visits of this kind. The same journey was a crucial part of the education of Velasquez, Rubens and Van Dyck, to name but three.

Of course, up till the foundation of St Andrews University in the early 15th century, all Scots had to travel if they wanted an education, and even after that, up until the mid–18th century, they naturally travelled for what we would now call their post–graduate years. Men like Michael Scot, Duns Scotus and George Buchanan travelled through universities in France, Italy and Spain and became great European scholars. One of Patrick Geddes's favourite heroes, the Admirable Crichton, seems to have had little other claim to fame than his attendance at a large number of universities around the Continent.

The Reformation certainly made it difficult for Protestants to travel anywhere in Catholic Europe, but even in the 17th century the break was not complete. From Scotland, the Earl of Lothian was collecting art in Paris before the Civil War,[4] and at much the same time young men were still travelling to France to complete their education.[5] But modern Roman art, the baroque style, was specifically associated with religious and political propaganda. This added a political dimension to the artistic equation. Not surprisingly, therefore, Italian baroque found few echoes in Scotland, and when it does appear in the ceiling painted by John Alexander for the Duke of Gordon, it is by a catholic artist working for a catholic patron. This was also a project that was conceived in Italy when both artist and patron were there.[6]

But to travel to find an education is not quite the same thing as to see travel as an education itself. That is surely a modern attitude and it was the essence of the aristocratic Grand Tour, a young man and his tutor setting out to see the world, their destination usually France then Italy. Perhaps one of the earliest examples of this kind of aristocratic grand tourist from Scotland is Alexander Stuart, illegitimate son of James IV, being sent to Italy to study at the beginning of the 16th century.

That was before the Reformation, and for all these continuities, it was still a watershed. Rome itself, and so the study of classical antiquity, represented a serious political problem, and not just for the travellers' reputation in the ecclesiastical politics of their homeland. There was always danger travelling as a heretic in a Catholic country. Even late in the 18th century, when the parish priests in Rome made their annual census before Easter, they often simply recorded the presence of a northern artist by noting the word 'eretico' in their book of the state of souls.[7] Wilkie bears witness to the reality behind these divisions. Although a son of the manse, when he first saw the catholic rite practised in a French church, as late as 1815, he was astonished by it.

It is remarkable, though, given these religio–political difficulties, how northern travellers did return along the path to Rome. It was the reputation of art that drew them, and it was the artists who led the way in making the visit an obligatory part of any liberal education. There was a large colony of northern artists in Rome throughout the 17th century. They had a reputation for wild living, artistic bohemians it seems. We do not know of any Scots among them in the first part of the century, but by the 1650s the Scottish educated painter, Michael Wright, was studying in Rome and was also dealing in pictures. He was followed a little later by the architect James Gibbs and his friend John Alexander. They were both catholics, but two other Scottish artists, William Aikman and John Smibert, were not. Aikman remarkably went not only to Rome, but on to Asia Minor. He was presumably using his family trading connections.

Aikman was relatively wealthy, at least he had an inheritance, though in a very modern gesture he traded it for the opportunity to study art and to go on the Grand Tour. But with Smibert and Alexander, we see a quite new phenomenon. They were only two among many artists of modest background and limited means who travelled because they saw it as essential to their professional education.

We see this increasingly in the 18th century. And for the genteel student too, music, literature, language, what at the time was called manners, were all part of the interest of Italy and to a less extent France. But art, modern and antique, was uppermost in their interest. It was the main part of the motivation in this history of pilgrimage. The sons of Sir John Clerk of Penicuik actually went to study painting in Rome in the 1730s, the younger brother Alexander coming back to Scotland to practise as a painter. The elder brother bringing back modern paintings for the family collection.

For a century or more, to visit the best antique sites and the studios of the leading contemporary artists, to collect if you were wealthy enough, these were the primary motives of the polite traveller seeking education. Would it be too much to say that modern tourism was founded on art, on the idea of the cultivation of taste?

Between Dorothea's dabbling in art, and romance, in *Middlemarch* in the last days of the classic Grand Tour in the mid–19th century, and the Baedecker tourism of *Room with a View* fifty years later (both spiced by romance) we move into the modern world. Though the continuity is striking, the difference is that in *Room with a View*, in spite of the romance, it has all become academic and impersonal. Everything is already streamlined for mass consumption. The grand tour has lost its grandeur.

Even so, as we look at this history, we can see very early on the first signs of an organised tourist industry. Published travel guides began to appear at the beginning of the 18th century. They had a classical model in Pausanias's guide to Greece. The first public museum in Europe, the Capitoline in Rome, was set up as a centre of study for the artists, art students in effect, who were coming to Rome in increasing numbers.

Colonies of expatriates grew up at the main centres to service the travellers, and an accident of history gave the Scots an advantage here.

As the heat went out of the Jacobite cause after 1746, the political exiles turned to culture for their living, acting as guides and agents for the increasing flood of visitors.[8] Andrew Lumsden, Prince Charles's secretary, and the Abbé Grant are typical. Scottish artists settled permanently in Rome too. Gavin Hamilton had spent fifty years in the city when he died there in 1798. In all that time he made only two brief visits home. He became a dealer and antiquarian as well as the doyen of foreign artists, presiding in effect over an extraordinary and informal multi–national art school.

This polyglot community was just like that in Paris a hundred and fifty years later. Riven with feuds and factions, it was nevertheless a melting pot of radical new ideas. Modern art was shaped there and as this happened, the Scottish input was vital.[9] It was through Rome that the most radical implications for art of Enlightenment thought were worked out, the ideas ironically that eventually undermined the authority of the Grand Tour itself. Homer, Ossian and a new primitivism were the ruling enthusiasms in the circle of young artists around Gavin Hamilton.[10]

Among these artists, were pioneers of this new imaginative art, men like Alexander Runciman, Henry Fuseli, Nicholas Abildgaard, J.L. David.[11] There were women too, like Angelica Kauffman and Catherine Read. Anne Forbes went out there as a student from Scotland in 1767, chaperoned by her mother. The old lady's correspondence gives a vivid insight into the life of the Scots community and the difficulties faced by a worthy Scots lady adapting to the familiar traveller's problems of foreign food, climate, language, money and all the rest.

And for all that it became so accepted, the journey was never a simple one. Though he took the overland route through France, Allan Ramsay still managed to be shipwrecked on the short part of the journey that he took by sea along the Ligurian Coast. The journey was not cheap, and the stay was always long. This was not a two week holiday. Artists regularly stayed for years. Perhaps they felt this was a once in a lifetime opportunity, though Allan Ramsay went three times and he was not unique. The time they took was surely also partly a measure of the importance of the task, of how much they had to learn, and that is reflected in the size of the investment that they made to get there. It was enormous in relative terms.

We know in some detail, the finances of Alexander Runciman[12] and of Anne Forbes. She was financed by a kind of family subscription, the large and wealthy Clerk clan all rallying round. But money was still a problem. Runciman went out to Rome when he was over thirty, an established tradesman painter, but not a rich man. He had patrons in Sir James Clerk and Robert Alexander. Like Gauguin, a century later, he gave up his business and raised all the money he could for his journey, but he was still broke within a year. Money could be made by copying and selling landscapes, but it was a struggle and the main source of feuding among the artists. Some of the lucky ones travelled as artists to some wealthy Grand Tourist, a kind of animate camera.

The same motive that took artists and travellers to Italy, also took them further afield. The reputation of Greece had never been completely eclipsed, though for long it was inaccessible. The first artistic explorers began to rediscover its remains in the late 17th century. But a new and powerful motive for the rediscovery of Greece, was provided by the analogy between ancient and modern democracy promoted by the Whigs. This was led, notably by the Earl of Shaftesbury who from the start saw this as an artistic analogy as well as a political one. In arguing for the historical importance of Greek society as the great precedent for modern British democracy, he also argued for the place of art in modern society. Significantly, he also dismissed any claim to culture by the Romans. It was vitiated by their imperial history. They were just showing the first signs of the dawning of some culture when 'by their unjust attempt upon the liberty of the world, they justly lost their own.'[13]

The Aberdeen philosopher George Turnbull developed this Philhellenism in an extended account of the history of Greek art and its superiority over any Roman imitations,[14] and he presented it as a model for the social role of art in present day society. His teacher in Aberdeen, Thomas Blackwell, had gone even further than this, to look beyond Greek antiquity to prehistory to argue that Homer was not a product of classical civilisation at all, but a natural poet from the preliterate childhood of mankind.[15]

Pioneering the artistic exploration of Greece, Robert Wood followed Blackwell to demonstrate the truth of his argument by actually comparing the landscapes Homer describes with the real landscapes of Greece. Thus he believed he had proved that Homer was indeed a 'natural' artist. Remarking as he did so that 'The Poetic Age of Homer differed from the age of his (Roman) critic Longinus ... as we do from our Gothic ancestors in the Age of Chivalry and Romance.'[16] A fundamental shift is heralded, not just from Rome to Greece, but from classical to romantic. Travel was beginning to find a new goal. Civilisation was perceived as having a quite different origin from the classical achievement of Rome.

The extension of the Grand Tour to Greece was logical, though. Rome had shaped Europe, but in Greece lay the true foundation of the humanity of western thought. With Blackwell and Wood something quite new had appeared. The subject of inquiry is no longer the civilised world. It is the world before civilisation from which civilisation had grown, but warped and twisted. To go back beyond the classical world was to search for a simpler original state from which to rebuild a new civilisation from first principles. The extension of the Grand Tour pointed to a profound change in values that eventually brought its end. But the journey remained a pilgrimage.

This argument was focused very clearly in a row that broke out among the community of artists in Rome in the 1750s. Allan Ramsay was there on his second visit, so was Robert Adam.[17] Ramsay was a friend of Robert Wood who was also there at the time. Ramsay took the new radical Greek line, but he went further to argue along with Shaftesbury that Rome's whole reputation was actually groundless. The Romans were a 'gang of meer plunderers...sprung from naked thieves and runaway slaves',[18] he said. They had usurped the culture and reputation of the Greeks. Piranesi, the champion of the Roman cause, countered with his superb etchings of Roman monuments. The Abbé Winckelmann followed Ramsay and Shaftesbury. Writing famously on the superiority of Greek art, he dismissed the 'so–called art of the Romans.'

But Ramsay had gone even further than this to argue that real civilisation, the political civilisation of modern democracy, had its origins neither in Greece nor in Rome, but among the ancient Goths. Theirs was the true civilisation. The classical was no more than 'an affectation of Italian elegance.' This was a radical attack on the central premise on which the reputation of Rome had been built. It was the Goths, after all, who were credited with the destruction of the Mother of civilisation.

Though the Grand Tour survived for another century, this was a significant straw in the wind. Radical change was beginning. At just the same moment, Thomas Blackwell's novel vision of Homer certainly influenced James MacPherson in his reconstructed interpretation of the Ossianic fragments of Gaelic literature that he converted into the poetry of Ossian. In the part that Ossian played in the fashion for travel to the Highlands, there is in turn a direct link between the origins of Highland tourism, the extension of the Grand Tour to Greece and its final demise.

Walter Scott's poetry and novels were of course central to this change, but there too it was a shift in the values dominant in high culture that was the driving force in the redirection of what was to become modern tourism. Scott was typical too in the way he set his poetry and his novels in the landscape. The Highlanders of Ossian, like the lowlanders of David Herd's Scots songs, were in and of the natural world that they inhabited.

Herd was one of the first systematic collectors of folk song. He published his *Scots Songs* in 1769 and in the preface he wrote of how the special distinction of the tradition of Scots folk song derived from 'the romantic face of the country and the pastoral life of the inhabitants'.[19] Herd was a close friend of Alexander Runciman, and in his 'Hall of Ossian' at Penicuik

House, Runciman laid special stress on the landscape. Thus these men clearly saw a direct relationship between this natural 'primitive' poetry and the landscape that produced it.

The poet Robert Fergusson was a mutual friend of Herd and Runciman. He sets the whole debate out with characteristic vividness. In these lines from 'Hame Content', written in 1773, he starts with an vision of the Grand Tourist setting out on his voyage fired with enthusiasm for the classic lands that are his destination, but he sets up a sharp opposition between their spurious charm and the authentic appeal of the native and natural:

> The chaise is yokit in a trice;
> Awa drives he like huntit' deil,
> And scarce tholes time to cool his wheel,
> Till he's Lord kens how far away,
> At Italy, or Well o' Spaw,
> Or to Montpellier's safter air:
> For far off Fowls hae Feathers fair.
>
> There rest him weel: for eith can we
> Spare mony glakit gowks like he:
> They'll tell where Tibur's waters rise:
> What sea receives the drumly prize,
> That never with their feet hae mett
> The Marches o' their own estate.
>
> The Arno and the Tiber lang
> Hae run fell clear in Roman sang;
> But save the reverence of schools!
> They're baith but doowy lifeless pools.
> Dought they compare wi' bonny Tweed,
> As clear as ony lammer–bead?
> Or are their shores more sweet and gay
> Than Fortha's haughs or banks o' Tay?
>
> Come, Fancy, come, and let us tread
> The simmer's flow'ry velvet bed,
> And a' your springs delightful lowse
> On Tweeda's bank or Cowdenknows,
> That, ta'en with thy inchanting sang,
> Our Scottish lads may round ye thrang,
> Sae pleas'd they'll never fash again
> To court you on Italian plain.

Soon will they guess you only wear
The simple garb o'Nature here:
Mair comely far and fair to sight
Whan in her easy cleething dight,
Than in disguise ye was before
On Tibur's or on Arno's shore.

Though the landscape is the setting, it is the people of his own country, their music and above all their language, which is the real subject of Fergusson's remarkable poem. But it was only a short step from this to see the landscape itself as inherently poetic and as offering the contemplative observer the same elevating feelings that he, and increasingly she, would find in the poetry that it inspired.

It was during these years of the middle and later 18th century and in the works of just this circle in Scotland that the idea of the importance, indeed the very existence of an inherently poetic, national landscape was born. Increasingly too it was not just national, but even more precisely local landscape that came to be celebrated for the history it had witnessed and for the associations that it held for the artist, poet or simple observer.

In 1817, Wilkie summarised the change. He wrote:

> Scotland is most remarkable as a volume of history. It is the land of tradition and poetry, every district has some scene in it of real or fictitious events, treasured with a sort of religious care in the minds of the inhabitants and giving dignity to places that in every other respect would, to the man of the world, be considered barren and unprofitable.[20]

This new vision of landscape replaced the long standing convention that Fergusson dismisses in his poem that only Italy, the classical landscape of the Grand Tour in fact, could be truly poetic. In 1790, in his *Essay on Taste*, Archibald Alison, a pupil of Thomas Reid explored these new ideas in a theoretical framework. He not only put forward the notion that our aesthetic feelings are always based on association, and that therefore the landscape that we know has a greater claim on us than any other, however beautiful. But he also argued that underlying our feeling for landscape in general, for nature, was our feeling for its creator. The contemplation of a wild and magnificent landscape, untouched by man, could not only be poetic. It could actually be a religious experience.

In spite of these changes, the Grand Tour continued to flourish throughout the 18th century and following pioneers like Wood, for the hardiest travellers it expanded to include Greece. Robert Wood himself travelled beyond Greece, further into the Middle East to 'discover' Palmyra, an event commemorated in a monumental painting by Gavin

Hamilton. In Greece itself, he was followed by an increasing flood of travellers. He personally assisted James Stuart and Nicholas Revett in their first expedition to the Aegean which eventually resulted in the publication of their monumental book, *The Antiquities of Athens*. A detailed and scholarly account based on measured drawings of surviving Greek buildings, it became the source book of the Greek revival. At the beginning of the 19th century, these two were followed by the Earl of Elgin on the expedition that famously brought back the Elgin Marbles, an expedition not without adventure as one boatload of marbles was sunk and the earl himself and his countess were both made prisoners of war by the French.

It was the privilege of rank that allowed Lord Elgin to make the journey at this time. For most people, the Grand Tour was out of the question during the 25 years of the Revolutionary and Napoleonic Wars. However it was not just because of this, that in the peace that followed, Rome was no longer quite the magnet that it had been. The changes in taste were already apparent. There was still a colony of artists there, and Rome was still the first destination for aristocratic travellers. But the dominant group in Rome were the German artists, called the Nazarenes, and significantly their interest was in medieval, not Antique or High Renaissance art. It was, what the eponymous English group who followed them, called Pre–Raphaelite art. This was the art of the 14th and 15th centuries, whose was not appeal of its high civilisation, but its lack of sophistication. We still occasionally use the generic term 'Primitive' to describe it.

But Scots continued to go to Rome too. David Scott and William Dyce were both in Italy in the late 1820s. They formed a link between the Nazarene group there, and their contemporaries in Britain. Lawrence Macdonald settled in Rome and made his career as a sculptor there. A large Scottish community of artists gave a dinner for Wilkie there in 1827. Wilkie was on his travels and these took him not only to Rome, but also to Spain, which for the rest of the 19th century became a favoured destination for artists following him. There he studied painting and became one of the first champions of Spanish painting among modern northern artists.

The counter–appeal of the natural, the primitive and the unspoilt was now clearly beginning to undermine the authority of the classic world. What Wilkie and those after him found in Spain, was the glamour of a heroic 'unspoilt' people. Their heroism was established in the popular mind by their prowess in irregular warfare in the recent Peninsular War. It gave us the word 'guerrilla'. But Spain's wild countryside and its colourful history were also part of this appeal. Altogether these were exactly the same qualities that put Scotland on the tourist map. They were also the precise opposite of the values once sought by the Grand Tourist in pursuit of 'civilisation'.

David Roberts and John 'Spanish' Philip were among the many artists who followed Wilkie to Spain. Then Roberts went on, further afield to the Middle East, Egypt and the Holy Land. The paintings he brought back made him famous and are still current as images of those places. Wilkie in turn followed him to Turkey and Palestine and died on the return journey. Wilkie's motive was important in this last journey. It was spiritual, to paint religious pictures recording the authentic people and places of the land of the Bible. He was seeking authenticity in its apparently unchanging population and landscape, and inspiration from the power of the unique associations with which it was endowed.

This was something new, and it revealed findamental changes in the motivations of the searching traveller or pilgrim. The artist Wilkie was surely motivated in the purest sense, still driven by an ideal goal and a moral search. Civilisation had come to seem tarnished and it was no longer its grand achievements that were the objective of the traveller, but whatever the question, it seems the answer was still to be found by travelling. Though now, almost the opposite of civilisation, it was the natural, the authentic and the unspoiled that the traveller sought.

In Spain, Wilkie looked for subjects among people who could be held to be untouched by civilisation, just as David Allan had sought them in the islands of Ischia and Minorca, among Allan Ramsay's gentle shepherds in the Pentland Hills, or in the Scottish Highlands.[21] It was this imagined quality that had been the huge attraction of Scotland as it was focussed by Ossian. We were looking deeper for our roots and our origins. And we were looking closer to home, to apparently unspoiled people and an apparently unspoiled countryside where we could imagine some continuity with our remotest origins, our primitive state. That had been the appeal of Ossian. It is a peculiar irony that the refreshing wilderness of the Highlands was in part at least a product of the very progress that had made civilisation seem so tarnished in the first place.[22]

The wild mountains of your native landhad become preferable to the landscape of the classics, and wilderness itself that had once been seen as barren and unprofitable could now be called sublime. We were no longer expected to search for humanity framed in the grandeur of civilisation, what the unknown artist from St Andrews had found so long before in the art of Rome. It was humanity reduced to its simplest form, one's self. The quintessential statement of this is towards the end of *The Secret Garden*. Archibald Craven, the father in the story, a lost soul, morally crippled, wanders alone in the wilderness of the Alps. There he finds himself. He rediscovers his moral nature in the contemplation of the beauty of a clump of forget–me–nots:

It was as if a sweet clear spring had begun to rise in a stagnant pool and had risen and risen until at last it swept the stagnant water away... Something seemed to have been unbound and released in him, very quietly.[23]

Wilkie died in 1841. It was just as the railway age was dawning and with it the possibility of mass travel. The idea of the holiday was born with it. The railway made possible the rare day's escape for the urban proletariat from the smoke and dirt and tedium of the industrial cities to the refreshment and cheerful forgetfulness of the seaside. This was physical, not moral regeneration. For many of us the annual holiday still serves the same purpose. From it has been born the cult of sun, sea and sand, the physical renewal of the old seaside day out vastly extended in time and space, but fundamentally unchanged. Though you could argue that it was an even deeper search for our primeval origins in the sea.

More cynically you could say that the cult of the sun tan is the ultimate solipsism, the pure cult of self in nature reduced to elementary, biological simplicity. Yet the old idea of pilgrimage runs deep and still persists alongside it. Tourists still follow the pilgrimage routes established by artists over the millenia. The layers of this long history can still be read in the itineraries of today's tourists.

The Author

Professor Duncan MacMillan is an Honorary Royal Scottish Academician, Curator of the Talbot Rice Gallery, and Professor of the History of Scottish Art at Edinburgh University. He is the author of several books, including *Scottish Art 1460–1990*, the most authority work ever written on the subject. He is also Chairman of University Museums in Scotland, the Scottish Society for Art History and the Edinburgh Galleries Association.

References

1. Macmillan D., *Scottish Art 1460–1990*, (pp 15–16), Edinburgh, Mainstream, 1990
2. Piccolomini's Diary, The Commentaries of Pope Pius II, trans. by Alden Spragg, Smith College Studies in History, Vol XXII, Oct 1936–Jan 1937, pp 19–20

3. Campbell, I., *Linlithgow's 'Princely Palace' and its Influence in Europe*, Architectural Press, 1995

4. Macmillan D., *Scottish Art 1460–1990*, (pp 63–4 & pp 68–70), Edinburgh, Mainstream, 1990

5. Thomson, D., *A Virtuous and Noble Education*, SNPG, 1971

6. Holloway, J., *Patrons and Painters, Art in Scotland 1650–1760* (pp 88), SNPG, 1989

7. These annual censuses are preserved in the Archives of S. Govanni Laterano in Rome

8. Skinner B., *Scots in Italy in the Eighteenth Century*, SNPG, 1966 for the pioneering account of this phenomenon

9. Macmillan D., *Woman as Hero: Gavin Hamilton's Radical Alternative*, in *Femininity and Masculinity in Eighteenth Century Art and Culture*, Perry, G. (ed), Manchester, 1995

10. Macmillan D., *Painting in Scotland: the Golden Age*, Chaps. 3 & 4, Oxford 1986

11. Skinner, B., *Scots in Italy in the Eighteenth Century*, SNPG 1996, for the pioneering account of this phenemenon

12. Macmillan, D., *the Earlier Career of Alexander Runciman*, Edinburgh University PhD, 1974 and Basil Skinner unpublished transcript of Forbes' correspondance from Aikman family papers, the Ross, Hamilton.

13. Cooper, A. A. (Earl of Shaftesbury), *'Advice to an Author' in Characteristicks etc*, (1711) ed John M Robertson (Ohio 1964), pp 143

14. Turnbull, G., *A Treatise on Ancient Painting* , London, 1740

15. Blackwell, T., *An Inquiry into the Life, Times and Writings of Homer*, London 1735

16. Wood, R., *An Essay on the Original Genius and Writings of Homer etc*, p.74, London 1769

17. Fleming, J., see account of this milieu, *Robert Adam and his Circle*, London, 1962

18. Ramsay, A., *A Dialogue on Taste*, London 1754

19. Herd, D., *Scots Songs* , 1769, (preface)

20. To Perry Nursey, 5 Nov. 1817, Dawson Turner Mss., Trinity College, Cambridge.

21. Macmillan, D., *Painting in Scotland*, Chap. 5

22. Hunter, J., *On the Other Side of Sorrow*, Edinburgh, Mainstream, 1996

23. Hodgson Burnett, F., *The Secret Garden*, p 256, First pub. 1911, London, 1975

Top: Arms of the Royal Burgh of Aberdeen, drawn in Art Deco style by Fenton Wyness (courtesy of the author). Bottom: the coat of arms granted to the Royal Society of Edinburgh in 1967. The symbol for DNA (desoxy–ribo nucleic acid) appears as a horizontal spital between the castle and the flaming sun (courtesy of Leslie Hodgson).

13

HERALDRY AND IDENTITY
From Knights to Corporate Branding

Gordon Casely

Identity is an inevitable part of the human condition. Nowhere in the world is it unavoidable; it has represented people, communities and corporations for millenia, and there is no evidence at all that the significance of it will decrease. We display an almost primordial need to express identity, both individually and as part of a group.

Much of this paper dwells on a particular but effective strain of formalised identity portraying nations worldwide; and it will conclude that mankind should maintain the strength of its embrace of the wondrous formality that is heraldry rather than be deluded by the witch-doctoral charms of logo merchants.

In July 1998, Althorp Park opened to the public for a two-month season so that visitors at £9.50 each may gaze on the island where Diana Princess of Wales lies buried. Pilgrims or tourists? They make a pilgrimage to pay their respects to a Princess who has been called 'an icon for her era' (BBC Television, 6 September 1997). The tourist path of these 150,000 expected visitors creates new sources of economic wealth for the Northamptonshire village of Great Brington. The object of adoration targeted AIDS, landmines and holiday playgrounds, showing herself as the quintessential 20th-century pilgrim-cum-tourist.

On view in Althorp are the arms of her father, the 8th Earl Spencer, borne by her throughout her lifetime. They, along with the Royal arms gained through marriage to HRH The Prince of Wales, form a backdrop in the museum created in the Palladian stable block at Althorp. The death of a princess creates a joint business of pilgrimage and tourism where heraldry becomes an essential item of presention, decoration and identification.

AN EXACT AND ANCIENT SCIENCE

Heraldry is the formal, structured method of identifying people, organisations and the communities in which they live. The science of armory marks, decorates and informs according to legal patterns. While heraldry is international, the governance of it is generally the lawful province of individual nations. In Scotland, heraldry is the only remaining national function which truly remains under Scottish control and for which the capital is Edinburgh.

A practical function of heraldry was the identification of friend or foe on the battlefield. Dressed to kill, men in fighting clothes were virtually unidentifiable. The invention of a method of marking men and their leaders started the creation of heraldry. Since the banner marked territorial position and the shield was a universal tool of offence and defence, it is on banner and shield that heraldry first appears in simple application of colour, cross and creature.

Since pre-heraldic times, groups of people have been associated with certain symbols: the eagle, king of birds, with Roman legions; and the lion, king of beasts, with the Assyrians. The origins of what has become heraldry reach back more than 1000 years to the reign of Charlemagne, the Bayeux Tapestry indicating that specific forms of personal symbols were evident at the time of the Norman Conquest. In Scotland, we accept the last quarter of the 12th century as being the dawn of our heraldry, when the science became applied by successive generations in hereditary fashion.

The success of heraldry as a method of visual communication, giving instant identification without the use of letters, was quickly recognised. The adoption of symbolic devices provided the key to its usefulness, for heraldry creates an instant message to the informed and the illiterate alike. This visual interpretation of a name led to its employment on seals; a document could be verified by the attachment of a seal with a recognisable coat-of-arms. Within a century, the system had spread across Europe. One of the earliest extant Scottish seals dates from 1177 bearing the *fess chequy* of the Steward of Scotland, a device still borne in the marshalling of the shields of many Stewart armigers today. Private letters were sealed with small seals, sometimes the impression being made by a ring. The signet ring of Queen Mary Stuart (1542–67) is an example of this method of authenticating documents and identifying the signatory.

To be effective, heraldry is best used in simplest form, that he who runs may read, that plain precedes complex. A banner had to be simple enough to be read by a man astride a galloping horse. 'In Heraldry the simpler the bearing be it is so much the purer', wrote the heraldist Sir George MacKenzie of Rosehaugh in 1633. Thus the national flag of Scotland incorporating a white diagonal cross on a blue ground is one of the simplest heraldic devices anywhere in the world, possibly rivalled only by the Rising Sun of Japan.

The essentially European outlook of Scotland led to strong influences of heraldic exchange. The *Armorial de Gelre*, prepared in Flanders circa 1380, has three pages featuring Scottish coats of arms. Late mediaeval Scotland was a relatively poor country where heraldry was sometimes the only form of decoration which could be afforded. Relative poverty did not prevent ability and skill in combining use of heraldry both to show ownership or kinship, and decoration. In Scotland, especially in the Lowlands, east coast and in the south west, the tradition still flourishes where buildings are decorated externally and internally with heraldic carvings, ceilings, windows and furnishing.

The control of heraldry in Scotland is vested in the Lord Lyon King of Arms, currently Sir Malcolm Innes of Edingight. He is chief of the heraldic and genealogical executive, who unlike the English Kings of Arms is not an official within a department but an Officer of State in his own right. Since 1542 he has by Royal Warrant borne sole authorisation for the granting of arms, standing as King of Arms in place of the Sovereign, and in recognition of the importance of his office is usually knighted shortly after appointment (Innes of Learney: *Scots Heraldry* 1956). His peculiar importance in Scotland is due to his incorporating the pre-heraldic Celtic office of High Sennachie of the ancient Royal line of Scotland, through which he continues to act as guardian and preserver of the Royal pedigree and family records. First mention of the office is in 1318 of a Lyon being inaugurated with the rank of knight at Arbroath Abbey. His Office is unique in that it is a court of law in daily session; it is also one of only two in Europe with judicial power, the other being in Spain.

In granting and matriculating arms, Lyon ensures that no person bears the same coat-of-arms, for in Scotland every coat-of-arms must be different: ' .... hereditary marks of honour composed of certain tinctures and figures granted or authorised by Sovereigns for distinguishing, differencing and illustrating persons and communities' (Alexander Nisbet: *A System of Heraldry* 1772). Arms are individual property: there is no such thing in Scotland as a 'family coat-of-arms', though in many European countries including England, it is possible to speak of 'family arms' since several persons of the same name may bear the same arms. Scotland gained early realisation that 'family arms' devalued the system if one man could not be identified from arms displayed by several others as well as himself.

Thus in 1592 during the reign of King James VI (1567–1625) the (Scots) Parliament passed an Act requiring the Lord Lyon King of Arms and his heralds to *difference* the arms of separate persons and to matriculate them in their books. This Act was followed by another of 1672 requiring all armorial bearings to be entered in the register of the Lord Lyon, now *The Public Register of All Arms and Bearings in Scotland* comprising some 80 volumes and maintained up-to-date since 1672. Scotland governs heraldry by the strictest laws in the world. Arms being heritable property, the representation as one's own of the arms of another person, community, company or organisation is theft, and is an offence seriously pursued by Lyon Court.

Qualifications for gaining a coat-of-arms vary considerably throughout Europe, and may depend on nobility or caste. Through the impact of the Celtic social system upon Scotland, the system is egalitarian, from the fundamental theory underlying clanship (and Lowland 'houses') that every member springs from the founder of the clan. Thus any person judged by Lyon to be *virtuous and well deserving* may be granted arms. The petitioner can be female or male, for Scotland has always maintained sexual equality in heraldry.

The time-honoured practice of heraldry is a modern growth business, what might be termed 'forward with the past'. As the 21st century beckons, there has never been a greater number of people and organisations pursuing arms as identity. The number of new coats-of-arms gained through Lyon Office in the past 30 years outstrips the number of grants and matriculations over the previous 300 years, with no indication of any diminution in demand. As a result, a new coat-of-arms appears every working day of the year.

The list of UK blue-chip companies who use or display heraldry on a daily basis includes banks, supermarkets, and major energy companies, businesses such as Tesco, Marks & Spencer, Barclays Bank, ScottishPower, Royal Bank of Scotland, BAA and the UK Atomic Energy Authority. The Bank of Scotland, founded 1695, employs its coat-of-arms every working day, just as it has done since the arms were granted in 1701.

Here in North East Scotland, Aberdeen Harbour Board, Clark & Wallace, Braemar Royal Highland Society, the Christian churches and both universities are immediately recognisable through arms, while Bluebird Coaches, though not possessing heraldry itself, makes a point of adorning its fleet with the Royal arms gained by Royal appointment.

Heraldry, the mediaeval survivor, has become a potent modern symbol.

THE CRUSADES

If the growth of religious evangelism created a market for pilgrimage, then the example of the First Crusade of 1095 led to a format for journeying to Jerusalem. The experiences of pilgrims inspired others to copy their journeys, with or without religious inspiration as driving forces. Thus mediaeval pilgrimage spawned early tourism. Both pilgrims and early tourists required visual identification to demonstrate status and country of origin, a need which provided impetus to the nascent business of heraldry. In turn, heraldry not only responded to the needs of the Crusades, but went further and drove the business of identification by becoming regulated.

From the time of the First Crusade in 1095, called for by Pope Urban II (1088–1099), those knights who set out to wrest the tomb of Christ and the surrounding territory from the 'unbelievers' of Islam stitched to their shoulders a cross made of strips of material; that is, they 'took the cross' The very name Crusade is based on the word 'cross'.

By the advent of the Second Crusade, the need for identification among legions of troops and followers became very strong. The unstructured evolution of early heraldry in the 12th century was given impetus towards some formal pattern by the urgent need among forces from different regions to attain visual recognition. Thus prior to the Third Crusade, King Phillipe II of France, King Henry II of England (1154–1189) and Count Philip of Flanders met at Gisors in North East France on 13 January 1188 to decide the particular colours to be worn by their men. These were agreed as white for the English, green for the Flemish and red for the French, the last because by this time the French had fought for over 60 years in red after the example of Hugh de Payens, founder of the Order of the Temple (Knights Templar). When he founded the Order circa 1119, de Payens was acquainted with the Assassins, a contemporary Muslim military order whose then course of action aided Templar policy. Assassin knights employed a distinctive livery of red caps and belts, and this may have influenced de Payens in his choice of colour of the Templar cross.

The Templars along with the Knights Hospitaller (of St John of Jerusalem), the Knights of St Lazarus and the Teutonic Knights (of St Mary of Jerusalem) formed the most powerful orders of chivalry to come from the Crusades. Templars today exist in the Portuguese Order of Christ, whose livery colour is red, while the colour of the shirts adorning England's international sportsmen and women is white.

Additionally, the Templar banner, called *Le Beausant* or *Bauceant* (Old French for piebald horse) is *per fess Sable and Argent*; black in the upper portion, white in lower. This was used together with a red eight-pointed cross (the so-called Maltese cross, whose eight points remember the eight

Beatitudes) usually depicted on lance pennons and guidons together with the *Agnus Dei*. *Le Beausant* hints that the Templars were 'fair and favourable to the friends of Christ, black and terrible to his enemies' (quoted, source not given, in *The Romance of Heraldry*, by C W Scott-Giles, 1929).

The Christian symbol of the *Agnus Dei*, also known as the *paschal lamb*, occurs in Scots and European heraldry, and depicts a haloed lamb *passant* holding a lance or staff at the upper end of which are both a cross and a white pennon charged with a red cross. The arms of the Royal burgh of Perth show a paschal lamb bearing a lance, with the banner of St Andrew replacing the cross and white pennon. A similar device appears on the civic bearings of the Royal burgh of Ayr.

Every crusader could now recognise the language spoken and territory of origin of a companion by the colour of the cross he wore. The wearing of the cross was not restricted to the strip of material worn by each crusader, but extended to wider uses involving many types of cross, differently shaped and with varying points.

In his crusade of 1146, King Louis VII of France (1137–80) adopted the fleur-de-lys as his personal emblem. The stylised Madonna lily (*lilium candidum*), ultimately the symbol of France, represents the purity of the Virgin Mary. It was also believed to indicate the crusading spirit, though followers of Louis VII loyally claimed that 'fleur-de-lys' was really 'flower of Louis'. Both as an armorial charge and as a means of heraldic ornamentation, the fleur-de-lys is ubiquitous because of the variety of forms in which it can be shown. So universal and popular did the heraldic lily become that within a century (c. 1225), King Louis' fleur-de-lys formed the centrepiece of the Welsh seal of Madog ap Knaytho. In the same century, the florin (from Italian *florina*, a little flower) was a gold coin first minted in Florence and named after the lily on the reverse. Florence is known as 'the city of lilies' from its coat of arms: *Argent, a fleur de lys Gules*.

The era of the Crusades (1096–1291) carries significance far beyond the actual campaigns in the Holy Land. Politically unrewarding they may have been, but the Crusades created strong cultural influences on the western world. The common sign was the cross, modified in form and colour as occasion demanded. The crosses incorporated in the national flags of Nordic countries from Finland through Faroe to Iceland are directly attributable to the territorial crosses of the Crusaders (Dr Ottfried Neubecker: *Heraldry - Sources, Symbols and Meaning* [Macdonald] 1988).

By the end of the Crusades, the power of the four great Crusading orders had grown to that of multinational companies. Consequently the use of their forms of identification in livery, emblems and symbols expanded beyond mere national allegiances. The lessons of identification arising from the Crusades were not lost.

SAINTS IN CIVIC HERALDRY

Saints and the Cross exert profound influence on Scotland's heraldry. Saints appear on or are referred to in 21 coats-of-arms of Scotland's 201 burghs; including St Adrian (Pittenweem), St Bryce (Kirkcaldy), St Cuthbert (Kirkcudbright), St Duthac (Tain), St Giles (Elgin), St Kentigern (Penicuik), St Lawrence (Forres), St Margaret (Queensferry), St Mary (Banff, Cullen, Lauder, Melrose, Selkirk and Tobermory), St Michael (Dumfries and Linlithgow), St Nicholas (Prestwick), St Ninian (Nairn and Whithorn), St Peter (Inverkeithing), St Ronan (Innerleithen), St Ternan (Banchory) and the very Saviour (Inverness). Three principal cities feature achievements of arms symbolising saints or their attributes: Edinburgh (St Giles), Glasgow (St Mungo) and Dundee (St Mary); while Aberdeen shows St Nicholas upon the so-called *sacred arms*. Aberdeen is one of only four burghs recognised by Lyon Office as possessing both civic and sacred coats-of-arms; the others being Kirkcaldy, Linlithgow and Montrose. The sacred arms in all cases highlight local patron saints.

Historic use of the cross is widespread, versions appearing on the burgh arms of Alyth, Ardrossan, Blairgowrie, Callander, Coldstream, Cove & Kilcreggan, Crieff, Dumfries, East Kilbride, Galston, Inverness, Kilsyth, Kinross, Lockerbie Milngavie, Markinch, New Galloway, Newburgh, Renfrew, St Monance, Troon and Wick. Few of these crosses possess direct if any link with pilgrimage, but ultimately are all drawn from religious association. Heraldic recognition of saints and their relics was maintained in the new civic heraldry arising from creation of regions and districts in 1975, and continued again in local government reorganisation of 1996. The practice continues to the present day in the arms granted this year (1998) to Aberchirder Community Council showing on the shield the crozier of the locally venerated apostle St Marnoch.

St Columba (521–597) existed six centuries before heraldry first arrived in Scotland, yet he in common with many European saints and even Christ himself has arms attributed to him, in his case a white dove on a blue ground. Among heraldic Columan representations in Scotland is the College of the Holy Spirit on Cumbrae (arms granted 1874, in which the saint appears in the 1st and 4th quarters: *Azure, St Columba in a boat at sea, in his sinister hand a dove and in dexter chief a blazing star all Proper*); and the Roman Catholic diocese of Dunkeld (arms granted 1990 showing the dove representing the saint: *Purpure, an open book Argent, binding and fore-edges Or, charged with three passion nails Sable conjoined and piercing a heart Gules, and perching upon the book a doves wings displayed holding in its beak and olive branch Argent*). The evangelism of St Columba led to Iona becoming a place of pilgrimage, initially as a burial place for Scotland's kings. The name *Iona* perpetuates an error, for the *n* was really a *u*, coincidentally giving a word which in Hebrew means 'dove'. Further coincidence occurs in the name Columba, for in Latin it also means 'dove'.

Columba the northern apostle might have become patron saint of the kingdom but for the rise in influence of St Andrew said to have begun in the reign of King Hungus Mac Fergus (752–61). The legend is related by the Scots historian John Spottiswood (1565–1639). In his *History of the Church of Scotland* quoted by McMillan and Stewart, he states that in the night prior to battle, the king had a vision of St Andrew: 'The history addeth that in the journey of the battle there appeared in the air a cross in the form of the letter *X*, which so terrified the enemies that they gave back .... ' John Leslie (1526–96) adds: 'That sa noble a victorie suld never be forzhett, when he (Hungus) was about to joyne with the ennimie S. Androis croce was ay borne before in the ansignze and armes of the cuntrey'. This legendary beginning of the cult of St Andrew has the result that the Cross of Andrew is now one of our five national symbols: Saltire, Royal Tressure, unicorn, lion and thistle. Thus veneration of St Andrew gradually replaced that of St Columba. King John Balliol chose St Andrew's Day 1292 for his coronation. When in the summer of 1385 the Scots prepared to invade England, Parliament decreed that every man should be identified by the diagonal cross: 'Item every man French and Scots shall have a sign before and behind, namely a white St Andrew's cross, and if his jack is white or his coat white he shall bear the same white cross in a piece of black cloth round or square.'

SYMBOLS OF DESTINATION

Places of pilgrimage today are no longer confined to religion: Jerusalem, Rome, Santiago de Compostela or Mecca. The crown room in Budapest has become a growing centre of Hungarian national pilgrimage since the return of the St Stephen's Crown from the United States of America in 1978. This sacred Magyar relic with its distinctive displaced cross surmounting the crown is still held by popular belief to be the insignium of St Stephen, first canonised king of Hungary, and used at his coronation in 1001. True or not, it certainly formed part of the regalia used to crown King Andrew III in 1290. The crown with displaced cross has surmounted the Royal arms of Hungary since 1849, the year of the failed Hungarian War of Independence. This coat-of-arms now forms the insignia of the president of Hungary, and is in widespread use.

An enduring symbol of pilgrimage is the shell, the heraldic *escallop*. It occurs as a charge on the burgh shields of Keith, Dufftown and Macduff (all of whose foundations are connected with William Duff of Braco, kinsman of the Duff earls of Fife), the London borough of Hammersmith and on scores of the arms of individuals in Scotland (House of Pringle, and more anciently the 13th-century seal of Lord Graham); England (Dacre); Ireland (Connolly); and Portugal (Pimentel). The escallop is the emblem of St James, patron of pilgrims, and regularly worn by pilgrims even today. However this was not always so, for towards the middle of the 13th century, Pope Alexander IV (1254–1261) prohibited 'all pilgrims who were not truly noble from assuming escallops as armorial ensigns' (Seton: *Scottish Heraldry* p.100). This arose because increasingly penitential pilgrimage was only being undertaken by the less well-to-do since the rich could commute it for alms-giving.

The escallop began as the badge of pilgrimage to the tomb of St James at Santiago in north west Spain, and is first mentioned in the eccentric *Liber Sancti Jacobi*, a kind of pilgrim's guide written around 1130. The guide records that shells were attached to pilgrims' cloaks; this at a time when a Jerusalem-bound pilgrim wore a cross, but few other emblems existed for pilgrimage, even to Rome.

If the scallop of Santiago remembers the politics of pilgrimage, then the heraldic ceiling of St Machar's Cathedral becomes at once the pilgrimage of politics, a place to visit to examine a unique record exactly encapsulating the picture of political and religious power in Europe at a time when it was about to change forever. Here in Aberdeen these 48 shields form one of Europe's greatest painted wooden heraldic ceilings, an illustrated lecture on the contemporary politics of Christendom about the year 1520, and a lecture strongly biased in favour of the Scottish nation.

CORPORATE BRANDING

The development in 1998 of *Scotland The Brand* represents an effort within Scotland to create national corporate branding, a move caused some bewailing of paucity of ideas and missed opportunities within the design community. Actually, it's not a bad name: pity about the logo. Where the greater sadness lies is in the blind eye turned to the widespread popular adoption of the Saltire.

Anyone recalling national sporting crowds over the past four decades will notice that whereas Scottish supporters once famously and erroneously fluttered the Lion Rampant, the same is not now so to any degree. The Saltire is asserting itself. At last we are learning that the Lion Rampant is the flag of our sovereign The Queen as head of state, and that the Saltire is the national banner able to be flown and flaunted by any Scot, anyone resident or domiciled in Scotland, or anyone with Scots interest or descent. It is the Saltire which leads our national teams; it is the Saltire which precedes Scotland's team at each opening of the Commonwealth Games. It is the blue of the Saltire which defines our national sporting colour (The inky hue of Scotland's rugby and football strip reflects the background navy of the Union Flag, a Hanoverian habit which ought to be erased forthwith).

The distinctive Saltire offers instant and international recognition. The marketing people of *Scotland The Brand* themselves point out that when products are perceived to be equal, country of origin is a significant factor in a customer's decision to purchase and national branding is an important influence. When a long-existing and internationally eye-catching item as the Saltire just waits to be flaunted, why do we so cringe from it that every new development in goods, services, lifestyle and culture is given a logo instead? While there may be evident beauty in the words *Scotland The Brand*, the decision to opt for tartan on the lettering renders the background colours meaningless in reproduction. What emerges is simply lettering in an undecided dark shade, a fusion of colour rather than the technicolour branding that tartan joyfully is. And in using the words *Scotland The Brand*, there is the presumption that the customer is literate, English-speaking and cognitive of Roman script.

A parallel departure into meaninglessness is the rebranding of British Airways. Thanks to the work of tail spin doctors, the rearmost upperworks of aircraft dissolve into patterns reminiscent of emerging Ruritania. When BA announced in 1997 that it was changing its image by replacing the BA coat-of-arms on tail fins with logos designed by 50 artists from around the world, there was immediate controversy. The resulting designs might appear fine on holiday T-shirts, but on aircraft the creeping complexity only serves to muddle otherwise clean flight lines.

BA works hard to tell us that in the interests of being 'global', 'caring' and 'multicultural', the heraldry on the tail has been dropped. Now a tailfin is a largely flat surface, and if it is to resemble its purpose in looking like a tailfin, then any symbol on it requires to be strong, simple, sharp and businesslike, something like a flag in fact. Which is what BA had. More precisely, it was a well-crafted coat-of-arms of which BA made splendid use everywhere. It appeared on aircraft, vehicles, stationery, furniture, fittings, uniforms, badges and banners. The *blason* (heraldic description) reads: 'Argent between a chief and a bendlet sinister couped Gules, a gyron issuing from the dexter, point in sinister, a chief Azure'. This is really clever stuff, for in appearance it creates the impression of being a segment of the Union Flag and gives literal truth to the marketing slogan 'Fly the flag'.

BA chief executive Bob Ayling advises that BA no longer wishes to be seen as a UK airline but rather as a global operator. In doing so, his company faces the danger of losing touch with the customer through an identity which confuses rather than clarifies. The identification of a BA aircraft at an international airport now enters the fantasy of a visual lottery; and there can be some sympathy for the Royal British Imperial Backwoodsmen whose howls of indignation about the new BA livery filled the correspondence columns of the London broadsheets. 'Disgusted of Tunbridge Wells' has more than a point: in Tony's Blair's new design era of Cool Britannia, here is an international carrier whose ambition of identity resembles the fashion of a honky-tonk republic.

Nor is BA entirely alone. In the rebranding of the RAC, the crown vanishes, causing *The Daily Telegraph* to remark: 'The Republican Automobile Club'. Additionally, the lower-case font making up the letters 'RAC' possess the charmless identity of a squeeze of toothpaste.

Television gains heraldry an audience of seven million people three times a day through the use of the BBC arms at the openings of the One O'Clock, Six O'Clock and Nine O'Clock News. The arms of the BBC were recorded in England in 1927, but the guiding hand of John Reith was all too absent, for no one at the BBC seemed to realise that this most original heraldry posssessed not a jot of legality in Scotland until matriculated here. Half a lifetime passed before this was done in 1958.

The ancient symbolism of heraldry illustrates broadcasting with splendid success, using a 70-year-old design which remains dateless. The atmospheric blue of the shield represents the ether, while the gold annulet encircling the globe symbolises the so-called Appleton Layer (of prime importance in early radio transmission). The globe and the seven stars describe the universal scope of the BBC, with the thunderbolt in the lion's paw crest indicating use of electricity. The eagle supporters highlight speed, while the bugles denote public proclamation. The seven stars plus Mother Earth add up to eight planets: there should be nine. The ninth planet Pluto wasn't discovered until 1930, three years after the BBC recorded arms.

The coat-of-arms of the UK Atomic Energy Authority (granted at the College of Arms 1955, matriculated Lyon Office 1972) is a remarkable piece of public relations, a statement of confidence through heraldry that the nuclear process is not only safe but can be quite properly controlled. The arms ranks as corporate favourites for two reasons, being attractive as heraldry, and encapsulating the story of the organisation they identify. Maintaining the simplest of classic design, the arms describe in colour and symbol how and why energy is produced through fission, as well as allusion to the work of nuclear pioneer Ernest Rutherford, and the place of uranium in the table of physical elements.

Which logo achieves all this? Logos only illustrate. Heraldry defines purpose, identity, decoration and history - as in the case of DNA (Royal Society of Edinburgh, Lyon Office 1967), or computers (British Computer

Society, College of Arms 1978). When does a logo accommodate a mission statement as succinct, concise and descriptive as *From Imagination, Reality*, the heraldic motto of the British Interplanetary Society?

Sometimes the roots of accepted insignia lie in a deeper past. At the end of the 13th century, Otto IV, Count of Burgundy announced that he had broken all ties with his emperor by surrendering his arms. He forswore his eagle, adopting a shield charged with a lion instead. This lion shield borne by his successors ultimately became the shield of Franche-Comte, the territory covering the original county of Burgundy. When the Peugeot car company established headquarters in the area last century, it adopted the lion as the corporate emblem. Thus if the Count of Burgundy had not quarrelled six centuries before, the emblem of one of the most developed car companies in Europe might have been an eagle rather than a lion.

Our home international football associations gladly eschew logos, choosing instead to flaunt heraldry on an everyday basis. The Scottish Football Association, 125 years old this year, recorded arms in 1951 with the lion rampant surrounded by 11 thistles. The Welsh Football Association similarly shows the red dragon among 11 leeks. (The English Football Association's three leopards of England are curiously encircled by only 10 roses. Evidently an English player has been red-carded and sent off).

All of which deserves to bring us closer to home. How is our new Scottish Parliament to be identified? There is no acceptable reason for it to be handed over to logo merchants to decorate willy-nilly with neither thought nor recourse to heraldry. Scotland has an established heraldic tradition, as our courts and custom houses throughout the land show, and it is correct and supremely fitting that the new Parliament is identified by means of the Royal Arms of Scotland. There is the handsome precedent of the rebranding of the Scottish Office four years ago, when the corporate identity used the Royal Arms of Great Britain as used in Scotland as the theme plus the words *The Scottish Office*. The finished concept pleases, and represents history, continuity and modernity.

The times we live in are exciting, for the growth of heraldry during this century has been nothing short of explosive. Heraldry extends into all spheres of life, spiritual and secular. It harks back to the past while providing a bond for the future. Yet heraldists remain far too modest in promoting themselves. Their ancient craft is proving one of Scotland's modern growth industries with downstream opportunity in design, print and manufacture. The underlying trend suggests that this growth will become even more pronounced in the 21st century. Heraldry is a dynamic practice; it moves to accommodate every purpose to which mankind strives. Heraldry is not only the shorthand of history; it becomes part of history itself in the manner in which it illustrates the recording of arms.

The Author

Gordon Casely OStJ FSAScot was educated at Hutchesons' Boys' Grammar School in Glasgow. He began as a journalist with D. C. Thomson & Co. in Dundee and Elgin before joining the *Evening Express* in Aberdeen. He is head of public relations for Aberdeenshire Council, and has held public affairs posts in Edinburgh, London and Glasgow. Until returning to Aberdeen, his was Assistant Director of the CBI in Scotland. He has twice managed the origination and launch of corporate identities: for Greater Glasgow Passenger Transport, and for Aberdeenshire Council. He writes and lectures on the subject of Scottish heraldry, and is an advocate for modern use and development of heraldry as identity. In 1977, he was one of the founder members of the Heraldry Society of Scotland. His published work includes papers delivered to the Society, and for the last six years has been writing a populist column on heraldry for the monthly magazine *Leopard*. Other activities include the Commonwealth Games Council for Scotland: sponsorship of the Scottish Team at Edinburgh 1986; press officer at Auckland 1990 and he is an Honorary Vice-President for the Lonach Highland & Friendly Society.

References

Bander van Duren, Peter: *Orders of Knighthood and of Merit*, Colin Smythe, 1995

Barden, Dr Patrick, *Heraldry in Scotland*, a brief resume for the Heraldry Society of Scotland, 1994

Briggs, Geoffrey, *Dictionary of Impersonal Arms*, Heraldry Today, 1971

Brooke-Little, J P, *Boutell's Heraldry*, Frederick Warne, 1970 (reprint)

Brooke-Little, J P, *Royal Heraldry: Beasts and Badges*, Pilgrim Press, 1994

Campbell. Colin, *The Scots Roll*, Heraldry Society of Scotland, 1995

Casely, Gordon, *The Heraldry of Science*, *The Double Tressure* No 20: Heraldry Society of Scotland, 1998

Cox, Ian (ed.) *The Shell*, Shell Transport & Trading Co Ltd, 1957

Drummond-Murray of Mastrick, Peter, *The Arms of Catholic Dioceses in Scotland*, *The Double Tressure* No 19, Heraldry Society of Scotland, 1997

Fitzgerald, Mairead Ashe, *The World of Colmcille*, O'Brien Press, 1997

Fox-Davies, A C, *A Complete Guide to Heraldry*, Crown Publishers, 1978 (reprint)

Friar, Stephen, *New Dictionary of Heraldry*, A&C Black, 1987

Innes of Learney, Sir Thomas: *Scots Heraldry*, Oliver & Boyd, 1956 (2nd edition)

Joubert, Pierre, *L'heraldique*, Editions Ouest-France, 1984

Laszlovszky, Jozsef, *A Magyar Cimer Toertenete*, Pytheas, 1990

Louda, Jiri, *European Civic Coats of Arms*, Hamlyn, 1966

Lovag, Zsuzsa, *The Hungarian Crown and Other Regalia*, Hungarian National Museum, 1986

Lynch, Michael, *Scotland - A New History*, Century, 1991

Machado de Faria, Antonio, *Armorial Lusitano*, Editorial Enciclopedia, 1961

Mackenzie of Rosehaugh, Sir George: *The Science of Heraudrie, Andrew Anderson's Heir*, Edinburgh, 1680

Mackie, Prof J D., *A History of Scotland*, Penguin, 1964

McMillan, William, *Scottish Symbols*, Alexander Gardner, 1916

McMillan and Stewart: *Story of the Scottish Flag*, Hugh Hopkins, 1925

McRoberts, David, *The Heraldic Ceiling of St Machar's Cathedral*, Friends of St Machar's Cathedral, 1981

Mericka, Vaclav, *Orders and Decorations*, Hamlyn, 1967

Neubecker, Ottofried, *Heraldry – Sources, Symbols and Meaning*, Macdonald, 1988

Nisbet, Alexander, *A System of Heraldry*, Edinburgh, 1722

Patton, David L H., *Arms of the County Councils of Scotland*, Argyll Reproductions, 1976

Paul, Sir James Balfour, *Heraldry in Relation to Scottish History and Art*, David Douglas, 1900

Paul, Sir James Balfour, *Ordinary of Arms Vol I*, Edinburgh, 1903

Pastoureau, Michael, *Heraldry: Its Origins and Meaning*, Thames & Hudson, 1997

Reid of Robertland and Wilson, *Ordinary of Arms Vol II*, Lyon Office, 1977

Lions and Thistles, catalogue of the Exhibition of Scottish Heraldry, Edinburgh, 1995

Seton, George: *Law and Practice of Heraldry in Scotland*, Edmonston & Douglas, 1863

Towill, Edwin S: *Saints of Scotland*, St Andrew Press, 1978

Urquhart, R M: *Scottish Burgh and County Heraldry*, Heraldry Today, 1973

Urquhart, R M: *Scottish Civic Heraldry*, Heraldry Today, 1979

Williams, David H: *Welsh History through Seals*, National Museum of Wales, 1982

14

LANGUAGE AND IDENTITY
Modern Sources of Written Scots

William Donaldson

The intelligent traveller looking for Lowland Scots, the language spoken by most Scots people, must, like the early pilgrims follow a neglected, overgrown route peopled by uncomprehending and unpredictable strangers. In this paper I look at some of the barriers encountered in my own search for Scots writing and suggest how we might provide a more clearly marked and hospitable route for the 21st century traveller.

People nowadays often regard Scots as a separate language, being more different from English than the Scandinavian tongues are from one another, but in the past it was more usually considered as a mere dialect of English. Patriots might insist that, if so, then it was in fact the oldest and purest form of English, uncontaminated by its southern counterpart's three-centuries-long collision with Norman French, a mood caught rather well by the poet Alexander Geddes when he wrote:

> Let bragart England in disdain
> Ha'd ilka lingo, but her a'in:
> Her a'in, we wat, say what she can,
> Is like her true-born Englishman,
> A vile promiscuous mungrel seed
> Of Danish, Dutch, an' Norman breed,
> An' prostituted, since, to a'
> The jargons on this earthly ba'!
> Bedek't, 'tis true, an' made fu' smart
> Wi' mekil learning, pains an' art;
> An' taught to baik, an' benge, an' bou
> As dogs an' dancin'-masters do;

Wi' fardit cheeks an' pouder't hair,
An 'brazen confidential stare
While ours, a blate an' bashfu' maid
Conceals her blushes wi' her plaid;
And is unwillin' to display
Her beuties in the face o' day.
Bot strip them baith-an' see wha's shape
Has least the semblance of an ape?
Wha's lim's are straughtest? Wha can sheu
The whiter skin, an' fairer heu;
An' whilk, in short, is the mair fit
To gender genuine manly wit?
I'll pledge my pen, you'll judgement pass
In favour of the Scottis lass.

IDENTITY AND REGISTERS OF USE

Scots is little used nowadays for public display, and is largely absent from the media. Even the maps are anglicised; you could visit Stuartfield or Fetterangus, King Edward or Foot Dee, without ever suspecting that you were actually in Crichie, Feshie, Kineddart, or Fittie. Visitors, finding themselves routinely addressed in English (however curiously accented), might reasonably presume that this was because Scots had ceased to be used. Not so. What they are experiencing is wholesale switching of register.

Scots speakers become skilled at this from childhood. There is one register for dealing with parents, another for siblings, and a third for friends. There are at least two in the classroom: one for classmates, another for addressing the teacher; an even more formal one for really important adults, like the headmaster, and a final tier in articulate children, which most closely resembles book-English and is reserved for use in social emergency, and dealing with God and the Queen. The more relaxed and intimate the communication, the more likely it is to be in Scots; the more public and formal, the nearer it is likely to approximate to Standard Scots English.

Spoken Scots is a relaxed and informal mode, used with insiders, used, indeed, to 'define' insiders. Many people having it as their preferred mode of communication, would not dream of using it in public settings with strangers. It would be considered a form of linguistic nudism, and therefore shunned. English and Scots do not, therefore, form the twin poles of a seamless continuum of usage, because they perform essentially different functions. Spoken English is a bridge between the user and the wider world, and Scots a bastion against it. The first is a means of including the user within a wider supra-national community, the second a means of excluding that larger community from the speaker and his circle and possibly also disrupting it. It looks very like what the Russian literary theorist Mikhail Bakhtin identified as the ceaselessly opposite pull between centripetal forces tending towards language centralisation and unification on the one hand, and centrifugal forces tending towards decentralisation and disunification on the other.

Everything depends upon the anticipated linguistic range and social standing of the listener. When the visitor, whether from different lands or a different class, is addressed, it will be in the way considered most likely to provide a comfortable linguistic and social 'fit', selected from a wide range of alternative possibilities. The reason for this is quite simple. The British state wants it to happen: it seeks to promote an English-dominated all-British consciousness and expends large sums of money in an attempt to achieve this goal. From the mid-Victorian period onwards, the elimination of Scots as a public medium has been a major objective of the Scottish education service. At the same time it is important to appreciate that the historic ability of the education service actually to deliver this programme may be rather limited.

THE RESILIENCE OF SCOTS

In the parish schools, Scots and Latin long formed the basic mode of instruction for able pupils, and the evidence seems to indicate that spoken Scots was highly resistant to the encroachment of book English. In any case, during much of the past two centuries, there was little actual instruction in English, exposure to that language being restricted to brief daily Bible reading, while in writing it was merely the medium into which Latin was translated. Inculcating spoken English was still more problematic. For example, there was serious debate in the School Board of Aberdeen during the 1870s about whether specialist elocution teachers might be hired for this purpose, in spite of the expense. This was because none of the city's school teachers, however able and learned otherwise, could speak English with any degree of plausibility.

Most Scots had little access to English as a spoken language until the end of the 1920s when broadcasting began, and it was several decades later before coverage began to become adequate on a Scotland-wide basis. In fact, the Scots were at least as likely to be affected by American English once talking movies arrived. The more so, perhaps, as they had a long established penchant for American dialect prose (spelt in such a way as to convey the pronunciation) from the pens of writers such as Josh Billings and Artemus Ward.

The spoken English heard in Scotland springs from a complex and expensive conditioning in the use of that language as a public medium. For the speaker it also represents a substantial personal expenditure of time and effort, especially in regard to those parts of the personality which have to be suppressed in order to accommodate its particular cultural set. What, then, of Scots as a written language and more particularly as a language of literature?

Most bookshops, to be sure, have substantial 'Scottish Interest' sections in them. Amongst the many volumes written in standard English, one can find books of poems in Scots, occasionally (although this is rather rare) discursive prose texts in Scots, novels with Scots dialogue, sometimes even plays in Scots. At first sight the heirs of Burns and Scott might appear to be in a reasonably flourishing condition. The culturally curious visitor cannot however refer to the annals of 'Scottish Literature' with unqualified confidence. For one thing, only a little of the canon is in print at any given time, owing to our failure to maintain a stable core of permanently available texts. Secondly, there is the curious way in which our literary tradition has been constructed. We cannot offer a coherent and systematic account of it. Reflecting the internal colonial ambience within which cultural producers in Scotland have long been obliged to work, our literary history achieves adequate definition only during those periods, such as the later Middle Ages, where Scottish texts require to be co-opted by our neighbours in the South to lend support to the idea that the distinguishing mark of Imperial English Literature is an unwaveringly high level of artistic achievement.

Successful academic careers tend to be Anglo-Scottish (with the emphasis upon the Anglo), and our existing institutions fail to provide support for an effective native intelligentsia. It should come as little surprise, then, to discover that rich periods in English Literature, such as the 17th and 19th centuries, are precisely paralleled by gaping holes in the contemporary Scottish account. The cultural inferiorism which grips the Scottish intelligentsia, then converts these gaps in knowledge into a damaging critique of Scotland itself as a civilised and culture-producing community. It is assumed that because little is known about these periods that there is, therefore, little to know, and that, consequently, Scottish tradition must somehow have been prevented from operating. Since 'traditions' are by definition continuous, there must be something fatally flawed about one which is not. Scottish cultural products are thus insidiously devalued by the very agencies which should support and defend them.

THE GAP THAT NEVER WAS

With regard to the 19th century, it has been usual to assume a gap nearly a century wide between the death of Scott and the coming of MacDiarmid, with nothing much except Robert Louis Stevenson in between. Commentators have described the Scott-MacDiarmid gap as evidence that 'the tradition seemed really to have come to an end, and not with a bang, but a whimper' and that Scotland had been 'all but emptied of native talents'. Where was the evidence? My earlier research in Scottish popular song had already made me doubtful about the assumption that a 'literary tradition' was something made of books or, at the very least upper-crust 'literary' periodicals. Armed with a research fellowship from the Leverhulme Trust, I began an intensive study of literacy and popular culture in 19th century Scotland, focusing on the popular newspaper press and what I found was rather interesting.

The all-UK bookmarket was dominated by England and by the powerful English circulating libraries. Scottish book novelists were compelled by the economic facts of life to address an English readership throughout the period, and therefore had to comply with English cultural prejudices and assumptions. Here, for example, is a *Blackwood's Magazine* reviewer on Huntly born novelist's George MacDonald's *Malcom*:

> Why will Mr. MacDonald make all his characters almost without exception, talk such painfully broad Scotch? Scotch to the fingertips, and loving dearly our vernacular, we yet feel it necessary to protest against the Aberdeenshire dialect ...which bewilders even ourselves now and then, and which must be almost impossible to an Englishman...It is poor art, and not truth at all to insist upon this desperate accuracy. Sir Walter's Scotch was never like this.

Or we might consider the remarks of S R Crockett, speaking in Galloway at a public dinner given in his honour:

> We authors...cannot always do just exactly what we would like. The publisher tells you to cut down the dialect because the English public does not understand it....The land that holds the heather and the sheep does not hold the money for the man who has to live by his pen.

The sheer cost of the case-bound book (a guinea-and-a-half for a first edition Victorian three-decker novel) meant that for much of the century book buying was the preserve of the relatively well-to-do. What the great majority of Scots read, tended not to be published in book form at all.

Major advances in popular literacy, and increasing affluence in the rapidly expanding upper working and lower middle classes, created a new reading public and a new mass popular literary market. So much so, that, during the 19th century Scotland experienced a virtual revolution in media communications.

REPEAL OF THE STAMP ACT

The automation of paper-making, mechanical typesetting, high speed steam driven rotary presses, and the growth of the railway network, combined to make cheap reading matter available on a hitherto undreamed of scale. With the repeal of the Stamp Act in 1855, prices of newspapers plummeted and the popular press experienced a period of explosive growth. By the end of the century there were more than 200 papers in Scotland. There were big city dailies like the *Glasgow Herald*, the *Scotsman*, the *Dundee Advertiser*, the *Aberdeen Free Press* and the great national popular weeklies like the *People's Journal*, the *Weekly News* and the *Glasgow Weekly Mail*. Then there were the regional 'county' papers, like the *Inverness Courier*, the *Banffshire Journal*, the *Perthshire Advertiser* and the *Oban Times*; then came the dozens of local weekly papers, such as the *Orcadian* of Kirkwall, the *Fraserburgh Advertiser* from Buchan, the *Hawick Advertiser* from the Borders, which were based on middling-sized burghs and circulated in their immediate hinterland.

Since these were Scottish enterprises they were not dependent upon English sales. They did not have to package Scotland for export, but could address a specific audience at national, regional or local level. Many papers supplied a whole range of recreational reading: original writing, poetry, prose, fiction, memoirs and reminiscences, biography, history, folklore and popular musicology, and they did it in enormous quantity. Little of this was ever published in book form, although some of the writing is of the highest quality. Buried in this apparently ephemeral source, therefore, is a great lost continent of Scottish prose, much of it being in Scots.

Why had this huge and important source been overlooked? Well, there is the assumption noted above that a literary tradition is something made out of books. This remains a difficult concept to overcome, even in a culture which affects to cherish its popular roots. Then there is the uncomfortable truth that newspaper research is hard work. The nature and location of the source material presents frequent difficulty. Newspapers are usually bound together in enormous annual slabs which are physically difficult to handle. Sometimes they are dirty. Often they are printed on cheap paper, which, unless storage conditions have been unusually good, is now disintegrating. There is also the fact that they are normally printed with battered second-hand type and arranged in dense columns which make reading a punishing experience, even more so since the advent of microfilm.

Some titles are still in the hands of their publishers who may or may not be willing to open their back files to the researcher. Local papers are held by local public libraries scattered all over Scotland. Holdings of the popular press in the big Scottish research libraries are distinctly patchy, since these institutions grew from professional or academic roots and tended not to subscribe to material deemed unsuitable for middle-class readers.

The only place that has nearly everything, is the British Library's Newspaper Library in Colindale, North London, housed in what looks like a superannuated power station up one of the grimmer reaches of the Northern Line. I well remember my first visit. I filled in the request slips, found a seat, and waited for my papers to appear. After a while, I began to notice that people who had gone up long after me were getting their newspapers, so after about 45 minutes I approached the desk and enquired if some oversight on my part had contributed to the delay. Riffling through the slips the attendant suddenly beamed and cried: 'Ow. It's your Scotch papers. Ain't no call for your Scotch papers, guv. Nah, if you'd wanted a London paper, you could 'ave 'ad it straight orff.' And he gave me to understand that, since there were 18 miles of shelves, and your Scotch papers were kept at the very end, a delay of 40 minutes or so between request and production might be considered trifling. Since I needed to see multiple issues of getting on for a hundred different titles, I could not entirely share this view.

TREASURES FROM NEWSPAPERS

Taking all of my research together, I discovered more than I could possibly have hoped for. I had gone looking for asses and found kingdoms. The newspapers of Victorian Scotland emerged as a major cultural source, and as by far the most important focus for writing in Scots during the period. Under the influence of the popular press, a new demotic prose, often of great orthographic inventiveness and freedom, had sprung up in all the major dialect areas, displacing 'book Scots,' (standard literary Scots), which was based on the usage of the Central Belt and enshrined in the works of Burns and Scott.

It could be found in every department of the paper leaders and features, correspondence, advertisements even, and was used for every kind of public discourse. All the leading issues of the age came within its scope, such as competition and materialism, free trade and deregulation, interventionism and state control, evolution and its consequences and the triumphs and tribulations of technological change. Above all, it was used for politics as exemplified below.

At the beginning of June 1877, the editor of the Dundee-based *People's Journal*, William Duncan Latto, sat down to write a piece on world politics. In it he presented a panoramic survey of the balance of power in Europe since the end of the Napoleonic Wars and dealt at length with the Imperial rivalry of Britain and Russia. Since the paper was advanced Liberal in politics and also Scottish, the tone of the article was strongly anti-imperialist. Amongst other things, it said this:

> We are feared for oor road to India, but hoo has it come aboot that we hae sic a deep interest in a road to India? Hoo did we get a haud o' India? Was it no by the sword? Ay, an' aften by the maist ootrageous proceedin's that were even seen or heard tell o' in this world! We got India by murder, treachery, an' stouthreif, an' we hae the cheek to blackguard Rooshia for annexin' her neebors! What did we do the ither day in the Sooth o' Africa? Did we no annex an independent republic ca'd the Transvaal? O yes, but it was for the guid o' the inhabitants. But that is juist what Rooshia says when she swallows up her neebors, an' she has as guid a richt tae say sae as we have. We winna hear o' Rooshia takin' possession o' Constantinople, because she wad then dominate the entrance to the Black Sea. But, of coorse, there's nae harm in Britain dominatin' the entrance to the Mediterranean by keepin' possession o' Gibralter. We've a perfect richt to clap oorsel's doon at Aden, an' so control the entrance to the Red Sea. Naebody has cause to complain o' oor keepin'a grip o' Heligoland near the mooth o' the Elbe. We are quite justified in squattin' oorsel's doon at Malta, at the Cape o' Good Houp, at Cape Coast, at Sierra Leone, at Hong Kong, at the Falkland Islands, at New Guinea– at scores o' ither places in a' pairts o' the habitable an' uninhabitable globe. But Lordsake, dinna let Rooshia get a grip o' the Dardanelles!

The local circulation of many of these papers encouraged the development of orthographically distinct forms of local Scots. There was an added incentive to this in the fact that the new breed of Scottish journalists were accustomed to use Pitman's shorthand as their everyday working tool. Since the basic principle of this was to give symbolic expression to the sounds of words, it was but a short step to a new phonologically-based demotic prose whose orthography showed with a high degree of accuracy how the various regional dialects of the language actually sounded. In this way they provided a reliable indicator of the phonology of Scots for more than a century before the advent of the tape recorder. Examples can be cited from the Northern Isles, Caithness, the North-East Lowlands, Dundee and Angus, the Central Belt and the Borders. One or two short extracts may help to illustrate this point. The first is from Orkney and dates from 1907–08. It occurs in a piece urging support for dialect teaching in schools, which indignantly contrasts the levels of support available for Gaelic as opposed to Scots:

> Ye'll a' ken dat ax an' twenty year sin', a neufangled ting ca'ad 'The Celtic Chair' waas begood i' the College aff sooth i' ald Reekie. Hid waas said tae be tae keep da Gaelic fae deean. Am seur miny a better ting's de'ed' at could be waar wanted...Guid kens foo muckle siller was begged, burrooed or staled tae pay for her wi'. Noo a' that waas seurly deun tae mak freens wi' da Ald Chiel, for hid's weel kent 'a Gaelic's the lingo dat's taaked i' da bad place, an' hid's a lingo ye maun tak' siccan moothfos o' as wad ding da yackles oot o' a yearald golt...Wir M. Pay jeust daves folk wi' 'is clatters aboot da trallers 'at am sheur never deud im ony herm, an' aboot ither poleetical faldaralls, fairilies an' lalls am dootin' he deusna ken ower muckle aboot...For Guid sake gae 'im sonting eusfil tae deu...Tell i' gin 'e winna voo tae hae wir dialec ta't i' the skeuls, there's naither a stirlin', auk, gruely belkie, selkie, scarf, crab, lempit, hobbler, yirning, wilk, sheep, mare or bluidy puddin'll vote for 'im. Sae might I trive dat wad gae da muckle ferrylouper a gluff gin onything wad fleg 'im.

Another example is from Buchan, from the pen of James Leatham, then editor of the *Peterhead Sentinel*, and one of the founding fathers of Socialism in Scotland. It expresses anxiety about the growing destructive potential of modern technology, unchecked by corresponding growth in human wisdom and restraint:

> Aw'm thinkin wir progress is some lopsidet. We mak great advances in mechanical science; but Aw'm nae sure' at humane an' kindly feelin's grouin in proportion. It's a dangerous thing ti pit great pooer inti the han's o' bad men. Aw'm fair terrafee't ti see the wy' at the pooers o life an' death are bein' multiplie't on ilky han'. An' it's nae only that Muckle hooses an' muckle toons, weers owreheid in a' direckshins, weers oondergrun' in pipes, electrick messages fleein' throu the air, electrick cars and mottircars rinnin throu the streets, tillyphones, tillygraphs, gramaphones catchin fat y say, an' reelin't aff again as lang's the record laists– weel, it's a' terrable bewulderin...

The third example is from Renfrewshire, from the Paisley popular miscellany *Seestu*, which reflects the rise of the leisure industry during the later Victorian period. This is from the mid 1880s:

Weel,' Jean says tae me the Friday nicht afore last–ye man ken Friday's yane o' oor coortin nichts. She says, 'Can ye skytcht, Jock?' I lucked at 'er an' says, 'skitch! Mighty me, whits that ?' 'Ye muckle gommerill,' says she, 'its scliden on the ice wi' yon airn things on yer buits.' 'Oh!' says I, 'skyten.' 'No', says she, 'skytchen'. 'Aw weel,' says I, 'skyten or skytchen, its a' yin, an' we'll let that flee stick to the wa'; but if its me that can skyte, ye shood jist ocht tae see me, ma certi.

I went looking for Scottish writing in 19th century Scottish newspapers and found that they contain enormous amounts of writing in Scots. At a conservative estimate, the Scottish Victorian press contains at least five thousand Scottish novels published as serials, original short stories in even greater numbers and a large body of folkloristic, autobiographical and social history writing, much of it in Scots. Taken together it amounts to a cultural achievement of massive proportions. According to the text-books, which have routinely assured us that discursive Scots prose died out in the 17th century, none of it ought to exist, and the fact that it does means that we must seriously revise our view of written Scots in the period since the Reformation.

I have drawn attention to the invisibility of much of Scottish culture, especially to the casual observer. Most of the reasons for this, as suggested, above, are institutional. The cultural institutions of the British state are not neutral. When we begin to grasp this, we can see why it is necessary to catalogue writing in Scots under 'English Literature'. It is why there is no category for Scots language or literature, or song or music for that matter, and therefore no appropriate sections to which readers can be directed on most library shelves. It explains why 'national' chains of bookshops respond with bewilderment to enquiries about books in Scots. So we can see the reasons why the recent reissue of *The Scots Musical Museum*, one of the foundation documents of modern Scottish culture, the greatest song collection assembled during the 18th century, with material gathered from all over Scotland by its effective editor, Robert Burns, and containing many original songs by him, is classified by the British Library as 'Burns, Robert 1759–1796, Songs in English'.

SCOTS AS A POSITIVE ASSET

It is clear whose cultural programme is being fulfilled, and it is not ours. What are we to do about this? The answer is not obvious but amongst the indicators of genuine change might be some of the following: when Scots resumes its place in the public domain; when skill in the Scots language becomes, like skill in English, a marketable commodity; when native Scots speakers become, like Gaelic speakers, valued and supported by the media; when our libraries and bookshops have clearly defined sections for writing in Scots; when the programme of cultural dispossession is halted in the schools; and when it is normal to hear Scots drama performed with some of the native rhythm and cadence of the language. Then, there are issues such as when the major 19th century source for Scots language, writing, history, folklore and music might be found in Scotland, not North London; when the agencies responsible for defining our cultural identity stop giving us a misleading and negative picture of ourselves; and when we have an account of our cultural past which is at the very least broadly true. Then, we may have begun to clear the way for cultural pilgrims, by doing everything in our power to ensure that their journey is worthwhile.

Scotland's long-standing cultural and commercial ties with her neighbours around the great communication highway called the North Sea, remind us that Scots belongs to the same family as the Norse and Germanic languages. It is no coincidence that some of the most important centres for the study of Scots language and literature lie outside Scotland. In Germany for example, we can find such centres at the Johannes Gütenberg Universität Mainz at Germersheim, with further centres of specialist interest at Bremen and Cologne. To many northern European visitors, Scots may be more accessible and reassuring than English, and its potential for development in the increasingly specialised and sophisticated arena of cultural pilgrimage may therefore be considerable. Perhaps this is the key which Scots language campaigners have so long and vainly sought. We know that, if the value of a thing is not able to be specified in accountant's terms, it has a tendency to disappear from the reckoning. If the Scots language lobby could demonstrate the importance of the language in wealth creation, they might find themselves knocking on an open door.

The Author

Dr William Donaldson is a cultural historian and a prize winning author. He was brought up in Buchan and obtained his PhD from Aberdeen University in 1974. A teacher and an Open University tutor, his research has been supported by the British Academy, the Leverhulme Foundation, the Carnegie Trust and the Scottish Arts Council. He is currently researching a book on *The Traditional Performing Arts in Scotland 1750–1950*. In addition to the titles listed below, he wrote *The Jacobite Song: Political Myth and National Identity* (1988). He won the Blackwell Prize for Popular Literature in Victorian Scotland.

References

Alexander, W., *Johnny Gibb of Gushetneuk,* introduction by William Donaldson, Tuckwell Press, 1995

Alexander, W., *My Uncle the Baillie,* Donaldson, W. (ed), Tuckwell Press, 1995

Craig, C. *et al* (eds), *The History of Scottish Literature*, 4 vols, Aberdeen University Press, 1987–1988

Dieth, E., *A Grammar of the Buchan Dialect*, Cambridge, 1932

Donaldson, W., *Popular Literature in Victorian Scotland: Language, Fiction and the Press*, Aberdeen University Press, 1986

Donaldson, W. (ed), *The Language of the People: Scots Prose from the Victorian Revival*, Aberdeen University Press, 1989

Fenton, A., *Craiters or Twenty Buchan Tales*, Tuckwell Press, 1995

Garioch, R., *Collected Poems*, Macdonald, 1977

Greig, G., *Mains's Wooin*, Aberdeen City Council, 1996

Grieve M. and Aitken, W.R. (eds), *Hugh MacDiarmid Complete Poems 1920–1976*, Martin Brian & O'Keeffe, 1978

Lorimer, W. L. (trans), *The New Testament in Scots*, Southside, 1983

Mc Clure, J.D. (ed), *Scotland and the Lowland Tongue*, Aberdeen University Press, 1983

McLellan, R., *Jamie the Saxt,* Calder and Boyards, 1971

MacLeod, I. *et al* (eds), *The Scots Thesaurus*, Aberdeen University Press, 1990

MacQueen, J. and Scott, T. (eds), *The Oxford Book of Scottish Verse*, Oxford, 1996

Milne W. P., *Eppie Elrick: an Aberdeenshire Tale of the '15,* Scrogie, 1955

North, J. S. (ed), *The Waterloo Directory of Scottish Newspapers and Periodicals, 1800–1900,* 2 vols., North Waterloo Academic Press, 1989

Scott, T.(ed), *The Penguin Book of Scottish Verse*, Penguin Books, 1970

Scott, A. (ed), *Modern Scots Verse 1922–1977*, Akros Publications, 1978

Wheeler. L. W. (ed.), *Ten Northeast Poets*, Aberdeen University Press, 1985

15

ACTION IN A LANGUAGE WAR
How The Kist/A' Chiste was Won

Robbie Robertson

Most things move on, or are moved by, the axle-tree of language. Destroy the axle and the language user's society is destroyed, and much else besides. It is the purpose and central principle of all Language Wars, understood by every combatant. *An Tir, An Canan, 'Sna Daoine*, The Land, The Language, and the People, were the principles on which the 19th century Land League of the Scottish Highlands and Islands stood, all three bound together into one cause: the defence of Gaelic culture.

In the Highlands and Islands the War was raging, use of English was growing, Gaelic was being obliterated – through education where Gaelic was not taught and, indeed, actively discouraged; through the switching allegiance of the middle classes; through the denial of the language as an official means of communication with government and its agencies; through the disparagement of its arts; through the creation of a sense of shame, a feeling that Gaelic was an inferior language lacking the grace and scope of English; and through a dozen other enfeebling strategies.

Such tactics are in the game-plans of all invader cultures, the League's cause is an ancient tale still being told in many versions around the planet. Destroying a language is the ultimate defeat of a people, their community, faiths and views on life generally. History as an organic experience vanishes, and a culture that was once alive becomes a ghost existing only through scholarship. In that defeat the land is drained of its meanings for the language provided a patterning of names, memories, associations and narratives from which the people drew major elements of their identity.

The replacement of one language by another means a new identity and new meanings. No language is a transparent account of the world, each provides more than a dictionary-load of words. The ideas and values which organise a world view come as an integral part of the package. When establishing English as the language of Indian education in 1835 Lord Macaulay wrote that 'a single shelf of a good European library was worth the whole native literature of India and Arabia.' Such delusions corrupted the responses of virtually all the educated classes of the day to the languages and sometimes major world literatures which the English, and their British allies, encountered in the quest for empire.

Delusions certainly flourished at home where Britain's Language Wars were first conducted and carried through most assiduously. The history of Scottish Gaelic has its parallels in the histories of the other Celtic languages, Irish Gaelic, Manx, Cornish and Welsh, in the suppression of the dialects of English, and in the continuing erosion of Scots.

Since only Manx and Cornish were totally destroyed as living languages (and Cornish is now showing a new sprig of green) the British campaign cannot be said to have achieved all its objectives, but, in the way of wars, there were casualties galore. The result of the War was survivor languages with chronic ailments which today's social engineering may not ultimately be able to cure. In a real sense, every Scot is among the walking wounded, since the War was also fought against Scots, Scotland's other native language.

THE SCOTS WAR CAMPAIGN

The history of Scots, and its relationship to English reflects so closely the histories of the Celtic languages that there is a temptation to read into them all some universal paradigm of how one culture achieves dominance over others through the destruction of their languages. Welsh and the two Gaelics are now at least protected and promoted. Like them, Scots was attacked yesterday, but Scots is still being attacked today and may well go on being attacked tomorrow. For Scots the War is still going on, and if you have not heard of the language, or are just a little uncertain about its nature, consider yourself the victim of some saturation bombing.

Scots is a close cousin of English and therefore more amenable to attack than the Celtic group which is composed, self evidently, of distinctive languages. For many centuries the wealth of England, its depth of resources and larger population have subjected Scotland and its languages to powerful fields of cultural force. Because of its nature, Scots also rides close to the international expansion of English and, like standard English itself, is easily colonised by the American side of the family. Although Scots has survived, it is far from healthy, and people of goodwill are already crowding its bedside looking grave.

Close to English in terms of appearance, and deeply interpenetrated by it, Scots may seem no more than another dialect of English, but it is a special case. A member of the West Germanic branch of the Indo-European family it is descended from Northumbrian and Anglian versions of early English not from Mercian (Midlands England), the language which gave modern English its deepest roots. Mairi Robinson, editor-in-chief of *The Concise Scots Dictionary*, sums up the case for Scots to be regarded as a language not a dialect:

> .... its linguistic distinctiveness, its occupation of its own 'dialect-island' bounded by the Border, its individual history, its own dialect variation, its varied use in a remarkable literature, the ancient loyalty of the Scottish people to the notion of the Scots language, as well as the fact that since the 16th century Scots has adopted the nation's name – all of these are attributes of a language rather than a dialect.

A recent pilot study, the absence of authoritative statistics is itself an indication of neglect, has shown that the language is probably spoken in varying densities by upwards of 65% of Scotland's population. The remainder, apart only from the most recent immigrants, have an English tinged with Scots idioms and words. On that basis some have argued that Scots, no matter how attenuated, should be seen as the common language of Scotland.

This language exists in a rich variety of dialects, each with its own distinctive character and history: in the North-east, Grampian Scots is called the Doric; in the Northern Islands, Shetlandic, Orcadian and the Norse are still the dominant elements; in the once heavily industrialised Central Belt, Glaswegian is peppered with Irish and Scottish Gaelic words placed there by the immigrant workers who sought the city's golden streets.

Counting dialects is a very imprecise science, but it would not be difficult to make a case for eight or so in Scotland, four are major dialect groups, even 42 has been claimed. All have quite different histories to those of English and its dialects. All are more or less mutually intelligible, one of the touchstones in identifying dialects whose clustering constitutes a language. Some are included in a thriving arts scene, a few are beginning to have educational materials written for them, and the young are becoming less self-conscious in using them publicly.

Yet, despite a complex history and a range and sophistication equal to that of any other European language, used by peasants and royalty, philosophers and poets, and a literature of great and continuing distinction, Scots must now be regarded as largely eroded. What produced this state of affairs? From a list of many campaigns five can be mentioned. All are obviously related:

Literary: From the 15th century onwards, writers in Scots (until the end of that century the language was called *Inglis*) began to include anglicised words and spellings in their writings, accompanied by a growing feeling that they were drawn from a superior language. From the beginning of the 17th century, the vast majority of published works were in English.

Religious: In the mid-16th century, the Reformation happened and the reformers were usually anglophiles. The English Bible was used in churches, worshippers heard only English, and Scots suffered because it lacked the stabilising influence of a common national text to authenticate the language and give it cultural resonance.

Political: In 1603, the Scottish court decamped en masse to London when James VI of Scotland became James I of Britain, and the culture lost its role models. In 1707, the Scottish and English parliaments were united and royal pronouncements, parliamentary processes and the enactments of Scottish law were expressed on the whole in English, although Scotland retained, and retains, a separate judicial system.

Linguistic: The first dictionary of Scots did not appear until the 19th century, and for this and other reasons Scots lacks a standard spelling system and a standard dialect, unlike English and other European languages. This has tended to promote neglect and a sense that Scots is of little worth.

Educational: Although in a system quite separate from England's, the discourses of Scottish education at every level were and still are conducted only in English. No Scots literature was taught in schools, children were punished for using the language, and Scots was actively despised.

The consequences were straightforward. Scots lost status and English became the prestige language. The more 'refined' social classes increasingly addressed each other in English. It was deemed polite to do so. To speak Scots became old-fashioned, socially a little unacceptable. People began to feel ashamed of using Scots, a second class language, with third rate qualities. The process took centuries and is still going on.

Speakers of broad Scots, especially older people, often feel a sense of inferiority when using it with English speakers and only a very few among the middle classes speak it within the family, more rarely in public. The language of Scottish mass media is English and, even in its heartlands, Scots is found only in the occasional newspaper column or radio programme on, usually, antiquarian or rural topics. It is very rarely used on television, except, obviously, for comedy. Within four centuries Scots has gone from being the national language to being a folk language and a bit of a joke.

Although most modern Scottish writers use English, there is, nevertheless, a robust tradition of Scots poetry, novels and stage drama, but now addressed to appreciative audiences who very seldom use Scots themselves. Out of such contradictions is a schizoid culture made. For example, no television soap opera exists in Scotland using the language of most of its potential audience. But it is that wealth of literature, and a literature of high distinction, which helps to justify that claim that Scots is indeed a national language. Writing in Scots has been a constant presence from the 14th century onwards, no dialect of English contains its depth and range, and it continues with its quality unabated. For example, Hugh MacDiarmid, a much admired 20th century poet at least of the calibre of Burns, wrote most of his best work in Scots, and James Kelman, a more modern writer, won a Booker Prize for a novel in an only slightly modified Glaswegian.

However, looking at this scene, a dispassionate observer would conclude that Scots, as a national language for the transactions and communications of the state, is moribund. The language of the majority of the Scottish people is given no place in the business of the country. This may seem crazy, but it is true. What to do about this state of affairs is a central social issue: if, indeed, anything should or can be done.

EDUCATION IN THE TRENCHES

When examining such issues, education is always put somewhere near the head of the queue for interrogation. Certainly, it has had a strong influence on the reduction of Scots and its abandonment as the common language of Scotland. Teachers have always been powerful proponents of the King's or Queen's English, yet their persecution of Scots was done as part of a general social policy.

The whole of Scotland did not wish the language to end, but powerful interest groups within British, including Scottish, culture certainly did. Members of the opinion-forming, Scottish population who had given the matter any thought must have considered it a commonsensical requirement for the future well-being of Britain. Those who talk as one will tend to think and act as one, permitting the ready passage of goods, ideas and peoples across the length and breadth of the country and creating the shared intentions and social cohesion which characterise a nation.

It is a plausible argument on which to base a War, and the formidable ideological forces which contributed to its naturalisation can be easily imagined – fashion, the prestige of England as a major world power, the incessant promotion of its culture's attractive richness and variety, its myths, the pleasures of its landscapes, narratives and way of life, its wealth... Replace 'England' with 'America' and Scotland's attitudes then becomes virtually any country's now. The result was the collusion of the oppressed with their own oppression. The professional classes certainly believed in such truths and schools and teachers, used as shock troops to produce results, were in the front line trenches of the campaign. Most of us (the writer also held a musket) were willing volunteers. How did the Language War go for education?

Initially, fairly well. The action against Scots had the same basic strategies as those adopted against Gaelic – rejection in the classroom; at one time corporal punishment for its use even in the playground; relegation of Scottish culture to the margins of the curriculum; the promulgation of disparaging myths about it, including the trivialisation of its history; the centralisation of standard English as a major focus of Scottish education.

This strategy based on lack of attention and neglect has worked to the extent that the curriculum is now delivered exclusively through English. Most Scottish pupils still leave their education knowing nothing of substance about the languages of their own country, and less about its literature. Until fairly recently this curriculum was considered perfectly appropriate, and the minority who challenged it – and opposition to the invasion of English was a constant presence over centuries – were easily marginalised.

But things have started to go wrong, a new spirit has emerged, a counter-offensive is under way, and the desertion rate from the armies of the English tendency have soared. Over the last twelve or so years, support has begun to appear in the examination arrangements of the Scottish Examination Board with Scottish dialects welcomed in creative writing, compulsory questions on Scottish literature, and real encouragement for the study of Scots and its dialects. Advice and guidance on Language, (Scotland has agreed frameworks rather than a statutory National Curriculum), produced by the Scottish Office Education and Industry Department (SOEID) now almost routinely promote Scots. The biggest trade union has pitched in with support.

Regional materials are increasingly being developed, there are more conferences on Scots, and teacher trainers are providing a growing element of pre- and in-service.

Conditions have been created where there is a clear basis for a general cease fire. No disagreement exists, for example, on the need to develop, promote and enhance skills in standard English. The British Isles clearly needs a common dialect to make easy communication possible between its different regions, and English would also appear to be rapidly becoming the world's language between nations. Indeed, English literature is among the world's finest, and well deserves study. What must now be agreed by all sides is that the inclusion of Scots in the curriculum of Language does not pose a threat to the mastery of English, but will in fact support it and at the same time do other kinds of invaluable business.

Central also to the story of Scots in the classrooms of the 90's has been the endorsement provided by *English Language 5–14* (published by SOEID). These national guidelines made possible the production of materials to familiarise children with both Scots and Gaelic. Collectively, they are known as *The Kist/A' Chiste* and their history, rationale, and intended effects are described below.

THE SCOTTISH LANGUAGE PROJECT

Changes in the profession's attitudes to Scots can be traced to increasingly obvious deficits in the policy to reduce Scots and Gaelic, but it should also be set within broader social considerations. Chief among them is a gathering sense of our Scottishness, a feeling that we are both a British and a European people with a culture sufficiently distinctive to constitute a unique community of interests. Although politicians now use and promote such ideas within Scottish domestic politics, it is unlikely that they did much fighting when the tide was going the other way.

There is also the demonstrable fact that the War against Scots did not work. Despite four centuries of educational effort, increasingly supported by nearly all the institutions of the culture, at least 65% of Scots still speak, as we have seen, some form of the language. This well represents what has already been described as 'the ancient loyalty of the Scottish people to the notion of the Scots language.'

Increasing awareness and knowledge have also undermined the War's principles and strategies. What is now known about the significance of the home language for the creation of self image, relationships and social identity compels a more sensitive teaching of the common dialect. Only the thinnest of partitions separate language and thought, and denying the home language may impede the development of logical thinking in some children. The so-called inferiority of modern Scots dialects has to be re-considered, since all languages are equally effective in meeting the communicative demands of their culture. What is known about language itself, its variations, and the significance of the social contexts in which they are found, also suggests that an ability to choose the appropriate language for a specific context, to code-switch, is more important than the production of an inflexibly unitary language.

Minority languages and languages composed of dialects are common place in Europe and throughout the world, and the European mood now is to offer support rather than mindless bombardment. This is because bilingualism can be attained easily by nearly all of a population, it has many advantages over monolingualism, and is a source of strength rather than weakness.

The Scottish Language Project which resulted in the set of national materials called *The Kist/A' Chiste* grew out of such knowledge. So too did the strongly supportive statements made about Scots and Gaelic in the government-produced *English Language 5–14* which for the first time in history officially set Scots within a national framework for curriculum development and assessment.

This seminal document reflected ideas on Scots contained in earlier publications and allowed teachers, schools and education authorities to re-consider attitudes. It also made a national partnership between the Scottish Consultative Council on the Curriculum (Scottish CCC), the government's principal advisers on the school curriculum, and the education authorities possible because it provided a common frame of reference. A period of consultation with the education authorities and other agencies settled the Scottish Language Project's outlines and approaches.

It was agreed that two related sets of materials would be developed for upper primary and lower secondary school classes: an Anthology of Scots and Gaelic, and a Teachers' Pack of related materials. The education authorities were to supply the texts in the anthology from the languages of their areas. They would also prepare most of the materials in the Pack.

Scottish CCC would be responsible for co-ordination and publication and would sell the materials to schools at a preferential price which fully recognised the authorities' contribution to the Project. There was general agreement that the materials should be presented in as colourful a way as possible to enhance the content, to give it status and to match the mass media experiences of its young readership. Scottish CCC went into partnership with a commercial publisher, Nelson Blackie, to ensure that end.

The Anthology contains prose, poetry and drama, about a tenth in Gaelic, the remainder in Scots, apart from three texts in English from the

Highlands where Gaelic mostly lost the War and Scots has not taken root. Photographs, songs, paintings, and comic strips provide additional texts for teaching. Texts in Gaelic are translated, those in Scots have a glossary. A majority are in simple Scots, although there is a gradation of difficulty to extend the skills of linguistically gifted pupils for whom Scots is a mother tongue.

In the Pack, each of the anthology texts is associated with a photocopiable three page pamphlet of classroom materials written by teachers. One page gives information on the text, its authorship, and cultural background, the others contain varied classroom activities for pupils of different abilities. These texts, and the activities surrounding them, have also been designed to supplement work in curricular areas other than Language. A set of audio tapes, recorded by the authorities, contains readings or performances of every print text in the anthology to let children hear the text in Gaelic and an authentic dialect of Scots. 'Hearing' words makes them more understandable, even although the Scots dialect itself and its spellings may be unfamiliar.

It was also clear that many teachers had been educated and trained during a time of War and were likely to carry misrepresentations of Scots or Gaelic in their baggage. A Teachers' Handbook was, therefore, a priority to provide accurate information about these languages, how texts in them might be taught, their history, and the positive qualities which give them a legitimate place in Scottish education. The Handbook was written by the Management Group of the Project, responsible also for general oversight, selection, editing and production. The Group was drawn from the education authorities, the colleges of education, the arts, publishing and Scottish CCC, and was chaired by the Professor of English Language at the University of Edinburgh.

The Kist/A' Chiste was published in late February, 1996. This paper is being written six weeks later, and take-up has proved very satisfactory. Two authorities have bought sets for all their schools.

The word *kist* (a chest or box) is found in virtually all modern European languages, in Latin and classical Greek. In the distant cousin languages of Northern India the word means a *boat*, an interesting parallel with the two meanings of *Ark*, a synonym of *Kist*. The international features of its name are appropriate because, in defending the present value of languages drawn from Scotland's past, in actively promoting them, there is no intention of closing down the claims of the future, blocking traffic between languages or denying the fundamentally unstoppable nature of language change.

The principles which underlie *The Kist/A' Chiste* celebrate diversity and provide an opening to the richness of all languages. Its rationale and structure might apply to all minority languages, all dialects, and how they might be used in classrooms dominated by the important concerns of a national, standard dialect. In that sense, *The Kist/A' Chiste* may well have unknowingly copied a previous design.

SOME TERMS FOR A CEASE FIRE

At times of festival, the same message of welcome to visitors is displayed many times along the length of George Street in Edinburgh, Scotland's capital, translated into important world languages. Gaelic is represented, Scots is not. The reasons for this oversight, conscious or unconscious, should now be clear. The absence, with its parallels in every aspect of Scottish life, suggests the scale of the task in bringing Scots to a point where it might once again be accepted as a language with the status of others.

Proponents of Scots range from the cautious, perhaps even timid, to the fiercely activist, perhaps even extreme. All groups in that range have their eyes fixed on approximately the same Golden City, but the battalions of the latter, the warriors, want Scots to be restored tomorrow, certainly no later than next week. The regiments of the former, the tacticians, are prepared to hasten slowly with short term objectives pursued over decades. Both have strengths but the ideas which underlie *The Kist/A' Chiste* are of the tactical persuasion.

Necessarily so, because education is a weak force. Even acting with the support of the nation's most powerful institutions, the educational army suppressed and damaged, but could not ultimately destroy Scotland's languages in four hundred years of very intensive warfare. Languages are beyond such crude attempts at control. They can be crippled but like rivers they pursue their own course, and the efforts of human engineering to tame and direct them usually prove ineffectual and on occasion destructive.

This is certainly the case in Scotland, where a now essentially bi-lingual majority, has been made uncomfortable with their Scots and equally uncomfortable with their English. They have been detached from Scottish culture by being given confused ideas about the language they use, a sort of jumble of misrepresentations of their history. Much of it is kitsch imagery from which is established a national identity, and a powerful sense, perhaps never uttered but always implied, that Scots is playing somewhere near the bottom of the fourth division in the league table of languages.

In such conditions, it is necessary to make slow progress. It has done without much social support, and to be in a situation where Scots can easily be ignored. We are in a country with no clear sense of its identity, surrounded by all the rubble of an inconclusive Language War, but dealing with an untameable force such as language. It must also be remembered that, although 65% of the population speak Scots, very few of them can write or read it with any aptitude. So far as Scots is concerned, the population must be regarded as functionally illiterate apart from a few experts.

Therefore, *The Kist/A' Chiste* has limited aims. They include to make children more aware of the richness of language generally by encouraging a wider variety in the classroom; to give them an understanding of the nature of dialects, slang, languages, accents, and their uses within culture; to help them appreciate the importance of a standard dialect; to provide a range of contexts which will allow children to value the Scots they may use at home, with their peers, in the community generally and to give them social confidence in its use; and, of crucial importance, to extend its range through speech, writing and reading.

The Kist/A' Chiste is set on the keystone of the bridge between primary and secondary education in the hope that it will be a positive influence on the language curriculum in earlier and later stages. The early stages are of particular importance. If children come to school and find that the language spoken at home is not a language that is acceptable to the school then they will feel naturally disadvantaged. Since the home language has become a mode of communication unrelated to learning, teaching and assessment, to education generally, children will sense, and will become increasingly aware, that their own language has been given an inferior status. Scots-speaking parents, themselves educated to malign Scots, will support that status. The effects and consequences of this unhealthy division can be traced throughout this paper.

Essentially, *The Kist/A' Chiste* is a supportive and very preliminary approach to achieving an enhanced awareness of the indigenous languages of Scotland. It emerges from a time of re-examination of the whole curriculum and its relevance to modern needs. It provides tasks that will let children develop a sympathetic relationship with the variousness of language through allowing them to use their own dialect of Scots, or indeed a dialect of English, in relaxed conditions in the classroom and on a regular basis. Use of these languages can only assist the development of skills in the standard dialect. Standard English and Scots are close cousins. Hence, skills acquired in one transfer readily to the other. Children can only be given a meaningful understanding of the importance of a standard, reasons why mastering it is of importance, if the value of their own language is acknowledged.

Without any understanding of Scots and Gaelic, of their histories, of the texts which justify a continuing awareness, and of the societies which produced them, there can be no basis for any meaningful recovery of

Scottish culture, no basis for a real sense of real Heritage. The token, and often deeply baffling experience of Burns, or other Scots writers, which children are still given usually once a year on his birthday is no effective foundation for developing that understanding. What is needed is a thought-through systematic approach to the curriculum at every stage. There should be an organised series of encounters and experiences which boost performance and competence and give the learner meaningful choices so that everybody will feel confident in whatever language they opt to use on a daily basis. One ultimate aim might be for a population which can code-switch easily between Scots and English and has a view of language sufficiently broad and well-established that none is stigmatised and all are accepted as being of equal worth.

These are large aims requiring a social consensus. It is certainly no part of the responsibility of education to bring them about without cultural support. However, education does have a duty to redress the damage it has done over centuries, and to help create the conditions where there can be an informed debate about the issues. At the moment, in a society riddled with misconceptions about Scots, and self-punishing attitudes towards the language that stem from ignorance, this is not possible. Only when knowledge is available, can an informed debate begin. Then, and only then, will the War be over.

The Author

Robbie Robertson is an Assistant Director of the Scottish Consultative Council on the Curriculum, the Government's principal advisers on the education of children, aged between 3 and 18. Helping to write national guidelines on the teaching of English, he focused his interest in Scotland's own indigenous languages and lead directly to the foundation of the Scottish Language Project. This partnership between this Council and every education authority in Scotland produced The Kist/A' *Chiste*, materials to familiarise Scottish children with Scots and Gaelic and to naturalise the place of Scots in the language curriculum. He co-ordinated the project, and the publication of the materials in February 1996 was the culmination of four years of intensive work. He has more recently been involved in reviewing elements of Scottish culture in the current school curriculum.

References

Aitken, A.J., *A History of Scots*, in: Robinson, M. et al (eds), *The Concise Scots Dictionary*, AberdeenUniversity Press, 1985

Daiches, D. (ed), *The New Companion to Scottish Culture*, Edinburgh University Press, 1993

Fladmark, J.M., *Towards a Trilingual Scotland*, in: Fladmark, J.M. (ed), *Sharing the Earth*, Donhead, 1995

Kay, B., *Mair Licht on the Mither Tongue: Scots as a National Language*, in Fladmark, J.M. (ed), *Sharing the Earth*, Donhead, 1995

Kay, B., *Scots: The Mither Tongue*, Alloway Publishing, 1993

Lorvik, M., *The Scottis lass betrayed?*, Scottish CCC, 1995

McClure, J. D., *Why Scots matters*, Saltire Society, 1988

Mac Pherson, J. A., *Beyond the Memories: Drawing strength from the Diaspora*, in: Fladmark, J.M. (ed), *Sharing the Earth*, Donhead, 1995

Niven, L. & Jackson, R. (eds), *The Scots Language: Its Place in Education*, Edinburgh, 1998

Robinson, M. et al (eds), *The Concise Scots Dictionary*, Aberdeen University Press, 1985

Scottish Office Education Department, *English Language 5–14*, SOED, 1991

Scottish Consultative Council on the Curriculum, *The Kist/A' Chiste*, Scottish CCC and Nelson Blackie, 1996

16

CULTURAL CAPITAL AND IDENTITY
Scotland's Democratic Intellect

Magnus Fladmark

The concept of identity has fascinated scholars for a long time: from the early Greek philosophers like Plato, to modern day sociologists and psychologists. Although it is tempting to pursue a lengthy discourse on the theoretical aspects of the subject, the approach taken in this paper is to look more pragmatically at lessons to be learnt from recent experience, including some personal reflections by the author, and then to examine some of the issues facing us today and in the foreseeable future.

Identity can be likened to a two-sided coin: on one side is the image we have of ourselves, on the other is the image of how we are perceived by others. These two images are seldom identical, the truth lies somewhere in between, and they change over time. Both are shaped by a complex set of forces largely beyond our control. Sometimes manipulation is attempted for deliberate effect, as in the past by the church, governments and dictators. Today, it is called branding, normally at the hand of spin doctors, as in the attempt at re-branding Britain as 'Cool Britannia' by our current government.

As for the process of cultural continuity, it is a complex system of interconnected parts, many extending into the past. These are exemplified by Isaac Newton's response, when asked how he had been able to roll forward the boundaries of science so dramatically. His paraphrased reply was: 'by standing on the shoulders of intellectual giants who preceded me' (cultural continuity defined in a nutshell). To tamper with this process, in the fragmented manner of today's spin doctors, is to tamper with the destiny of cultural advancement.

A visit to economic theory reveals that the resource factors of production are normally defined as land, labour, capital and entrepreneurship. Capital is defined as all man made aids which further production (Lipsey, 1972). When applying these factors to the heritage industry, it is helpful to distinguish between economic capital and cultural capital, the latter comprising intellectual assets which underpin identity and further production.

In this paper, culture is broadly defined to embrace the intellectual dimension of most areas of human endeavour. Increasingly, every sector is acquiring an intellectual dimension with its own epistemology. The value of such intellectual assets is governed by primacy and confidence, as perceived by both the holder and the beholder. Their stability is determined by two main factors: intellectual cohesion and cultural continuity. Other factors governing value are scarcity, authenticity, quality and accessibility.

What follows focuses on Scotland, set in the wider context of the UK. The main narrative is built around the intellectual legacy of Patrick Geddes (1854–1932), which was much concerned with the formation of cultural capital. Viewed from the standpoint of his philosophy, it is concluded that the main threats to cultural cohesion and continuity are reductionism and modernism. Reductionists live in pigeonholes and wear blinkers to avoid exposure to the wider picture. Most modernists are dedicated to self-expression and denial of history.

The general conclusion is that we have on many counts betrayed the ideals of both Geddes and his successors, the last guardians of the Scottish 'democratic intellect'. Cultural continuity and convergence as philosophical ideas are being replaced by their opposites in what can be called 'the trap of discontinuity and divergence'. By drawing on others who came after Geddes, like C P Snow and Eric Ashby, we find confirmation of an increasing failure to communicate across disciplinary boundaries. The consequences of this are highlighted in two concluding case studies of valued natural assets.

ON THE SHOULDERS OF GEDDES

Who was Patrick Geddes? His main academic discipline was biology, and he was professor in this subject at Dundee University. He spent time under the tutelage of the scientist, T H Huxley, who did so much to popularise Darwin's theories, but his contact with John Ruskin, the humanist, was equally significant in stimulating his polymath approach to learning.

The three professions of ecology, sociology and town planning claim him as their founding father. He was also a landscape architect, philosopher, educationalist and community activist. His biographer, Philip Boardman (1978), referred to him as 'part-time professor and full-time generalist'. For an introduction to his life and work, Murdo Macdonald's contribution to this volume is recommended as prior reading, along with this author's opening chapter in *Sharing the Earth* (1995), which touches briefly on some relevant aspects.

To Geddes, there were three inescapable precepts governing formation of cultural capital and human identity. The first was his idea of cultural continuity, believing that each successive generation must respect and build upon the achievements of preceding generations. Then there was his belief, which he practised himself, that cultural progress is made through the convergence of ideas from different disciplines and walks of life. The arts and the sciences stood together for mutual benefit, as did intellectuals and workers. Third, was his fundamental principle that human destiny is inextricably linked to the way we treat the natural world: sustainability in today's nomenclature.

In his interpretation of history, the other factors to shape Scotland's cultural identity were a spirit of enterprise, scholarship and egalitarianism. He felt that that these were traits of which Scots should be proud, and by implication argued that they were what gave us a competitive edge as a nation, both intellectually and commercially. The culture in which they were rooted, he traced back into history beyond the Renaissance, but showed that they first came to be seen as representing the hallmark of our cultural identity during the Age of Enlightenment in the 18th century. Although some find it tempting to follow a nationalistic line of argument to show them as uniquely Scottish, he regarded this as historically incorrect.

The flourishing of humanism during the Renaissance and subsequent scientific advances were inspired by international exchange of ideas which were seen at the time as manifestations of a wider culture. Indeed, the strength of the Geddesian vision of Scotland was to explain our heritage and identity as a nation in the wider context of European culture. This deep awareness of an umbilical cord that feeds our national psyche is the fourth Scottish trait which can be referred to simply as internationalism.

Although the 18th century was a time of great changes, there was also a strong sense of continuity and the four traits were proudly embraced as the common currency of a robust and convergent culture. They were regarded as virtues shared by all disciplines, and familiarity with both the humanities and science was expected from any accomplished scholar. Geddes identified with a tradition where the inventor, entrepreneur and scholar spoke the same language, and it was the spirit of this integrated culture with few barriers that he embraced and sought to continue into his own time.

He had great admiration for the interdisciplinary fellowship of intellectual giants in the 18th century, an example of which was the 1776 obituary tribute by the economist Adam Smith to his philosopher friend David Hume (Flew, 1962). Evidence that Geddes was not alone in showing healthy disregard for subject boundaries can be found in a book edited by J Morley from 1878. Entitled *English Men of Letters,* this contains an lengthy study of the life and work of David Hume by the scientist T H Huxley.

In many of his projects, Geddes attempted to carry forward into this century the spirit of the learned societies founded during the Age of Enlightenment. According to Sapin (1993), The Royal Society of Edinburgh, when founded in 1783, was intended to serve as a broad cultural fellowship to cater for all aspects of scientific and literary knowledge. He states that 'the social bond between Scottish men of science and aristocrats was regarded as a compliment on either side'.

Thirty years earlier, in 1754, the English had founded what is today commonly known as The Royal Society of Arts (The RSA). Its full name was and still is 'The Royal Society for the encouragement of Arts, Manufactures and Commerce'. The objectives set by its founding members were 'to embolden enterprise, to enlarge science and refine art, to improve our manufactures, and to extend our commerce'.

However, the mood changed towards the end of the 19th century, and we begin to see Geddes reacting against the emergence of self-sustaining professions. The nature of politics began to change from a calling to a paid occupation. Although the learned societies manfully adhered to their holistic ethos, the sciences and the arts started to drift irretrievably apart. Each established its own academic territory, governed by distinct value systems, separate languages and exclusive professional bodies.

As Geddes grew to maturity, he found an increasingly fragmented culture of divergent sectors and a declining desire to communicate. Although he campaigned against it with the encouragement of people like John Ruskin and T H Huxley, they failed collectively to stem the tide. For example, the philosophy of cultural continuity underlying the Arts and Crafts movement was entirely swept aside by modern art and architecture which rejected all things traditional.

The author's own experience in the 1960s, as a student of architecture in Edinburgh, demonstrated how deeply the divisions had become entrenched by then. He had expected to learn at least something about the cultural identity of Scotland as reflected in its built environment. This is not how it turned out. Educational philosophy dismissed the past and glorified individual expression. Teaching was dedicated to modern technology and designed to instil admiration for modernist architecture, mostly better suited to other cultures and climates.

This disregard for cultural continuity in professional training was the main reason for widespread destruction of priceless architectural heritage in many historic towns, since much regretted. It certainly ran contrary to what Geddes had said about human identity and the evolution of urban fabric in towns. His approach was not demolition and rebuild, but what he called 'conservative surgery'.

In conclusion, it can be said that Geddes has won a partial victory on the environmental front. Although not in the holistic manner he would have wished, his concern for the natural world is now embraced by all. In respect of the built environment, his ideas have largely fallen on deaf ears, and the principles of cultural continuity and convergence have only limited currency today. Our future priority is to ensure that the other Geddesian pillars of cultural identity, as seen by him in enterprise, scholarship, egalitarianism and internationalism, stand firm to sustain us into the next millennium.

THE DEMOCRATIC INTELLECT

Our educational system is designed to produce the nation's intellectual capital, and a difficulty today is that academic governance of this capital has suffered from fragmentation brought about by increased specialisation. This has happened imperceptibly over the last 75 years, as we have abandoned the spirit of democratic intellectualism and turned our back on the integrative philosophy of Geddes.

For a full discourse on democratic intellectualism, readers are referred to texts by George Davie. This philosophical concept is concerned with values associated with retaining a broad approach to the acquisition of knowledge, so central to Scotland's educational tradition. Its relevance to the arguments in this paper has been aptly articulated by Murdo Macdonald (1993):

> The point about Democratic Intellectualism is not that non-experts have a right to scrutinise the work of the expert, but that the work of the expert is only complete in the light of such scrutiny. The expert is thus valued as part of a community and it is recognised that his or her value as an expert can only be fully realised if it is accepted that blindspots within that expert view are an inevitability, and that others in the community, by virtue of their lack of expertise, have a responsibility to comment on these blindspots.

The author's personal stance on the need for striking a proper balance between the generalist approach and specialisation was first inspired by reading C P Snow's *The Two Cultures and the Scientific Revolution* (1959) and Eric Ashby's *Technology and the Academics* (1958). The situation we have today is that when politicians look for cultural input from the universities, they have to knock on many doors. Behind each door there is likely to be a highly focused specialist, rather than a generalist with a strategic and integrative view of culture.

We see the mirror image of this when looking at the system of government. When academics go to politicians for advice on priorities and support, they are passed around the houses of a vast array of central departments, quangos and local authority officers. Each is likely to be responsible for a specialist function, but it will not always be clear how particular functions fit into a larger strategic framework, if indeed such a framework actually exists.

Like Geddes, Snow regarded himself a product of an integrated cultural tradition, but found himself inhabiting two separate worlds in order to pursue his twin careers as scientist and novelist. As scientist, he worked and mixed with a certain set of people. As novelist, he spoke another language and moved in an intellectual circle which subscribed to a different cultural value system. His analysis showed that this cultural dualism pervaded all sectors, and he concluded that this mutual exclusivity represented a destructive tendency for both our cultural and economic capital.

Eric Ashby, another scholar in the Geddes mould, foreshadowed the problem we are now facing: two academic cultures, represented by a two-tier system of 'ancient' and 'new' universities. This problem goes back almost a century to a time when new universities of technology were being promoted, but ended up becoming our 'central institutions' (Strathclyde, Heriot-Watt, Napier and Robert Gordon). To the consternation of some, these have now been granted university status, and the natural reaction of the ancients has been to claim the high ground by seeking to promote a two-tier system. Ashby foreshadowed this in 1958, when he said:

> Round every Senate table sit men for whom the word university stands for something unique and precious in European society: a leisurely and urbane attitude to scholarship, exemption from the obligation to use knowledge for practical ends, a sense of perspective which accompanies the broad horizons and the distant view, an opportunity to give undivided loyalty to the kingdom of the mind. At the same Senate table sit men for whom the university is an institution with urgent and essential obligations to modern

society; a place which society regards as the pace-maker for scientific research and technological progress. And so universities find themselves searching for a compromise.

If allowed to consolidate, a two-tier system is likely to accentuate the drive towards increased specialisation and a dual set of values for higher education. It would be unwise to endorse the desire of one tier to occupy the high ground of learning, and to banish the other to second class status. Their separate value systems would perpetuate an 'elitist' tendency in direct contravention of Scotland's tradition of egalitarianism. Admission to the ancient ivory towers (Ashby's 'kingdom of the mind') would become a privilege rather than a human right, and our cultural identity would suffer further fragmentation. An obvious alternative to avoid this happening is the merger of institutions, as debated in the media at the time of writing (Fraser, 1998).

NEW PIGEONHOLES

The preoccupations of academics often mirror, indeed ought to mirror, what goes on in the rest of society. According to Snow in 1959, the two-culture syndrome had already spread to our entire system of government and business. Since then we have witnessed several new groups emerge, and two of these have developed and consolidated their position to the extent of qualifying a self-sustaining entities, each securely ensconced in a new pigeonhole. They are associated with the environment and the world of business.

Geddes would have been saddened to observe how the culture of environmentalism has been cornered by scientists, and to see that his own legacy has been discarded in favour of a doctrine imbued by the arrogance of science. This new spirit runs through its entire philosophy and operational ethos, and there is now a host of assertive voluntary organisations representing the green movement. They span in time from 1887, when Royal Society for the Protection of Birds was established, to 1971 when Friends of the Earth came into being. Their strength has been reinforced by legislation, leading to the creation of agencies like the Nature Conservancy Council in 1948, and to English Nature and Scottish Natural Heritage in 1992.

It is widely felt that their core philosophies assign a lesser moral position to other groups, and they have their own language which all sensible people are expected to use and understand. Although the modern concept of sustainability was developed by pioneering environmentalists like Patrick Geddes, today's environmentalists treat it as their own invention.

The term 'sustainable development' has spread like wildfire to all sectors, and is now used to lend respectability to any project you may care to mention without regard to substance and deeper meaning.

In turning to the intellectual pedigree of industry and commerce, it can be seen that the culture of business studies has grown out of economics, management and politics. It is now sustained through the educational input from our modern business schools. The establishment of an independent academic discipline started with the Harvard Business School in 1908, the model for a world wide network of such schools. Their MBA graduates now emerge from a scholastic environment on a par with other disciplines of longer standing, and the theoretical principles of management, marketing and entrepreneurship are drawn on by others. Indeed, the coming of age of this new discipline is reflected in current controversies about the practical relevance of teaching and research at Harvard itself.

Although the history of economics goes back as long as taxes have been levied, politicians first embraced the subject in a serious way when government became directly involved with business through public sector intervention to speed economic recovery in the 1920s. The role of economists was further enhanced when it was decided to provide state assistance for post-war regional development. The private sector response was to establish bodies like the Scottish Council Development & Industry in 1931 to articulate its own role, and to facilitate communication with the apparatus of government.

The shift from government intervention to partnership between private and public sectors came in 1975 with enabling legislation for the Scottish Development Agency, now Scottish Enterprise. This gave the enterprise sector official blessing and a firm footing in Scotland. Accordingly, the business community today is in the happy position of having its own academic discipline and language, taught in university schools, and with a network of 'local enterprise companies' to provide government support.

The author has had two personal encounters with the forces of divergence in areas straddling professional boundaries. The first as a postgraduate student when the concluding battles were fought in the struggle to separate town planning from architecture and to make it into a new discipline of the social sciences. A disheartening experience for followers of Geddes who fought so hard in his own time for a professional confederation of architects, landscape designers and town planners.

The other encounter was on entering the Scottish Office in 1967, at a time when there was then a strong commitment to the operational integration of physical and economic planning. The two functions were for a short spell discharged through the same department under one minister, but the honeymoon was short lived. Economists and environmental planners

226

cared little for sharing the same minister, showed little inclination to speak the same language, and a new department was created in 1970 so that the two disciplines could enjoy equal status (Fladmark, 1988). It is now called the Scottish Office Education and Industry Department.

Another issue of identity is the political neutrality of the civil service, which has always been regarded as a fundamental virtue of our system. Although resisted by civil servants, political posturing is becoming more frequent by those who aspire for senior appointments. The malaise has also reached local government where chief officers have been known to gain or lose posts for political reasons. Related to this is the intellectual neutrality of 'the generalist' administrator in the civil service. Representing qualities associated with Ashby's 'sense of perspective which accompanies the broad horizons and the distant view', the role of the generalist remains an important balancing factor in a stable system of good government.

EXPERTS WITHOUT MORALITY

A sense of broad perspective is certainly absent from the interface between science and government. Our confidence in the advice given by scientists is regularly shaken, principally because of the narrowness of approach taken in research and the degree of specialisation cultivated by the scientific community itself. An example is the frightening flaws recently identified in the storage system for atomic waste at Dounreay. Here, one group of scientists had worked out an 'absolutely' safe method of storage, or so we had been led to believe, until another group of later vintage came along to tell us about the potential danger of a major disaster due to the explosive mixture of different types of waste in a single shaft.

C P Snow had a deep concern about scientists abrogating their moral responsibilities, referring to science without morality, and he had this to say about interdisciplinary communication and collective comprehension:

> It is dangerous to have two cultures which can't or don't communicate. In a time when science is determining much of our destiny, that is, whether we live or die, it is dangerous in the most practical terms. Scientists can give bad advice and decision-makers can't know whether it is good or bad. At present we are making do in our half-educated fashion, struggling to hear messages, obviously of great importance, as though listening to a foreign language in which one only knows a few words.

We have certainly denied Geddes, and it can be argued that we have moved backward rather than forward since Snow wrote in 1959. His warning was given at the height of the Cold War, and it may be said that the problem no longer exists. Indeed, military confrontation between East and West has gone, but we now have other and equally pressing problems of a different kind. We ignore his warning at our own peril, and there are several urgent issues we need to tackle if we are to avoid finding ourselves walking, not just blinkered, but blindfolded into the future.

Judging from the author's own experience in government service and academia, the crux of the matter is that we tend to communicate in two modes without realising it. Within each group, communication is done in a 'deep' mode, and between groups it is done in a 'shallow' mode. The deep mode is value specific, and is therefore likely to be contentious when extended beyond disciplinary boundaries. The shallow mode is relatively value free and only suitable for dealing with constructs raised to a level of generalisation which often render them meaningless.

When we gather for multidisciplinary exchange, we tend to 'speak in tongues'. It sounds good, and it makes us feel good to put up a show of togetherness. We pretend to understand each other, but the substance often escapes us through lack of comprehension. Indeed, individual groups have made progress at the expense of collective comprehension, and both cultural identity and moral values have been blurred. A reversal of this tendency can only be achieved if we take proper cognisance of the difference between shallow and deep communication.

The concluding section illustrates what can happen when single sectors and shallow communication are allowed to override philosophical and moral content in strategic policy. In relation to preceding sections, an interesting case is 'Scotland the Brand' initiative. The full potential of this important project, in terms of enhancing both cultural capital and identity, has been blunted by a perception that it is too narrowly focused on commercial objectives. A broader alliance of partners, allowing substantive input by cultural and environmental organisations, would have been more likely to deliver a more flexible and enduring product.

This lesson is important, if it is decided to replicate Panel 2000 and its Cool Britannia products north of the Border, as reported in the media at the time of writing (McGinty & Smyth, 1998). Deep public scepticism about such ventures was reflected in the sub-title carried by *The Sunday Times*, which referred to 'Scotland the Cool: Rebranding the nation that brought you haggis, porridge and Lulu'. If such scepticism is to be proved misguided, it would be necessary for a planned 'Cool Caledonia' campaign to have all its contributing partners come out of their pigeonholes, and to require their adherence to the principles of convergence enshrined in the philosophy of democratic intellectualism.

SQUANDERED HERITAGE

Two case studies have been selected to show what can happen when traditional respect for our land and culture is abandoned in conflict between divergent sectors, the likely outcome being a permanent loss for both the nation and modern pilgrims in search of 'real' Scotland.

The first and most important issue concerns our propensity to squander irreplaceable assets. Our new way of thinking and working in compartments has had devastating consequences for many of our most precious historic townscapes and valued cultural landscapes. The following is the author's selective catalogue of irretrievable losses:

> Partial destruction of Victorian Glasgow according to the Bruce Plan of 1945 and the Highway Plan of 1964, loss in Edinburgh of St James Square and George Square, removal of the Dundee Green Belt to allow urban expansion, destruction of a potential World Heritage Site by building a new industrial estate beneath Stirling Castle, quarrying at historic Dunsinane to build more roads, allowing gold mining near Tyndrum of questionable viability, despoliation of the Strathspey valley by attempting to make Aviemore into 'St Moritz in Scotland', wanton destruction of hallowed scenery steeped in history by building the road bridge to the Isle of Skye, and the proposed handing over of Drumkinnon Bay on Loch Lomondside for permanent destruction by property developers.

Two of the above have caused much recent controversy: Aviemore and Drumkinnon Bay. Aviemore had been a charming and quintessential Scottish resort town at the foot of the Cairngorm mountains until the 1960s, when it was decided to make it into Scotland's answer to St Moritz as the premier national skiing centre.

In the absence of an adequate system of planning control on the lines found in national parks, the area was developed in a style which made it look like a theme park lifted out of an urban conurbation. Whilst the town has expanded, the built fabric has become shabby with age, and tourists have become more discerning, Aviemore is increasingly seen as an obvious mistake. And having permanently spoiled part of the Strathspey valley, a second mistake may now be about to be made on the mountain by building a funicular railway which will convey visitors to the top of Cairngorm, especially during the summer season.

Unspoilt scenic beauty is Scotland's greatest asset, but also its most vulnerable resource. It is the very foundation of our tourist industry, but here we have two sides acting out their parts as if they came from different planets. One represents economic development agencies on behalf of the hard pressed tourist industry, which might have been expected to resist further despoliation for the sake of self-preservation and long term survival. However, the attitude seems to be that, as the mountainside is already cluttered with snowfences and chairlifts, let us go the whole hog and build a railway.

The other side is led by a government agency, Scottish Natural Heritage, which holds the three statutory protection cards of access, amenity and conservation. Through some mysterious logic known only to themselves, it would appear that they chose to play only the nature conservation card when first objecting, and then withdrawing their objection to the proposals. Following their decision in 1996, the Vice Chairman of the agency, Christopher Smout, used the letter columns of *The Scotsman* to express his personal opinion on the case:

> An unsatisfactory proposal of this sort, rushed through in an atmosphere of controversy, is the last thing that should be foisted on one of the most important mountain areas in northern Europe. Only very good quality tourist development will ever succeed in bringing business or prosperity to the Highlands. Pushing the summer-time equivalent of Blackpool Tower up Scotland's second highest mountain at extreme public expense is not it. We are likely to be faced with another economic, political and planning disaster; it is for those charged with surveillance over economic development to take action now to stop a fiasco of this kind.

As for the battle of Drumkinnon Bay, it was lost in 1998 with the granting of outline planning permission. This project represents another illuminating case of divergent action within the public sector. One agency is seeking protective status for Loch Lomond as a National Park, while another quango is actively promoting commercial development which will undermine the integrity of one of the nation's most valued landscape assets. In 1996, Dumbarton Enterprise placed the following advertisement in *Building Design:*

> Loch Lomond is one of the most famous places in the world. It is also one of the most beautiful, with a rich history blended with myth, legend and romance. As yet there is nowhere where its visitors can be orientated, its stories interpreted and its urban communities connected to it. There is only one area, at the south-west tip of the Loch, where all these things can be realised. In Abercrombie's visionary Clyde Valley Regional Plan it was said, 'Here should be the great reception point for tourists; an area where

they should be accommodated and suitably introduced to the attractions of the North.' Building on Abercrombie's vision, following in the footsteps of Patrick Geddes, and continuing a Scottish tradition of sensitively planned places we wish to establish a planning and design framework to guide the area's development and to inform an outline planning application.

The reader might have been forgiven for thinking that this had been written and issued by the park authority. The language and images are those normally associated with heritage conservation, but the game is given away in the next paragraph where the wolf in sheep's clothing declares:

The focus of the framework will be an area of approximately 100 acres which will include a key orientation/interpretation centre, a landscape setting and public realm of the highest quality, an hotel, speciality retail and housing. The framework will require to link the core site over the River Leven to Balloch Castle Country Park and reflect the aspiration for the paddle steamer, Maid of the Loch, to sail again.

The intention here is to bring a piece of Costa Brava to the bonny banks of Loch Lomond at a time when Spain is realising its mistakes. The Scottish nation is fiddling while the bonny banks are burning, without a word of protest. Abercrombie would have been horrified to know that his words were to be used to justify a major new hotel development and speculative housing amounting to the equivalent of a small new town. As for Geddes, he would have turned in his grave at such blasphemous use of his name.

CULTURAL CAPITAL

So much for squandered natural heritage. The concluding question is whether the same can happen to our cultural assets. Most Scots will observe the loss of irreplaceable environmental assets with some alarm, but they will take comfort from assuming that it could not possibly happen to our cultural heritage. We are an old nation with well established traditions. There has always been a separate legal system, education and church, and we are soon to have our parliament back. These assets, combined with the national traits of enterprise, scholarship, egalitarianism and internationalism, make the strength of our cultural capital seem unassailable.

The author's answer to the above question is that there is little cause for complacency. What is being done to the environment is also being done to our cultural heritage. It was suggested in the introduction to this paper that the value of cultural assets is governed by primacy and confidence, as perceived by both the holder and the beholder, and that their stability is determined by two main factors: intellectual cohesion and continuity. Sadly, much of what we do today represents the opposite of intellectual cohesion, and lack of confidence in our own past is undermining cultural continuity.

In the educational sector, we see the virus of divergence being nurtured by two emerging academic cultures, as our universities are becoming split between the value systems of the ancient and the new. Academic point scoring is starting to take precedence over constructive dialogue with local colleges, schools and employers, and too little attention is given to closing the gap between vocational and academic education.

Divergence has gone beyond C P Snow's two cultures. We now have many additional groups striving to qualify as self sustaining disciplines, with their own territory and competing objectives, including their own academic pigeonholes and language. Whilst helping internal communication, there has been a breakdown in interdisciplinary communication and regression into blinkered professionalism, with a consequent reduction in mutual understanding and tolerance.

This has given rise to what might be called 'educated philistines'. Although we have access to better qualifications in business management, there are now fewer cultured business managers. Likewise, our environmental managers are better trained, but there are fewer cultured environmentalists. There is too much respect for discipline boundaries and a monocultural tendency in career planning. Both our cultural life and economic prosperity would benefit from more movement across sector boundaries.

The mirror image of this can be seen in today's approach to government. When we go to politicians and officials for advice on priorities and support, we are passed around the houses of a vast array of central departments, quangos and local authority officers. Each is likely to be responsible for a specialist function, but it will not always be clear how these fit into a larger strategic framework, if indeed such a framework actually exists.

Many of these organisations produce glossy annual reports, and they are frequently entitled 'A Strategy for Scotland' or such like. You think you have found what you were looking for, but then discover that each is confined to a specific aspect of culture. The point is that such corporate strategies do not provide the pieces to make up a complete jigsaw of the grand strategy for Scotland's cultural heritage.

The making of such a strategy is one of the great challenges facing us as we go into the 21st century. The footsoldiers of cultural divergence should be asked to stand back, and the scope of the strategy should be governed by the principles of democratic intellectualism founded on Patrick Geddes' philosophy of cultural convergence and continuity.

To guard against repeating the kind of mistakes described above, these principles should be made a core element of educational curricula in schools, the universities and in vocational training for the professions. They represent the glue that can bind our fragmented identity together into a progressive image combining the best from the past with the best of the new.

The threats to our cultural capital are omnipresent, and the forces of cultural incomprehension should not be underestimated. An example is the suggestion that the Welsh dragon be replaced with a more modern image on the national flag of Wales. Indeed, some associated with the 'Cool Britannia' campaign suggest that the cross of St Andrews is similarly unfit to fly over the new parliament in Edinburgh. They forget that the Saint has been woven into the cultural fabric of Scotland for a very long time. His bones came here in the year 732, and the Saltire was first seen in the sky above Athelstaneford in 750.

The Author

Professor Magnus Fladmark served in the Norwegian army, worked in journalism, and studied horticulture, architecture and town planning. After a spell in the Scottish Office, he directed an ODA programme at Edinburgh University (1970–76), where he was made an Honorary Fellow. As Assistant Director of the Countryside Commission for Scotland (1976–92), he established a new research division which provided the impetus for many initiatives in national heritage policy. A former Chairman of the RTPI in Scotland and Governor of Edinburgh College of Art, his advice has been widely sought overseas. In addition to drafting many government policy documents, he has written or contributed to several books. He started the Heritage Unit and masterminded a new MSc in heritage management at the Robert Gordon University. His contribution to Scottish affairs recently earned him an Honorary Fellowship from the Royal Incorporation of Architects in Scotland.

References

Ashby, E., *Technology and the Academics*, Macmillan, 1958
Boardman, P., *The Worlds of Patrick Geddes: Biologist, Town Planner, Re-educator, Peace-Warrior*, Routledge & Kegan Paul, 1978

Davie, G., *The Democratic Intellect*, Edinburgh University Press, 1961

Davie, G., *The Scottish Enlightenment*, The Historical Association, 1981

Davie, G., *The Crisis of the Democratic Intellect*, Polygon, 1986

Davie, G., *The Importance of the Ordinary MA*, in Macdonald, M. (ed), *Democracy and Curriculum*, Edinburgh Review, 1993

Donaldson, W., *Popular Literature in Victorian Scotland: Language, Fiction and the Press*, Aberdeen University Press, 1986

Dunbarton Enterprise, *The Loch Lomond Project*, advertisement in *Building Design*, 23 February, 1996

Fladmark, J. M., *The Planning Framework*, in Selman, P. H. (ed), *Countryside Planning in Practice: The Scottish Experience*, Stirling University Press, 1988

Fladmark, J. M., *The Wealth of a Nation: Heritage as a Cultural and Competitive Asset*, The Robert Gordon University, 1994

Fladmark, J. M., *Introduction*, in Fladmark J. M. (ed), *Sharing the Earth: Local Identity in Global Culture*, Donhead, 1995

Flew, A. (ed), *Two Biographical Documents: Letter from Adam Smith to William Strachan*, in *David Hume on Human Nature and the Understanding*, Collier Macmillan, 1962

Fraser, D., *Universities in merger talks to beat cash squeeze*, in *The Sunday Times*, 5 April, 1998

Lipsey, G. L., *An Introduction to Positive Economics*, Weidenfeld & Nicolson, 1972

Huxley, T .H., *Hume*, in Morley, J. (ed), *English Men of Letters*, Macmillan, 1878

Macdonald, M. (ed), *Patrick Geddes: Ecologist Educator Visual Thinker*, Edinburgh Review, 1992

McGinty, S. & Smyth, J., *And now for 'cool Caledonia'*, in *The Sunday Times*, 26 April, 1998

Sapin, S., *Science*, in Daiches, D. (ed), *The New Companion to Scottish Culture*, Polygon, 1993

Smout, C., *'Unsatisfactory' Plan for Cairngorm*, in *The Scotsman*, 10 May, 1996

Snow, C. P., *The Two Cultures and the Scientific Revolution*, Cambridge UP, 1959

17

FOOD IN FOLK TRADITION
How Scotland Celebrates the Seasons

Catherine Brown

Revelling in the daft days:
many festivals, one spirit.

From Christmas Eve, through Hogmanay, and into the first days of January, Scotland celebrates. It is a week to ten days of festivities, when not many employers expect much work to be done and some close down and give everyone a holiday. For what has happened in the late twentieth century festive calendar is a revival, with some modern alterations, of the old pre-Reformation 'Daft Days'. Originally styled on the French 'Fête des Fous' when winter solstice celebrations began with a religious Christ's mass of thanksgiving in church, followed by a gathered-family festive meal at home, overflowing into secular revels, satirical plays and community gatherings in the streets when 'drouthy neebors, neebors meet'.

It looked for a while as though the TV screen would become a substitute for the street, but the failure of the box to replace the live experience appears to have saved the old festival from extinction. Now there has been a recovery of the old Hogmanay traditions of secular, social, public-in-the-street partying and first-footing round the neighbours, most notably in Edinburgh, where of people street-party around the centre of the town in what is reputedly the largest communal New Year gathering in Europe.

It also looked for a while, during the first half of the twentieth century, as though Scots might continue to reject popish Christmas. Seen by the Reformed Scottish church as a Church-of-Rome affair, the habit of heavy feasting was also out of tune with their calvinistic ethics. As recently as the late 1950s, most Scots still worked on Christmas Day, shops stayed open, life went on as normal. A miserly two days holiday were given at Hogmanay. Throughout the 1920s and 30s, my Dundonian father, and his six brothers and sisters, hung up their stockings for Santa's presents on Hogmanay, and their father opened his tea and coffee merchant's shop and worked on Christmas Day.

It has been, ironically, the power of secular, commercialised Christmas which has caused its revival, providing Scots with a chance to stretch the two festivities into a more satisfying period of midwinter feasting. It is a bright period in the middle of cold wintertime when Northerners can revel in special luxury eating and drinking, have fun with family and friends, as well as express goodwill among the wider community. Two days will not do. It takes a week, preferably a fortnight, to unwind, to celebrate vigorously, to recover, to start all over again: to catch again the old spirit of the Daft Days.

THE CYCLE OF LIFE

For Northerners, winter feasting has always had special significance. While primitive people worried about their survival and the survival of their race, nature mysteriously provided them with food. The sun shone, the crops grew, the animals thrived, the harvests were gathered. Certainly, there was a pattern to this rhythm of the earth, but also huge uncertainty. In one growing cycle things would go well and there would be plenty to eat, while in another there was disaster and death. So at critical times of the cycle, like midwinter, when it looked as though the sun might disappear forever, sacrifices were made and symbolic acts performed to encourage the sun to treat them kindly and return to the earth. When it did, they believed that their actions had been correct. Superstition, sacrifice, myth, magic and folklore, relating to nature, was their religion.

Though they were simple nature-worshippers, indulging in what are now regarded as naive practices, their emotions about nature were extremely powerful. They were not just happy when winter ended and spring began, or sad when summer faded into autumn, they worshipped this progress of the earth's cycle. It was a cause of adoration and reverence, that life should be followed by death, followed by rebirth. The cycle of life, death and resurrection gave them their faith. It also established times in the cycle when intense worship was essential for survival, each racial group making its own consensus of what seemed to be the best time and the most effective rites, ceremonies and feastings.

Living on the islands which now make up the UK, there was an amalgam of racial strains of primitive peoples in different permutations, and in different proportions, which eventually created four distinct nations within a comparatively small area. In Scotland, the predominant racial strain was Celtic. There was also a strong mixture of Scandinavian blood from the Norse colonies in Caithness, Orkney and Shetland plus a few 'pirate nests' in the Hebrides and along the coasts. Although there were other racial strains (Northern English, Flemish and Norman), there were no wholesale conquests in this primitive period of Scottish history, and so the great festivals of the ancient Celtic and Norse people in Scotland became firmly established and nationally distinct.

While the Norse sea-reivers followed the movements of the sun and the moon, celebrating their festivals according to the solstices and equinoxes, the romantic, mystical, poetical Celts divided their year according to the movement of flocks from lowland pasture to highland pasture and vice versa. In the Celtic calendar, Beltane (1 May) was the beginning of summer while Samhuinn (31 October) was the beginning of winter. The Celtic New Year began at sunset on 31 October.

It is a variation in the division of the year which continues, with differences between the Scottish and English calendar: the Scottish quarter days occurring in February, May, August and November while in England they are in March, June, September and December.

Among the ancient Celts, the most influential nature-worshippers were the Druids, though Christian missionaries discovered several others, as well as many popular superstitions and magical practices which pre-dated the Druids. But compared with the early beliefs of other primitive peoples, Druidism was a sophisticated, civilizing force, practising divine worship and involving powerful, esoteric priests who were regarded as philosophers and theologians. They took on the management of order in the community, educating children as well as taking responsibility for settling disputes and deciding rewards and penalties. Unlike non-Celtic Europe, which had polytheistic systems, the mystical nature-worshipping Celtic Druids were much more compatible with the new Christian faith which arrived in Scotland with St Ninian at the Isle of Whithorn (fourth century) and St Columba on Iona (sixth century).

To begin with, the primitive Christian church had very few festivals. In the first century, only Sundays, Easter and Pentecost were celebrated. In the second century, Lent was initiated and in the fourth century there was the institution of Saints' days. Though the Nativity of Christ is mentioned in the second century, it was not until the sixth century that it became a universal celebration.

Christian priests, during the early days of their mission, had great difficulty converting the people from nature-worshipping to worshipping a God of love and forgiveness who had nothing to do with the practical needs of day-to-day survival. Of course the people carried on with the old familiar rites and ceremonies, which is hardly surprising considering that these customs had long been regarded as vital to their survival. Eventually Christianity accepted defeat and decided to keep the times of the nature-worshippers festivals as well as some of their rites and ceremonies. The proviso was that they would all be given a Christian significance.

And so Yule, the northern nature-worshipper's midwinter festival would become a celebration of the Nativity of Christ, while midsummer's day would celebrate the life of St John the Baptist instead of the radiant Norse sun god Baldur. The celebration of the Celtic spring goddess Bride, would become Candlemas Eve, when the church would celebrate the Purification of the Virgin. The Beltane rites in May, marking summer's beginning, would be dedicated to the Holy Cross. Lammas in August would continue to celebrate the grain harvest, but the rites would be in Christian churches with loaves of bread. And the most deeply significant festival of the Celtic nature-worshippers which came at the end of summer, Samhuinn, would become a night when all the Christian saints would be hallowed.

CELEBRATING SUMMER'S END

Samhuinn, and the spring festival of Beltane, had been the most important feasting periods for the early Celts who divided their year, simply, in half. The two festivals marked out winter and summer symbolizing darkness and light, the ebb and flow of the tides, the death and resurrection of nature. While Beltane was celebrated at first light, with fires lit at sunrise on hilltops, Samhuinn, summer's end, marked the beginning of the Celtic year and was celebrated in the dark, with fires lit at sundown on sacred sites of standing stones or graveyards. Today, on 31 October, guising, bonfires, fireworks and communal partying are first and foremost good fun, especially when they hit that scary nerve, but their roots go deep into ancient rites which celebrated the natural rhythm of life and death on earth.

At the beginning of November nature was disturbed, the earth was decaying and the sun dying away in the sky. Of course there was cause for thanksgiving in the recently gathered harvest of crops, but it was believed that on this night of seasonal change all sleeping spirits of good and evil were awakened. For one night only, they came alive and the powers of darkness were in the ascendant. Good spirits came back to visit their relatives, while those with less honourable intentions – witches, ghoulies, ghaisties, warlocks, bogles, kelpies, gnomes and trolls – the whole unhallowed clamjamfrie of the netherworld, came back to do as much harm as they could.

Since fire was a cleanser and purifier, as well as a sun symbol, lighting a bonfire was a means of burning the evil spirits which hovered above the flames. Burning an effigy of a witch on the bonfire became a symbolic attempt to destroy all agents of malevolence. While there was panic and terror in their minds, and though this was essentially a festival of the Cult of the Dead, the festivities also involved a great deal of fun and frolicking. Their communal celebrations not only released pent-up tensions with wild behaviour, but also at a deeper level they included worship, when there was joyful thanksgiving for the soul's immortality.

Halloween guising continues as one of the frolics of this festival. It is thought to have originated in the folk-memory of Druidic feasts when a mask was used to avoid being recognized by the spirits of the dead. They also believed that the hazel tree, the Golden Bough was imbued with magic because wizards considered it the root and symbol of wisdom. The apple tree, the Silver Bough, was the talisman which admitted favoured mortals into the Otherworld, giving them the power to foretell the future.

Today, the apple rite of dooking for apples is linked to the Ordeal by Water. To get to the land of the Silver Bough you had to pass first through water and then fire. Obsolete in its original form, but still enduring in suspended treacly scones which must be caught and eaten by the guisers, the ordeal by fire entailed fixing an apple and a lighted candle to either end of a rod. The rod was then hung from a height and twirled, while participants attempted to grab a bite of the fruit without being burnt by the candle.

Magic continues to fascinate. Many customs and superstitions have been handed on from one generation to the next, the remnants continuing whether in simple lucky charms or symbolic stones hung in pouches and worn round necks, or charms worn on bracelets. All have their origins in primitive nature-worship, as do the ring, thimble, button and silver coins which are put into cakes or dumplings as 'surprises' for children. In Scotland, a variety of eating traditions developed in connection with lucky charms at Halloween.

In some parts the lucky charms were buried in a large pot of 'champit tatties' (mashed potatoes) while in others they were put into a 'clootie dumpling' (a spicy fruit pudding boiled in a cloth). In the Highlands the hiding-mixture was whipped cream with oatmeal known in Gaelic as 'fuarag' The young people (sometimes blindfolded) sat in a circle round the pot, each with a spoon, supping until it was empty. Part of the fun was the supping, but there was even greater hilarity when everyone disclosed what their fortunes were to be. Who finds the most valued ring will be the first to marry; a silver coin, will be wealthy; the button or thimble, will not marry; the wishbone, will have their heart's desire; the horseshoe, will have good luck.

Today, children are the most enthusiastic revellers at Halloween as they continue – despite the attractions of more sophisticated entertainment – to catch the spirit of its spooky merriment. Their imaginations, encouraged by enthusiastic adults, are excited by the innocent fun of guising, dooking for apples, catching be-treacled scones or finding a lucky charm in a clootie dumpling.

CELEBRATING SUMMER'S BEGINNING

While Christianity chose April as the springtime festival of rebirth, marking the end of Lent, and now established in Scotland as Easter, the nature-worshipping Celts had originally celebrated a month later at the beginning of May with Beltane. 'Ne'er cast a cloot till May is oot', say canny Scots, meaning that cold winter can still come hurtling back when farther south it is already well into warm summer. A longer spring, shorter summer, and therefore later growing cycle made the festive times different in nature-worshipping Scotland.

Easter was formerly known in Scotland as Pace, Pasch or Pesche, from the Latin 'pascha', itself from the Hebrew 'pesach' passover (Gaelic 'Caisg' from the same root), its name later conforming with English to become Easter after a Saxon goddess of spring 'Eastre' or 'Ostara'. The egg-symbol of new life had been the nature-worshippers' analogy with the miracle of the earth: apparently lifeless, then dramatically coming alive. In the mystical and magical religion of the Druids, eggs were sacred and their priests wore symbolic egg-shapes round their necks to denote rank.

Their 'Feast of the Eggs', had involved rolling eggs downhill to symbolize the movement of the sun. So the Christian church took the custom and related it to an imitation of the stones rolling away from Christ's tomb. Today, children continue to egg-roll at Easter, with the lucky ones those whose eggs roll the farthest without breaking. While symbolic egg-feasting has primitive native origins, other eating traditions like hot-cross buns and simnel cakes come from other cultures. Commercialized Easter may have taken its grip, yet Celtic Beltane has not been entirely abandoned. Like the revival of street-partying at Hogmanay, there has been a symbolic rebirth of the old midsummer sun-worshipping event. The Beltane fires which died out in the early years of the century have been re-lit in the 1990s on Calton Hill in Edinburgh with a wild night of feasting and dancing, including a symbolic dance of the Beltane bride (the earth) and bridegroom (the sun).

As with the end of October, the beginning of May marked a time when the earth was in turmoil, but this time with new life. Once again the spirits of the netherworld were disturbed from their sleep and came alive to do good or evil. While in October there was thanksgiving for the earth's harvest, in May there was supplication for protection from the ill luck of bad weather, crops failing and animals dying. Many rites and customs relating to nature's birth were practised round the daybreak bonfires which were often surrounded by a wide circular trench, within which the people gathered.

Because the earth's rebirth required moisture as well as heat and light, Beltane celebrated water as well as fire. The water from sacred wells took on magical powers, and pilgrimages were made to certain wells. There are still about 600 sites of wishing wells in Scotland. One of the best known is the Clootie Well just outside Inverness where people nail a piece of cloth to a nearby tree for good luck. But the most sacred water for nature-worshippers was the early-morning dew collected on the first of May and used by Druids in secret rites. The superstitious custom of washing faces in the May dew remains a popular tradition with parties of young women still following the ritual climb to the top of Arthur's Seat on 1 May. In 1934, the *Daily Record* reported 'About two hundred young women climbing to the top... to bathe their faces in the May dew.'

Besides the Celtic fire and water rites, the first of May festivities have also been influenced by the Roman floral festival known as 'Florilia'. A springtime flower festival which was predominant in Europe, even in areas which had never been occupied by a Roman legion. When parts of southern Scotland became de-Celtisized, Florilia was grafted onto Beltane. In some of the burghs, the maypole became the focal point of the festivities with games and dancing and the election of a May Queen and King. The maypole was decorated with flowers, houses were filled with flowers, and newly green branches of protective trees (rowan, juniper and elder) were taken into the house. Meantime, people in the more strongly Celtic areas of the north continued to light the Beltane bonfires on hilltops, visit sacred wells, gather the May dew and wash faces in it. On the special Beltane hills around the country, where huge bonfires had been burnt year after year for many centuries, geologists have identified a thick stratum of charcoal underneath a covering of fine loam.

Among the eating traditions recorded at Beltane, the most symbolic was a custard-type mixture of eggs, milk and oatmeal, known as 'the Beltane caudle' which was cooked on the Beltane bonfire. Some of it was poured symbolically onto the ground so that the hens would lay plentifully in the coming year, the cows give abundant milk and the fields a rich harvest. The remainder was either eaten or poured over the Beltane bannock.

'These cakes or bannocks, as we call them in Scotland,' says Sir James Frazer in *The Golden Bough*, 'were oatcakes baked in the usual way, but washed over with a thin batter of whipped egg, milk, and cream.' The nature of the festive bannock appears to have varied throughout the country with some bannocks remaining in the form of large round inch-thick cakes of barley or oatmeal while others took on a triangular shape. A Beltane bannock on the Isle of Mull is recorded in *British Calendar Customs* by M M Banks, as being a large round cake with a hole in the middle, through which the cows were milked on 1 May for good luck. In Ross-shire they were called hand-cakes (Gaelic, dearnagan) because they were entirely worked by hand, not rolled out on a board or table. After baking, they were put immediately into the hands of the children to eat.

The Beltane bannock survived on the Isle of Lewis at least to the beginning of the twentieth century, where it is recorded as being made with barley meal, spread over with a mixture of switched egg, oatmeal and milk and toasted before the fire. The ritual bannock, in its most sophisticated form, appears to have been made with a batter coating of flour, cream, eggs and sugar which was cooked onto the already baked bannock. A layer of about a quarter of an inch was spread on one side and this was put to toast at the fire. When that had browned, another layer was added and the procedure repeated. Several layers were built up on each side of the bannock, each toasted separately before the fire in the same way that Germans make their *Baumkuchen* (tree-cake) on a revolving spit before the fire while the layers of thick batter are cooked onto it.

In many parts of Scotland a newly made sheep's-milk cheese was specially prepared for Beltane. It was cut and laid on the Beltane bannock and eaten before sunset. According to the sixteenth-century poet Alexander Scott, other festive foods included;

> Butter, new cheise, and beir in May,
> Connan [rabbits], cokkelis, curds and quhey [whey].

MIDWINTER AND HOGMANAY

Throughout the Middle Ages, as the Christian Church in Scotland took over 25 December, it also took over Twelfth Night or 6 January, known as 'Uphalieday', the feast of Epiphany, or the day on which the holy days were up. Throughout the long period of Catholic Scotland, before the Reformation in 1559, Epiphany was a great court festival with plays, pageantries, guising and revels involving much parody and mocking of the authorities such as the sixteenth-century play *Ane Satyr of the Thrie Estatis*, which has been revived several times at the Edinburgh Festival. Though it exposed the corruption of both the monarchy and the church, it was originally performed before the King and Queen at Linlithgow as a finale to winter feasting. It was the Scots in an irreverent, jokey mood, when relaxed hilarity and goodwill took the stage – at least for a night.

For most of Scotland, however, the Reformation meant the loss of both religious dedication at Christmas as well as satirical fun and games during the twelve Daft Days. In 1649, a century after The Thrie Estatis was performed before king and church, the church's General Assembly had banned both Christmas and the Daft Days. Abolishing this annual and only holiday for those who worked on the land, church ministers were advised to make checks on their congregations, with special house visits to make sure that everyone was at their work and nothing festive cooking-up on the family stove.

Of course people continued to celebrate, prohibition being a powerful incentive to rebel, and stories are recorded of people hiding the roast goose under the bed when the minister called. Attention moved, however, to the 'hinner end o' Yule' and to New Year's Night, untainted by the Church of Rome, therefore religiously more acceptable to the narrow-minded church hierarchy. What happened was an amalgam of the old festivities of Christmas, Yule and Twelfth Night or Epiphany, into what has now become known as Hogmanay. From its early beginnings, Hogmanay brought together the forbidden customs from other festivals (hence the reason for my father hanging up his stocking for Father Christmas at Hogmanay), and the new celebration took a particularly strong grip on the emotions of the Scottish people, which shows little sign of abating.

A possible derivation of the name, according to the *Scottish National Dictionary*, is from the French 'aguillanneuf', a street cry for gifts on New Year's Day. It appears to have come into the language from early Franco-Scottish connections, the cry altering and changing from the seventeenth century onwards until it was eventually modified into a cry of children and beggars who knocked on doors looking for a gift of food, such as an oatmeal bannock or some money:

> Get up, good wife, and shake your feathers,
> And dinna think that we are beggars;
> For we are bairns come out to play,
> Get up and gie us our hogmanay. (1847)

The transfer of the word to the communal celebrations lasting several days, appears to have developed during the eighteenth and nineteenth centuries with people celebrating at stone circles or mercat crosses. Though now a universal celebration throughout the country (except in Shetland where Up-Helly-Aa prevails), in its early days Hogmanay was most enthusiastically celebrated in the strongly Protestant areas of the country, such as the Covenanting South-West, and least observed in the Catholic 'belt' beyond the Grampians and in Aberdeenshire and the North-East, where Episcopalian influences were strong and Christmas was still an acceptable time to feast.

While townspeople will gather at a clock in the town centre, the rural tradition is to 'see in the bells' at home before taking off first-footing and partying in houses. In the Highlands and Islands, where the 'ceilidh' tradition survives, there are several nights of dusk-till-dawn entertainment plus drinking and eating, as the ceilidh moves each night round neighbouring communities.

In the area of Wester Ross where I have spent most Hogmanays in the last thirty-five years, the spirit of Hogmanay past is still alive and well, but with its own peculiar quirks. First-foots do not carry a piece of fuel for the fire, or a festive orange, shortbread or cake, as they might do in other parts, but no one is without a bottle of whisky. They are welcomed throughout the night in every house where a light continues to burn and will first be given a small communal 'dram' glass. (A remnant of the days when a Highland crofter was unlikely to have owned more than one glass in the house.) They will fill the glass from their own bottle, and then go round the gathered company, refilling the glass before they offer it to each person with the toast: 'Slainte, Bliadhna Mhath Ur' (good health, happy new year).

A sideboard of cold meats, oatcakes, cheese, shortbread, pancakes, soda scones and clootie dumplings are among the most usual fare for the night. Favourite meats are a cold haunch of venison or leg of mature mutton, a thick slice placed on a crisp oatcake. At other northern Hogmanay revelling, the festive food might involve pots of hot stovies, served with pickled beetroot and oatcakes or a bowl of Scotch broth. Black bun may be served instead of clootie dumpling. Compared with a sit-down, gargantuan Christmas feast, Hogmanay fare is modest. Nothing is over-rich, nothing obligatory. Huge amounts of energy are required during the night in walking from house to house, often a distance apart, so that food is welcome sustenance and never the cause of over-eating.

UP-HELLY-AE AND THE CLAVIE

While Hogmanay remains the strongest communal celebration in mainland Scotland, in the remote Shetland Islands, more deeply Norse in their ancestry than any other part of Scotland, the Lerwick fire-festival of 'Up-Helly-Aa' (when holidays or 'helli' days are up) marks the end of the twenty-four days of 'Yule'.

For five hundred years (ninth–thirteenth century) during their occupation of a large part of Scotland, the Vikings feasted vigorously, danced, joined hands and whirled in a circle round the fire-worshipping bonfires. Though they were eventually defeated at the battle of Largs in 1263, and many converted to the Celtic Christian church, the spirit of the Viking Yule remains strong on the islands where its roots are deepest. In the nineteenth century, and for some time into the twentieth, Yule Day in Shetland, continued to be celebrated, not on 25 December, but on 6 January, which was according to the old calendar, originally changed to its present form in 1752.

'Auld Yule' was a period of a whole month, the Merry Month, which began seven days before Yule, and ended twenty-four days after on Up-Helly-Aa, the last Tuesday in January. Yule Day itself was traditionally a time for feasting and vigorous exercise, a practical and healthy means of keeping warm, when men played a game of traditional football with a specially made Yule Ba. The remnants of this activity remain in the game of Uppies and Doonies, now played on New Year's Day in the main street of Kirkwall in Orkney when the two teams, relating to the top and the bottom of the town, engage in a heaving mass of disorderly scrum, as the ball goes either up or down the street.

But in Shetland, Lerwick's Up-Helly-Aa is a more organised event developed from an old festive midwinter custom of burning tar barrels. In 1881 the tar barrels became torches and a committee was formed to run the festival. By 1889 the idea had developed of burning a longship and creating a pageant for a day in the town. It's a community festival which has grown in the last hundred years into one of the largest winter fire-festivals in Europe.

It begins in the morning with a pageant of a full-sized Norse galley with a dragon's head and a fish's tail and is accompanied by Guizers dressed as Norsemen. The galley spends the day in the town while the Guizers visit hospitals, schools and homes for the elderly. In the early evening they take part in the spectacular torchlit procession of several thousand people to a playing field where their torches are thrown into the galley, igniting it, and sending the whole ship blazing up into the night sky.

When the flames have died down, the merrymaking continues throughout the night in halls and hotels, with Guizers turning up to provide entertainment and receive hospitality. During the day, the halls have been organized by hosts and hostesses who sell tickets for their hall and who provide food and entertainment, often until dawn. To sustain the revelry, gallons of soup are made. Much of it is flavoured with reestit mutton: a salt and sugar cure, still available in butcher's shops on the islands, where the brined meat is hung on a special frame or 'reest' to dry out, then stored on hooks on rafters. In addition there are large quantities of home-baking as well as home-made toffee for children. It is twenty-four hours of fire, frolic and feasting based on myth, history and innovation which has become firmly established, and greatly loved by the people.

Another survivor of the Auld Yule fires of Norse ancestry, which at one time blazed all along Scotland's northern and eastern coasts, is the fire festival at Burghead on the Moray coast where the community gathers each year on 11 January to burn 'The Clavie'. The word appears to be a corruption of the Gaelic 'cliabh' pronounced 'clee-av', meaning the basket which is used for carrying the fire. While the Sheltanders converted their blazing tar barrels into a longship, the people of this small fishing village continue with the older tradition of a half barrel fixed to a stake which is filled with tar-soaked wood and set alight with a live peat. When it is well alight it is carried through the town by the Clavie King and his followers until it reaches the Doorie, a large grassy knoll reputed to be a centre of Druidic fire-worship, where it is fixed to a pillar with a spoke.

The fire is revived with more tar, poured onto the glowing mass, and there is a tremendous cheer as the flames shoot up into the black night, throwing their glow onto the crowd of up-turned faces. When it has died down, the clavie is dismantled and there is a mad scramble for a piece of what's left of the barrel, an ember from a sacred Druidic fire, bringing good luck for the rest of the year.

FASTING FROM FEBRUARY TO APRIL

The period after riotous midwinter feasting was a natural time to sober up, hibernate, slow down, conserve energy – and fast. A time of denial during the bleakest period of empty, late-winter larders which was adopted by the early Christians as the time for religious atonement. Never mind self-denial being good for the soul, fasting was as expedient as war-imposed rationing, and the church simply fashioned it with its own doctrines.

Depending on which historical timewarp you choose, religious abstinence from food might have meant no meat, fish, eggs, milk, butter, cream and cheese. Had the medieval church been in control, the full-blown denial would have been forty symbolic days of bread and water, only after sundown. Sounds grim. But before it began there was a final fling of pre-Lenten merriment, starting at the festival of Candlemas, on 2 February, involving dressing-up and street processions.

The fun and frolics ended on the Tuesday in February after the first spring moon, known as 'Fastern's E'en', 'Fester E'en', 'Shreftis E'en', or 'Shrove Tuesday' which marked the beginning of a period of 'shriving,' or shrivelling when pre-Lenten pancakes were made with the remaining eggs and milk in the larder. The Scots version of Lenten pancakes were known as 'bannocks' and were made with oatmeal, eggs, milk or beef stock and cooked on a girdle. There was also the custom of making a special milk-brose or gruel to eat with the bannocks, so that the festive night was known in different parts of the country as Bannock Night, Brose Day (Brosie for short), or Milk-Gruel Night.

While there was communal merriment, the night's ritual also involved gatherings of young people round the family hearth for superstitious rites and customs pre-dating the Christian church. It would start with fortune-telling. Then there was the ritual pouring of batter onto the hot girdle by one person, while another turned the pancakes and a third removed them when they were ready, handing them round the assembled company. When the bowl of batter was almost empty, a small quantity of soot was added to the mixture to make the large 'sooty' bannock, also known as the dreaming-bannock. The magic soot, a relic of the ancient sun-worshippers symbolic fires, perpetuated the belief in the magical properties of the fire's ashes.

A sooty bannock filled the whole girdle. Symbolic charms were dropped into it: button (batchelor); a ring (married); thimble (old maid); farthing (widow); scrap of material (tailor); straw (farmer). Once the bannock was turned and cooked through, it was cut into bits and put into the baker's apron for people to take their lucky dip. At the end of the evening, a piece of the sooty bannock was put inside a sock and placed under pillows where the dreamer hoped to dream of their future partner.

In today's pre-Lenten pancake culture, Scots no longer believe in the power of a sooty bannock hidden under their pillows, but they continue to make thick spongy pancakes on a girdle for Shrove Tuesday, rather than thin tossable French crepes in a frying pan. Like the soot, the large bannock with charms also appears to have been abandoned and pre-fasting pancakes have shrunk to small rounds about four to six inches across. They are the pancakes which are still to be found at continuous-girdle-bakings, often run by the WRIs in tents at Highland shows and other gatherings. A communal and sociable event as people stand round waiting for each batch to come off the girdle, buttering, sugaring and squeezing with lemon. The ritual remains.

ST ANDREWS AND ROBERT BURNS

St Andrew's Night dinners, on 30 November, are the time to honour the patron saint first of Pictland and eventually of all Scotland with the toast: 'To the memory of St Andrew, and Scotland Yet.'

Andrew was a doer-behind-the-scenes. A quiet, self-effacing apostle who went off and found the loaves and fishes for the gathering on the shores of the sea of Galilee. He was martyred on a cross decussate, X-shaped rather than the usual T-shaped cross, which eventually became recognized as the Scottish national emblem first appearing on the royal seal in 1290.

'Sanct Andra's Day', 'Andyr's Day' or 'Andermas,' all older Scottish forms, is celebrated as a patriotic festival at home and abroad by expatriate Scots. Dinner menus usually contain a selection of national dishes, though not always a haggis.

Blasts of January chill find Scots deeply involved in steaming haggis puddings, warming toasts of whisky and many spirited addresses to the haggis. But for Burns suppers on 25 January, the ugly old pudding might never have made it into the nineteenth century, let alone survived the twentieth century's fast-food revolution.

It is now 200 years since Burns's death, yet thanks to him this ancient method of stuffing an animal's innards into its stomach bag remains more or less intact. Developments with plastic casings notwithstanding, we still eat the same old pudding which inspired him to write his 'Address to a Haggis' in the winter of 1786.

It appears to have found its way to Scotland via Ancient Greece, Rome, France and England, but until Burns there was nothing particularly Scottish about it and recipes appear in English cookery books at the same time as Burns was writing the 'Address'. But he strikes a celebratory note, dear to Scottish hearts, while at the same time honouring something which has little, if any, visual appeal. It was entirely appropriate that he should choose a haggis. Do not judge by appearances, he says. Honour the honest virtues of sense and worth, not in French ragouts and fricasses, but in a more democratic dish which makes the least attractive parts of an animal into something worth celebrating.

It was a challenge, firstly to Scots, but as it has turned out, also to the rest of the world, with Burns supper celebrations taking on a universal meaning. Yet at the same time its influence on the national food image has been extremely powerful. 'An assertion,' says James Kinsley, 'of peasant virtue and strength, expressed in harsh, violent diction and images of slaughter.' Just as there is no escape from reality in life, there is no escape in Burns's poem. The image is of a nation celebrating in hospitable and open-hearted ways a hearty, wholesome, unsophisticated yet highly distinctive food at a unique occasion.

In 1801, five years after his death, the first Burns Club was formed in Greenock. In 1805 Paisley had formed a club, and two years later Kilmarnock. The Edinburgh literati, including Sir Walter Scott and Alexander Boswell, son of the biographer James Boswell, had their first Burns celebration in 1815 and resolved to have one every three years. In

London, Scots along with some English poets had a Burns anniversary supper in 1819. But it was not until the centenary in 1859 that the idea of an annual 'Nicht wi Burns', or Burns Supper, on 25 January, first developed.

In the two centuries since his death a worldwide cult has developed with deep roots founded on the poet's appeal, not just to the literati, but to everyone. Though there may be greater poets, but none have so far surpassed Burns in expressing the spirit which bonds people of all nations, creeds and colours. For Scots, he is among a handful of makars who have written from the heart in their own tongue, adding an emotional nostalgia to Burns suppers with the colour and character of the rarely heard native Scots language.

The Author

Catherine Brown is a Glaswegian journalist, food writer and author. She studied Food and Nutrition and her early career involved both teaching and professional cooking in hotels and restaurants. During a period of post-graduate research at Strathclyde University, she wrote the thesis which was published in 1976 as *British Cookery*. In the early 1980s, she began to write a food column in *the Herald* which she continues, as well as writing for a number of national magazines. In both 1989 and 1995 she was awarded Glenfiddish Food-Writing Awards for her columns in the *Herald* and was recently awarded the Scottish Chef's Association 1996 Achievement Award. Her publications are listed in the Reference section below.

References

Banks, M. M., *British Calendar Customs Scotland*, Folk-Lore Society, 1941
  Vol. 1: *Moveable Festivals*.
  Vol. 2: *The Seasons, The Quarters, Hogmanay, January to May*.
  Vol. 3: *June to December, Christmas, The Yules,*
Barz, B., *Festivals with Children*, Floris, 1984
Brown, C., *Scottish Regional Recipes* Drew, 1981
Brown, C., *Scottish Cookery* Drew, 1986
Brown, C., *Broths to Bannocks*, John Murray, 1990
Brown, C., *Food Trails of Scotland (1) Dumfries and Galloway (2) Tayside*, Hamely Fare, 1996
Brown, C., *A Year in a Scots Kitchen*, Neil Wilson, 1996
Carey, D. and Large, J., *Festivals Family and Food Hawthorn*, Stroud, 1995

Irvine, J., *Up-Helly-Aa*, Shetland Publishing, 1992

McNeill, F. M., *The Scots Kitchen Blackie*, 1929

McNeill, F.M., *The Silver Bough*, MacLellan, 1957

   Vol. 1: *Scottish Folk-Lore and Folk-Belief*

   Vol. 2: *A Calendar of Scottish National, Festivals, Candlemas to Harvest Home*

   Vol. 3: *Hallowe'en to Yule*

   Vol. 4: *Scottish Local Festivals*

Whyte, H. and Brown, C. (eds), *A Scottish Feast Argyll*, Glendaruel, Argyll, 1996

Celebrating Hogmanay in Glasgow in 1826, from drawing by William Heath (courtesy of the author).

251

Top: photo from 1878 looking east towards the Los Angeles River with the Plaza and the old Catholic Church on the left and Pico House on the right. Bottom: view looking west of the Plaza today with Pico House in the foreground and Los Angeles City Hall behind.

18

THE MEETING OF CULTURES
El Pueblo de Los Angeles

Jean Bruce Poole

El Pueblo de Los Angeles Historical Monument is the most historic area of the City of Los Angeles. It is a 44 acre site encompassing 27 buildings of varied architectural styles and dates ranging from 1818 to 1926. Four are open to the public as museums, and several others are used for commercial purposes. The buildings surround a central plaza with huge Moreton Bay fig trees which were planted in the 1870s. At a right angle on the north side of the plaza lies Olvera Street, a colourful one block Mexican marketplace which is one of the city's major tourist attractions.

For almost four decades from 1953, when all the properties in the area were acquired by eminent domain, the Monument was administered under a Joint Powers Agreement signed by the State of California and the City and County of Los Angeles. It was a State Historic Park, run by the City with oversight from the State, but nobody was happy with this arrangement. Eventually, in 1992, it was agreed that the City of Los Angeles should take over. The City created a new department for E1 Pueblo, and a seven member commission was appointed in 1994 to administer it. The Commission's task is to develop and restore the buildings and sites in the Monument and to achieve this without causing a financial burden to the City.

At present, the Monument is self-supporting, its funds being principally derived from the rentals of stalls and shops in Olvera Street and the parking lot fees. Unfortunately, E1 Pueblo's yearly income is not currently adequate to provide funds for restoration and for creation of state of the art historic exhibits. It will therefore be necessary to invite developers to pay for the cost of restoring and developing the buildings and sites on the south side of the Plaza. They, in turn, will expect to make a profit on their investment, which could mean that there will be less space than would be desirable for historic interpretation. This could have an effect on the types of visitors who come to the Monument, as it seems to be the case that well preserved and restored historic sites are more attractive to tourists and pilgrims than areas that are mainly commercial in their uses.

El Pueblo de Los Angeles sobre el Rio de la Porciuncula was founded in 1781, on the orders of King Carlos III of Spain who desired to colonise Alta California for fear of encroachment by Britain or Russia. The Spaniards ordered the establishment of three types of settlements: missions to be run by the Franciscan order, *presidios* or army forts, and *pueblos* or small towns to grow crops to supply the presidios. The 44 *pobladores,* or settlers arrived over the summer of 1781 in parties escorted by soldiers at a site that had been selected by Felipe de Neve, the military commander, following a recommendation for settlement made by an expedition 12 years earlier.

The settlers found good land for agriculture with a copious river and a village of friendly Indians nearby. Although all of the *pobladores* were Spanish subjects, they were of mixed ethnic origins, with two pure blooded Spaniards, two men described as *Negros, and* nine *Indios.* The rest were *mestizos* or *mulatos.* Today, African Americans are proud of the fact that 26 of the original 44 settlers had some degree of African American ancestry. This marked the beginning of Los Angeles as a multi-ethnic city.

By 1800 the population of the pueblo had increased to 315. In 1821, Mexico declared her independence from Spain and after that, as all the land no longer belonged to Spain, successive Mexican governors made outright land grants to different individuals. The Avila Adobe and the Plaza Church remain from the Spanish and Mexican periods.

What was known as the pastoral or ranchero period now began. Vast estates were amassed, and the main activity was the raising of vast herds of cattle, slaughtered for their hides and tallow rather than for meat. Some foreigners came to the pueblo during this period, including Americans, French and Italians, many of whom were vintners who produced highly regarded wine. There were also a couple of Scots, one of whom, Hugo Reid, married an Indian woman and wrote interesting articles about the Indians and their customs. In order to be eligible to own land, the settlers had to take on Mexican citizenship and many of them married daughters of local rancheros.

The Mexican American War broke out in 1846 and ended in 1848. Los Angeles was taken by United States forces in 1847, although the city remained Mexican in language and custom until the 1870s. Many new settlers from abroad now began to arrive. Of a population of 4,399 in 1860, 400 were French. In the same decade, several Chinese settled in the Calle de Los Negros, a street northeast of the Plaza where the poorest inhabitants lived. Partly because of their unusual appearance, and partly because the residents believed that the hardworking newcomers would take their jobs away, the Chinese were not well accepted and racial tensions grew. A terrible massacre erupted in 1871 when 19 Chinese and one American were killed. Later, a series of Exclusion Laws made their lives even more difficult.

In 1870, the Pico House, which was the city's first elegant hotel and first three storey building, was completed in the Plaza by Don Pio Pico, last governor of Los Angeles under the Mexican rule. In order to raise funds to build the hotel, he sold his extensive landholdings in the San Fernando Valley. But sadly, he lost it to foreclosure ten years later, and a three storey theatre built the same year on the south side of the hotel also ran into difficulties. Directly across the Plaza, Olvera Street, formerly known as Wine or Vine Street, was renamed in 1877 in honor of Agustin Olvera, first judge of Los Angeles County. In the 1880s there was a building boom and several new structures were erected which are still standing today, including the city's first firestation. After that, the area began to decline as its business and residential heart moved southwards. Other populations that suffered during the last half of the 19th century were the Native Americans and the Mexicans. By the end of the century the Native American population had been decimated and many of the poorer Mexicans had moved to an area known as Sonoratown, north west of the Plaza.

By the early 1900s, the Plaza area itself had greatly deteriorated and a number of the buildings began to be used for light industrial purposes. The old Mexican families such as the Avilas and the Lugos who lived in homes around the Plaza had moved away. Others, including many Chinese, had taken their places.

In the 1920s, leaders of Los Angeles began to make plans to build an enormous railway station to service the three competing railroads which used the city as a terminus. A special election was called in 1926, and citizens were asked to choose one of five sites for the construction of the station. Overwhelmingly, they picked the Plaza area. Fortunately, by 1931, the city leaders had moved the site for the station slightly to the east and thereby sparing most of the historic buildings at El Pueblo.

A few years earlier, a woman named Christine Sterling started walking through the Plaza area and was appalled by the condition in which she found the historic buildings. The Avila Adobe, the oldest house still standing in the city, was a slum with a condemnation notice on the door and Olvera Street was an unpaved alley with an open sewer running down the middle. With great effort, she persuaded five civic leaders to contribute $5000 each towards the closing of Olvera Street in order to transform it into a Mexican market place which was opened on Easter Sunday in 1930.

It is important to recognise the context in which Olvera Street was turned into a Mexican marketplace. The 1920s and 30s saw a major Spanish Revival movement in Southern California, which manifested itself in Spanish style buildings and architectural features, and in events with romantic Spanish themes, many of which were inspired by Helen Hunt Jackson's novel *Ramona*. This was the story of a young and handsome Indian named Alessandro who fell in love with Ramona, the beautiful daughter of a Spanish don and married her, against the wishes of her family. Tragedy ensued, and Alessandro was killed.

Another influence may have been the phenomenal growth of the Hollywood movie industry, where exotic experiences could routinely be produced and where an authentic historical set could be constructed almost overnight. This was the perfect background for the creation of an authentic Californian historic place. And now, more than 65 years later, Olvera Street is, by Los Angeles terms, historic. It is an authentic 'inauthentic' place. However, in the process of transforming a slummy alley into a Mexican marketplace, while not historic, it created an environment which allowed for the celebration of the Mexican culture in Los Angeles. Prior to the 1930s there was no place for this to exist.

Olvera Street has thrived and the 70 plus merchants who operate its shops and puestos or stalls, many of whom are children or grandchildren of people who started businesses there in the 1930s, have a very strong stake in what happens to the Monument and its administration. The merchants are protected by long term leases and have an Advisory Committee which has been established so that they may provide advice and recommendations to the Commission. The Los Angeles Convention and Visitors' Bureau estimates that over one million Southern California residents and tourists from all over the world come, each year, to visit this historic site and, especially, Olvera Street.

El Pueblo itself, as distinct from Olvera Street (which is certainly its best known component), is a recreation centre and traditional meeting place for the Hispanic/Latino residents of the city. It is the scene of major celebrations of traditional Mexican holidays such as Cinco de Mayo and Mexican Independence when as many as 10,000 people, of whom 90% are Latino, participate each day in a three day weekend fiesta. In fact, the popular conception is that El Pueblo is a totally Hispanic place. However within the last ten to fifteen years, there has been a great resurgence of interest in El Pueblo by groups whose history has been intimately involved with this area. These include the Chinese, whose original Chinatown was in and around the Plaza, particularly on the east side; the Italians who owned or used five of the 13 buildings in Olvera Street; and, to a lesser extent, the French, who were responsible for building or using seven other buildings in the Plaza area.

While many of the Olvera Street merchants applaud the plans to create, in one of E1 Pueblo's Chinese buildings, a museum relating to the history of the Chinese settlers in Los Angeles, and in another building, known as the Italian Hall, to develop a museum interpreting the history of the Italians in Los Angeles, others are vocal in their disapproval. They are not the only dissenters, as shown by the vandalising of plaques on buildings which briefly describe their history where the word 'Chinese' has been scratched out wherever it occurred.

Who are the present day pilgrims to E1 Pueblo? Certainly the Chinese and the Italians who have formed groups of 'Friends' to record and preserve their heritage. Others are the people who come to look up their roots in the birth, marriage and burial records at the Plaza church, and also the thousands of worshippers at the church on Sundays who traditionally stroll along Olvera Street after Mass. Another group is Los Pobladores 200, whose members must all be descended from the settlers who originally founded the pueblo in 1781. Over 200 of them came forward at the time of Los Angeles's bicentennial in 1981, and every year on the first Monday in September they re-enact the founding of the pueblo by walking nine miles from Mission San Gabriel to the Plaza where they are welcomed by city officials and actors dressed as historic personages from Los Angeles' history and an appreciative audience. Recently, too, a group of Mexican/Latino people, many of whom are academics involved with the history and culture of Mexican Los Angeles, and another group of people who are concerned with the Spanish heritage of the city, have formed organisations at El Pueblo.

Others include teachers who bring their history, or historic preservation classes to El Pueblo because of the spiritual experience it provides as the only place that represents the founding of Los Angeles, even though it is not the original site as nobody knows where that was. It is the closest thing the city has to a historic heart. What distinguishes all these people as pilgrims is the degree of their passionate concern about El Pueblo, or some facet of it.

Often spiritual issues are tied to political issues, and El Pueblo is deeply enmeshed in political issues. Many of the civic leaders also feel strongly about El Pueblo, but for different reasons. Some care more about the predominance of the Mexican culture as reflected in the Monument's traditions and events; others are interested in the actual history of the buildings and in that of all the ethnic groups which have been involved over the years. Still others are concerned about the accurate preservation and restoration of the buildings. The current and proposed uses of the buildings do not always reflect their history.

Whether or not alternative new uses can be found for the buildings which reflect their history remains unknown, at least an effort should be made to find something suitable for what has been determined as the prime period of each building. An example might be the Pico House, mentioned earlier, of which the prime period has been determined as 1875–6. At that time the hotel boasted a French restaurant with French chefs and menus printed in French. The plan has been to reinstall a French restaurant in the hotel. This caused an outcry among some of the community who were not aware of the actual history of the building.

If a French restaurant is ultimately to be installed in the Pico House, some effective public relations efforts will be needed to explain why it is important to tell the history as it happened. This will depend to some degree on how the management of the Monument sees fit to interpret the history. But this may not be easy. In addition to the Commission and the staff, other players who could have influence over decisions made at El Pueblo, include the Mayor and the Los Angeles City Council and the California State Office of Historic Preservation. The latter has an interest 'in perpetuity' in buildings for which El Pueblo has at any time received a grant of financial aid. Other interested bodies include the City's Cultural Heritage and Cultural Affairs Commissions and concerned community groups.

Other myths that have been perpetuated at El Pueblo include the fate of the Simpson Jones Building, which was originally built in 1894 as the home of Moline Automobile Engines, and then of Gregory Engines (selling farm equipment) and later the Soo Chow Restaurant (selling Chinese food). The building also housed the Diamond Shirt Company. In 1959, the Simpson Jones Building was altered to look like a Mexican banco, and a plaque on the wall outside proclaims that this was the 'first unit completed' at El Pueblo de Los Angeles. Next door is a Mexican restaurant where women are seen hand-shaping the tortillas used in the meals. Neither a Mexican banco nor a Mexican restaurant were ever tenants of this building, so the impression that this is an authentic historic restoration is inaccurate at best. These activities have more to do with the perception of Olvera Street as a Mexican marketplace.

Another interesting case is the basements under the Pico and Garnier Blocks on the south side of the Plaza. A tunnel was dug under the street between the two blocks in the 1960s to provide service access from Los Angeles Street to the Pico House. This tunnel connected the basements under the Merced Theatre, built in 1870, and those under the Garnier Building, constructed in 1890. But stories keep surfacing in the press about the 'historic catacombs' under these buildings. The legend is that the oppressed Chinese would move from building to building underground, and would go by tunnel all the way to Union Station to escape their persecutors. Neither did it matter that the connecting tunnel was only constructed in the late 1960s, nor that Union Station was not completed until 1939, and that there is a fairly steep slope from the Plaza down to the site of Union Station, so that in wet weather any tunnels would have filled with water.

Catacombs are generally thought to be historic burial places, but the Chinese did not bury anyone in these basements, preferring to send the bones of their dead ancestors back to China for burial or to inter them in a cemetery in East Los Angeles. Despite the fact that these are not catacombs, visitors are eager to see the basements and when they do, they often come away disappointed. Should we perhaps create interesting displays in the basements and make something exciting where previously nothing existed? The problem is that, even if things did in fact happen, we have no knowledge of them.

An interesting change of attitudes at El Pueblo has been caused by a 18 by 80 feet mural named *America Tropical*, painted on the Italian Hall in 1932 by David Alfaro Siqueiros, who, along with Jose Clement Orozco and Diego Rivera is regarded as one of the three great Mexican muralists. When it was unveiled, its subject matter caused immediate controversy. The title might suggest a man in a large hat sitting under a palm tree waiting for the dates to drop in his lap. Instead, Siqueiros said that he had painted an Indian peon crucified on a double cross above which 'the eagle of the American gold coin' stretched out its talons. Behind them was a Mayan temple, a huge twisting tree, two sharp-shooters aiming at the eagle and other symbolic characters. The artist's six months visa was not renewed. He was deported and the portion of the mural that was visible from Olvera Street was whitewashed. A few years later the whole mural was painted over.

This mural did not fit in with the theme of Olvera Street, where the impression that leaders wanted visitors to receive was one reflecting what were believed to have been the halcyon days of the Dons when fiestas and fandangos continually took place. In 1977, the mural began to emerge from under its whitewash thanks to the fierce sun, wind and rain on the south-facing wall where it was painted. Although faded and deteriorated, it is now regarded as a symbol of Mexican American pride, and as an internationally significant work of art. The Getty Conservation Institute is assisting with a multi-million dollar project to conserve the mural, build a protective shelter and install state of the art exhibits to interpret its story to the public.

When this major project is fully funded and its various phases are accomplished, it will tremendously increase tourism to the Monument and thereby improve the economic situation at Olvera Street. If it is also possible to bring a good development project to on the south side of the

Plaza, and the seven buildings there are restored and opened to the public, then the whole tourist picture will improve dramatically.

That said, it is essential for the Monument's administration to be aware that El Pueblo's most important attribute is its history. There is an urgent need for an imaginative and creative vision to ensure that the Monument will fulfill its extraordinary potential. The way to do this is not only to restore the buildings with integrity and skill, but also to interpret the history to reflect its varied and multi-ethnic past by developing a good interpretive programme enhanced by really outstanding exhibits. When this happens, we will be able to attract a far wider range of visitors who are looking for a deeper educational and historical experience.

As may be appreciated, working at El Pueblo may not be easy, but it is always interesting. Among the many lessons I have learnt there, the following are the most important:

1. historical knowledge of a place goes beyond the place itself and the people who live there, and extends to knowing something about the individual cultures and places the people belonged to before they arrived;
2. our vision of history is governed by more than facts, and it should be remembered that perceptions of the past change over time;
3. a multicultural environment means many masters, it demands an inclusive rather than exclusive approach, and requires political sensitivity;
4. a varying mixture of authenticity and creativity is required to give life to interpretive programmes;
5. you cannot always rely on the public purse, and profitable commercial development is often necessary to provide the necessary funds for conservation work.

The Author

Jean Bruce Poole was appointed Historic Museum Director for El Pueblo de Los Angeles Historical Monument in 1992, following long service as the Monument's Senior Curator. She is head of the El Pueblo History division and museum programmes, and is very involved with historic restoration and research projects. She is also actively working with the Getty Conservation Institute on the conservation of *America Tropical*, a mural painted by David Alfaro Siquerios. She previously served for five years as Southern California director of the California Historical Society, and taught a graduate class in historic preservation at UCLA from 1980–82. A co-author of the Historic

Structures Reports on the Plaza Substation and the Italian Hall at El Pueblo and co-editor of *A Guide to Historic Places in Los Angeles County*, she is currently completing a book on the history of the buildings and sites at El Pueblo. In recognition of her outstanding contribution, she recently received awards from the California Historical Society and the Historical Society of Southern California.

References

Bancroft, H.H., *History of California*, 7 vols. Santa Barbara, Wallace Hubbard,1996

Beilharz, E.A., *Felipe de Neve, First Governor of California*, San Francisco: California Historical Society, 1971

Cleland, R.G., *The Cattle on a Thousand Hills*, San Marino, Huntington Library, 1969

Davis, M., *City of Quartz: Excavating the Future in Los Angeles*, Los Angeles: Verso Publications, 1990

Griswold del Castillo, R., *The Los Angeles Barrio, 1850–1890: A Social History*, Berkeley

Harlow, N., *California Conquered: War and Peace on the Pacific, 1846–1850*, Berkeley and Los Angeles, University of California Press, 1982

McWilliams, C., *Southern California: An Island on the Land*, Salt Lake City, Gibbs M. Smith, Inc., Peregrine Books, 1993

Newmark, H., *Sixty Years in Southern California*, Los Angeles: Zeitlin and Verbrugger, 1970

Owen, T., The Church by the Plaza, *Quartely of the Historical Society of Southern California*, XLI, March/June 1960

Sterling, C., *Olvera Street, its History and Restoration*, June Sterling Park, Long Beach, 1947

Treutlein, T.E., *Los Angeles, The Question of the City's Original Spanish Name*, *Southern California Quartely*, LIII, Sept. 1971

The mural called 'America Tropical', painted on the Italian Hall by David Alfaro Siqueiros in 1932.

19

RELIGIOUS LIFE AND ART
St Mungo Museum in Glasgow

Harry Dunlop

There are three topics of conversation which tend to be banned from family gatherings in Glasgow: politics, religion and football. Given that religion is indeed a difficult subject to discuss owing to the passions it arouses, it is not surprising that most museums tend to shun the subject. Although there are great museums around the world full of religious objects, these tend to be interpreted from an art historical perspective or are sometimes dismissed as exotic fetishes, however religion, cannot be ignored and is crucial when considering the nature of human society and how people throughout time have tried to make sense of their lives. The St Mungo Museum is an attempt to do just this.

The St Mungo Museum of Religious Life and Art opened on 1 April 1993. The building was not designed as a museum, but was erected by the Society of Friends of Glasgow Cathedral as a visitor centre, for those wishing to explore the history of the cathedral and make use of much needed facilities including toilets, café and, of course, the all important gift shop. The project was financed by the Society of Friends of the Glasgow Cathedral, The Scottish Tourist Board, Glasgow Development Agency and the European Regional Development Fund, Glasgow City Council and many individual and corporate sponsors.

The building, designed by Scottish architect Ian Begg in the Scottish Baronial style, may please the tastes of the Prince of Wales who laid the foundation stone, but more locally is referred to by taxi drivers as 'Weetabix castle' because of the bran-coloured stonework. In 1990, the building was taken over by Glasgow City Council, when the project ran into financial difficulties. The Council provided cash for the completion of the building and paid off debts incurred by the Society of Friends.

The Director of Museums agreed to take on the management of the building, and various ideas were suggested for an appropriate subject in such an historic and sensitive site. One was a museum of medieval world drawings on the reserve collections of the Burrell Collection. This gave birth to the suggestion of a museum, which would not only examine medieval Christianity, but would also look at the importance of religion in people's lives across the world and across time. In a city which has a history of religious sectarianism, this idea seemed wholly appropriate and aimed at fostering mutual understanding and respect between people of different faiths and of none.

The museum stands beside the medieval Cathedral Church of St Mungo, Patron Saint of Glasgow, in the heart of the old city. It draws around 150,000 visitors a year, a large proportion of whom are European tourists. The present cathedral, dating from the early 13th century, is used by the Church of Scotland for Presbyterian worship, although the actual building is Crown property and maintained by Historic Scotland. The cathedral was built on the traditional burial site of St Mungo, situated in the magnificent Lower Church of the cathedral. With its forest of Gothic columns and vaults, the early 13th century Lower Church is for many tourists the highlight of their visit. Most of the nave dates from the 14th century in a simpler style of Gothic, probably as a result of money shortages during the time of the Scottish War of Independence.

St Mungo also known as Kentigern, was probably born on the east coast near Culross in Fife in the 6th century. He established a monastic settlement on what is now the site of the present cathedral, and is believed to have been the first Bishop of Glasgow. As his 'Life' was written hundreds of years after his death, it is very difficult to separate fact from fiction, although there are many beautiful legends about his miracles and monastic journeys. However, the legend of his mother is not so pretty. St Thenew or St Enoch is described as the daughter of King Loth of the Lothians who was raped and cast adrift into the Firth of Forth in a small coracle without any oars. The little boat was miraculously guided across the river by seals and landed at Culross where she gave birth to St Mungo on the shore. They were rescued by monks from a nearby monastic community and St Mungo was raised in the monastery under the guidance of St Serf, abbot of the community. Some of the emblems on the City Coat of Arms relate to miracles performed by the young saint during his time in the monastery.

St Mungo's tomb lay directly below the High Altar of the early 13th century choir and sanctuary above, and became a focus of pilgrimage. In the Middle Ages, St Mungo's relics were exhumed and placed in a silver shrine behind the high altar which became a focus of pilgrimage. Pilgrims to the shrine, to which the Pope later attached indulgences, included Edward I who left an offering of candle wax to be burnt at the saint's tomb. The shrine and other 'relicks of popery' were of course swept away by the Protestant Reformation in the 16th century, but happily the building remained intact.

Only the Cathedral and Provand's Lordship, a 15th century prebendal manse, remains of the pre-reformation precinct. In the 19th century, the political, educational and commercial centre of the city move westwards leaving the cathedral in isolation. Indeed, the principal reason behind the visitor centre proposal was to encourage tourists to visit the cathedral as part of a multi-million pound re-landscaping of the area by the architects Page and Park. The museum itself is built on the site of the Bishop's Castle or Palace which was begun in the 13th century. The castle, which was in a ruinous state by the late 18th century was eventually demolished in the 1790s to make way for the neighbouring infirmary.

The cathedral precinct is dominated by the necropolis, a large graveyard lined with grand tombs and monuments reflecting the wealth of the city in the 19th century. A large statue of John Knox, at the top of the hill, pre-dates it and was erected in the 1820s, possibly as a symbol of local Protestant resistance to the proposed Catholic Emancipation Bill of 1829.

Glasgow is a city of diverse religious traditions with a history of religious intolerance. This makes the museum all the more relevant to the life of the city. As well as targeting tourists to the cathedral, the museum was aimed at reflecting the religion of local people to create a feeling of local ownership of the displays. Importantly, the museum also includes references to sectarianism as an issue which has been part of the history and identity of the city for some time. Since the 1870s, the city has grown into a multi-cultural, multi-faith city with Jews, Muslims, Hindus and Sikhs opening their own places of worship.

These groups are represented in the museum, not only in the Religious Life gallery but also in the Scottish Gallery where we highlight Glasgow as a city of many faiths and traditions which shocks some of our visitors who would rather see only Christianity represented in a 'Scottish' context. The museum is divided into four main galleries: the Gallery of Religious Art, the Religious Life Gallery, Scottish Gallery and a temporary exhibition space.

The art gallery contains beautiful religious works carefully chosen to reflect something of the meaning of the religious faiths which inspired their creation. This was designed as a quiet reflective space which allows people to explore the objects and their meaning, and more importantly what they mean to them. For example, Salvador Dali's 'Christ of St John of the Cross' purchased by the city in 1951 was chosen to represent

Christianity, reflecting as it does, the centrality of the crucifixion in the story of salvation.

Most of the objects come from our permanent collection, but some pieces were specially purchased in areas where objects were lacking. The large imposing figure of Shiva Nataraja, the Lord of the Dance was specially purchased to represent Hinduism, but unfortunately suffered damage in May 1993 from a Christian visitor who managed to topple the huge bronze sculpture. Both Shiva and Dali's painting, damaged twice in the past, sadly bear the scars of a city divided by religion.

Leading from the Art Gallery is the gallery of Religious Life. Various ideas where discussed concerning how this gallery should be approached. Our original ideas were object-centred and revolved around a set of themes including 'holy books' and 'altar equipment'. These ideas were felt to be to cold, uninspiring and failed to communicate the more human aspects of belief and practice. Instead, we decided to explore the importance of religion in the human life cycle from birth to death, across the world and time. This allowed us to bring together a wider variety of material to provoke discussion.

The objects in this gallery range from high quality works of art to everyday objects used by people in their devotions. A plastic shrine clock in the shape of the Lourdes Grotto purchased from a Glasgow market might be aesthetically repellent for some people, but for others it is a way of communicating with the sacred and reminding them of their faith and identity. This clock incidentally chimes the 'Ave' at 18.00hrs which we felt could be the ultimate museum interactive.

Another important aspect of this approach was the inclusion of oral testimony from people of different faiths and opinions. These are included in audio-hand-set form and in written quotes inside the displays. These injections of human emotion, ranging from stories of tragic death to one woman who hopes that there is no smoking in heaven, allow people to empathise with the issues being raised in a deeply personal way.

Another aspect of this gallery are six individual displays which look at particular religions in more depth. These are Buddhism, Christianity, Hinduism, Islam, Judaism and Sikhism, commonly regarded as the world's major religions. Here we bring together a range of objects, photos and quotations to communicate to our visitors the essence of each particular belief system. All of the displays are introduced by a key statement which aims to communicate their meaning. These are presented in Urdu, Punjabi, Gaelic and Chinese: the main languages other than English spoken in Glasgow.

As most people have an opinion on religious issues, both the Religious Life Gallery and the Scottish Gallery have 'talk-back' boards, designed so that visitors can add their own opinion to the displays. These have proved extremely successful and visitors love having a good read and an argument with each other.

The Scottish Gallery on the third floor looks at the importance of religion in the culture of the west coast of Scotland. The displays are thematic rather than chronologically lead, because of a shortage of material to represent the pre-reformation period, and analyse issues which we felt communicated the main characteristics of religious development in the area ranging from the past to the present, including, sectarianism, charity, missionaries and immigration. The gallery is probably the most disappointing for visitors in terms of content, many feeling that not enough emphasis is paid to the unique role of Protestant Christianity in the realms of education and social responsibility. Since opening, we have been in dialogue with representatives from various groups to improve this space, adding more information panels and possibly in the future changing some of the displays.

Outside this gallery are displays which provide visitors with information about the history of the site, the cathedral and of course St Mungo. This area also provides a panoramic view over the cathedral and necropolis and the Zen garden in the ground below. This was designed by a group of professional Japanese Zen gardeners, and is meant to communicate aspects of Buddhism, and the interrelationship between human beings and the beauty of the natural world in which we live.

The minister of the cathedral, Dr William Morris said to me that, although the collapse of the visitor centre idea came as a bitter blow, he is now of the opinion that God had other purposes in mind. The museum, standing beside Glasgow's oldest religious building, reminds visitors why the cathedral was built in the first place and provides a context for exploring its wider history and religious significance. It is our hope that local people and tourists visiting the museum leave with a greater understanding of the importance of religion in people's life, and with a lasting spirit of respect and understanding for different cultural beliefs and practices.

The Author

Harry Dunlop read history and sociology at the University of Glasgow, specialising in social anthropology and medieval religion and undertook postgraduate studies in museology at the University of Leicester. He was appointed curator of the St Mungo Museum of Religious Life and Art in 1989, following a varied career engaged in research and development work associated with museums. This included projects on politics and poverty in Glasgow and 'Glasgow's Good News' at the People's Palace. He has won various awards for his work, including the Scottish Museum of the Year, and is a popular contributor to conferences and publications.

Further Reading

The Lives of Ninian and Kentigern, Llanerach Enterprises, 1989
Dunlop H., Carnegie L. and Lovelace A., *The St Mungo Museum of Religious Life and Art*, Journal of Museum Ethnography no.7, 1995
The St Mungo Museum of Religious Life and Art, Chambers, 1993

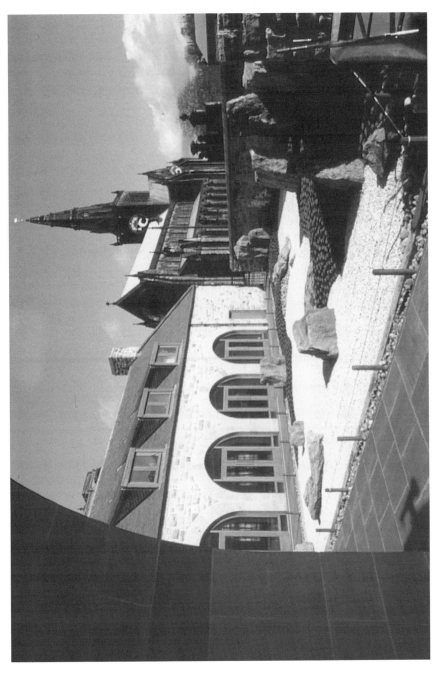

Courtyard at the St Mungo Museum with Glasgow Cathedral in the background.

MUSEUM OF NEW ZEALAND TE PAPA TONGAREWA

20

A MUSEUM CHALLENGE
The Iconography of New Zealand

William Tramposch

The anthropologist Robert Redfield once observed that it is often those newest to a culture who are best able to describe it.[1] We see such instances of this in the writings of many early visitors to the colonies of America in the 18th and 19th Century, *Democracy in America* by Alexis de Tocqueville being perhaps the most well known of them all. Being fresh-landed in a culture does enable one to observe and delineate the differences between home and away in ways that often surprise those who have lived in the 'away' for years. Since my arrival in New Zealand, I have been very interested in those aspects of culture here that are revered by kiwis, specifically those places that are pregnant with symbolic as well as real value for those who dwell here. In short the places to which one journeys for sacred or other kinds of intrinsic edification. As Director of Museum Resources, at the soon-to-be opened National Museum of New Zealand Te Papa Tongarewa, I too have a professional interest in such matters. Our department oversees the Museum's extensive collections and the scholarship that underpins the interpretations of these treasures.

Many of Europe's central places of pilgrimage are well known to most of the world: The Vatican, Canterbury Cathedral, Notre Dame, The Louvre, The Eiffel Tower, etc. Even the United States, though a much younger country, has quite a galaxy of places of pilgrimage. Usually these are monuments of a less religious and more political nature: Independence Hall, Mount Rushmore, Vernon, Monticello, The Alamo, Wounded Knee, to name out a few. Many of America's icons are also museums or public parks like Colonial Williamsburg, Mount. Rushmore, the Grand Canyon etc.

271

The symbolic power of place struck me when I worked for The Colonial Williamsburg Foundation in Virginia. Williamsburg was the capital of the colony of Virginia. Today, this restored 18th century city plays host to almost one million visitors a year. It is America's largest outdoor history museum, and the centrepiece of this restored city is the reconstructed Royal Governor's Palace surrounded by acres of gardens. Walking through these gardens one afternoon, I noticed quite a concerned-looking man with a box under his arm. He wandered from one flower bed to the next, and his behaviour led me to approach him to see if I could help. While first hesitating to talk with me, he at last confided that it had been his mother's last wish to have her ashes spread somewhere within the gardens of Williamsburg's Royal Governor's Palace. Shyly, he asked if I knew of any policy that would preclude him from carrying out such a wish. Had there been such a policy, I said, it had no right existing, and with our blessings he spread the contents of his sacred parcel amidst the blooms.

Thereafter, whenever I walked the grounds of Williamsburg, or those of any other shrine for that matter, this story returns as a reminder of the hold that such places can have on our imaginations. How powerful are some places in our national souls. The Alamo, for example, is another such place in the landscape of America's culture and myth. This mission-fortress is the most thoroughly recreated shrine, where Davey Crockett made his last patriotic stand against (we are told) Mexican aggression.

Visitors to the Alamo are not asked but told, that if they must speak at all to speak in hushed tones. Here, hats must come off in respect for those gallant Americans (Texans and others actually) who died here in the name of 'democracy' (really manifest destin). History's interpretation may be revised, but neither change nor the years are seen to dim the ever growing significance of such shrines. Such iconographic places are by their nature open to various interpretations, but regardless of any such interpretation, each is a place of pilgrimage and safe harbour for the visitor's deep affections. Even Elvis's Graceland secures a place among America's most revered places as Paul Simon explains:

> The Mississippi Delta was shining,
> Like a National guitar,
> I am following the river,
> Down the highway,
> Through the cradle of the Civil War.
> I'm going to Graceland,
> Graceland,
> In Memphis, Tennessee,
> I'm going to Graceland,

Poorboys and Pilgrims with families,
And we are going to Graceland.

Collecting items of real and symbolic significance is at the heart of a museum's work. Half a world away from Williamsburg and the Mother Country, the new Museum of New Zealand Te Papa Tongarewa (Te Papa) is actively engaged in selecting, collecting and interpreting the symbols of an Oceanic culture. It is a young culture by comparison, but it is a culture that has grown very quickly. Captain James Cook was just sighting these South Pacific islands when the American colonies were in the midst of demanding repeal of the Stamp Act, and when talk of revolutions was in the air. By his third visit just eight years later, the American colonies had separated from England. The Maoris that Cook met in his explorations had not been there long by European standards either, having arrived at about the time the mortar was setting at Westminster Abby.

Surely no built icons like England's Westminster grace the landscape of Aotearoa New Zealand, so what then does such a relatively recent culture tend to adopt as its cultural symbols? Early Maori buildings were impermanent and none survive from the days of the first encounter and these structures built by the first mid-19th century settlers from England and France were not much more permanent. Thus, there is little in New Zealand's built environment that can serve as significant places of pilgrimage. What is it then, that kiwis revere and, they themselves, tend towards when they 'longen to go on pilgrimage'. More importantly, what do these icons suggest about New Zealanders? To this newcomer there seem to be at least four key places in the hearts of New Zealanders, and each place contributes to an understanding of the country's unique national identity. These thoughts have been verified by countless kiwis during the last several months. Most agree thoroughly with the choices listed below; and most appreciate the fact that these places of pilgrimage, when considered together, make New Zealand culture unique. Not surprisingly, each of these real yet symbolic places finds a substantial home within Te Papa. These are The Great OE, The Bush, The Marae, and Home. However, Before beginning a discussion of each of these places in the heart, it is necessary to introduce the key concepts of Te Papa.

OF WAKAS AND WAHAROAS

The concept of 'journey' is central to an understanding New Zealand's cultural identity. Remarkably, the first Maori settlers arrived in canoes (waka) following a 1,000 mile voyage from the north, almost one thousand years ago. The various hapu (tribes), though impressively consistent in the use of language and tradition, were quite war-like and the need for protection influenced settlement patterns markedly. The connection to ancestors is so strong that today's Maori often recite their pepeha (family history) right back to the first canoe on which the forebears travelled. Neither the importance of the journey nor the whakapapa (genealogical table) can be overestimated among today's Maori. Their place in this lineage is their place to stand.

The 'journey' is also a very important concept for the cultures that came to New Zealand from England and elsewhere. Even today, many modern 'Pakeha' (until recently, chiefly English immigrants) recite the story of their emigration from 'home' to an antipodean clime. Oftentimes, the home that they left behind is romanticised through the story's telling, and this is a topic of discussion later in this paper.

Similarly, 'journey' is also a concept at the geological bedrock of this island culture. Only one hundred and thirty million years ago (young in geological terms), New Zealand was just a part of a major land mass which is today referred to as Gondwana Land, while only eighty million years ago these islands broke away from this super-continent to drift continually east. Even today, New Zealand continues to move inexorably east across the Pacific Earthquakes,[2] volcanoes, and persistent winds all serve to remind, Maori and Pakeha alike, that their country is very much still in the making, still journeying.

The Museum of New Zealand Te Papa Tongarewa seems more a part of this national journey more than it does a museum. When opened, it is to be a 'forum for the nation' to discuss its developing and independent identity. Exhibits and programmes will focus on the journeys that all New Zealand residents and their landscapes have been making and continue to make. The chief concept of the museum will be that of 'waharoa' (a Maori term meaning gateway) into which, and out of which come and go the thoughts and people that make a culture.[3] It follows that this purpose-built 36,000 square metre building will only be part of what the nation will come to consider 'its museum'. This place will also 'reach out beyond its walls', as the concept document states, to the Marae (meeting grounds of the Maori), to schools, to homes and to other museums throughout the country. The new museum will open in February of 1998 on the waterfront of Wellington, the nation's capital city. As this paper describes the four places of pilgrimages mentioned above, it will also strive to describe how these places in the nation's soul will be highlighted in the Museum.

THE GREAT OE

A recent Air New Zealand advertisement claims the company to be 'airline of the world's greatest travellers'. The high value placed upon journeys, coupled with thoughts of England traditionally have led thousands of New Zealanders back to their roots. For many New Zealanders, a return to England, is considered an integral part of one's upbringing and education, and trips back to the homeland can be positively medieval in length, tending to last many months if not years. With each successive generation, though, the 'home' about which parents have talked becomes more and more of an abstract notion. Today, home for an increasing number of kiwis is simply where they have been living all of their lives, New Zealand. Thus, the need to return to a place that was never truly intimate to their experiences decreases with each successive generation. What England does have to offer many kiwis, however, is a chance to advance their talents and education conveniently within the Commonwealth system. Many modern New Zealanders travel abroad for the simple reasons of gaining valuable experience in business or of enhancing their cultural educations. The accountancy firm, Peat Marwick, insists that its young executives leave the New Zealand offices, if they ever expect to be promoted, emphasising that the overseas experience will be an invaluable component to their advancement. In short, 'overseas experience' (OE) broadens skills as well as provides young kiwis with the opportunity to visit the places that serve as cultural icons in their English heritage. But with the growth of multiculturalism and national identity, the importance of this experience naturally diminishes.

Even so, the importance of symbolic connections to the homeland is apparent on almost a daily basis at Te Papa. The press often seizes upon the opportunity to point out the risk inherent in the Museum undervaluing the country's English heritage when developing future exhibitions. They fear instead that the emphasis on New Zealand or, worse, Maori culture might be 'overemphasised', whatever that may mean. A recent cartoon featured a couple walking by the new museum site. Spotting a tiny outhouse on the construction site of this huge museum, the woman said to the man: 'I suspect that is where they will be putting all of their European art'. One collection of colonial period furniture, the Elgar Collection, will not be shown (as it has been) in its entirety. Consequently, the press coverage insists that the Museum is overlooking a very important aspect of it the country's heritage, implying that most New Zealanders left households replete with such fine furnishings. While the criticism is valid, the suggestion is not to forget English heritage, and the remarks are more than slightly tinged by a romanticism of the past run wild.

The gradual separating from English tradition, which is occurring in New Zealand, is somewhat reminiscent of the pulling-away that occurred during the so-called 'American Renaissance'.[4] Writers and artists began to realise the importance of the native themes available in their new abode, yet most were still unwilling to separate completely from the Mother Land. New Zealand arts and culture have tended to increasingly demonstrate a startling uniqueness that comes from biculturalism and life in a strikingly different world from that represented by the past. More importantly, the people of New Zealand are beginning to realise the particular significance of their cultural contributions to the world as evidenced by rapidly increasing art prices and the growth of international loans and exhibits of New Zealand art.

Not coincidentally, Te Papa is serving as a place for the expression of national identity in the making. Realising that national identity is emerging more and more confidentially each year, the Museum takes its role as a forum for these discussions quite seriously. Several major programmes and exhibits will feature the distinctive styles that characterise the visual arts in New Zealand, while a special exhibit will focus on the central article of government, the unratified Treaty of Waitangi which was written by English (Pakeha) and signed by many Maori 156 years ago. The treaty is under constant reinterpretation, and it sits at the roots of most of the modern conflict between Maori and Pakeha. Admirably, the Museum takes its responsibility as a forum for such national debates very seriously indeed and is developing a most provocative exhibit as a result. Yet another exhibit (with the working title, 'Exhibiting Ourselves') will interpret the ways in which New Zealand has chosen to represent itself more independently to the world. Such interpretations will help kiwis to draw comparisons of national self-identity over the ages.

Yet, even with these several key exhibits that are intent on interpreting national identity, the Museum is careful to afford ample space for the exhibition of European cultures. Such special exhibits are always of great interest to New Zealanders. *The Queens Pictures* exhibition, featured paintings from The Queen's Picture Gallery at Buckingham Palace, was among the most popular programmes ever offered by the Museum, in spite of the fact that the crowds gathering to see the Queen diminish greatly with each successive visit.

THE BUSH

While Air New Zealand might claim to serve 'the world's greatest travellers', increasingly the world is traveling to New Zealand because of its singular natural beauty. The overseas visitation to these islands has increased 15 percent in the past year and more than doubled in the past decade. Airports, once ample for the numbers travelling, are now groaning under the weight of visitors. Both Auckland and Wellington are currently expanding their facilities radically. The New Zealand landscape is not only the focus of interest for overseas travellers, it has also been of greatly increasing interest to those who dwell there. It is clearly the most common place of pilgrimage in this country that has few ancient landmarks. On any given weekend, regardless of the weather, the footpaths of most reserves are well-worn by New Zealand families out for a 'tramp'.

The natural history of the country is unique in the world. Having serparated so early from Gondwana Land, the islands carried with them many forms of plant and animal life that were present when dinosaurs roamed the earth. The Tuatara, for example, is one of the most ancient lizards on the face of the earth; while tree ferns still common today, once stood eye high to these prehistoric creatures. So fiercely protected are these environments today that the penalties for illegal importation of animals and agricultural goods are quite severe. Pets remain in quarrantine for six months, and camping gear is confiscated at the border unless proof of a recent cleaning is presented. Travellers, in fact, are sprayed inconspicuously with an insecticide as powerful as Black Flag prior to getting off the plane, a process that was far more obvious to visitors in the 1980s as flight attendants walked awkwardly up and down the aisles with a spray can in each hand.

Although the means of environmental protection might seem quite severe, no one can argue with the ends. Thusfar the country has kept such dreaded diseases like rabies from its doorstep, and the rates of native animal extinction have been slowed dramatically during the past several decades. In turn, the world and New Zealanders are becoming increasingly aware of the treasures they have in this distinct landscape with ancient lizards, rare flightless birds like the kiwi, expansive bush tracks and fiords. The waiting list to take South Island walks like the famous Milford Track is up to seven months long.

Writing of the importance of the bush in kiwi life is an effort bound to fail here. Its depths and particular gifts must be experienced at first hand. One need only hear the sound of the rare Kokako or the night cry of the kiwi or Blue Penquin to realise the near-spiritual significance that these places have for New Zealanders. The bush is where most choose to go when they seek 'recreation', it is a central focus of pilgrimage for this nation, and it is all around. Even the capital city of Wellington is surrounded by it.

So significant and symbolic is the bush to New Zealanders that the Museum will be bringing the outdoors inside. When visitors first enter the giant central core of the Museum in 1998, they will be greeted with extensive natural history exhibits featuring giant Nikau Palms grown hydroponically, and with abbreviated bush walks that take one from the alpine regions to the sea in a matter of minutes. In addition, a large adjacent, outdoor Harbour Park, accessible only from within the building, is being constructed and will include such items as swing bridges, hundreds of native trees, caving experiences, and a fossil dig. In yet another gallery, natural forces that have made, and continue to make New Zealand will be interpreted. The heat that makes volcanoes and earthquakes as well as the 'modifiers' like wind and rain, will be highlighted in very interactive exhibits. Finally, on the same floor, one of several 'dark' theme rides will carry one through a thoroughly researched prehistoric setting, interpreting the sights, sounds and smells one might have encountered when dinosaurs and giant Moas were afoot. The bush is a central icon in New Zealand culture and this is why it will receive such thorough attention as a centrepiece of the exhibits in the new Museum.

THE MARAE

Directly above the vast natural history exhibitions in the new Museum, will be a national 'Marae'. This is an enclosed ground or meeting place for Maori, but the Museum will be opening, with the help of the nation's tribes (Iwi), a Marae that will serve as a meeting place for the entire nation. This feature is at the heart of the 'forum' concept that is To Papa. In Maori and Te Papa culture, the Marae is a place of challenge, a place of worship, and a place for sharing deep emotions. It is the centrepoint of Maori life and the place where Maori are in closest contact with their whakapapa or heritage. It is their place of pilgrimage. The recent movie, *Once Were Warriors*, emphasises the importance of the Marae eloquently. It also stresses how adrift modern Maori society is without such connections to tradition and ancestors.

At any successful museum, teaching is not only didactic, it is also emotive. The Halocaust Museum in Washington D C, for example, teaches us in very emotional terms about our Jewish kin who for a short while succeeded us in this world. Here it is not uncommon to witness visitors in tears amidst the exhibits. Without reservation, Te Papa will stress our emotional ties to heritage and culture as well as our intellectual ones. The Marae will be central to this effort. It will be a very challenging and emotional place and unlike any other place in the museum world. One of the charges of the Museum is to 'change the perception people have of museums'. We intend the Marae to be a key factor in the achievement of this goal.

Adjacent to the Marae, will be the wing of the museum that features the central taonga (artefacts) of the Maori collection. Many of these pieces travelled with the *Te Maori* exhibition that toured the United States in the mid-1980s. Since the return of the taonga, there has been a renewed and reinvigorated interest in objects Maori, and the new museum concept was in no small part spawned during this period when enthusiasm about Maori heritage and legacies were at a peak. Since that time, Te Reo Maori (Maori language) has become an official language of New Zealand, and Maori scholarship has grown tremendously. In the midst of all of this interest and change, the Marae remains remarkably the same as it was in the 19th century. While the national Marae itself will serve as a forum for discussion and emotion concerning an emerging national identity, its strong institutional tradition will serve as a reminder of the consistency that is Te Maori. To succeed, it must be not only understood, but embraced as a place that will be central to the values of all New Zealanders, not just Maori. Only then will it be a place of pilgrimage for all visitiors, as it currently is for Maori life and culture.

A QUARTER ACRE OF PARADISE

Having described the OE, the Bush and the Marae, perhaps no single place serves more as a place of pilgrimage than one's own home. This, of course, is a central feature of many cultures, but in New Zealand it is carried with admirable extreme and to the degree of a practicated art form. Wellington freatures thousands of modest bungalows, tightly packed next to one another because of the steep hills surrounding the city and the limited amount of buildable land. Yet, despite the tight proximity of housing, most sections have been worked in such ways as to provide its owners the privacy of the bush, the retreat and protective value of the Marae, and the conveniences and culture of 'home'. Oftentime referred to as 'quarter-acre paradises', more money and time is spent in these domains than on overseas travel and bushwalks combined. Give a kiwi a fine weekend, and the garden gets preened, the lawn gets hoovered. If there is time, the house and its eves will also get a firm powerwashing. Owning and caring for such a property is held in very high regard indeed. Paying off the mortgage as soon as possible is considered a sign of even greater independence and self-identity.

These aspects of independence, self-reliance, and ingenuity figure quite prominently in New Zealand myth and culture. The notion that kiwis can fix anything with 'fencing wire', is so ingrained in the culture that even a modern computer company unwisely boasted that it could make computers with such methods, not a very persuasive sales pitch. Modest, but neat housing, very controlled gardens, and ingeniously planned privacy characterise New Zealand domestic life, and such qualities will figure clearly in the exhibits about New Zealand character, especially in an exhibit called 'Passports'. It interprets the making of a life in this new country, the setting-up of one's home, and how that effort contributes to an individual's and country's self-identity.

As an American now resident in New Zealand, it is very clear to me that the home is often a reverential space in this South Pacific country, and the quarter acre oftentimes serve as little daily reserves, or bush retreats, during the weekdays and often on fine weekends. If this were not so, why is working on one's quarter acre and improving such a constant focus for many? It is because it has this ritualistic quality about it, which is so important for the human spirit and its well-being.

CONCLUSION

Most New Zealanders will understate their emotional attachments to the land, to their Marae, or their homeland. Understatement is itself a national characteristic. But each of these places carries varying sacred values with it. Each is a place to which New Zealanders go on regular pilgrimages, and each is a place charged with symbolic and reverential meaning for its pilgrims. Because of their values, the Museum of New Zealand Te Papa Tongarewa has chosen each as a focus of some of its major exhibits. Together these four places in the hearts of kiwis help to make their culture distinctive and unique.

The Author

Dr William Tramposch is Director of Visitor Programmes and Services, and prior to that, Director of Museum Resources at the Museum of New Zealand Te Papa Tongarewa. He was formely President of the New York State Historical Association, Executive Director of the Oregon Historical Society, and a director at The Colonial Williamsburg Foundation in Virginia and Old Sturbridge Village in Massachusetts. He has served as Vice Chairman of the US National Committee for the International Council of Museums and held two Fulbright Fellowships to New Zealand. His special interests are in professional training and the educational role of museums and historical societies.

References

1. Redfield, R., *The Little Community: newpoints for the study of a human whole*, University of Chicago Press, Chicago, 1955
2. Bishop, N., *Natural History of New Zealand*, Hodder and Stoughton, Auckland, 1992
3. The Museum of New Zealand Te Papa Tongarewa, *Statement of Intent for the Financial years ending 30 June 1998*, Wellington, 1995
4. Matthiessen, F.O., *The American Rennaissance: art and expression in the age of Emerson and Whitman*, Oxford University Press, New York, 1941

'BYDAND'
THE GORDON HIGHLANDERS

FROM
BUCHAN to BURMA, St. CYRUS to CYPRUS
FORMARTINE to FRANCE, GARIOCH to GERMANY
KINCARDINE to KENYA, MAR to MARETH, MEARNS to MALAYA
STRATHISLA to SWAZILAND, ZETLAND to ZANZIBAR
IT'S
'A GORDON FOR ME'
Apply : Army Information Office, 36/40 Market Street, Aberdeen

Regimental recruitment poster from the 1960s, stressing local identity and the opportunity for overseas travel.

21

A REGIMENTAL SHRINE
The Gordon Highlanders Museum

Stuart Allan

So long as Mist rolls down the Ben
So long as Water runs down the Glen
Shall the Memory of the Brave Remain,
And be Health and Victory for ever
With the Lads of the Marquess of Huntly

> Translation of Gaelic toast used by the Gordon
> Highlanders

In common with Scotland's nine other regimental museums, the Gordon Highlanders Museum in Aberdeen deals as much in tradition and reputation as it does in the facts of history. In contrast to other history museums, and notwithstanding a developing and laudable social history approach in our regimental museums, it and its counterparts carry a heavy responsibility to commemorate and to celebrate their subject: an obligation which rather weighs against dispassionate, balanced analysis and interpretation of the historical processes and contexts in which the regiments developed. For all that, the Gordon Highlanders Museum seeks, both for altruistic and commercial reasons, to educate and entertain the widest possible audience, it remains essentially a place of homage, both for the local visitors to whom it presents itself as a focus of communal pride, and for the tourist visitors who seek to connect with the cultural inheritance, often a family inheritance, which the museum represents to them.

This initial assessment is by no means intended as a criticism. By their very nature, regimental museums belong to their parent regiments, drawing their financial support from private regimental funds and from the Ministry of Defence. It would be curious indeed, to find a regiment not in the business of self-promotion. Formed from collections amassed over decades by regimental officers for the adornment of their mess rooms, the museums were first conceived as a focus of pride for the use of the regiments themselves, to foster regimental identity and to impress guests.

From this inward looking beginning the focus gradually turned out towards the general public, as the Ministry of Defence recognised the regimental museums' utility for public relations and recruitment purposes (Wood, 1993, 271–273). Present day Ministry of Defence policy requires regimental and corps museums to 'make the public aware of the regiments and corps, their roles and achievements thereby contributing to the projection of a positive image of the Army' (Ministry of Defence, 1998). In this respect, the role of regimental museums, and the historical interpretation presented there, might be likened to the historic family house or the whisky distillery visitor centre, both telling a celebratory story and, certainly in the latter case, promoting a product in the present day.

Much as published regimental histories tend to approach the history of a unit in isolation from the external forces shaping its experiences, and seek (perhaps subconsciously) to show the subject regiment in the best possible light, so traditional interpretation in regimental museums takes as read much of what is commonplace in service life, in order to concentrate on the extra-ordinary in the regiment's story, on its feats in battle, on deeds of individual heroism, on great commanders and memorable 'characters'. In victory the regiment is magnificent, though war itself is not necessarily glamorised and a sense of the personal cost is present; in defeat the regiment is indomitable and acts of defiant gallantry and sacrifice predominate the story (Thwaites, 1996, 150).

In recent years, much soul searching within, and on behalf of, military museums has tended to deem this traditional approach, with its inherent concepts of glory, pride and the romance of war, to be outdated, inferring that in order to remain relevant and attract new audiences, interpretation in regimental museums should instead concentrate on the social aspects of military history, examining the day to day lives of those who served (Wilkinson & Hughes, 1991). In the late 1990s, in the wake of acute defence budget cuts and consequent reduction in Ministry of Defence funding for museums, relevance and new audiences might well become a matter of survival for many. However, the experience of the Gordon Highlanders Museum since 1994 suggests that, with some adjustment and improvement, the traditional regimental museum can sustain and develop a role as a cultural attraction not only while retaining its shrine-like quality but, what is more, by deliberately emphasising it.

Survival was certainly much in the minds of the museum's governing regimental trustees when, in 1994, the regiment itself fell to amalgamation in a reduced British Army, shrunk by the government's 'Options for Change' defence review. With the Ministry of Defence unwilling to support two regimental museums for the new regiment created by amalgamation, The Highlanders (Seaforth, Gordons and Camerons), it was only by virtue of a highly successful public fundraising campaign organised by the trustees (some £1.3 million raised, including a Heritage Lottery Fund grant) that the museum was able to survive and develop as a financially independent concern with charitable trust status.

The funds raised allowed the creation of a new museum, extended on its original site, with facilities which other regimental museums would be hard pressed to match. In addition to new exhibitions, these include an audio-visual/conference room, tea room, gift shop, gardens, toilets, collection stores and offices. Uniquely among Scotland's regimental museums, the trustees employ a professional curator, supported by a small staff, and the museum operates by virtue of the involvement of a remarkably large number of highly motivated, unpaid volunteers.

As it must rely heavily on income from visitors for its survival, the museum necessarily seeks to maximise its appeal in a way not yet incumbent upon equivalent museums elsewhere in Scotland still in receipt of core public funding. These are, in some cases, located within historic properties (Edinburgh Castle, Stirling Castle, Fort George) which themselves attract large numbers of visitors. Yet in the process of planning new exhibitions interpreting the Gordon Highlanders' two hundred year history, curatorial assessment of the museum's potential market appeal as far as image and interpretative message were concerned was not in conflict with the regimental trustees' own desire to present the traditional story of the regiment's renown and honour and to promote the set of values which they took this story to embody.

Consequently, although its presentation techniques are modern, and while every attempt is made to make the story accessible and clear to those with little or no knowledge of military matters, the approach taken to interpretation is very much in the traditional mould and the new museum ultimately represents a tribute to that intangible quality, the Spirit of the Regiment, much as did the original mess collection of the regiment's officers. In differing ways, many of the museum's visitors today come to pay a form of homage to that ideal.

It is characteristic of the British Army's regimental system that individual regiments are identified with particular geographical areas, and this tendancy is nowhere stronger than in Scotland. The Gordon Highlanders were deemed the local regiment of the north east of Scotland and so became, and remain, a symbol of local pride to the people of the area, whether or not these people had a personal or family connection to the regiment. The notion of the local regiment as champions for the whole area has over the years been sanctioned by numerous civil authorities through the award of burgh freedoms, not least in the city of Aberdeen which counts the Gordon Highlanders 'among our illustrious institutions' (Wyness, 1993, 193).

To the museum's staff and volunteers, it is clear that many local visitors take pride in the story that is presented in the museum, and commonly bring with them visitors from outside the area in order to parade this part of their local heritage. Indeed, the museum owes its very existence at least in part to local communal support, since donations from local individuals, groups, institutions and businesses made up a considerable proportion of the sums raised to rescue and develop the museum in 1994. The literature issued to promote the fund-raising appeal naturally made much of the local dimension, raising the spectre of a potential act of sacrilege: the likelihood not so much of the possible dispersal or mothballing of the museum's collection as of its removal from the traditional regimental area and the concomitant damage to local heritage (The Gordon Highlanders, 1994). Furthermore, the appeal drew on networks of local support generated in the remarkably successful, but ultimately doomed, mobilisation of public opinion to 'Save the Gordons' from amalgamation.

While the local origins of the regiment are perfectly genuine, the Gordon Highlanders were raised by the Duke of Gordon in 1794 and recruited largely from his estates in the north and north east of Scotland, the local identity of a British Army regiment is a very deliberate and careful construction. Regiments did attempt to recruit where possible from their original localities, yet competition from other regiments, corps and services meant that recruits were sought where they could be found, in the major population centres and as regiments and their detachments travelled the country, so producing a numbers of non-local and non-Scottish recruits in Scottish regiments. These soldiers were led by officers of whom local origins increasingly became the exception rather than the norm.

Only as a result of army reforms in the 1870s and 1880s did infantry regiments formally become 'territorial' in organisation with demarcated regimental areas for recruitment purposes. The local image which this fostered proved a potent element in mass volunteering, conscription and national service in the twentieth century. In attracting young men to fill their ranks, and in cultivating valuable support form the civilian world, regiments have found it to be very much in their interest to stress their local character.

A twentieth-century phenomenon as it may be, popular feeling for the Gordon Highlanders in the north east of Scotland is undoubtedly genuine.

Its pervasiveness may be explained in statistical terms with the example of the First World War, where in four years some 50,000 men served in the regiment. Even allowing that a sizeable portion of that number came from outside the area, the links to local families and communities which such a total represents must have verged on the universal. The fact that, of the 50,000 who served, some 29,000 were killed or wounded serves to underline the poignancy of the connection (Falls, 1958, 271). 'Family' is an important word in regimental parlance, not merely because male members of the same family tended to follow one another into service with the local regiment, but because, at least since the early twentieth century, the soldier's loyalty to his regiment was shared and often championed by his dependants and relations, to whom the regiments increasingly reached out (Henderson 1993, vii).

Since the 1960s, regiments have commonly appointed a Families Officer, and like other regiments the Gordon Highlanders has a Regimental Association dedicated to the welfare of tourism talisman of tartan and piping has the greatest authenticity. It was principally in the highland regiments of the British Army that highland dress and piping survived the 1746 Disarming Act. In the 1880s the adoption of highland dress distinctions by lowland Scottish regiments did much to establish highland dress as the national costume of the whole of Scotland, while the maintenance of pipers in Scottish regiments has helped to establish a national cultural icon as well as a national music (Thorbum, 1970).

In the past, regimental museums had no over-riding incentive to appeal directly to tourist visitors (who constituted neither potential recruits nor influential civilian support) and the opportunity to attract and engage overseas visitors was not grasped. Happily, recognition of this potential from tourism and museum agencies (Adams, 1995, 199) and a timely co-operative approach from the regiments themselves has prompted the beginnings of new marketing activity with the Scottish Tourist Board and Scottish Museums Council's backing of the 'Scotland's Regimental Heritage' promotional campaign in 1996.

The Gordon Highlanders Museum also participates in the 'Grampian's Treasures' marketing consortium, backed by Grampian Enterprise, which endeavours to attract visitors to the north east by jointly publicising leading cultural attractions. Indeed, since so many of Scotland's historic monuments and sites are military in nature, it seems possible that the bodies which control them together with the regimental museums could do more to promote themselves under a common theme. In reasonably close proximity to the Gordon Highlanders Museum in Aberdeen is the fine military collection at the National Trust for Scotland's property at Leith Hall, the battle sites of Harlaw, Alford, and the scenes of Robert Bruce's harrying of Buchan in 1308, not to mention the story of the

Marquis of Montrose's sacking of Aberdeen in 1644, now largely lost from public memory.

Equivalent examples may be found in every area of the country. In a nation which boasts such marvellous military monuments as the castles at Edinburgh and Stirling, as Fort George at Ardersier, as Culloden and Bannockburn, it is a matter of regret that so many sites lie forgotten or unmarked. In 1995–96 enormous interest was aroused beyond these shores by the various 250th anniversary commemorations of the 1745 Jacobite rebellion. Yet scenes of earlier spasms of Jacobite military activity, having much of the pathos and romance of a Culloden, such as the site of the 1690 rout of the highland army at the Haughs of Cromdale in Speyside, are silent to the visitor.

As past of a larger story in Scottish heritage, the story of the absorption of highland identity into Scottish and British identity, and of Scotland's place within the Union and the British Empire, Scotland's regimental museums are of no small significance. In the current political climate of impending constitutional change, historical evidence of Scotland's separate existence from the other parts of the United Kingdom is very much de rigeur, as in the language of the 'restoration' of the Scottish parliament and its siting at Holyrood. Acknowledgement of the prominent part taken by Scots in British imperial expansion and administration over three centuries does not sit comfortably with the current search for a devolved Scottish identity. Yet a visit to any of Scotland's regimental museums with their souvenirs and trophies of campaigns in India, Africa, North America and the Far East can leave the visitor in little doubt of how Scottish the British Empire was.

The manner in which Scotland's soldiers were championed by her own people as national and imperial heroes rather gives the lie to any suggestion that Scots were continually manipulated into the martial service of the Empire against their inclination or interest. Whatever view of Scottish identity is taken to complement the institutional adjustments of the late twentieth century, it would be an ill-informed view without this knowledge. It is also possible that the 'Britishness' of Scotland's regiments, and particularly of the highland regiments, might not easily register with some overseas visitors, familiar with the much peddled and seductive image of the oppressed and tragic highlander of Glencoe and Culloden. They will find a very retired Gordon Highlanders and their families.

The existence of this regimental family, stretching back over decades, is apparent in the context of the museum. Visitors commonly have a family connection to the regiment, though it may be two or three generations distant, which they are keen to narrate to the museum's volunteer staff. Many are eager to learn more about their relatives' service and indeed the museum receives a dozen or more written research enquiries every week from descendants of Gordon Highlanders and other enthusiasts. The museum's gardens have taken on a commemorative character, as visitors contribute to museum funds in return for the opportunity to dedicate a garden feature or plant to the memory of a loved one, ancestor or, in some instances 'to all Gordon Highlanders'. The volunteer staff which the museum has assembled is itself a manifestation of the regimental family, comprising some who served in the Gordon Highlanders, some with relatives who served, and some without a direct connection but who take pride in what the museum represents.

Perhaps the most telling evidence of the museum's ministration to this amorphous family lies in its collecting activity. For exhibition and reference purposes, it naturally seeks the most interesting and enlightening artefacts along with examples of the typical material culture of the individual Gordon Highlander. Yet it also collects artefacts which are not needed for such purposes in order to satisfy the strong desire of the donors to see their own, or their relatives', belongings become part of the collection even if they are unlikely ever to be displayed. This is particularly true of the museum's medal collection which, alongside many significant awards and groups, includes large numbers of standard campaign and service medals. Their personal association with the individual recipients aside, these are essentially duplicates. Yet recognising its role as a form of reliquary, the museum invariably accepts for preservation any medals awarded to Gordon Highlanders and so satisfies the donors wish to see the medals safely 'home' to the Regiment's care, preserved and available for future generations.

Families of course migrate, and the family connections to the museum stretch far beyond Scotland and the United Kingdom. Ex-soldiers, widely travelled and perhaps holding a broader view of the world's opportunities, often settled overseas and this particular diaspora brings their descendants as visitors to the museum from North America, South Africa and the Antipodes. By virtue of more general migration patterns, these same places of course have sections of their populations which take great interest in things Scottish, and particularly things highland Scottish, and so supply a significant element of Scotland's tourist visitors.

Indeed, there still exist a number of 'highland regiments', affiliated to the genuine articles in Scotland, in what once were called the White Dominions, not to mention the highland societies which thrive in these countries and in the United States. Whether or not they claim any specific connection to the Regiment, many overseas visitors to the Gordon Highlanders Museum undoubtably feel they have come closer to their roots. Despite already having paid an admission charge, they are often ready to contribute to museum funds to help ensure that the museum's work for their heritage continues.

The story of the Scottish soldier, and more particularly the image of the highland soldier, also carries a powerful attraction to overseas visitors who do not claim a connection to the country, to the highlands, or to the regiments themselves. In kilt and feather bonnet on the field of Waterloo, as the gallant piper on the frontiers of India or in the trenches of the First World War, he epitomises the romantic image of Scotland with which, for all we may hope to promote more modern and sophisticated images, many visitors to this country are familiar and comfortable. What is more, it may be argued that it is in the context of Scotland's military heritage that the different highlander in the museums of Scotland's highland regiments.

As a military museum, arguably 'the most harshly political of museums' (Wood, 1987, 65), the Gordon Highlanders Museum will inevitably invoke a range of reactions from its visitors according to their own experiences and opinions. The traditional approach taken in interpreting the regiment's story leaves it open to accusations that it glorifies war and ignores potentially contentious issues inherent in British military history.

It is certainly true that the museum's displays make no attempt to deal with the 'whys' of the regiment's story and that the enemy is barely visible other than as a generic term, usually on the receiving end of something heroic, if rather traumatic for the recipient. This is quite deliberate since analysis of the political reasons behind the British Army's presence, as aggressor or defender, in any particular campaign is no more the business of a regimental museum than it was the business of the officers and men of the Gordon Highlanders who fought the battles. A critique of British foreign and imperial policy over three centuries is surely beyond the scope of what is possible or desirable in the regimental museum setting, and, if it can be done at all, may be left to national military museums to tackle as they see fit.

A small proportion of visitors to the Gordon Highlanders Museum, justifiably sensitive to the fate of the Indian 'mutineers' of 1857 for example, or to the arduous and often brutal life of the common soldier, might thus experience a rather extreme attack of what has been described as 'dissonance' in heritage interpretation (Tunbridge & Ashworth, 1996). Yet in light of the museum's function as a place of commemoration and celebration, any attempt to present a 'revisionist' view of the regiment's story, or to deconstruct the traditions and ethos inherent in the story, would surely create far greater dissonance in a manner that many visitors would find deeply offensive. Furthermore, the existence of regimental museums in the traditional mode preserves the story of Scotland's regiments as they themselves understood it to be and as it was accepted by civil society in the past. The survival of such museums in their true form surely contributes to contemporary understanding of the regiments' place in our military and cultural heritage.

A more subtle criticism of the traditional regimental museum would be that it tells the regiment's story according to the officers, not the ordinary soldiers, and that the experiences of the rank and file are therefore viewed rather partially. The concept of dissonance in heritage contends that heritage interpretation is selective and that those in control of the interpretive process may, in creating heritage in their own image, disinherit groups in the past and present who cannot exercise any control over the process. With the obvious class differences and very deliberate separation between commissioned and non-commissioned ranks which exists in the British Army, regimental museums might be a prime example of this tendancy.

As we have seen, their collections have typically grown around a core of objects aquired by generations of regimental officers for the decoration of their mess rooms, while the material culture of the officer, by virtue of its quality, is more likely to have been valued and preserved in the past, resulting in a preponderance of objects associated with officers in the museum collections, particulary in relation to the regiments' earlier histories. The officer bias is also characteristic of published regimental histories, which tend to have been written by retired officers, about officers, for officers. Regimental history is also used instructively, to induct new recruits into the traditions of the regiment, to set an example of the conduct expected of the rank and file by the officers, and to promote a sense of corporate responsibility for maintaining the good name and reputation of the regiment.

It would nevertheless be naive to imagine that a regiments' soldiers would otherwise simmer with a desire to replace the officers' fine tales and traditions with an alternative history of poor pay, corporal punishment, disease, danger and boredom. Soldiers are, as a matter of course, fiercely loyal to their regiment, proud of its symbols and traditions and so of its museum. While they might add a touch of irony in their own telling of the official version of the story, by and large they subscribe to it at least as fully as many officers, particularly in its presentation to outsiders, not least to soldiers of another regiment.

In describing the nature of the Gordon Highlanders Museum as a shrine patronised by a large and multifarious regimental family, one must leave a question mark over the long term sustainability of such museums. Any burial ground of a good age will supply evidence of family shrines fallen into disrepair and neglect as families grew distant and died out. As the British Army continues to shrink and become less local in its organisation, the emotional links between regiments and local communities are likely to weaken. The process is already underway. It might also prove to be that dissonance in interpretation of warfare, and particularly colonial warfare, is likely to increase with the passing of generations.

The more questioning approach of our post-modem age might indeed deem archaic the values such as courage, pride, loyalty and sacrifice which exude from regimental museums, while elements of the story, such as the general absence of women from it, will perhaps increasingly seem peculiar. In search of audiences in years to come, and with the prospects of continuing Ministry of Defence financial support looking uncertain, it might be that regimental museums will be forced down the social history road after all.

Yet having attempted to show in this paper how such an approach diverges from what the museums represent in essence, a less radical alternative may be posed here. Attitudes might indeed continue to develop away from those values and symbols for which the museums stand, but who is to say that this very difference might not make them more interesting and challenging places for visitors of all opinions? The picturesque and sympathetic highlander of the Napoleonic Wars, Robert Burns' 'poor and honest sodger', stands today as a benign and attractive image. The distance of time renders the cause in which he fought less pertinent and emotive than might apply for example to his successors in Victorian colonial campaigns and the First World War which, for the time being, are subject to a style of revisionist scepticism.

Might it not be that as Scottish and British culture gradually comes to terms with its imperialist inheritance, and as distance allows historical events and attitudes to be viewed by contemporaneous rather than contemporary standards, fascination with the story of Scotland's regiments will endure, come what may in the British Army of the future? For where other than in our military museums will the visitor find so many ordinary and extra-ordinary Scotsmen, with an overt Scottish identity, participating in the dramatic set pieces of world history, such as a Waterloo or an El Alamein? The Scottish soldier will not leave our cultural iconography without a fight.

The Author

Stuart Allan is exhibitions curator at the Scottish United Services Museum, Edinburgh Castle, Scotland's national museum of armed forces history, which is currently undergoing a major gallery development. From 1995 to early 1998 he was curator of the Gordon Highlanders Museum, Aberdeen, which re-opened under private regimental ownership in 1997. He was previously on the curatorial staff of the Scottish Record Office, Edinburgh, and worked with regimental museums in Scotland and Canada. He is a graduate of Edinburgh

University and holds the University of Leicester's post-graduate diploma in museum studies.

References

Adams, G., *Access to a Nation's Asset'*, in Fladmark, J.M., (ed), *Sharing the Earth*, Donhead, 1995

Burns, Robert, *When wild War's deadly Blast was blawn*, in Kingsley, J., (ed), *The Poems and Songs of Robert Burns*, 3 vols., Clarendon, 1968

Falls, C., *The Life of A Regiment Volume IV*, The Gordon Highlanders in the First World War, 1914–1919, Aberdeen University Press, 1958

Gordon Highlanders, The Gordon Highlanders 200th Anniversary Museum Campaign, privately printed brochure, 1994

Henderson, D. M., *Highland Soldier 1820–1920*, John Donald, 1989

Henderson, D. M., *The Scottish Regiments*, HarperCollins, 1993

Ministry of Defence, *Executive Committee of the Army Board MOD(A) Policy Towards Regimental and Corps Museums*, 1998

Thorbum, W. A., *Uniform of the Scottish Infantry 740–1900*, HMSO, 1970

Thwaites, P., *Presenting Arms: Museum Representation of British Military History*, 1660–1900, Leicester University Press, 1996

Wilkinson, S. & I. Hughes, *Soldiering On'*, in *Museums Journal*, November 1991

Wood, S., *Military museums: the national perspective*, in *Museums Journal*, September 1987

Wood, S,. *At their countr's call*, in Fladmark, J.M., (ed), *Heritage*, Donhead, 1993

Wyness, J., *The Heritage of Aberdeen*, in Fladmark, J.M., (ed), *Heritage*, Donhead, 1993

Looking down from the upper gallery at the scale model of the Murchison oil platform suspended above visitors as they enter the Museum (photo Mike Davidson).

22

A CITY HARVESTING THE SEA
Aberdeen Maritime Museum

John Edwards

Aberdeen faces the North Sea and straddles what was once the River Dee estuary. With these simple geographical facts the casual observer can conclude that this city's history, industry, commerce and social interactions all have a key linkage to maritime affairs. This factor ensured close ties with the ports of the Baltic, Scandinavia, the Low countries, France and England from the late medieval period when communication by land was both time consuming and treacherous. The sea gave Aberdeen access to finished goods and commodities while providing an outlet for the main produce of the city and its hinterland.

Through the years the port developed from a simple quayhead at the bottom of Shiprow to a busy Victorian harbour marked by the improving engineering skills of Smeaton and Telford. During the last 200 years, the quays and docks we know today were established and the industries of shipbuilding and fishing flourished. The mechanisation of the fishing industry through the steel steam trawler gave the shipyards a new outlet for their engineering skills. Great clipper ships of unsurpassed speed and grace were soon overtaken by the steamships of not only the fishing trades, but cargo and passage vessels as well.

From the 1830s, steamers provided scheduled services from Aberdeen to Leith, London in the south and northerly to Orkney and Shetland. These time-honoured routes provided much needed communications, not only for the transport of goods and live stock, but also for passengers: a vital lifeline especially for those in the Northern Isles. Ships like *St Sunniva* were also used for summer cruises in the late 19th century to Norway and even the Mediterranean. The local shipyards produced especially well appointed staterooms for vessels whose everyday tasks would be the transport of ships and cattle.

The 20th century witnessed a consolidation of the traditional industries of shipbuilding and fishing, up until the 1960s, when a long decline in the city's maritime fortunes seemed to be an inevitable prospect. Rusting trawlers lay for weeks in the Upper Dock, and shipbuilders saw order books dwindle. However, the harbour welcomed its first seismic survey vessels during this period and soon drilling oil rigs were working over the eastern horizon. With the development of the astonishingly abundant, high grade oil and gas fields in the North Sea, Aberdeen once more saw the harbour prosper in the way witnessed during the trawler boom 100 years earlier. This development coincidentally would also ensure the establishment of a world ranking maritime museum in the city.

MATERIAL CULTURE AND MARITIME HISTORY

There is the perception that Aberdeen's Maritime Museum came together in the early 1980s and the bulk of its collecting was done from then. In fact, the material culture of objects, paintings, models, drawings and photographs, came together over a considerably longer period. The first item collected was the exquisitely detailed cased half model of the *S.S. Thermopylae*, presented to the city by the owners, Messrs George Thompson & Co in 1895. From this promising start, other ship models, instruments, shipbuilder's tools, fishing equipment and paintings came to the city's museum, largely by way of donation.

The collecting policy during the first half of the 20th century appears to have been passive; that is the museum simply waited for donations to be handed in. The written catalogue of the period reflects the haphazard nature of maritime acquisitions, and there is no evidence of active collection: actually seeking out items to record the history of the day or recent past. Because of this, the collection is surprisingly weak in a number of important fields, and these weaknesses are reflected in the present museum displays. For example, no one saw fit to collect the shipyard drawings and block models which existed before 1945 which are known to include many of the world's most famous Tea Clipper ships. The loss of this information is incalculable and means that we often have to rely on a few photographs or ships' paintings to portray one of Aberdeen's finest achievements.

Similarly, very little was collected from the decades of intensive activity in the fishing industries. Not only are there few objects relating to the fishing itself, but the important fish processing trade, coaling and icemaking ancillary trades are under represented.

Part of the reason for these gaps was, the lack of a dedicated space to display the maritime collections. Without a public face for the subject, its importance would appear to be relatively insignificant compared with the city's important public art collection. Indeed, Aberdeen was unique among cities of its size for placing greater emphasis on its art gallery than its historical collections. The policy not to establish a Museum of Aberdeen had the legacy of creating fragmented collections and a lack of public provision in may key areas of history, archaeology, and social history, for example it is interesting, that the 'Granite City' has no granite museum to tell its citizens how Aberdeen was built, and this also helps to explain, why in 1998, the city's history museums have had to introduce admission charges while the Art Gallery remains free.

Maritime collecting has become much more pro-active since the appointment of a full-time Keeper (Curator), when key gaps in the collection were identified and efforts started to concentrate on these areas. The ship model collection was weakest in subjects such as colliers, coastal steamers, fishing, line boats and certain tall ships, and models were commissioned to fill these gaps.

As publicity for the maritime section grew, so did public awareness and with it some major private collections. The Duthie family of shipbuilders gave legacies of important sailing ship paintings, builders' models and even a turn of the century ship's deck house. The Aberdeen Shipmaster Society, established in 1598, lent its historic collections, including the votive 'Schip' model (1689), a Scottish Warship painting (c1660), its treasurer's box (1602) and several paintings of Aberdeen sailing ships. Several very large oil platform models came from oil majors, while key trades like drilling, oil supply vessel fleets and helicopter companies contributed material, documentation and illustrations. This actively lead to the establishment of a permanent, stand alone maritime museum within the city.

THE MARITIME COLLECTIONS

The first displays of maritime history were in the Industrial Museum which later became the Regional Museum sited in the Cowdray Hall adjacent to the Art Gallery. This museum contained a vast array of objects from sea shells and fossils through to stone axes, medieval pottery and the occasional ship model. Although it is still remembered with fondness by some, one can hardly say it contained a logically arranged exhibition interpreting the history of Aberdeen's connections with the sea, been largely cases with labels and little graphic material to aid understanding of the displays.

This changed radically in the 1970s, when the maritime collections were reorganised and a new interpretative display installed in the Cowdray Hall basement. This afforded the first overview of the maritime history of Aberdeen and the North Sea with objects, models and art works placed together and properly interpreted through graphic display panels. The site was not large and was tucked away from the Art Gallery, but nevertheless it demonstrated the potential of the collection, so that by 1979 efforts to find a dedicated site for a maritime museum were being made, Provost Ross's House being one option considered.

The House, built in 1593, stands on the Shiprow, the main road between the harbour and the commercial city centre in the Castlegate, making it a highly appropriate location for a maritime museum. Furthermore Provost Ross, after whom the building was named, was an 18th century shipowner with trading connections with Holland and other North Sea countries. The house overlooked its subject, the harbour and had the potential of interpreting many aspects of the port and its marine industries development. The building was acquired by The National Trust for Scotland in 1953, which then restored it, from a very dilapidated condition. The Trust had no plans to develop the building for its own purposes, and it was a relatively straightforward procedure to reach an agreement with the City Council to use the building for a new maritime museum.

A design feasibility study was carried out in 1980, and it confirmed that the building could be converted to a museum. A professional museum design company was brought in to deal with the difficult nature of the building and the need to engage people with good contacts in the display contractor sector. The museums department had not attempted such a project before and did not have the in-house expertise to tackle such a large design scheme. There had been some resistance to the scheme when presented to Council, as some felt the house was far too small to accommodate the subject and the large collections. This feeling would later have the effect of encouraging the expansion of the museum with plans for a 'Phase II' development being laid as early as 1984.

Meanwhile, the Phase I development in Provost Ross's House moved along with the acceptance by the Council of the design study and the appointment of contractors with a view to an opening in early 1984. The design would utilise the three floors of the house entirely for exhibitions, and a small shop. No office or storage space would be provided in order to maximise the limited space available. A major 'Reserve and Study Collection' facility was also planned to be inaugurated in 1984 and this environmentally controlled building would house all material not on display.

Offices for the Keeper, exhibitions and marketing staff were also off site, so as to save valuable potential exhibition spaces and enable close contact between all curatorial and display staffs who were based at the Art Gallery or in nearby James Dun's House. The fact that a curatorial presence was rarely on-site would have significant impact on the running of the new museum, making the building merely an exhibition centre remotely controlled from a distance of half a mile. The author believes it is preferable to have a curator on site to attend to any detailed questions regarding the exhibits and oversee management of the museum, and this view prevailed when considering the Phase II plans years later.

The new Aberdeen Maritime Museum opened in Provost Ross's House in April 1984. The ground floor provided direct access off the Shiprow, and this area contained the shop, toilets and a small introductory display. Significantly, this was the only area accessible by wheelchair users, given the problems of attaining planning permission to build a lift in an historic building and the number of levels within the house. This fact also spurred on the Phase II development's urgent need for improved disabled access.

The lower ground floor was used for temporary displays during the winter months and by the National Trust for Scotland in the summer months for their information centre and shop. The middle floor included displays of a 19th century shipowners office dubbed 'The Duthie Room' in tribute to the many artefacts provided by that local family. A paintings gallery, display room on the North Boats and a harbour and fishing gallery completed this level. The top floor devoted two rooms to the development of the clipper ship, while the final room was devoted to the story of North Sea oil and gas. This last display included a then state-of-the-art three projector slide tape presentation and the 4m x 4m x 3m engineering model of the 'Murchison' oil platform.

Clearly, there was a great deal of subject matter packed into the museum, and visitors often had just one complaint: it was all very good but far too small. Well over 50,000 people came to this free museum in its first year, demonstrating that it had a large audience eager to learn about Aberdeen's maritime past, and demanding more.

It was recognised that the museum would be very tight for space years before it opened its doors, and efforts were made to locate premises for expanding the museum from its base in Provost Ross's House. The Trinity Congregational Church down the hill from the House became available in 1983, and was purchased from the congregation in 1984. The agreement stated explicitly that the church building could only be developed as part of the Maritime Museum Phase II project. The first step in a 13 year expansion process had begun.

THE PHASE II PROJECT

Experience gained during the 1980s, through surveys and temporary exhibitions in Provost Ross's House, confirmed the need not only for enlarged exhibitions on the themes covered already, but for visitor facilities including a larger shop, high quality café, auditorium, dedicated staff facilities, office accommodation and a research library. In human terms, it was vital to increase the curatorial staffing to include Assistant Keepers of Maritime History and later of education as well as on-site clerical support and a much expanded provision of museum assistants.

All the design efforts and budget levels pointed to two separate buildings with a courtyard area between. A shop and access stairs were to be built in the space between the two buildings but visitors would have to brave the elements to go between the two sites. The church building would be converted to museum purposes using the existing floor plans of basement, church and balcony thereby keeping building costs to a minimum. The church would house a large display on the North Sea oil and gas industry as well as the facilities outlined above. Little, if any changes, would be made to the displays in Provost Ross's House.

If this plan had been implemented, over half of the museums total display area would be dedicated to oil and gas exhibitions and no further development of the traditional industries of fishing and shipbuilding would have been provided. In the light of experience this would have brought an imbalance to the overview of maritime history in the museum. Consequently, one can argue that it was beneficial that the original concept did not go forward and the Phase II project was put on hold until the 1990s.

The catalyst for getting the project underway was an unlikely combination of oil and sailing ships. During the late 1980s, there had been a proposal to establish an 'Oil Experience Centre' on the Aberdeen beach front with a drilling rig sited just offshore. This bold concept recognised the fact that the 'Oil Capital of Europe' did not have a showcase for showing visitors to the city the enterprise and technological aspects of the offshore industry. Even the families of oil workers had little idea of what offshore work was really like, and this centre would redress this shortfall for them and many thousands of visitors.

There were many meetings held among the business community, City Council and Grampian Enterprise aimed at building the Centre. The City would donate the land, but the bulk of the funding would have to be found from private sources. Over the years, the estimate cost of the project rose from several million pounds to ten million and finally to twenty million. The economic viability of servicing the facility required some

300,000 paying customers every year, clearly a remarkable challenge given the size of Aberdeen.

Concurrent with the ups and downs of this project came the proposal to bring the Tall Ships Race ships to Aberdeen. The City Council backed this venture and successfully bid for the 1991 event. The Race had a good record of attracting enormous crowds and generating substantial income for the local economy wherever it had gone. Excellent preparations were made for the Aberdeen section of the Race, but no one was fully prepared for the huge impact the Tall Ships would make on the city, its citizens and visitors. Helped by sunny warm conditions the four day event witnessed hundreds of thousands of visitors swarming over the ships and the quayside. All of Aberdeen had caught 'Tall Ships Fever' and there was genuine regret when the ships sailed out into the North Sea. But the second key strand of the Phase II project had been given a major boost by the event.

In November 1992, Aberdeen City Council and Grampian Enterprise met to discuss the prospects for progressing the 'Oil Experience Centre'. It appeared that the project would not be started and yet both parties wished to see a permanent oil exhibition in the city. Attention was drawn to the concept studies done for the Maritime Museum, and it was argued that the site already existed for such a project, as well as the expertise to develop it. Grampian Enterprise gave a strong indication that they would assist funding of the project and officers were given instructions to develop the scheme. A further commitment was that, if the Phase II project were to be built, it would have to be operational by the time the Tall Ships Race visited Aberdeen again: probably in 1997.

During 1993–97, the profit the project became locked into a long series of deadlines. Given the structure of local government and the number of Council departments involved, the project progressed in a very ordered manner. Many deadlines were dictated by working back from the opening date to 1993 and allocating the necessary time to get each individual task completed. All key officers meet fortnightly to discuss all issues connected with the project and to keep to the overall timescale.

DESIGN AND THEMES

The Phase II project of the 1980s had a capital expenditure allocation of about £1m, which, would have converted the church and provided outdoor access between two distinct buildings. With all the experience gained over the years, it was felt that a more ambitious scheme would be needed. The major spending commitment likely from Grampian Enterprise (£950,000) meant that the museum officers could investigate a concept, physically linking two buildings and thereby bridge the gap site. This proposal was attractive in not only providing a third extra space for exhibitions, but also the prospect of filling a gap in the Shiprow streetscape. A bold new building would immediately suggest to visitors a modern and exciting museum within and would make a statement about new directions in architecture.

By early 1993, museum designers had been appointed to draft a new design feasibility study. This study became the blueprint for the future museum and would be used as a concept model for all initial discussions with Council departments, funding partners and external bodies. It was also the basis on which the Council and Grampian Enterprise approved funding in the summer of 1993. The importance of such a study carried out by respected professionals cannot be underestimated. If the plan is well developed then a museum project has every chance of achieving success. The consultant's study therefore merits closer examination to explain the basic themes and concepts of the Aberdeen Maritime Museum. The following extract from the report, details the curatorial requirements and the designer's ability to incorporate these needs within the proposed complex. The report was written in close conjunction with museums staff and reflects the stated aims and objectives of the museum. The themes were to be: North Sea oil and gas, fishing, ship building, age of the clipper, Aberdeen at war, and the harbour. The curatorial requirements of the developed museum, as listed by the author in 1993, were for the enrichment of displays to complete a comprehensive coverage of Aberdeen's maritime history as follows drawn from report by Robin Wade $ Partners

NORTH SEA OIL AND GAS

1. 'Murchison' Oil Platform model with addition of the underwater 'jacket' which supports the platform.
2. Remotely Operated Vehicles which serve as camera platforms and/or undersea work stations equipped with manipulator arms, capable of being animated or even visitor controlled.
3. Aviation to the Rigs. Helicopters, large and small, which fly from the world's busiest heliport in Aberdeen.
4. Drill head set-piece which shows the conditions on board an exploration rig.
5. The products of petroleum. How our lives are dependant on oil and all its hydro-carbon cousins. Environmental concerns could be addressed here.
6. Life and work on the rigs. An opportunity to tell the day-in-the-life story of oil workers and the impact on those left on shore.

FISHING

1. Expanded general displays.
2. Display major fishing equipment including trawl gear, gallows and nets.
3. Model ships and fishing techniques.
4. Fish processing from smoking to the herring cure.
5. Life and work on a trawler. Through personal accounts, tell the story of one trawler of the past, how the crew worked the ship and fished, and the conditions on board.
6. Display some of the internal features of a trawler including a typical cabin.

SHIPBUILDING

1. An opportunity to utilise the large collections relating to Aberdeen's principal shipbuilders. The collection includes thousands of ship drawings, models, books and tools.
2. Ship sections could be installed in the museum displays, showing how a ship is framed and plated.
3. A steam engine could be installed and even animated to give the feel of a ship underway.
4. The personal stories of many great shipbuilders could be related here. For example, Thomas Blake Glover who went to Japan in 1860 and helped found the shipbuilding skills of that country. Or, the life and times of the Hall or Duthie families.

AGE OF THE CLIPPER

1. Enhance the displays by including the stories of those who sailed these fine ships, utilising diaries and pictures.

ABERDEEN AT WAR

1. Tell the history of Aberdeen's contribution to the war efforts of 1914–18 and 1939–45 when many ships were built in the city for the navy and others were converted for the admiralty.
2. Aberdeen's own warship, the cruiser HMS 'Scylla' deserves a place in the museum. We will have an eight foot long scale model of the 'Scylla' in the near future.

HARBOUR

1. Links between the development of the city and the harbour.
2. Life and work in the harbour.

USE OF THE CHURCH

Our 1985 report referred to the desirability of stripping out the building for the insertion of new floors. The deterioration of the building since then now dictates the need for such measures, enabling the insertion of two new floors. The previous report also suggested that the church be used to house the North Sea Gas and Oil displays. Now that a link building is proposed, whose modern character is so appropriate for a contemporary industry, the church can more suitably be employed or other purposes as follows.

1. *Ground Floor:* A cafeteria or coffee shop with direct access from Shiprow, together with kitchen (with services' access from outside) and public toilets. This would be capable of opening out of Museum hours, without encroaching on the security of the Museum buildings, or possibly as a service available in the evenings when the AV auditorium on the floor above is in use.
2. *First Floor:* Audio visual and lecture auditorium seating 70 people together with an assembly or entertainment area where organised groups can be briefed, etc. A platform in front of the high lancet windows affording views across the harbour.
3. *Second Floor:* Shipbuilding displays and a section devoted to Aberdeen at War. A reference library and computerised access to the extensive photographic archive, both for public access.

PROPOSED CORE BUILDING

A physical link between the church and Provost Ross's House was necessary in order to provide:

1. A central entrance space, approachable from any direction, containing reception, shop and a vital introduction to the Museum complex.
2. An indoor link between the two buildings, the floor levels corresponding with those in the church and ramps to reach the floor levels in Provost Ross's House.
3. A central system of vertical circulation:
    i) Avoiding multi lifts and stairs and changes of level.
    ii) Giving means of access for the disabled to the upper two floors of Provost Ross's House. There are two positions in the gable wall where openings could be made.
    iii) Shared fire exits from both buildings, probably further allowing the removal of the unsightly, external iron staircase and upgrading of Provost Ross's House.
    iv) Relieving the pressure of increased visitor numbers over all three floors of Provost Ross's House.

4. A rational sequence of display themes.
5. The insertion of a modern structure would make a positive and dramatic contribution to the street-scape. With a glass front and internally lit it would announce the presence of the Museum and invite people to enter.
6. The view inwards from the street would be most especially attractive since it is proposed that the giant model of the 'Murchison' Oil Platform be extended to its correct height above sea level (to scale), resulting in a central display feature some 8,5 metres tall.

PROVOST ROSS'S HOUSE

1. Ground Floor: The National Trust Shop remains in situ but may well have its own direct access to and from Shiprow. Space for an administrative office.
2. First Floor: The Harbour display to be fully developed.
3. The picture gallery and Duthie Room remain before.
4. Second Floor: The gallery will be devoted to full coverage of the Fishing Industry, including aspects of related social history.
5. The Age of the Clipper Ships gallery to remain unaltered.

Many of the above points of detail were altered during the ongoing design process which continued until the project drawings were finalised in early 1995. Nevertheless, the broad themes of the museum were established by the summer of 1993 and the location of each of the exhibition spaces and facilities was set.

This process was not done in isolation. The Arts & Recreation Department was the 'client' department with the City Architect's Department (later Property and Technical Services) as the prime organisation for designing the buildings, infrastructure and leading the project through the many contractual processes. The third element of the design team were the specialist museum consultants who were responsible for both 3-D exhibition design and graphics. This team worked on a daily basis with the client department serving as the main section for driving the project on.

There were tensions between many of the groupings largely due to the complex nature of the project and the desire to produce the best design. This lead to compromise on some occasions and in others the need to firmly restate requirements. However, the fact that the team did produce the museum demonstrates the professionalism of all involved.

MEDIA

Another factor in the museum design was the desire to incorporate modern computer display solutions into the galleries. The designers and curators had experience of 'interactive' displays and consulted widely on the array of options available. An Aberdeen-based specialist audio visual company and was contracted to develop the multimedia elements of the exhibitions, and one of the advantages of utilising a local was their experience in producing promotional training and educational videos for the oil industry. This meant that they had stock footage of every aspect of offshore activities or the right contacts to enable new footage to be shot at virtually no cost to the museum. This factor enabled savings and made many of the programmes relatively straightforward in their productions. Curators worked with the firm to develop the scripts, reviewing the material available and discussing the fine details of how each of the 24 programmes or AV elements would work. Again team work with the architects and designers was essential to produce a seamless end product between the multimedia displays, graphics panels and exhibits.

Experience has shown that the decision to have independently operated computers was a prudent one. Each of the programmes was on a separate, stand alone computer rather than a networked system working from a single site. The disadvantage of the latter is, if a fault occurs, it causes the entire network to 'crash', leaving blank display screens throughout the museum. Stand alone systems mean that each station works independently of each other and if a fault occurs in one system the others are unaffected. At worst, only one or two presentations are down at any one time, and in practice this has been for a very limited time.

INSTALLATION AND OPENING

For the concluding stages of the implementation programme, it would be true to say the project elements literally came together in the final few months before the opening date. By early 1997, the project steering group were confident that the building and exhibitions would be ready by mid May and a public opening date of 15 May was set.

The building contract ended in mid January and was officially handed over to the Council. In a variation to what is often normal museum practice, the installation of cases and fine joinery work was done in the final building period rather than after the finish of the main works on site. This speeded up the process, but meant a thorough clean of the entire building and contents was necessary prior to objects, computers, graphics and paintings being accepted on-site.

Concurrent with this installation phase off-site tasks included the hiring of staff, preparation for the marketing campaign, production of all print including a full colour catalogue, arranging for familiarisation visits by special interest groups and the testing of the interaction of all systems in the building.

Although two curators had been working on the project since 1995, it was not until January 1997 that the budget allowed for the hiring of an Assistant Keeper of Education. This post had been programmed to start much earlier, but revenue budget constraints across the department meant this post could not be filled until close to the opening date. This was not the ideal as the advice of a trained educationalist would have been valuable when developing the exhibitions, text, and printed materials. In practice the education officer was able to develop a school's programme, handling seminars, activities sheets and a teacher's pack in the four months prior to the opening. This proved invaluable, especially as a total of fifty schools visited the building in the first six weeks of operation.

The education post was seen as very important by Grampian Enterprise recognising the key educational role of the museum and important linkages to schools and young people. For the Council, this marked a change in attitude as previous posts would be labelled 'interpretation' or 'extension services'. This was due to the legacy of education provision being based in the regional authority with the City Council not being responsible for this service. Consequently, all education was felt to be the remit of a separate authority with the attitude being that the former District Council need not pay for educational services. This proved cumbersome and unhelpful in previous years, but with local government reorganisation in 1996, education came back within the city, thus smoothing the museum's path to appoint an education officer.

All elements of the final installation came together in good time for the May opening. These included the main exhibits, set pieces, models, restored objects and equipment from contributing sponsors. Although cleaning, case dressing, and labelling continued right up to the official opening, there were no gaps in the exhibitions or presentations on day one. The museum was launched with a series of special events, TV advertising and blanket media coverage. In the first six weeks the museum welcomed 35,223 visitors as well as many schools, special groups and evening corporate entertainment parties. This was naturally a very exciting and gratifying period as the reaction to the museum was very favourable. It provided time to catch up on many points of detail and trouble-shoot areas such as computer programmes, lighting and general building maintenance prior tot the influx of visitors anticipated during the visit of the Tall Ships Race.

With the return of the Tall Ships during 11–15 July, the Maritime Museum project had come full circle. An idea which had been given a much needed boost by the 1991 Tall Ships visit had now come into being by their return. The museum was filled to capacity with 10,036 visitors during the five day event with many visitors seeking the top floor with its superb views over the assembled vessels.

LISTENING TO THE CUSTOMER

During the first nine months of operation, a number of visitor surveys were carried out in order to assess the needs and desires of the visitor and build a profile of who comes to the museum. The findings confirmed a very high level of customer satisfaction with all aspects of the museum. Most critical comments reflect individual's personal interests and their wish for a different balance in the exhibition themes. For example, some would prefer less on offshore oil in favour of more on fishing. Others would like more information on the natural history of the North Sea, and on environmental issues, whilst others have voiced a desire to see special exhibition themes as diverse as pirates and the 'Titanic'.

A further test of customer satisfaction came with the introduction of admission charges on 1st April 1998. The City Council faced a cut of 18 million pounds from its budget with Arts & Recreation facing a massive 25% cutback. The option of eliminating the tradition of free admissions to all museums was decided by elected members and introduced with a view to gaining much needed income. Initial response has shown no change in the visitor numbers into the building where shop and café remain free. However, only 50% of those people then pay admission into the exhibitions, a figure which is well down from the previous eleven months of operation. Further efforts will be made to build on the existing audience, but enhanced marketing will be required in this new economic climate. Given the ability to face the multiplicity of tasks in the Phase II project itself, we are confident that Aberdeen Maritime Museum will meet this new challenge.

The Author

Dr John Edwards attended Dalhousie University in Halifax, Nova Scotia, graduating with a BA in history in 1973. As a student, he was employed by Parks Canada as a researcher and interpreter at Signal Hill National Historic Park, St John's, Newfoundland, when he also wrote papers on the recently discovered Norse settlement at L'Anse aux Meadows and an early native archaeological site at Port au Choix. Having attended the course in museums studies at the University of Leicester, he held curatorial posts at St Helen's Museum and with the Museums Service of Dunfermline District Council in May 1975, which included, the Pittencrieff House and Inverkeithing Museums. In 1984 he was appointed to the post now called Keeper of Maritime History in Aberdeen, with responsibility for the Phase II development outlined in the above paper.

References

Kemp, Peter and Ormond, Richard *The Great Age of Sail, Maritime Art and Photography*, Phaidon, Oxford, 1986

Lubbock, Basil, *The Colonial Clippers*, Brown, Son & Ferguson Ltd., Glasgow, 1948

Lubbock, Basil, *The Last of the Windjammers*, Brown, Son & Ferguson Ltd., Glasgow, 1948

MacGregor, David R., *Merchant Sailing Ships 1850–1875*, Conway Maritime Press, 1984

MacGregor, David R.,*The Tea Clippers, Their History and Development 1833–1875*, Conway Maritime Press, 1983

Robinson, Robb, *Trawling, the Rise and Fall of The British Trawl Fishery*, University of Exeter Press, 1996

Wynes, J., The Heritage of Aberdeen, in Fladmark,J.M.(ed), Heritage, Donhead, 1993

Documents available from Aberdeen Maritime Museum:

1. Reports to Arts & Recreation Committee, August 1993 and August 1994, providing details of the Design Feasibility Study and indicative costings of the project.
2. Full working drawings of the building and exhibition designs showing the evolution of the design from the 1985 concept to 1997. Details include structural design, exhibition layout, case design, computer interactive scripts and finishes of display areas.
3. *In The Pipeline*, Arts & Recreation Department, Aberdeen District Council, 1993. Promotional folder to launch and update the media and sponsors on the development up to 1997.
4. *Aberdeen Maritime Museum*, Aberdeen City Council, Arts & Recreation Department, 1997, catalogue with introduction and essay by John Edwards.
5. *Aberdeen Maritime Museum*, Teachers' Pack 1997. Compiled by Ann Scott, Assistant Keeper (Education).

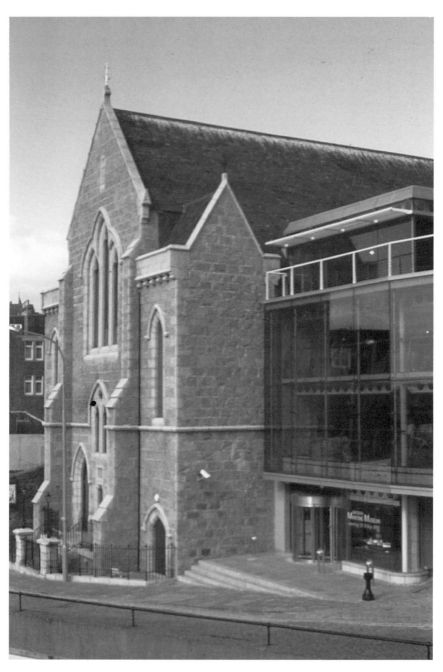

Old and modern parts of the Museum side by side on Shiprow, overlooking Aberdeen harbour (photo Mike Davidson).

23

SOUTH INDIAN FOLK HERITAGE
Breaking New Ground at Dakshinachitra

Deborah Thiagarajan

South India is a culturally rich and diverse region with beautiful beaches, tropical forests, enchanting mountain ranges and vast stretches of agricultural areas dotted with small villages. It is home to more than 200 million people. The South is divided into states according to the boundaries of language: Tamil Nadu for the Tamil speaking people, Kerala for the Malayalam speakers, Karnataka for Kannada speakers, and Andhra Pradesh for Telugu and Urdu speakers.

The culture of the people is extremely diverse within each state, and the states are very different to each other. A Keralito and a Tamil are as dissimilar as an Englishman and an Italian. Part of the reason for this wide diversity lies in the differing ecologies of the region which tied the people to the exigencies of the land and tended to isolate people into local clusters.

Migrations, invasions, international and national trade, limited communication and mobility and the traditions of rulers, also helped to shape this diversity. Special crafts, performing arts, festivals and architectural forms evolved over centuries differently and simultaneously in many localised regions of the South.

Tourism is new to South India. Most foreign tourists who come to India go to the north: to Delhi, the Taj Mahal in Agra and the palaces in Jaipur. Rajasthan has become a major destination, but South India has experienced relatively few international tourists and is a region waiting to be discovered.

In the South, the joy of travelling today lies not only in the beauty of its extensive architectural heritage, but also in the openness, friendliness and unstinting hospitality of the South Indian villager. Accustomed, according to their religion and life philosophy, to receive a guest as a blessing to their home, the villagers today will still gladly welcome an absolute stranger into their home.

For years, I have been travelling through the countryside and villages of South India, stopping the car wherever something attracts me and wandering through a village, and into homes and temples to see how people live, worship and entertain themselves. It has been a most humbling and enriching experience. This quality of the South is perhaps the most fragile to the impact of tourism.

THE AIMS OF DAKSHINACHITRA

It was through these years of travel and study that the concept of Dakshinachitra emerged. Myself and a small group of like-minded people banded together in 1985 to form the Madras Craft Foundation, a non-profit making society whose goal is the documentation, preservation and promotion of the arts and culture of South India.

Aware of the ever increasing trend towards change and modernity, the Foundation felt that a concentrated effort had to be made to research, archive, and preserve the traditional architecture, craft skills, performance knowledge, folklore and artefacts of a broad spectrum of traditional South Indian cultures before they disappeared. The physical focus of these efforts is Dakshinachitra, a centre of ten acres located 21 kilometres from Madras city along the Bay of Bengal, on the heavily travelled road to the 7th century seaport of Mamallapuram.

Dakshinachitra is a centre for the architecture, crafts, folk performing arts and the life styles of the people of each of the four Southern states, presented in a setting of authentically reconstructed homes and village spaces of the turn of the century. In 1996, the centre was opened with the Tamil Nadu and Kerala areas complete. Karnataka and Andhra are still to be built.

Even before the construction of the centre began, the Foundation had been actively engaged in research and had acted as a resource centre in bringing the diversity of the Southern arts, particularly the folk performing arts, into the Madras community. Unfortunately, urban India is nearly as ignorant about the multitude of traditions in its midst as is the foreign tourist. The Foundation's major goal is to engender an understanding and appreciation of these cultures among domestic Indian tourists.

TOURISM AT DAKSHINACHITRA

The Foundation regards tourism as the means to propel the institution forward and sustain the deeper objectives of the organisation. There are a great many questions that tourism poses to an organisation like ours. We have been asked whether tourism will eventually override our basic objectives and reduce the centre to superficial clichés, as we attempt to give the tourist an experience.

The Dakshinachitra centre has multiple target groups, foreign tourists being one. The educated Indian tourist is another. The educated Indian resident of Madras, and his guests, as well as school children, are also our targets. School children are a primary target, and like most museums abroad, the Foundation lays emphasis on outreach education and has hired expertise for organising children's programmes. Besides introducing children to their heritage, the programmes should raise questions about the relationship of culture to ecology and the direction in which society is going.

Foreign tourism to Dakshinachitra is based on another assumption that is important to our goal. The Foundation feels that foreign appreciation and interest in local culture could help to generate pride and appreciation in that culture by the local inheritors and practitioners of the culture. It is hoped that this pride will motivate talented local persons to continue their artistic traditions, or at least see the inherent values in traditional art forms even in a modern society.

Dakshinachitra then becomes a testing ground to see how the projection of traditional values to all tourists can affect the view of the local tourist towards his own culture. Can appreciation of a culture by foreigners help to legitimise that culture for locals? Will this projection have any long-term effect on the thinking of the local or Indian tourist? If so what will its effect be? These are questions Dakshinachitra intends to address in the years ahead.

The Indian tourist has a different set of interests and perceptions from the foreign tourist. For the urban Indian under the age of 50, our centre represents a glimpse into traditions of his youth, observed in his own home, or more likely in his grandparents' home. Chances are that he has distanced himself from these 'old world' traditions and is trying to embrace modernity: which means Western dress, living in an urban flat or westernised bungalow and assimilating changing mores in food, socialisation and work orientation.

India has jumped from British rule, which for four centuries rejected Indian aesthetics and values as inferior to a Christian-based society, to the 21st century. Increased communication, with satellite television, cellular phones, electronic mail, commercialisation, growing materialism and access to global ideals of youth are the reality in urban India. These trends may irrevocably change and eventually destroy the traditional culture of South India. The few intervening years between British rule, independence in 1947 and today were hardly long enough for even one generation of Indians to re-explore and re-affirm their own history and values as seen from their perspective instead of from a non-Indian perspective. The result is a certain ambiguity in understanding or appreciation by many Indians of their own heritage.

Dakshinachitra is primarily for this tourist: for him to re-affirm the legitimacy and the place of his roots and his own sense of identity. As Dakshinachitra is new, the Foundation is not yet able to gauge how urban India will respond or what number will be attracted to the centre and from what social strata. To date the centre has only been open by selective invitation. Only half a kilometre away is a modern amusement park, three times the cost of a visit to our centre. The park is full. We will have to see what fraction of that crowd will be attracted to a centre of traditional culture.

EARLY WESTERN INFLUENCE IN INDIA

Although the concept of Dakshinachitra is not new in most countries around the world, it is new in India. In India, the conservation of heritage is itself new. In a nation that views life as an endless natural cycle of birth, growth and decline, the idea of intervention in this process is seen as very Western. India has several hundred thousand buildings and sites dating from the 1st century BC to the early 18th century deserving of preservation. Less than 10,000 are protected by law. These monuments are protected by the Archaeological Survey of India, and the state archaeological departments. The list of monuments was drawn up by the British in the early 20th century and has changed only little since then. Luckily, many early monuments are in stone. It is the fragile, historical ambience of the cities and towns which are immediately threatened.

Heritage tourism is also a new concept. People are so busy with the pressures of daily life, both financial and physical, that few people have thought about the presentation of their past. The population explosion in urban India which makes city land among the most expensive in the world mitigates against the preservation of heritage. Financial constraints are another problem.

Government officials and business men often ask me: 'Why should India preserve 19th century colonial buildings in its cities no matter how attractive they are, when land is at a premium and new buildings are more efficient in their use of space? What is the point of preserving a traditional temple environment with its traditional Brahjain enclave when the owners themselves want to develop their property and India no longer wants to be reminded of past elites with their unequal hierarchy?'.

India has not yet realised how fast change is occurring and how quickly the past is being obliterated. Indians are still too close to their past to romanticise it or to link it to their future. Dakshinachitra is one small step in raising the awareness of the people in their heritage and the need for heritage preservation.

The future for heritage tourism in India for all tourists, foreign and Indian alike, will depend on the local Indians. If they perceive a need for heritage tourism for themselves or as part of an entrepreneurial opportunity, they will respond. This process has begun.

HERITAGE AND MODERN TOURISM

In the past, Indian tourism has been primarily religious pilgrimages to temples. However, as the middle class in India grows, Indians have begun to spend money on their leisure and travel unrelated to religion. In the South, it is only in Kerala that tourism is beginning to come of age.

The first to understand the importance of the local heritage was a young German entrepreneur. He built a hotel with a distinctly local ambience by constructing cottages from the traditional wooden homes of South Kerala. The success of his venture stimulated Indian hotels to expand his concept. As the backwaters become a tourist destination, local people have also begun to fabricate traditional boats into floating hotels and many are seeking to preserve their traditional homes. Local crafts are also flourishing. Kerala's performing arts are vibrant, but yet untouched by major tourism. Tourism like this, involving the people and their heritage, is ideal.

Kerala is like Bangkok and its backwaters 30 years ago. To sustain its environment, the necessary legislation must be passed in Kerala to prevent overbuilding and destruction of the natural beauty of the waterways. How will such laws be passed unless the population sees the necessity? Awareness will have to grow at a much faster rate than it is now. Real estate development and tourism are at odds with each other in an uneven race.

Bombay and Hyderabad are the only cities in India to have passed heritage legislation. The municipalities have persevered with these initial laws through many court cases against them. Other cities are slow in following suit, and pressure groups from local organisations like the Indian National Trust for Art and Cultural Heritage, need to be strengthened and this can only be done through local awareness.

International and Indian tourists themselves can aid this process by proclaiming what they would like to see. External pressure groups for India's heritage would make a difference. Tourism which focuses on heritage and which brings in money to the states may have a faster and a more enduring impact on heritage preservation than the efforts of local heritage groups. Most state governments in India have not yet realised the significance of tourism. As yet, they do not understand its potential for employment or income.

Too often, the goal is simply to get the largest number of tourists to a particular place without regard to the carrying capacity or environmental fragility, and special interest tourism is not yet understood either. Tour operators still have continual problems with government regulations. Only the ever growing number of five star hotel groups seem to be able to plough their way through the maze of officialdom.

Tourists comments could make a difference. The Foundation would be happy to serve as a clearing point for comments on heritage and heritage preservation from tourists and tour groups coming to India who have statements to make. We will pass on all views to the relevant government departments for their action and present the views at major tourism meetings and conferences. India has some of the world's most magnificent heritage sites, and it is possible that tourism will be the agent to keep them preserved by drawing attention to them after centuries of neglect.

KEEPING TRADITIONS ALIVE

The Foundation has two other very different target groups who are integral to its working, folk performers and the craftsmen. The introduction of folk performances to the audience is not only for audience entertainment. The Foundation works to introduce the performing artists to different situations within the urban setting and to give them exposure to urban tastes, and helps, where possible, with costuming and with repertoire. Most performing arts were used in India to disseminate values as told through the epic tales of the *Ramayana* the *Mahabaratha* and other Puranic tales. They were the primary means of education and entertainment, and were usually performed as a part of a major festival.

Programmes were often up to ten hours long each evening and spanned several nights. Helping performers to detach their age old traditions from their ritual context to make them suitable for non-village audiences and changing village tastes, or for audiences outside of their region, is fraught with problems. The Foundation sees this as the only alternative for them to survive in their changing society, but there are limits. The authenticity and perceived essence of the performance by the performers and the

316

village will not be changed even for tourism or for the appeal of drama or sleekness.

Dakshinachitra remains a living tradition, and this is what distinguishes it from other similar site museums today. The craftsmen at Dakshinachitra, who are representative of many hundreds of similar craftsmen in the region, make their living from their skills. They are also being marginalised by the changes occurring in the economy. The Foundation has a mandate to help them in their product development and with the marketing of these products. The interaction of the tourists with the craftsmen and their crafts at our craft shop and the performing artists and their performances is seen as beneficial to both groups.

There is no way that the foreign tourist on a short visit to the South, particularly as part of a group, can experience the hospitality, diversity or richness of the culture of the common Indian. Unless the group is an adventurous one, the tourist may not even experience Indian villages. He or she will leave without an understanding of the aesthetics or life style of the traditional South Indian home.

Dakshinachitra is based on the assumption that foreign tourists want an experience and want to be informed about what they are seeing. With the complexity of the cities and towns, first time tourists often miss much and misunderstand what they see. The onslaught of so much that is different on the senses, tends to leave little time for in-depth reflections of the visual stimulus. Dakshinachitra will give tourists time to pause by presenting them with an authentic environment, information and an interaction with craftsmen, performers and personnel at the centre. For the foreign tourist the experience at Dakshinachitra will include an insight into how Indians regard their life through their daily activities and rituals.

The Author

Dr Deborah Thiagarajan was educated at Smith College and the Universities of Pittsburgh, Rochester and Pennsylvania. She obtained her PhD from the University of Madras where she studied ancient Indian culture and archaeology. She is President of the Madras Craft Foundation, and played a key role in the establishment of the Dakshinachitra Centre. As well as being Convenor of the Tamil Nadu State Chapter of the Indian National Trust for Art and Cultural Heritage, she is a popular lecturer and prolific writer.

References

Thiagarajan, D., *Social Stratification of Harijans in Tamil Nadu*, Madras Institute of Development Studies, 1971

Thiagarajan, D., *Food Habits and Beliefs of Pregnant and Lactating Mothers in Coimbatore District*, Tamil Nadu Nutrition Project, 1973

Thiagarajan, D., *Wood Craft in Tamil Nadu*, in *Crafts of Tamil Nadu*, Mapin Publications, 1991

Thiagarajan, D., *The Craft of Derala*, Mapin Publications, (forthcoming)

Traditional rural buildings from South India, reconstructed at Dakshinachitra.

24

AFRICAN HERITAGE
The Assets of Sierra Leone

Arthur Abraham

Sierra Leone is remarkably well endowed with heritage resources, relative to its size, be they natural, mineral, cultural or historical. Yet, it is ironical that a country whose GDP growth rate in the decade after independence was higher than the world average, has been caught in a vicious circle of decline since the 1980s. Scarce resources have led to neglect and consequent loss of heritage assets, which in turn have given rise to official and public apathy. Efforts made during the colonial and early independence periods, now seem almost lost in the face of continued low priorities being accorded to heritage matters in national resource allocation.

That heritage assets form the foundation for tourism development is a lesson yet to be learnt. Thus, the enormous potential which the country possesses remains largely unharnessed, with the contribution of tourism to the economy being very low. Although the enforced exodus caused by the slave trade was a cultural and human catastrophe, we are fortunate to have identified distinct communities in the South-East of the United States who are descendants of Africans exported from Sierra Leone. This connection represents an obvious focal point for developing cultural tourism in response to their search for identity and cultural roots in African heritage. Tourism could be developed around this theme and the revenue generated ploughed back into heritage conservation and management, thereby arresting the current spiral of neglect and decline.

This chapter is an eclectic review of some of the heritage resource potential for tourist pilgrimages. I examine the rise and demise of heritage management initiatives, mounted at different times in Sierra Leone, and conclude with some proposals for possible solutions.

THE BACKGROUND

Sierra Leone is a small country occupying part of the western bulge of West Africa, measuring 73,326 square km in area and with a population of 4.3 million. Its Atlantic coastline of beautiful beaches and mangrove swamps with indented lagoons, river estuaries and natural harbours, is 340km long and has a continental shelf of 25,000 square km. The diversity of its eco-systems also includes savanna woodlands and tropical forest. Half of the country is low-lying plains rising to a hilly plateau, with several important peaks, and there is a richness of mineral and water resources.

There are two distinct seasons: the dry season from December to May, and the rainy season from June to November. Annual rainfall varies from 120–200 inches on the coast to 80–100 inches inland. The mean annual temperature is 27 degrees C, with high humidity of 90% in the rainy season and 60% in the dry season. The hottest months are March and April.

Sierra Leone comprises eighteen ethno-linguistic groups, most of which show a remarkable degree of socio-cultural similarity in institutions and values. The youngest ethnic group, the Krio, are a direct consequence of the Atlantic slave trade. The Krio are descendants of a multitude of West Africans, who were actually enslaved in the Americas or were recaptured by British war-ships during the process of exportation in the early 19th century and brought to Freetown to be liberated on land that had been acquired for the purpose in 1787. Until the end of the American civil war in 1865, frequent accretions from re-captives and migrants from the interior led to the expansion of settlements and by the last quarter of the 19th century, descendants of all these groups came to be called Krios with a distinctive language and culture. The dynamic growth and spread of Krio has made it the lingua franca of Sierra Leone, and it is now a national language.

The hinterland was declared a Protectorate by the British in 1896, while the territory occupied by the Krios was ruled directly as a Crown Colony since 1808. Sierra Leone gained independence in 1961 as a unified country and became a Republic in 1971. During the 1960s, economic performance was encouraging with GDP growing at 4.3% per annum as against the world average of 3.7%, indicating a good standard of living. This economic growth slowed down during the 1970s, making way for stagnation in the early 1980s, and actual decline since then, such that

320

people today are economically worse off than they were at independence. The World Bank Structural Adjustment Programme, in place since 1991, has exacerbated social hardship and the situation has been compounded by a run-away inflation. The UNDP Human Development Report of 1994 rated the country as the last but one in terms of human development.

The political priorities of the regime which came to power in 1968 helped precipitate an engulfing economic decline, and the situation was worsened by a rebel war which spilled over from neighbouring Liberia in March 1991. Since then, each one of the twelve administrative districts has been physically hit, mercifully excepting the Western Area where the capital is located. Even this proved illusory when in May 1997, the national army invited the rebels to join them overthrow the one-year old democratically-elected government in a bloody coup, destroying much of the city's infrastructure and unleashing a regime of anarchy, mayhem, and pogrom. In February 1998, the international community supported the use of force to remove the junta from power and restore the government. It is clear that the entire population has been affected, with over a million being killed, internally displaced, or becoming refugees.

This state of affairs has compounded the fact that heritage issues which were considered important in colonial times, have gradually lost steam since independence. Economic decline has led to parsimonious budgets which are ridiculous in real terms today, and public interest has shifted away from the potential value of the nation's heritage assets. This has left a legacy of gross under-funding which has made it impossible to sustain any serious programmes to promote public awareness, education, management and planning for the future.

THE ENDOWMENTS OF NATURE

Beautiful sunny beaches, mountains, rivers and lakes, tropical rain forests and savanna grasslands all provide for potential tourism. However, tourism has only been promoted in relation to the white sandy beaches found almost everywhere along the entire 340km of the Atlantic coast. Although only an estimated 10% of the original closed canopy tropical rain forest of Sierra Leone remains today, the country boasts of at least 2000 plant species, 78 of which are found only in Sierra Leone, including one entire genus.

Control over flora and fauna is vested in the Forestry Division of the Ministry of Agriculture under the Wild Life Conservation Act of 1972. The Ministry can declare reserves and prosecute offenders. Four non-hunting reserves have been declared, and twelve types of bird and sixteen types of mammal and reptile have been proclaimed prohibited animals. Five animals are listed as 'genera of which the young are specifically protected'. But the Division is under-staffed and under-equipped and can hardly carry out its duties.

There are 15 species of primates. These comprise chimpanzees, ten species of monkeys including baboons, three strange creatures, two galagos and the potto. There is a large antelope family with 18 species. Forest elephants can still be found. With its well watered system of rivers, Sierra Leone affords an ideal place for water safaris to view river wildlife comprising mammals, reptiles and birds found in the water, on the rocks and beaches as well as in trees along the river banks. In the dry season when the river currents slow down and the water becomes clear, vast schools of tilapia can be seen underwater.

An inviting menu for the eyes includes the palm-nut vulture, the West African fish eagle, the Senegal thick knee, the Hadada ibis, the hammerkop, collared pratincole, the endangered pygmy hippo, crocodiles, monitor lizard (or iguana), and many fish species including the Nile perch, African pike, catfish, electric fish and lung fish.

The savanna woodland areas display the spectacular lophira trees which are very fire resistant, with the red flowers of the locustbeans hanging like fireballs from the stems, and are dotted with termite mounds, elaborate mud castles, sometimes over 2 metres high. Here dwell the nocturnal aardvark, three members of the hog family, the African civet or bush cat, the leopard, etc.

In the tropical forest, much of the activities demonstrating life occur far above the observer's head. However, ants are immediately obvious on the ground. Birds cannot be easily seen but their singing is almost omnipresent, with the shining dongos, three types of greenbuls, the black-headed oriole, the chestnut wattle-eye, three species of large hornbill, etc.

At present, there are five areas of reserves that are capable of offering the most to wildlife tourists. The Western Area and Guma Valley Trails are part of the non-hunting Forest Reserve of the Western Area which afford excellent outings and scenery, with 299 species of birds. There is also the Mamunta-Mayosoh Wildlife Sanctuary established in the Tonkolili District in 1980. Although only 20 square km, this area provides an important sanctuary for waterfowl and the endangered short-nose crocodile, as well as a staging-post for over 240 species of birds, most of them migratory to and from North Africa and Europe.

The Outamba-Kilimi National Park in the northernmost part of the Bombali District was established in 1983. It covers an area of 980 square km of woodland, boulder-covered hills, pockets of swamps and forests, offering a variety of habitats for both dry savanna and forest birds and animals: chimpanzees, elephants, waterbuck, wart-hogs, genets and over 260 species of birds. The Loma Mountains Non-Hunting Reserve occupies

330 square km in the Koinadugu District, a granite massif with several peaks including the Bintumani (1945m) which is the highest mountain in West Africa west of Cameroon. This is home to leopards, bush cows, and several primates, as well as 245 species of birds including the Sierra Leone prinia, a species found only here.

The Gola Forest Reserve in the South-East is part of the great swathe of tropical rain forest stretching eastwards into Central Equatorial Africa. It harbours 222 species of birds, 178 species of trees, 46 mammals including monkeys, chimpanzees, leopards, elephants, and golden cats, and a great number of animals yet to be discovered. Here live a number of endangered species such as the white-breasted guinea-fowl, the whitenecked picathartes (bare-headed rock fowl), the bongo and the zebra duiker.

The Tiwai Island Wildlife Sanctuary, declared in 1978, is located in the lower reaches of the Moa river near Potoru in the Pujehun District. One hundred and fifty species of trees have been identified, some with canopies over 50 metres high. Within the 12 square km area of the island, there are eleven species of primates, a large number of mammals, 120 species of birds, over 800 species of butterfly. The initiative for conservation here was led by the local community itself, five years before government declared the island a wildlife sanctuary.

There are very serious environmental threats to these areas which have given rise to conservation concerns. The lack of support and underfunding by government means that the Conservation Branch of the Forestry Division of the Ministry of Agriculture, charged under the 1972 Wildlife Act with responsibility for these activities, remains a lame duck. In response to this state of affairs, the Conservation Society of Sierra Leone was born in 1986 as a voluntary organisation. The society carries out awareness programmes, and supports research and environmental management activities. Although the Society receives co-operation from international agencies, it still has very limited resources to run all its programmes.

MONUMENTS AND RELICS

The Monuments and Relics Commission was set up in 1947 'to provide for the preservation of Ancient, Historical, and Natural Monuments, Relics and other objects of Archaeological, Ethnographical, Historical or other Scientific Interest'. In 1962, an amendment to the law defined 'ethnographical article' as any item made or fashioned before the year 1937. By far the most important change was made in 1967. The original corporate status of the Commission was lost as it was now placed under the supervision of the Minister of Education, who provided an annual subvention for its work. Equally significant was the fact that the Commission was allowed to acquire, maintain, and administer the Sierra Leone Museum founded in 1953, which remains to date the only Museum in the country. During 1948–65, the Commission identified and declared 19 monuments, the most famous being:

1. The De Ruyter Stone of 1664;
2. Bunce Island;
3. nomoli or stealite stone figurines;
4. John Newton's House and Slave Factory on Plantain Island;
5. the original Fourah Bay College Building.

The Commission also erected memorial plaques to historic buildings in Freetown, three in 1958 and three in 1960. The Commission is so underfunded that it has hardly functioned as envisaged in the enabling legislation, and has taken no advantage of research findings. Archaeological work is characterised by a series of scattered, scanty and limited excavations with few published results. By far the most important work was done by John Atherton (1969 and 1972). He provides details of Later Stone Age material cultures based on excavations at the Kakoya Rock Shelter near Musaia in the Koinadugu District, Yengema Cave in Kono District, Kamabai Rock Shelter in Bombali District and Yagala Rock Shelter near Kabala in the Koinadugu District. Work based on these sites has established that neolithic populations existed in Sierra Leone since about 2500 BC. A significant shift in material culture occurred between the 7th and 8th centuries AD manifested by the introduction of iron working, which was probably related to the empire building activities of the Western Sudan in the medieval period.

THE NATIONAL MUSEUM

The founding of the National Museum was due to the initiative of two colonial governors. In 1954, Sir Robert de Zouche Hall suggested to the Sierra Leone Society, a cultural and historical organisation, that a museum 'can contribute towards the growth of a national pride in what is past and what is traditional, by collecting and preserving objects and making them available for contemplation and study'. Consequently the old cotton-tree railway station was acquired for the purpose.

On 10 December 1957, the new governor, Sir Maurice Dorman, officially opened it as the Sierra Leone Museum. Outlining the objectives, he stated that the Sierra Leone Society wanted 'to collect, to put in order and to preserve the work of men's hands, both what remains of the records of the past, what is disappearing from our lives now, and what is the common artefact of today'. He stressed that the museum should be a place 'where an illiterate man can be inspired by the display of what is best in his culture both in the past and in the present. We want not only to delve into the past but we want to keep for our children a record of this rapidly developing Sierra Leone.'

The Sierra Leone Society formed a Museum Committee with the late Dr MCF Easmon as the first Chairman and Curator. By 1964, the Sierra Leone Society had become defunct, and in 1967 the Monuments and Relics (Amendment) Act handed the Museum over to the Monuments and Relics Commission. Present needs and financial constraints made the museum inadequate. With only 1,059 square feet of original floor space, there was insufficient room for any kind of acquisitions and expansion. A German grant in 1987 remedied this somewhat, by providing a new building with a total floor space of over 2000 square feet. The tiny library was located in the Curator's office, which has also become partly a store room.

Funding for the activities of the Museum in the past two decades has declined in real terms by nearly 150% from the equivalent of US$ 9000 in 1975/76 to 3,700 in 1992/93. Such budgetary limitation makes new acquisitions impossible and the Museum has had to rely purely on donations. Consequently, it has lost the opportunity to acquire important items of national importance, with resultant official apathy.

When the colonial railway was phased out in 1968, the government sold off all the tracks, rolling stock, engines and all, and not even a museological set was preserved. The same fate befell our double-decker buses which, for over twenty years previously, provided the main means of public transportation in Freetown. British colonial style telephone booths and post boxes have all been discarded without any of them being preserved. In 1977, Nigeria organised FESTAC, the second World Black and African Festival of Arts and Culture, at which Sierra Leone participated. The Museum's most valuable pieces were put on display there, having been borrowed by the Ministry of Tourism and Cultural Affairs. Those pieces never came back and have been lost for ever.

It is certainly the case that the Museum has not been able to fulfil its role as a centre of humanistic expression. Its lack of resources and facilities has also made it impossible to manage and keep even what it already owns. In 1984, an antique bronze cannon was also stolen from Bunce island, itself a declared national monument. Apart from pilfering, the loss of heritage assets in a situation of civil war whereby countless towns and villages have been wilfully burnt down, can better be imagined than described. Indeed, the nation has paid a heavy price for ignoring my *Cultural Policy in*

Sierra Leone, published in 1978 and my calling for an exhaustive inventory and documentation of cultural resources.

However, the desperate financial plight of the Museum has not prevented it from rendering useful service to the public and the international community. The Museum's collection of historic, ethnographic and archaeological items attracts people from all walks of life. School children are allowed to visit the Museum one hour before it is open to the public. A sample attendance taken for the year 1975/76 showed an average of 858 visitors per day, with an annual estimate of over 309,000. This has dropped considerably, and in 1994/95 there were only 32,100 local visitors, roughly 200 per day. 1,784 foreign visitors from 61 countries signed the visitors' book in 1975/76, while in 1994/95, there were 2,100 foreign visitors from 35 countries.

BUNCE ISLAND

Bunce Island is a small deserted island, 10.5 acres in area lying strategically in the Rokel river estuary, some nine nautical miles from the largest natural harbour in Africa at Freetown. It is one of forty European forts built on the West African Coast during the period of the Atlantic slave trade and it was declared a National Monument in 1949. It was the entrepot from which slaves and captives were shipped to North America, making it different from its rival forts on Goree Island in Senegal and at El Mina in Ghana, which shipped out slaves mainly to the West Indies and Brazil.

In 1672, the Royal African Company was established in England and started to build a fort on Bunce Island. From that time, English companies operated from there until to 1806. Piracy and an extension of European hostilities overseas saw the destruction of the fort in 1704, 1728, 1779, and 1794, but it was rebuilt each time. After the abolition of the slave trade, the island was used successively during the 19th century as a recruiting station (1811), a saw mill (1820), a trading post (1850s), and eventually at the end of the century, as a quarantine station for African troops returning from the Ashanti wars.

From the late 1750s onwards, the owners of Bunce Island shipped slaves regularly to the ports of Charleston in South Carolina and Savannah in Georgia. The staple crop in both colonies was rice. An important historical fact to note is that this part of Africa was then dubbed the 'Grain Coast' because rice had been grown there probably from about 2000 BC. Slaves from the Grain Coast were experts at rice growing, and consequently the planters were ready and willing to pay consistently high prices for these skilled slaves. These latter contributed immensely to the prosperity of the two colonies. In South Carolina and Georgia, the descendents of these exported Africans are called Gullahs. The language and culture of the Gullahs have been anthropologically proved to be directly related to cultures of the Grain Coast, including Sierra Leone.

Today, Bunce Island exhibits relics of its turbulent past. There are ruins of the residence of the Chief Agent or Governor, called the 'great house' fortification with iron cannons; a large open air slave enclosure and an undercellar cave or prison; a powder magazine; store rooms and dormitories; watch-towers; two cemeteries (one European and one African) etc. Apart from a single effort led by this author to rehabilitate the island in 1976, no other constructive attempts have been made. Vegetation is destroying the ruins, while tourists are allowed to take away whatever they want, including the bronze cannon referred to above. The Monuments and Relics Commission stands helpless as it has no means to control or supervise activities relating to the island.

The US National Park Service did a rehabilitation feasibility study in 1989, and Gullahs made a visit there the same year. A Gullah Heritage Society was formed, 'devoted to increasing the knowledge of the historical, cultural, spiritual and linguistic linkages between African-Americans and Sierra Leoneans'. One of its major goals is the preservation of Bunce Island as a historical site. But public apathy manifested in lack of sufficient government commitment and political will has discouraged these initiatives. Little effort has been made by government to exploit the Gullah Sierra Leone connection and to help raise the US $2.5m project cost estimated in the feasibility study, although the prospects of raising the necessary funds are promising.

There are incidentally, several monuments representing the heritage of the slave-trade and slavery experience. Nearly all the 'Colony Villages' in the rural areas around Freetown were founded for recaptured slaves after the British abolition of 1808. These villages still evince a romance of their own in life styles and architectural designs of the Victorian era. Those who settled or established these villages must have passed through 'King's Yards'.

When the British captured slave ships bound for the New World after 1808, they brought them to Freetown for adjudication. The slaves on board the ships were housed in large compounds known as 'King's Yards', while awaiting the court proceedings and eventual liberation. The largest in Freetown was where the present national referral hospital, the Connaught Hospital, stands. The gateway to the Lower Dispensary bears this inscription: 'Royal asylum and hospital for those rescued from slavery by British valour and humanity'. This Gateway to the King's Yard was declared a national monument in 1949, along with Bunce Island.

THE PUBLIC ARCHIVES

The Public Archives which originated in the Colonial Secretariat, were moved to Moyamba during World War II, and brought back to Freetown afterwards and dumped in some army huts at New England. In 1950, Christopher Fyfe was appointed Government Archivist and he undertook a systematic arrangement of the holding. By the time of his departure in 1952, the archives were moved to Fourah Bay College campus on Mount Aureol, then a constituent College of the University of Durham in England. Honorary Government Archivists were subsequently appointed from staff of the College.

It was not until 1965 that the Public Archives Act was passed to make provision for the appointment of a Director of Archives whose duties were to 'make provision for the custody, preservation, arrangement, repair, rehabilitation, and for such duplication, reproduction, description and exhibition of archives including the preservation and publication of inventories, indexes, catalogues and other finding aids or guides facilitating their use'. To date, no Director has been appointed. There are also official archives and records maintained at the administrative headquarters of the twelve administrative districts and the three administrative provinces.

The Public Archives housed at Fourah Bay College occupy four large rooms in two separate buildings. The bulk of the archives in the repository date from 1788 to 1919, and a total of about 63,000 linear feet of records are held on dexicon shelves. By far the largest amount of documents relate to the slavery experience, abolition, and the establishment and development of the Krio Society. The archives operate under 'the thirty-year rule'. The most numerous and regular group of searchers come from the university community with the United States and Britain accounting for the greatest number. Local use is limited mostly to digging for information with regard to chieftaincy elections and land disputes.

In 1965, UNESCO undertook a study of the organisation of the archives and recommended the creation of a Record Centre. In 1970, UNESCO again provided assistance for microfilming and a mobile unit was able to deal with a small collection of 200 items. In 1978, The British Ministry of Overseas Development sponsored a one-week seminar on records management while the Commonwealth Secretariat and the Nulfield Foundation funded a project in 1991. This project set up a temporary Records Centre by clearing semi-current and non-current records in selected government Ministries, and provided training in records' management.

By far the most fundamental problem is the lack of government and public support. The ad hoc manner in which government has set about organising the archives has led to an unstable situation. Temporary housing has seen the archives shifting domicile on several occasions. This is most unsatisfactory as it leads to deterioration, while the current Fourah Bay College hosts need their spaces and have in the recent past threatened the archives with eviction.

The gross under-funding has been exacerbated over the years, going down in real terms from the equivalent of US$ 30,000 in the mid 1970s to an insignificant US$ 3,300 in 1992/93, a drop of over 800%. Accordingly, the Archives cannot get permanent accommodation, nor can the full complement of staff be employed. Of the six staff employed currently, only two have received para-professional training. The archives lack everything from space to stationery. The documents therefore suffer from continuous damage and destruction. Fungus attacks caused by high humidity are compounded by convenient breeding grounds for termites and silver fishes. There are neither de-humidifiers nor airconditioners. There are no restoration and reprographic units thus subjecting original documents to unacceptable wear and tear. Even the bindery is under-equipped. There is no vehicle to transport archives from District and Provincial offices to the national centre.

Much has been lost or destroyed. When the national archives were originally set up, documents deposited were only up to 1919. Documents from 1920 onwards remained in the Colonial Secretariat. In the late 1960s, they could not be traced. In response to inquiries, the author was informed that a cleaning exercise in the Secretariat had seen those documents in flames.

As for District and Provincial archives, no control has been kept over them. Researchers had unfettered access, and as no photocopying facilities are available in the interior, they are able to take away as much as they please, apparently without anybody caring. This is perhaps because none of these offices has any archivists or records officers. Only clerks are put in charge who do not know the value of the documents as cultural assets. Civil disturbances led by students against the government in 1977 saw the burning down of some district offices together with their archives. To crown it all, the rebel war which started in 1991 has physically devastated all administrative districts in the country. Countless government buildings have been burnt down or otherwise destroyed or vandalised. The exact nature and extent of this destruction can only be assessed when the war is over.

SIERRA LEONE STUDIES

The publication of *Sierra Leone Studies* was an important element in promoting heritage awareness and conservation. It was established by Governor R.J. Wilkinson in 1918. He expected administrative officers to learn something of the language and customs of the people over whom they had authority, including judicial powers. Additionally, the Governor felt that this would stimulate 'an active interest in one's work and one's surrounding' and asked for any contribution connected with ethnography, linguistics, history or natural features, life and customs of the people, flora and fauna, geology and resources, etc. The Governor hoped that 'in the course of years the sum-total of these *Studies* will be of great scientific value'. How very right he was.

The journal was interrupted by World War II, but another enthusiastic governor, Sir Robert de Zouche Hall, was instrumental in reviving it on the basis that the journal had 'preserved a mass of information of permanent value which might otherwise have been lost'. The main force behind the establishment of a museum in Sierra Leone, Governor Hall provided funds in 1953 to start a 'New Series' of the journal, the editing of which was transferred from the Colonial Secretary's Office to the University. The journal was taken over by the Institute of African Studies on its establishment in 1963, and publication continued till 1970 when it ceased, and has not been revived since. Here, for once, the blame cannot be put on government because it has kept money voted for its publication in annual budgets since then. The challenge now lies with Fourah Bay College, which presided over the demise of the journal, and now faces the task to get it resurrected.

THE INSTITUTE OF AFRICAN STUDIES

Fourah Bay College is the oldest University College in tropical Africa. It was founded by the Church Missionary Society in 1827, and became affiliated to the University of Durham in England in 1876. As a constituent college, it offered Durham degrees until 1969, when it became part of the new University of Sierra Leone. The original building of the College, located near the harbour in Freetown, was constructed of red-stone, and dates back to 1845 when the first coloured Governor, an Afro-West Indian, Staff Sergent Major William Fergusson, laid the foundation stone. In his address at the ceremony, he tearfully drew attention to the fact that 'on the very spot where they were preparing to erect a building from whence it is hoped that spiritual freedom would be imparted to many Africans, there stood, forty years ago, a slave factory'. It was opened in 1848 and was in use for a century until the outbreak of World War II. The college campus was transferred to Mount Aureol after the War, and the original building was declared a national monument in 1955. This educational lead earned for Sierra Leone, the epithet of 'The Athens of West Africa.'

African studies came to Fourah Bay College in 1963 when the Institute was founded, and immediately took over publication of *Sierra Leone Studies*. The Institute's programme was largely to do research and undertake publication. Its remit was ambitious, including a long-term interpretative study of political and constitutional history. It was also to 'collect, assemble and collate' from all sources, materials on the history of the peoples of Sierra Leone; research into all aspects of Sierra Leonean life and thought and promote archaeological work; establish a 'Depository Library-cum-Museum' of African (including Afro-American, Caribbean, and Latin-American Negro) history, culture, music, art, etc. undertake studies of language, religion, customary law, music and art, ethnography, philosophy, politics etc.

A British government grant enabled permanent housing to be erected in 1969, and with a two-year planned expansion in 1970, a Government White Paper even proposed that the Institute be made an independent organisation. But anticipated funds never materialised, and the Institute never realised any of its objectives, lost its grandeur and attraction for academic pilgrimage and today it functions like any other teaching department of the University.

THE WAY FORWARD

Sierra Leone has all the potentials for developing into an important attraction for modern pilgrims in search of heritage. To achieve this, there is a need to start tackling issues which will improve standards of heritage management, remove national apathy and public neglect and make the necessary resources available. Unregulated access and theft have all conspired to generate and perpetuate a cycle of decline, which has not only led to loss of extremely valuable heritage assets, but is depriving the government of income that could be earned from cultural tourism development. It is high time that Sierra Leone became a party to the 1970 UNESCO convention on the Means of Prohibiting and Preventing the Illicit Import, Export and Transfer of Ownership of Cultural Property, as well as to the 1972 Convention Concerning the Protection of the World Cultural and Natural Heritage. Thus the government could strengthen its position in seeking international assistance for the restoration of stolen property, or preservation of cultural heritage.

Tourism and heritage affairs are interdependent activities and close collaboration between these two functions is necessary for success. At present, heritage affairs are scattered over a number of government ministries, but there is no link with the Ministry of Tourism. There are thus enormous challenges to be addressed and the following suggestions aim to create a new sense of identity and corporate national pride.

An integrated approach is envisaged whereby heritage assets will be used to attract tourists. This would generate revenue which could in turn be used to develop further heritage resources and attract a much wider interest in cultural tourism. It is hoped that when these solutions are implemented, heritage tourism will develop into one of the major revenue earning sectors of the economy thereby eliminating the neglect from which our heritage assets have suffered for so long.

First, I propose that the Ministry of Tourism should be reorganised to incorporate all matters of cultural heritage as far as possible, and should be renamed the Ministry of Heritage Affairs and Tourism or as appropriate. It should work for Sierra Leone to accede without any further delay to the 1970 and 1972 UNESCO Conventions on Cultural Property and Cultural and Natural Heritage. Under the new ministry, the Monuments and Relics Commission should be given a new lease of life by granting an adequate budgetary allocation, and it should undertake the following immediate tasks:

1. Seek assistance of agencies such as UNESCO, the International Centre for the study of the Preservation and the Restoration of Cultural Property in Rome, the West African Museum Project, and ICOM, to carry out an inventory and documentation of heritage assets/cultural resources.
2. Develop a strategy for management and promotion of all identified national monuments such as the archaeological sites of Kamabai, Yagala, Kakoya and Yengema.
3. Rehabilitation of Bunce Island as a top priority, and collaborating with the Gullah Heritage Society, funding should be sought to implement the National Park Service study recommendations so that it can become the centre of pilgrimages from America, the operation being part of a larger strategy including conservation and promotion of the Colony Villages.

Second, the Museum services should be planned in light of the changing role for museums. It should not only be concerned with conservation, but also with research, dissemination and education. This requires a reorientation of methods and activities with flexibility and involvement in the community. One museum cannot serve the needs of a whole nation either intellectually or geographically. I therefore recommend that the national museum service be organised around a series of specialist areas. Premises should be provided preferably by rehabilitating those that qualify for the status of National Monument, there being numerous ones which would qualify. Decentralisation is the way of the future and regional and local museums should be established, along with school and private museums. At national level, I proposed the following areas of specialisation:

1. Museum of Popular Art;
2. Museum of Ethnography and Traditional Culture;
3. Museum of Colonial History;
4. Museum of Science and Technology
5. Museum of the Slave Trade;
6. Museum of Archaeology;
7. Museum of the Rebel War;

Third, a National Arts Council should also be established under the new Ministry. It would work hand in hand with the museums service and should coordinate, promote, revive, develop, and encourage literary, visual and performing arts. The single National Dance Troupe is inadequate. At least three troupes should be organised by the new Ministry to meet the needs for local and international engagements, and Regional decentralisation should be encouraged.

Galleries and craft centres should be encouraged as cooperative community initiatives with particular attention paid to women in the rural areas. Gara tye-dying, textiles, ceramics, fibre and wicker-work, leather products, carvings, soap-making, etc., are examples of cottage industries that not only create a cultural tourist market, but also help improve rural incomes. Fourth, the old Fourah Bay College Building at Cline Town, itself a national monument, should be made the permanent home of the public archives. The new Ministry of Heritage Affairs and Tourism should then make budgetary provision and seek external assistance to purchase basic equipment. All government ministries and administrative offices should appoint Records Officers to be responsible for proper organisation and care of archival material. Fifth, Heritage publications such as *Sierra Leone Studies, Journal of the Historical Society, Bulletin of Religion* and others should be revived through appropriate funding and responsibility given to qualified persons in the University who can be expected to deliver high quality products. The Institute of African Studies should be made to design and offer appropriate training programmes in heritage interpretation and management. Sixth, Nature and Wildlife Reserves should be developed with appropriate safari facilities to encourage ecotourism. This would require an agency with responsibility for governing both conservation and access. It would work closely with the Forestry Division of the Ministry of Agriculture.

Bold measures such as these can restore the Athens of West Africa to its rightful place among proud nations with a regime of heritage management that will enable it to become a premier tourist destination on the African Continent.

The Author

Professor Arthur Abraham holds a PhD in African Studies from the University of Birmingham, and has experience of teaching and research at universities in Europe, Africa, and the United States. A member of several professional bodies, he has been a Development Consultant since 1986. He has published several books and monographk, numerous articles, and a large number of study reports and unpublished papers covering a broad range of development, historical, educational and cultural issues and topics. He was one time Minister of Education, Youth and Sports, as well as Minister of Trade, Industry and State Enterprises in Sierra Leone. He holds the Chair of African Studies in the University of Sierra Leone, is Director of the Institute of African Studies, and Dean of the Faculty of Social Sciences.

References

Abraham, A., *Cultural Policy in Sierra Leone*, UNESCO, 1978

Abraham, A., *Quo Vadis African Studies?* Director's Address at the African Studies Week. Fourah Bay College, February 1994

Abraham, A., *Easmon, M. C. F.* in *Encyclopedia Africana Dictionary of African Biography*, Vol. II, Algonac, 1979

Abraham, A., *Sierra Leone Studies in the School Curriculum*, Working Document and Keynote Address, Seminar at National Curriculum Development Centre, Department of Education, Freetown, July 1994

Abraham, A. and Fyle, C. M., *Report of Bunce Island Rehabilitation Camp*, *Africana Research Bulletin*, VII, 1, 1976

Abraham, A and Gaima, E .A .R., *Ethnographic Survey of the Kalantuba Limba of Kalansogoia Chiefdom, Tonkolili District, Northern Province, Sierra Leone*, Freetown, Institute of African Studies Occasional Paper No. 5, 1995

Atherton, J., *The Later Stone Age of Sierra Leone*, Oregon University PhD thesis, 1969

Atherton, J., *Excavations at the Kamabai and Yagala Rock Shelters*, Sierra Leone, *West African Journal of Archaeology*, 2, 1972

Ayandele, E A., *Country Programme for Sierra Leone, 1993–1997: Proposals for Projects in Cultur Dakar*, UNESCO Regional Office for Education in Africa, 1991

Field, G .D., *Birds of the Freetown Peninsula*. Freetown, 1974

Foray, C .P., *An Outline of Fourah Bay College History*, Freetown, 1979

Fyfe, C., *Short History of Sierra Leone*, Longman, 1979

Fyfe, C., 1787–1887–1987: Reflections on a Sierra Leone Bicentenary, *Africa*, 57 (4), 1987

Hall, R. de Zouche, *A Museum for Sierra Leone?*, *Sierra Leone Studies*, NS 3, December 1954

Kouroupas, M. P., U.S. *Efforts to Protect Cultural Property*. *African Arts*, Autumn, 1995

Reynolds, D. et al., *Recommendations for the Protection and Management of Bunce Island National Historic Site, Sierra Leone*, Report by U.S. National Park Service for U.S. Peace Corps, 1979

Seisler, P. and Gyorgy, A., (eds.) *Wildlife and Nature Reserves of Sierra Leone*, Freetown, Conservation Society of Sierra Leone, 1993

Serageldin, I. and Taboroff, J. (eds.) *Culture and Development in Africa*, World Bank, 1992

Sierra Leone Studies, Introduction and Editorial Notes, *Sierra Leone Studies*, June, 1918

Wilkinson, R. J., Foreword, *Sierra Leone Studies*, June, 1918

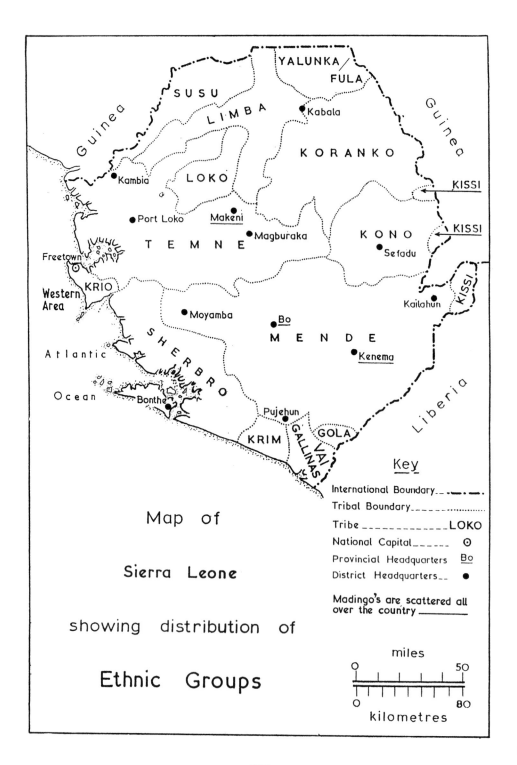

Map of

Sierra Leone

showing distribution of

Ethnic Groups

Key

International Boundary —··—··—
Tribal Boundary ············
Tribe ——————— LOKO
National Capital ———— ☉
Provincial Headquarters Bo
District Headquarters —— ●

Madingo's are scattered all
over the country ————

25

ECHOES OF AFRICA
Jamaica's Musical Heritage

Olive Lewin

MEK WE WALK AN TALK

Verse 1:   Dis long time gal me nevva see you
            Come, mek me hol' you han

Refrain: Peel head John Crow siddung pon tree top
            Pick off the blossom
            Mek me hol you han gal
            Mek me hol you han

Verse 2:   Dis long time gal me nevva see you
            Come mek we walk and talk

Verse 3:   Dis long time gal me nevva see you
            Come mek we w'eel and tun

Coda: Mek we w'eel and tun till we tumble dung
            Mek we hol you han gal
            Mek we w'eel and tun till we tumble dung
            Mek me hol you han gal

This traditional greeting song has been passed on by generations of Jamaicans for at least one hundred and thirty years. We older Jamaicans cannot remember when we learnt it, or who taught it to us. It is as though it was 'blowing in the wind', and we caught it. Sing it now and thousands of Jamaicans scattered in continents and islands worldwide join in.

We knew what it said: meet, greet and dance together, but it was not until in the 1960s that the meaning of the refrain became evident at a 'reasoning' session between this researcher and villagers, varying in age from 40 to 80. The John Crow mentioned is a scavenger bird, never likely to sit on tree tops picking blossoms. So the refrain invites friendship (hol you han) until John Crows pick blossoms, till the seas run dry, forever. Originally, this song would have been used by workers in the plantation system, where life was hard and remained so after emancipation in 1838. Low wages and substandard living conditions continued even after the birth of Jamaica's first labour union one hundred years later. Occasions for socializing and having fun would have been grasped eagerly. Singing and dancing always played their part and were used with gusto.

Often it was death ceremonies that were used for what would now be seen as secular recreational activities. This fitted into the old belief system whereby death was seen as the door allowing the spirit of the 'departed' to proceed to another phase of life. It meant reunion with ancestors and loved ones 'gone before', and release from earthly cares, sorrow and pain. Many reasons for rejoicing.

Other occasions (all out of doors) involved similar celebrations. These included cropover dances at the end of the main sugar cane harvest and moonshine dahlins, when workers and villagers of all ages, gathered to 'eat drink and be merry' by the light of the moon. She still is sometimes referred to as the parish lantern, greatly appreciated for giving such beautiful bright light in non-electrified places.

Moonshine dahlins, as well as informal cane field and/or backyard parties were utilized for keeping children happy, active and occupied. Story telling, ring games, hopscotch, stone passing and clapping games, riddles and so on were the norm in these settings. Sometimes before, but chiefly after the children were shooed to bed, adults indulged in quadrille dancing, telling jokes and tall tales, singing games and the indigenous mento song/dancing for their recreation. In the extended family and cluster style of living, 'bed' would have been within walking and watching distance of the party. Grandparents or other elders would escort and stay with children who lived farther away.

'Dis long time gal' was ideal for such occasions. It was suitable for lusty mixed or single sex singing and appropriate for children to join in. Unlike quadrille and set dances, it gave scope for varied and improvised movements accompanied by rhythms clapped and/or played, or sticks, graters or any such things at hand. However in spite of its suitability for a wide range of performance styles, it should be noted that this song was used only among social peers, friends, fellow workers and siblings. Has the time come for the boundaries to be stretched: for barriers to be dismantled?

338

HERITAGE TOURISM

The 20th century is ending with some serious concerns regarding the fate of planet Earth. This means that the heritage of today's youth, and of succeeding generations also, might be in jeopardy. The time seems ripe for freeing the spirit of 'Dis long time gal' and for letting it dissolve whatever has been inhibiting willingness to 'walk and talk'. Today's adults can and must learn to 'meet, greet and dance together' to give friendship a chance, to let it flow, day by day 'til peel head John Crow siddung pun tree top pick(ing) off de blossom'. Doing less, means missing opportunities to take discussions about heritage and about tourism from the realms of theory to practice, the only route to success.

Tourism seems ideally poised to set in motion a worldwide initiative for helping individuals to increase their respect for and understanding of the diverse cultures that they can experience in their travels. The arts have long been recognised as holding the key to the heightening of transcultural awareness. This paper focuses on the role of Heritage music in this quest.

> Lend me the stone-strength of the past,
> And I will lend you the wings of the future
> *Jeffers*

Jamaica's musical heritage reflects the several ethnic and cultural groups that came there after Columbus, our first recorded pilgrim. This travelling in our region began as part of the 15th century gold rush which culminated in the seizure of land and peoples. After the initial rush, travel was not that of people anxious to make their fortunes, but of people from Africa shipped across the Atlantic to work as slaves, or bonded labour from the poor of the British Isles. There also were felons transported, Indians escaping from famine, and Chinese. Jews fleeing the Inquisition had been members of Columbus' crews. Other Middle Eastern peoples, and Germans came later, as did some voluntary labourers from Africa.

Each group adds aspects of its own heritage to an increasingly rich and varied tapestry of beliefs and their expressions. However as over 90% of Jamaicans are of African ancestry, the music of our heritage is predominantly African in spirit and in rhythm. Ancient melodic and harmonic styles, instruments, instrumentation and performance practices also hark back to the sounds and the customs of Africa. These have been passed on orally for centuries. The time has come for heritage to be seen and used to build bridges of respect and understanding between peoples of diverse backgrounds and cultures.

FROM INDIAN INHABITANTS TO AFRICAN IMPORTEES

We have been told that the first inhabitants of Jamaica were Amerindians. Older Jamaicans knew of them as Arawaks. Recently they have been identified as Tainos. By whatever name, they were gentle, and peace loving people.

In 1494, Christopher Columbus and his crews landed on the north coast of the island. Led by their Cacique, the inhabitants greeted the visitors with music and gifts. This picture soon changed, when the visitors proved to be adventurers in relentless pursuit of gold, and easy living. The Amerindians' life of self sufficiency and peace among themselves, supported by reverence for nature and harmony with their surroundings, became one of enslavement to the new settlers. Torn from their ancient traditions, they suffered severe cultural displacement. Unaccustomed diseases brought by the Europeans cost many lives, as did cruelty and overwork. Despair and depression leading to suicides and infanticide increased their wretchedness.

This work-force dwindled to uselessness by the turn of the century. Brandon (1961) tells us 'They (native Indians in the New World) died drunk, they died insane, they died by their own hands. They died they said, because their souls were stolen'. According to the Historian Clinton Black, those who survived escaped to Jamaica's rugged protective hills. Today, their record lies in small remnants of their language, in clay pots and vessels for storage, in a few cooking styles, some archaeological finds and in a few grave sites. They had 'vanished in such numbers that African labourers could not be shipped in fast enough to take their place'.

Our African forefathers were first shipped to Jamaica in the early 16th century by means of the trans-Atlantic trade in human beings. They were captured and sold, sometimes by their own people into the slave system that became a shameful example of 'man's inhumanity to man' (Burns). Though in some cases conditions in their homeland were substandard, it was worse to be snatched from familiar surroundings and loved ones, for shipment under dreadful conditions, into the unknown. They were taken empty handed, but within them they had deeply ingrained cultural traditions; memories which cruelty and suffering engraved rather than erased; knowledge of arts and skills that were one day to enrich their new homeland and the lives of descendants for incalculable years.

COMMUNICATION DENIED AND CREATED

The ships' human cargo was collected from different cultural areas. From the traders' points of view it was an advantage that differing languages limited the ability to plot and plan against their masters and the system. However, the slaves' common lot prompted the forging of a language understood by them all, but largely beyond the masters' ken.

The oral language evolved into today's Jamaican Creole, with more than a sprinkling of words and phrases with recognizable sources:

Buffoo	Twi-abofuru	Lazy, good for nothing
Cas cas	Twi-kasa kasa	Contention
Macca	Carribbean and Arawak Indian – macca	Prickle
Pinda	Congo – mpinda	Ground nut
Susu	Ewe– susu Twi–susukwa	Gossip
Unu	Ibo–unu	You – plural
Kench	Old Scottish and Irish –kench	Small amount
Schub	German – schub	Push, shove
Should can	Old Scottish – should can	Ought to be able
Must can	Old Scottish – must can	More emphatic of above

Songs combining words with music and supported by strong rhythms were even more powerful in bringing the diverse imported people together, and in sustaining ancestral connections, visible and invisible. Hoeing, pounding produce and breaking stones on the one hand, whilst communicating with the Creator/supreme God ancestral gods and spirits on the other, these invisible links were unaffected by the distance between the motherland and the new settings. Singing helped to reinforce old beliefs, to maintain spiritual loyalties, to fulfill obligations to ancestors. Since singing often helped work to go better, and therefore increased the masters' wealth, it was allowed even when drumming and gatherings were banned. Therefore, it aroused no suspicion in the ever watchful ever fearful owners, although it bonded the workers together in common plight.

According to people of Yoruba descent still living in western Jamaica, 'Amasunduwa, Tahta Lu', is a gentle song handed down from their ancestors. In this the presence of the Creator Tahta Lu has been invoked by several generations of Yoruba speaking slaves and their descendants. Members of certain other groups, now seriously endangered, also for centuries, have used songs and flat footed dancing in rituals and ceremonies to honour and communicate with Mother Earth, the provider of all material needs.

Songs and their supporting rhythms are still vital in maintaining, and when necessary, re-establishing harmony with the Creator, and all levels of life. Neglect of this results in dis-ease: social, spiritual, mental and/or physical. Between peers, songs have been used to pass messages and secret information, often under the guise of singing just to lighten labour or to enliven the day; to help to relieve stress and to keep hope alive.

Human beings, needed also to sustain respectful contact with the worlds of animals, plants and the elements, important constituents of life in its entirety. Only by careful attention to communication with all levels of life could the displaced people continue to maintain both ancestral links and their own place as human beings within the Creator's cosmic plan. For this, music played a crucial role. In particular its rhythm has helped people to keep in touch with the all-pervading rhythm of life always present and operative even when its physical location appears inanimate: a leaf, earth, a stone.

The slaves, items of property like cattle or sugar cane, were required to work wageless and in total submission to produce wealth for their owners. They also were goaded into producing offspring to replenish the stock of labourers and provide bodies to meet plans for expansion and for sale in the slave markets that thrived for over 300 years.

Owners changed from Spanish and Portuguese to English in 1655, but requirements from the workers remained essentially the same. Any form of revolt or infringement of orders, explicit or otherwise, could bring swift and sometimes brutal punishment: 'The bodies remained (hanging and) stiffening in the breeze till the court martial had provided another batch of victims. Workhouse Negroes came in the evening with carts and took them away to cast them into a pit dug for the purpose, a little distance out of town' (Bleby, 1853, referring to revolts between the end of the slave trade in 1808 and the abolition of slavery in 1838).

The slaves, then ex-slaves and later unbonded labourers realized how they were viewed by perpetrators of the plantation system. There was cruelty and there were confrontations, with predictable results, as reflected in a folksong referring to the 1865 post emancipation uprising and massacre.

> Soldiers from Newcastle come dung a Monklan
> Wit gun an sword fe kill sinna oh

342

However it was, less dangerous and destructive of life and property to circumvent the system. Ways were found to do this, many recorded in song. They were mainly:

1. escaping from the grasp of life on the plantation
    > Run Moses, run
    > Missa Walkler da come
    > If you buck you right foot,
    > Buck you lef foot
    > Try doan look back

2. avoiding work and/or overwork, 'Sally' is a song for hauling houses has 4 phrases, only 3 of which are used for the hauling. The other is used for resting. In an 8 hour day, 2 hours' (one out of 4 phrases) rest made a difference. The workers dared not stop to rest, but out of sight, the sound of their worksong allowed the owners and their overseers to feel confident that work was proceeding 'happily'.

3. evading punishment and most of all retaining one's 'subtle, mystic pride' (Brandon) as human beings in the Creator's cosmos, in spite of the difficult and inhumane conditions of life and labour. Singing 'happily' to mask suffering; making fun even of the man, probably black, standing nearby with a whip.

The outward existence as a submissive nobody in the masters' world had to be reconciled with the inward life as a free and distinctive member of the Creators' world. To this end, cultural resources, especially music and movement used with 'imagination, courage and cunning' (J Hope Mason, 1991) became powerful weapons and indispensable invisible assets. They are still available to assist in solving the persistent problems relating to human interaction at the end of the 20th century.

BRIDGES OF RESPECT

Tourism creates countless opportunities daily for improving or impairing human relationships worldwide, therefore can help to halt or even just lessen tensions and misunderstandings born of prejudice, intolerance or only an innocent inability to allow people of diverse cultures, whether home folk or visitors, as much freedom as possible to be themselves: an inability to accept and respect differences without feeling the need to thwart or destroy. Any bias or bigotry can be multiplied thousands of times every day wherever in the world the recreation industry flourishes.

Situations fraught with hidden dangers can arise and grow all too quickly into unpredictable monsters. Robert Burns' wise words should be noted, but even he would probably now be willing to concede that we need to put effort and work behind this wish:

> Oh wad some power the giftie gives
> To see oursels as other see us!
> It wad frae monie a blunder free us
> An' foolish notion.

It is necessary to take Robert Burns seriously if bridges of respect, or at least tolerance, are to be built in time to save this planet for ourselves and for future generations. Tourism needs to work at balancing people motives with profit motives. It is an industry in which much time, effort, thinking and most of all, cash and kind are invested. Without profit it fails. There must therefore be many, investors small and large, who are primarily interested in receipts. These include air lines, hotel chains and producers of their needs, whether technology, staff, food, furniture or mass-produced curios. Included too, are the makers of hand-crafted items, farmers selling small quantities of seasonal crops or produce unique to their areas, prostitutes pushers of drugs. The needs of the second group are more likely to be buying food for the family, shoes to go to church, bus fares for the children to go to school and medicine for grandma. No doubt everyone mentioned sees him/herself as providing essential goods and services to the tourism industry.

How do they see each other? How do visitors and home folk assess each others' roles? In one scenario, words like exploiters, pimps, molesters, law breakers quickly come to mind. They suggest suspicion, selfish unhealthy competition, alienation and fragmentation. Profit is the pre-eminent goal, with self at the centre. Marya Mannes (*Life*, June 12, 1964, p.62) wrote: 'In the race for money, some men may come first, but man comes last.'

Many of the suppositions may be incorrect, but this makes them no less potent, no less dangerous. A way or ways must be found to change the attitudes and opinions that cause and support them. For example at two International Music Festivals, the Jamaican Folk Singers found that music opened doors that led to camaraderie, cooperation and respect between groups from differing linguistic and cultural areas.

At the 1990 Drummondville Festival of Folklore in Canada, an Inuit group was heard singing a Jamaican Folksong that had recently been performed by the singers from Jamaica. The two groups, with no linguistic means of communication got together and worked quite successfully on preparing a joint presentation of the Jamaican song. Accents, body language and performance styles were different, but the spirit of cooperation and mutual respect were powerfully present. What is more, subsequently individuals met and learnt more about each other's arts: Inuit sculpture and Caribbean dance styles mainly. Before the music encounter we had been strangers to each other. After it, there were always smiles and cordial greetings.

Furthermore, the Jamaican Folk Singers were invited to perform and compete in the International Eisteddfod of South Africa. There were 28 nations participating, the Jamaicans being the first non-African blacks to take part in the event. Many languages were spoken in the Eisteddfod village, and performance styles were truly diverse.

The Jamaicans were asked one evening to prepare a 15 minute package for a joint performance with the large group of vibrant Gabonese singers. Both groups performed their songs with eloquent movements. The styles were poles apart, both in voice production and in use of bodies and of space. The Gabonese were Francophone, the Jamaican Anglophone. There were two hours only for rehearsal, and an hour's break to don costumes and so on, before having to standby backstage. An audience of up to 8000 visitors and fellow performers might be waiting. The leader of each group chose three songs, discussed harmonization, dynamics, dramatization where appropriate, choreography and staging. Each group learnt the other's songs (in a language new until then) and then staged them with all the trappings. The finale would be 'Kumbya'. After two hours everyone felt fairly confident and determined to make the performance a success. We were in it together, like old friends.

There had been no rehearsal on the performance stage, but on cue we entered as though each of us knew exactly where to stand. The performance went well. After what seemed like a year of silence, the audience broke into wild applause. They gave us a standing ovation. There were tears backstage, and had been in the audience too, we were told. People had thought it miraculous that virtual strangers, so far removed culturally as well as geographically, had sent such a clear message of harmony and supportiveness to an audience even more varied than the performers. The teamwork and rapport had been established in record time. Music had transcended as many man-made barriers as could have been in place; language, politics, religion, colour, class, race.

Was this just a flash in the pan, or could it be duplicated, again and again? Did it spell hope? Might there really be peace and civilized problem solving one day? Is music underutilized in today's technologically galloping world? Has its role changed? Both, perhaps.

One can safely say that in all phases of the industry, music plays an important role. Music designed to entertain, to please and to attract those who are expected and encouraged to spend. Up to twenty or so years ago, in the Jamaican situation, performing groups often ruined their chances of being engaged a second time, because their first presentations were considered inappropriate. Visitors looked and listened. They paid attention. They did not chatter, laugh, buy drinks, let down their hair or sound happy. This did not please management. It spelt success for the performers and even brought invitations for overseas engagements, but caused frustration to the local promoters.

For the latter, musical entertainment, which always had a movement dimension was to tickle and titillate in order to further commercial aims. There was a time too, when performers of folk music were required to change into costumes in car parks, rest rooms and passage ways, not again. They are now seen as allies in the industry that means much to Jamaica. There is more respect for them and the music that they present. Organised pop musicians have long been treated as peers in another profit conscious industry. Although there are hopeful signs regarding the use of traditional music in performances, we have moved far away from the role of our traditional music in everyday life. Music to communicate and encourage cooperation and togetherness, for therapy and healing is disappearing fast as 'development' and death overtake its proponents and their way of life.

Our work songs, singing games, songs for death ceremonies and festivals all put communal needs at the centre. Firth puts it clearly (*Human Types* 64–65, 1958) when he says, 'It is sometimes imagined that the main drive to the economic activity of tribal people is their immediate desire to satisfy material wants...... In the first place, it is a socialized and not an individual response. It is seen then in the second place, that many of the wants upon which their economic life is based is of an immaterial type.'

Sowande, in *The Quest of an African Worldview* (1974, p.84) mentions another aspect. 'For the traditional African, a discourse involves as likely participants, not only those of his fellow human beings who are in his immediate vicinity or within reach, but also his gods and goddesses, his ancestors and heroes, the departed members of his society, the forces of the elements, the spirits of nature and *Mother Earth*.'

These two excerpts may take us beyond our vision for the 21st century, or might even seem to take us backwards into ages and civilizations past. However, we can hardly not agree that today's remarkable and ever rapidly changing scientific advances have outstripped our definitions of human development. Perhaps we do need to include, wants 'of an immaterial kind' in our quest for economic well-being. And, with the increasing recognition of ours as One World, and a shrinking one at that, our considerations need to go beyond 'fellow human beings in (our) immediate vicinity.'

Tourism and education are already taking us in that direction. The populations of many schools worldwide provide children with classroom neighbours from countries thousands of miles away. They may not always speak any one language, yet their lives must touch.

Children may not be the most visible or numerous visitors in this industry, but they are our chief concern, long term, and will be the next generation of tourists. Let music give them the chance to play together. Similarities already exist in games played in different parts of the world. Starting with the familiar will make it easier to introduce the unfamiliar, and probably induce some of the young ones to share their own playtime activities with their new pals. On returning home, they might be willing to pass on what they have learnt to their own home, school and community peers. This will help their chums to travel in imagination, and also spark interest in actually visiting other countries.

In fact, as part of the product development for the new millennium there could be countless possibilities for children's music and heritage games to be accessed via the internet. In days gone by, before the bulk of our population had the benefit of formal education or communication through the written word and when there were no electronic media, our people had their own very effective ways of preparing the young for life.

Movement, music and stories played a big part in this, helping to develop the children's bodies through play, giving them emotional security through being cuddled, rocked and sung to, helping their minds to grow through games that taught concentration and expended their imaginations and skills. It was also important for children to recognise the limits within which they could operate. Loving concern includes ensuring that the loved one does not grow like a weed. Good habits and good manners need to be engendered; discipline learnt from within. A song like *Manuel Road* helped and incidentally could help to pass on valuable messages.

> Go down a Manuel Road gal and boy
> Fe go bruck rock stone
> Bruck dem one by one; gal and boy
> Bruck dem two by two; gal and boy etc.
> Finga mash no cry; gal and boy
> Memba a play we dah play, gal and boy

This is a stone game played by both adults and children. Grown ups playing it, move large stones with such vigour that fingers can indeed be crushed: 'mash'. Little ones, though using smaller stones, also play energetically and need to concentrate and co-operate with the rhythm of the song. Therein lies the discipline. One submits to the rhythm and enjoys the game, or one doesn't and spoils it. Break the rhythm, and apart from running the risk of being unpopular with the other players, there is a distinct possibility of having fingers crushed. But, as the song says, 'finga mash no cry, memba a play we dah play'. It is only a game so one must accept it good naturedly. The message is clear. Co-operate, concentrate, put your whole heart into the game and we shall all have a lot of fun. Be careless, un-cooperative and scatter-brained, and you might end up with an injured finger and no sympathy.

Older Jamaicans who had the privilege of growing up in homes where stories were part of the training can recall being told, for instance, 'don't tease', it can cause life long worries just as it caused hog and dog to break friendship and not agree all these years, 'till now'. The story would follow: Times were so hard that hog had to accept work from rat. This was humiliating enough, but when his laziness caused rat to dismiss him, hog was mortified. Dog on the other hand was well placed as guard at the market gate. Not wanting to attract attention, hog was sneaking by one day when dog, laughing out loudly, ridiculed him. Hog never forgot or forgave, and the animosity has continued till today.

> Time get so hard
> Hog an' all a look work
> Dog siddung a Market Gate
> An' a laugh after hog distress

So sang 80 year old Miss Ada in the mid sixties, adding the warning that we should always resist the temptation to 'make game', ridicule.

Adults should not be excluded, but as children are most at risk, they could be given priority. However, adult travellers should be encouraged, to be participants in entertainment packages, and not just passive onlookers. Less formal programmes should be designed to make it easy for them to 'touch' homefolk as well as other visitors through music. If too shy to sing they, surely then can clap their hands or tap their toes. In addition, attendance at local and international Eisteddfods and Festivals of the Arts whether as performers or audience should be sought and seen as fertile means of learning and sharing with fellow travellers on planet Earth.

Print, as well as electronic media should be pressed into service. Some media specialists would no doubt quickly see the advantages of being involved. Documentation and packaging of heritage music from field or platforms worldwide would transform local material and performance styles into world resources. Tourism would have begun to balance people motives with profit ones and to advance the chances of our making One World, in human terms, a reality.

Bob Marley, Jamaican reggae star, became more than an entertainer in his comparatively short career. He took a message of Peace and 'One Love' worldwide, borne on the rhythm of reggae, but even more so on his sincere efforts to make his vision into reality. Hovever, his efforts would have been in vain, had his unique style of singing not inspired and stimulated the necessary response in many language areas where his words were not understood.

The explanation seems to be that it was the spirit of his songs, and intangible values that he himself projected, that affected his listeners. All this was in addition to his ability to entertain people of all ages. He was top of the charts in Japan, Turkey, the Americas and in many European, African and Caribbean countries. He proved music to be capable of bridging cultural, linguistic, geographical and generation gaps.

Tourism can only benefit from aiming at using music in a similar way. Since heritage music is born of human needs rather than created to meet specific criteria or to satisfy passing popular taste, it is more appropriate to the task. One of the many apt phrases which Marley set to music was: 'in this great future, you can't forget your past.'

Only when we begin to interact trans-culturally, and local heritage assets become accessible to all, will we really move towards appreciating each other's past and our shared global heritage.

The Author

Dr Olive Lewin was educated at Hampton School for Girls in Jamaica and read social anthropology and ethnomusicology at Queens University, Belfast, where she obtained her PhD. She has been engaged in comparative research into Jamaica's music and folklore since 1967, and founded the Jamaica Memory Bank in 1981, holding the position of Director until 1989. She is the founding director of the Jamican Fold Singers, which she has led to many overseas countries, and of the Jamaica Orchestra for Youth. She has compiled five biiks of Jamaican Folk Songs, published by the Organisation of American States and the Oxford University Press. Lecture demonstrations, workshops and papers have been presented for schools, colleges, universities and international conferences in Sweden, France, the United States of America, the United Kingdom, Japan, India and Caribbean countries. Her articles on arts and culture have appeared in several publications, including *Grove's*

Dictionary of Music and Musicians, and the *Yearbook of the International Folk Music Council*, and other journals in Cuba, Germany, Spain, the United States of America and Jamaica. She is a Fellow of Trinity College, London, and Associate of the Royal College of Music, and of the Royal School of Music and the Royal Academy of Music. Her honours include Chevalier dans l'Ordre des Artes et Lettres (1986); Gold Musgrave Medal (1987), and Jamaica Foundation (New York) for Excellence in the field of Education (1991).

References

Black, C., *History of Jamica*, London & Glasgow Collins Clear Type Press, 1958

Blacking, J, *The Aesthetic in Education*, Oxford Pergamon Press, 1984

Braithwaitee, K., *Kumina in Jamaica*, Journal 42, 1978

Carter, H., *Language and Music of Kumina*, In ACIJ Newsletter 12 Institute of Jamaica

Cassidy, F. G., *Jamaica Talk*, London MacMillan, 1961

Cundall, F., *Historic Jamaica*, London: West Indian Commitee for the Institute of Jamaica, 1915

Jekyll, W., *Jamaica Song and Story*, London Folklore Society, London University, 1907

Seaga, E., *Rivival Cults in Jamaica*, In Jamaica Journal 132, Institute of Jamaica Publication, 1969

Tanna, L., *Dinki Mini*, In Jamaica Journal 202, Institute of Jamaica, 1987

26

MAKING MINOR PLACES
Dilemmas in Modern Tourism

Dean MacCannell

Conversation between two young men, strangers to each other, working out on an indoor plywood and metal bolt rock climbing wall in a sporting goods shop in California:

> Uh, have you ever climbed outdoors?
> No man, have you?
> No.[1]

My first field of study was social or cultural anthropology. I arrived at Berkeley as an undergraduate in the fall of 1961, the week that Alfred Kroeber died, and I was among a handful of people, the last to be taught by a faculty hand-picked by him.[2] So this was to be my heritage. My rebellion was immediate and so total that I did not even recognise it as rebellion. The idea of peoples, defiant by virtue of their mere presence, successful in terms entirely different from the ones I was supposed to accept as my own, was and is very precious to me. The notion of heritage is highly ironic. We speak of 'embracing heritage'. But no heritage can survive as such unless it is also the object of opposition through the generations. Thus I regard current controversies over 'whose heritage' as a blessed gift. Otherwise what we call heritage could not be distinguished from anything else: all of life and culture would be unresisted self-congratulation; undifferentiated time-space.

Certainly I could not imagine myself involved in attempts to further the programme of anthropology by repeating the methodological gestures of ethnography, either functionalist or salvage. I was interested in the forces, including anthropological investigation, that were killing off hunting and gathering peoples; peoples more remote than ancient civilisation, but in many ways more curiously like ourselves; peoples whose life situation might qualify as the only common human heritage. I thought that the greatest contribution anthropology could make would be to turn its powerful methods of observation back onto the observers, to do an ethnography of the global modernisation process. In holding these opinions and beliefs, I thought I was merely being a good student; that the whole field of anthropology was turning to these new objects of investigation and that I was simply turning with it. Mine was a kind of delusion which is quite common, but for which there is no clinical term. It is a mirroring of paranoia: you form the mistaken belief of not being followed; rather, that you are following someone or something when you are not.

So I did not become an anthropologist. In the process of not becoming, I learned a lesson: heritage is not what the dead did and thought, it is more their manner of speaking to the living. After my Berkeley studies, no matter how far they were broken down, for me cultural elements will always have a material aspect; all cultural ideas are embodied and transmitted in forms (myths, songs, dances, decoration, settlement pattern, practical method, etc.) which are subject to interpretation and misinterpretation. My interest in tourism and in heritage comes down to questions about the ways cultural objects operate on the mind and vice-versa. Is that Kroeber speaking?

If I may move quickly ahead, almost to the end of this story, I have concluded that culture cannot simply reproduce itself. If anyone undertakes simply to reproduce culture, it dies. All of us have had the experience of trying to persevere in a dead institution, university department, marriage, social class; of going through the motions of a living relationship, but eventually realising it is useless to try to continue; of experiencing the near death of one's own soul. The solution is not always a matter of breaking free. Sometimes it involves the re-discovery of the desires which gave rise to the social form in the first place. At the base of every vital cultural arrangement, there is a dialectic of creativity and tradition. If tradition lives, it is because every generation succeeds in not copying it, in creating it anew. The persistence of heritage is an illusion that covers enormous creativity, and masks the difference between creation and death.

Now I am way ahead of myself. I got the idea to study tourists and tourism in the summer of 1965. I had just finished my Master's degree in Rural Sociology at Cornell University and was in western Puerto Rico, preparing the way for a larger team of professors and graduate students who would come in the fall. Their plan was to study agricultural productivity, rural markets, and the causes of the diffusion of agricultural

352

innovations: mainly new technologies of production invented in American universities. I understood the goals of the study, the research design, and the theory behind it, but I was only 'the advance person' who would leave when the full study team arrived and not be involved in the actual research. My role was conceived as a way of saving time and money so the full team could 'hit the ground running'. I located and gained access to government data, found farmers using innovative methods and farmers using traditional methods, sampled, found housing for the team, etc. But I kept noticing the resort hotels rising on the beaches near the study area. I could not keep the thought out of my mind that tourism was about to have a greater impact on local cultures and economies than whether or not the farmers adopted new agricultural technologies.

THE TOURIST

The graduate research library at Cornell was, and is, one of the best in the world. When I returned in late summer of 1965, I searched for social, cultural and economic reports on the impact of tourism on Third World Development and found fewer than ten articles on the subject of tourism, and no books. I proposed a comparative study of tourism on a global base as my PhD dissertation, but it was flatly rejected by my committee. I was angry at the time, but in retrospect the judgement of the committee was correct. My professors told me that it was a great idea and they thought I could pull it off, but it would take at least ten years to do it, and they did not want me hanging around in graduate school for that long. *The Tourist* appeared on schedule ten years later in 1976, still the first book on the subject, beating Valene Smith's and Nelson Graburn's books into print by a matter of months.[3] During the same decade, tourism had risen to dominate the global economy.

I tried to treat tourism with a great deal of respect; as more powerful and important than any other institutional force and any potential science of it; as the only unifying grounds for modern culture and consciousness. I argued that 'the tourist' is the best metaphor we have for modern man in general, alienated absolutely from his own life, condemned to search endlessly for authenticity in the lives of others or in his own past. The tourist attractions, for their part, the things gotten up for display to tourists, are literally object lessons in the post-modern system of mythic values consecrated to Peace, Liberty, Authenticity and Tradition, and everything else that modernity claimed to hold in the highest esteem while destroying it. In their totality the attractions constitute a catalogue or guide to the deep structure of modern society and the compromised and tortured psyche at the end of modernity.

For example, so-called eco-tourism or 'sustainable tourism development' in very remote mountainous or rain forest regions of the world responds to the substantial anxiety of postmodernites that they can never really get away from it all, a need to touch the untouched, to experience 'the unspoiled' at the incredible instant just before ones own presence spoils it. This kind of tourism, not incidentally, also functions beautifully as the cutting edge of global capital: using the passions of travellers, who actually do see themselves as pilgrims, to change forever the values of the last isolated systems of barter exchange, agricultural self sufficiency, local land ownership, and traditional forms of hospitality.

I suggested that the arrangement of tourist attractions, large and small, on a global base was the closest thing modern peoples had to the sacred texts of agriculturally based societies. All of this pre-supposed three things:

1. a system of attractions which were assumed to stand outside the world of economic exchange and social differences, objects of ultimate worth requiring preservation, which should be accessible to everyone equally: in short, a human heritage that reaches into modernity;
2. an embodiment of values in quasi sacred object-place relationships or 'site specificity';
3. a requirement of 'being in the presence of the attraction' in order to maximise the benefits of its mysterious powers.

I did not suggest that there were no mediated experiences of tourist attractions such as souvenirs, travelogues, etc, only that mediated experience was not a substitute for being in the presence of the real thing, and that the bigger the aura of mediated representation of any given attraction, the more powerful the attraction.

There is almost no discussion in *The Tourist* of two kinds of activities that are classified as 'tourism' but which I discounted as trivial in the context of the global expansion of modernised consciousness, or the establishment of a new cultural set-up on a global base.

Firstly, I did not treat recreational leisure non-activities such as sun bathing, fishing, etc. If there is a sense that the beach itself, or the river, is only important because it delivers the necessary recreational ingredients, the experience is non-site-specific, and this particular beach or river on this occasion is not a tourist attraction in the meaning that I am trying to bring to the term, even if there are hundreds of tourists playing there. It should not be necessary for me to remark that I am not trying to belittle such recreational experiences. At the level of the tired psyche they are most important. I was focused on the 'culture of modernity', how it insinuates itself into consciousness, and spreads.

In this context, I was only interested in non-substitutable experience where there is an unbreakable prismatic moment in one's life, linking a specific attraction to the feelings and meanings that can only be refracted in 'that' moment in 'that' place through 'that' consciousness. The attractions are, to use Lacan's term, 'points de capiton' of meaning. One of the tourists I quoted said: 'When I saw the Eiffel Tower for the first time, I burst into tears.' Of course, not every attraction has the power to do this, not even the Eiffel Tower does it to everyone. I was fascinated to discover how broadly powerful many of the global attractions had become and how even small attractions could insinuate themselves into touristic consciousness, namely, beyond the local. In sum, I found that recreation and sightseeing had nothing in common beyond the fact that they both might be accomplished while on vacation.

The second kind of tourism which I did not entirely dismiss, but definitely classed as 'derivative' was visits to commercialised attractions, theme parks, etc. My argument was that if they were set up to profit a single individual or company, they were, perforce, inauthentic or not directly reflective of deep collective problematics. Even though all sights are completely dependent on sightseers, an authentic sight can never *seem* to be dependent on sightseers, economically or otherwise. It must always 'appear' as existing beyond the reach of time and economic exchanges; as worthy of marriage with Nature itself; as capable of enduring stupidity and neglect, if only as a magnificent ruin. Conversely, any sight where the seers are made to pay to the point where profits accrue to narrowly defined private 'interests', always appear faked up, tacky or 'promoted'.

DREAMWORKS BY INSTALMENTS

It should be clear enough in the manner in which I am reporting on my own book that I now regard it as an anachronism. It is based on assumptions about human subjectivity and character which are theoretically and perhaps historically no longer tenable. I wrote *Empty Meeting Grounds* partly to address the following issues which substantially altered global cultural arrangements and the situation of the tourist.[4]

The first issue relates to the revolution in electronic media which began almost immediately after the publication of *The Tourist*. This revolution launched an aggressive assault on all distinctions between originals and copies. Jean Baudrillard has authoritatively pronounced that in the post-modern world every important object has been overwhelmed by its copies. So now we no longer have origins, foundations, or primacy, but only simulacra of origins. In *The Tourist*, I made an absolute distinction between the attraction and souvenir copies of it. Not only was every tourist capable of making this distinction, and making no mistakes about it, it was also the structural basis for their motivation to travel. They worked their way 'backwards' from the simulation of the attraction, or from the copy, the representation on the travel poster or in the guidebook bought at home, back to the attraction itself.

The enormous energy expended in touristic travel was generated by an inversion of the sequencing of consciousness in the relationship of memory to experience. In several senses, the tourist pays for collective memory on the instalment plan: he gets the memories up front and pays them off over time by visiting the places 'remembered' in advance. When the souvenirs of a place precede the experience of it in consciousness, the touristic subject is incomplete, or in debt, until it has travelled there.

Suppose we lose our faculty of distinguishing a memory of a memory from a memory of an actual experience. Or suppose that actual experience comes to be regarded as inferior to synthetic memories, to the point that manufactured 'collective memory' becomes 'enough'. Baudrillard's thesis has chilling implications for tourist travel as theorised in *The Tourist*, and not incidentally also for those responsible for managing heritage sites.[5]

The second issue is that the ascent of tourism to a pre-eminent position in the global economy did not go unnoticed by the global corporations. Tourism must have visited a certain horror on the corporate consciousness. In tourism's original form, it did not exist by virtue of being promoted and sold. It existed in and of itself. People from all over the world would walk across the desert to visit the Egyptian Pyramids even if no one ever advertised them. In fact, at the time of the publication of *The Tourist* there was a strong inverse correlation between the amount of money a destination spent advertising itself to tourists and its tourist dollar revenues. It was still a 'word of mouth' industry, and therefore operated mainly outside of corporate control. An airline could develop a route to fly tourists to the Pyramids. A hotel could build an establishment nearby. But business could not turn the appeal of the pyramids on and off, or force a tourist to become a repeat visitor, or prevent the tourist from desiring food from the local bazaar. The airline can buy the hotel and build its own 'clean' and 'ethnic' restaurant, but it is still dependent on the destination, not vice versa. So long as there are elements of site specificity and authenticity involved in travel decisions, the corporations do not completely control the tourist or the tourist economy.

The corporate solution to this problem was swift and dramatic. After 1975, there has been a massive, global attack on site specificity and authenticity. This takes several forms.

First, actual attractions are moved from their locations. Some of these moves have been short as in the case of the Liberty Bell, taken from Independence Hall in 1975 and set up in a shrine of its own down the street. Others have been dramatic. London Bridge now spans a man-made lake in the Arizona desert. In 'Little World', a Japanese ethnological museum and theme park, entire villages (American Indian, Greek, French, Thai, Korean, etc) have been purchased, packed, and re-assembled, where they and some of their original inhabitants serve as objects of study and touristic visitation.

Second, objects which achieved fame during the early phase of tourism are copied, cloned, and re-constructed in places very far from the original. Disney was certainly an early innovator in this area with his 'Seven Great Rivers of the World' ride at Disneyland, and, of course, his plaster Matterhorn. There are plans currently in Japan to recreate Mount Rushmore. Every major shopping mall in North America has its thematised references to famous attractions elsewhere. New Orleans's Bourbon Street has been reconstructed in West Edmonton Mall. This drive has reached its highest stage of development in the construction of new Casinos in Las Vegas after the airlines and international hotel chains took over the gambling industry from the mob.

The current casino-hotel under construction is called 'New York, New York', designed to appear from middle distance as the New York skyline, with New York style street level vendors, cafés, etc. in the lobby. Ditto the most recently finished hotel named 'The Paris Experience'. The Egyptian Sphinx and Pyramids are also hotels in Las Vegas, complete with an authentic reproduction of King Tut's tomb and treasure in the basement. Visitors from Hawaii and other parts of the Pacific region comment favourably on The Paris Experience; on the convenience of having a Paris experience without having to go to Paris, or even to leave the casino. The aggressiveness of these gestures is nicely manifest on the billboard in San Francisco which advertises Las Vegas with the slogan: 'Accept No Substitutes'.

Third, increasingly, entire residential neighbourhoods and shopping districts in the middle class areas of world cities are built to resemble corporate leisure environments.[6] In short, manufactured generic otherness suggestive of vacation leisure has become the design motif for new urban and suburban domestic space. In North America, this usually means, minimally, that a line of palm trees will be planted. Sometimes it means much more. The largest scale urban housing development now under construction in the United States is Playa Vista, built on a salt marsh wetlands area just north of the international airport in Los Angeles. Playa Vista is a speculative real estate venture put together by Stephen Spielberg, former Disney CEO Jeff Katzenberg, David Geffen (owner of

Geffen Records), Bill Gates, Paul Allen who was co-founder with Gates of Microsoft and current owner of the Portland Trailblazers and Ticketmaster. At the heart of Playa Vista will be the 'campus' of Dreamworks which is an electronic media and technology company owned by the investors.[7]

What is interesting are the plans for the homes to be built there. According to one plan, they will be 'work-live' spaces for artists and technicians and will be built in the first place as stage sets like the old studio back lots. Only this time the 'lot' is also the homes and neighbourhoods of the Dreamworkers. Thus, you may be able to live on a street corner in a simulated Paris, New York, Cairo, etc, and be a bit-player in a movie as you go about your daily routines. It is especially interesting to contemplate what a child growing up in this neighbourhood will eventually regard as his or her heritage.

A BAG OF DIRTY LAUNDRY

Given these historical shifts, would I recommend abandoning the vision of *The Tourist*? Not necessarily. But I would certainly correct its aim. Today it reads not so much as an ethnography of modernity, but rather as a manifesto for minor places. I want my notion of 'minor places' to retain a ring of irony. We must after all begin to count among 'minor places', the Matterhorn, the Egyptian Sphinx, Mount Rushmore and every other attraction which has been made passé by its better organised corporate copies.

It is only after capitalism completes its global sweep and has absorbed all other economic and cultural forms that we will be able to see its real contradictions, the one that Marx foresaw, and some new ones. We seem to be hurtling toward this moment. In that moment I see a deep divide between tourists who willingly stay within the horizon of capital's 'definition' of tourism on the one side, and a kind of tourist desire that cannot be contained in the frame of capital's definition on the other: the war between the tourists.

First, capital's children and their heritage. I have already suggested that advanced, technology-driven capitalism has begun to resemble a kind of hyper-kinetic feudalism. One is not supposed to think of oneself as different from, or other than one's place in an organisation. As organisations become larger and more powerful, and as every community is increasingly composed of de-contextualised, generic symbols, everyday life devolves into a frenzy of boredom. After work, or even during work at breaks, the workers subject themselves to exercise racks, or run in place like caged gerbils. Any identity that is not contained in the organisation is composed of micro-fragments that mirror demographic projections of consumer behaviour: heterosexual-white male-feminist-jogger-vegetarian. The imagination is lost to individuals who become dependent on the corporation to do their dreaming for them: 'Dreamworks'.

Under this regime, individuals in their 'free time' become pure consumers, spending billions of dollars and ending up with nothing to show for it. When a tourist from California travels to Japan to 'take in the sights', the act leaves no tangible trace, except perhaps in his conversations: 'Oh, yes, I've been to Japan.' It is possible to travel world-wide, seeing all the important sights, spending enormous quantities of money, and return home with nothing but a bag of dirty laundry. Where does all this money go? It is invested in 'moving things' around to re-create them in new locations. It fuels the global displacement of every symbolic form that once had a certain dignity derived from its local specificity. The drive of capital to de-stabilise what is local, extends to very intimate details of life. In the United States today there is a campaign by cosmetic makers to convince white anglo women that they should attempt to make their eyes appear somewhat 'Asian' and their lips, somewhat 'African'. The human face itself has become the empty meeting ground of postmodern cultural 'differences' which no longer make a difference.

An obvious question here has to do with sustainability. Tourism that is militantly disconnected from local heritage would seem to be self-destructive. When every destination comes increasingly to resemble every other destination, when every destination is just another pastiche of displaced cultural elements, why leave home? The answer is not obvious and requires a logic of its own, a postmodern logic. Tourism literally makes one's own place, one's 'home' into the ultimate destination. The tourist's home may be without style or distinction, just another postmodern box with styling affectations reminiscent of some former style of some remote region. Moreover, this home may not even be different from any of the places on the tourist's itinerary, except for its singular designation as the point of origin and final destination. In such a world, rigid and homogeneous, leaving home is the only way to mark it as distinct from every other place; it may not be different from other places, but at least it is 'the place one is from'. If you cannot change your social place or position, at least you can travel as a kind of imbecile literalisation of mobility.

The postmodern tourist operating within the framework of definitions of 'travel experience' provided by advanced capital may discover that 'home' is only arbitrary even if it seems to be the point of origin and final destination. This would not necessarily weaken the desire to travel. It can also serve to make postmodern touristic travel all the more frenzied. What better way of marking status differences in a world in which everyone is required to 'stay in place' than to visit just about every place?

MINOR PLACES VERSUS DREAMWORKS

So what about people whose travel desires cannot be contained in capitalist dreamworks? If any such people exist, it is not because the curators of minor places have been doing a superb job of representing heritage. For the most part, the tourist is either over-whelmed or under-whelmed by the sight-marker combination in the presence of significant objects. I do not think that this is just an issue of too much or too little text, though often there are problems here. More often, the problem is taking the matter of 'presentation context' too literally. The visitor to minor places is overwhelmed with authenticity and goes blank.

Here at the end, I want to recommend that in addition to the goals of authenticity, there should be a second goal of opening up 'the space of creativity'. By this I mean representing creation, geologic and/or human, which went into the making of the place in such a way that the visitor is not overwhelmed by the accomplishment of others, but rather is invited to participate in that accomplishment. Every display should also be a place which has been made safe for continued creativity. Museums which combine art and science in interactive exhibits are exemplary. How can this kind of energy and freedom be brought to a heritage site? Let me suggest the following ways:

1. Those who are responsible for minor places should be working to break down the tourist/local distinction. Local people should be involved in the development and management of all minor places. Ideally, they should be crawling all over the place with the tourists, speaking about the significance of history and heritage for them and making the tourists aware of contested heritage. The second battle of the Alamo which is now taking place between Anglos and Mexicans in Texas is exemplary.

2. The minor place should be set up in such a way as to engage faculties other than sight. They should go beyond sight and the other senses and involve the major virtues: vision, integrity, honesty and sympathetic understanding. They should not be ethically levelled or diluted. Properly managed, a minor place should contribute to the demise of the notion of 'sightseeing' itself, or at minimum cause the visitors immediately to sense that they are engaged in something more profound than mere sightseeing.

3. Minor places should have residency programmes. Specialists should be brought to live at or near the site and to interact with it, to engage in projects while in residence. These residences should be non-obvious. Scientist should have residencies in art spaces and artists in science museums, etc. Those who are responsible for minor places should be eager to find out what a strange resident might do or think there.

What sort of things might happen? I would be interested in trying to link specific aesthetic displays of heritage to investigation of 'memory' and 'value'. Visitors involved in questioning the nature of memory and value, where they are first introduced to objects which they are 'supposed' to remember and value, might be able to get beyond the brass plated armour that has been applied to heritage and which set up tourism for its corporate takeover in the first place. Investigations of different forms of 'virtual reality' and their implications for human consciousness could be combined with heritage reconstructions. Every virtualised bit of reality can teach us something about the constitution of the actual object, as opposed to the virtual one, as well as something about the constitution of experience. The ability of tourists to 'see through' Disney can only be developed at a counter-attraction, at a minor place.

Such experiments will necessarily involve strange crossings of disciplines, as well as being expanded to include odd-feeling contextual surroundings. But they might lead to knowledge of heritage entering the touristic consciousness along with new and innovative methods for understanding creative processes, memory and its vicissitudes, the connection of display to psyche, and the techniques that are used in the corporate takeover of the human soul. In sum, I am suggesting that the next battle in the tourist war be fought as a guerrilla campaign with the initiative coming from minor places.

The Author

Professor Dean MacCannell is based at the University of California at Davis where he holds the Chair in Environmental Design and Landscape Architecture and is Adjunct Professor in Sociology. Qualified in anthropology and rural sociology, his pioneering work on tourism in modern society has gained him an international reputation, and he has held visiting professorships at the American College in Paris and the Universities of Rutgers and Cornell. A former Executive Director of the Semiotic Society of America, he is the recipient of many honours, including an Award from the

California Legislature and Fellowships of the Humanist Institute and Society of Davis and Cornell. A prolific writer and popular lecturer, he contributed to the 1996 BBC Television Series, *The Tourist,* and its associated publication. As befits a polymath, his research and teaching interests are listed as cultural issues emerging between the ex-primitive and the postmodern; effects of hyper-modernisation on tourism, agriculture and community life; and subjects such as critical theory, semiotics, psychoanalysis and consumer cultures.

References

1. Overheard and reported to me by Timothy Webb.
2. Alfred Kroeber (1876–1960) was one of the most influential anthropologists of the first half of the 20th century, whose primary concern was to understand the nature of culture and its processes. He made valuable contributions to American Indian ethnology, the archaeology of New Mexico, Mexico, Peru and to the study of linguistics, folklore, kinship, and social structure. His career coincided with the emergence of academic, professionalised anthropology in the US and contributed significantly to its development.
3. *The Tourist,* New York: Schocken, 1976 and 1989
4. *Empty Meeting Grounds,* London: Routledge, 1992
5. One detects in Baudrillard a little nostalgia for authenticity and originality, but not enough to hang a culture on. His vision is of an electronic feudal system where the serfs subsist on virtual reality and the elite go to the Holyland, or 'Holy-wood', in search of the silicone grail. In California now, after the Silicone Valley computer graphics companies succeeded in making virtual actors and selling their creations to the motion picture industry, we speak of 'Sili-wood'.
6. This has been explored in detail in Michael Sorkin's excellent edited volume, *The City as Theme Park.*
7. Here I am indebted to Linda Roberson's unpublished Senior Thesis, *Diluted Realism,* department of Environmental Design and Landscape Architecture, University of California at Davis, 1996.

27

SERIAL SOAP ADDICTION
From Screen Viewing to Pilgrimage

Patricia Sterry

Coronation Street is a serialised television drama about a fictitious working class community located within a terraced street in a suburb of Manchester. It comes complete with corner shop, pub and cloth cap image, and commands the largest television audience every week in Great Britain with an average of 18–19 million dedicated fans of all ages and classes who watch each episode.[1] The growth in popularity of serialised television drama, especially 'soap' operas, has been phenomenal and dominates viewing statistics. Full of humour, strong characters, vitality and often unrealistic plots, such programmes become an addiction for some people. The phrase 'soapalcoholics' is quite appropriate, as obsessive viewing takes over their lives.[2] For others, 'soaps' provide an engagement of interest that is characteristic of any popular programme. Storylines become the talking point at family gatherings, and in offices or with friends, as viewers are drawn into the myth of the narrative.

A visit to places associated with a favourite television 'soap' is for many people a deep spiritual quest, fulfilling a need through association, though often dismissed as parochial and pedestrian. *Emmerdale, The Last of The Summer Wine, Dr Finlay* and *Coronation Street* are just a few of the many successful television serialised productions that have fuelled demand for tourist excursions to places associated with or portrayed during the programme. The venues of televised costume dramas, as in the recent serialised production of *Pride and Prejudice,* and locations from films such as *Rob Roy, Braveheart* and *Highlander,* have also been much in demand.

Opportunities to 'cash in' on this contemporary trend of visiting film and television locations has generated new cultural heritage sites of significant economic and social benefit, but not without some discord, as former tranquil areas are mobbed by new wave tourists searching for a glimpse of their favourite character. Whether it is Holmfirth (*Last of the Summer Wine*), Auchtermuchty (*Dr Finlay*), or the fictitious Wetherfield (*Coronation Street*), the significance of location enables the 'serial' tourist to interact and engage in the public consumption of familiar signs and symbols in a environment which both dislocates and relocates the myth of a programme's narrative.

This paper discusses three interesting examples which demonstrate that popularity of location has little to do with local culture, which is transformed by the pseudo narrative of the television programme with which they are associated. Although focused on sites in my own locality the significant growth of such sites can be found throughout Great Britain.[3]

The underlying concern must be that if television 'does not produce impressions based on truth; it can be used to create a fantasy world,'[4] then it would be reasonable to conjecture that some visitors might not be able to draw distinctions between myth, truth and reality. Television is a powerful communicator, and there is clearly an inter-relationship with certain serialised programmes and people's perception and cognition of working class culture, heritage and identity, which is more often than not based on myth and without real substance. Are 'serial' tourists simply being seduced by a nostalgic rural vision and narrative based on popular non-elite culture and fabricated for television viewing? Does this matter? The paper situates present day serial tourists as pilgrims within an historic framework of sightseeing and cultural tradition.

A CONTEMPORARY PILGRIMAGE

Manchester is not a name that immediately springs to mind as a major destination of pilgrimage, as does perhaps Canterbury, York or Chartres. But just as earlier medieval pilgrims journeyed to their sacred place to pay homage at the end of their journey, so do millions of contemporary pilgrims visit the Manchester based, Granada Studios Tours, with the specific intention of seeing the Coronation Street television set. Here, the myths and legends of a television 'soap' opera based on working class life in neighbouring Salford, (called Wetherfield in the programme) become reality as the 'Street'. Here its heroes are presented for public consumption, midst the incongruous glitz and glamour of a very small (just 3 acres) American Theme Park. The link between Granada and Universal Studios Tour in the USA is of course, tenuous.

It is clear that Coronation Street, now celebrating 35 years on screen in four weekly episodes, is the enabling mechanism for this new major tourist attraction. What does it matter, asks one commentator, if some viewers think Coronation Street is real, or whenever a house comes up for sale, people write in and ask to buy it, on the understanding they are given a part in the programme, or that two offers of £68,000 cash was made when The Rover's Return was on sale in the programme recently.[5] Although clearly a fictional story, viewers identify with the strong female characters and the fairly innocuous world they inhabit: '...all these people are doing is trying to buy into a delicious fantasy, the kind of world we would all like to inhabit, a world which has never existed, in which no one's dog ever fouls the pavement, neighbours rally round in a crisis and everyone meets in the local pub afterwards.' [6]

A restored bonded warehouse provides the setting for the backstage studios tour.[7] This is not the real studios where filming takes place, which are perhaps 100 yards away, but a facsimile made especially for the tour. Numbered groups of visitors are guided around sets of makeup and wardrobe departments, they can volunteer to read the news, are shown a few tricks of the trade, and see a few of the interior sets of Coronation Street (again these are not real sets but mock ups specifically made for the tour) and sets of other famous productions made at the Granada Studios, including a walk along Downing Street, pausing to be photographed with the policeman outside No 10.

After the backstage tour is complete, visitors can make their own Grand Tour of Sherlock Holme's residence along a full size set of Baker Street, complete with Victorian Music Hall, calling in to the Houses of Parliament (where you can join in a debate), and to the jewel in the crown, Coronation Street itself. Visitors are invited to 'walk the hallowed cobbles of the very street where the series is filmed' [8] (true), pausing at the entry to visit the flower filled grave of Stanley Ogden, a street resident who died aged 62 years (myth).

Photography is encouraged, and it is interesting to watch the excitement in the Street itself where people are anxious to be photographed outside buildings with which they are familiar from the television serial: the Kabin, the Corner Shop or the Rover's Return. Urry suggests that 'to photograph is in some way to appropriate the object being photographed. It is a power relationship',[9] and it does appear that fans of this extremely popular soap opera have taken the characters very much to heart. They peer through the windows and letterboxes of the houses as if expecting to find the street characters at home. The buildings are all television sets, facades of front and back, and so of course cannot be entered. Lights are left on in upstairs rooms, and windows left slightly ajar to hint at the possibility of the occupants being at home.

There is a variety of other attractions on site, including eating places ranging from an American Diner to a facsimile of The Rovers Return and associated shops where modern day pilgrims collect, not the cockle shell emblem so beloved by medieval pilgrims to Santiago de Compostela in Northern Spain,[10] but other just as significant memorabilia such as plaster flying ducks, (a familiar symbol of the Ogden household), a selection of Bet the Barmaid's earrings or perhaps a video of themselves talking with their favourite character.

Coronation Street is described as 'comfort food, like the sausage and mash of bitter winter nights or the porridge of frost-sharded autumn mornings. It is a hot water bottle in a cold world. Like dropping in on favourite relatives, you always know what you are going to find: warmth, humour and a nice cup of tea, luv'.[11]

It is possible that attractions generated by successful television programmes like Coronation Street provide the symbols by which modern people give their lives meaning ', and seek an authentic understanding of their world'.[12] Coronation Street celebrated its 35 birthday in 1996, so many of its viewers have grown up with the programme, and the characters are more like family. Over twenty million people tuned in on the day the barmaid Bet was leaving. Perhaps the need to visit the television set might be fulfilling a need to find a traditional and familiar way of life and to find stable 'roots' in the face of an increasingly uncertain future.[13]

Of course the staged set for sightseeing tourists in nothing new, MacCannell described staged back regions of tourist space as 'a kind of living museum for which we have no analytical terms.'[14] He characterised stage sets as 'unique among social places...designed to reveal inner workings of the place...there is a staged quality to the proceedings that lends to them an aura of superficiality'.[15] Staged sets are constructed only for sightseers whose consciousness is a desire for authentic experiences, yet it is difficult to tell if the experience is authentic '...what is taken to be entry into a back region, is really entry into a front region that has been set up in advance for touristic visitation ...and in which tourists are allowed to peek'.[16]

Visitors to the Studios Tour can peek at 'real' Salford history if they choose just half a mile away or simply walk round the corner to the restored, renovated, and regenerated Castlefield site, in which the tour is based. Interpretation of this 'authentic' historic site into Britain's first Urban Heritage Park has been a challenge with many aspects open to criticism.

CASTLEFIELD

The Castlefield site, not far from Manchester City Centre has been developed to play a dominant role as a major tourist attraction of the region with its cluster of restored and renovated buildings of historic, architectural and cultural importance. The Bridgwater canal has been restored, there are hotels, a first class museum and art gallery, a visitor centre and meeting area, all developed for leisure pursuits and cultural entertainment. Castlefield is bordered by the GMex Conference Centre and highly sought after housing developments. Such clusters of complimentary spatial association are the acknowledged prerequisite for sound cultural tourism, and are recognised as leading to a greater appreciation of the cultural-historic heritage of an area.[17 & 18]

Castlefield is a site of significant historic importance, from its early period as a Roman fortress, although the Roman mural depicting the site under the railway viaduct alongside a reconstruction of a gate from the Roman fort is of very poor quality. The heady days of 19th century industrialisation with warehouse, canal and rail links to Manchester's thriving cotton industries can be found amongst many examples of original buildings, from early warehouses to Victorian market halls. The Liverpool Road Station, opened in 1830, was the first modern passenger railway between Liverpool and Manchester and is preserved on its original site within The Museum of Science and Industry. The museum forms a major attraction, as does Granada Studio Tours, within Castlefield.

THEMES AND DIVERSITY

So why include a three acre American Style Theme Park within an historic site with 2000 years of 'real' history? This example has demonstrated the diversity of contemporary tourist development. The commodification, and some would say exploitation, of such historic sites for consumption as a heritage package with a variety of different attractions, has become increasingly typical over the last decade and is replicated throughout Britain. 'Theming', it appears, 'has swept Britain to a point of saturation and staleness...and in the selection of a theme...areas are choosing to ignore, suppress even their real and natural multivariate personalities and their features.'[19]

For some critics, the Studio Tours would appear to fulfil the criteria of the perfect recipe for 'day out' heritage: first catch your history (old house, castle, etc), chuck in a bit of pastness (jousts, bygones, etc) with whatever else is to hand (crafts, tubeslide, etc), stir to remove integrity and allow eclecticism to surface, and then simmer until tacky, with froth on top'.[20] Fans of The Street, however, would argue that the Tour is rich in cultural heritage and a destination that is just as meaningful for them as the 'authentic' history round the corner within the Castlefield site.

THE TELEVISUAL EXPERIENCE

Locations associated with television programmes have provided both a market and a product. Stunningly beautiful countryside is enjoyed not in its own terms but with the name of the associated television programme: 'The Last of The Summer Wine Country,' 'Emmerdale Country' and many others, each supported by a wide range of services, books and memorabilia to suit all pilgrims. The guide to Emmerdale Country suggests that the 'soap' serial *Emmerdale* 'mirrors modern-day life, ...tackling issues like divorce, child abuse, addiction, single parenthood, and lesbianism, ...and has more deaths per annum than any other soap'.[21] It follows on to say that, 'although Emmerdale exists only in the minds of its creators and the millions of devoted fans of the series', it is its scenery and landscape that is the reality: a captivating landscape of wilderness and softness, of dark grit stone crags, white limestone and lush pastures criss-crossed with dry stone walls which sweep up the heather moorland and the high Pennine Fells.[22]

Esholt is the pretty, picturesque village in Yorkshire where filming of Emmerdale takes place and is now included in a heritage trail that encompasses, Haworth (Bronte Country), Harrogate and The Dales. To increase the viewing figures of this farming community 'soap', (complete with The Woolpack pub, café and corner shop), the scrip writers included 'the largest stunt this side of Hollywood' creating an airliner crash in the village with all its dramatic possibilities. The programme was scheduled for viewing at the same time as the anniversary of the Lockerbie disaster, which created much additional publicity and discussion. Topically, a Heritage Farm was created for tourists within the programme, complete with costumed gamekeeper.

The filming of the extremely popular *Last of the Summer Wine* in 16 series, over almost 24 years of production, has changed the small, quiet Pennine town of Holmfirth to a busy centre geared to tourism based on its association's with the television drama serial.[23] Holmfirth appears to have lost its own identity, to have been in a way devalued as it is mobbed by pilgrims searching and hoping for a glimpse of their favourite characters from the series, rather than simply enjoying the intrinsic beauty of the town with its alleyways, river and weaver's cottages. There is Sid's Cafe in the courtyard outside the Parish Church, which is the haunt of the programmes chief characters, where you get a certificate to prove you have you have been there. There is The Wrinkled Stocking Café, a reference to Nora Batty, (a distinctive character in the series) and the television home of the character Compo, as well as a museum dedicated to the programme and a town centre almost like a theme park as visitors seek out familiar buildings and landmarks. There are also souvenir shops which supply a diverse range of memorabilia. Holmfirth appears to fulfil 'the search for authenticity of experience that is everywhere manifest in our society.' [24]

These examples appear not to be a superficial, contrived tourist experience [25] where a tourist is playing a passive role, but are a genuine attempt of the soap tourist to sightsee in an environment within which they can locate familiar sights and buildings, and can share with family and friends as a collective remembering of events, stories and situations.[26]

Television locations are just another of the many and diverse destinations that have been attractive to tourists throughout history. They appear to fulfil a need for present day pilgrims to share in an experience, albeit fantasy or myth, of people and place that has initially been consumed two-dimensionally, into a deeper and more meaningful experience and one in which they can locate themselves.

GRAND TOURS AND PILGRIMAGE

There is a link between the need of modern day pilgrims to visit hallowed sites and that of pilgrimage in the past. The Grand Tour is one of the most frequently cited phrases in the history of tourism.[27] It is associated with aristocratic young gentlemen in the early 18th century taking an extended pleasure journey throughout the principal cities and places of interest of western Europe for a cultural education. They acquired art treasures, classical antiquities, a love of picturesque scenery and other booty on the way, to adorn galleries in their country houses throughout Great Britain. In the later 18th century there is evidence that middle-class professional people often travelled with their families on a Grand Tour.[28]

The Grand Tour was a product of a particular social and cultural environment,[29] just as pilgrimages in the medieval period were part of the irresistible forces that controlled peoples lives.[30] Community, identity, popular piety, the veneration of saints and the cult of relics were as much a part of the social makeup then as they are today.

During both periods a tourist industry evolved to meet the demands of the travellers. There is evidence of an extensive but informally organised range of services which could be adapted to meet the requirements of the Grand Tourists, including accommodation, transport, banking and guides.

It is suggested that the motive behind a pilgrimage is similar to that behind a tour: both are quests for authentic experiences.[31] Indeed, just as contemporary concerns are fixed on the problems associated with authenticity and the need to provide access to tourists, the same was true but not always achieved throughout history. For those who did the Grand Tour, many purchased works of art which may or may not have been authentic, much of the classical statuary they bought was not. There are recorded incidences of classical figures being made up of diverse broken pieces. Towner describes a whole class of artists called 'scarpellini' who were working in Rome exclusively for the tourist trade.[32]

Similarly, in the medieval period, the unprecedented demand for bodily relics for the consecration of churches meant that demand exceeded supply. Many relics bought were of doubtful authenticity. Theft of relics was commonplace, as were counterclaims of who held authentic remains.[33] A miracle was considered the only proof of authenticity of relics, and these too were often fabricated in order to attract pilgrims.

THE ULTIMATE FAKE

Throughout history the need for sightseeing, of visiting new locations and collecting souvenirs to 'authenticate' the visit, has been a confirmation of self and a necessity which has fulfilled different needs. It is recognised that sightseeing 'is a form of ritual respect for society and ...tourism absorbs some of the social functions of religion in the modern world'.[34] It is not surprising that contemporary society with its overwhelming use of media images should generate a desire to participate in modern day pilgrimage associated with television viewing. If the opportunity 'for fantasy, diversion and colour are necessary to people's lives',[35] then locations associated with favourite television programmes are meeting the challenge.

Television, it appears, is the provider of a renewable cultural heritage resource, which can be packaged, presented and exploited indefinitely as new programmes catch the public's imagination. Some would argue that the result is synthetic cultural heritage developed with little integrity, and marketed simply for commercial gain which devalues the location from its inherent culture and heritage.

Others perhaps empathise. If serial tourists are willing to part with their cash for a product that is 'a satisfying activity at a desired destination' [36] then commercial gain is a reasonable exchange for such enjoyment and entertainment. Consequently, the locations of television programmes would be the catalyst for seemingly unlikely places to become successfully promoted as tourist destinations and as places of pilgrimage, an invaluable resource for the tourist industry. Indeed, the two appear to be deeply interdependent. The response to television locations as spectacles for consumption is a celebration of popular culture venerated by present day-out serial pilgrims, perhaps not addicted but simply fans, and should not be underestimated.

However, a new development is, I feel, a cause for concern. The Coronation Street set has recently been cloned in Blackpool, the ultimate theme park, directly across from the Pleasure Beach. This must call into question the very logic of authenticity and cultural heritage representation where even the copies are copied and the fake becomes reality as it is dislocated from its origins. Ultimately such developments fuel and support current critique that 'it may be too late for Britain to be other than a theme park.' [37]

The Author

Dr Patricia Sterry is a Senior Lecturer in Design History at the University of Salford and is course leader of a new postgraduate MA degree in Heritage Studies, which focus on interpretation, presentation and design, within the Faculty of Art, Design and Technology. She obtained her PhD at Manchester Metropolitan University in 1994 on the subject of *Heritage Centres: Design and Visitor Response. She* has presented papers at conferences in Great Britain, Europe and America on heritage interpretation issues, heritage design and visitor studies, and most recently at the Trends in Leisure and Entertainment Conference in Maastrict. She is currently establishing an international forum of designers compiling guidelines to integrate visitor studies data within the heritage design process of leisure environments.

References

1. Audience for Coronation Street, quoted in Little, D (1995) *The Coronation Street Story,* The Book People Ltd, Surrey
2. Landesman, C., 1996 Get Albert Square Out Of Your Head, *The Sunday Times,* 10 March 1996. Article describes 'Jack Duckworth Memorial Clinic' in Newcastle set up to help soapalcoholics which doesn't exist!
3. Vauxhall Movie Map, *Film and TV Locations in Britain.* 1996, BTA
4. Inglis, J., and Curtis, N., (1990) Its Scotland's Oil. Museums, Heritage and National Consciousness, in Baker, F. 7 Thomas, J. (eds.) *Writing The Past in the Present,* Pub. St David's University College, Lampeter

5. Graham, A., (1995) 'Many Happy Rovers Returns', *Radio Times* 2–8 December. Article asks what it is about this Northern saga that keeps the lives and loves of its stars at the top of the ratings
6. Graham, A., (1995) ibid
7. Urban regeneration in and around the Castlefield site has been substantial, especially in terms of warehouse restoration and renovation. I would recommend Williams, M and Farne, D (1992) *Cotton Mills in Greater Manchester*, Carnegie, Preston for a detailed description of individual buildings with a comprehensive bibliography
8. *Publicity Leaflet.* Granada Studio Tours, 1995
9 Urry, J., (1990) *The Tourist Gaze*, Sage, London pp 138 – 40, 1990
10. Sumption, J., (1975) *Pilgrimage*, Faber and Faber, London. An excellent account of the Great Age of Pilgrimage
11. Graham, A., (1995) op cit
12. MacCannell, D., (1976) *The Tourist : A New Theory of the Leisure Class*
13. Inglis, J and Curtis, N (1990) op cit
14. MacCannell, D., (1973) Staged Authenticity: Arrangement of Social Space in Tourist Settings, *American Sociological Review*, Vol 79, pp 589–603
15. ibid
16. ibid
17. Urry, J., (1990) op cit pp 117–118
18. Dietvorst, A., (1994) 'Cultural Tourism and Time – Space Behaviour' in Ashworth, G & Larkham, P (1994) *Building a New Heritage*, Routledge, London, pp 69–90
19. Boniface, P.,(1994) Theme Park Britain, in Fladmark J (ed.) *Cultural Tourism*, Donhead, London, pp 101–113
20. Fowler P (1992) *The Past in Contemporary Society: Then, Now*, Routledge, London
21. Taylor, D., (1995) *Inside Emmerdale*, Trail Publishing in conjunction with Yorkshire Television, Leyburn, Yorks A behind the Scenes look at the Village and characters of the programme
22. ibid
23. Burgess, C., (ed) (1995) Welcome to Summer Wine Country, pub Express and Chronicle Newspapers, Holmfirth
24. MacCannell, D., (1973) op cit
25. Boorstin, D., (1961) The Image: A Guide to Pseudo Events in America, Harper and Row, New York
26. Edwards D and Middleton D (1986) Joint Remembering: Constructing an Account of Shared Experience through Conversational Discourse *Discourse Process*, vol 9, pp 423–459
27. Towner, J., (1985) The Grand Tour: A Key Phase in the History of Tourism, *Annals of Tourism Research*, Vol 12, pp 297–333
28. ibid
29. ibid
30. Sumption, J., (1975) op cit

31. MacCannell, D ., (1973) op cit

32. Towner, J., (1985) op cit

33. Sumption, J., (1975) op cit

34. MacCannell, D., (1973) op cit

35. Boniface, P., (1994) op cit

36. Lickorish, L., (1991) *Developing Tourism Destinations*, Longman Ltd, London

37. Boniface, P., (1994) op cit

Select Bibliography

Corner J., and Harvey S , (1991) *Enterprise and Heritage: Crosscurrents of National Culture*, Routledge, London

Granada Studios Tour (1996) Presspack

Hughes H., (1987) Culture as a Tourist Resource – a Theoretical Consideration, *Tourism Management*, vol 8, 3, Sept, pp 205–216

King M., (1990) Theme Park Thesis, *Museum News*, 65, Sept/Oct, pp 60 – 62

Mills S., (1990) Disney and the Promotions of Synthetic Worlds, *American Studies International*, vol 28, 2, Oct, pp 66–79

Prentice R., (1993) *Tourism and Heritage Attractions*, Routledge, London

Sudjic D and Bussel A., (1988) Hordes at the Gate, *Blueprint*, Oct, Issue 51, pp 33–36

Tighe A., (1985) Cultural Tourism in the USA *Tourism Management*, Vol 6, 4, Dec pp 234–251

Vandermey A., (1984) Assessing the Importance of Urban Tourism, *Tourism Management*, vol 5 2, pp 123–135

Wickham-Jones C (1988) The Road to Heri-Tat, *Archaeological Review*, vol 7, 2, pp 185–193

28

IN SEARCH OF BRAND IDENTITY
The Makers of Wales Campaign

John Carr

The people of a nation are its strength. All their efforts have a lasting value, for good or ill, and remain in an evolved culture, whether as language or art form, castle or cottage, field wall or wharf, myth or music. 'Makers of Wales' is about people. It explores and celebrates their actions and achievements over time. The acts of exploration are intended to build cumulatively to a festival for the Millennium; to establish a community of intent, a partnership at all levels, whether national, regional or local; to fashion a special identity for the nation which is sustainable in a competitive market place long into the next century. That can best be achieved through widespread participation and commitment to forging a new and vibrant sense of self, of place and of pride in the past, the present and the future by building on a cultural inheritance of enormous breadth, richness and distinctiveness.

THE GENESIS OF THE MAKERS OF WALES

It all began with the wish to establish a strong, sustainable campaign for the promotion of the 131 ancient monuments in the care of the Secretary of State for Wales. For more than a decade the numbers of visitors to this remarkable portfolio had been in structural decline. Following the Investiture of Prince Charles as Prince of Wales in 1969, and the world-wide media coverage it received, Caernarfon Castle achieved visitor numbers approaching half a million, many from the core markets of western Europe and North America.

The nature of holiday-taking in the UK in the 1970s was such that England's north-west and Midlands' Wakes Weeks poured thousands of annual holiday makers into North Wales. Numbers at the three Edward I castles of Harlech, Beaumaris and Conwy were buoyant on the back of the fourth Caernarfon. Between them they contributed about 60 per cent of the circa 2.1 million visitors who then regularly attended the sites in State care until the late 1970s. The south-east was a Mecca for coach trips, particularly travelling through the Wye Valley to Tintern Abbey, and towards Monmouth via Raglan Castle; and the west contributed through Kidwelly and Carreg Cennen Castles and St Davids Bishops' Palace. Rural mid-Wales where there were and are few monuments in care of any high profile, was and remains a heritage tourism desert.

By October 1984 when Cadw Welsh Historic Monuments was created, the all-Wales numbers had declined to 1.289 million, producing a gross revenue of £989,000. The Castles of Edward I in Gwynedd still fed some 58 per cent of visitors towards the total. Caernarfon contributed about 320,000, Harlech and Beaumaris about 115,000 each and Conwy roughly 200,000.

The purpose of creating Cadw was not simply to ape what was happening in England, where English Heritage became a Non-departmental Public Body (NDPB) or quango, carved out from the Department of the Environment. Cadw was a collation of several inchoate elements of the Welsh Office. Its publicly-stated primary task was to inject some vigour into the presentation of the heritage of Wales, and to contribute handsomely to the country's overall tourism product. This was to be achieved while at the same time creating a statutory body responsible for the application of the law as it related to historic buildings and ancient monuments.

By 1987 total visitor numbers had increased to nearly 1.6 million, and revenues to circa. £2million. In 1988 Cadw devised and launched a major campaign to celebrate the 800th anniversary of The Journey Through Wales of Giraldus Cambrensis (the Anglo-Norman-Welsh churchman, travel writer, politician and gossip). This campaign largely achieved its objectives of increasing or stabilising visitor numbers for 1988–89. It attracted larger numbers to south and west Wales, but could not stem the endemic decline in Gwynedd.

The Gerald of Wales initiative was not alone in temporarily stopping the rot. In 1983 the Wales Tourist Board imaginatively staged a pan-Wales promotion, Cestyll '83 (Castles '83). It, too, had the effect of gaining more visitors into Wales and into monuments in State care. However, the relative surge created by both these campaigns was short-lived. Within 18 months the drift downwards was once again apparent. By 1991 Cadw numbers had decreased to 1,3 million, albeit with revenue rising to £2,3 million. Hence the wish to create a sustainable image for heritage and a platform for revenue growth.

The first idea was to stage a three-year onslaught through the medium of the more prominent properties: the now World Heritage sites of the Edward I Castles and Town Walls in Gwynedd, the world-renowned ecclesiastical romantic ruins of Tintern Abbey and St Davids Bishops' Palace, the Roman remains of the Augustan Legion at Caerleon and the Castles of the Welsh Princes, again dominant in Gwynedd. This would be supported by consolidation of the growth already achieved in the west.

That concept did not, however, fit comfortably with the gradually emerging change in Cadw's policy towards the presentation and promotion of the totality of the Welsh built inheritance. Emphasis was increasingly being given to financial, marketing and, in some cases, presentation support to all structures in an even-handed, all-Wales approach. This was evident through the encouragement of the historic buildings and conservation areas grant schemes; the town schemes; and through a deliberate concerted effort to grant-aid owners of scheduled ancient monuments to care for the less-noticed and undervalued field monuments.

The original *raison d'être* of Cadw had gradually moved towards an emphasis on the promotion of the ideal of protection, preservation and promotion of the historic legacy at large as an integral part of the wider tourism infrastructure. The monuments in care were increasingly seen as elements within communities, assets to be developed with an eye to supporting local economies.

Through discussion within Cadw, the obvious, but overlooked point emerged: that the built heritage had influenced the landscape of Wales; and that equally the landscape had influenced the human footprint upon it. They were inseparable. Each had contributed, and was still contributing, to the essence, the culture of Wales: socially, linguistically, economically, artistically, militarily, industrially.

THE CONCEPT OF BRAND IDENTITY

The original idea of a three-year, castle-orientated blockbuster thus grew wings. The idea was no longer solely concentrated upon the promotion of Cadw's majestic estate, nor with the built heritage in general. It had become a possible vehicle for the promotion of the culture and essence of Wales as a whole. The campaign might be sustainable over several years. Then realisation dawned: the Millennium was approaching. Given a separate, fresh title or subject for each of the seven years leading to the year 2000 or 2001, it might be possible to create an enduring image for Wales through the medium of several, interlocking themes for each year; and to use these building blocks to create a distinctive identity of and for a nation which had no immediately recognisable identifier. But how to test that concept of brand identity?

With some nervousness, Cadw presented its proposal to what were perceived to be associated and conceivably like-minded bodies in Wales: the Countryside Council, the National Museum, National Library, National Trust, Council of Museums, Royal Commission on Ancient and Historical Monuments, the Prince of Wales' Committee, Wales Tourist Board, Welsh Development Agency and the British Tourist Authority.

All were enthusiastic. Cadw was agreeably surprised. The loose-knit group resolved to form a progressing committee. After testing the concept on focus groups throughout Wales, the title and logo of the campaign emerged: 'Makers of Wales'. The themes for each year were agreed:

1. Chieftains and Princes
2. Arts and Literature
3. Shaping the Landscape
4. Myth, Faith and Religion
5. Transport and Communication
6. Conflict and Settlement
7. Industry, Energy and Enterprise.

Through these themes, every member of the committee would be able to contribute in one or several of the years. With imagination and a degree of lateral thinking, they could, it was felt, participate in every year. As important, here was a vehicle for encouraging other participants: the smallest civic or historical society, communities in the Welsh heartland, major industries, environmental bodies, farmers, museums, galleries, landowners. Indeed, it included anyone who saw, or who could be persuaded to see, advantage for him or herself and for Wales in taking part in an all-Wales promotional enterprise.

But how to implement a campaign with such widespread potential in a country with, then, 45 local authorities, 80 civic societies, more than 100 tourism associations of variable energy, more than 800 community councils, an active voluntary sector and a history of unwillingness to subsume individual identity in cooperative partnerships?

The original committee became the National Partners' Steering Group. Many pledged core-funding support to pay for a coordinator and for promotion; all signed up to a Heads of Agreement (the majority, being public bodies, could not sign into a corporation); and in September 1995 the Campaign Coordinator was appointed to pull together all activities within what had become the Makers of Wales Millennium Festival Campaign. While much had been achieved through the staging of exhibitions and publishing of books by Cadw and its first non-national partner, Gwynedd County Council, there was still a vast store of untapped potential.

THE CONTEXT: A NATION DIVIDED

Wales lacks a single, strong national identifier. England exploits its Beefeater image through the Tower of London, ceremonial State occasions and gin. Scotland's kilt and 19th century renaissance of tartan stands dominant alongside the water of life. Of the three United Kingdom territories, Scotland possesses arguably the most distinctive national promotional branding, known and respected the world over: whisky dressed in bottles with tartan emblems and thistles. England appears indifferent to such branding. Perhaps it is the arrogance of certainty. Possessing the British capital, the hub of transatlantic air travel, the centre of international finance in the City of London and regional identifiers such as Sheffield's cutlery, Nottingham's Robin Hood, Manchester's cotton, Wordsworth's Lakes, England can, perhaps, afford to be aloof. And England is a synonym for the British Isles in the outside world.

The tourist milk-run from Bath to Stratford-upon-Avon and back to London by way of York captures the bulk of first-time international business, and possibly an unfair proportion of the home market. English history dominates schools' curricula; the English language has bested French internationally, except perhaps still in diplomatic circles, former colonies and Quebec.

Wales, often addressed by transatlantic cousins as 'Wales, England', stands in the western shadow of its Act of Union partner. Its 'popular' identity is still shrouded in coal dust and the noxious fogs of primary industry (despite nearly two decades since the first signs of collapse of industrial Wales), of harps and male voice choirs. That is the problem. Internationally, Wales has given its names, and therefore its language, to many countries of the world: expert industrialists to towns in Russia (Hughesovski); Bryn Mawr in North Wales, to an exclusive girls' college in prosperous Pennsylvania; to townships named Jonesboro from Arkansas to Oregon, via North Carolina and Maine. Morgan features in South Africa, Antarctica and Queensland, while Evans the Mounts are found as far afield as Alberta and New Zealand.

The people from Wales (like their cousins the Scots, but less dominantly) have permeated throughout the world. There are Welsh societies in every continent. St David's Day is celebrated with *gymanfa ganu* wherever two

379

Welsh people happen to bump into one another. Yet Wales as a separate nation, with its distinctive language and its preserved culture, stands almost unnoticed by the world's increasing number of tourists. Those from overseas who have learned to know Wales return regularly because of its outstanding landscape and heritage and the unique identity of its culture, still vibrant through its language. They have learned something of the Makers of Wales by exposure; the campaign aims to enhance and formalise that learning within them and within the wider international community, whose dollars and yen are so important to the future economy of the country.

Apart from the regional and racial slur of spinning pit-head wheels and shining eyes through blackened miners' faces, the other images of Wales are found in horticulture and myth: daffodils, leeks and dragons. The first have been commandeered by the Dutch; the second, while tasty and nutritious, and eaten wherever they will grow, are more an apt point of ridicule for Falstaff or Max Boyce than truly symbolic of nationhood. The red dragon (*Y Ddraig Goch*) is splendid and mythical, but somehow this vibrant symbol has failed to gain widespread recognition; somehow it lacks substance as an international identifier for Wales, however eagerly and universally it is displayed. And it is, and has been since the time of the founder of the Twdwr dynasty, Henry VII.

Had the Act of Union unified Wales, then perhaps the centuries would have produced a more distinctive and characteristic identifier. As it is, Wales, not unlike England's North and South divide, or Scotland's Highlands and Lowlands, is a nation divided within itself. Even the bond of a shared language, probably the most vital and certainly unique among all European minorities, creates an irritable schism between the 'Gogs' (*gogledd*) of the north and their Cardi cousins in the west, both of whom scorn the 'champagne' utterances of the Pobol Pontcanna (the chattering Welsh equivalent of London's Hampstead and Highgate) and the alleged incomprehensibility of their 'received' BBC and S4C Welsh. Indeed, the Gogs and Cardis sometimes even refer to their southern countrymen as *saesneg* (foreigners).

The nation is also divided by geography and history. South of the imaginary line of the Landsker (a string of Norman castles protecting the fertile lowlands and coastal areas of Pembrokeshire from the native Welsh, driven into the rapidly-rising, bleak Preseli hills) lies 'Little England Beyond Wales', where Welsh is barely heard and even the place names owe more to Viking, Norman, Irish and Flemish origins than to the 'language of heaven'.

The West, between Cardigan Bay and the central uplands, from the Brecon Beacons to the foothills of Snowdonia, is concerned with quiet farming and taking a living from the sea. While the North, in the mountains of Snowdonia, Eryri (Eagle), in Gwynedd, remains the proud, unconquered fastness of Welsh princes, ringed into subjection by the mighty fortresses of Edward I for the past seven centuries.

The North-east, on the English side of the Clwydian Hills and their dominant hillforts, looks more to Liverpool and Chester than into the historic heart of Wales; and the populous South-east, from Swansea to Newport and hemmed in by the Valleys and the Severn Sea, is where the former industrial action rests and the hi-tech factories of Japanese, American and Korean inward investors are supported by an ever-burgeoning financial services sector and grants from Europe. Even the roads and railways are orientated east-west to the North and South; and the quickest way from Gwent by road or rail is via England.

Despite the clearly identifiable regional differences, and despite having been overrun by various incursions (some hostile like the Romans and Normans, Vikings and Dark Age Irish; others bent on work, like the English Midlanders and another wave of Irish into the satanic revolution of the industrial Valleys) there is nonetheless a homogeneity, a fellow-feeling of unity, despite good natured insults, of separateness from the rest of Britain and of nationhood. That there is also warmth and sympathy felt to others on the Celtic fringe is not surprising: not simply because of cooperation in the face of the imperialist overlords, but perhaps because Welsh-speaking Celts once dominated much of Britain, as evidenced in the prefix Aber to many place names in Scotland, such as Aberdeen and Aberdour.

THE TOURISM CONTEXT

Wales has been a tourist country since the Journey Through Wales by Giraldus Cambrensis in 1188, George Borrow's tour through Wild Wales, the forays by the Brothers Buck in search of romantic ruined material for the first picture postcards in the 17th century, and J.M.W. Turner's evocative landscapes in the Picturesque period after Napoleon put an end to the fashionable Grand Tour in Europe.

However, the product has been, and is, diffused. The North Wales beaches attracted thousands of Midlanders and Mancunians during the annual wakes' weeks to Rhyl and Prestatyn, Llandudno and Conwy; the West was holiday haven for South-east Englanders seeking beaches and countryside relatively unspoiled by the kiss-me-quick magnets of Barry Island and Porthcawl (the Brighton and Blackpool of South Wales). Swansea and the Gower Peninsula vied with South Pembrokeshire for the environmentally aware. Many of these thousands were and still are temporarily housed in the ubiquitous caravan and chalet parks or in Bed and Breakfast establishments. Only over the past ten years has there been growth in numbers and standards of starred hotels in response, perhaps, to the Marbella syndrome which raised expectations in an increasingly discerning market.

It was that syndrome in the 1970s and 1980s that contributed to the depletion of bulk numbers of tourists (coupled with the Chernobyl fall-out and Libyan terrorism). Between 1979 and 1989 Wales experienced a 50 per cent fall in long-holiday (that is, more than four nights) inward tourism as a result of Britons seeking the sunshine and new experiences of Spain's Costas and Balearic islands and the get-away-from-it-all lure of Greece, Cyprus, Rhodes and other smaller offshore islands. In real numbers, that represented a drop in tourism visits to Wales from 3.8 million to 1.9 million, against an increase in the numbers of Britons travelling overseas from 5 million in 1965 to 15.5 million in 1979 and 31 million in 1989.

Even the attractiveness of the heritage product to overseas visitors to the United Kingdom has not had a marked effect on actual numbers into Wales. These have remained relatively static at around 640,000 for a decade. Research indicates that Wales, on the western edge, is principally discovered by those who are making their second or subsequent visits to Britain. These tend to be the more discerning, the better-educated, those with an orientation to 'lifestyle' and the joys of the environment; in other words, largely the AB sector with relatively high levels of disposable income, although the Dutch tend to disappear into the mountainous hinterland with back-packs, bikes and low budgets.

Table 1: Overseas visitors to Britain

	Nr. of visitors (000)		% change	Prop. of total (%)	
	1979	1989	79 to 89	1979	1989
North America	2196	3481	+ 59	17.6	20.1
EC	6605	8960	+ 36	52.9	51.7
Non EC	1268	1728	+ 36	10.2	9.9
Australasia	497	658	+ 32.4	4.0	3.8
Japan	140	505	+ 261	1.1	2.9
	10706	15332	+43		
World Total	12486	17338	+38.9		

As Table 1 shows, there has been dramatic growth in North American visitors to Britain between 1979 and 1989 (+ 59 per cent), with a 36 per cent increase from Western Europe (including EC and non-EC), and 32.4 per cent uplift from Australasia. Staggeringly, but from a low base of 140,000 in 1979, the Japanese posted an increase of 261 per cent at 505,000 in 1989.

For different reasons, both North America and Japan are exceptionally devoted to heritage visits: the Americans perhaps seek a stability in the past, adding to their own short history that of their perceived origins, while the Japanese may assuage their guilt about taking holidays by filling them with cultural pursuits, an acceptable means of justifying time taken from work.

Within the context of assessing Makers of Wales potential markets, the BTA's Digests of Tourist Statistics show (See Figure 1) the dominance of heritage and museums as the principal reasons for visiting Britain. Extrapolated for Wales, that is a market not to be ignored. Comparatively small though the actual numbers may be, 640,00 represents more than 33 per cent of all long-stay visits in Wales. And, significantly, Cadw sites attract between 23 and 27 per cent of this market (150–172,000), with research data showing that an average of two sites are visited in any one stay (c. 310,000).

Further research demonstrates that 45 per cent of those visiting Wales from the UK (all sources) are attracted by heritage and landscape. This represents a pool of some 6.5 million visitors, of whom roughly 3 million come for the special characteristics of Wales: scenery which represents a microcosm of the variety of Britain's landscape; an abundance of heritage (there are more than 500 officially recorded castles and fortified sites in the nation's 21,000 square kilometres); and a distinctive cultural identity.

With greater international mobility and a sustaining of interest in heritage world-wide, allied to the newly won freedom of the Wales Tourist Board to promote the country overseas (a case of power but little cash support) it is possible to suggest that visits to Wales will benefit from the forecast growth in visits to Britain from key markets (Figure 2).

Thus, there is an existing and potentially growing pool of tourists. There is already a national identity, however unexploited. And there is a product whose attributes have barely been exposed in any cohesive or coherent way to a market segment which seeks less of the razzmatazz, being more attuned to seeking absolution in a wasteful world and realising that the vogue concept of sustainability of the environment, however difficult to define, is of paramount importance for the future.

One little-recalled finding of the Rio conference, which a government in tune with political reality touched on in its *This Common Inheritance: Britain's Environmental Strategy*, is the emergence of Local Agenda 21. This places an obligation on local authorities to set out their stalls for measurable sustainability of all aspects of the environment: social, economic, physical and cultural. Little is evident in the public media of how that remit is being fulfilled. However, with the emergence of unitary authorities throughout Wales, there is a growing understanding at local government level that sustainability is not just about finite resources, but that the quality of social and economic environments must also be improved; that those improvements should be built on and kept at levels which avoid erosion of attitude, habitat and cultural identity.

Thus Makers of Wales may be seen as a forum for assisting the stabilisation of society as well as contributing to the economic future of Wales. At the same time it may instil or nurture a sense of self and of place. These circumstances combined have set the agenda for the Odyssey for a Brand Identity.

THE CAMPAIGN OBJECTIVES

The campaign has the following principal objectives:

1. to help to create an enduring image for Wales, by encouraging community, regional and national organisations to preserve and to promote inherited assets and the overall environment of Wales.
2. to help to promote Wales as a distinctive destination for both tourism and inward investment.
3. to enhance the knowledge and enjoyment of residents and visitors.
4. to increase people's appreciation of the value of their cultural, built and natural inheritance and of the need to protect and preserve it.
5. to increase the number of visits to museums, historic properties and landscapes which are open to the public.
6. to foster strong and mutually supportive partnerships for the protection and enjoyment of the cultural, social, built and natural environment of Wales.
7. to help to promote sustainable development in Wales.

There is little surprising in this list of interrelated objectives. It would perhaps be surprising if there were. Evident within them are two main strands: preservation of cultural assets and economic advantage. The first of these embraces the understandable aims of fostering and sustaining the environment; the second stresses the importance of cohesion of effort and identity in order to provide a solid and sustained partnership effort which cumulatively would build to a commonly-pursued purpose. Linking and permeating each strand is the aim of grasping long-term economic advantage for the benefit of the next and succeeding generations of the people of Wales. For what is the purpose of a brand identity unless it is to help market a distinctive product? Simplistic truism, yes; but nonetheless true.

ACHIEVING THE OBJECTIVES

The question most frequently asked is *How*? The *Who*? is not a problem. The *What*? is evident to any one who lives in Wales: heritage litters the landscape. If the *Why*? has to be voiced then the campaign is talking to the wrong people. *When* is now, and for the next five years, conceivably, if momentum is sustained, beyond deep into the next millennium.

Behind the *How*? are the next questions: which of the themes is relevant? Are themes from previous years no longer available? The answer to both is that the themes are pointers to each year; they do not become unavailable or obsolete simply through the passage of time. The original intention remains: to present and retain all themes year-on-year and to use them as building blocks to create an increasingly revealing and interesting product, for tourism and for community involvement.

It is possible to take a heritage asset and to exploit its attributes by building on each theme cumulatively over the life of the campaign. Most villages possess a church or chapel, or both. Many have grand houses, ruined castles or priories. All have roads and footways, many continuously travelled since prehistory; all provided livelihoods for their people; all sprang up or were altered in times of peace; all related to the surrounding landscape, influencing and being influenced by its characteristics. Table 2 randomly lists subjects for potential exploitation in each of the themes; many cross-refer to previous or subsequent themes.

TWO CASE STUDIES

Two examples serve as illustrative case studies of outwardly dissimilar built heritage sites: Tintern Abbey and the village of Templeton in South Pembrokeshire.

Tintern Abbey sprang from the Cistercian faith (Theme 4: Myth, Legend and Faith). Its Abbot was a powerful Marcher Lord, a Prince of the Church, imposing his will and disposing his leadership over the whole of the vast diocesan area, treating with serf and with royalty (Theme 1: Chieftains and Princes). The arts of writing, illuminated manuscripts and advanced masonry skills were developed here (Theme 2: Arts and Literature). The choice of the Abbey's location at the base of a sheltered valley was not a chance happening: seclusion fed the practice of faith and provided some comfort from the elements; similarly, the fertile valley floor alongside the Wye provided sustenance from corn and sheep and fish (Themes 3 and 7: Shaping the Landscape and Industry, Energy and Enterprise). As the Abbey developed, so did the dependence of the less-advantaged populace nearby, thus bolstering power and wealth (Theme 1). The landscape influenced the Abbey's place of foundation; its shelter from the worst buffeting of the seasonss winds, gave some small worldly comfort to the monks. The pilgrims' paths led over hills and valleys to the place of succour, of body and spirit, and produce had to be taken to market (Theme 5: Transport and Communication). Agricultural development was heavily influenced by the monks whose needs of more advanced implements influenced the skills of blacksmith, cooper and wheelwright (Theme 7). The Abbey was created after the Norman Conquest and fell beneath Henry VIII's anger over Papal intransigence (Theme 6: Conflict and Settlement), and gained new importance during the Picturesque period of J.M.W. Turner (Theme 2) and as a contributor to the tourism economy (Theme 7).

These snapshots of how the themes without much effort, can be made, to interweave are similarly applicable to churches at community level. Many were founded by invading lords. They dominated the community through patronage and learning, giving what little education they could to an illiterate population and, by osmosis, absorbing into the local Christian canon the more respectable elements of folklore which had developed from prehistory and the Dark Ages, borrowing beliefs and language, artistic and poetic culture from the several separate waves of invasion. Many such churches were founded on early post-Roman sites; their incumbents were fed by tithes from industry; they were built by skilled men whose arts had been developed in Europe, and they were places of haven in times of conflict. Thus the sublime nature of Tintern can be mirrored in every Anglican parish throughout Wales.

Templeton bestrides a locally important route from Narberth to Tenby. Superficially, it has no residual cultural or commercial importance. And yet it has a history of great richness. Nearby is the Iron Age camp of Molleston (Theme 1). Two hundred yards from the road stands Sentence Castle, a Norman motte and bailey, and one of the possible sites of the Princes of Arberth who figure so dominantly in the Mabinogion. That collection of myth and legend reveals much about Dark Age and early-medieval belief and chivalry, culture and society. It is also elusive in its deepest origins: Celtic? Irish? Roman? Prehistory? Dark Age? Norman? (Theme 2).

The village itself sprang from the lord in the motte. Along a single street, curiously rather inconveniently steep, burgage plots lead geometrically back from street-front house platforms to meet the ageless boundaries of enclosed pasture (Theme 3). The 19th century church stands high and modestly handsome above and distant from the motte. Why? A good question without apparent explanation, but it is thought to have been built on the site of a medieval hospice founded by The Knights Templars (Themes 4 and 5 could reflect Templeton's contribution to the Crusades). There is further association with Theme 5 through the village's position on the Knights Way, a route from coastal Amroth to the important mill at Blackpool and on to Haverfordwest, with a slight detour to Slebech where the Commandery of the Knight's Hospitallers was founded.

Farmsteads known as Poyers and Templeton bear witness to mid-17th century evolution of the agricultural landscape (Themes 3 and 6). The most drastic rearrangement of the environment came with steam power and the railways (Themes 3 and 7) in the second half of the 19th century. The railway, originally used for industrial production only, serviced the new brickworks industry in 1868. Limestone quarries scarred the countryside and the fuel came from the modest coalfields of South Pembrokeshire (Theme 7). The railway station is no more, but Templeton had a short and possibly more dramatic life in the 1940s when an airfield (still operational) was sited immediately outside the village (Theme 6).

While virtually every community possesses assets which may be incorporated into a melange of thematic development, clearly some assets dominate others; and, equally clearly, historical data is a variable commodity, thus limiting the number of productive story lines which may be developed. Nonetheless, given imagination and some flexibility it is possible to build a special selling point for each settlement of any size through a combination of research and folk memory.

Indeed, the South Pembrokeshire Partnership for Action in Rural Communities (SPARC) has so wholeheartedly embraced the concept of Makers of Wales that it has successfully bid for LEADER II financial support from Europe. Every hamlet, village and town in the SPARC area is busily auditing its cultural and heritage assets and producing leaflets on the interesting and unusual. These build cumulatively to integrate into a generic area marketing brochure and an already-established but now expandable series of trails (foot, cycle and combustion engine) to encourage visitors to recognise and enjoy the peculiar characteristics of the region. At the same time, having branded its region so firmly with the Makers of Wales identifier, SPARC is actively integrating the range of other visitor attractions within its boundaries with an improving and expanding accommodation base, thus providing further ammunition for inward investment to what is a beautiful but economically unstable rural area, dependent largely on agriculture and tourism. Such efforts are already showing encouraging signs of a stemming of rural depopulation and providing sustainability, thus engendering a greater spirit of hope in the future.

Much of this text has concentrated upon the built heritage. In mitigation, the concept did begin in a built heritage agency, but the initial presentations could not have excited the museum curators had they not seen their collections as keys to unlocking understanding of the achievements of men and women over time.

Each museum discipline has much to offer: archaeologists finding, curating and interpreting the human imprint of what has been unearthed; geologists explaining the formation, forces, disadvantages and potential of landscape in the limestone, coal, slate and iron industries; botanists and biologists analysing the contents of graves and middens to cast light on dietary habits leading to evidence of agricultural practices as they developed during and following waves of immigration over extensive periods, both in prehistory and post-Roman; philologists tracing the evolution of language, with its borrowings from Irish, Latin (pont = bridge as in Pontardawe, the 'bridge over the Tawe'), French (eglwys = eglise = church); architectural historians; Keepers of Manuscripts (the Mabinogion, White Book of Rhydderch) and Bishop Morgan's first commitment to paper of the Bible written in Welsh; and of Pictures (the Brothers Buck, Horner, Sandby, Turner): numismatics (coinage from Rome and the Mints at Aberystwyth, Aberdulais and Dyfi Furnace); metallurgists and their expertise in lead, iron and gold mining (c.f. the Roman goldmines at Dolaucothi in the foothills of the Black Mountains of Powys); telecommunications (Marconi on Flat Holm in the Bristol Channel, offshore from Cardiff), and sundry other disciplines and sub-disciplines.

EDUCATION POTENTIAL

Here is a mine of information which may be quarried to meet the requirements of the National Curriculum. Artefacts, buildings, the environment at large are all capable of providing source material to whet the appetites of both teachers and pupils in a structured way. Indeed, as the matrix at Figure 3 shows, an historic structure can be used as base material for the teaching of a wide range of academic subjects. If they are selected to reflect the special inheritance of Wales they would give force to recognition of the Makers of Wales campaign as early as the nursery school and certainly into adult education.

All the material for inculcating a deeper knowledge, and understanding and enjoyment of the special nature of the history and culture of Wales exists, spread widely through various institutions. In its Odyssey for a brand identity, the Makers of Wales campaign is faced with the twin challenges of encouraging people to unlock their storehouses and to recognise that, if the parts are summed to the whole, they will produce a collation of fascinating information about the origins of the people of Wales and create a true festival leading to the celebration of Wales in the next millennium. There is the added prospect of perhaps pointing to their future as a nation on the fringe of Europe. But that is another story to be written by future Makers of Wales.

The Author

John Carr now runs his own consultancy, specialising in heritage, tourism and interpretation developments, as well as in marketing, promotion and public relations. He was the first Director and Chief Executive of Cadw: Welsh Historic Monuments (1985–95) which has responsibility for the built heritage of Wales and for the conservation, presentation and marketing of 131 monuments. During his tenure, Cadw won awards from the Civic Trust, Prince of Wales' Committee, Campaign for Rural Wales and the Society for the Interpretation of Britain's Heritage. He initiated and oversaw the 'Gerald of Wales Journey Through Wales' 800th Anniversary project (1988) and the 'Makers of Wales' Millennium Festival Campaign (1994–2001). He remains honorary chairman of the festival's Steering Group. After reading English, Archaeology and Anthropology at Cambridge University, he spent 20 years in newspapers, as journalist and general manager on *The Sunday Times* and *Times* Newspapers. In 1982, he was appointed Director of the Neath Development Partnership to take charge of economic regeneration of an area severely affected by the collapse of primary industries. A writer and frequent media commentator, he was elected a Fellow of the Royal Society of Arts in 1994 and was awarded the CBE in 1995.

References

Ashworth, G.J., *Heritage Planning*, Geo Pers. (undated)
Carr, J., in *Heritage Sites: Strategies for Marketing and Development*, Herbert, D. T., Prentice, R. T., Colin J., (eds) Avebury, 1989
Carr, J. and Hood, A., *Does Heritage need IT?* in Stevens, T. and James, V., (eds), *The Future for Europe's Past*, Proceedings of COMETT Workshops, Swansea Institute of Higher Education, *et al*, 1995

Carr, J., *Cadw: Its Aims, Role and Programme*, in, The Proceedings of a Conference held by the Cambrian Archaeological Association 1985, St David's University College; Lampeter *et al*, 1986

Fladmark, J.M., *The Wealth of a Nation: Heritage as a Cultural and Competitive asset*, The Robert Gordon University,Aberdeen, 1994

Gantz, J., *The Mabinogion*, (trans) Penguin Classics, 1976

Gaunt, P., *A Nation Under Siege: The Civil War in Wales 1642–488*, HMSO and Cadw: Welsh Historic Monuments, 1991

Jenkins, J.G., *Getting Yesterday Right: Interpreting the Heritage of Wales*, University of Wales Press, 1992

Kenyon, J. R. and Avent, R., *Castles in Wales and the Marches*. University of Wales Press, 1987

Kightly, C., *A Mirror of Medieval Wales: Gerald of Wales and His Journey of 1188*, Cadw: Welsh Historic Monuments, 1988

Rees, S. (ed), *Guides to Ancient and Historic Wales*, Dyfed (1992), Glamorgan and Gwent (1992), Gwynedd and Clwyd and Powys (1995), all HMSO

Robinson, D., *Heritage in Wales*, Macdonald Queen Anne Press, 1989

Robinson, D., (ed.), *Guidebooks to Ancient Monuments in the care of the Secretary of State for Wales*, CADW, 1985–1996

Secretary of State for the Environment *et al*, *This Common Inheritance: Britain's Environmental Strategy*, Cm 1200, HMSO, 1994

Thorpe, L., *Gerald of Wales: The Journey Through Wales/The Description of Wales*, (trans) Penguin Classics, 1978

Whittle, E., *Historic Gardens of Wales*, HMSO, 1994

Williams, G., *Renewal and Reformation Wales c. 1415–1642*, Oxford University Press, 1987

Williams, G., *The Welsh Church from Conquest to Reformation*, University of Arkansas Press, 1993

Williams, G. (ed), *Swansea: An Illustrated History*, Christopher Davies, 1990

Theme Matrix for National Curriculum Subjects

Subjects	Prehistory	Roman	Abbeys	Castles	Industrial	Townships
Humanities Sociology Anthropology	Social Organisation	Social Economic Colonial	Social Economic	Military Social Economic Townships	Migration Social Engineering	Markets Settlement Inter-dependence
Art& Design	Rock Art Craving Military Forts Flint, Iron, Toold, Objects	Artefacts Mosaics, Painting Decoration	Writing Music Sculpture Painting	Music Painting Decoration Sculpture	Mines Bridges Machinery	Municipal Design Parks
Architecture	Hill Forts Design of Settlements, Camps	Forts Houses Temples Fora	Styles Techniques Symmetry	Motte to Concentric Swelling & Stronghold	Mills Factories Aqueducts Railways	Self-explanatory Multi-Period
Archaeology	Tools Vessels Weapons Art	Tools, Coins Vessels, Glass Weapons Roads	Burial Rites Artefacts	Lifestyles Construction Artefacts	Post-reformation Adaptation	Planned Design: Roman, Norman Vicorian
Biology	Diet (from archaeological analysis)	Diet (from archaeologic al analysis)	Diet Agriculture Animal - Husbandry	Diet Deer Parks Animal Husbandry	Nutrition	Diet Crop/Farming Increased yealds
Botany	Farming Crop Development	Imported Plants Indigenous	Imported Flora, Crop-development Local Flora	Imports via Crusades Colonising Flora on ruins	Ferrous loving Species	Import of Alien Flora
Geology	Caves Capstones Iron, Copper Mines	Gold, Lead Copper, Coal Mines	Choice & Use of Stone Mineral Extraction	As Abbeys	Mining: Coal, Slate, Copper, Iron, Lead, Tin	Pit, Mill, Slate Worker Villages
Geography	Migration-Multi Phase	Empire Spread in Britain	Spread of Manastic Houses	Development of Estates, Land Tenure	Power, Trade Areas & Minerals	Distribution: Topographical Influence
History	Various Strands Migration Settlements	Numerous Topics	All-pervasive Influence	Military,Social Economic Pan-Europe	Social Economic Military	Social Economic
Language Literature		Latin Classics, Legends, Myths	Latin, French Bible Laws	Latin,French Patronage Myth	Miners' Institutes Beard Schools	
Mathematics	Planetary Orientation Trade	Trade, Building Houses, Roads,Arena	Trade Architecture Design	Architecture	Technical Innovation	Schools, Universities
Physics Chemistry	Building Forts Burial Chambers Medicine	Building Construction Ballistae Medicine	Building Tanning Dyes Milling Weaving	Building Techniques Weaponry	Technical Innovation Medicine	
Religious Education	Burial Rites	Gods Christianity Temples	Self-explanatory	Chapels in Castles Churches Patronage	Methodism Baptism	Henges Church Chapel, Mosque, Synagogue

Building Blocks for the Main Campaign Themes

1	2	3	4
Chieftains & Princes	**Arts & Literature**	**Shaping the Landscape**	**Myth, Legend& Faith**
Prehistoric Burial	Stone Carving	Historic Landscapes	BurialChambers,
Hill Forts	Architecture	Clearance	Barrows Chapels,
Roman Forts	Individual Structure	Field Boundaries	Cathedrals,
Civil Towns	Townspeople	Land Management	Pre-Christian
Welsh Castles	Planned Housing	Monastic Agriculture	Roman gods
Welsh Prince's	Sculpture	Coastal Fortifications	Early Churches
Castles	Literature	Land Reclamation	Parish Churches
Marcher Lords	Poetry	Enclosure	Private Chapels
Norman Mottes	Painting	Farming	Abbeys
Anglo-Norman	Music	Homesteads	Monasteries
Castles	Crafts	Hill Forts	The Reformation
Abbeys	Furniture making	Castles	Nonconformist Methodist,
Monasteries	Eisteddfodau	Abbeys	Baptist,
Hywel Dda-	Illuminated MS, Books	Mines	Congregational
Prince & Lawmaker	Stone Masonry	Forestry	Welsh Saints
The Lord Rhys	Joinery	Parks & Gardens	Lundy, Caldey, Bardsey
Owain Glyndwr	Blacksmith	Pilgrims' Ways	Islands
Llewellyn	Pottery	Roman Roads	Bible Translation
Edward I	Patronage - by Kings,Princes,	Nature Reserves	Hymn Writing
Bishops (as Princes	Prelates,	National Parks,	Education
of the Church)	Magnates,	AONB	Bishops & Ministers
Industrial Magnates	Gentry	SSSI	Evangelists
(Bute, Crawshay,		Nature Reserves	Holy Wells
Guest...)		Ancient Woodlands	Celtic Crosses
Mayors, Council		Estuaries	Pilgrimage
Chairmen, MPs,		Moorland	Synagogues,
Government		Wetlands	Mosques
Ministers		Commoners' Land	
		Industrialisation	

5	6	7
Transport & Communication	**Conflict & Settlement**	**Industry,Energy & Enterprise**
Trackways	Hut Circles	Flint Factories
Drovers's Roads	Hill Forts	Bronze Age Mining
Road Building -	Roman Military & Civil Towns	Roman Mining
Roman to present	Walled Towns	Coal, Iron, Slate, Limestone, Lead Agriculture
Fords/Stepping	Farmsteads	Forestry
Stones	Urban Design/	Building,
Bridges	Planning	Construction
Tunnels	Defences	Charcoal Burning
Ports & Harbours	Villages	Copper Smelting
Coracles	Medieval Villages	Iron Working
Shipping	Ribbon Development	Steel Making
Tramways	Estates/ Great Houses	Iron Masters
Railways	Religious Communities	Shipbuilding
Beacons	Llysœdd/Maerdrefi	Ports & Harbours
Supply Routes	(early Welsh Administrative	Factories
Motor Vehicles	Areas)	Japanisation
Rivers & Estuaries	Edward I	Foreign Investment
Two SevernBridges	Civil War in Wales	Cardiff Bay Project
Canals	Owain Glyndwr	Marquess of Bute
Marconi	Urbanisation	Great Houses
Radio & TV	Garden Cities	Tourism
		Hydroelectricity
		Nuclear Energy
		Renewable energy
		Sustainability

393

Roadside sign in a wine growing village of Alsace.

29

THE HERITAGE OF ALSACE
Trails For The Imbibing Tourist

Dragan Crnjanski

With just over 1.6 million inhabitants on 8000 square km the Alsace region represents 3% of French population and 1.5% of French territory. Extending over 200 km from north to south, it forms the eastern border of France, in osmosis with the pan-European river connection Rhine–Main–Danube. Alsace has two international airports, in Strasbourg and Basel-Mulhouse.

It is important to be aware of the main historical periods of this region, in order to fully understand its complex and interesting cultural identity. Alsace became Gallo-Romanic and assumed strategic military significance after the victory of Julius Caesar over different Germanic peoples in 58 BC. From then on, the Rhine river served as the frontier between the Roman Empire and the. The military camp of Argentoratum later became the town of Strasbourg. The military presence led to agricultural development and craft industries, and wine growing was introduced in the first century AD, three centuries before the Christian era.

The frontier line was breached under the assault of the Germanic peoples at the beginning of the 5th century, with the settlement of the Alamans who impose their language on the indigenous Gallo-Romanic population. The Alamans were then vanquished in 496 by the Francs, the result being confirmation of the area's military significance and the extension of Christianity.

The name Alsace first appeared in the 7th century AD. After the reign of the Carolingians (8th–9th century), when cultural and spiritual life flourished with the building of abbeys at Murbach and Wissembourg,

Alsace was in 870 integrated into the Eastern Frankish kingdom, which became future Germany.

Alsace thus remained part of the vestiges of Charlemagne's Holy Roman Empire until the 17th century. Indeed, throughout the 12th–15th centuries, the Alsace and the Rhine valley represented the centre of cultural gravity of the former Empire, especially in regard to the heritage of Romanesque art. The Habsbourgs conquered the southern part of the area at end of the 13th century.

This period was followed by the 'golden century' of the Renaissance, when Alsace was one of the main centres of Rhine humanism, with a Latin school in Sélestat, Gutenberg staying in Strasbourg, and the extension of the Reformation to the towns of Strasbourg, Colmar and Mulhouse.

Following the Thirty-Years' War, a deep economic depression struck the region, and more than half of its population disappeared. Starting from 1648, Alsace was progressively integrated into the French kingdom, and the Rhine river became an international border in 1697. The strategic significance of the region was again reinforced by Vauban's military fortifications along the Rhine and in Belfort.

The 18th century was characterised by cultural renaissance and prosperity, and a bilingual culture started to develop. There were improvements and diversification in agriculture, emergence of industrialisation, and strong expansion in transit trade through the Rhine valley. The name Alsace disappeared with the French Revolution, when the area became part of two departments, and the Protestants and then Jews were granted civic and professional equality.

The 1870 War led to the annexation of Alsace by the German Reich, which started a period of strong traumas for the region, and the nationalistic rivalry between France and Germany continued until 1945. However, development of the European Community is allowing Alsace once again to assume its central role in the affairs of Europe.

Today, it draws on its collective memory steeped in two cultures. One was born from the division of its territory between the Latin and Germanic worlds, and drawn along a north-south line of the Vosges mountain massif. The other came from the integration of southern Alsace to the Habsbourg Empire from the 13th to the 17th century, the separation line being that dividing the Departments of Bas-Rhine and Haut-Rhin today.

THE WINES OF ALSACE

The area of the Alsatian vineyards is situated at the piedmont of the Vosges mountains. It stretches over a distance of 120 km and extends to over 13000 hectares, representing 1 % of French wine growing territory. The vineyards are among the steepest in France, covering hills between 200 and 400m in altitude. Wine growing accounts for 5% of agricultural land and 25% of the agricultural gross product of Alsace.

Sheltered by the Vosges mountains from oceanic weather fluctuations, with an orientation to the south and east, the area enjoys a semi-continental climate, with dry, sunny and hot summers. Alsace, together with Champagne, is the premier wine producing area in France. It also has the least rainfall, barely 500 mm per year, favouring slow and long lasting grape maturation.

Due to the geomorphology of the massif formed by the Vosges and sediments from the Black Forest in Germany, the soil of Alsatian vineyards is a rich mixture. The main varieties of Alsatian vines, allowed to use the legally protected label of 'Appellation d'origine géographique controlée de Alsace' are:

1. *Sylvaner* covering an area of about 2500 hectares (20%), a vine brought from Austria at the end of the 18th century;
2. *Pinot Blanc* covering an area of about 2500 hectares (19%), brought from Northern Italy;
3. *Riesling* covering an area of about 2700 hectares, the oldest variety known in Alsace;
4. *Muscat d'Alsace* covering an area of about 375 hectares;
5. *Pinot Gris* (or strangely Tokay) covering an area of 680 hectares;
6. *Gewurtztraminer* covering an area of about 2500 hectares;
7. *Pinot Noir* with 870 hectartes, brought from Burgundy and producing the only rose or red wine of Alsace.

With an average yield of one million hectolitres per year, Alsatian wine production represents about 20% of French white wine production under the controlled origin system, representing 7% of overall controlled production. In 1995, a fairly good year for Alsatian wine growing, the average yield per hectare was about 85 hectolitres. Out of 8000 individual wine growers, 20% produce their own wine, which account for 40% of the wine growing area. Several hundred of these independent operators have their own promotion and sale outlets located directly on and along the Wine Route. It is estimated that about 30% of Alsatian wine production is sold directly to Wine Route visitors.

TOURISM IN ALSACE

The present accommodation capacity available in Alsace is about 107 000 beds in the following categories:

1. 44 000 beds in hotels;
2. 35 000 beds in camp-sites;
3. 13 000 beds in rural or 'green' tourism facilities;
4. 15 000 beds in 'associative tourism' facilities such as vacation camps, youth hostels and others.

For a total permanent population of 1.6 million, this capacity corresponds to a tourist function rate of 6.6 (number beds per 1000 inhabitants) of 6.6. To this capacity, one should add the secondary residences, which total about 100 000 beds. As a whole, the administrative space of the wine growing communes representing the Wine Route, offers an accommodation capacity of 21 000 beds for a population of 104 000. This corresponds to a tourist function rate of 19.81.

In 1997, there where 12 million tourist nights in Alsace as a whole, out of which an estimated 2.3 million were in the Wine Route area. A total of about five million excursions or daily outings were made, comprising visitors from neighbouring regions, trans-border visitors, and tourists in transit and staying in non-commercial accommodation.

An overall preliminary evaluation of the economic impact of regional tourism trade gives a global turnover of 20 billion French Franc (direct, indirect and induced), and an employment of 30 000 persons. The direct turnover, corresponding to tourist expenditures, is estimated at 6,4 billion Franc, out of which about one billion is generated by tourists staying in Wine Route accommodation.

Our market assessment, including surveys carried out in 1988 and 1995 and based on a sample of 1500 persons staying in tourist accommodation, has enabled us to draw up an overall typology of tourists visiting Alsace, divided in five groups of relatively homogeneous profiles:

1. new clients 'seeking a different cultural experience', representing 29% of the sample and coming to Alsace to discover the region and its cultural uniqueness;
2. visitors who already know Alsace and who has 'adopted' its culture, representing 27% of the sample;
3. short stay visitors seeking change and relaxation, representing 17% of the sample and coming mostly coming from nearby regions and countries;
4. regional visitors looking for 'active relaxation', representing 14% of the sample;

5. professional/business tourists, representing 14% of the sample.

This confirms that the motivation for cultural discovery is a dominant factor. Over 50% of visitors come, either to discover specific features of Alsatian culture, or to visit Alsace again after having been attracted by its culture and traditions in the first place.

From a qualitative point of view, the behaviour of national and international tourist markets has become increasingly characterised by cultural motivation for travel, with a growing tendency on the part of tourists to move from a contemplative to an active mode of discovery. In parallel to this motivational evolution, we have seen a move towards vacational fragmentation into several short-stay holiday breaks for active cultural leisure as opposed to few and longer stays for passive rest.

The indications are that tourism behaviour is becoming increasingly unpredictable and impulsive, which will make it necessary to take a more flexible approach to product development, promotion and marketing tools. On the assumption that this trend is here to stay for a long time, a likely consequence is that air transport will have to be further deregulated to provide easier movement across regional boundaries and more convenient access to the cultural heritage of this continent.

Within such a context, it is to be expected that competition will be fierce. This is likely to apply less between countries than between regions with a strong cultural identity, as it is the heritage assets underlying this identity that will be used for brand development and image building. In Alsace, we intend to take full advantage of what we have to provide a robust tourism infrastructure for the future.

As for future predictions, the most recent forecasts by the World Tourism Organisation indicate an increase of 50% in tourist flows visiting Europe over the next 10 years. Based on the actual state of the tourist capacity in Alsace, there is a real prospect of the region being able to attract a volume of 18 million tourist nights by the year 2007. This estimate excludes any hypothesis for a new and international scale tourist project in Alsace, such as for instance a very high capacity scientific and cultural leisure theme park.

Out of this volume, at least 50% would be represented by active and demanding visitors, wanting to discover and understand the region's cultural and historical heritage, deciding about their precise place of stay at the last moment, and being ready to abandon Alsace for another destination if any one of their requirements could not be fully satisfied.

In light of this market evolution and mutations in the behaviour of visitors before and during their stay, it will be necessary for the cultural tourism products offered by Alsace to be re-conceived, re-branded and re-targeted accordingly. The basic ingredients for such a 'revolutionary strategy' do exist, however abundant and sporadic they may appear to the visitor today. If anything, the Wine Route has shown in a rather spontaneous manner without much planned development, the value of providing the backbone of a system for contemplative tourist discovery. It has demonstrated it role as a vital plank in the strategic infrastructure of Alsace, and the challenge for the future is to ensure its complementarity with other tourism products and themes offered by the region.

Indeed, as stated in the introductory paragraphs, the cultural heritage of Alsace owes its density and character to the historical fact that it was and still is part of the 'civilising corridor' of the Rhine Valley. This is reinforced by the fact that the corridor overlaps the fracture line between the Latin and Germanic cultures, a real 'cultural tectonic faultline'.

In other words, it is ideally located in space for interpretation of several European regions. Alsace is where their cultures meet, and the challenge for us is to develop a tourism strategy to harness this cultural dynamism. The two basic features of duality and dynamism of cultural life are what makes the region so attractive to tourists. This combined with the proximity of markets put us in a strong position.

ROUTES TO ALSATIAN HERITAGE

The presence of the Wine Route has demonstrated its ability to attract and to absorb a major share of tourist flows visiting the region along a corridor marking the boundary of Alsace's three geographical and cultural entities: the Vosges mountain massif, the vineyards and the Rhine valley. This has resulted in a strong concentration within the corridor of high quality accommodation, as well as a high degree of tourism animation during the peak season, over the period of when the Wine Route is 'open' from mid-April to the end of October.

The only strategic tourism product we offer in this well endowed region to channel tourist flows along a continuous itinerary of discovery is the Wine Route, with 119 wine growing villages over 170 km of waymarked route. However, it is not yet able of fulfil its expressed objectives: firstly, to improve the quality of visitor appreciation across the range of the area's cultural and historical heritage, secondly, to improve awareness of and increase visitation at other centres of tourist interest in the region. For these reasons, since 1991, Alsace Regional Council has developed an integrated strategy of developing on-site thematic tourist signage in order to improve awareness and 'readability' of certain heritage assets and tourism products on offer: cultural landscapes, historical monuments and cultural attractions, religious shrines and the arts, and river based activities. Steps are also being taken to develop a network of supports for the management and distribution of tourists within the region.

Moreover, the strategy has made provision for action to identify places for thematic initiatives to harness synergies between regional and local tourism operators, the basic aim being to encourage and support the production and marketing of new and more comprehensive tourism products. The first step in this direction was to plan the 'Romanesque Route of Alsace', a cultural discovery trail running from north to south and identifying some twenty major heritage sites, most of them churches. This was don within an integrated process, starting with an inventory audit, evaluation of the visitor potentialities, and a costed programme of implementation.

The form of the on-site signage for this cultural route is a post, presenting on one side, the site in question. On the other side is a mapped invitation to discover selected cultural and historical sites in the surrounding area. The written communication is trilingual, and the same design concept is developed in a brochure presenting the whole of the Romanesque Route. The scheme of signage has been implemented and actions are underway for the creation of a network of thematic information and exhibition centres located at some of the twenty heritage sites. Following the launch in 1994, there has been a yearly festival of medieval vocal music called *Voices on the Romanesque Route*, and the project is now concentrating on developing tourism products focusing on a dominant cultural theme related to the Romanesque heritage.

The same concept was applied to the Wine Route in 1994, when seeking to lift its profile in connection with celebrations of the 50th birthday of this route. It consisted of creating a logo to give the route a clear identity, and this is used on posts at the entrance of vineyard villages and on road signage. We also designed and erected a dozen on-site tourist information posts, placed at the heart of the vineyard country, and indicating rest areas, panoramic views and picnic sites along the route. Present on one side in three languages is the historical, cultural and wine growing heritage of the locality. On the other side is shown the different cultural and historical sites to be discovered off the Wine Route.

The third application of the same concept has been done for signage of the river tourism network, the physical aspect of the supports having been treated in a contemporary design style. This signage informs tourists using river boats about the different cultural, historical and natural heritage landmarks situated in an area 10 km wide on either side of the canal. It also provides information about tourist and other services available in the harbours and other stopping places along the river tourism network. An essential part is illustrated information about the technical and engineering heritage of the waterways bridges, tunnels and gates. This project went through pilot application stage on a section of the Marne to Rhine canal, including a survey of tourists which allowed us to ascertain their judgement of the quality and the adequacy of the new signage system.

The purpose of this 'three pronged' strategic initiative, initiated by Alsace Regional Council in 1991, was to provide good quality and up to date information on the historical and cultural heritage of interest to the travellers of today and tomorrow. The philosophy was that this would help them acquire knowledge of the region's past and cultural identity, and thereby encourage them to go for more in-depth discovery of specific sites. Another objective was to achieve a more balanced distribution of tourist flows throughout the regional territory.

TOWARDS 'TERROIR' IN TOURISM

The wine-growing area of Alsace has special potential for an interesting concept in tourism promotion, thanks to its *terroir* dimension. This notion of *terroir* offers the basis for development of a unique type of tourism products, enabling a more active dialogue of positive conviviality between the visitor and the host. The word *terroir* is that untranslatable French term for the unique combination of site, soil and climate which defines each vineyard and is an article of faith for every French *vigneron*. As expressed forcefully by one of the best known Alsatian wine growers:

> Our wines do not only express our terroirs but also our identity. My wish is that clients, once back home, when they opens a bottle of my wine, they can see me and can feel able to tell the story of that wine. It is in this cultural and convivial exchange that we have to place our future and not in the supermarkets. Until now, we have trained our men, improved our vineyards and transformed our enterprises. It is time now to learn how to transmit what we are and what we have been doing. This is indeed the magical ability of wine to express place and time.

The general tourist image of Alsace is of an opulent region with a colourful countryside comprised of neat and well gardened villages, where food and wine are plentiful and living is easy. This, combined with the next door presence of affluent visitors from Baden Wurtenberg, Switzerland, has led to an apparently stable economic situation of the tourism sector. Therefore, no special efforts have been necessary to run the tourism industry of the region.

Indeed, Alsace can justifiably be considered as one of Europe's prime tourist destinations, in which the relative abundance and variety of heritage resources have kept attracting contemplative and now ageing market segments. This continuous flow of daily visitors has fed the operation of catering and leisure facilities without showing apparent need for improvement of tourist accommodation, some of which now faces serious structural problems in terms of modernisation, absence of leisure and sports facilities, adequate customer care and facility management.

Prevailing supply constraints and the new trends in international markets, as briefly outlined above, mean that there is now an urgent need for regional tourist operators to respond flexibly to new and constantly changing requirements. It call for 'instant product tailoring' within a strategy of supported initiative for creating and marketing 'active' tourism products.

It is proposed that a possible approach is to apply the concept of *Tourist Terroir*; in the sense that *terroir* is defined as a unique combination of a given soil, a given climate, a given vine variety and traditional local know-how, as well as the ceremony and festivity associated with harvesting and production. Such a definition could be applied to the conception of tourist products.

The author suggests that such an approach could help rejuvenate the image of Alsace, and enable it to enhance its position in key market segments. We are all having to face up to the new notion of geography where physical distances no longer exist. Air travel time and accessibility will increasingly be the criteria to govern future travel patterns. Industrialised farming will progressively replace traditional methods, and only where these are rendered viable through a tourist interest will economic viability continue. The *terroir* approach could allow the 'vineyard' resource to develop all of its facets, transcending beyond the stage of wine tasting and buying.

A strategy of access through itineraries, combined with *terroir*, could allow visitors to reach the heart of the 'vineyard' heritage, provided the required synergy is developed among the different operators still functioning separately in their respective fields.

It is expected that trails bringing tourists into the vineyards of Alsace will deepen and branch off into more secluded parts sought by travellers eager to learn and understand. They will find out about wine growing and tasting, but they are also likely to be drawn to other and lesser known features of the region. This may include the giant and mysterious 'pagan wall' found in and around the pilgrimage site of the Sainte-Odile Mountain, the unexplained Telluric forces of the Vosges forests, and, why not, the witches of Scharrachbergheim, and many other villages where wine, history and culture have met and melted together for many long years.

This paper has sought to identify some of the major issues facing Alsace, as well as other tourist destinations in Europe, and the author has attempted to explain some of the strategic initiatives implemented. We all need to brace ourselves for dealing with major changes both in supply and demand. Some of these are likely to remodel parts of the tourism industry as we know it today. For example, new communication technology has not only added virtual reality, but it may also paradoxically help to stimulate the interest of tourists in 'the real and authentic', the *terroir* of future tourism. To make progress, it will become increasingly important to for us to maintain an international dialogue for exchanging knowledge and experience.

The Author

Dragon Crnjanski is Director of Tourism for the Alsace region, where he has pioneered several inter-agency initiatives. He has been engaged on many international assignments and is participating in the inter-regional collaboration project 'Destination Christmas: Peace on Earth' in partnership with Bethlehem, Lapland, Turku, St Petersburg and Naples. At the time of publication, he was on secondment in Yalta under the TACIS Programme of the European Union to advise on future tourism development in Crimea.

References

Banquis-Gasser, I., *L'Art et la Vigne: Route des Vins d'Alsace*, Le Verger, 1994
Tourisme Alsace, *The Alsace Wine Route*, Comite Régional du Tourisme d'Alsace, undated leaflet
Tourisme Alsace, *Route Romane d'Alsace: A Heritage to be Discovered*, Comite Régional du Tourisme d'Alsace, undated leaflet

30

HISTORIC NORWAY
Identity and Issues in Heritage Policy

Hild Sørby

As far as I know, research into who actually visits ancient monuments has not been undertaken in Norway, but those of us working in the heritage business know from experience that they were until recently the same kind of people who go to classical concerts, and to galleries and museums. Traditionally, people from a working class background visited neither medieval churches nor manor houses. Such places did not belong to their world. They were strange places without interest, or perhaps even intimidating, and therefore places never contemplated as a day out. Perhaps they found the entry price too expensive, perhaps they did not feel themselves having the necessary cultural competence to gain something from the music heard or the sights seen. To sit quietly for hours listening to Mozart, or to pay a large amount of money to look around an old building was felt to be rather meaningless. There was a clear division in society between those who preferred so called 'high culture', and the others who preferred a more easily accessible and more entertaining culture, or so called 'mass culture.'

This division is to some extent still in existence, as confirmed in research done by the French sociologist Pierre Bourdieu. His contention is that cultural participation is dictated by the existing system of class diversity. In his opinion, economic capital has a corresponding symbolic capital and value. The groups which own cultural capital, correspond to those which possess or have command over economic capital. He argues that this economic and cultural capital is passed from one generation to the next. However, it can be seen that the situation is not quite stable. During recent decades, new participation groups have been moving across into the traditional arena of high culture. Indeed, these groups have displayed a strong interest in our indigenous cultural heritage. This may be due to the fact that indigenous culture is regarded as least alien, and is therefore more accessible for those without further education.

A large number of people have achieved a higher standard of education in recent years and now enjoy a better quality of living than before. Although education in itself does not necessarily provide a sufficient basis for individuals to appreciate Kandinsky, and even less chance to enjoy contemporary composers such as Stockhausen and Boulez, it can stimulate an interest in the history of our culture. The contemporary arts, whether it be music, art, literature or theatre, require a different type and degree of cultural proficiency which makes it difficult for the ordinary public to gain a rewarding experience from participation.

CULTURE AND IDENTITY

With indigenous culture it is different. Here education, historical knowledge and cultural consciousness come together to form a springboard. As part of higher education, comes the need to learn to know one's own history, to find one's own identity in society, and to understand oneself. My impression is that many people visiting historic sites, such as ancient rock carvings, stave churches, and old buildings and monuments, represent the first generation to have received higher education. They are also often the ones to fight for the preservation of an old school building and who work eagerly to convert the local textile mill into a museum. Many come from a background in agriculture or other rural industries, and it is as important for them to learn about their own working class heritage as it is to learn about bourgeois culture.

A change in priorities took place in the 1970s when 'cultural democracy' became the slogan of the time. The heritage of no single social group or class should be considered more important and meaningful than any other. Factories and the workplace should be taken care of alongside manor houses and castles. This broader view of heritage helped individuals to define their own place and position in society. Most people are interested in where they come from, to be able to see what kind of house their grandparents lived in and what kind of factory they worked in. I think this change in attitude has been a factor in making the past more relevant than ever. Cultural heritage is of increasing significance as a creator of identity for a steadily growing number of people. Through education and increased awareness, they experience how important it is for understanding their own culture and identity.

406

Heritage in this sense also functions as an entry to the wider arena of high culture. You do not need as much specialist cultural knowledge to enjoy old houses and buildings, boats, quays and bridges, as you need for full appreciation of the finer points of high culture. Just the opposite. Recognition is perhaps the most fundamental aspect of appreciation. The simplicity or pomposity of a dwelling is compared to your own home, the old church is compared to the one where you yourself were baptised, the workplace of the old factory is compared to your own place of work today etc. All the time, you compare your own situation and culture to that which is portrayed from the past. Recognition and self reflection are central to this process.

It can therefore be seen that the modern culture seekers are a very complex mixture of people. In Norway, they are mainly comprised of an urban elite with long cultural traditions. But there is now a steadily expanding group of first generation culture seekers, people with agricultural and working class origins. In addition, there are also many older people with no further education who only go to places which are of special interest to them. For example, they go to a sardine canning museum, but would be unlikely to go to an art museum. We also know from a recently published study (1993) that most of the overseas tourists visiting Norway are well educated.

The interest in cultural heritage in modern times came with the national romantic revival and establishment of the bourgeoisie in the 19th century. For a long time, culture was something that only interested experts and an educated bourgeoisie elite. Although there was no government sanctioned heritage protection until 1912, already in the 1840s the landscape painter I C Dahl took the initiative to establish a society whose aim was to take care of stave churches and other monuments from the Middle Ages. He lived in Germany, as it was impossible to make a living from painting in Norway at that time. He was a member of the well established 'Altertums-verein' conservation society in Dresden, and on visits to his native country he noticed with concern that many of the beautiful old stave churches were being destroyed. Among his teachers was the German Romantic painter Caspar David Friedrich, and he thus became influenced by the aesthetic philosophy of the Romantics which was concerned with the history, the religion, the mystique and atmosphere of the Middle Ages. Dahl therefore understood the importance and need to take care of the heritage from this vital period of Norwegian history before it was too late.

PROTECTION FROM 1844 ONWARDS

As one of the first non-governmental heritage organisations in Europe, The Society for the Preservation of Norwegian Ancient Monuments (Foreningen til norske Fortidsminnesmerkers Bevaring, or 'Fortisminne-foreningen' for short) was established 1844. On its first board was a historian, an architect, two painters, a musician and a member of the royal household. Until 1912, when the Directorate of Cultural Heritage (*Riksantikvaren*) was established in response to its lobbying, this voluntary body was the premier heritage institution in Norway, similar in purpose and significance to the National Trusts in Britain. It did an invaluable job at drawing attention to buildings of historical and architectural importance and worthy of preservation. Many medieval buildings were drawn and measured, and others were bought by the Society if they could not be protected in any other way. Today, it is still as active as ever, and is the owner and keeper of 42 properties, eight of which are stave churches.

After World War II, government departments became increasingly engaged with questions concerning heritage conservation. In 1973, responsibility for heritage was moved from the Department of Education to the Department of the Environment. This transfer underlined that heritage was part of our common cultural environment and was to be treated as a part of our physical planning system. Another milestone was the European Year of Architecture in 1975. From then on, it was not only single buildings of important historical or aesthetic interest that were to be protected. Henceforth, it was not only the main building on the farm which was to be protected, but also the cow sheds, the barns and other utilitarian buildings. It was no longer a matter of merely the manor house, but also the workers cottages and industrial buildings. Whole streets of vernacular architecture can now be listed. In other words, heritage assets were to be judged on a new social and cultural conception. It was no longer only the magnificent and impressive culture of the upper class that was regarded as heritage, it would henceforth also embrace the familiar and most common.

Cultural democracy achieved its breakthrough in Norway during the 1970s. As a consequence of this new ideology, responsibility for heritage conservation was in 1990 devolved to the 20 county councils which are in effect democratically elected regional authorities. The only exceptions are medieval heritage and churches more than 90 years old, which come under the jurisdiction of the Directorate of Cultural Heritage. Each county has two or three experts to give technical advice, but it is the local politicians who have the decision making authority. This is how heritage conservation in Norway has become decentralised and politicised.

Although this working arrangement has advantages, it has some weaknesses. Local county politicians very often have little sympathy for and a low competence in heritage conservation. Heritage issues are usually given a low priority compared to other concerns in society. Not least, can this be seen in cases of urban development. If the county politicians wish to make the local hospital bigger, it matters little if the heritage experts say that the small villas in the area around the hospital should be preserved. The villas, built in the period 1915–40, are perhaps the only ones remaining in place from this period. Therefore, the experts consider it important that they are protected as important heritage assets. If not, there will be no local examples left of architectural styles in art nouveau, national romantic, classicism or functionalism. Normally, politicians believe hospital buildings to be more important than anything else. A well equipped health service is a high priority for the public, and to have a high profile in health politics gives the politicians prestige, popularity and, quite obviously votes.

Our heritage assets therefore have few friends. Indeed, there is no a higher authority to get help from, as the politicians themselves are the county's supreme heritage authority. As stated above, the Directorate of Cultural Heritage has authority only over medieval monuments; churches over 90 years old and heritage of national importance. Nobody is able to argue that an area of 20–30 small wooden villas from the period between the wars has national interest. Accordingly, there is no doubt that many communities will loose an important part of their architectural and cultural history.

SOME ISSUES

For me policy makers are not only members of Parliament and those working in the Ministry. The problems are perhaps greatest for those working in the decentralised heritage offices of the counties, and for those who manage and administer local heritage. The heritage legislation states that anything older than 1537, when the Reformation took place Norway, is automatically listed for protection. It also holds that heritage assets and the cultural environment should be taken care of as part of the nation's common inheritance and identity, and they should be regarded as being part of a complete environmental and resource management system. The law states that it is a national responsibility to look after these assets as the source material forming the foundations for the experience, self understanding and activities of present and future generations.

The legislation also states that heritage shall be an integral part of the collective system of environmental protection. Just as the Norwegian people has the right to a well developed health care system which takes care of you when you are ill, they also have the right to be surrounded by meaningful heritage. As a source of knowledge about the past, heritage awareness leads to the creation of a feeling of identity and provides cultural roots in an otherwise quickly changing world. In other words, heritage has a clear and useful value. The functions of protection and restoration are regarded as a public enterprise because heritage is seen as a common good for society. It is a human right that everybody shall have the opportunity to share in the nation's heritage.

All this sounds fine, but it can sometimes be a little problematic. What do we mean by heritage and the cultural environment? In fact, what is our heritage? Can heritage be a universal or unifying concept which all Norwegians may share whether they live in Oslo's West End or in a fishing village in the Lofoten islands, in the far North? And what about immigrants, who come from foreign cultures, can they turn into Norwegian citizens who will identify with our national heritage? Indeed, is there a common heritage which represents our collective identity to provide the foundations for the experience, self understanding, and activities of present and future generations?

Current heritage legislation now defines heritage as 'all traces of human activity in our physical environment'. The cultural environment is defined as 'those areas where heritage is a part of a larger totality or association'. The definition is open and relative. Everything surrounding us that can be preserved is in fact heritage. But clearly we cannot preserve every trace of human activity. There would be no space for new buildings, and it would be too expensive. But most importantly, it would be completely absurd as we would turn the whole the country into a museum.

The German writer Hans Magnus Enzensberger has already said that Norway today is the greatest folk museum in Europe. Perhaps we should take him at his word and remain a folk museum. Economically, it might perhaps be a good thing. It is often said that the country is going to survive on tourism anyway, but we cannot preserve every house, every bridge and every boat in the country. The legislation also specifies that it is structures of cultural and architectural value which represent special importance that are to be preserved. But this qualification does not help very much, as different people will assign special importance to different things.

It was much easier with the previous heritage legislation which said that it was objects of antique importance that should be preserved. And what were these? These were monuments that the professional experts on antiquity said were important. Today, these experts do not have the decision-making power any longer. They now recommend which monuments should be preserved, and it is the democratically elected politicians who finally decide. They are a diverse group of individuals belonging to various social groups and different political parties. Their opinions about what is important can be correspondingly different. For some, the first immigrant shop in Oslo's East End will have a higher heritage interest than a jewellery shop with an authentic art deco interior in the city centre. If they have to prioritise preserving one, it is an open question which might be chosen.

It is also the case that the heritage experts are not always in agreement about what should be preserved. Indeed, they are not as unified a profession as they once were, simply because they also have different social and professional backgrounds, and many now answer to politician masters. An art historian will often prioritise differently from an ethnologist or an architect. However, when experts do prioritise, we do normally get well formulated arguments for their decisions. That is not always the case when the politicians decide. Then a great variation in motives can lead to unpredictable and diverse decisions.

What is of great importance for the politicians today, is the role of heritage in tourism. Apart from the pilgrims to Nidaros in the Middle Ages, the first tourists to visit Norway came mainly from Britain in the 19th century to fish for salmon. Later, they also came for other reasons, such as to walk in the mountains or go by cruise ship on the fjords. What both domestic and overseas tourists had in common, was that they were travelling to experience the natural environment. It was mainly the fjords of the west coast, with the salmon rivers and the glaciers that were attractive, not so much old farm houses and churches. Edvard Munch and Gustav Vigeland have always had some admirers, so have the Folk Museums at Bygdøy and at Maihaugen in Lillehammer. But natural scenery has to this day always been the most important tourist attraction in Norway, confirmed by the 1993 *Tourist Report*.

THE NEW VIKING CENTRES

Today we realise that being able to experience the natural environment alone is no longer enough. People want something more, and heritage has a strong appeal to many. The tourist industry is especially eager to market Norway as the homeland of the Vikings. Accordingly, all tourist areas have in recent years searched for traces of the Vikings and started constructing Viking centres. A place did not need many traces before it was enough to construct a 'Viking Land'. At one time we were planning about 30 Viking centres throughout the country. Some of these are now completed, others are held on ice, some went bankrupt before they were completed. Some were built in collaboration with archaeological museums.

I must say that I find it difficult to understand how it is possible from traces of post holes in the earth to reconstruct the walls and ceilings of a complete house, although I must defer to the expertise of the archaeologists. But it is not merely that the factual foundations for the reconstructions are sometimes fairly flimsy. My fear is that, the eager wish to satisfy the entertainment needs of the modern culture seekers, can skew the historical authenticity of heritage sites. For the politicians, the important thing is that the Viking town gives people an experience, that the children can play Vikings and have fun, and that the tourist has seen something tangible.

To the politicians, as Arne Lie Christensen has indicated, heritage is not a goal in itself, but a means. It is a means to attract tourists to the place, and to create jobs and incomes. Therefore, qualities such as the authenticity and the historic value of the heritage in question, are of less consequence. What is meaningful is that the community has a heritage site where something happens and which will attract people. As pointed out above, legislation tells us that heritage should not only give people identity and roots, but it should also give them an experience. Today, an experience is seldom connected with reflection and contemplation; an experience is regarded as being associated with entertainment. Indeed, the art of entertainment is something the custodians of heritage sites and museum workers have had to teach themselves in the fight for customers.

The politicians give financial support to an initiative according to the number of visitors it is likely to attract. People go to places where something happens, where they can buy nice souvenirs, and where they can taste good coffee and waffles. Old houses, churches and cloisters are no longer enough in themselves; something must happen there. The outcome is that we now find all sorts of theatrical performances amongst the ruins during the summer season. A buzz of activity can be heard in all old houses to the sound of crackling fires, the clanking of tools used by craftsmen, and guides walking around in medieval costume. All these things are done so that the visitors can gain an impression of how people lived in the past.

Museums were until recently known as places where one could gain knowledge of historical authenticity. The museum exhibitions were based on research and historical knowledge, and interpretation was made by people with appropriate qualifications. But their product or the picture of reality they presented was not always fun. The tourists seek an experience, they are attracted by the great, the beautiful and the dramatic: things that give them entertainment. The constant pressure to attract new visitors makes heritage institutions feel obliged to present something which will give the visitors such entertainment. Instead of a guide telling a factual story, we now have small plays performed at the site.

When historical material is to be dramatised, it is necessary to concentrate on those parts of history which will have the greatest appeal to the public. Thus, knowledge is gradually skewed towards what people find entertaining. In this way truth and authenticity shrink, and the difference between traditional museum presentations and the new heritage industry is no longer so great. Some will be of the opinion that this is not a matter for concern. What is being presented can easily be changed, and next time it can be told in another way. However, a serious issue arises when money is only given by political direction to sites which attract the most people, and other sites are neglected in spite of having a greater historical value. I would argue that we have gone to far when politicians allocate generous funds to build a Viking centre which is pure fake, but do not grant the necessary money for the proper upkeep and promotion of historic buildings and monuments.

HAMAR

What has happened at Hamar, is a good example of an issue which has been much debated. In the Middle Ages, this small town north of Oslo, had one of the country's five cathedrals. After the Reformation, the cathedral was destroyed, and it has since lain in ruins. The remains of the Romanesque arches, set among the trees on the shores of Lake Mjøsen, were a popular scene for the 19th century painters of the National Romantic School. The ruins became the most important historic monument in Hamar and served to give the towns and its inhabitants identity.

Over the years the ruins have steadily deteriorated. Most of the experts were of the opinion that the only way to preserve the remains of the shattered ruins, was to build a protective structure over them. An architectural design competition among architects was held, which was won by the well known firm of Lund and Slaatto. Their idea was simply to place a glass cover over the remaining structure in the form of a large edifice roughly the size of the original cathedral. The cost was estimated 50 million Norwegian Kroner, about £5 million. This was more money than could be found at the time, and the years passed without the project being implemented. Indeed, many of us were happy about this, as we believed it would be madness to use that amount of money on a single ruin, while other heritage sites were being neglected due to lack of finance.

However, the project was given a new life in 1995 when an old American lady bequeathed 10 million Kroner, about £1 million, towards the cost of the protective structure. Both experts and local politicians have been lobbying for the state to make up the difference, and last year the money was delivered. The archaeologists will get an interesting workplace protected from the weather, and the politicians will get a heritage attraction which will draw people from all over the world. Many countries have discussed placing glass covers over their most valuable heritage objects, but as far as I know it has not yet been done in Europe. The project will thus be a European pioneering project, and people will come to Hamar, not so much to look at the old ruins, but to gawk at the new building.

Personally I feel that to use public funds in this way places the bond between knowledge and the heritage institutions in an absurd light. We have a fairly free attitude to authenticity and facts, by building copies and tolerating fake solutions at many heritage sites. But at Hamar we propose to spend 50 million Kroner to preserve ruins which are in no way unique. I do not believe it is informed decision making in relation to heritage conservation which is at stake here. The case argued by the specialists is only hiding the real motive: to get the eyes of the world on Hamar. Sometimes we must accept that ruins go back to earth, and let us use our money more sensibly.

BORGUND STAVE CHURCH

A problem in the field of cultural tourism is that some of the most popular heritage sites are overrun by tourists. This is the case at Borgund stave church, one of our most beautiful and best preserved stave churches. Every year 60 000 people visit this tiny wooden church, and most of them come during the summer season from June to August. The result of this is enormous wear and tear, not only on the church itself, but also on the surrounding cultural landscape. Another consequence is that so many people in the small church makes it impossible to have a true and spiritual experience when inside this medieval shrine. The outside view of the church itself is often obscured by the many tourist busses parked against the graveyard walls.

The Borgund Church is owned and managed by the Society for the Preservation of Norwegian Ancient Monuments, and to take care of it in the best possible way is their primary concern. It does not seem right to raise the price of entry in order to reduce the number of visitors. A few years ago we held an architectural design competition for a service building. This will include a café, toilets, shop, museum and an exhibition area. The idea is that this building, to be placed 400 meters from the church, will have a medieval exhibition to show aspects of life in the

Middle Ages and how a stave church was built etc. Visitors will receive information and acquire knowledge that will hopefully enhance their experience of the church itself. It is also hoped that the interpretive presentation in the new building will be so comprehensive that many tourists will feel that it is enough to visit the centre and view the church from the outside. Our concept is that perhaps only those who are especially interested will venture in, whilst the rest will sit in the café or see the video. In this way, the Society intends to give the visitor a better deal, and ensure that the church is subject to less wear and tear.

In this paper, I have touched upon diverse issues that are presently under discussion in Norwegian heritage politics. I imagine that many of the problems mentioned are similar to those in other countries. The modern culture seekers (culturists) provide the opportunity to protect and positively manage more heritage sites than previously. But this also leads to the pressing question of which sites and objects to save. I am therefore concerned, and must conclude with the question: do eager heritage managers falsify history on the altar of tourism? This is a difficult issue, and I personally believe that authentic heritage should take precedent over manufactured heritage. In authenticity lies, not just historic source material, but also aesthetic values and a peculiar aura that only an old, used and worn cultural relic can have. A heritage site without authenticity has lost both its meaning and its magic.

The Author

Hild Sørby is Associate Professor of art history at the Stavanger College. Her speciality is 20th century Norwegian architecture. She has written books on Norwegian painters of the 19th and 20th century and on the history of Norwegian prefabricated houses. She has been Chairman of the Society for the Preservation of Norwegian Ancient Monuments, an organisation which owns 42 old buildings, including eight stave churches. She is curently Vice Chairman of the National Council for Cultural Heritage and a board member at the National Gallery.

References

Christensen, A.L., *Kulturminnevern i klemme*, in *Fortidsvern 2*, 1995
Christensen, A.L., *Vernebygger – økonomisk ruin*, in *Fortidsvern 4*, 1995
Lidén, H.E., *Om sogespel og kulturminner*, in *Fortdidsvern 2*, 1994

Linén, H.E., *Fra antikvitet til kulturminne*, Universitetsforlaget, 1991

Lyngnes, S., *Kulturminner på billigsalg?*, in *Fortdisvern 2*, 1994

Myklebust, D., *Monuments & Sites*, Universitetsforlaget, 1988

Sørby, H., *Klar Ferdig Hus: Norske perdighus giennom tidene*, Gyldendal, 1992

Sørby, H., *Velkommen til Museum Norge*, in *Fortidsvern 2*, 1995

The stave church at Borgund as pictured by British pilgrims in an engraving
published in 1985

31

POLAND IN TRANSITION
The Spirit and Identity of Cracow

Jacek Purchla

Cracow lies at the very centre of Europe, being situated three to four hundred kilometres from Prague, Vienna, Bratislava, Budapest and Warsaw. Its location as the former capital of Poland, between Scandinavia, the Adriatic, and the Baltic, and between Western and Eastern Europe, has insured its pivotal role in the affairs of the nation since early times.

In the history of Cracow, known as the 'heart of Poland', there are at least three major epochs of close connections with Europe: the medieval, when the Hanseatic city on the Vistula was part of the network of great European commercial emporia; the Jagiellonian, when the flourishing royal metropolis influenced the extensive territories of the multinational state; and the nineteenth century, when modern Cracow flourished in the favourable atmosphere of liberalism, a high level of civilisation, and the creative decadence of the great Hapsburg monarchy in its last days. During these periods, Cracow combined the role of the principal city of Polish politics with that of an important element in the multinational network of Central European cities. Throughout this time, external factors and its role as a bridge between the different parts of central Europe determined the course of Cracow's development.

The unique position of cultural heritage had become a problem peculiar to the development of Cracow by the first half of the 19th century. In the period of the so-called first Austrian occupation from 1795–1809, Cracow's gradual decline and provincialisation reached its nadir. Formerly, Cracow was retained as the capital of the Polish State until the end of the eighteenth century, but the main royal residence and the seat of parliament had already moved to Warsaw in the first half of the 17th

417

century. This fact, paradoxically, helped to preserve intact the historical fabric of Cracow from its heyday: from the times of the late Middle Ages and the epoch of the Renaissance.

During the era of Romanticism, it was possible to revive the myth of Cracow, the old capital of Poland, as a symbol of the magnificent historic past of a nation deprived of independence, a sacred place for Poles. The solemn funerals of the heroes of Napoleonic times, Count Josef Poniatowski and Tadeuss Kosciussko, in 1817 and 1818, confirmed the function of Wawel as the national Pantheon. Cracow was perceived not only as a history book but also as a protoplast city, 'The Polish Rome', and at times 'The Polish Troy'.

In the latter half of the nineteenth century, Cracow quickly recognised the uniqueness of its situation in comparison with the Russian-occupied sector of Poland. It was gripped by repression and grief after an uprising, and undergoing progressive Germanisation. The city quickly took on the role of the nation's spiritual capital, a place integrating all Poles. This was possible due to the autonomy that Galicia, the Austrian part of the Polish lands, enjoyed from the 1860s. Wawel Cathedral became the venue for symbolic royal funerals. The municipal district, supported by private investors from all over Poland, took on the role of surrogate for a non-existent state. In this situation, beset by many contradictions, Cracow also became the major centre of Polish thinking about the past and its heritage.

It was towards the end of the 19th century that Cracow actually began the attempt of taking advantage of its past heritage to revive the city gradually from its decline. On the threshold of autonomy, Cracow reviewed the whole of its past, reinterpreted it and consciously adopted it for its contemporary and future existence. There was no such second city in the whole of Central Europe which would comprehend its past so deeply and concentrate on it so strongly. The creation in Cracow of a peculiarly historic industry concurred with the initiation by Jan Matejko, the greatest Polish historical painter and a Cracovian, of the mature phase of his work in the mid-1860s. It went to the heart of this new stage in Cracow's development during the era of the first presidents of Cracow, Josef Dietl and Mikoaj Syblikiewics. This is one of the reasons why the phenomenon of Matejko combined so organically with the phenomenon of Cracow in the 1870s and 1880s.

Reaching towards national tradition in its broadest sense, which was most fully and deeply symbolised by Cracow, became for the 'Sta csyks' (Cracow conservatives of vital political importance in Galicia) a tool for validating the existing *status quo* and for the defence of old values. Their natural inclination towards the past, as a *sine qua non* condition of conservatism, lent itself to the Cracovian cult of historical heritage, and provoked a search for new symbolic meanings. On this basis, the peculiar process of national conservation focusing on Cracow, consciously implemented by the Polish gentry, took place in the latter half of the nineteenth century. At that time the city also became a place of pilgrimage. Masses of Poles journeyed to the 'heart of Poland' from all partitioned areas of the country and from émigré countries.

A gradual decline of the phase of 'Small Cracow', the Sarmatian 'Reserve of Polishness', occurred in the early 1880s. This 'Reserve of Polishness', which so shocked, for example, guests from Warsaw, slowly thawed. The prosperous economic situation in the 1880s, resulted in the rapid development and modernisation of the city, which continued into the next decade. By 1900, Cracow had 10,000 inhabitants, and 150,000 with neighbouring suburban boroughs. The city's social structure underwent transformation. The rapid population growth led to a continual strengthening of the liberal middle class. The model of Cracow as a closed enclave engaged in reinterpreting the past, created by the 'Sta csyks' on the threshold of the autonomy, was on the way out.

The death of Matejko, in the autumn of 1893, almost coincided with the opening of the monumental Municipal Theatre in Cracow. This fact has a symbolic dimension, and the year 1893 can be seen as a clear turning point in the history of the city. The new theatre foreshadowed a new era of capitalist modernity and spirit which was knocking at the door of the city. This was reflected, amongst other things, by the installation of electricity in the theatre. It predated the construction of a municipal power plant in Cracow by a decade or so. The conflict between Matejko and Cracow's City Council over the location of the theatre, which occurred towards the end of the artist's life, had a wider context. The Council's decision broke the past convention of almost unlimited reverence for the past. It was conscious interference in the medieval structure, which was easier to preserve on Matejko's canvas than in reality.

This conflict also symbolises today's dilemma Cracow 'heritage or development'. However, let us say at the outset that in the present situation this is only an illusory dilemma, as the cultural heritage accumulated at the foot of Wawel is one of the principal determinants of Cracow's position on the map of Europe and of its identity. This is why the argument currently going on in Cracow, between the 'destroyers' and the 'defenders of the past' should lead us to seek an intelligent compromise which will effectively protect the cultural heritage of Cracow during a period of rapid and unavoidable change. This requires a new, active philosophy of preservation, which should become an integral part of Cracow's new development strategy.

The shape of Cracow's town centre and its historic complexes today was formed in the nineteenth century by a dedication to urban design and the conservation of monuments. Protection of the nineteenth century heritage is thus a protection of the historic value of Cracow as a whole. This characteristic 'merger' took place not only at the aesthetic, ideological and material levels, but also at the functional level. In the nineteenth century, many of the existing historical buildings were adapted to new functions. A symbolic example of such reinterpretation of existing monuments is the restoration of the Cloth Hall by Tomass Prylinsviski in the years 1874–1879. This Gothic-Renaissance building, which over and above being the 'Palais du Commerce', constitutes the heart of the city, became a 'Temple of Art' that housed the collection of the first, newly founded, Polish National Museum. Restoration of the Cloth Hall went hand in hand with its reorientation as urban design and a change in the function of the Market Square.

The functional metamorphosis of the historic centre of Cracow that took place at the turn of the century made it possible for the core of the city, shaped before 1914 within the inner ring-road, to serve successfully today as the service centre for the city. Protection of nineteenth century Cracow is in effect the preservation of many urban service functions created at that time in the central area.

The organic penetration of nineteenth century architecture into the medieval city centre was enhanced by the overwhelming and enduring dominance of historicism in Cracow. Large-scale restoration work also played an important role in the integration of Cracow's historicism with the existing urban substance. For a long time, the whole architectural complex of Cracow's city centre has been subject by law to conservation protection. So there is certainly no longer a threat from the 'destroyers', in terms of ideology and modern conservation doctrine. However, this is not necessarily sufficient as an effective system of protection for the whole urban fabric and individual buildings.

The extent of the threat is a result of a combination of several adverse factors associated with the post-war development of Cracow, of which ecological disaster is the most obvious and most often mentioned. It was brought about by Stalinist industrialisation, which came to be symbolised in Cracow by the construction of Nowa Huta and the great metallurgic plant. However, it is not environmental pollution of recent decades which has caused deterioration of the urban complex in Cracow, comprising about 5,000 buildings. The key to understanding this process and, above all, to finding a prompt remedy, lies primarily within the legal, constitutional and economic spheres.

The removal of the natural mechanism of land lease, and more generally, of the economic foundations of the city during the last forty years has become an invisible enemy of the historic monuments of Cracow. This has caused a gradual decapitalisation of the whole city's building stock, including historic monuments. Paradoxically, it has passed unnoticed by the general public who considered the more perceptible environmental pollution as the main threat to the city's historic monuments.

Immediately after World War II, bourgeoise Cracow became one of the enemies of the new authorities. The fight with private property owners was chosen to be a basic tenet of the officially declared class struggle. Administrative decisions limiting ownership rights, and advocating liquidation of the housing market served this purpose. The incapacity of the property owners, without the compensation of adequate public spending on communal services, had resulted in significant decapitalisation of the housing stock by the 1960s.

This phenomenon gradually assumed a more widespread character, which may be called cultural degradation, and it also affected the cultural heritage of the city. Among other things, this degradation resulted in the rearrangement of the social composition of tenants in the deteriorating houses, coupled with a dispersal of the internal furnishings accumulated over generations. Architectural details also started to undergo destruction: entrance halls, staircases and the apartments themselves. The process could not be stopped by the obligatory overhauls carried out by the management. These were commonly accompanied by the so-called modernisation of the buildings, which was often focused on altering the nineteen century structures and spatial arrangements.

Towns summarise civilisation. This very obvious truth has not been properly understood in recent decades, neither in Poland nor in the other former communist countries of the region. Urbanisation has been treated mainly as a consequence of the process of industrialisation. The domination of the Marxist approach has led to a vulgarisation of the concept of the city as a very complex and highly sophisticated organism. Urban studies have been understood mainly as town planning, completely isolated from the economic and social context of the city. At the same time, our cities have lost their legal suzerainty. Jane Jacobs, in her classic study: *Cities and the Wealth of Nations, Principles of Economic Life* makes a very interesting remark concerning our joint central European reality:

> When the Soviet Union took under its economic control Gdansk, Warsaw, Cracow, Prague, Bratislava, Budapest, part of Berlin and other cities of East Germany, it acquired an additional supply of city earnings to drain for transactions of decline. The chief trade-off for these cities has been export work destined for inert economies in the Soviet Union. Far from continuing to develop, the economies of these cities have been arrested.[1]

Communism as a centralised system of ideology separated from the economic calculus, in the free-market meaning of this term going back to

Adam Smith, was conducive to conservation successes. Above all, it made it possible to carry out reconstruction on a large scale. This was one of the reasons why a huge market for conservation work was created and a great army of excellent conservators was created in Poland. Indeed, a great conservation potential was established, as was symbolised by the well known reconstruction of Warsaw. However, this formula for managing historic cities also brought about many negative effects, as it interfered with the social fabric. A look at Warsaw Old City centre shows that its reconstruction was not only separated from the natural economic mechanisms, but also from the social arrangement enforced by the authorities. Of course, this was combined with the significant increase in the symbolic functions of the historic monuments which occurred after World War II. In this new reality, the historic monument also became an important tool for the legitimisation of the new authorities which had implications far beyond the framework of the urban economy.

Detachment from the economic base became evident after the War, primarily in those historic cities which were not destroyed, precisely in such centres as Cracow. The fabric and historical core of these cities, were either frozen in their functions and in natural development mechanisms, or were subjected to gradual decapitalisation. This was one of the reasons for the paradox which occured over the last 50 years. On the one hand, one could note spectacularly great achievements of conservators in the field of reconstruction. On the other hand, the new system could not altogether cope adequately with seemingly much easier situations such as the maintenance of the authentic historic structure of cities like Cracow which survived war destruction.

This deepening discrepancy between conservation achievements and the less and less effective protection of whole urban complexes was a simple result of the diseased economy of the whole system. This disease affected the fabric of many historic cities which underwent a process of rapidly progressing decapitalisation and degradation, especially in the 1960s. In Cracow, this degradation was counteracted by the restoration which started in the late seventies. It was carried out and funded through a centralised system of administration. However, this conservation work was again separated from both the economic and social contexts. It clearly departed from what is an important determinant of historic cities and a component of their value: from the natural, spontaneous process of the city's life and authenticity of its social fabric. Only a few years ago, restoration in Cracow led to a peculiar 'modelling' of the city. Subjected to costly conservation work, buildings were deprived of authentic dwellers, and quite often of their past functions.

This was a special paradox in Cracow, the only large Polish historic city to have survived the tragedy of World War II physically and socially intact. The absurdity extended to economists from the Academy of Economy being busy over the city map, specifying service functions for particular shops. What should have been regulated by the free market under the supervision of the conservation services became a subject of pseudo-scientific studies. This example is a good illustration of the helplessness faced in approaching the conservation problems of a historical city at the final stage of the communist economic system. This road led to nowhere, as it was based on thinking which regarded the city as a static rather than a dynamic phenomenon.

The utopianism of this approach was conclusively laid bare in 1989, when the cities of Central Europe found themselves in a wholly new political and economic reality. The manifestation in each country varies across the region, depending on the range and character of systemic transformation. Polish cities, after the Balcerowics and local government reforms of 1990, historical cities in the Ukraine, and cities in the Czech Republic and Slovakia, all experienced it differently. The key starting point for seeking new solutions to the management of historic cities is however primarily the regaining of independence by them. This has happened through the decentralisation of the state and restoration of local government at the grass roots level.

Another factor of changes was the 'unfreezing' of economic mechanisms. My own experience in 1990–91, when I directed the city's policy of historic monument protection, is very instructive. 'Defrosting the fridge' in which Cracow had been prior to 1990, above all brought about spontaneity in urban processes. Cracow played a pioneering role in Poland, for it preserved the pre-war ownership structure. In communist times, it was embraced by autocratic state administration which significantly restricted the rights of owners, and deprived them of income. This contributed to the decapitalisation of the urban fabric, but it did not deprive them of their right of property ownerships. This is why, when the state administration over private property came to an end in 1990, the owners regained their full and sovereign rights. In a short time, this changed the functioning of the historical city. It was soon necessary to start searching for new legal instruments to provide effective conservation measures for the free market forces at the heart of the historic city (*Gründerseitfiber*).

This has highlighted the need to abandon static thinking about the historic city, and to assume a dynamic approach to the complexity of town planning. Systemic transformation and conflicts of interest among various social groups in historic areas are compounding such complexity. These conflicts are very evident today, and can be seen in the Market Square of Cracow with conflicting interests of different lobbies. They recognise the advantages to be had from the attractiveness of such places, and they use this attractiveness to advertise and promote their products. The only remedy to cope with the chaos and spontaneity of this process is a fundamental change in the approach to the city's economy and the management of its historic parts.

This is how Central Europe is now moving into a development phase with which conservators of historic monuments in Western Europe and elsewhere are familiar. This happened several decades ago in the USA, where the dynamics of urbanisation forced conservation to be part of the wider process governed by 'the management of change'. This means an attempt to control and regulate the rigid planning of urbanisation processes. The cities of our region are in the process of continuous systemic transformation and they are now laboratories for experiment and testing on the living matter of historic cities. This applies to various conservation doctrines and policy as well as to the economy and city management. Replacement of a totalitarian economic control by a system based upon structural and economic freedom and on liberalism provides opportunity for effective protection, but it also poses considerable risk. The establishment of a clear distinctive link between the cultural landscape and the socio-economic system is essential during the transition period.

The first symptoms of change were gaudy advertisements in the historic areas of our cities against which conservationists had no defence. This is not only a sign of change in the system of ownership and leaseholding, but also evidence that past instruments of heritage protection are inadequate. They were efficient within a system based on economic stagnation and total control, but they fail today when confronted with a new and dynamic style of urban living.

Protection to deal with the architectural heritage of the last two centuries has thus become a complicated matter. It has forced a change in the philosophy of protecting cultural heritage. The problem of heritage protection in this part of Europe is symbolised by Berlin, Cracow, Prague or Saint Petersburg. Their problems call for a new strategic formulation of protection which would lead to the effective revitalisation of the large housing developmemts of more recent date. In this process of total protection, the only guarantee of success would rest on inclusion rather than exclusion of cultural heritage into the new economic model. This in turn requires that a balanced compromise be found between the doctrine of preservation, the needs of everyday life and the laws of economics.

Comprehensive cultural heritage protection should embrace what the Germans call a *Kulturgesellschaft*, and by acknowledging the fact that the cultural sector also has its economic dimension, which was lost sight of under the former regime. It is through culture that we communicate our economic and social life, and one cannot maintain effective protection of the historic parts of our great cities without adequately embracing environmental, economic and social policies in urban heritage management. One of the key issues here is the problem of how to deal with often dilapidated historic districts. The efficiency of this protection is best guaranteed by creating a suitable image of the city. Its attractiveness largely depends on its cultural potential and on the extent of the preservation of the built heritage. It is frustrating that these issues are so slow to reach the consciousness of political and economic decision makers.

The historic cities of Central Europe have another potential resource, which should feature more prominently in future strategies. This factor is the human potential of the artistic and intellectual circles living in our historic cities. They work mostly in the state sector, still based on an outdated system of funding, and their full potential is only partly used. Creating a market for cultural tourism, including great festivals of art, should be an element of heritage strategy in its broadest sense. A very positive experience in this respect was the Cracow programme for the European Cultural Month, a great festival of European art organised in 1992 by the International Cultural Centre.

When describing the place of medieval art in the rehabilitation of the monuments of Cracow, Lech Kalinowski notes the persistent survival of the medieval urban core in spite of its changing function.[2] Similar conclusions may be drawn from looking at the art of more recent times, and expansion of protection of cultural artefacts ranging over the whole of the last two centuries implies a change of strategy. Even cities with roots deep into the Middle Ages are today dominated by the cultural fabric of the nineteenth century. The types and magnitude of the problems require a fresh and holistic approach to protection policies.

When discussing strategies for the overall protection of the historic city, one has to differentiate between the transition period and the final structural model. This is a consequence of transition from the centralised system of a command economy in which the town was denied any political and economic freedom, to the system in which Cracow will become a fully independent and self-governed municipality. This painful process of transformation often carries many serious risks, including monument protection.

In respect of the built heritage, it is characterised by the crisis of the state budget, which so far has monopolised the financing of monument conservation in Poland. It is accompanied by the appearance of a new type of player, usually aggressive capitalists and profit motivated investors, for whom the existing cultural heritage, especially the most recent, is something difficult to comprehend. It has no value, and often stands in the way of their plans. The first symptoms of this phenomenon were gaudy advertisements that in a short time changed the appearance of Cracow's historic centre. The fact that there is no way to keep them under control was the first warning. It could not be opposed using normal administrative methods, which were successfully applied under the former system.

This transitional period should be used to construct a new policy towards the functioning of the historic city. A key issues is to find a new approach to revitalise the city's nineteenth century housing complexes. They are today dilapidated, but represent a huge potential. They constitute an essential component of development in the coming decades. This is why the city should immediately formulate an explicit policy based on the restoration of private property, introduction of cheap mortgage loans, and a gradual placing of the nineteenth century housing stock on the market. Their condition and perceived cultural values represent an attractive commodity for the revived Polish middle class. Foreign experience may be helpful in this peculiar 'gentrification' of the nineteenth century city.

A different approach is required to save the urban structure of the Kazimiers district which is primarily nineteeth century building stock. The uniqueness of the area comes predominantly from the need of a systematic solution to the property question. More than 90% of pre-war house owners in this district were Polish citizens of Jewish origin. Nearly all of them became victims of the 1939–45 Holocaust. This fact requires the local government to solve the property problem comprehensively within international law. It requires cooperation between the Polish government and Jewish organisations.

Only clear policies for the problem of properties left by Jews may open the way to attract international capital to revitalise Kazimiers. The municipality should take over abandoned properties, and create a trust fund for the whole district to meet possible claims from Jewish heirs dispersed around the world. It will also be the municipality's task to identify a new function for Kazimiers by preparing a physical master plan for the district. It should become a starting point for seeking foreign credit and investment in order to revitalise the area.

The effectiveness of city-wide heritage protection, as well as that of an individual monument, relies on an appropriate fit between operational utilisation of a building and its functional purpose. Proof of this thesis may be found in the relatively well preserved historic church architecture of Poland.

Martin Krampen points out that a change of 'ideology of city functioning', as is happening in Poland, results in a change of meaning for the whole city's environment. This change is reflected, according to him, in the 'repertory of architectural objects'. New types of buildings, when replacing old ones, represent not only new town functions, but also a whole new social organisation. A good illustration of this phenomenon in

Cracow is the historic stock exchange building. Its architecture was well suited to the needs and taste of the communist authorities, which after World War II turned it into the regional Communist Party headquarters. Today, this building has returned to its stock exchange and financial function which reflets the magnitude of the changes which are occurring in Cracow.[3]

In many instances, particularily for those related to nineteenth century architecture, protection should take a more flexible approach to the original functions of buildings. The best illustration of this phenomenon within Cracow is undoubtedly the building of the Sowacki Theatre. Its construction in 1893, resulted mainly from a deep understanding of the cultural and community forming function of the theatre in the development of the city. Effective protection of this edifice today must consist in extending its function not only to cover opera performance, but also to house prestigious international congresses and conferences.

Only a solution like this will secure the financial means to carry out a comprehensive overhaul of the theatre and its subsequent use. The conservation and renovation of this most prominent example of historicism in Cracow has an additional a positive motivating effect by promoting recognition of the value of nineteenth century architecture. Furthermore, a broader urban design context is also essential in this case by bringing order to the critical transition zone between the medieval centre of the city and its nineteenth century continuation towards the railway station. Timely completion of the renovation work, not only saved this historic structure from its progressive deterioration, but also brought benefits by enhancing the image of Cracow.

The merging of artistic and intellectual vigour with economic viability, represents the basis for cultural revival of our historic cities. Abandonment of the static model of protection is the most important issue to come from our seven years of experience in transforming the historic towns in Central Europe. One can talk about various types of historic city, and about their different size, character and functional models. The experience of Cracow is not only one of a historic city, but also of one that has always developed with particular reverence for its past. At the same time, it is a city with a heterogeneous functional pattern of land use.

The conflict between form and function will remain a fundamental and controversial issue in the management of historic cities, as will be the tension between situation on the ground and conservation doctrine, as well as separation of economic policies from conservation strategies. The remedy is to regard the whole economic mechanism as an indispensable co-determinent of efficient protection. The heritage industry is an opportunity for many of our historic centres, but it also poses many threats, among which tourism is often mentioned.

It is still very difficult to estimate to what extent our cities, as well as our consciousness of the meaning of cities, have been devastated. However, there can be no doubt that a general philosophy of the city should once again be based on the traditional and universal values of well regulated private ownership, a free market economy and local democracy. This should include formulation of new goals and policy measures to facilitate the process of efficient revitalisation of the more recent housing complexes. In this process, the only guarantee of success may lie in the wise incorporation of cultural heritage into the economic equation. This in turn requires that a balanced compromise be found which will combine conservation doctrine, the needs of everyday life and the local economy.

Comprehensive cultural heritage protection should be viewed also from the perspective of creating *Kulturgesellschaft*, acknowledging the fact that the cultural sector is an economic asset. One cannot speak about the effective protection of the historic districts of great cities today without adequate city management policies for the urban economy. A key issue here is the problem of implementing appropriate urban functions. Cracow has a long tradition of preserving the past, its citizens having had a special respect for their cultural heritage over more than 150 years. The experience of nineteenth century Cracow, which based its economy on the meaning of its cultural heritage is also significant for its future.

The Author

Professor Jarek Purchla is Director of the International Cultural Centre in Cracow and leads the Department of Urban Development at the Cracow Academy of Economics. A writer on urban development and social art history of the nineteenth and twentiesth centuries, his work includes books on: *How the Modern Cracow originated* (1979 and 1990); *Wien-Krakau im 19.Jahrhundert* (1985); *Jan Zwiejski, Turn of the century architect* (1986); *House under the Globe, (1988); Non-economic factors of Cracow's development in the period of Galician home-rule,* (1990 and 1992*); Krakau unter osterreichischer Herrschaft 1846–1918: Faktoren seiner Entwicklung* (1993); *Das Theater und sein Architect* (1993); *The Duke Aleksander Lubomirski Foundation* (1993). Editor of *Cracow Yearbook* and Vice-President of the Society of Friends of the History and the Monuments of Cracow, he was Deputy Mayor of Cracow 1990–91, participated in the Eisenhower Exchange Programme in 1991, was a Fellow of the Alexander von Humboldt Stiflung in 1992–93, and served as General Coordinator of the European Cultural Programme in Cracow in June 1992.

References

Jacobs, J., *Cities and the Wealth of Nations*, Penguin, 1986, p 200

Kalinowski, L., *Miejsce sstuki redniowiecsnej w rewalorysacji sabytkw Krakowa (The Place of Medieval Art in the Restoration of Cracow's Historic Monuments)*, Acta Universitis Nicolai Copernici, Nauki Humanistycsno-Spo ecsne, Vol 226, 1991, pp 53–56

Krampen, M., in *Meaning in the Urban Environment* (1997, p 69) writes that when urban ideologies change, the meaning of the urban environment as a whole also changes

Early photograph of Patrick Geddes as a young man.

32

SIR PATRICK GEDDES
Pilgrimage and Place

Murdo Macdonald

... when he spoke on the interrelations of geography and history he illustrated his thesis by reference to the Thames, with its English capital city, London, and its sacred place of coronation, Westminster, paralleled by the Tay with its Scottish capital, Perth, and its sacred place of coronation, Scone. As one listener said, Geddes at his best made one think of the lines in Kubla Khan:

> For he on honey-dew hath fed
> And drunk the milk of Paradise.[1]

Early in his childhood Patrick Geddes's family moved to a cottage on the slopes of Kinnoull Hill overlooking the city of Perth. It is no overstatement to say that it was on Kinnoull Hill, complete with its tower-topped outlook crag, that Geddes laid the basis of his life's work. The value of such a natural environment as a playground to the boy who was to become a professor of Botany and who would write articles on biology for the *Encyclopaedia Britannica*, is obvious. But in emphasising the importance of Perth and Kinnoull Hill to Geddes, we must go further.

His pioneering appreciation of the relations between city and region has often been presented in the context of Edinburgh and Lothian, but the roots of this thinking lie in his appreciation of the interdependence of Perth, Strathearn and Strathtay. And the basis of his understanding of those inter-relationships was laid during his boyhood on Kinnoull Hill. That is the background to his Edinburgh Outlook Tower, which he used to unite direct visual perception of the surrounding buildings and hills with an appreciation of the history and potential of the city and the region. [2]At the end of his life he built another Outlook Tower overlooking the city of Montpellier in the South of France, and the link between the towers of Kinnoull Hill, Edinburgh, and Montpellier, is but one simple demonstration of Geddes's practical internationalism.

GEDDES THE MAN

Patrick Geddes lived at Mount Tabor Cottage from the age of three until he was twenty (1857–74), the formative years of his life. He grew up to be a polymathic genius of international reputation, which has its heart in Scotland but extends worldwide. As his disciple Lewis Mumford said: 'Geddes's Scotland embraced Europe and his Europe embraced the world'. So many of the things he concerned himself with a century ago, ecology, town planning, heritage issues and community arts are now on everyone's agenda. The context for all his thinking was an understanding of the creative interdependence of the local, the regional, the national and the international. This is an approach we need more than ever today, and Geddes is not simply a person who deserves to be remembered and studied, he is someone who has relevance now and for the future. The awareness he gained in his Perth childhood of the relationship of a city to its region was fundamental to all that he undertook in later life. He is famous for his Outlook Tower in Edinburgh, but the inspiration for this tower came directly from his youthful rambles to the tower on Kinnoull Hill.[3]

But who was Patrick Geddes? This ecologist, botanist, theorist of cities, advocate of the arts, community activist, publisher, town planner and educator was born in Ballater in Aberdeenshire in 1854. He died at the Scots College he had founded in Montpellier in the South of France in 1932.[4] His life is one of extraordinary vitality, variety and interest. On the one hand, as a biologist and social scientist, he studied evolution with T H Huxley. He thereby came into direct contact with Darwin in London, and he also became one of the founders of the Sociological Society. On the other hand, as a cultural activist, he was a moving force behind the Scottish Celtic Revival in literature and the visual arts.

In 1888, he was appointed Professor of Botany at University College Dundee. Thirty years later, he became the first Professor of Civics and Sociology at the newly established University of Bombay. But he is often thought of today primarily as a pioneer of community-sensitive town planning and as a theorist of the relations between city and region. Indeed, it has been the planners who have kept a little of his thinking alive within academic teaching.[5] He carried out some of the first studies on the conservation and regeneration of urban environments in places such as

Edinburgh, Jerusalem, Dunfermline and Dublin. He also developed an evolutionary analysis of the growth and decline of cities which was adopted, and adapted, by Lewis Mumford.[6] From 1914 onwards, he also carried out major studies in India.[7]

Geddes regarded education and cultural activity, in the broadest sense, as the necessary complement of planning, and he knew that these two aspects acting together could yield a truly civic approach. As an educational reformer, he initiated university residences in Edinburgh and London, run by the students themselves, which revitalised the medieval tradition of universities as democratic institutions. He also pioneered interdisciplinary 'summer meetings' in Edinburgh, early examples of the summer schools now taken for granted world wide. He had the ability to attract a wide range of people to debate in the context of an understanding of history, arts, geography, and biology. Both radical thinkers like Kropotkin and the Reclus brothers and Scottish aristocrats like Lord Rosebery and Lord Pentland came together under Geddes's influence. He advocated an open-textured approach to education and community, non-exclusive and generalist in ethos.

THE ECOLOGIST AND CULTURAL PILGRIM

There is at present a growing recognition of Patrick Geddes's importance, and we can understand why from the wonderfully concise statement of his ecological vision;

> How many people think twice about a leaf? Yet the leaf is the chief product and phenomenon of Life: this is a green world, with animals comparatively few and small, and all dependent upon the leaves. By leaves we live. Some people have strange ideas that they live by money. They think energy is generated by the circulation of coins. Whereas the world is mainly a vast leaf-colony, growing on and forming a leafy soil, not a mere mineral mass: and we live not by the jingling of our coins, but by the fulness of our harvests.[8]

At a time when ecology is becoming a matter of popular concern, the ability Geddes has to make it popularly accessible is exemplary, and it must be stressed that Geddes's ecological vision is matched by his cultural engagement. This volume is concerned with the legacy of pilgrimage and its relevance to tourism, and in a book published in 1920 we find Geddes exploring just this area. It is at first sight surprising to discover that a chapter entitled 'Holidays and Pilgrimages' should occur in Geddes's biography of his friend, the Indian physicist and physiologist, Sir Jagadis Chandra Bose (1858–1937), yet it should not be surprising.[9]

As usual, Geddes is stating the obvious when everyone else was tending to forget it, namely that the 'ever-widening cultural sympathies' which can be developed through well planned holiday travel, both at home and overseas, are central to an effective life, not luxuries tacked on to it. For Geddes, Jagadis Chandra Bose is an example of a cultural pilgrim who is a better scientist as a result. Of course in our over specialised world, proving that Bose was in fact a better scientist as a result of his cultural awareness of his place and his planet, is impossible. But such proof is not the point. What concerns Geddes is to advocate a society in which this pilgrimage aspect of the holiday is recognised and valued. If this is valued, in Geddes's view, society will value itself more. Furthermore, it will have people able to make the necessary links to other cultures and other idea systems. This will in turn lead, not only to a stable and harmonious world, but also to a world which facilitates the creativity and productivity of the scientist and the artist, and hence the well-being of every community.

Geddes brings in the example of the need for such holiday pilgrimages to facilitate the rebuilding of Europe after the first world war. It should be noted that this is not just some pious concern of Geddes, it is an historically informed view, for Geddes had predicted the inevitability of war several years before it started. He writes;

> The reunion of Europe, then, can most strongly, even if slowly, be made through the education of travel. Not merely in the recent tourist spirit, at least in the cruder forms; but in that combining of the best of modern cultural travel with something of the old spirit of pilgrimage which that helps effectively to renew. The Brownings and Ruskin in Italy were examples of this union in their day: why not renew it more widely? As Europeans grow more tolerant and more sympathetic, like the Indian travellers we have been following, our scheme of educational travel will grow and spread into fuller pilgrimages, which should be on the Indian scale – throughout Baltic and Mediterranean lands alike, from Scandinavia to Spain, and thence to Greece and beyond. Why not east and west, from Russia and Ireland, indeed to America as well? – with ever increasing appreciation of all their regional and civic interests, the natural, the spiritual, and the temporal together, and in aspects historic, actual and incipient. Does this seem 'Utopian'? It is after all but what the tourist and the wandering nature-lover, the art-student, and the historian have long been doing, and what the regional agriculturalist and the town planner are now in their turn doing. Today it lies with re-education, with reconstruction, and with re-religion as well, to organise these contacts more fully.[10]

The idea of a unified but culturally diverse Europe, a Europe in which 'contacts were more fully organised' was an idea close to Geddes's heart, and like so many of his ideas it looks both to history and to international comparisons for its inspiration. At the same time it looks to the future, and the relevance of these views, published almost a century ago, is obvious for us today, when many of the developments Geddes envisaged as possible within Europe are coming into being. Geddes was one of the pioneers of the idea that close attention to the well-being of local, national and regional identities within a wider European framework was the only way forward politically. He argued that political control should be held at appropriate levels within that structure. Successive UK governments have found this principle difficult to grasp, but the European notion of 'subsidiarity' expresses it, at least in theory.

Here one must be aware of Geddes's interest in medieval Europe, in which there was a culture of pilgrimage to places as diverse as Iona, St Andrews and Santiago de Compostela. In a real sense, Geddes saw this as a factor of European unity. While we cannot recreate medieval culture, he considered it important to be aware that the human impulse to pilgrimage is still with us;

> Neither Cook's tourists or American ones may strike us as models of reverence; but none the less it is their element of reverence which has sent the bulk of them – so far therefore on true pilgrimage – to the historic places of the world. Much more so is this reverence persistent in India. So for both East and West; as real and living education vitalises or replaces the traditional official or commercial sorts, the socio-religious education of travel will grow up into a very real revival of the pilgrimages of old, however largely we may as yet prefer to describe it in more secular-looking terms, as of the wander-years of higher education.[11]

FROM LOCAL TO INTERNATIONAL

There are few people who cannot find some aspect of Geddesian thought worth exploring, whether it is from a local perspective or from an international point of view. For example, in the immediate local context of Perthshire, the work of Geddes the botanist resonates with the achievement of Scone-born David Douglas, the outstanding naturalist who gave his name to the Douglas Fir, as well as with that of Charlie Macintosh, the Dunkeld amateur naturalist and postman who inspired Beatrix Potter. But in the case of the latter, this is more than a mere resonance, for we find Geddes in 1923 contributing the introduction to Henry Coates's biography of Macintosh.[12]

It is easy to see why Geddes was happy to associated with this biography. On a local level, Macintosh was an exponent of just the type of generalist virtues that Geddes valued. He spent his life as a post-runner around Dunkeld, and made of his work an opportunity to observe and classify the flora of the area. So much so that Henry Coates observes, in one small group of fungi alone, Mackintosh 'added six species to those previously known to occur in Britain, besides two which were entirely new to science.'[13] Coates also describes Mackintosh as: 'at once botanist, zoologist, geologist and meteorologist. But he was more than all these for the study of man and of his history from remotest times fascinated him always, so that archaeology became another of his favourite subjects of research.'[14]

In addition to these scientific accomplishments, Macintosh was also a fine folk musician whose grandfather had been taught the fiddle by the legendary Neil Gow, whose portrait by Raeburn is one of the most distinctive icons of the Scottish Enlightenment period. Macintosh is thus very much an example of a person who had a strong awareness of his local environment both scientifically, musically and historically. And this generalist awareness is the context for his wider significance, whether it be seen in terms of his scientific achievement, or in his influence on Beatrix Potter. It should be noted that an awareness of her regard for and understanding of Macintosh's work gives us a much more rounded view of Beatrix Potter herself, and we come to understand that the success of her children's stories owes a great deal to a serious study of nature.

It should also be noted that the great John Muir of Dunbar, founder of the National Parks movement in the United States, was an exact contemporary of Charles Macintosh, for both were born in the late 1830s.[15] Accordingly, there is great potential for exploring issues of cultural and ecological significance for today, and in a popularly accessible way: through a network of figures such as Patrick Geddes, David Douglas, John Muir and Charles Macintosh. It brings together natural heritage and cultural heritage, in a way that is valuable and generative at local level, national level and international levels.

As a strong advocate of the visual arts and photography, Geddes's work also relates to other great figures with Perthshire links such as David Octavius Hill, John Ruskin, and J D Fergusson. Perth-born Hill is best known for his collaboration with the chemist Robert Adamson which led to pioneering documentary photography work in the 1840s, particularly of the people of Newhaven. Geddes and his colleagues in Edinburgh were keenly aware of the usefulness of the camera as a tool of urban analysis, and their work can be seen as part of a tradition initiated by Hill and Adamson.

PATRICK GEDDES AND JOHN RUSKIN

Although John Ruskin was born in London, he was in spirit and ancestry more Scottish than English, as affirmed by Frederic Harrison in his biography of Ruskin;

> John Ruskin, born in London, was a Scot of the Scots, his father and mother being grandchildren of one John Ruskin of Edinburgh. Both parents and he himself passed much of their early life in Scotland, where he had many Scotch cousins, and whence he ultimately took a Scotch wife. He talked with a Lowland accent, and his dominant tone of mind was a mysterious amalgam of John Knox, Carlyle, and Walter Scott.[16]

In an even earlier biography, Ruskin's secretary W G Collingwood observes;

> If origin, if early training and habits of life, if tastes, and character, and associations, fix a man's nationality, then John Ruskin must be reckoned a Scotsman. He was born in London, but his family was from Scotland. He was brought up in England, but the friends and teachers, the standards and influences of his early life were chiefly Scottish. The writers who directed him into the main lines of his thought and work were Scotsmen – from Sir Walter and Lord Lindsay and Principal Forbes to the master of his later studies of men and the means of life, Thomas Carlyle. The religious instinct so conspicuous in him was a heritage from Scotland; thence the combination of shrewd common-sense and romantic sentiment; the oscillation between levity and dignity, from caustic jest to tender earnest; the restlessness, the fervour, the impetuosity – all these are the tokens of a Scotsman of parts, and were highly developed in John Ruskin.[17]

By 1912, the view of English commentators on Ruskin was beginning to change, and E T Cook wrote: '... the reader need not be troubled with any of the researches which biographers too often push to the point of tiresomeness about the remoter ancestry of their hero.'[18] By 1949, when Peter Quennell's published his book on Ruskin, Scotland had become a place of old aunts rather than intellectual influence. By the time of Peter Fuller's *Theoria* in 1988, it is not really there at all. Even a writer with a high degree of consciousness of the culture of Scotland finds himself in 1994, referring to: 'the very British John Ruskin' as a contrast to a Scottish/Celtic position.'[19]

However, it is worth bearing in mind that even to describe Ruskin as British is a somewhat radical Celticising move in itself in the light of comments such as: 'And in that learning we may have a glimpse of the mind of one of the greatest of English writers; a man whose extraordinary ambition was to give England a kind of nineteenth-century Renaissance, a critic whose culture, learning and experience of art was exceptional for his time, and for ours.'[20] This view is not without validity, but what it lacks is cultural context, and part of that context for Ruskin is not simply Scotland, but Perth. Not Perth as a tourist destination, but Perth as a place to which he was linked by family ties and upbringing. Paradoxically enough, it is Cook who had been somewhat dismissive of Ruskin's ancestral links with Scotland, who provides a good description of his Perth childhood;

> In these homes at Perth, we may picture Ruskin as a child dabbling in the pools of the Tay, or gazing at the hills of Kinnoul, or playing with his cousins on the meadow. But it is needless to continue, for all of these things are inimitably told in *Praeterita*, and here and there in *Fors Calvigera* there is an additional touch as when he describes a summer evening by the edge of the North Inch, where the Tay is wide, just below Scone, and the snowy quartz pebbles decline in long banks under the ripples of the dark clear stream.[21]

Indeed, as an expatriate, Ruskin's idea of Scottishness becomes for him a kind of moral touchstone;

> You will find upon reflection that all the highest points of the Scottish character are connected with impressions derived straight from the natural scenery of their country. No nation has ever shown, in the general tone of its language – in the general current of its literature – so constant a habit of hallowing its passions and confirming its principles by direct association with the charm, or power, of nature. The writings of Scott and Burns – and yet more, of the far greater poets than Burns who gave Scotland her traditional ballads, – furnish you in every stanza – almost in every line – with examples of this association of natural scenery with the passions.[22]

Geddes clearly found in Ruskin a powerful linkage between culture and nature of a kind that was inspiring to him. In addition to this, Geddes was one of the first thinkers to advocate Ruskin's economic theories.[23] It is therefore intriguing to reflect that Patrick Geddes the boy might even have met John Ruskin the man roaming on Kinnoull Hill.

THE CELTIC REVIVAL AND THE SCOTS RENAISSANCE

Patrick Geddes's powerful but unacknowledged cultural influence has led Duncan Macmillan, who has done more than any other scholar in recent years to raise public awareness of Scottish art, to see Geddes as fundamental to the understanding of Scottish art in this century. He writes of:

> ...the belief expressed so forcefully by Patrick Geddes a hundred years ago that art is part of a nation's vitality and a measure of its well-being; it should be modern and international in its horizons, but it should also be the product of a nation's own values, of its confidence in itself and of its awareness of its history.[24]

In this context, attention has been drawn by The Fergusson Gallery in Perth to the Celticism of the great Scottish Colourist painter, J D Fergusson.[25] Whether Fergusson and Geddes ever met, I do not know, but they shared a strong commitment both to Celticism and to the links between Scotland and France, as did their mutual friend, Charles Rennie Mackintosh.[26] We almost hear Geddes, when Fergusson wrote: 'If Scotland, or Celtic Scotland would make a new alliance' with France, not political like the auld alliance but cultural, it would perhaps put Scotland back on to the main track of her culture ...' Fergusson emphasises here and elsewhere the significance of traditional culture within an international context.

Fergusson wrote these words in *Modern Scottish Art*, published by Maclellan of Glasgow, as one title in a group of 1940s publications . These also included the early booklets of George Bain on different aspects of the Pictish school of Celtic Art. When Bain gathered his work together in the classic *Methods of Construction of Celtic Art*,[27] we find ourselves again linked both to the local and the international. The book contains a design by Bain illuminating a poem by Douglas Young written to mark the death of that fine Perth poet, William Soutar,[28] as well as a letter from Ananda Coomaraswami, in which the renowned art historian expresses strong interest in Bain's 'excellent booklets on Celtic Art'.[29] As one begins to develop an awareness of this cultural milieu, its local roots and international links become increasingly significant.

Another link between Fergusson and Geddes is Hugh MacDiarmid, whose *In Memoriam James Joyce*, was illustrated by Fergusson. MacDiarmid's admiration for Geddes led him to devote a significant section to their friendship in *The Company I've Kept*.[30] Two themes emerge here for further exploration: the Celtic Revival and the Scots Renaissance which was given impetus in the 1920s and 30s by MacDairmid, Soutar et al. Again, Geddes the Scots-speaker, resonates both with the work of the William Soutar Fellowship in Perth and that of the Scots Language Resource Centre in the same city. The fact that Patrick Geddes came from a family in which Scots, Gaelic and English were understood, and with Scots as the main language, contributed greatly to his later awareness of the importance of different cultures and the significance of local tradition.

The Scots language can be considered to be one of the elements at the heart of Geddes's thinking.[31] This can be seen explicitly in his admiration for Allan Ramsay's collection of Scots poetry, *The Evergreen*. It was adopted by Geddes as the title of his own interdisciplinary magazine where a number of poems in Scots were published. A further resonance can be found in the whole notion of 'Scots Renascence', for it was an essay by Geddes with that title (in the *Evergreen*, 1895) which used this phrase for the time in the sense of something applying to contemporary society. It can therefore be justifiably argued that Geddes is one of the people who prepared the ground for the current revival in Scots in which Perth and Perthshire have played a significant part.

The fact that Scots is now recognised as a European language within the European Union, could be no better endorsement of Geddes's belief in local and international interdependence. His knowledge of Gaelic suggests wider cultural partnerships and also links him to that Perthshire-born philosopher of the Scottish Enlightenment, Adam Ferguson, widely acknowledged as the founding father of sociology. It is of course no accident that these two men, Geddes and Ferguson, who helped to create the comparative and international approach to the study of societies which we now take for granted, should both have come from multilingual backgrounds.

THE SCOT IN EUROPE AND BEYOND

Patrick Geddes, the Scot-in-Europe, addressed many of the issues that are being re-run at present in the European Union. All these aspects: cultural, environmental, geographical and historical are brought together in Geddes's triad of 'Place, Work and Folk'. Geddes the ecologist was aware of the great environmental challenges which face us today. His relevance ranges from the personal to the geopolitical dimension, and there are a number of relationships between Scotland and Europe to be explored in the context of the Geddesian canon. These include links such as Geddes's long term commitment to France (Roscoff, Paris and Montpellier in particular), not least in the context of the Auld Alliance. Key aspects of his ideas relevant to the European situation today are;

1. the promotion of ecological thinking;
2. the analysis of cities and regions;
3. the cultural interdependence of the local and the international;
4. the idea of Europe-wide educational and cultural interchange.

If Geddes is considered from these points of view, rather than as a figure of merely historical interest, one begins to see more clearly why one of Europe's leading contemporary architects, Giancarlo De Carlo of Urbino,[32] cites Geddes as a primary influence on his own work. Beyond Europe, his wider links, not least with India, where he did work of great distinction, are also avenues of considerable potential. There is also considerable interest in his work in Japan, particularly in the Yamaguchi Prefecture, representing opportunities waiting to be developed.

Geddes's holistic approach to heritage in its many forms is highly relevant in every sector of contemporary society from schools to tourism. His wide ranging achievements on behalf of Scotland is a matter of pride and represent a challenge for all of us, who are committed to fight for a healthy and happy future together, in a world of rich cultural diversity. This challenge can be summed up in two of Geddes's own mottoes: 'By leaves we live' and 'By living we learn'. His assertion that culture and ecology are interdependent is one of the great messages that Geddes can give to us, whether in the context of everyday life, or in that of journeys we may make as tourists or pilgrims.

The Author

Professor Murdo Macdonald holds the Chair in History of Scottish Art at the University of Dundee. As a former lecturer, he retains links with the Centre for Continuing Education at the University of Edinburgh, where his main subjects of teaching and research were in the field of Scottish Cultural Studies. He studied painting at the Hammersmith College of Art in London and philosophy and psychology at the University of Edinburgh. He gained a First in Psychology and followed this with PhD research into the relationship between art and science. He has published a number of papers on the work of the polymath Patrick Geddes, and on wider issues of art and ideas, as well as being an art critic. He was editor of the literary and philosophical journal *Edinburgh Review* 1990–1994.

References

1. Stewart A. Robertson, *A Moray Loon*, Edinburgh: Moray Press, 1933
2. The Outlook Tower in Edinburgh was one of the most developed examples of Geddes's thinking. It is located at a key point within the psychogeography of the city, between the symbol of state power, the castle, and the then symbol of rejection of the authority of that state in matters spiritual, the Free Church College (now New College of the University of Edinburgh). Furthermore it is within easy view of the headquarters of the Bank of Scotland, and it stands on a ridge of rock coextensive with the remains of an extinct volcano which we now call Arthur Seat. For Geddes this was an ideal outlook from which to begin thinking about the evolution of cities, regions and cultures, in terms of the interaction of geographical, economic and social factors. Through this Outlook Tower one could learn, not just through words and images but from direct experience, about a multiplicity of aspects of Edinburgh, Scotland, Europe, and the world, all of which had a bearing on how people made their lives through their work in a particular place, and here Geddes emphasised the categories (adapted from the work of the French sociologist Frederic Le Play) of Place, Work and Folk as essential to any analysis. This idea of the importance of place, both historically and geographically, comes across in one of the most simple devices in the Outlook Tower, namely the geographical indicator inscribed in the stone of the parapet. But unlike most such indicators, this is a place indicator of Scotland, rather than a way of making sense of the view. Thus much of what is indicated cannot be seen, thus shifting the viewer from his or her direct perception to the idea of the region and the country as a whole. Among places ranging from Tain via Stornoway to Oban we see inscribed two which have special place for Geddes: 'Iona' the inspirational key to his Celtic Renascence and 'Perth', the site of inspiration for his entire life. The Outlook Tower was described in its heyday as the world's first sociological laboratory and Lewis Mumford identified it as the point of origin of the Regional Survey Movement. It was an assertion of the importance of all areas of knowledge, all arts, all sciences, all religions, within the context of a real place, explored in terms of the unity of the local and international
3. Also see Philip Boardman's description of this period of Geddes's life in chapter 1 of *The Worlds of Patrick Geddes*
4. The college as such did not survive World War II, but there is still a significant interest in Geddes's work in Montpellier, which seems set to grow rather than diminish
5. A good introduction to this side of Geddes's work can be found in Peter Hall's *Cities of Tomorrow*, 1988. Especially Chapter 5 'The City in the Region'.

6. See *The Culture of Cities*, p. 284. In Mumford's works his debt to Geddes is fully acknowledged. An illuminating section of *The Condition of Man*, (p.381–390) is devoted to Geddes

7. Norma Evenson, in her 1989 book *The Indian Metropolis* (pp.114–115) comments: 'Unlike the British engineers who had directed most municipal public works in India, Geddes had a sympathetic appreciation for Indian townscape.' And again: 'His common sense approach was ... difficult to fault. He approached his investigations with receptivity to the local scene, seeking to understand the nature of the Indian settlement, and making no attempt to impose a foreign conception of urban environment.' See also, in particular, *Patrick Geddes in India*, a selection of Geddes writings edited by Jacqueline Tyrwhitt, 1947

8. Reported by Amelia Defries, *The Interpreter: Geddes*, London: Routledge, 1927, p. 175

9. Patrick Geddes, *An Indian Pioneer of Science: The Life and Work of Sir Jagadis C. Bose*, London: 1920

10. *Ibid.* 118

11. *Ibid.* 111

12. Henry Coates, *A Perthshire Naturalist: Charles Macintosh of Inver*, London, T. Fisher Unwin, 1923. The short introduction is signed by Geddes and his former pupil and colleague Prof. J. Arthur Thomson of Aberdeen

13. Henry Coates, *Charlie Macintosh: Post-Runner, Naturalist and Musician*, London, T. Fisher Unwin,1924,139

14. *Ibid.* 136

15. John Muir (1838–1914). Charles Macintosh (1839–1922)

16. Frederic Harrison, *John Ruskin*, London: Macmillan, 1902. 3–4

17. W.G. Collingwood, *The Life of John Ruskin*. London: Methuen, 1893, 3

18. E.T. Cook, *The Homes and Haunts of John Ruskin*, London: George Allen, 31

19. Timothy Neat, *Part Seen, Part Imagined: Meaning and Symbolism in the Work of Charles Rennie Mackintosh and Margaret Macdonald*, Edinburgh: Canongate, 1994, 26

20. Tim Hilton, Foreword to *John Ruskin*, London: Arts Council of Great Britain

21. E.T. Cook, *Op. Cit.* 35

22. Ruskin, *The Two Paths*, London: Smith Elder, 1859, Lecture I. Section12. He adds a footnote at this point: The great poets of Scotland, like the great poets of all other countries, never write dissolutely, either in matter or method, but with stern and measured meaning in every syllable. Here's a bit of first-rate work from example: *Tweed said to Till, | 'What gars ye rin sae still?' | Till said to Tweed, | 'Though ye rin wi speed, | And I rin slaw, | Whar ye droon ae man, | I droon twa'*

23. *John Ruskin, Economist.* (1884)

24. Duncan Macmillan, *Scottish Art in the 20th Century*, Mainstream, Edinburgh, 1994, p 1

25. See, e.g., Kirsten Simister, *Celtic Spirit*, leaflet accompanying exhibition at Fergusson Gallery, Perth, April–October, 1994

26. See Thomas Howarth, *Charles Rennie Mackintosh and the Modern Movement*, London, Routledge and Paul Keagan, 1977, esp. 229–232, and Murdo Macdonald. 'Art and the Context in Patrick Geddes's Work'. *Spazio e Societa* Milan, October/December, 1994

27. George Bain, *The Methods of Construction of Celtic Art*, William Maclellan, Galsgow, 1951

28. *Ibid.* 122

29. *Ibid.* 20

30. For example, MacDiarmid quotes Patrick Geddes's son Arthur: 'I well remember the day in Montpellier when in *Les Nouvelles Litteraires*, we first read a few of MacDiarmid's poems and my father wrote to him straightaway; the friendship began with poems and response to them!'

31. I have noted this in print on at least two occassions (i) *Patrick Geddes e l'intelletto democratico*, Spazio e societa, no.68, Milan: Gangemi Editore, 1994, pp.28–42. (ii) *Patrick Geddes in Context: Glossing Lewis Mumford in the Light of John Hewitt*, Irish Review, in press

32. Giancarlo De Carlo said in a recent interview: 'Here in Scotland, in Scottish culture, from what I have read and I have studied, I think you have one educational pillar which is very important. It is what you call generalism. I think this is peculiar to Scotland, this idea that you have to have a general view of something in order to understand it. Specialisation, specialists, I consider in a way to be an accident of our present time. I think we should go back to the idea of the general view, and in Scotland you have a good grounding in this approach, not least because of the work of Patrick Geddes...'

33

NEW PILGRIMS OLD TOWNS
The Historic Burghs of Scotland

David Cameron

> Sir, said Christian, I am a man that am come from the City of
> Destruction, and am going to Mount Zion; and I was told by the man
> that stands at the gate at the head of this way that if I called here you
> would show me excellent things, such as would be a help to me in my
> journey.

> from the *Interpreter's House* in *Pilgrim's Progress* by John Bunyan.

Obviously Bunyan is illustrating an approach to life by way of an
allegorical pilgrimage. In past centuries to be a pilgrim was both
adventurous and noble and was no doubt rewarding to the spirit. There
were famous routes throughout Europe to the resting places and
reliquaries of important Saints, and Scotland was an internationally
important destination with the bones of St Andrew. To suggest
pilgrimages are similar to today's tourist trails makes me feel
uncomfortable but clearly there are for instance the same practical needs
for accommodation en route. Dare I even mis-use a common expression
that how you travel is often more important than arriving.

Also to hint that cities are places of destruction is unfair. However, it is
true that many have in the process of growth destroyed much evidence of
their small town origins. Of Scotland's four cities, Dundee and Glasgow
were substantially rebuilt and expanded in the 19th Century but
Aberdeen and Edinburgh in particular retained at least the pattern if not
always buildings of earlier periods in the centre. This heritage is now
accepted as an economic as well as a cultural resource and Edinburgh's
Castle and Old Town has become the visitor gateway to other parts of
Scotland. However, tourists are often attracted more by Scotland's unique

landscape, especially the Highlands, than by the cultural wealth of its many historic burghs and towns.

With changing work patterns and increased mobility many burghs now are threatened by retail and employment competition from cities and larger towns. Although some burghs have adjusted to or have a niche in the new 'market place' a number have lost their *raison d'être* and have become dormitory towns albeit pleasing in a picturesque way. The physical condition of older areas can often be run-down and there are problems with unsympathetic alterations.

Although sometimes laudable efforts have been made to revive them, some measures such as the design and materials of traffic calming schemes are most unconvincing. Considering that they are a physical manifestation of Scottish culture, it is a great pity that not all burghs are the best they can be for both their inhabitants and visitors. However, I believe the wealth of our historic burghs has the potential of giving visitors to Scotland a rewarding experience of cultural discovery:

1. to see at first hand how Scottish towns have been planned and built since medieval times in response to local conditions;
2. to find out how imported ideas and styles have been adapted to create a uniquely Scottish architecure of great variety and richness;
3. to feel the hand of history in accommodation which may have provided shelter for generations of travellers;
4. to enjoy a wide range of leisure pursuits in historical surroundings.

Who are the likely pilgrims to Scotland's burghs today? The list would, I am sure, include in no particular order; families on school mid-term; students on bicycle tour; prematurely retired pensioners by rail; coach parties on cultural outings; artists looking for inspiration; backpackers from the Far East; expatriots researching their roots; conference delegates on half-day off; golfers going to the nineteenth. Will they see and get: a' the best frae Scotland? Not always, as yet, and that is why the Historic Burghs Association of Scotland came into being.

HISTORY AND IDENTITY

The most complete scheme of national, regional and town planning in Scotland began in 1124 on the accession of David I. Robert Naismith in his book *The Story of Scotland's Towns* explains:

The King's plan comprised four elements: (1) the introduction of the feudal system; (2) the establishment and maintenance of law and order; (3) the reorganisation of the Church as the national vehicle for religion, culture, scholarship and science; (4) the promotion of local and foreign trade.

The third component of the King's plan was provided by the churches and monasteries. Many of the religious establishments having been built close to the towns to supply religious teaching and education, they enhanced the visual quality of the burghs by the fine architectural quality of their buildings.

To achieve the fourth objective, the promotion of trade, the planning of a network of towns became vital. David I and his successors up to the end of the thirteenth century applied themselves to this enterprise with masterly effect. They distributed the new chartered towns in locations over the whole part of the country where agriculture was practicable, so that the benefit of the plan would reach all the King's subjects, not just those living in Scotland's south-east.

St Margaret, wife of Malcolm Canmore, King of Scots, had begun introducing Norman clerics into Scotland and her son David I accelerated the process. This meant that the less well organised Celtic Church (or Culdees) gradually declined, and their saints were often supplanted by those acceptable to Rome. Thus some early Scottish saints were replaced, such as St Blane by St Lawrence, and the popularity of others, like St Ninian, St Fillan and St Kentigern diminished. St Giles was adopted for several new burgh churches being the patron saint of merchants. Fortunately, St Columba of Iona did not lose his place. Although there were pilgrimages to local saints, the importance of St Andrew, being the 'first-called' of the disciples, put Scotland on the European pilgrimage map. Monasteries were usually established just beyond the walls of towns and so were not strongly integrated in layout terms, but contributed to the townscape skyline and identity:

> Towers, turrets, kirnels, pinnacles hie
> Of Kirks, castells, and ilke fair citie,
> Stood painted, every fyall, fane and stage,
> Upon the plain ground by their own umbrage.

from *Aeneid* by Gavin Douglas, 1513

It is thought that the Flemish skill in new town building was a major influence, as the burgh layouts are more linear and are quite unlike the English models and French gridiron types. Eventually, there were over 80 Royal Burghs in Scotland, each with its own unique character. In addition, there are former Abbey Burghs and Burghs of Baronies, as well as newer towns arising from the industrial era. Plans of the 12th and 13th centuries, as for example in Forres, Stirling and Perth have features in common and yet with interesting differences. Forres has the more familiar linear High

Street, while Stirling has a much wider market area, and Perth has two parallel streets giving a virtually square shape to the boundary.

The new Royal Burghs were often sited on rising ground at a place where routes converged such as a ford in a river. Each plot of land or burgh feu was pegged out by Sheriff Officers along the street using the burgh rod (about five metres), and the depth of the site was marked by a ploughman's furrow. A typical feu for a burgess would be one rod by 25 rods, and he would build the house gable-end on to the market place. At the foot of the feu, he was obliged to construct his part of the town wall or dyke, and possibly also a defensive ditch beyond. Confined by these defences through time, the entire strips of land were developed, and the buildings crammed in also increased in height and the population density grew. Sometimes, the street building lines were encroached upon. Colin MacWilliam, in his book *Scottish Townscape*, captures the identity of the whole ensemble:

> Houses hug their allotted length of street front, to which the richer houses present their long sides, the less privileged (with narrower plots) their chimneyed gable ends. The contrasting motifs of level eaves and pitched gable become the standard profile of the Scottish street, indefinitely repeated and varied. Gables are crowstepped; the eaves may depart from the straight line and sprout into gabled dormers of one and sometimes two storeys, or even pretend to be gables themselves so as to provide more chimneys at the wall head. Slates cover the better houses, and the majority, as Slezer shows, are thatched until pantiles become more easily available in the early eighteenth century. Thatch is still seen at Glamis and Auchtermuchty.
>
> On street level the angular jostle of houses is mitigated by bold curves and chamfers to minimize damage by animals and carts or avoid too tight a squeeze between the packed buildings of a close; above it, rounded corners return to the square as quickly as possible, or the squared angle bulges into a round turret. Many a turnpike stair has a little room at its head, and so that you can get into that, another stair turret with snuffer top is pushed out (as are the walls themselves) into the shrinking air space overhead.
>
> This is a style so intimately connected with function that it can hardly be called a style at all. If you took it away, you would take away the useful parts of the building. It has the abstract quality of all useful things, and this is almost everywhere enhanced by the use of harl, a rough rendering thrown on to rubble walls. Functionally this is a continuous weatherproofing coat over walls that are mostly built of rough or field stones and soft lime mortar, the available freestone being saved up for the margins and openings, or more exceptionally for sculptured trimmings like skewputts, or initialled and dated lintels. Abstractly, harling is an enveloping, neutral blanket which has the effect of making a building into sculpture.

Trade in a Royal Burgh was in the open air market place, the centre piece of which was the Mercat Cross (incorporated within the Association's logo). The burgesses had specific rights to buy and sell merchandise, and to administer their burgh. Some burghs also had a castle for the King's Sheriff to control the surrounding land.

Rural depopulation in the aftermath of the Industrial Revolution saw some burghs expand considerably in response to new work opportunities and agricultural reforms. The first official census in 1801 showed a national population just over 1.5 million, with 40000 in Edinburgh and 80000 in Glasgow. A few towns, such as Paisley, Dundee and Aberdee had reached about 30000. Perth stood at 6000, but most ranged between one and two thousand.

Scotland was changing from being a separate country to becoming an integral part of the United Kingdom. The Scottish Enlightenment brought new ideas, including more regular and rectilinear town plans influenced by Continental practice in the neo-classical style. Nevertheless, the dramatic appearance of earlier castles and burgh architecture was respected and appreciated.

The rise of the Victorian middle classes led to a new role for some towns as holiday destinations. Places such as Ayr, Helensburgh, St Andrews, Grantown-on-Spey and Strathpeffer flourished. Royal presence at Balmoral inspired, and Scots baronial buildings were popular models for the large number of new hotels and public buildings. Many architects drew strength from the traditional Scottish burghs and castles, in particular Sir Robert Rowand Anderson and later Sir Robert Lorimer. Even Charles Rennie MacIntosh has strong overtones of the Scottish vernacular in his buildings.

In the process of expansion, town walls were demolished and some burghs did lose much of their valuable heritage. In the 1880s, Sir Patrick Geddes was to demonstrate the merits of 'conservative surgery' and an holistic approach to reviving run down areas with the active involvement of the local community. His work in Edinburgh's Old Town, including Ramsay Gardens, remains as a testament to his approach which is as valid now as it was then. Indeed, his philosophy gained and still has an international reputation.

Obviously, the significant changes in transportation with new railways, trams and major road improvements created both opportunities and threats for towns. Pollution from industry and the burning of coal produced a not inconsiderable health problem, and also discoloured buildings

THE HISTORIC BURGHS ASSOCIATION

All of these burghs and towns today have a heritage of trade, cultural history, planning, buildings and materials worthy of study and conservation. Too little is made of their historic townscapes, and many tourists bypass them for better promoted visitor attractions. Much could be done to make their heritage assets more accessible through improved local interpretation. Although exaggerating the point, David Milstead's description of a fictional town in Perthshire brings out the issue:

> Indeed, if you are aware of the town at all, it is likely to be as 'that rather twee place on the A9, with the pretty gardens'. Although it cannot be said of Craigfieth that if you blink, you miss it (the 30mph limit sees to that, or should do) it is certainly not likely to remain imprinted on the memory, and despite the artfully placed notices at either end of the town, Welcoming Careful Drivers and exhorting them to Haste Ye Back, it is unlikely that many people do, unless they be hastening somewhere else. Craigfieth does a modest summer trade in golfing holidays for mature gentlefolk who pass a placid fortnight in one of its clean guest houses or in the one unexceptional hotel, and take moderate exercise on the well-maintained though undemanding links.

By having an Association to focus on their needs, it is hoped that the local identity of burghs will be reinforced and action encouraged to promote the well-being of both inhabitants and visitors. Indeed, our historic burghs and towns need a collective voice to speak on their behalf and to promote their cause. To that end, the Association has produced two publications, one on vitality and transportation philosophy, and the other on a retail viability in seven larger Scottish towns. A recent study looked at the economic development and character of 17 smaller towns, including three on the Isle of Man.

These reports, and the 'family' of others to follow, may seem a tall order for an organisation which was launched as recently as February 1995. However, there is clearly strong support, as both the inaugural conference on 'Vitality and Quality' and a seminar on 'Places for People' were both over-subscribed. The 1997 conference in Kilmarnock was on 'Health of Town Centres: Symptoms and Solutions', and the 1998 event in Montrose was on 'Caring for Scotland's Historic Burghs: Identity, Investment and Improvement'.

The primary objective of the Association is to promote and reconcile quality of life and conservation in historic towns throughout Scotland, with particular emphasis on Scotland's Historic Burghs. To achieve this, the Association sets out to:

1. promote dialogue between local authorities with responsibility for the management of historic burghs, towns and cities, as well as with other public, private and voluntary agencies.
2. organise seminars and conferences to discuss issues of common concern, and produce publications of use to member towns.
3. encourage a partnership approach to the management of historic towns and exchange information of mutual interest.
4. formulate a collective approach to issues which are likely to affect the interests of historic towns generally.
5. establish links with the European Union, the Council of Europe and other appropriate European historic towns, cities and agencies.

Initially, the Convention of Scottish Local Authorities approached the Scottish Society of Directors of Planning, proposing that a Scottish equivalent of the English Historic Towns Forum be explored. The idea found favour with other national bodies, including the Institute of Historic Building Conservation, the National Trust for Scotland, the Scottish Civic Trust and The Saltire Society, which all supported the formation of a steering committee. Since then, local authorities, universities, companies and individuals have shown much interest and membership is open to all. The first AGM took place in October 1997, so we are now a properly constituted organisation with an Advisory Council chaired by Professor Sir James Dunbar-Nasmith.

There is a strong desire that the Association should serve as the focus of a co-ordinating network concerned with needs and future trends. Therefore, contact will be maintained with organisations such as departments of The Scottish Office, the Association of Town Centre Management, the Scottish Burgh Survey (Archaeology), local community and commercial interests, as well as with the English Historic Towns Forum and a future forum for Wales. We intend our output to be professionally sound advice, especially for local authorities, planners, surveyors and architects. In addition, participation by educational and research institutions will be encouraged.

None of this would obviously be possible without sponsorship. We have been most fortunate to date and have had the backing of Donaldsons and Colin Buchanan & Partners, plus other bodies in our formative stages. In 1966, sponsorship approaching £50k was achieved for the Seven Burghs Survey, some of the findings of which are covered in this paper. Last year, further finance was given for the Small Towns Study. We are particularly grateful for the support of the new local authorities and to Scottish Enterprise and the Local Enterprise Companies.

THE SEVEN BURGHS SURVEY

When chapman billies leave the street,
And drouthy neebors, neebors meet,
As market days are wearing late,
An' folk begin to tak the gate.

Tam o' Shanter, Robert Burns

The vitality and viability of town centres are a matters of considerable concern with so much competition from out-of-town shopping centres and discount warehousing. In anticipation of National Planning Policy Guidelines on Retailing being issued by The Scottish Office, the Historic Burghs Association mounted a survey of seven burghs during 1996, focusing on a 'health-check' of their their town centres. That meant involving local authorities, Local Enterprise Companies, local traders and others. The work was ably carried out by Donaldsons Surveyors and Colin Buchanan and Partners regarding movement and 'footfall'. The towns covered were Inverness, Stirling, Dunfermline, Berwick-upon-Tweed, Hamilton, Kilmarnock and Ayr.

There is a full report of findings, and the following resume of the visitor survey results is relevant here:

The dominant reason for trips to Scottish Burghs is to shop (an average of 50% were visiting for this purpose). This is similar to the findings of a similar English Historic Towns Forum study of English historic cities which found that on average 58% of visitors were visiting with the primary aim of shopping. The Study indicates that a similar proportion of visitors are in the towns to shop for food and household groceries (26%) whilst on average 24% of visitors were shopping for non-food goods. The findings indicate that food shopping is still an important draw for visitors to most historic towns but there is clearly a threat of major diminution in this type of trade from out of town stores.

The purchasing patterns of visitors inevitably reflect the types of goods that are on offer in a town centre. Convenience shopping dominates purchases made in Scottish towns and just under half of visitors to the Historic Burghs (49%) purchased food during their trip while just 39% purchased clothing and footwear. In view of the fact that almost as many visitors (24%) intended to purchase comparison goods as convenience goods (26%) in the town centre, the figures suggest that the comparison offered in the town has no always succeeded in fulfilling shoppers' requirements. Deviations from the average for individual towns are quite substantial and in one town the comparison offer is so poor that just 18% of its visitors purchase clothing and footwear whilst there.

Linked trips are clearly important in established town centres both in terms of proportion of overall trips and the potential turnover of a town

452

centre that they represent. On average 51% of visitors intended to link their primary trip with another activity in the town. This is a slightly smaller proportion and was found in the EHTF Study where an average of 58% of visitors undertook linked trips during their visits to town centres. Linked trips involve visits for work, meetings with friends or relatives, personal business (doctor/dentist/lawyer, etc), conference and business meetings, as well as tourist visits. The proportion of visitors surveyed in town centres in connection with tourism is extremely low at 1% whereas the EHTF Study indicated that 13% of visitors were on tourist trips in English towns. Clearly there is potential for considerable improvement in business generated from tourists in Scottish Burghs.

There are wide variations in mode of travel to the Scottish Burghs surveyed with an average half of all visitors travelling by car with a large proportion (31%) travelling into the town centre by bus and a further 15% arriving by foot. Other modes of transport include train (2%), bicycle (1%) and taxi (1%).

In all of the Scottish towns surveyed, an average of 30% of visitors returned to the town centres during the evening and this pattern is broadly replicated in all of the Historic Burghs. Evening visitors come for a variety of different reasons including going out to eat or drink, visiting nightclubs and playing bingo and on average more than three-quarters of all evening visitors stated that they returned for these purposes. Just under half of evening visitors (47%) indicated that they came back to the town centre to visit the cinema or theatre and 15% said they returned to the town to make use of the leisure facilities.

Visitors' attitudes to a wide range of qualitative issues were recorded, including pedestrianisation, safety, accessibility, facilities, environment, and activities such as the performance, where appropriate, of town centre management in upholding and promoting the attributes of the burgh. The Historic Burghs Association study of the size of town surveyed has shown that:

1. It is possible to measure selected vitality and viability indicators on a comparable basis.
2. The *health-check* process is a useful tool to help identify key priorities for the town centre and it involves all the main players in the process.
3. Historic towns in Scotland are generally reasonably strong local shopping centres within a local catchment, but have potential to attract more visitors and trade by promoting their historic character.

The Association would encourage other towns to do similar studies for further comparison and would like to see the results monitored and updated at regular intervals. Also the Association carried out a similar survey with adopted methodology in 1997 of a representative number of smaller burghs which are less significant district shopping centres and perhaps rely more heavily on tourism and their heritage.

THE WAY AHEAD

So, will the new pilgrims be attracted in greater numbers to our ancient burghs steeped as they are in history? I believe they will need to be given more suitable information, focused promotion and effective interpretation, including a gazetteer of the towns. My suggested figure-of-eight tour of Scotland's historic burghs is illustrated at the end of this paper. If this caught on, visiting all the burghs might be seen as a similar challenge to climbing the Munros (all Scotland's mountains over 3,000 feet high). This would be an authentic cultural and educational pursuit into which hopefully 'Brigadoon' and 'Braveheart' themes would not intrude. Ideally, there should be a Scottish Burghs Interpretation Centre, probably in Stirling, with possibly sub-centres in certain other burghs around Scotland.

Will this influx be against the interests of local inhabitants? I do not think that well-handled, the prospect of increased tourist trade (although there will eventually be an upper limit) and the considered and well executed restoration of our towns can be anything but welcome. In the process sensitive design standards for new infill buildings and traffic calming measures will be devised as sadly there have been too many examples of what not to do in terms of scale and/or materials.

Nevertheless there have been outstanding award-winning schemes and the work, of for instance, the National Trust for Scotland with its *Little Houses* restoration scheme is admirable.

The issues for Scottish towns can be seen throughout Europe albeit that ours have different characteristics coming from a northern and often windy climate. Clearly transportation policies; the 'changing market place'; the constraints and opportunities of the historic urban forms; the numbers of visitors, attractions and Listed Buildings; the conservation action plans and other town centre management schemes all have a part to play in tackling the increasing concerns. There is no doubt that the effects of edge-of-town developments and traffic congestion in town centres are leading to the lowering of quality for the pedestrian and are limiting the range of uses and choice of activities in the heart of our historic burghs. Generally we need to remind ourselves of what we have lost in our burghs as well as what we have gained and make sure that the new Scottish Parliament will have the right agenda for their future. For instance, there is a great need for an overall design policy – Norway has its Norskform and Scotland needs a Scotform!

454

Our burghs are potentially a string of individual pearls of which any nation should be proud and should want to share with others. Each is individually shaped and moulded by topography and time and set as they are in Scotland's outstanding natural scenery, they are incomparable. In the past many were on routes of famous pilgrimages and some are awaiting rediscovery by today's visitors. I will leave the last words to Rosaline Masson writing in Scots:

> I ken a toon, wa'd round, and biggit weel,
> Where the women's a' weel-faured, and the me's brave and leal,
> And ye ca' ilka ane by a weel-kent name;
> And when I gang to yon toon, I'm gangin' to my hame.
>
> I ken a toon, its gey grim and auld;
> It's biggit o' grey stane, and some finds it cauld;
> It's biggit up and doon on heichts beside the sea;
> But gif I get to you toon – I'se bide there till I dee.

The Author

David Roderick Cameron is an architect planner and Director of AUI Ltd (Architects and Urbanists International), and is Convener of the Historic Burghs Association of Scotland. He is Chairman of the Sir Patrick Geddes Memorial Trust, Convener of the Saltire Planning and Environment Committee and the Charles Cameron Campaign (St. Petersburg), Vice-President of the Clan Cameron Association, Scotland and a member of the National Trust for Scotland Council. He was previously Depute Executive Director of Planning for the City of Edinburgh District Council (1983–96), Project Manager for the European Union, ECOS funded Kazimierz Action Plan for Krakow (1993–95) and Chairman of The Saltire Society (1990–95).

References

Masson, R., *Scotland the Nation*, Nelson, 1934
Hurst, R. and Reiach, A., *Building Scotland*, Saltire Society, 1940
Fladmark, J. M., *The Wealth of a Nation*, Robert Gordon University, 1994
Adams, I. H., *The Making of Urban Scotland*, London, 1978
McWilliam, C., *Scottish Townscape*, Collins, 1975
Naismith, R., *The Story of Scotland's Towns*, John Donald, 1989
Moody, D., *Scottish Local History*, Batsford, 1986
Moody, D., *Scottish Towns*, Batsford, 1992

Middleton, M., *Man Made the Town*, Bodley Head, 1987

Harrison, P., (ed), *Civilising the City: Quality or Chaos in Historic Towns*, Nic Allen, 1990

Engwicht, D., *Towards an Eco-City: Calming the Traffic*, Envirobook, 1992

Milstead, D., *The Chronicles of Craigfieth*,Mainstream, 1988

Milstead, D., *Market Forces*, Mainstream, 1989

Donaldsons, *Town Centre Health Checks*, HBAS, 1994

Scottish Office, *Retailing*, National Planning Policy Guideline No. 8, 1996

English Historic Towns Forum, *Townscape in Trouble*, EHTF, 1990's

English Historic Towns Forum and Civic Trust, *Traffic Measures in Historic Towns*, EHTF & CT

Davis, C., (ed), *Edinburgh Streetscape Manual*, Lothian Region and Edinburgh District Council, 1995

McKean, C et al., *Illustrated Architectural Guides to Scotland*, RIAS/Landmark Trust, 1980's and 90's

Torrie, P. et al, *Archaeological Surveys of Scotland's Historic Burghs*, Historic Scotland/Scottish Cultural Press/Centre for Scottish Urban History, University of Edinburgh

Covers, K., *A Vision of Scotland: The Nation observed by John Slezer 1671–1717*, National Library of Scotland, 1993

LIST OF SOME OF THE HISTORIC BURGHS OF SCOTLAND

ROYAL BURGHS (R) = Significant Early Royal Burgh (+) =Also Important Bishopric	DATE OF FOUNDATION CHARTER	POPULATION HMSO 1971	OUTSTANDING CONSERVATION AREA STATUS
Aberdeen (+) (now City)	1124–53	182,071	x
Airth	1195–1203	1,027	
Annan	1532	6,051	
Anstruther Easter	1583		x
Anstruther Wester	1587		x
Arbroath	1599	22,586	x
Auchterarder	1246	2,446	
Auchtermuchty	1517	1,475	x
Auldearn (Earn)	1179–82	405	
Ayr (R)	1203–06	47,896	x
Banff	1189–98	3,723	x
Berwick (R) (presently in England)	1119–24		
Brechin (+)	1641	6,578	x
Burntisland	1541	5,699	
Campbeltown	1700	5,960	x
Canongate (now in Edinburgh)	1128–1343		x
Clackmannan	1153–64	3,248	
Crail (R)	1150–52	1,075	x
Cromarty (R)	1264	484	x
Cullen (Invercullen) 1189–98	1,207		x
Culross	1592	523	x
Cupar	1327	6,603	x
Dingwall (R)	1227	4,232	
Dornoch (+)	1628	838	
Dumbarton (R)	1222	25,640	
Dumfries (R)	1186	29,382	
Dunbar	1445	4,611	x
Dundee (now City)	1191–95	182,204	x
Dunfermline (R)	1124–27	49,897	x
Dunkeld	1704	273	x
Dysart	1594		
Earlsferry	1589	895	x
Edinburgh (R) (now City)	1124–27	453,584	World Heritage
Elgin (R) (+)	1136–53	16,407	
Falkland	1458	896	x
Forfar (R)	1184	10,499	x
Forres (R)	1130–53	4,718	x
Fortrose (+)	1590	1,081	x
Fyvie	1264	405	
Glasgow (+) (now City)	1611	897,483	x
Haddington (R)	1124–53	6,502	x
Hamilton	1549	46,349	x
Inverary	1648		x

Inverbervie	1341	850	
Inverkeithing (R)	1153–62	5,861	x
Inverness (R)	1153–65	34,839	x
Inverurie	1195	5,437	
Irvine (R)	1372	3,019	x
Jedburgh (R)	1124–53	3,874	x
Kilrenny	1592	3,037	x
Kinghorn (R)	1165–72	2,146	
Kintore	1187–1200	835	
Kirkcaldy (R)	1644	50,360	
Kirkcudbright	1330	2,502	x
Kirkwall (+)	1486	4,617	x
Lanark (R)	1124–53	8,700	x
Lauder	1298–1328	604	x
Linlithgow (R)	1138	5,684	x
Lochmaben	1440	1,261	
Montrose	1124–53	9,959	x
Nairn (R) (Invernairn)	1190	8,037	
New Galloway	1630	338	
Newburgh (Fife)	1631	2,062	x
North Berwick	1425	4,414	x
Peebles (R)	1124–53	5,884	x
Perth (R)	1124–27	43,030	x
Pittenweem	1541	1,518	x
Queensferry	1636	5,172	x
Rattray	1564	5,553	
Renfrew (R)	1124–47	18,595	
Rosemarkie	1590		
Rothesay	1401	6,595	x
Roxburgh (R)	1119–24		x
Rutherglen	1124–53	24,732	
St. Andrews (+)	1620	11,630	x
Sanquhar	1598	1,991	x
Selkirk	1328	5,684	
Stirling (R)	1124–27	29,776	x
Stranraer	1617	9,85	
Tain	1439	1,942	x
Tarbert	1329	1,391	
Whithorn (+)	1511	988	x
Wick	1589	7,617	
Wigtown (R)	1292	1,118	

The Historic Burghs Association of Scotland does not confine itself to the above list. It is equally interested in Abbey Burghs, such as Dunblane and Paisley, and in Burghs of Baronies, such as Thurso and Musselburgh as well as in later towns. Whether or not a town is one of the original Royal Burghs, or developed out of the Industrial Revolution, it is part of Scotland's unique built heritage.

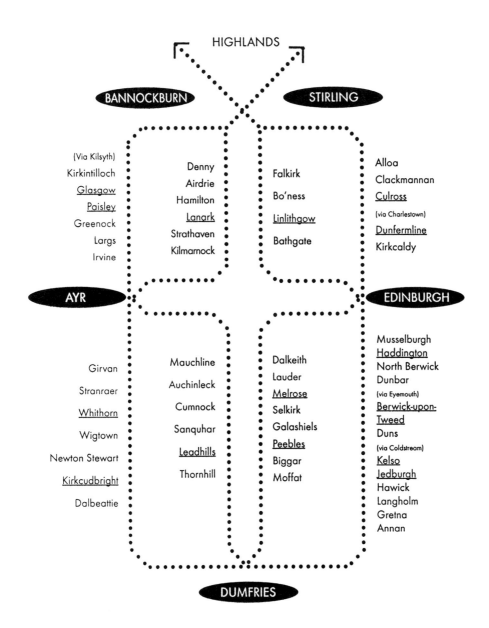

Figure 1 Southern part of a tour of Scotland's historic burghs with coastal and inland choices of long or short circuits. A figure of eight, saltirewise, through Stirling is suggested. Major stops are shown in capitals, and those convenient for longer breaks are underlined. The inland routes are shorter, but are hilly and scenic, and an infinite set of options are possible by combining coastal and inland sections between major towns. It is hoped that local councils, area tourist boards and the churches might collaborate to produce a 'pilgrim passport' for the historic burghs.

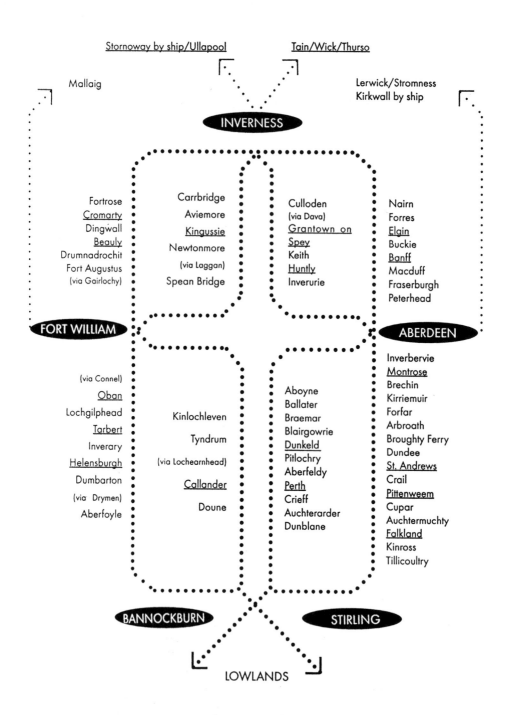

Figure 2 Northern part of tour of the historic burghs with coastal and inland options for long or short circuits.

34

SCOTTISH MERCAT CROCES
Their Spiritual and Secular Significance

Lindsey Thomson & Dennis Urquhart

Market crosses (*mercat croces* in Scots) are historically tied into travel due to their religious and trading associations. They have traditionally been the focal point of Sxcotland's historical burghs or small towns, and have significant value historically, culturally, architecturally and as a heritage asset. Local authorities could seek to raise the profile of the market cross to visitors in the promotion, interpretation and development strategy for our historic town centres, and also develop their awareness of the risks posed to such monuments by environmental impact. The writer is building a risk assessment model in order to develop an improved management framework for this monument type, as well as proposing an enhanced role for the market cross in promoting the heritage of Scotland's burghs.

HISTORICAL SIGNIFICANCE

The function of the market cross was mainly as a symbol of the burgh's right to trade. This privilege was granted by the crown, or by a local baron or monastery, and the taxes exacted from this trading activity lined the pockets or coffers of the burgh patron. Occupying a central position within the market place, they formed the physical focus of trading activity during markets and fairs held in the late- and post-medieval periods.

Their prominent site, as well as civic associations, also made them a landmark associated with other official burgh business. As such, they were used as the point from which proclamations were made to the burgh population, and frequently as the site of punishments and even executions. A visible reminder of this is exhibited by the shafts of some examples which still bear the remains of the town jougs, an entrapment device for the punishment of petty wrongdoers, such as. at Inverkeithing and Kinross. Burgh records vividly illustrate the involvement of the market cross in a variety of public events. On occasion, the more elaborate constructions at Aberdeen and Edinburgh were even specially decorated with gilding, garlands and tapestries, and for royal visits in the 16th century wine was engineered to flow from the gargoyles.

We know from historical evidence that market crosses were erected from at least the 12th century in Scotland. They were first mentioned in association with King David I's ambitious 1124 plans to establish numerous new towns to help foster trade and generate more taxable income. These early examples have left no physical trace, and it is thought that they were constructed of timber. Our surviving market crosses date from perhaps as early as the 14th century, such as in Inverkeithing, although 17th and 18th century examples are more common.

The earliest ones are the most simple in construction, consisting usually of a stepped base, surmounted by a polygonal shaft crowned with a capital and finial, as illustrated by the example at Old Rayne in Aberdeenshire. A few of the later examples were larger constructions, consisting similarly of a shaft with capital and finial, but surmounted upon a more substantial understructure, as illustrated by the example at Elgin. This latter type obviously required greater resources to construct, usually coming from a prominent burgh patron. They generally consisted of a small polygonal room containing a staircase spiralling around the central shaft. The stairs allowed privileged access to a rooftop platform, which afforded some protection from the mob to heralds, burgh officials, VIP's and even royalty when occasion demanded. This design is uniquely Scottish.

Symbolic, to more recent generations, of the Scottish urban heritage, market crosses have continued to be erected even into the present century. The Victorians erected a few elaborately carved market crosses in the Gothic Revival style with pinnacles and crocketting, such as the example at Cullen. Following the First World War, it was thought that the market cross lent itself well as a model on which to base the design of certain new town memorials to the dead, for example at Abernethy and Kelso. In yet more towns (e.g. Gretna), war memorials of various styles stand upon the site of former market crosses. In these later monuments, we see concepts of community foci and 'pilgrimage' preserved through site continuity. In an unusual instance, the Corstorphine market cross was made by five trees set out in cruciform, a design recently replanted in a park.

Although the word 'cross' bears witness to their early historical origins, it is a misnomer today in that religious iconography features little in surviving examples. They are mostly secular monuments whose finials comprise heraldic devices, sundials and other ornamented and abstract forms. Often the finial is a sculpture of a lion or unicorn, usually clasping heraldic arms. The parapets of larger examples are also adorned with these devices, as in Edinburgh, which features a series of painted and gilded arms, and at Aberdeen with its series of royal portraiture and arms. These devices were no doubt intended to symbolise and legitimise the domain of civic authority within the market place and within burgh machinations generally.

SPIRITUAL ORIGINS

Evidence of pilgrimage and of trade and exchange extends from prehistory through to the present. There are various types of evidence for this early travel, including documentary records, archaeological finds and even influences upon building styles. For example, Scotland had significant trading links with Dutch and French ports and this architectural influence can be seen today in some of the Scottish burgh architecture (Howard 1995). The recovery of non-local items including, for example, pottery and other items such as personal ornaments and pilgrims' souvenirs, is a very useful indicator of travel and trading links.

Further back in time, it is possible that certain of the megalithic monuments and associated stone alignments in prehistoric times attracted a kind of pilgrimage activity, for veneration of gods or ancestors. Exotic materials found at ritual and burial sites indicate trade and exchange, their use being bound up with ritual and the expression of status. Evidence of conspicuous consumption of 'exotica' is notable in many excavated sites of the iron age in Europe, indicating long-distance trade for example between Britain and the Continent.

Pilgrim routes in the early Christian period did have 'wayside' crosses to serve the spiritual needs of the traveller, as sites for prayer and contemplation. It has been suggested that early market crosses were of this type, and that the idea of the market cross developed from a tradition of using wayside and churchyard crosses for making deals and oaths in the early medieval period (Drummond 1860 & Hutcheson 1900). Documentary evidence shows that in certain cases regular markets were held in churchyards during past centuries until the practice was eventually stamped out in the 18th century, and market crosses still stand in churchyards in Moray, e.g. Dallas and Duffus. Deals might have been considered more binding if made before a holy symbol, and it has been suggested that the deal-striker may even have placed a hand on the cross while giving his word, for added emphasis (Drummond 1860).

Such crosses would also, no doubt, have acted as prominent landmarks useful as places of meeting or assembly. Compared with today, the open market was a vital trading space such that the market cross formed part of the necessary outdoor furniture. Thus, the concept of the market cross might have developed from a religious tradition and came to be constructed in town centres by the 12th century.

If the market cross evolved from wayside or other Christian crosses, then the iconography of the finials evolved from the 'Cross Ecclesiastic' to alternative themes of heraldry, time-telling and other plainer and even abstract terminals at some time during or prior to the 17th century. Most of the surviving finials post-date the Reformation and are secular in theme. However, there is some uncertainty with regard to the effect of the Reformation upon market cross iconography, due to the lack of evidence for finials pre-dating this.

Hutcheson (1900), claimed that the market cross was a monument whose erection ran chronologically in parallel with the Cross Ecclesiastic for four hundred years preceding the Reformation, and that it had previously come to be differentiated from the Cross Ecclesiastic due to the civic uses for which it was required. However, it is likely that the 1581 Act passed against pilgrimage to 'some chappellis, wellis, croces, and sic vther monumentis of Idolatrie' (some chapels, wells, crosses and such other monuments of idolatry) discouraged the use of religious themes in the design of market crosses. The few examples which still incorporate religious imagery of pre-Reformation origins include that at Banff. Its finial comprises a calvary scene and is a replica of the original which dates from the early sixteenth or possibly even the fifteenth century.

Parallels have been drawn between the Scottish market cross and other monument types in Continental market places. Their function and appearance is considered to be very similar to that of Belgian perrons (d'Alviella 1914; Black 1928), and the function of German Roland statues has been recognised as similar to that of Scottish market crosses (Hamilton 1914). Some authors have even envisaged a broad ancient link between the functions of market crosses and these European equivalents on the one hand, and that of prehistoric monoliths of the pre-Christian era on the other (Hutcheson, in Small 1900; Hamilton 1914).

It has been suggested that the practice of using market crosses for oath-making, proclamation, assembly, and for meting out punishment may stem from an ancient tradition. According to this idea, the use of prehistoric monoliths was subsequently endorsed by adherents to the Christian faith, sometimes visibly by carving a simple cross onto them, and there are certainly plenty examples of these early wayside crosses. As such, the pre-Christian concept of using pillar stones for arking points, bargaining and punishment may have persisted through time, manifested in the Middle Ages by the market cross. This line of argument sees a pagan tradition, christianised, and then secularised.

Thus, whether either or both of the origin theories for the market cross evolving from the Christian cross and from prehistoric monoliths are correct, it is clear that the market cross evolved and developed thoroughly within the context of early travel. Certainly from the 12th century they were erected for the purpose of encouraging trading activity at each site, thereby stimulating regular travel to such centres.

TOUNS AND *CROCES* AS HERITAGE ASSETS

Numerically, the survival of Scottish market crosses is quite substantial, with around 146 examples standing today, including some fragments and 20th century examples. Market crosses survive in most Scottish burghs, in some cases heavily repaired or reconstructed, and they do represent an important cultural element of our urban heritage with potential as focal points in local interpretation strategies. Most surviving examples are located in the south and east of Scotland, largely reflecting the distribution of burghs historically.

In the rural Highlands and Islands, a rather different set of socio-economic relationships prevailed as a result of the clan system. Livestock, agricultural produce, labour and military assistance were important alternatives to hard currency, settlements were more remote and more self-sufficient, trading activity was less organised and specialist goods might be bought from a pedlar. In Scotland overall, there were at least 300 burghs in existence by the beginning of the eighteenth century, although these do not all survive today. Many planned towns were built and existing ones developed between 1730 and 1830, particularly in the north-east of Scotland, as the result of a programme of 'new town' building to promote economic development (Rodger 1983).

A key issue today is the question of how local communities might stay competitive, and how tourists could be attracted away from the traditional Scottish 'honeypots' to allow a more even distribution of the economic benefits brought by visitors. Recent initiatives to improve the environment and to promote the cause of our historic burghs are to be welcomed, such as establishment of. the Historic Burgh Association of Scotland (Cameron, this volume). Another is the Small Towns Initiative, complemented by Planning Advice Notes (The Scottish Office PAN 52, 1997). It is important that the role of the market cross be given due consideration in future strategies.

Most burghs are quite small towns, concentrated in the south and east of Scotland. Smaller towns have clearly been undergoing significant changes in recent decades, due to population change, economic restructuring, displacement of employment and services, traffic growth and insensitive development. For example, changes in the traditional industries and markets have required towns to seek new roles with regard to economic development and employment, populations have tended to migrate or commute to larger towns, the increase of motor vehicles has demanded the upgrading and widening of roads and building of new ones, recent conversion of properties and construction of new buildings has often corrupted the traditional character and appearance of the area.

Attracting tourism is one avenue which offers some prospects for smaller towns in the current social and economic climate. Similar lines of development have been pursued in Ireland in the 'Heritage Towns' scheme (Browne 1994). The historical attractions, traditional characteristics and charm of the Scottish burgh could be further promoted as a heritage asset, in combination with interpretive aids and a variety of innovative and appropriate visitor facilities. In the field of rataling, there is a need to be sensitive to what tourists are looking for and to maintain high standards of product quality.

Existing examples of such developments include that at Culross, where the National Trust for Scotland's 'Little Houses Scheme' has enhanced the 16th and 17th century remains of the historical burgh. The Trust has saved and created an aesthetically pleasing yet informative time-warp, very popular with tourists, and preserved structures include the market cross.

An alternative approach is that adopted for St Andrews where it was decided to improve visitor orientation and interpretation facilities (Glen 1994). This initiative began with a heritage audit of the town and a consideration of the existing and potential visitor market, vehicular traffic systems, environmental capacity, tourist advice in the town and the visitor potential of the hinterland. Interpretation and signage followed five broad themes perceived to be formative in the identity of the town. One of these focuses upon the medieval heritage of the *'mercat toun'*, the remains of which still thrive as a retail centre. The market cross no longer survives, but its vivid history nevertheless features in the interpretive material as the site of the burning of the martyrs. The strategy also sought to promote lesser known attractions in the town and surrounding area.

Market crosses are today still a significant component of the burgh resource, representing an importrant historical and cultural asset. With regard to their iconography and heraldic devices, market crosses in a sense convey the spiritual and secular identity of each historical town and the surviving examples are each unique in design. They represent important assets which could be used as icons to convey the colourful, romantic and dynamic picture of Scotland's urban heritage. In terms of developing brand images of localities, they represent sites of enduring spiritual significance reaching back into the mists of time, often associated with:

1. highly emotionally charged historical scenes of secular outbursts and corporal punishment;
2. crowded sites of public celebrations, some relating to historic and national themes;
3. noisy points of contact and communication between public authority and local communities in an age predating mass media;
4. bustling scenes representing the focus of local enterprise and trade.

There is a re-emerging desire to retain the traditional character and use of historical environments wherever possible (Wood 1995, p125). In Britain, we have frequently given the motor vehicle priority in urban layout. The car has modified urban quality and we seem to have less public recreation space in town centres than our European counterparts. Historical market areas could be reconverted to public space through the removal of vehicular traffic and environmental enhancement schemes. To attract public use of the space, appropriate building uses should be encouraged. Planners should recognise the need for people in towns 'to come together as a community for meetings, to buy and sell, to see justice being done, to protest, and to celebrate; they need to feel that they belong to the human pack' (Conzen 1978, in Wood 1995).

A public space should be the natural focal point of a town, and traditionally the market cross is the focus of this. Market crosses could be given a new lease of life if they were given a stronger focus and more attention in the provision of information and interpretation about the burgh and its history.

STONE DECAY AND PREVENTION

The decay of carved stone is a subject of current concern and research in Scotland, and one which is central to the writer's current research into this monument type. Although market crosses are standing in many Scottish towns, closer investigation reveals that, in fact, many of their stone components do not date from the original construction. Most market crosses are built of sandstone which can be quite vulnerable to weathering in certain circumstances.

A good example is the Banff market cross, a shaft-upon-steps type of construction and originally erected in the late fifteenth or early sixteenth century. The shaft was replaced in 1627. In 1768 the monument was purchased by the Earl of Fife who erected the shaft and finial onto a dovecot at a site one mile outside of Banff, while some other carved stones from the market cross were built into the wall of a Banff house. It was moved again in 1900 to the Plainstanes in Banff town, and the shaft and finial were erected upon a new base. In 1994, the shaft and finial were finally moved into Banff Museum and replica parts now take their place on the Plainstanes. The former parts have suffered substantial weathering, probably aggravated by the salty, coastal atmosphere. This is merely one example which demonstrates the complex history of intervention which these monuments have undergone and the risks from erosion that they face.

With regard to environmental decay agents, stone decays naturally due to factors of temperature, sunlight, moisture and natural salts, which interact and synergise to cause physical and chemical weathering. Stone decay is measured by fragmentation and material loss. Locational factors such as climate and proximity to the coast (atmospheric salt) affect the type and rate of weathering. Even the morphology of the monument itself and the degree of surrounding shelter affect the micro-climate around a monument, contributing to the weathering pattern.

Many decay problems are indirectly anthropogenic in source, such as air pollutants from traffic exhaust fumes and from domestic and industrial emissions. As monument morphology, siting and the built context are determined by man, these could also be considered to be indirect anthropogenic causes of decay. However, with the possible exception of siting, these factors can generally not be altered today. It is also possible for well intentioned restoration and conservation projects to pose a risk in certain cases, particularly if less-experienced individuals are involved. It is likely that the practice of moving many of the market crosses may have accelerated damage in some cases.

Inappropriate conservation materials or methods may also introduce new sources of degradation. For example, many repairs in the first half of the 20th century made use of cement mortar which has introduced problems in moisture retention in the stone and caused increased erosion of stone at masonry joints. Iron brackets have also caused the fracture of stone where they have been subject to corrosion and expansion. There are also risks from sporadic vandalism, but this does not appear to be a significant problem. In practice, environmental and anthropogenic decay factors interact as a set of conditions in the weathering process, where one aggravates the effect of the other.

The writer is currently undertaking a risk assessment of Scottish market crosses with the aim of producing a framework for improved management of this monument type. A mapping method is being developed for detailed recording of the condition of the market crosses, which will take account of the specific changing compositions and environments of each surveyed example since its construction. This will provide base-line data for future monitoring of their condition. An analysis of the collected data will allow a model for risk assessment to be established with regard to various environmental and anthropogenic factors.

Parameters for decay, and conversely for the relative stability of condition, will be postulated for a representative sample of the market crosses, with a view to identifying ideal and achievable conditions for their survival. Stonework notoriously experiences a build-up of stress to a threshold point, beyond which decay can generate drastic and visible effects of surface material loss.

Conservation is usually a remedial reaction to processes which have exceeded this threshold, conditions which can be difficult to spot in advance. Arising from the risk assessment, it is intended to explore the possibility of gauging criteria for intervention based upon the prevailing stone condition, on the general premise that preventative conservation is better than cure. With regard to the cases which seem particularly at risk, potential funding sources for conserving market crosses include the 'Townscape Heritage Initiative' in Scotland recently launched by the Heritage Lottery Fund, or European Union grants such as the Raphael Programme.

The Authors

Lindsey Thomson is currently undertaking research for her PhD with the Masonry Conservation Research Group at The Robert Gordon University. Her research focuses upon developing a risk assessment model for Scottish market crosses, in collaboration with Historic Scotland. Her background is in archaeology, heritage management and conservation. Since graduating with an MA with Honours in Archaeology from Glasgow University, her contracts have included excavating at various archaeological sites, interpreting archaeology from aerial photographs, including the recent English Heritage Monuments at Risk Survey, and archaeological reconstruction. She is a Fellow of the Society of Antiquaries of Scotland and member of the Pictish Arts Society.

Dennis Urquhart is a consultant building pathologist and conservation scientist, formerly Reader in the School of Construction, Property and Surveying and Director of the Masonry Conservation Research Group at The Robert Gordon University. He has extensive experience in the field of stone masonry conservation research and is author and co-author of numerous publications. His recent work includes biological growths and biocide treatment of sandstones, sandstone and granite cleaning, consolidant and water repellent treatments, market crosses in Scotland and access to historic properties.

References

d'Alviella, G., 1914. *Les Perrons de la Wallonie et les market-crosses de l'Ecosse.* Hayez, Brussels

Black, W. G., 1928. *The Scots Mercat 'Cross': An Inquiry as to its History and Meaning.* William Hodge & Co Ltd, Glasgow and Edinburgh

Browne, S., 1994. *Heritage in Ireland's Tourism Recovery.* In Fladmark, J. M. (ed) *Cultural Tourism.* Papers presented at the Robert Gordon University Heritage Convention 1994, Donhead Publishing Ltd, London, pp 13–25

Drummond, J., 1860. *Notice of Some Stone Crosses, with Especial Reference to the Market Crosses of Scotland.* Proceedings of the Society of Antiquaries for Scotland 4, 86–115

Glen, M. H., 1994. *Interpreting St Andrews.* In Fladmark, J. M. (ed) *Cultural Tourism.* Papers presented at the Robert Gordon University Heritage Convention 1994, Donhead Publishing Ltd, London, pp 261–273

Hamilton, P., 1914. *The Boundary Stone and the Market Cross.* Scottish Historical Review, October 1914, p24–36

Howard, D., 1995. *The Architectural History of Scotland: Scottish Architecture from the Reformation to the Restoration, 1560–1660.* Edinburgh University Press

Hutcheson, 1900. *Introduction.* In Small, J. W. 1900. *Scottish Market Crosses.* E Mackay, Stirling, pp i–xi

Rodger, R. D., 1983. *The Evolution of Scottish Town Planning.* In Gordon & Dicks (ed) *Scottish Urban History.* Aberdeen University Press, pp 71–91

The Scottish Office Development Department, Planning Services, April 1997. *Planning in Small Towns.* Planning Advice Note PAN 52

Wood, L., 1995. *The Conservation and Management of Historic Urban Space.* International Journal of Heritage Studies 1 (2), pp 111–125

The Mercat Cross in Banff, being one of the few pre-Reformation examples to survive, showing the recently restored crucifix.

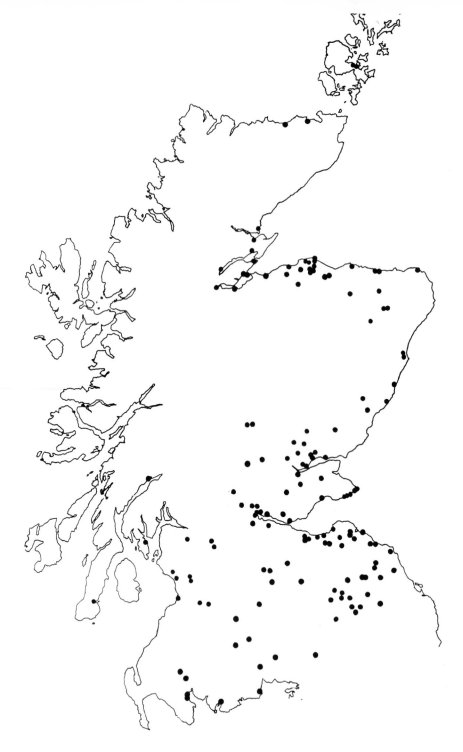

Map of Scotland showing distribution of surviving mercat crosses.

35

READING THE CITY
Approach and Orientation

Brian Evans

A city can only exist,
when it is inhabited in the imagination of its citizens
Alistair Gray

Why is it that some cities have clear and accessible form and others are confused and perplexing? How is it that sophisticated and expensive applications of modern technology to orientation and provision of information for visitors can sometimes be immediately understandable and on other occasions be totally indecipherable? To answer these questions for the future, we need to start in the past, and in his anthology, *The Power of Place*, James Swan states that:

> The art and science of environmental planning and architecture have been an integral part of human life since even before King Solomon's temple. Geomancy (divining the right action for each place, present and future) is a parent of the modern environmental design process. At the core of geomantic wisdom everywhere is the assertion that not all places are alike.(Swan p2).

Swan observes that, in the modern world, the fate of places is settled in lengthy hearings when proposed developments are weighed against the environmental and cultural impacts. While modern science and technology enable sophisticated analysis of all the variables involved, geomancy asserts that there is correct action for each place. To determine the best course of action through reductionist scientific thinking by weighing the perceived costs and benefits is in direct contrast to the ancient view of examining the *spirit of the place* to determine what is best. In Swan's words, 'to know the spirit of place would seemingly be essential to the art of planning, designing and building sustainable societies'. In reality, the issue of how nature influences consciousness is left almost entirely to artists, poets and writers, even although statistics show that we are drawn to special places to recreate, and our unconscious voices call us to visit special places even though we are not sure why (ibid).

The growing consensus among scientists, designers and politicians is that we need to make the next few decades count in terms of increased environmental awareness and balance or there will be no future for mankind. A fundamental part of this process is the recovery of the meaning of place, but in the recent past, guidance on livelihood and creativity has come from economics, technology and the media. The ancient awareness of place was set aside in favour of progress, development and growth. It is not that technology is evil and anti-ecological, but that the forces which shape it are unconnected to the natural and intuitive wisdom which springs from place and nature (ibid p3). As cities stress more and more their unique character and qualities in an effort to become successful business and tourist centres, the issues identified by James Swan become increasingly relevant to modern city planning.

Whereas no modern architect or planner would contemplate rejection of all the favoured technology, techniques and professional tricks for a simple consultation with the shamans or 'old ones', there is no doubt that during the latter half of the this century, architects and planners have become increasingly aware of and concerned with the importance of the *spirit of place*, the *genus loci*, and the need to build this into the decision making process about design, urban intervention and the interpretation of the city for residents and visitors alike.

Respect for place is the new mantra in urban design. This paper is in three parts. The first reviews the development of thinking about place in the twentieth century. This is followed by an examination of two case studies which illustrate the application of this thought in practice: (1) to the preparation of a strategy for the public realm, the streets and spaces, of the city centre in Glasgow; and, (2) to the design of a direction and interpretive sign system for the same area.

TWENTIETH CENTURY THINKING

Differences between the attributes of here and there have always been of great interest to architects, geographers and planners because it is precisely the differences between places that generate the movement of goods, people, and information (Gould & White p15).

The study of preference for place is a reasonably recent pursuit, but during most of the 20th century scholars have thought about the images that people have of their local environment. Interest has focused on the way in which people perceive landmarks, routes, boundaries, and neighbourhoods. One of the first to comment on the subject was Charles Trowbridge in 1913 who recorded that some people in a city seemed to have a good sense of orientation, whereas others are confused about direction when emerging from theatres, etc. Trowbridge postulated that some people had informal maps in their heads centred on the location of their home whereas others saw direction in relation to their own position at any particular point in space (ibid p28).

In the 1950s the anecdotal work of Trowbridge was followed up by Kevin Lynch. Lynch studied environmental perception by asking people how they felt about prominent landmarks in Boston, Jersey City and Los Angeles in the USA and questioned them about major routes and areas of the city which they used to navigate their way around the city. In this way Lynch built up a general view of the city that highlights the key elements of the urban landscape. His book *The Image of the City* first published in 1960 is a seminal work for planners and urban designers. It sets out for the first time a language of the way people perceive the key elements of the urban landscape.

In Lynch's words, *The Image of the City* is, 'about the look of cities, and whether this look has any importance, and whether it can be changed' (Lynch, 1960, preface). Lynch recognised the urban landscape as something to be seen, remembered and to delight in. He recognised that giving form to the city is a special kind of design problem and his book set out to describe a method to deal with visual form at the city scale and offer some first principles of city design. Kevin Lynch was one of the first to realise that moving elements in the city, not just traffic, but people and all their activities, are as important as the urban fabric itself. Lynch argues that not only is the city an object which is perceived by very many people of widely differing character and class, it is also the product of many builders who are constantly modifying the city for their own reasons and therefore while it may be stable in general, it is constantly changing in detail. Only partial control can be achieved over its evolution and development, no final outcome, but a continuous succession of changes (ibid, p3). One of Lynch's key contributions was to recognise that shaping the city for its enjoyment, urban design, is an activity quite separate from architecture on one hand and the arts on the other, learning from them but not imitating them.

At the centre of his work was the study of the mental image of the city held by its citizens and the concept of *legibility* i.e. the ease with which parts of the city can be recognised and organised into a coherent pattern. Acknowledging that legibility is not the only important property of a beautiful city, Lynch nonetheless stressed its special importance in considering urban size, time and complexity and that to understand these things it is essential to consider not just the city as an entity in itself, but as an entity, image and organism being perceived by its inhabitants and by extension by its visitors (ibid p4). With these few concepts, Kevin Lynch changed for good the perception of urban design related only to the understanding of the buildings and townscape of the city, extending far beyond to the way in which buildings, streets and spaces are used and perceived.

Lynch's method is quite simple and involves the understanding of legibility through the application of five simple elements. The simplicity is a key to the value of the method. Lynch concentrates on the effects of physical, perceptible objects while recognising that there are other influences on legibility and image including the social meaning of an area, its function, history and, in certain circumstances, its name. Hidden in the text is an important statement which can bear frequent repetition:

> It is taken for granted that in actual design, form should be used to reinforce meaning, and not to negate it.
> (Lynch 1960, p46).

His five elements are:

> *Paths:* the routes along which people move. They may be streets, walkways, roads, cycleways or railways. People observe the city while moving through it and, as a consequence, relate other elements to this movement;

> *Edges:* linear elements not considered as paths, but as boundaries between parts of the city, lateral references rather than axes of movement, e.g. shores, boundaries of a campus, railway or motorway cuttings;

> *Districts:* areas or neighbourhoods of the city recognisable as having a common identifiable character, the observer is either 'inside' or 'outside' of districts;

> *Nodes:* strategic spaces in a city that the observer can enter, the principal foci to and from which people travel, places of

convergence and gathering, e.g. major public spaces, major junctions, transport termini;

Landmarks: external distinguishing elements whether distant or near that are easily recognisable and used by people for navigation. At the city scale they are spires, towers, major bridges and, at the local scale, a shop, clock or sign.

(Lynch 1960, pp 47–48)

These elements can overlap or have a dual function, e.g. a motorway can be a path for drivers and an edge for pedestrians. Application of the method begins with the division of the city into different elements, but ends with reintegration using the elements to describe a whole and coherent image. The elements are the ingredients of the city environment and it is the overall pattern, with networks of paths, clusters of landmarks, that provides the accessible and meaningful description of the city. Used in design, the elements should reinforce and support one another and the meaning of the city. Thus a new landmark should demarcate an existing district and the principal nodes within it. Equally the method can be used in reverse to diagnose problems with existing city form where the principle of reinforcing the meaning of the city has not been observed and as a result creates an ambiguous image, e.g. if a tall building is unmistakable in the city-wide panorama and yet unrecognisable at its base, then a chance has been lost to pin together the image of the city at two different levels.

It is the simplicity, adaptability and flexibility that makes this method such a powerful tool for urban design analysis.

In his later work, Lynch moved towards exploration and development of normative theory. In *Good City Form*, Lynch built on his analysis of good city form from the analytic techniques of *The Image of the City* through normative studies, e.g. Le Corbusier, *the City as Machine* and Geddes, *the City as Organism*, towards his own theoretical approach characterised by five performance: *vitality* (life), *sense* (perception), *fit* (form & use), *access* (movement) and *control* (management) modified by the further principles of *efficiency* and *justice* (Lynch 1980, p118).

The importance of place in architecture, design and planning has also been explored by Christian Norberg-Schultz. In *Intentions in Architecture*, Norberg-Schultz had analysed architecture scientifically by 'employing methods from natural science' (Norberg-Schultz, p5). While continuing to believe in the value of this approach, his later book, *Genius Loci*, establishes a complementary and more existential approach on the basic relationships between man and the environment and focuses on the task of the architect 'to create meaningful places' (ibid). The work emphasises understanding *the loss of place* on one hand and *the recovery of place* on the other by embracing experiential and qualitative techniques in architecture, design and planning as advocated by Lynch.

An early application of Lynch's work in the United Kingdom, took place in Birmingham where, with the assistance of the *Birmingham Post*, people were asked to collaborate in a study investigating their perception of the city centre. Readers were asked to send maps or sketches that conveyed the key impression of the area drawn by themselves without the assistance of published maps, a quick unaided impression to convey the basic pieces of information that people keep in their heads and which they used in moving around the centre of the city. The large response reflected the willingness of people to become involved in the planning process. The responses were synthesised and a composite image of the city centre was built up based on people's perceptions:

> The composite image displayed a marked emphasis for things at the human scale. Some of the tall, skyline features were not nearly as prominent as expected, while others such as the Cathedral Yard and the Bull Ring were singled out as desirable 'oases' in the bustling urban scene. Many specific shops were mentioned because of their street-level interest, while other areas were almost blank
>
> (Gould & White p30)

The resultant image taught the planners quite a lot about the way in which Birmingham people perceive the city and has influenced urban designers.

This work helps to illustrate the intuitive understanding that citizens have about good and bad neighbourhoods in a city – the extent to which people are 'street-wise'. The information that goes into building a mental image will reflect more than the knowledge of landmarks and routes. Cities can be highly stressful and dangerous places. In an area of Philadelphia, a seminal study plotted a large sample of people's fears creating a map of places to be avoided (e.g. the headquarters of gangs and of drug dealing) and other places of greater safety creating a widely known but unpublished map that citizens use in finding their way about in safety (ibid).

Terence Lee was one of the first post-war planners to consider the neighbourhood as a planning concept for modern urban living. What Lee discovered was that social space and physical space are so tightly linked that most people do not distinguish between the two. People define their neighbourhood as an area whose size is independent of the density of people living in it. Inner city and suburban neighbourhoods are perceived by their residents to be about the same size. In other words, people do not think of their neighbourhoods in terms of the number of people who live there, but as a comfortable and familiar space around them (ibid p34). The concept of neighbourhood is an important perceptual image for people and for the planners and urban designers who aspire to provide for people's needs in the city. Today the work of the *Urban Villages Forum* in the United Kingdom and the *Congress for a New Urbanism* in the United States concentrate on the cohesiveness of the urban neighbourhood as the key to understanding the coherence and legibility of the city.

Using the knowledge that people have of their neighbourhood and city can be a good way of interpreting and revealing that knowledge to others. For example, a 1970's study of Los Angeles revealed expected but nonetheless startling differences between different ethnic groups in the city. Upper class white residents had a detailed knowledge of the extensive city and the wide and interesting areas within and around it. Black residents had a much more restricted but detailed view of the main streets and the city centre whereas other districts were 'out-there' somewhere, unrelated and unlinked to the city core. The situation was most extreme among the Hispanic minority whose mental map of Los Angeles covered only their neighbourhood, the City Hall and the major transport termini (Gould & White pp 34–37). The lessons of awareness from this story of privilege and exclusion can be used by designers in designing sign systems to help people orientate themselves in the city.

Leaving aside the social comment that this study reveals about the stratification of different groups in the city, the detailed mental image of a city can be used by urban designers to provide a simple understandable map to reveal, interpret and assist people with orientation and navigation around the city. In this way the knowledge and familiarity of the city can be shared, not only with strangers and visitors, but also with the disadvantaged of the city who through the process of getting to know their city better may feel a little less alienated and more able to participate in the corporate identity of the city.

These techniques were used by Gillespies first in understanding the city centre of Glasgow, secondly in preparing a strategy for the public realm, the squares and streets, of central Glasgow and thirdly in designing a pedestrian sign system to help residents and visitors orientate themselves, navigate around the city centre and interpret the environment through which they pass.

THE PUBLIC REALM IN CENTRAL GLASGOW

In the study of urban design, practitioners talk of the 'legibility' of the city by which they mean the extent to which ordinary people, residents and visitors alike, can *read* the city or, in other words, the ease with which they can orientate themselves and find their way about. Some cities and towns are, because of their plan and prominent features, more naturally legible than others. In general, towns and cities with radial plans are easier to read than those with a regular grid for the simple reason that all major routes tend to lead to the centre whereas one intersection of a grid can look very similar to the next. A prominent skyline is equally helpful to legibility and orientation, consider the value of Edinburgh's heroic skyline in this respect.

The belief that a city should be intuitively legible has informed the design work of Gillespies, a landscape and urban design practice which believes that the essence of good urban design is born out of an understanding of the character of the place and the culture of its people and that the qualities of the city should be clearly but subtly revealed to contribute to vitality and coherence in the city whilst celebrating the diversity among cities. Kevin Lynch has been an important influence on the philosophy of Gillespies, the author's practice, who have sought to build his ideas together with those of Gordon Cullen and Christopher Alexander into a coherent application of urban design principles in their home city of Glasgow as well as many others.

In the 1990s, the Practice was asked by the public authorities in Glasgow to prepare a strategy to guide interventions in the public realm of the city centre, i.e. the streets and spaces which make up the public space of the city. The document is in four parts (Gillespies, 1995). The first describes factors influencing the city centre during the recent history of urban regeneration in Glasgow including area initiatives and landmark property developments. The second part describes the urban analysis undertaken to understand the environment of the city centre in order to identify a hierarchy of streets and spaces: a structure of the public realm of the city centre for the purposes of guiding public investment. The third section establishes principles and guidelines for achieving quality in the design and construction of public spaces and the fourth section identifies early action projects, selected to demonstrate visibly the quality intended for the city centre as a whole.

We are concerned here with the analysis in the second part. The attempt to understand and reveal the character and quality of Glasgow city centre in a visible, understandable, clear and coherent manner. The techniques used owe much to the Practice's evolving philosophy of urban design and draw on many techniques used widely in urban design analysis including techniques of figure-ground analysis by Christopher Alexander and Gordon Cullen. But it is the Practice's belief in the meaning of place, understanding, revealing and interpreting the meaning of the city physically and culturally, allied to interventions of lasting quality which is the overarching principle guiding the work and which sees the application of the principles and techniques discussed earlier in this paper. The *sense of place* of Glasgow City Centre was examined through:

1. the inherent character of the urban form and townscape;
2. the way people use, perceive and inhabit the City Centre; and,
3. transport needs to service the business, resident and visitor requirements of the City Centre (ibid, p17).

The analysis begins with an examination of the history of the place, the inherited townscape and the nature of Glasgow's grid. Figure-ground techniques are used to illustrate the historical development of the grid and topographic studies reveal the nature of this regular grid laid out over the underlying geomorphology of a drumlin field . This combination gives the city its distinctive character of rising vistas terminated in the sky and falling views beyond the immediate confines of the street to neighbouring rooftops and skylines. The consistency of Glasgow's grid can cause confusion. As a result corner blocks become very important aids to orientation. Additional legibility comes through the shape and form of the streets which vary between the more intimate character of the older Merchant City and the broad Georgian Avenues of the Blythswood new town. The grid gives Glasgow a unique quality which distinguishes it from Scotland's other cities. Despite generations of modification the grid retains the geometric and distinctive morphology which is a major contributor to Glasgow's identity.

This analysis provided a firm understanding of the form of the townscape in the city centre of Glasgow. However, the analysis and distribution of institutions, open spaces, pedestrian movement, land use change and character areas complement the townscape analysis and reveals even more about the way Glaswegians use and perceive their city. Our undersrtanding of this is a fundamental precursor to the design of interventions in the public realm and later, in designing a sign system which is intended to reveal and interpret the character of the city centre for residents, businesses and visitors alike. The city is fortunate in having some streets of striking character and renown which are a key part of the City's identity. The final element of the urban design analysis is an examination of the need to move goods and people around the city centre by vehicle and by public transport.

These three analyses were combined to prepare a synoptic understanding of the character of the city centre revealing an ordering principle for the streets and spaces of central Glasgow, not a rigid hierarchy, more an interpretation device to consider the inter-related nature and relative importance of streets and spaces and a means to consider interventions into the public realm. The identification of principal, major and minor streets was derived by applying the following criteria:

1. the importance of urban form – historical, architectural and urban design attributes;
2. the presence and use of institutions and attractions;
3. the importance for retailing, office and residential use;
4. the importance as a pedestrian route; and,
5. the importance as vehicle thoroughfare.

This analysis and resulting perception of the structure of the city is now used as a guide in the control of development by the City Council and in the design of interventions into the public realm such as the re-design of Royal Exchange Square, Candleriggs and the re-planning of Buchanan Street as the City's major urban thoroughfare.

In conferring the Royal Town Planning Institute Silver Jubilee Cup, the UK's premier planning award on the Public Realm Strategy and the associated demonstration projects, the judging panel commented:

> The establishment of a set of principles for the creation of a high quality public realm to which all those responsible for its promotion, provision and aftercare subscribe is, in itself, a significant achievement.

The analysis and understanding of Glasgow city centre prepared for the Public Realm Strategy was also used to provide the underlying perception of character in the design of a pedestrian sign system intended to reveal, interpret and provide orientation for visitors, businesses and residents.

DESIGN OF THE GLASGOW PEDESTRIAN SIGN SYSTEM

To become completely lost in the city is a rare experience for many, given the help of other people and the presence of way-finding devices including maps, street signs and numbers, route signs, direction signs and bus destination signs. In the process of way-finding, Lynch observed that:

> The strategic link is the environmental image, the generalised mental picture of the exterior physical world that is held by the individual. This image is the product both of immediate sensation and of the memory of past experience, and it is used to interpret information and to guide action. The need to recognise and pattern our surroundings is so crucial, and has such long roots in the past,

482

that this image has wide practical and emotional importance to the individual. A distinctive and legible environment not only offers security but also heightens the potential depth and intensity of human experience.

(Lynch 1960, pp 4–6)

The intuitive use of architectural features, natural topography and the town plan as a means of orientation is referred to by psychologists as cognitive. It is common for planners and urban designers to provide clues for people to assist them with the process of reading and orientation. The oldest, most common and most enduring form of this assistance is the map or perspective plan. It can be held in the hand and compared with the features of the city.

As manipulators of the physical environment, architects and planners are interested in the factors which affect the environmental image. Lynch's work encourages professionals to concentrate on collective or public images, the mental pictures common to large numbers of a city's inhabitants, the areas of agreement representing a common culture.

In the early 1990s, following two decades of successful urban regeneration, the City of Glasgow was attracting some 3 million visits each year. In response to this success, the city authorities established a partnership for tourist development to provide information, infrastructure and managed support for those who visit the city.

One of the first exercises carried out by the Tourist Development Partnership was to study the ease with which visitors could orientate themselves within the city, travel to and find Glasgow's principal and other attractions. Surveys revealed that the city centre is somewhat lacking in legibility for the visitor. The metropolitan nature of Glasgow gives a character of great vitality and interest but the regular grid can make orientation and way-finding difficult. Street intersections which are subtly different to local people tend to appear identical to the visitor causing confusion and frustration with people losing their way easily. It was resolved, therefore, to provide an urban signing system for pedestrians which would provide directional information and, if possible, interpretive detail about key features along the route. Gillespies was appointed to design the signs, prepare an indicative network, procure a prototype sign and construct a pilot project.

Both residents of and visitors to cities use pedestrian signs to find their way about. For residents, such signs serve as reminders or confirmation of a chosen route whereas for visitors, the sign system provides primary orientation and directional information. However, a sign system is only one of several mechanisms that is used, often concurrently, by people moving about the city. Printed maps and plans are perhaps the most popular method and are frequently supplemented by verbal confirmation from passers-by. On occasion, people rely on 'instinctive' wayfinding using familiar landmarks.

Pedestrian signs must provide useful and meaningful information, but the system need not be designed to cover all the eventualities that may be anticipated. Indeed, the success of the system depends on the selection of the minimum level of information necessary to direct people effectively and to ensure a maximum degree of simplicity and clarity. Furthermore, the requirements for the level of information vary throughout the city. For example, key arrival points such as transport termini require extensive information to be provided, including public transport links and general visitor information as well as directions to adjacent attractions and facilities. In other locations simple directional signs to a single destination may be all that is necessary. It is possible therefore to identify a hierarchy of sign locations throughout the city and this in turn necessitates a hierarchy of physical sign types to accommodate different levels of information.

It is also clear that the destinations identified on the signs are of many different kinds, ranging from broad geographical areas (e.g. West End, South Side), to specific attractions (e.g. Kelvingrove Museum, City Chambers), and supporting facilities such as phones or toilets. The destinations also vary considerably in their level of importance, some being of international renown (e.g. Glasgow School of Art) and others which would be unfamiliar to visitors.

By ranking the information on the signs, levels of detail can be varied as required. Rationalising the manner in which information is presented to people in this way can enhance the quality of information provided whilst retaining a high degree of simplicity.

The first level of information is represented by the broad geographical areas that make up the city, City centre, West End and South Side, for example. The next level comprises widely recognised neighbourhoods, major streets and key city landmarks. The third tier of information deals with specific attractions or facilities with the information for a specific location being announced at an appropriate distance in advance of that location. Further detail directing people to toilets, phones and so on forms the final tier.

Two of the four signs can hold up to 44 distinct pieces of information and the principal signs in the system can accommodate several sizes of type and graphics so that key information can be larger than subsidiary information. There was concern that ordinary people would not understand the hierarchy. However, the designers argued successfully that in fact lay people would not notice it. The argument was won with a simple analogy – if a pencil is well designed, the user concentrates on what he or she is drawing, not on its shape, and in a sign programme, if a hierarchy is well devised, people can access the information they want when they need it (Diebler-Finke, p37).

Four sign types direct visitors through the streets of Glasgow. Key orientation signs, posted at principal public spaces, are broad two sided signs with large maps, transport and interpretative materials. Secondary orientation signs, sited at key junctions and other important locations, are narrower four-sided structures with local area maps, interpretive material and directional prompts.

Directional signs located at important junctions are two-sided, and provide a hierarchy of directional information. All three sign types allow for a hierarchy of graphics and type size in order that key information can be larger than subsidiary information.

The fourth and most minor sign type is a blade sign. It gives users a final prompt to turn off a major route reassuring them that they are approaching their destination.

Anxious to avoid spurious historicism and unnecessary ornament, the design team was concerned to establish clear objectives for the signing project which would lead to the design and construction of a signing system closely related to the needs of the visitor and resident and appropriate to the city of Glasgow. The Steering Group agreed that the Victorian look popular for signs and street furniture was inappropriate for Glasgow. Nor was the limited size of small pole-mounted 'finger signs' used in most UK cities to direct pedestrians appropriate. Instead of simple names and arrows, the Design Team set out to provide residents and visitors with maps, directions, public transport information, interpretive historical information and cues related to self-guided tours in tourist authority literature. This type of sign should not be small or quaint It needed to be bold and contemporary.

The Design Team and the Steering Group was determined to avoid the British trap of designing something for the needs of today as if it had been conceived of hundreds of years ago. The Glasgow sign system intends to fulfil the needs of the day with the look of its time in the hope that this will continue to be relevant tomorrow by contributing to the continuity of our towns and cities. This approach is unashamedly European, taking clues from Italy and Germany where old is reserved for repair and new benefits from high quality contemporary materials. Design is not venerated today in the United Kingdom and is often seen as fashion or taste, whereas design principles have a rationale tried and tested far beyond the choice of style and colour (Diebler-Finke, p38). Ultimately, a series of functional and aesthetic objectives were established to meet these aims and the relevant statutory regulations (Gillespies, 1994).

The signs have been designed to be:

1. readable, meaningful and reliable;
2. able to accommodate variable size and type of information
3. flexible, to allow for changing information;
4. suitable for erection on a variety of surfaces; and
5. easy to erect, avoiding interference with pedestrian and vehicular movement.

Programme, funding and location in a robust urban environment meant that the signs required to be:

1. straightforward to manufacture;
2. durable, easily repaired and vandal resistant; and
3. easy to maintain.

Finally, the signs are highly visible components of the streetscape and therefore aspire to:

1. avoid clutter in the street;
2. suit a widely varying architectural context;
3. present a strong image for Glasgow reflecting the city's goals for quality in design and the environment;
5. be simple and stylish – classic rather than classical design; and
6. enhance subtly the city centre streetscape.

Resolution of three key issues guided the design and production of the sign system: *urban design and hierarchy*, clarification of the relative importance of the information to be displayed, the significance of the sign structures in the streetscene and the design of a clear and meaningful network; *graphic design* – the expression and identity of the signs themselves; and, *product design* – the use of simple, repeatable technology with reliable, durable materials.

The intention was to create signs that would endure both physically and aesthetically. Simple tough materials were selected and the design concept sought to reflect the nature of Glasgow as a robust city, and one with a demanding environment. In a review in the US Journal *Identity*, Gail Deibler-Finke noted:

> The word that all involved in the Sign Program use repeatedly is 'robust' in the British sense of strong, healthy and vigorous. It's a word that describes Glasgow, once a shipping and industrial capital and now facing the future head on as the industrial age winds down. It also describes Glasgow people, a mix of working-class and

white collar men and women who hit the pubs as well as the ballet. The new sign program had to stand up to them as well as to weather and pollution.

Although the sign system is a unique design for Glasgow, it is not unique technically. A proven low-technology system was chosen for easy construction and assembly. Full-sized 'mock-ups' were made and the presentation took place outside in the street. The modular sign faces at the basis of the system are manufactured by the London based HB Sign Company. Gillespies worked closely with the client group to develop the sign hierarchy and information, and with the sign manufacturer on the detailed product design.

The implementation of the system began with a pilot project erecting a small number of signs along one street to study maintenance, durability and public perception. Seven signs were erected along Sauchiehall Street, one of Glasgow's busiest shopping streets and a demanding urban environment. Unchanged other than for a few very minor details, the system went into production early in 1994 with two major phases which were completed late in 1995 giving coverage of the entire city centre. The value of the sign system to visitors and residents has been studies by a graduate student from Bulgaria (Botsmanova, 1996), who found that:

> The interpretive and direction information, logic and design of the signs recognises the concept of the implied reader. The 'narrative' is understandable in this communication where the techniques create both a sense of identity and a point of contact with the 'reader'. In other words, the message in these 'printed texts' is obvious although the mode of address is impersonal. There is no obstacle for the 'reader' and the feeling is one of being spoken to. ...Designed for people, they meet their needs and expectations, so they are user-friendly for visitors to Glasgow and a pride and joy for Glaswegians.

In 1995, the Glasgow urban signing system won the award for best direction signing from the Sign Design Society, the fledgling European body and youthful counterpart of the prestigious US based Society of Environmental Graphic Design. In their citation for the Award to the Glasgow project, the judges noted:

> This programme won on its visual integrity, its potential durability, and its relationship to the environment in which it is placed. The judges liked the substance of it. We felt that it was going to stay the course.

CONCLUSION

The significance of place is ancient and transcendental. Increasingly architects, urban designers, geographers and planners recognise the importance of the cultural and existential analysis of place in addition to the physical and functional. The principles of cognitive mapping and the writings of Kevin Lynch in particular remain valid for contemporary practice in urban design. Examples in Glasgow illustrate how the application of these principles in practice can greatly enhance the understanding of the city in preparing strategies for design of public spaces and in designing direction sign systems to reveal and interpret the qualities of a place for visitors and guide their orientation within the urban fabric.

The Author

Brian Evans was born in St Andrews and educated at the Universities of Edinburgh and Strathclyde. An urban designer and planner, he is a partner of Gillespies, the multidisciplinary design practice with offices in Glasgow, Manchester and Oxford. He has worked extensively in the fields of urban design, urban regeneration and landscape planning and has carried out assignments in the Netherlands, Scandinavia and Italy. He is a visiting lecturer at the Scott Sutherland School of Architecture at the Robert Gordon University, Aberdeen.

The author is indebted for advice and support to his colleagues at Gillespies and to Penny Hudd, Graphic Designer and Head of Graphic Design at Kingston University (formerly with the Glasgow School of Art and The Architects' Collaborative, Boston, Massachusetts).

References

Botsmanova, Magdelena, *Glasgow's Blue Orientation Signs*, unpublished graduate study, University of Strathclyde, 1996

Deibler-Finke, G., *Robust Signs for a Robust City, Identity*, Feb 1996, pp 36 – 41

Evans, B. M., *Respecting the Town*, in Brogden, W. A. (Ed) *The Neo-Classical Town: Scottish Contributions to Urban Design since 1750*, the Rutland Press, 1996

Galloway, M. P. & Evans, B. M., *Glasgow City Centre, Urban Design Quarterly* no. 36, June 1990

Gillespies, *Establishing a Tourist Transport System for Glasgow*, unpublished report to the Glasgow Development Agency et al, 1993

Gillespies, *Glasgow City Centre & the River Clyde: Continuing the Renaissance*, unpublished report for the Scottish Development Agency, 1990

Gillespies, *Glasgow City Centre Public Realm : Strategy & Guidelines*, Strathclyde Regional Council, Glasgow City Council & Glasgow Development Agency, 1995

Gillespies, *Glasgow : Approach, Orientation & Arrival*, unpublished report to the Glasgow Development Agency, 1992

Gillespies, *Pedestrian Sign System for Glasgow City Centre*, unpublished report to Glasgow City Council et al, 1994

Gould, P. & White, R., *Mental Maps*, Pelican, 1974

Katz, P., *Towards a New Urbanism*, Congress for the New Urbanism, 1996

Lynch, K., *The Image of the City*, MIT Press, Cambridge, Massachusetts, 1960

Lynch, K., *Good City Form*, MIT Press, Cambridge, Massachusetts, 1981

Mulvagh, G. Y. & Evans, B. M., "Creating the Context", *Architects' Journal*, May 1990

Norberg-Schultz, C., *Genius Loci : Towards a Phenomenology of Architecture*, Rizzoli, New York, 1980

Schama, S., *Landscape & Memory*, HarperCollins, 1995

Swan, J. A., *The Power of Place : Sacred Ground in Natural & Human Environments*, Gateway Books, 1993

Urban Villages Group, *Urban Villages*, Urban Villages Group, 1992

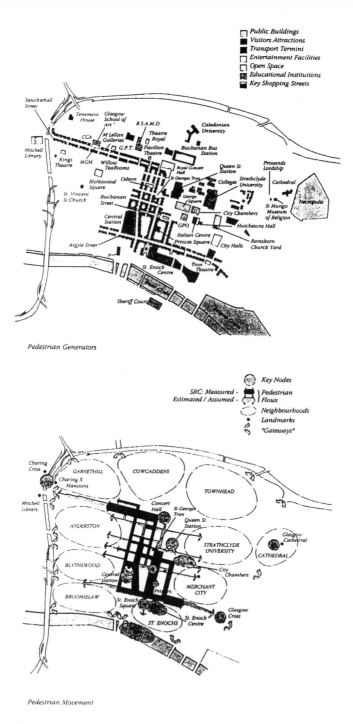

Figure 1 The application of Lynch's techniques of cognitive mapping applied to Glasgow city centre, showing status of institutions on the left, and pedestrian movement on the right (source Gillespies).

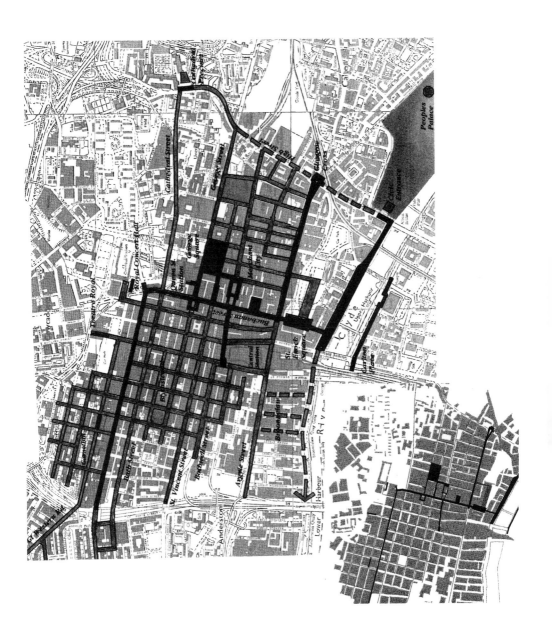

Figure 2 The grid of central Glasgow, with a public realm hierarchy of streets and spaces (source Gillespies).

491

Primary Information Point

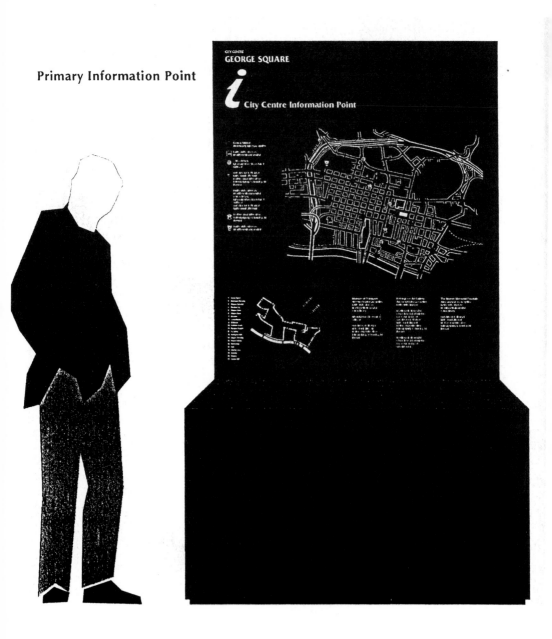

Figure 3 The Glasgow pedestrian sign system, showing the design for a primary information point (source Gillespies).

Figure 4 Map of the central city pedestrian sign system, showing distribution of the interpretative information points for visitors and residents derived from cognitive mapping studies (source Gillespies).